MARVEL
1602

writer
NEIL GAIMAN
illustrator
ANDY KUBERT
digital painting
RICHARD ISANOVE
lettering
TODD KLEIN
cover artist
SCOTT MCKOWEN
Dark Dimension Art in Part 8,
Page 33-34 by Steve Ditko

editors
NICK LOWE & JOE QUESADA
special thanks to
KELLY LAMY & NANCY DAKESIAN

collections editor
JEFF YOUNGQUIST
assistant managing editor
MARK D. BEAZLEY
assistant editor
JENNIFER GRUNWALD
director of sales
DAVID GABRIEL
production
JERRY KALINOWSKI
book designer
MEGHAN KERNS
creative director
TOM MARVELLI

editor in chief
JOE QUESADA
publisher
DAN BUCKLEY

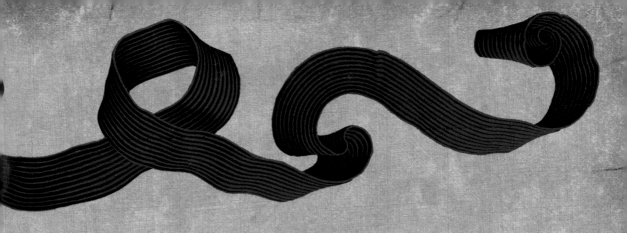

For Stan Lee and Jack Kirby and
Steve Ditko, with infinite admiration.
For Jonathan and Lenny, comics fiends.
And, of course, to Todd,
for making it necessary.
-*Neil*

For Stan Lee, Jack Kirby and Steve Ditko...
for giving us the characters with the stamina of
time, that we could take them back in time.
For Neil Gaiman and Joe Quesada...
for having the faith in me.
And for my father, Joe Kubert...for showing me how.
-*Andy*

For Catherine.
For Florian, Sophie, Quentin and Mathieu.
-*Richard*

To Neil, for keeping me in mind.
-*Todd*

To Marge, who first put pencil and paper into my
chubby little hands. Many thanks.
-*Scott*

TIME AFTER TIME: FROM 1602 TO 2004
by Peter Sanderson

Many admirers of the work of Neil Gaiman must have felt confounded on learning that he was writing a comic series about Marvel super heroes. Gaiman, after all, had first achieved fame through creating his Sandman comics series for DC Comics. *Sandman's* cerebral, contemplative mood, its sophisticated prose style and thematic content, and its somber title character would seem to have nothing in common with the dynamic fight scenes, fervid melodrama and vividly colorful costumed characters one associates with Marvel super hero books. Gaiman has followed much the same route in his novels and screenplays. Was writing a super hero story taking a step—or a whole series of steps—backwards?

But a unifying theme in Gaiman's work is his interest in mythology. In Sandman, Gaiman devised a contemporary mythology of his own, incorporating existing DC Comics characters, even DC's previous Sandmen, who were super heroes.

It should therefore be no surprise that Gaiman is interested in exploring the mythic underpinnings of Marvel's super hero mythos as well. The result, *1602*, is a surprising reinterpretation of Stan Lee's classic Marvel characters in Gaiman's style, superlatively illustrated by Andy Kubert. The familiar heroes and villains in *1602* are still recognizably Stan Lee's co-creations, and yet they would not seem out of place wandering into one of Gaiman's other stories.

Gaiman's basic device for penetrating to the heart of these characters is a simple one: what if these familiar Marvel heroes had existed in early 17th-century England instead of originating in 20th-century America? Gaiman narrowed his focus to the characters featured in the Marvel Comics of the 1960s, "the Silver Age of Comics." This is the period when editor/writer Stan Lee, together with Jack Kirby, Steve Ditko and other artists created, scores of characters who remain leading figures of the fictional "Marvel Universe" to this day.

People think of the super hero as a creation of the 20th century, but it is really a modern guise for character archetypes that have endured throughout the history of literature. In reconceiving these classic Marvel heroes and villains in terms of Renaissance England, Gaiman shows us what remains the same about each character in such different circumstances. In other words, Gaiman demonstrates the timeless essence of Stan Lee and his collaborators' greatest creations.

For those readers who may be unacquainted with the core Marvel characters upon whom Gaiman based much of his *1602* cast, introductions may be necessary.

One may seem more at home in the past than in the present day: the wizard Doctor Strange. Another would easily find a role to play in any time period: the soldier turned spymaster, Nick Fury.

Most of you are surely familiar with Stan Lee's most celebrated co-creation, Spider-Man, swinging exuberantly amid Manhattan skyscrapers on his webbing. But in *1602* Gaiman presents his version of Peter Parker as he was before he was bitten by the irradiated spider: a studious, introverted youth grappling with questions of moral responsibility.

Lee and Kirby's first Silver Age heroes were the Fantastic Four, a team of explorers of the unknown, linked by ties of blood, marriage and comradeship into a family. Their leader, Reed Richards, is a scientific visionary whose mind reaches beyond the knowledge of his time just as he has the power to stretch his physical body. His wife, Susan Storm, can take on ghostly invisibility, while her brother, Johnny, the Human Torch, resembles an elemental being of fire. Their best friend, Ben Grimm, is a tragic figure, a man transformed into a superhumanly strong, grotesque monster, the Thing.

The Irish-American Matt Murdock was blinded by radiation that, as if in compensation, greatly heightened his other senses. This paradox enabled him to become the vigilante Daredevil, who has been portrayed both as a witty, acrobatic modern-day swashbuckler, and as an implacable "devil" serving the cause of justice.

From Norse mythology comes Thor, thunder god of the Vikings, who, in Lee and Kirby's version, took on frail, human form to walk among the mortals he protects.

Another of their creations, Bruce Banner, unquestionably served his government superiors in creating a new form of weaponry, and ended up being transformed into a living embodiment of its destructive power, the marauding Hulk.

There were not only individual superhumans emerging on Earth, but an entire race of mutants, hunted by humans who feared them. From among this persecuted minority two leaders have arisen. One is Magneto, who believes that mutants constitute a master race whose destiny is to supplant humankind. The other is Professor Charles Xavier, a teacher and prophet of a vision of peaceful coexistence between the races. Xavier has gathered about himself a community of young disciples, the mutants he calls his X-Men.

Into this new wave of super heroes Lee and Kirby reintroduced a hero from the 1940s: Captain America, the everyman who became the guardian of his country and its democratic ideals.

And there are many more characters whom Gaiman transplants into this 1602 setting. Two are of particular importance. One is Richards' archenemy and only intellectual rival, Doctor Victor von Doom, a sinister genius whose armored mask hides his ravaged face.

The other is Uatu the Watcher, an alien version of the Man in the Moon, who observes the struggles of humanity like a god peering down at Earth, yet has vowed never to intervene in their lives.

In 1602 Gaiman's versions of these fictional characters interact with iconic figures from history. There is the elderly Queen Elizabeth I, the last of the Tudor line of monarchs, and her successor, James I of Scotland. England's early settlement in America, the Roanoke colony, was real, as was Virginia Dare, the first person of British descent who was born in America. In actual history, the Roanoke colonists mysteriously disappeared, but legends arose about Virginia Dare, who was alleged to have survived.

From this melding of fictional fantasy and historical reality, Gaiman has crafted a saga with perhaps unexpected thematic richness. Gaiman examines the role of the older generation in guiding the younger. He also deals extensively with religion, showing how it can be warped into a rationale for repression. In contrast, there is Reed's belief that God means people to fulfill the potential of their talents.

The cast of 1602 find themselves in the early years of a new century, as we do now, and within such a short time their world and ours have changed radically. Like today's America, 1602's Britain finds itself threatened by terror from abroad, resulting in the invasion of a foreign tyrant's domain.

Moreover, with the death of good Queen Elizabeth, the years of stability to which her subjects became accustomed come to an abrupt end. A new ruler, James, sacrifices people's lives and livelihoods in asserting his power. Loyalists to the previous regime find that "their" England is no more. Have their lives been wasted? What does one do when your world collapses around you?

Like characters in past Gaiman works, certain persons in 1602 must decide whether to change their vision of right and wrong to adapt to an altered world. When does moral principle become blind, destructive absolutism? How far can they compromise with evil in order to achieve a greater good? Watch in particular as one major character, fallen into despair, paradoxically reemerges through both betrayal and self-sacrifice to stand revealed as the series' unexpected hero.

1602 demonstrates that the classic Marvel characters have a universality that enables them to work in any time or place. But, in yet another of the series' paradoxes, Gaiman also uses 1602 to show us how distinctly American these heroes are.

One way in which Marvel revolutionized the genre is in depicting super heroes as outsiders and even outlaws. Unable to return to James's newly repressive England, many of the 1602 heroes immigrate to America, there to help found a nation free from monarchs, where people, fleeing political, religious and racial oppression, can start their lives anew. It is a nation where everyone, no matter how different—even mutants and monsters—can live together in peace and prosperity. 1602 thereby ties together Xavier's dream with that of the Founding Fathers. Super heroes are icons of the freedom of the individual; a community of super heroes becomes a metaphor for democracy itself.

On the surface 1602 is about Britain in the 17th century. In reality, 1602 is a remarkable work about America, and it is about now.

PETER SANDERSON is a popular culture critic and historian specializing in comics. He was Marvel Comics' first archivist, is the author of Marvel Universe (Harry N. Abrams), and reviews graphic novels for Publishers Weekly. Mr. Sanderson begins teaching "Comics as Literature" at New York University in the fall of 2004 and writes the weekly online column "Comics in Context" for IGN FilmForce.

IN WHICH WE ARE INTRODUCED TO CERTAIN OF OUR PLAYERS

1602

PART ONE

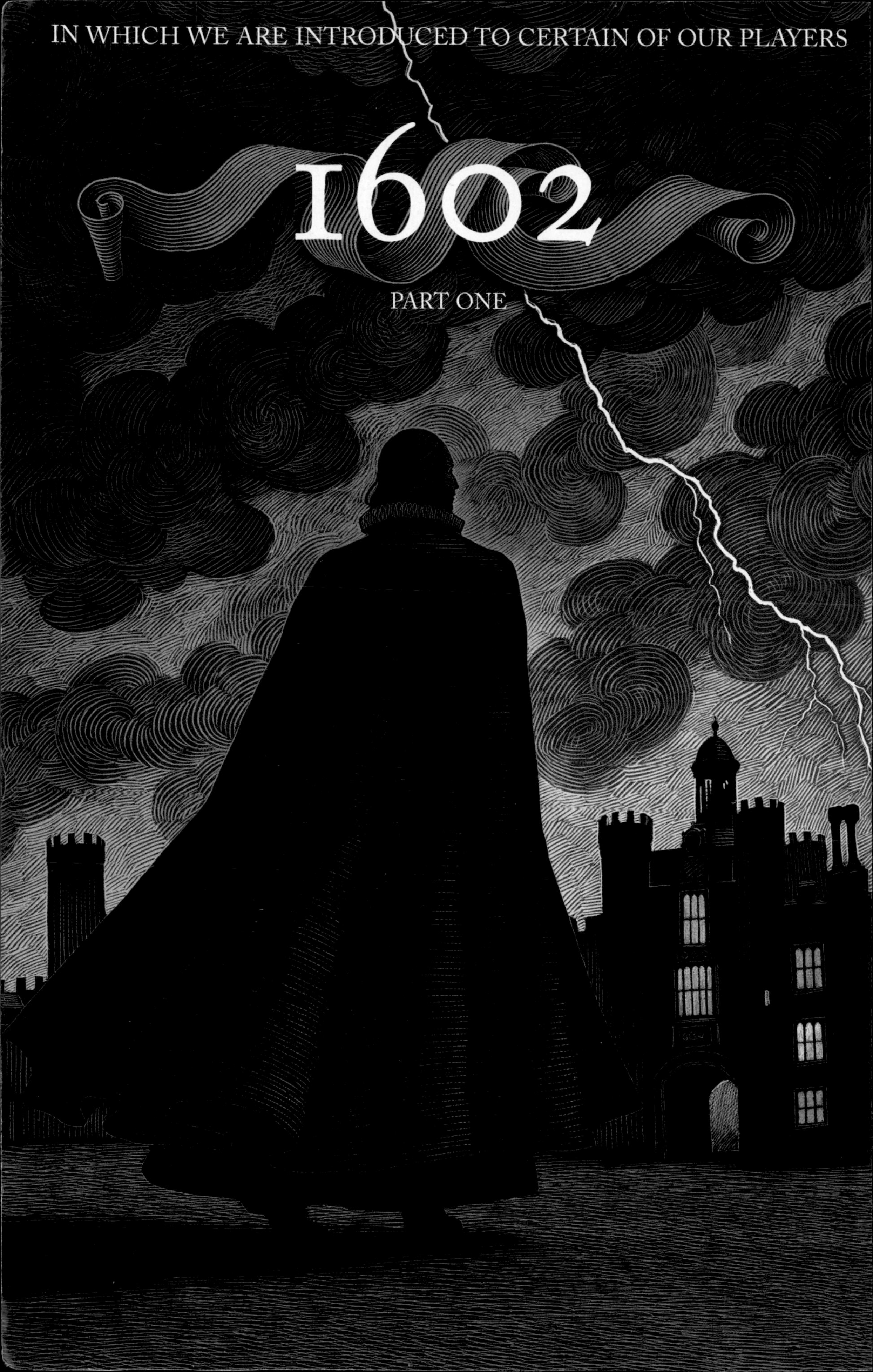

- 1602 -
March. Hampton Court. England.

"For a whole week the skies over London have been *blood red* at noon. We have reports here from all over our *kingdom.* Reports of *thunderstorms,* with thunder-claps loud enough to *deafen,* and *lightnings* that strike churches and towers alike, but not one *drop* of rain that falls.

"Look at *this--*

"Where did I put it?"

"Ah yes. *Look. Earthquakes* tumbled our city of York. The fens are *flooded.* And from what you are saying, such things are happening across Europe--perhaps across the world."

Yes, Majesty. I believe so.

You understand, Sir Nicholas, there are those in court who say that this---*koff! koff!*---means we are entering the *final* days. That the *world* will end in fire and darkness soon enough. What do you say to *that?* Eh?

I'm afraid Armageddon is rather outside my *department,* Majesty.

Ah, the good Doctor. Right on time.

What say *you* then, good sir Doctor? Is the *world* truly *ending?*

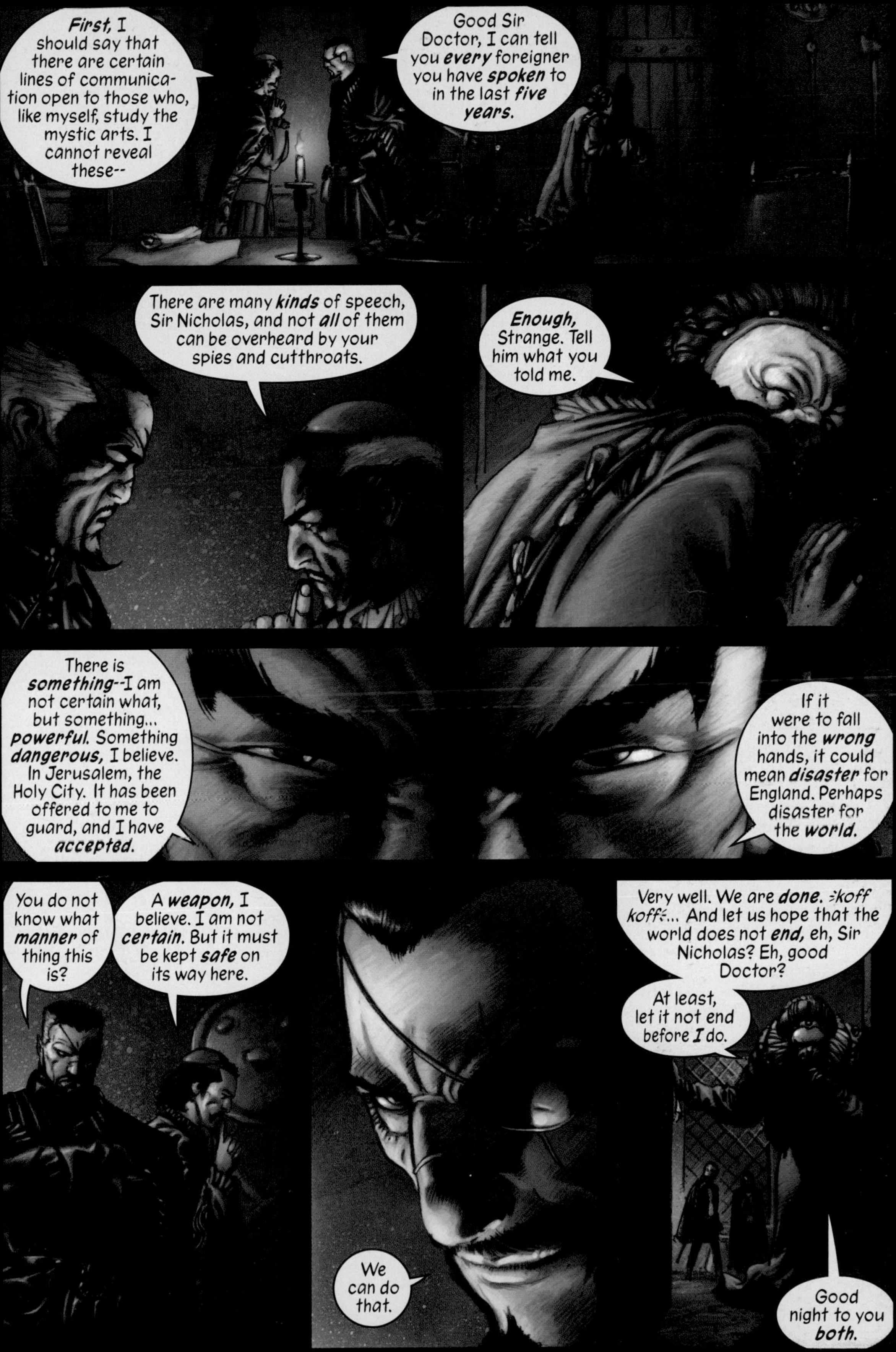
First, I should say that there are certain lines of communica-tion open to those who, like myself, study the mystic arts. I cannot reveal these--
Good Sir Doctor, I can tell you every foreigner you have spoken to in the last five years.
There are many kinds of speech, Sir Nicholas, and not all of them can be overheard by your spies and cutthroats.
Enough, Strange. Tell him what you told me.
There is something--I am not certain what, but something... powerful. Something dangerous, I believe. In Jerusalem, the Holy City. It has been offered to me to guard, and I have accepted.
If it were to fall into the wrong hands, it could mean disaster for England. Perhaps disaster for the world.
You do not know what manner of thing this is?
A weapon, I believe. I am not certain. But it must be kept safe on its way here.
We can do that.
Very well. We are done. *koff koff*... And let us hope that the world does not end, eh, Sir Nicholas? Eh, good Doctor?
At least, let it not end before I do.
Good night to you both.

The High Tower in the Palace of the Inquisition. Domdaniel. Spain.

Yesterday, they burned a *Jew*. He was a secret Jew--his grandfathers had converted to Christianity to stay in Spain--but still, he did not work on the Sabbath, and he ate no pork, which was how they found him out.

I could *smell* him burning from up here.

A stench of woodsmoke and burning hair, then a smell of meat, cooking. There were *screams*. He called on his God to protect him.

Last night--my captors told me as if it was not important--a heretic died, being tortured. They were *disappointed*. A waste of a death.

They have not tortured me. Not *physically*.

I have been left here, chained in this tower, able to feel the winds on my face and skin. Sometimes they ask me questions.

They ask as friends, enquiring after my health and livelihood:

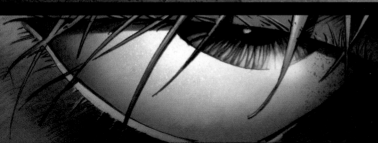

Who *hid* me as I grew? Who *protected* me? Did I kiss the Devil's *rump* before I grew my wings? Do I have *friends* who are *witchbreed*?

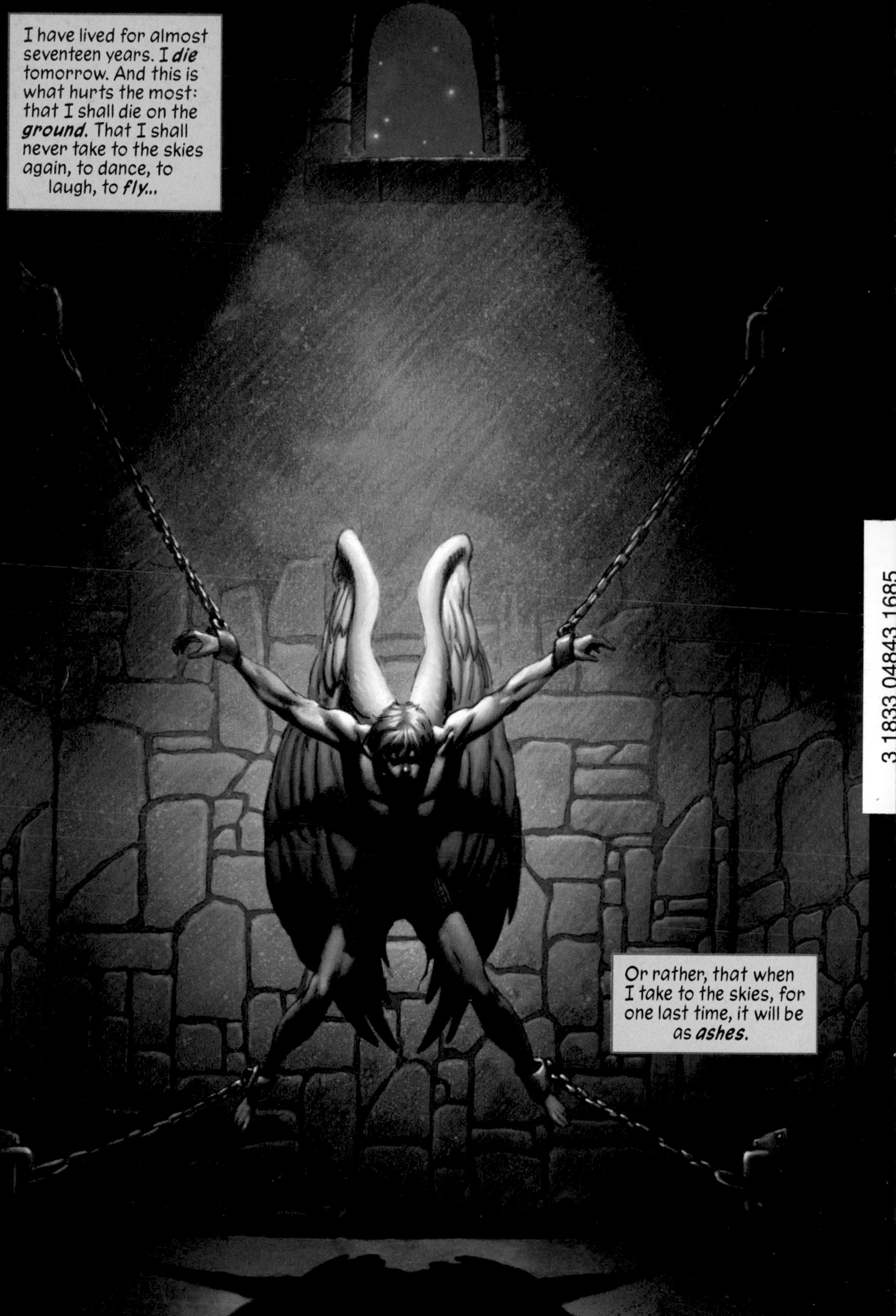
I have lived for almost seventeen years. I *die* tomorrow. And this is what hurts the most: that I shall die on the ***ground***. That I shall never take to the skies again, to dance, to laugh, to ***fly***...
Or rather, that when I take to the skies, for one last time, it will be as ***ashes***.

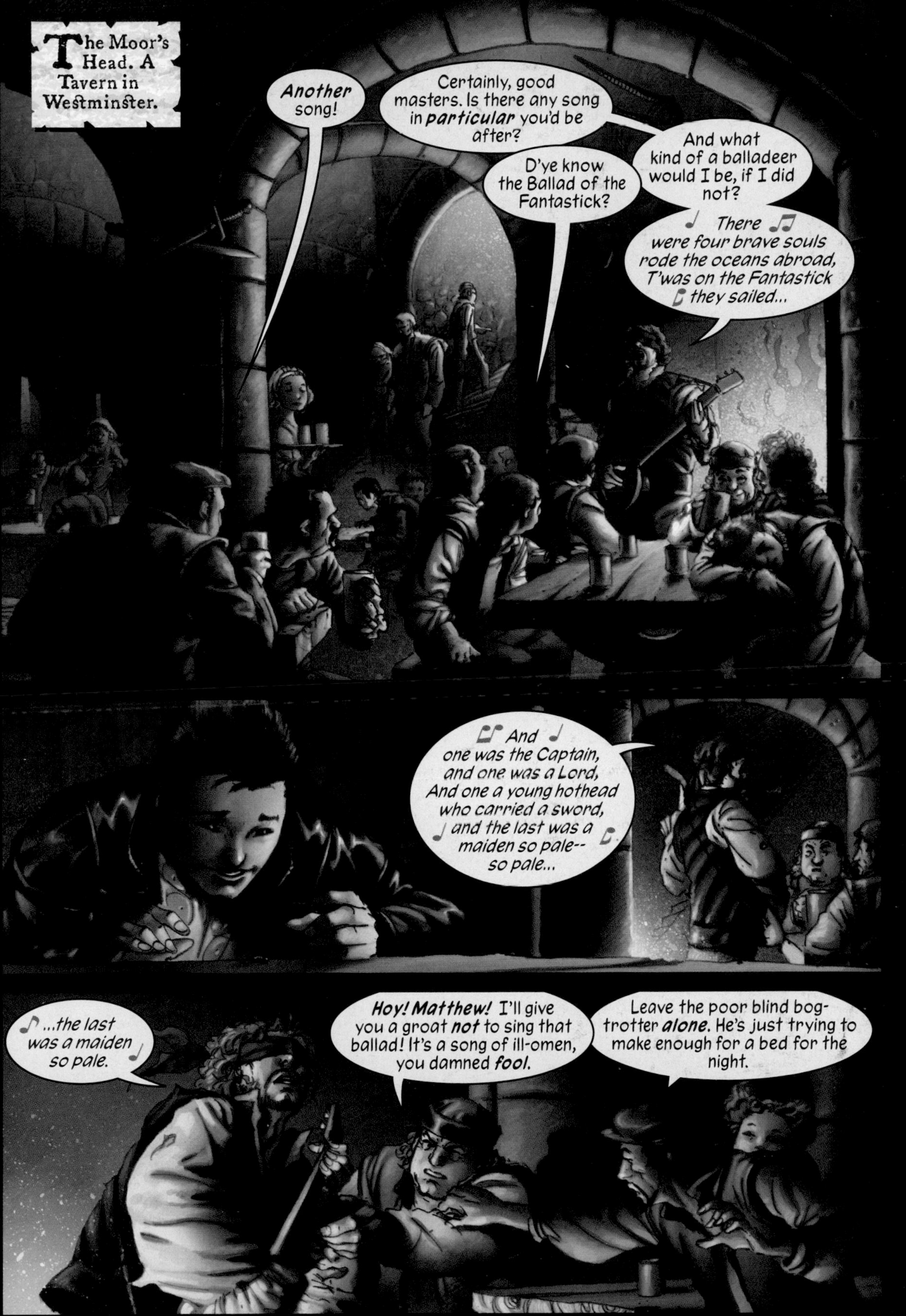
The Moor's Head. A Tavern in Westminster.
Another song!
Certainly, good masters. Is there any song in *particular* you'd be after?
D'ye know the Ballad of the Fantastick?
And what kind of a balladeer would I be, if I did not?
♩ *There* ♫ *were four brave souls rode the oceans abroad, T'was on the Fantastick* ♪ *they sailed...*
♫ *And* ♩ *one was the Captain, and one was a Lord, And one a young hothead who carried a sword,* ♩ *and the last was a maiden so pale--* ♪ *so pale...*
♪ *...the last was a maiden* ♩ *so pale.*
Hoy! Matthew! I'll give you a groat **not** to sing that ballad! It's a song of ill-omen, you damned **fool.**
Leave the poor blind bog-trotter **alone.** He's just trying to make enough for a bed for the night.

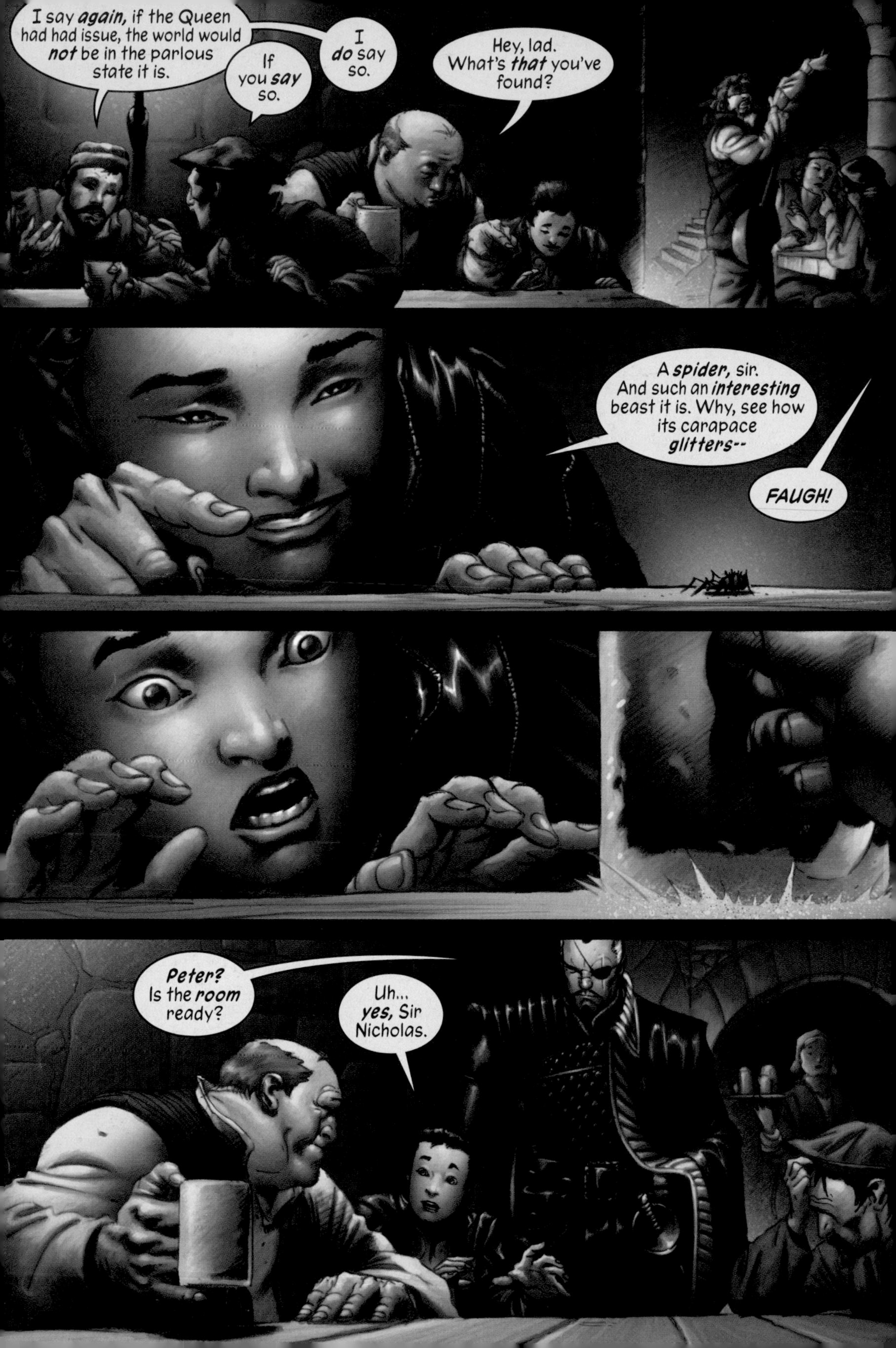

I say *again,* if the Queen had had issue, the world would *not* be in the parlous state it is.
If you *say* so.
I *do* say so.
Hey, lad. What's *that* you've found?
A *spider,* sir. And such an *interesting* beast it is. Why, see how its carapace *glitters--*
FAUGH!
Peter? Is the *room* ready?
Uh... *yes,* Sir Nicholas.

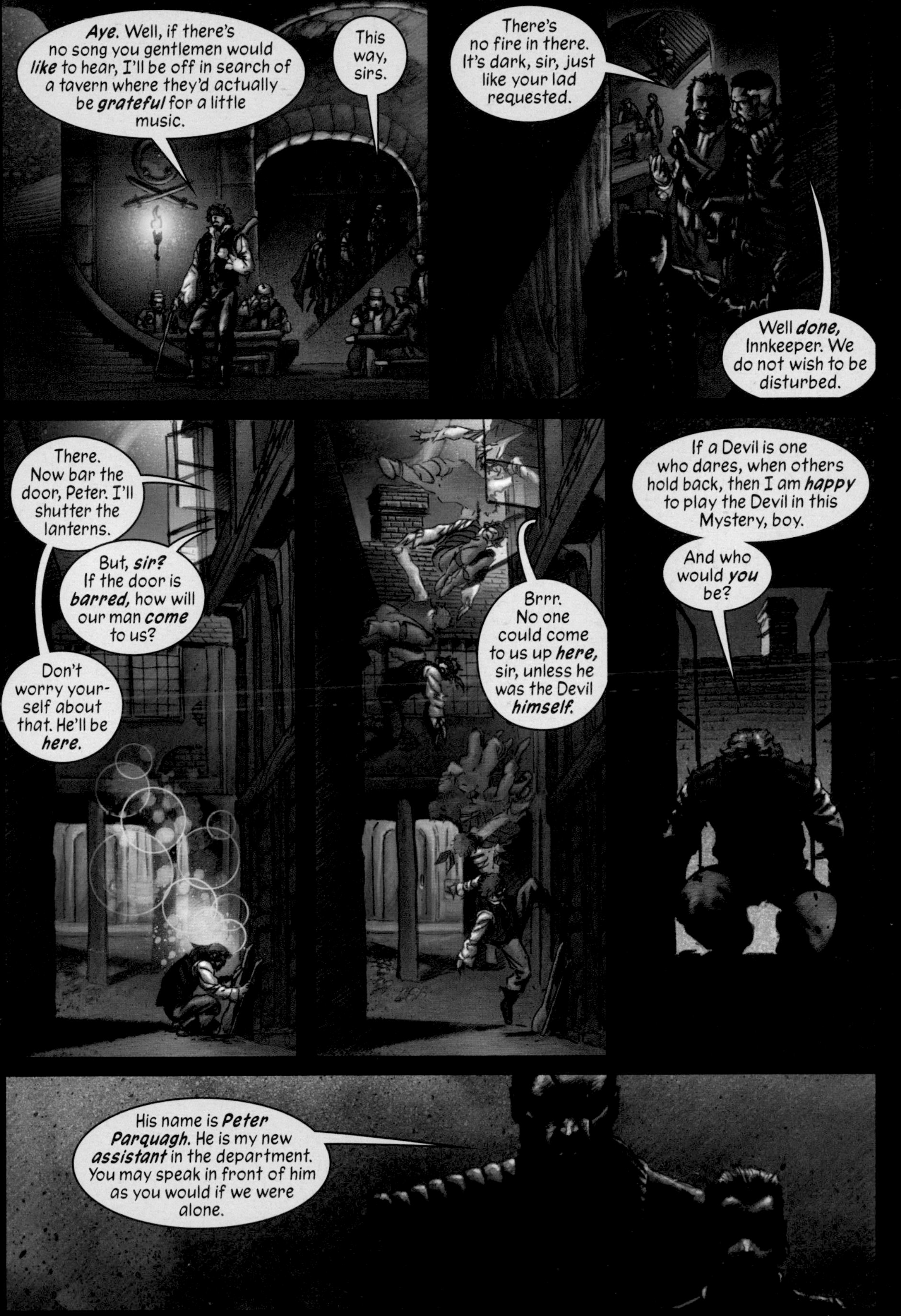
Aye. Well, if there's no song you gentlemen would like to hear, I'll be off in search of a tavern where they'd actually be grateful for a little music.
This way, sirs.
There's no fire in there. It's dark, sir, just like your lad requested.
Well done, Innkeeper. We do not wish to be disturbed.
There. Now bar the door, Peter. I'll shutter the lanterns.
But, sir? If the door is barred, how will our man come to us?
Don't worry yourself about that. He'll be here.
Brrr. No one could come to us up here, sir, unless he was the Devil himself.
If a Devil is one who dares, when others hold back, then I am happy to play the Devil in this Mystery, boy.
And who would you be?
His name is Peter Parquagh. He is my new assistant in the department. You may speak in front of him as you would if we were alone.

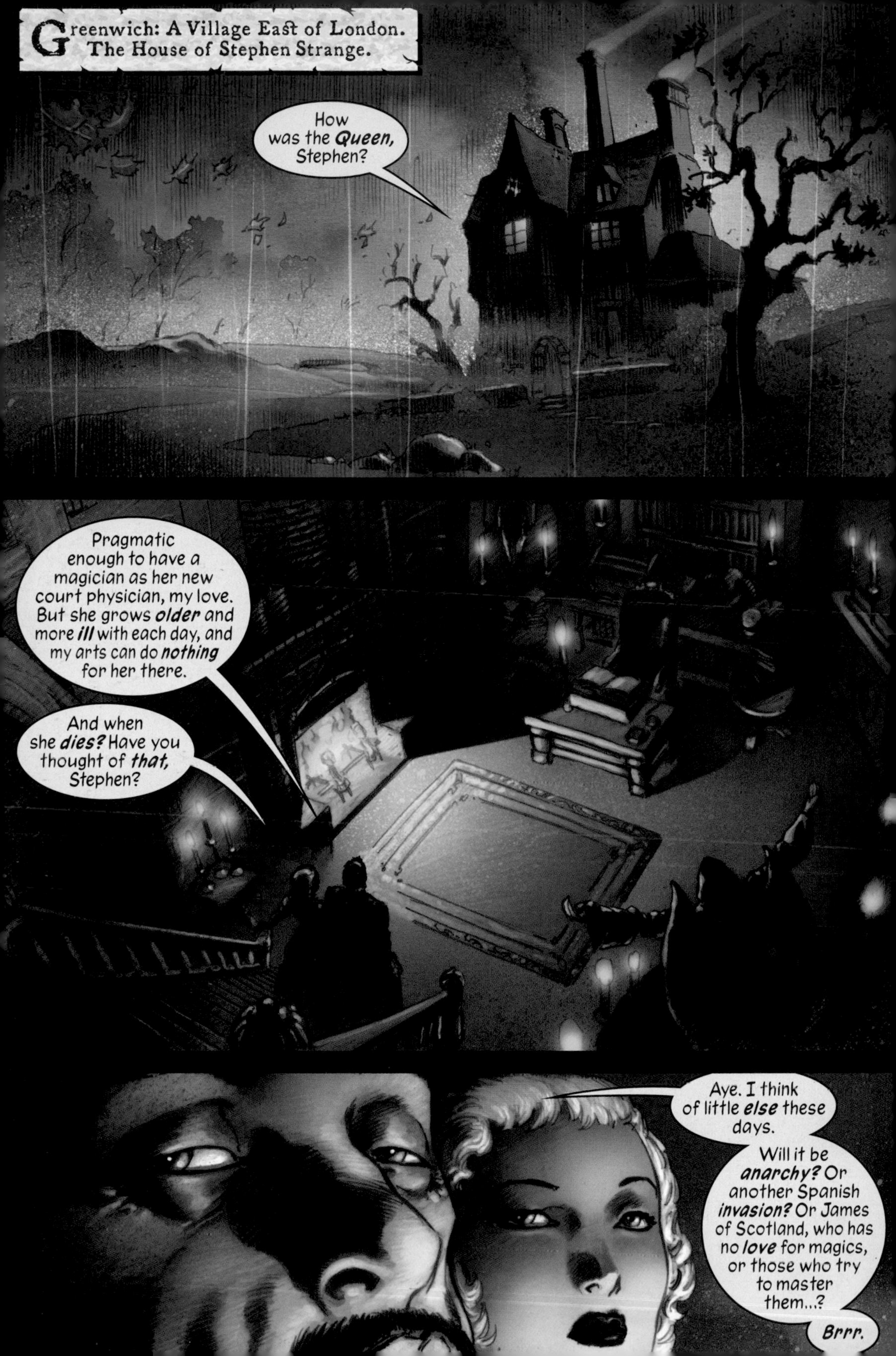
Greenwich: A Village East of London. The House of Stephen Strange.
How was the Queen, Stephen?
Pragmatic enough to have a magician as her new court physician, my love. But she grows older and more ill with each day, and my arts can do nothing for her there.
And when she dies? Have you thought of that, Stephen?
Aye. I think of little else these days.
Will it be anarchy? Or another Spanish invasion? Or James of Scotland, who has no love for magics, or those who try to master them...?
Brrr.

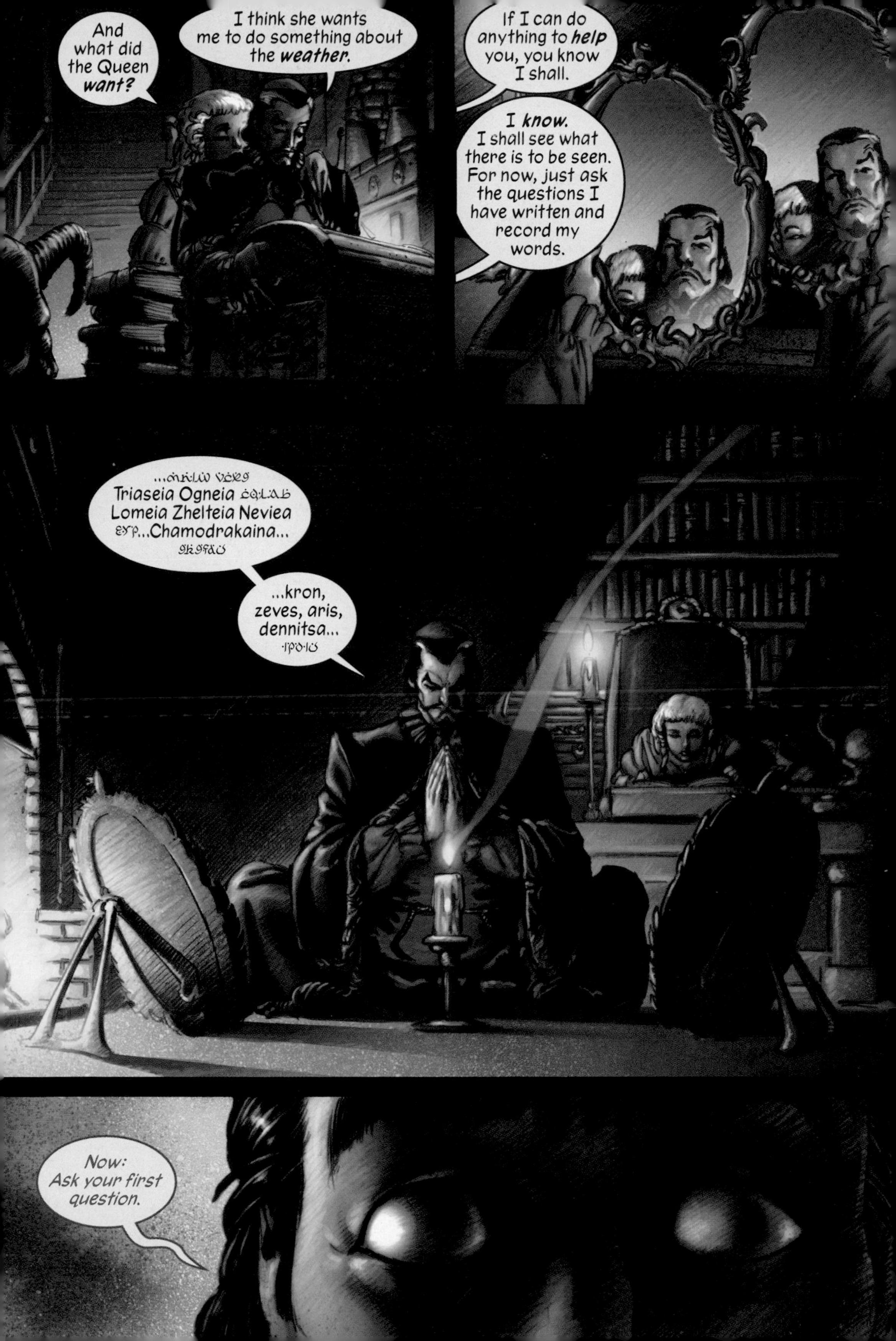
And what did the Queen *want?*
I think she wants me to do something about the *weather.*
If I can do anything to *help* you, you know I shall.
I *know.* I shall see what there is to be seen. For now, just ask the questions I have written and record my words.
...Triaseia Ogneia
Lomeia Zhelteia Neviea
...Chamodrakaina...
...kron, zeves, aris, dennitsa...
Now: Ask your first question.

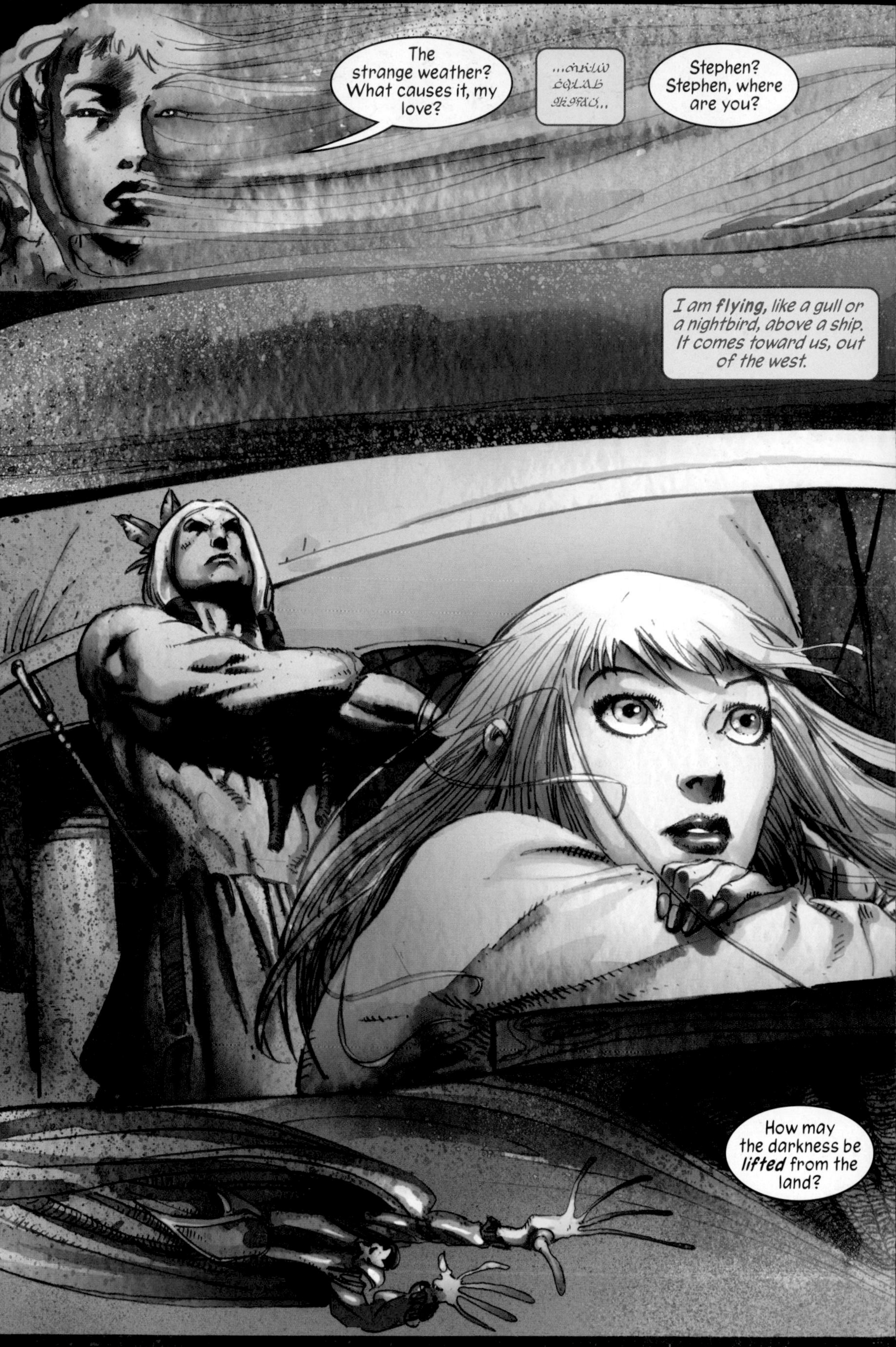
The strange weather? What causes it, my love?
Stephen? Stephen, where are you?
I am **flying**, like a gull or a nightbird, above a ship. It comes toward us, out of the west.
How may the darkness be ***lifted*** from the land?

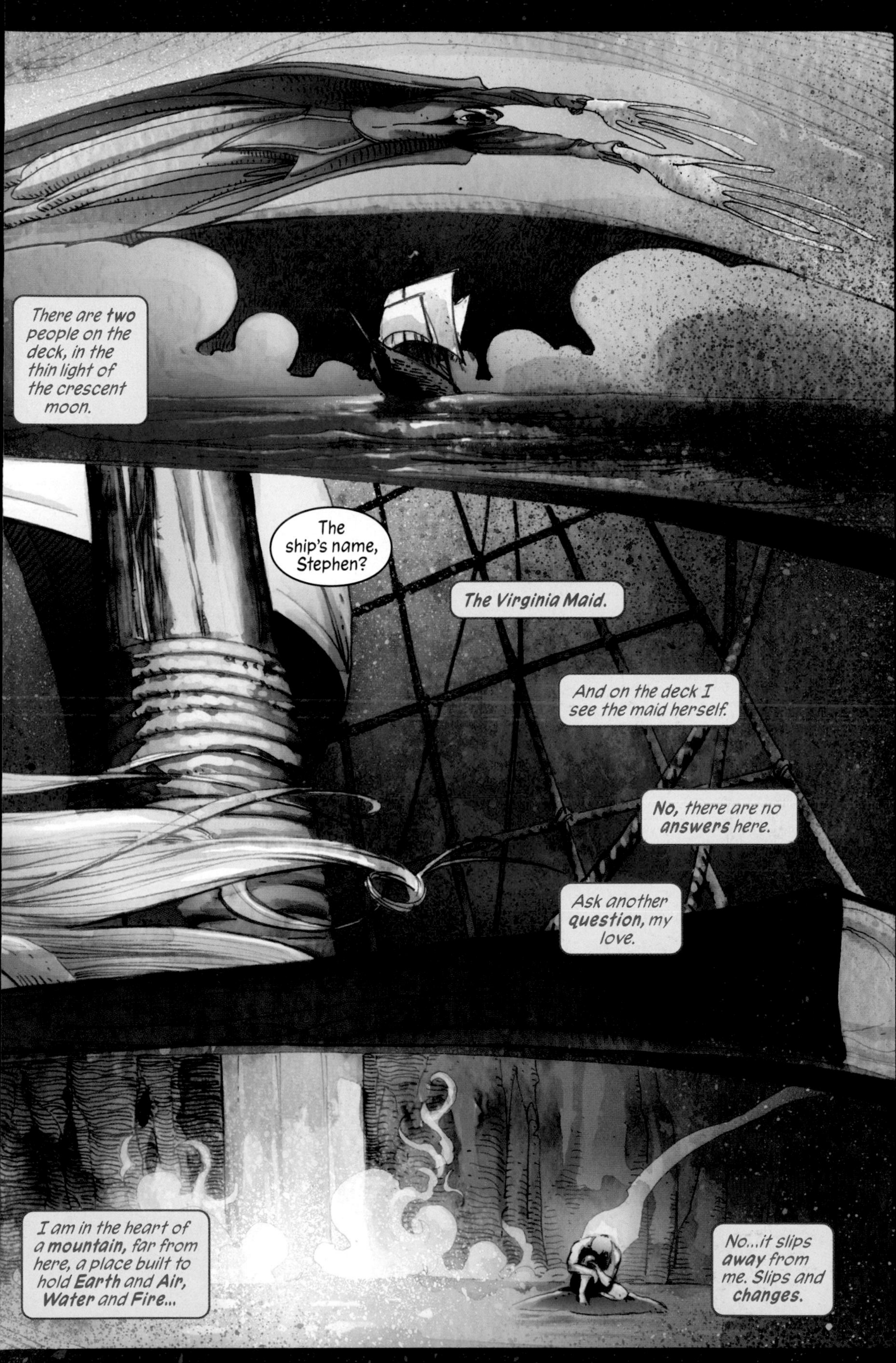
There are two people on the deck, in the thin light of the crescent moon.
The ship's name, Stephen?
The Virginia Maid.
And on the deck I see the maid herself.
No, there are no answers here.
Ask another question, my love.
I am in the heart of a mountain, far from here, a place built to hold Earth and Air, Water and Fire...
No...it slips away from me. Slips and changes.

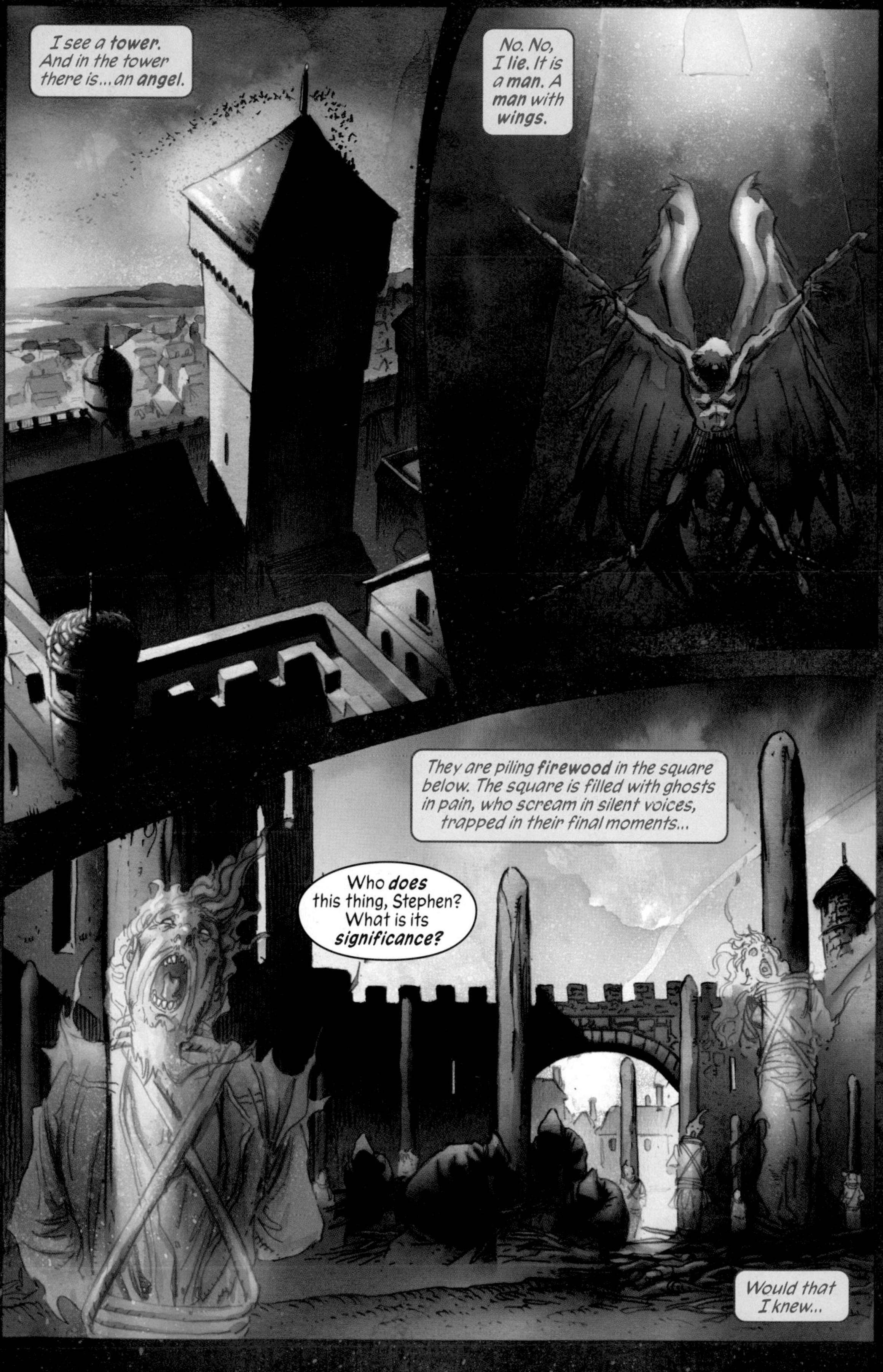
I see a tower. And in the tower there is...an angel.
No. No, I lie. It is a man. A man with wings.
They are piling firewood in the square below. The square is filled with ghosts in pain, who scream in silent voices, trapped in their final moments...
Who does this thing, Stephen? What is its significance?
Would that I knew...

Nothing, Grand Inquisitor. Perhaps...perhaps I simply *imagined* it.

I *doubt* it.

No, it was *Javier.* I have no doubt on *that* score.

Petros? Send a message to the guard: they must be *extra* vigilant at tomorrow's burning.

Yes sir.

You may *leave* us, Sister Wanda.

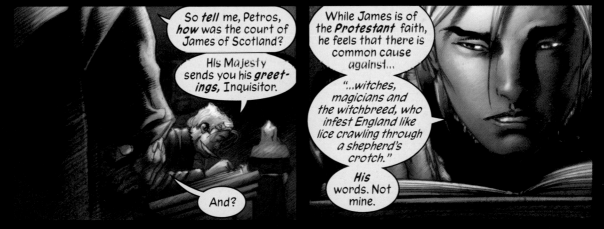

So *tell* me, Petros, *how* was the court of James of Scotland?

His Majesty sends you his *greet-ings,* Inquisitor.

And?

While James is of the *Protestant* faith, he feels that there is common cause against...

"...witches, magicians and the witchbreed, who infest England like lice crawling through a shepherd's crotch."

His words. Not mine.

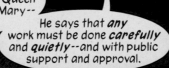

So is there room for an *alliance?*

He told me that the English have *long* memories. They have not yet forgotten Queen Mary--they call her Bloody Mary--and her burnings.

He says that *any* work must be done *carefully* and *quietly*--and with public support and approval.

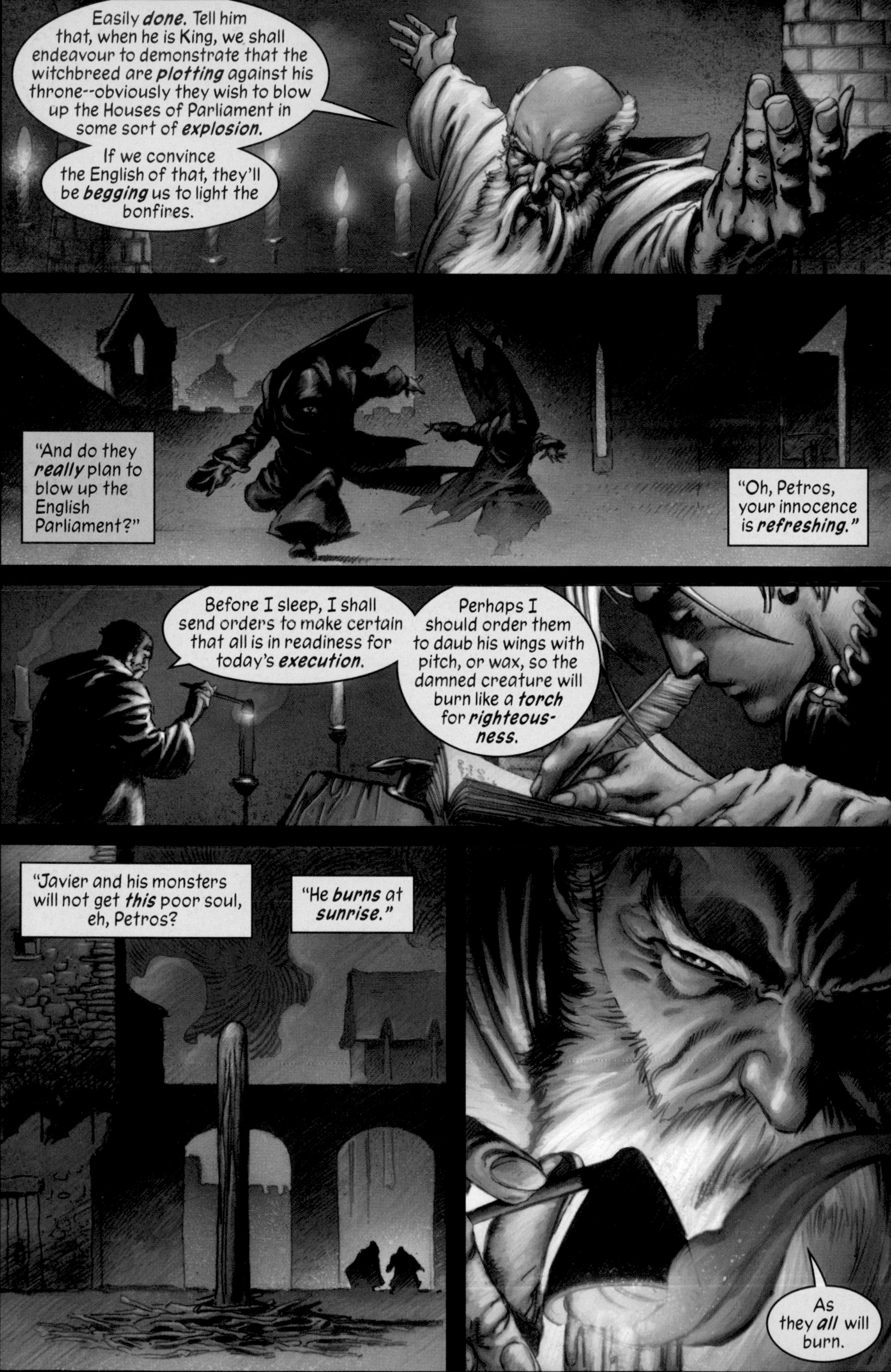
Easily *done*. Tell him that, when he is King, we shall endeavour to demonstrate that the witchbreed are *plotting* against his throne--obviously they wish to blow up the Houses of Parliament in some sort of *explosion*.
If we convince the English of that, they'll be *begging* us to light the bonfires.
"And do they *really* plan to blow up the English Parliament?"
"Oh, Petros, your innocence is *refreshing*."
Before I sleep, I shall send orders to make certain that all is in readiness for today's *execution*.
Perhaps I should order them to daub his wings with pitch, or wax, so the damned creature will burn like a *torch* for *righteous-ness*.
"Javier and his monsters will not get *this* poor soul, eh, Petros?
"He *burns* at *sunrise*."
As they *all* will burn.

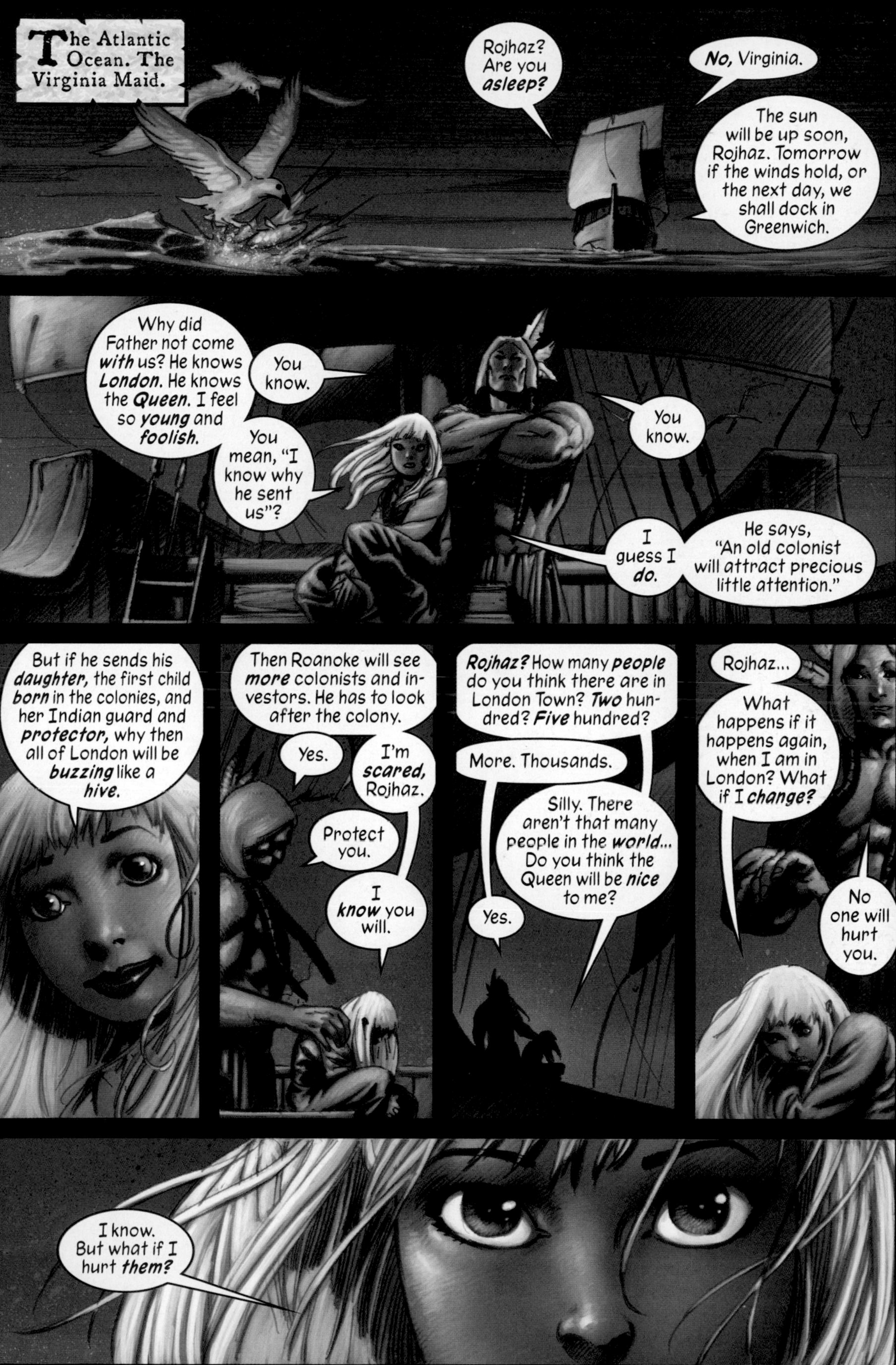
The Atlantic Ocean. The Virginia Maid.
Rojhaz? Are you *asleep?*
No, Virginia.
The sun will be up soon, Rojhaz. Tomorrow if the winds hold, or the next day, we shall dock in Greenwich.
Why did Father not come *with* us? He knows *London.* He knows the *Queen.* I feel so *young* and *foolish.*
You know.
You mean, "I know why he sent us"?
You know.
I guess I *do.*
He says, "An old colonist will attract precious little attention."
But if he sends his *daughter,* the first child *born* in the colonies, and her Indian guard and *protector,* why then all of London will be *buzzing* like a *hive.*
Then Roanoke will see *more* colonists and investors. He has to look after the colony.
Yes.
I'm *scared,* Rojhaz.
Protect you.
I *know* you will.
Rojhaz? How many *people* do you think there are in London Town? *Two* hundred? *Five* hundred?
More. Thousands.
Silly. There aren't that many people in the *world*... Do you think the Queen will be *nice* to me?
Yes.
Rojhaz...
What happens if it happens again, when I am in London? What if I *change?*
No one will hurt you.
I know. But what if I hurt *them?*

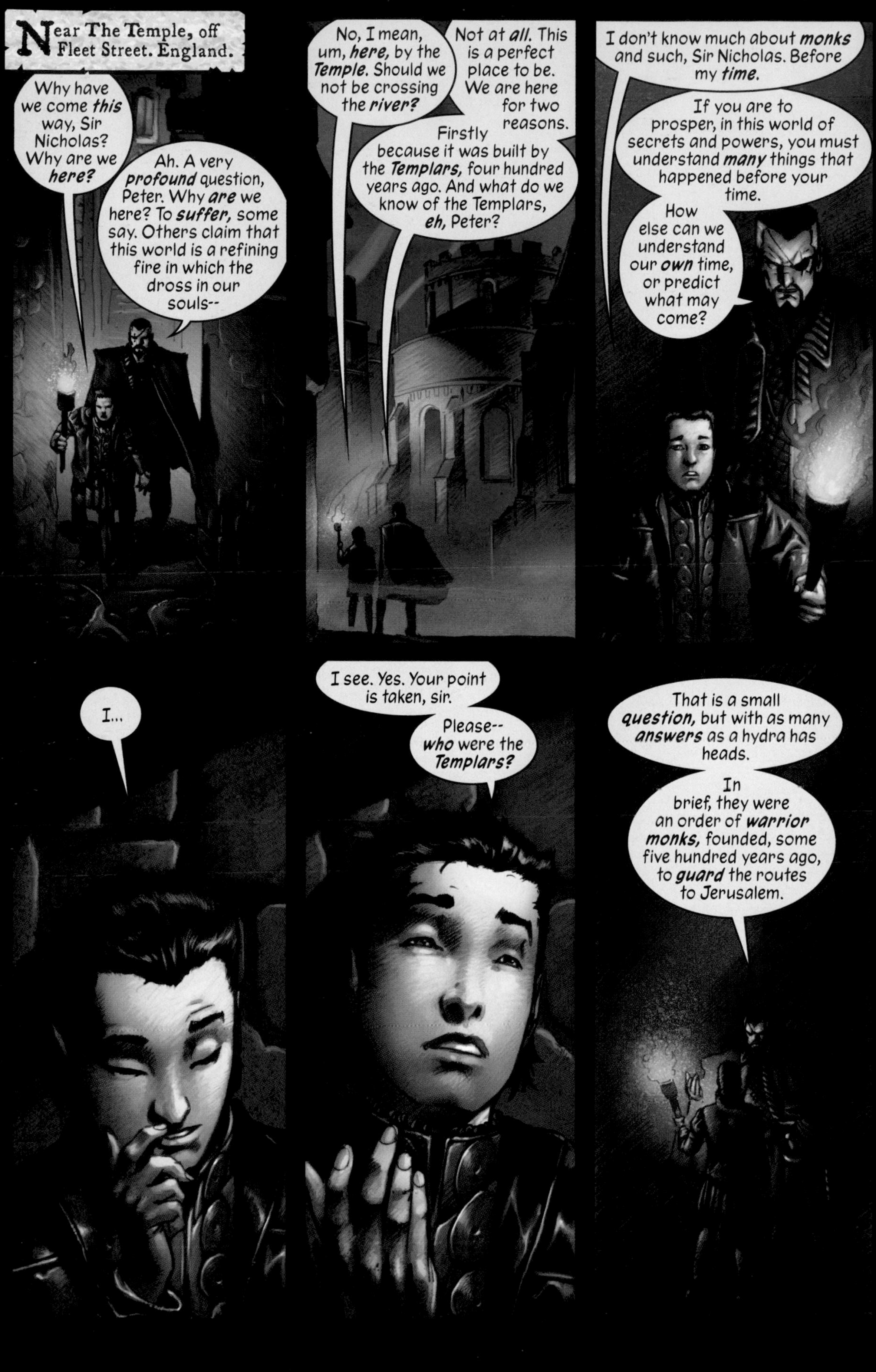
Near The Temple, off Fleet Street. England.
Why have we come this way, Sir Nicholas? Why are we here?
Ah. A very profound question, Peter. Why are we here? To suffer, some say. Others claim that this world is a refining fire in which the dross in our souls--
No, I mean, um, here, by the Temple. Should we not be crossing the river?
Not at all. This is a perfect place to be. We are here for two reasons.
Firstly because it was built by the Templars, four hundred years ago. And what do we know of the Templars, eh, Peter?
I don't know much about monks and such, Sir Nicholas. Before my time.
If you are to prosper, in this world of secrets and powers, you must understand many things that happened before your time.
How else can we understand our own time, or predict what may come?
I...
I see. Yes. Your point is taken, sir.
Please-- who were the Templars?
That is a small question, but with as many answers as a hydra has heads.
In brief, they were an order of warrior monks, founded, some five hundred years ago, to guard the routes to Jerusalem.

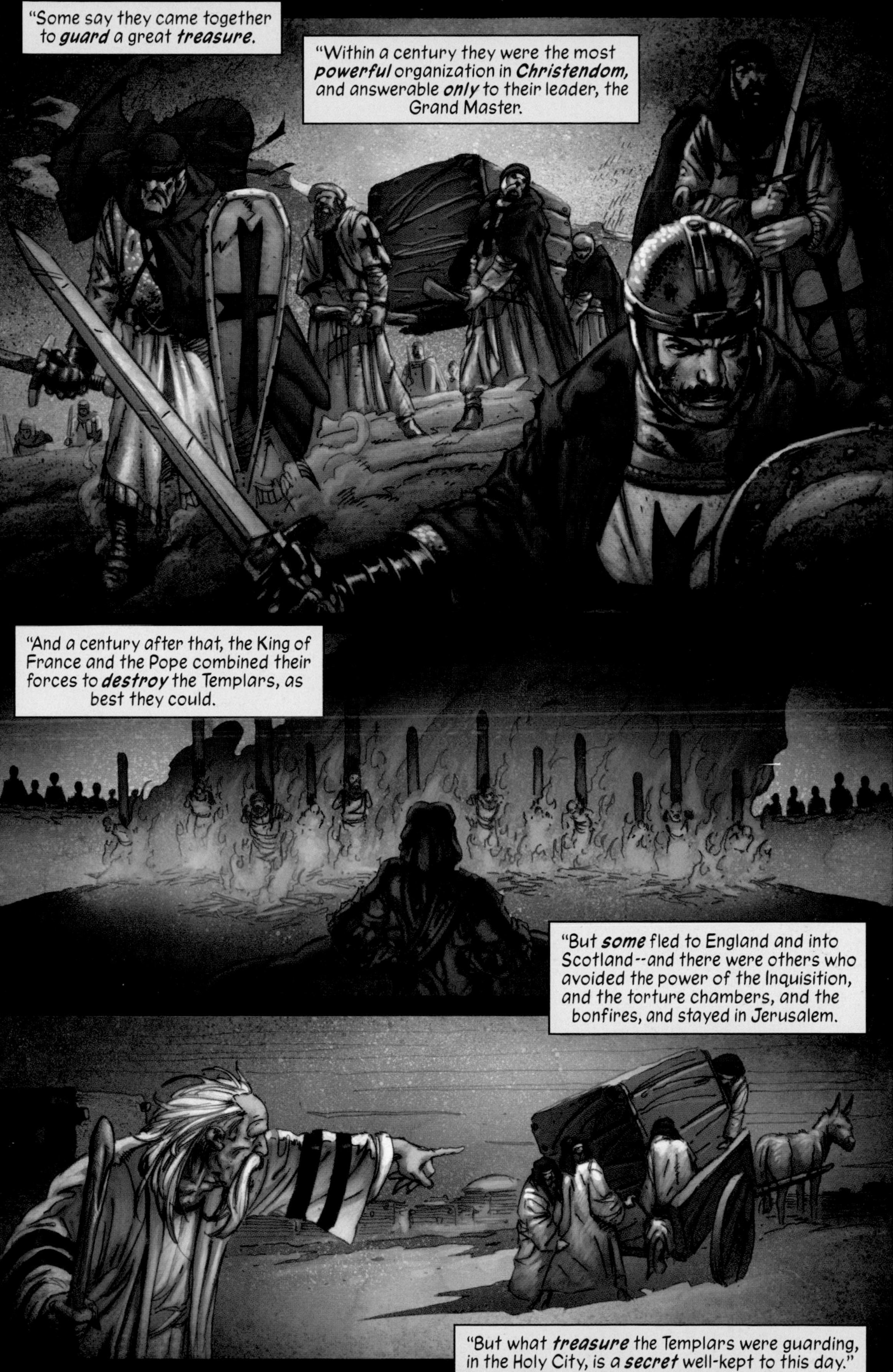
"Some say they came together to guard a great treasure.
"Within a century they were the most powerful organization in Christendom, and answerable only to their leader, the Grand Master.
"And a century after that, the King of France and the Pope combined their forces to destroy the Templars, as best they could.
"But some fled to England and into Scotland--and there were others who avoided the power of the Inquisition, and the torture chambers, and the bonfires, and stayed in Jerusalem.
"But what treasure the Templars were guarding, in the Holy City, is a secret well-kept to this day."

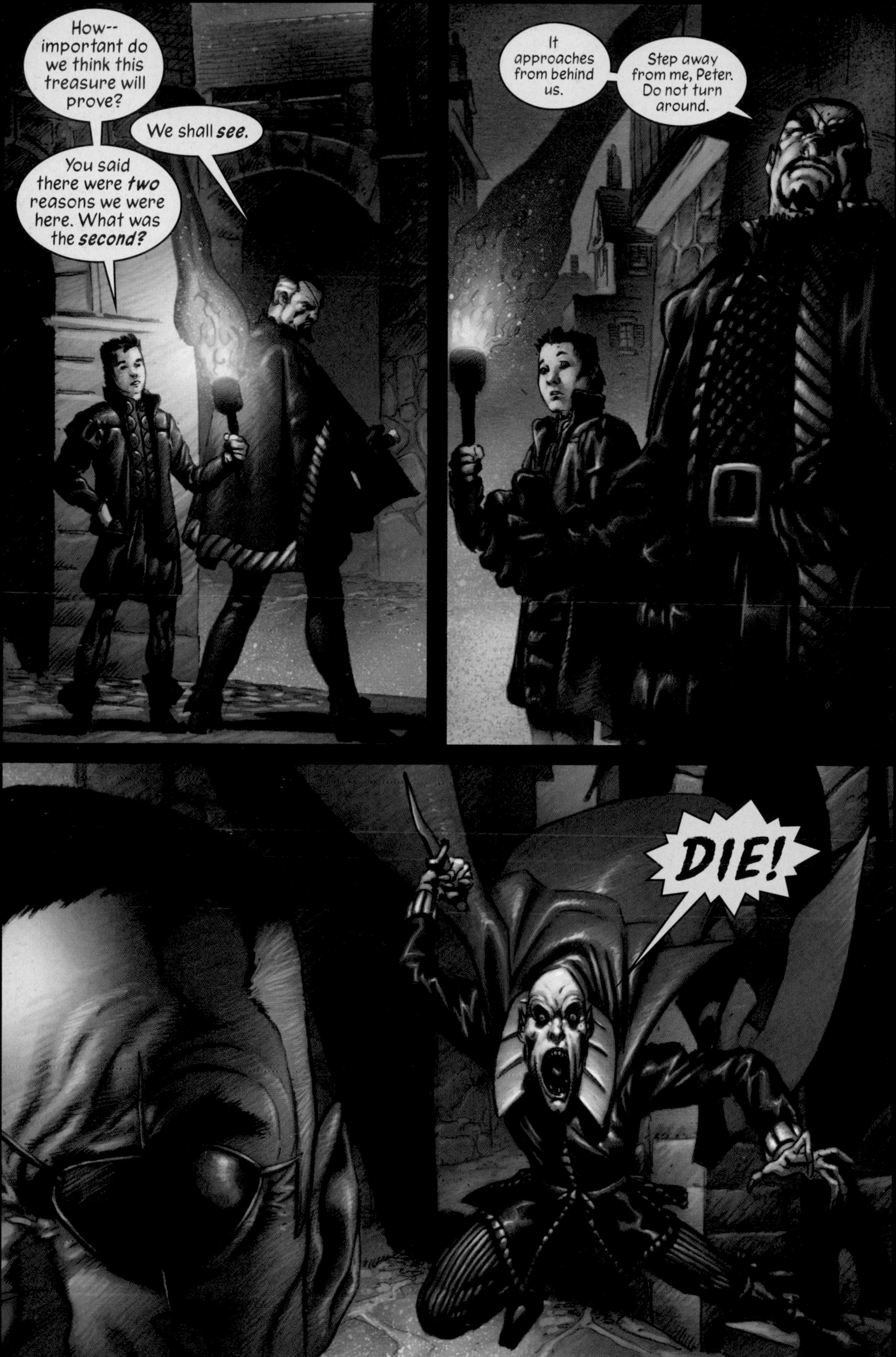
How-- important do we think this treasure will prove?
We shall see.
You said there were two reasons we were here. What was the second?
It approaches from behind us.
Step away from me, Peter. Do not turn around.
DIE!

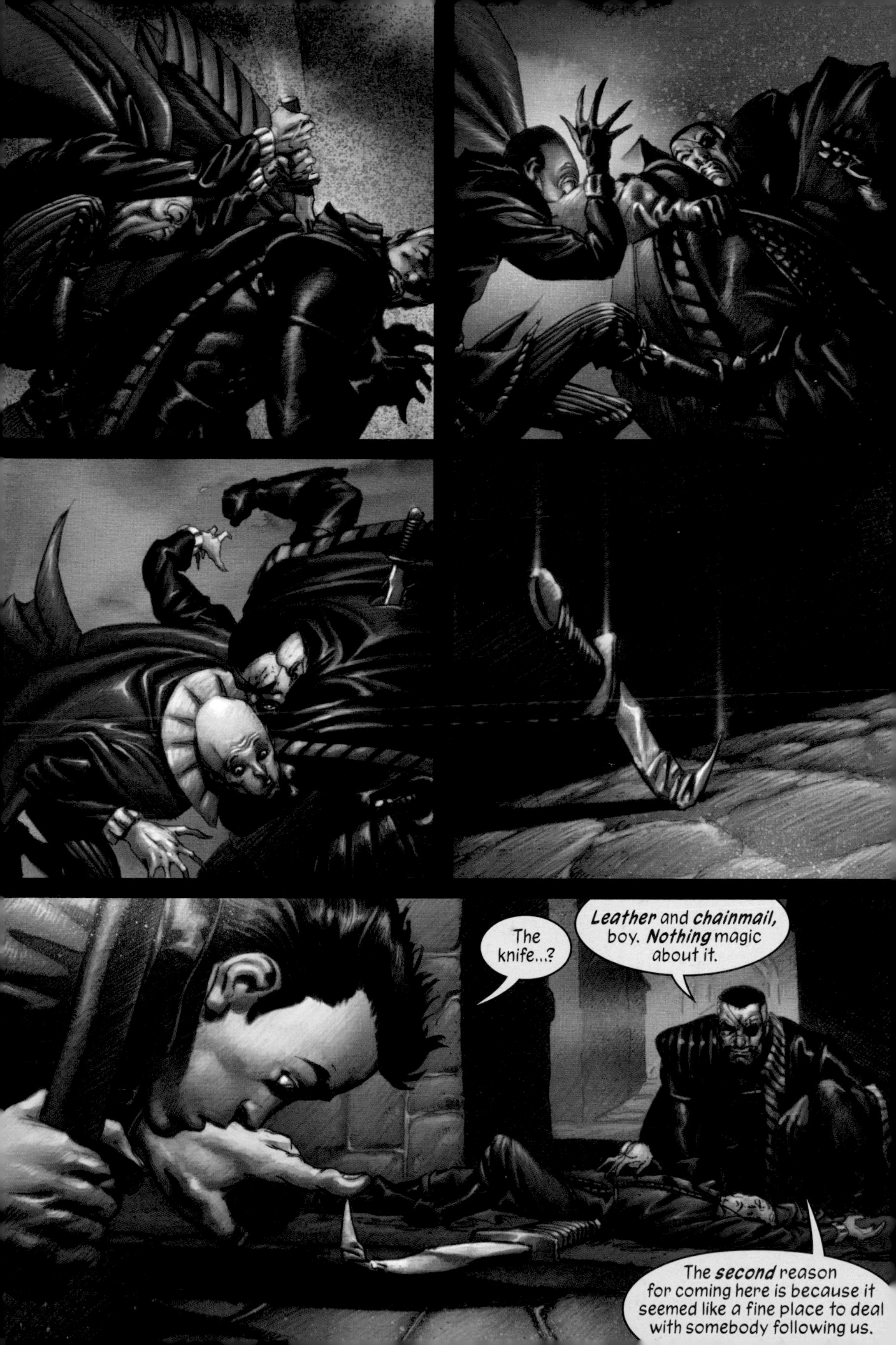
The knife...?
Leather and **chainmail,** boy. **Nothing** magic about it.
The **second** reason for coming here is because it seemed like a fine place to deal with somebody following us.

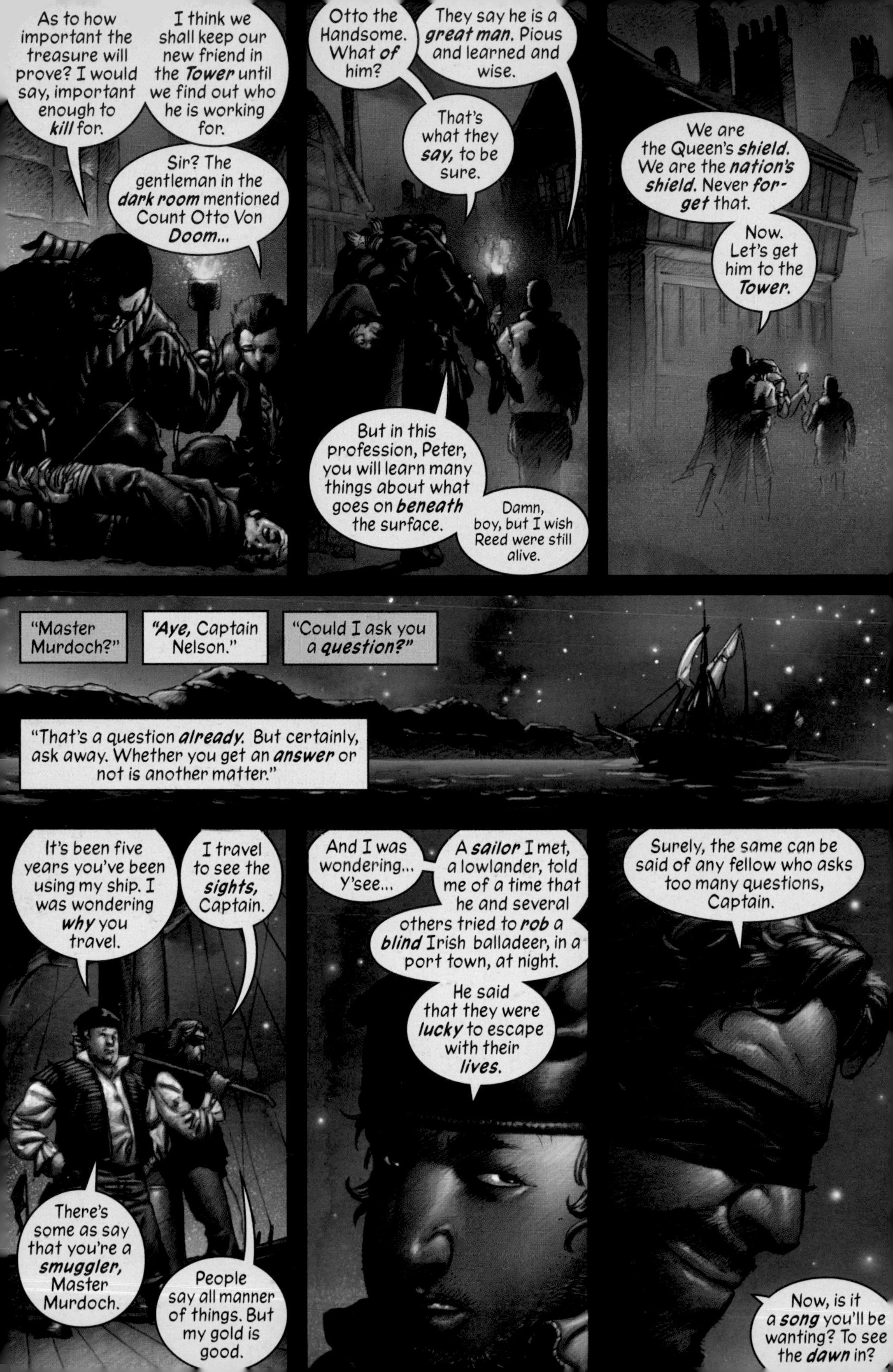
As to how important the treasure will prove? I would say, important enough to **kill** for.
I think we shall keep our new friend in the **Tower** until we find out who he is working for.
Sir? The gentleman in the **dark room** mentioned Count Otto Von **Doom...**
Otto the Handsome. What **of** him?
They say he is a **great man.** Pious and learned and wise.
That's what they **say,** to be sure.
But in this profession, Peter, you will learn many things about what goes on **beneath** the surface.
Damn, boy, but I wish Reed were still alive.
We are the Queen's **shield.** We are the **nation's shield.** Never **for-get** that.
Now. Let's get him to the **Tower.**
"Master Murdoch?"
"**Aye,** Captain Nelson."
"Could I ask you a **question?"**
"That's a question **already.** But certainly, ask away. Whether you get an **answer** or not is another matter."
It's been five years you've been using my ship. I was wondering **why** you travel.
I travel to see the **sights,** Captain.
There's some as say that you're a **smuggler,** Master Murdoch.
People say all manner of things. But my gold is good.
And I was wondering... Y'see...
A **sailor** I met, a lowlander, told me of a time that he and several others tried to **rob** a **blind** Irish balladeer, in a port town, at night.
He said that they were **lucky** to escape with their **lives.**
Surely, the same can be said of any fellow who asks too many questions, Captain.
Now, is it a **song** you'll be wanting? To see the **dawn** in?

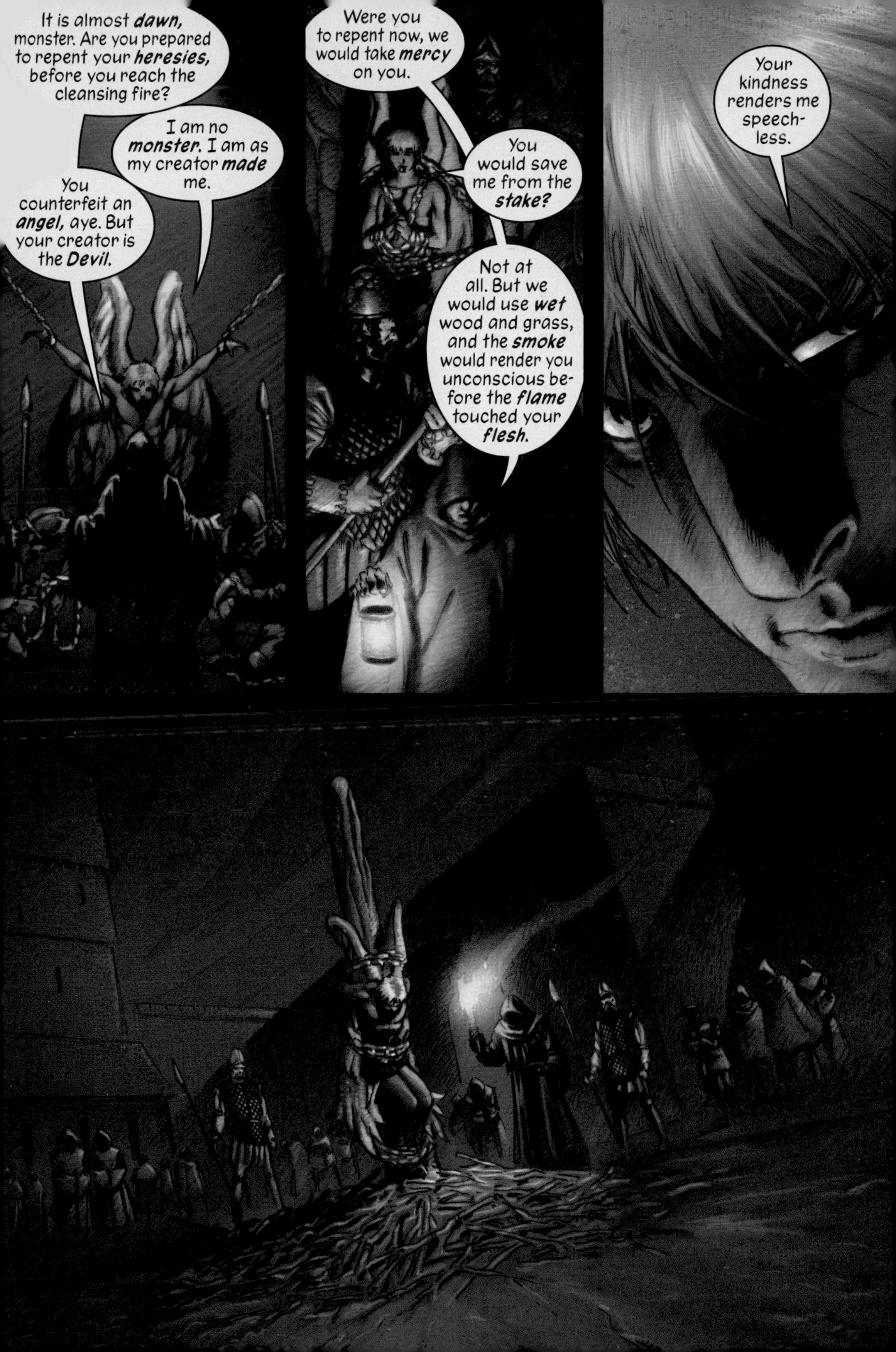
It is almost *dawn,* monster. Are you prepared to repent your *heresies,* before you reach the cleansing fire?
I am no *monster.* I am as my creator *made* me.
You counterfeit an *angel,* aye. But your creator is the *Devil.*
Were you to repent now, we would take *mercy* on you.
You would save me from the *stake?*
Not at all. But we would use *wet* wood and grass, and the *smoke* would render you unconscious be-fore the *flame* touched your *flesh.*
Your kindness renders me speech-less.

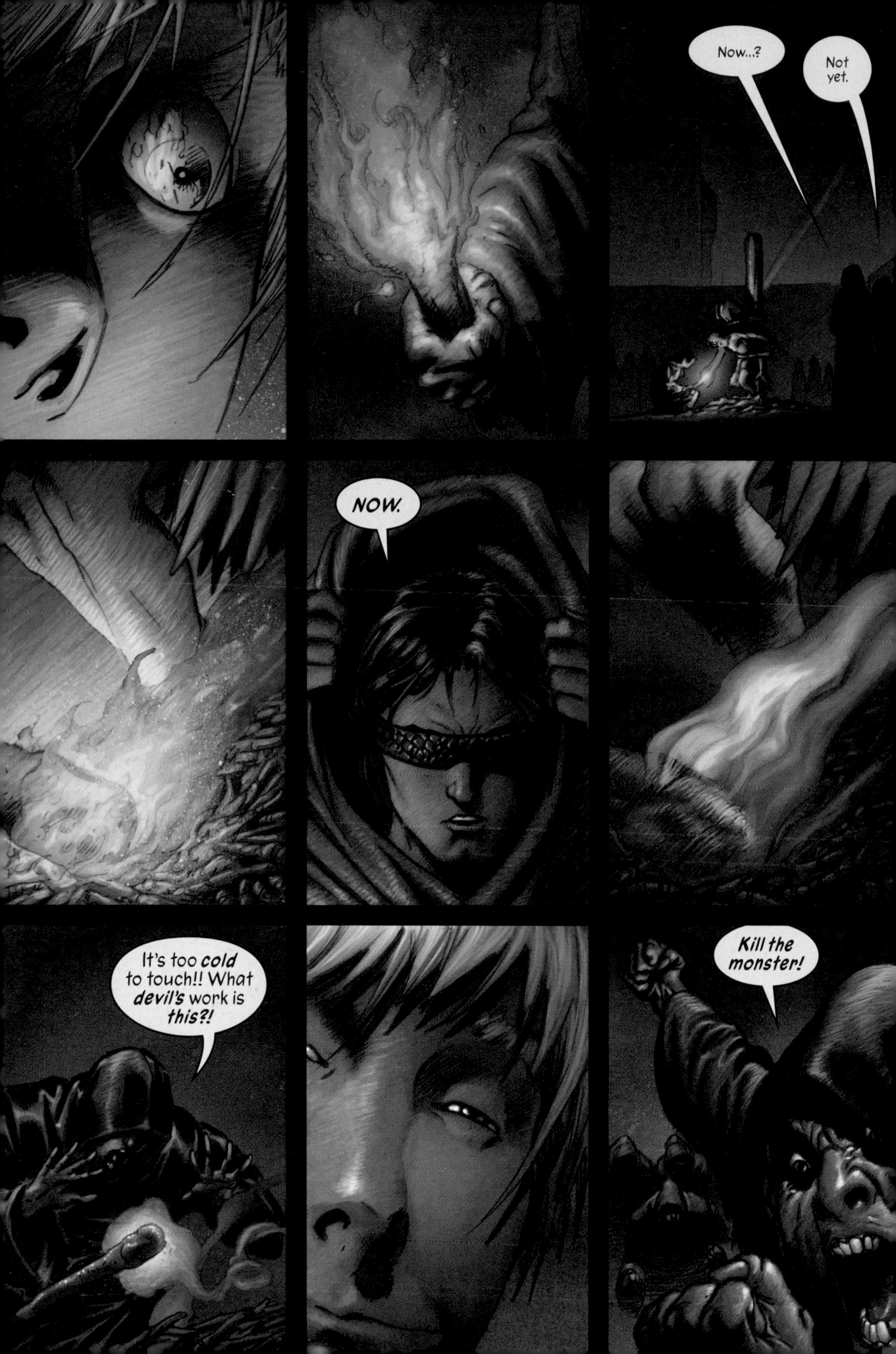
Now...?
Not yet.
NOW.
It's too *cold* to touch!! What *devil's* work is *this?!*
Kill the monster!

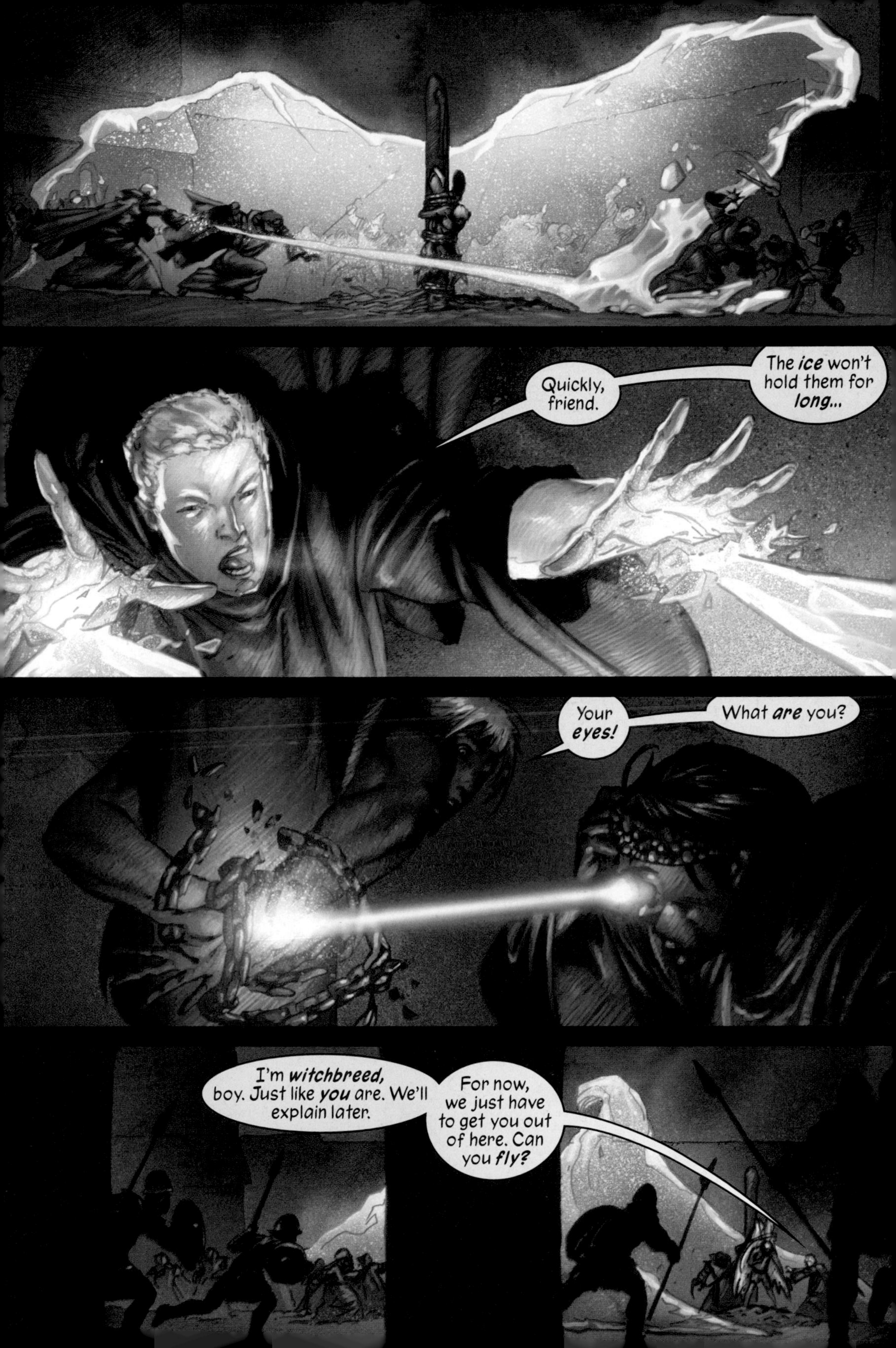
Quickly, friend.
The *ice* won't hold them for *long...*
Your *eyes!*
What *are* you?
I'm *witchbreed,* boy. Just like *you* are. We'll explain later.
For now, we just have to get you out of here. Can you *fly?*

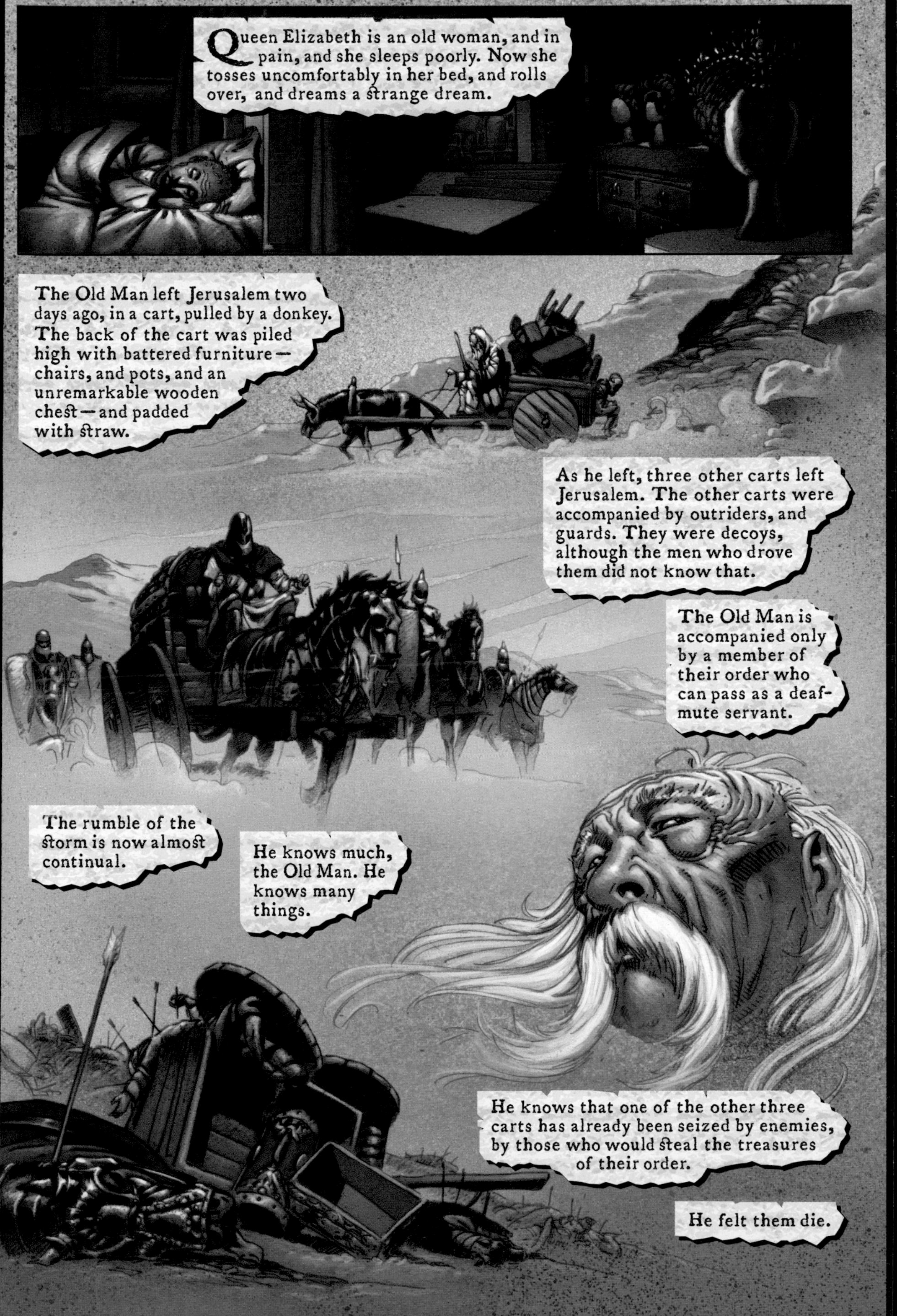
Queen Elizabeth is an old woman, and in pain, and she sleeps poorly. Now she tosses uncomfortably in her bed, and rolls over, and dreams a strange dream.
The Old Man left Jerusalem two days ago, in a cart, pulled by a donkey. The back of the cart was piled high with battered furniture—chairs, and pots, and an unremarkable wooden chest—and padded with straw.
As he left, three other carts left Jerusalem. The other carts were accompanied by outriders, and guards. They were decoys, although the men who drove them did not know that.
The Old Man is accompanied only by a member of their order who can pass as a deaf-mute servant.
The rumble of the storm is now almost continual.
He knows much, the Old Man. He knows many things.
He knows that one of the other three carts has already been seized by enemies, by those who would steal the treasures of their order.
He felt them die.

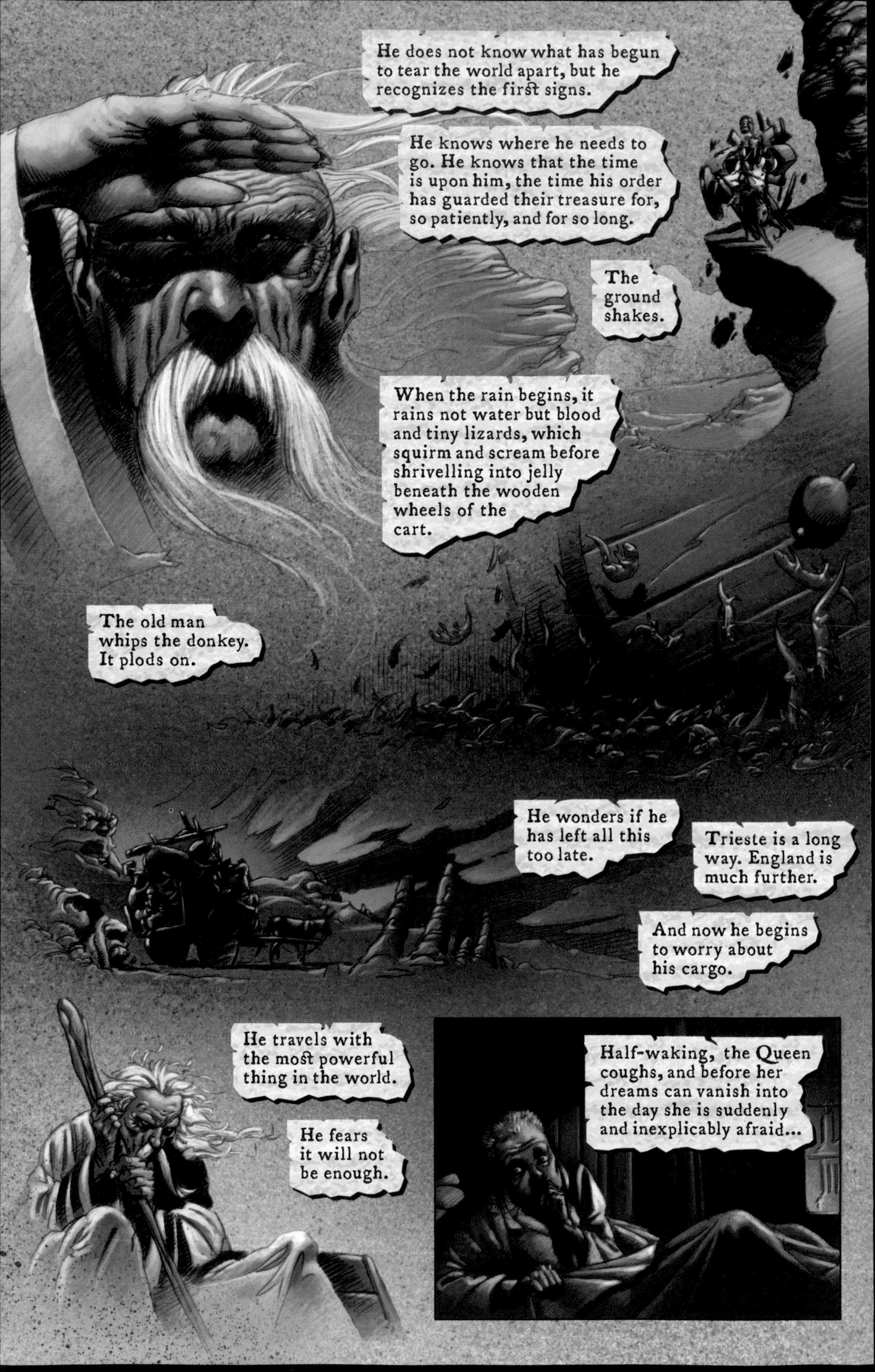
He does not know what has begun to tear the world apart, but he recognizes the first signs.
He knows where he needs to go. He knows that the time is upon him, the time his order has guarded their treasure for, so patiently, and for so long.
The ground shakes.
When the rain begins, it rains not water but blood and tiny lizards, which squirm and scream before shrivelling into jelly beneath the wooden wheels of the cart.
The old man whips the donkey. It plods on.
He wonders if he has left all this too late.
Trieste is a long way. England is much further.
And now he begins to worry about his cargo.
He travels with the most powerful thing in the world.
He fears it will not be enough.
Half-waking, the Queen coughs, and before her dreams can vanish into the day she is suddenly and inexplicably afraid...

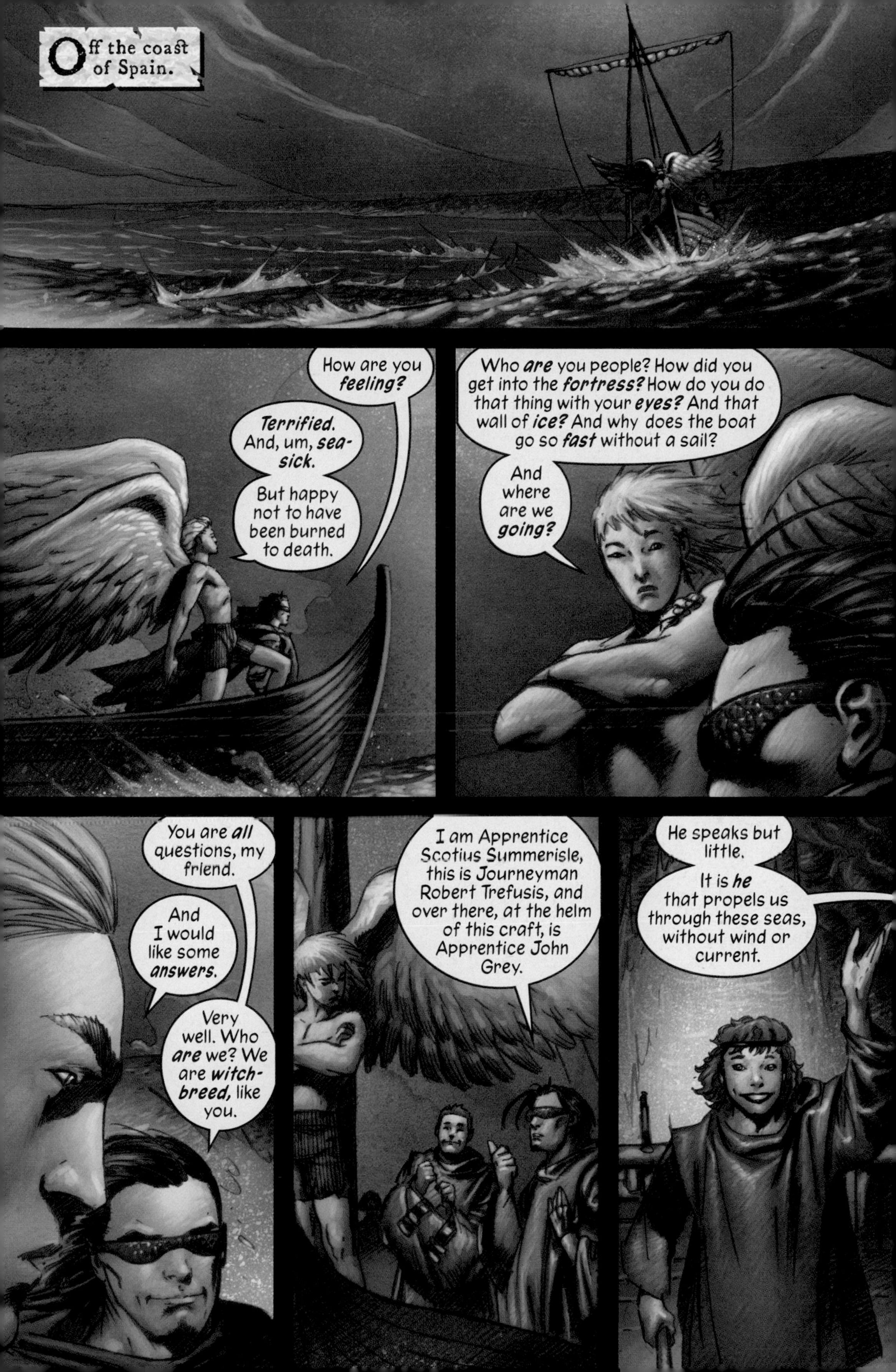
Off the coast of Spain.
How are you *feeling?*
Terrified. And, um, *sea-sick.*
But happy not to have been burned to death.
Who *are* you people? How did you get into the *fortress?* How do you do that thing with your *eyes?* And that wall of *ice?* And why does the boat go so *fast* without a sail?
And where are we *going?*
You are *all* questions, my friend.
And I would like some *answers.*
Very well. Who *are* we? We are *witch-breed,* like you.
I am Apprentice Scotius Summerisle, this is Journeyman Robert Trefusis, and over there, at the helm of this craft, is Apprentice John Grey.
He speaks but little.
It is *he* that propels us through these seas, without wind or current.

IN WHICH THINGS BEGIN TO CHANGE

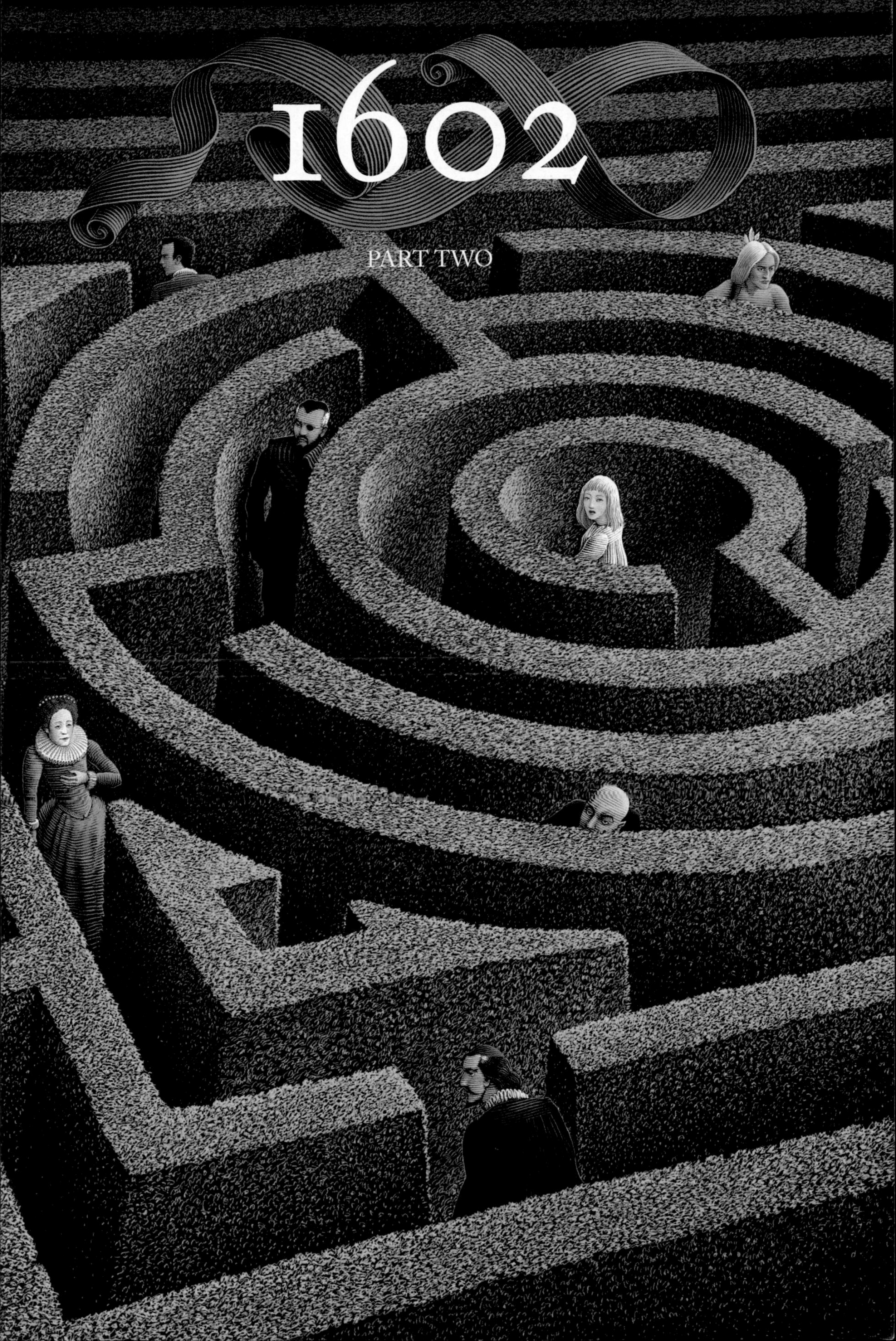
1602
PART TWO

From Sir Nicholas Fury to Her Majesty Elizabeth, By the Grace of God, Greetings.

Madam,

Since last we spoke, I have despatched my finest agent to the continent. He journeys to meet the Old Man, the Head of the Templars, who has smuggled the treasure of the Templars out of Jerusalem. My man, whom I have only encountered in darkness, will bring him and his treasure to our shores safely.

The strange weather continues, putting many in fear of their lives.

Today, Miss Virginia Dare, the first born of Your Majesty's Colony in Roanoke, will be presented to Your Majesty. I have entrusted my attendant, Master Parquaugh, with her safety.

I will not be there, alas. It has become imperative that I speak to the learned Carlos Javier, whose educational establishment I have discussed with you on many prior occasions.

I shall take pleasure in ensuring Your Majesty at all times knows what transpires.

And have the honour to sign myself,

Sir Nicholas Fury

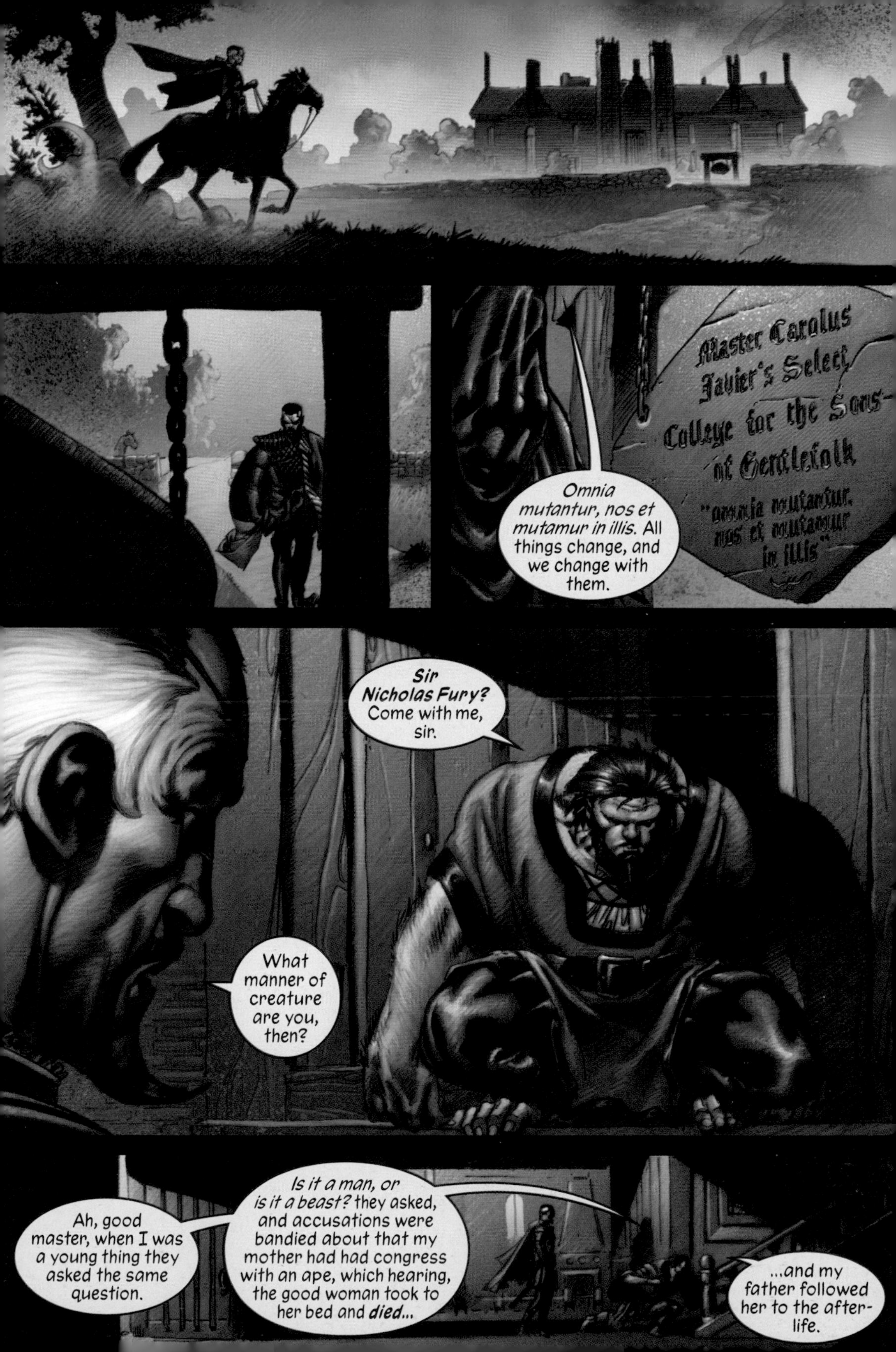
Master Carolus Javier's Select College for the Sons of Gentlefolk
"omnia mutantur, nos et mutamur in illis"
Omnia mutantur, nos et mutamur in illis. All things change, and we change with them.
Sir Nicholas Fury? Come with me, sir.
What manner of creature are you, then?
Ah, good master, when I was a young thing they asked the same question.
Is it a man, or is it a beast? they asked, and accusations were bandied about that my mother had had congress with an ape, which hearing, the good woman took to her bed and ***died...***
...and my father followed her to the after-life.

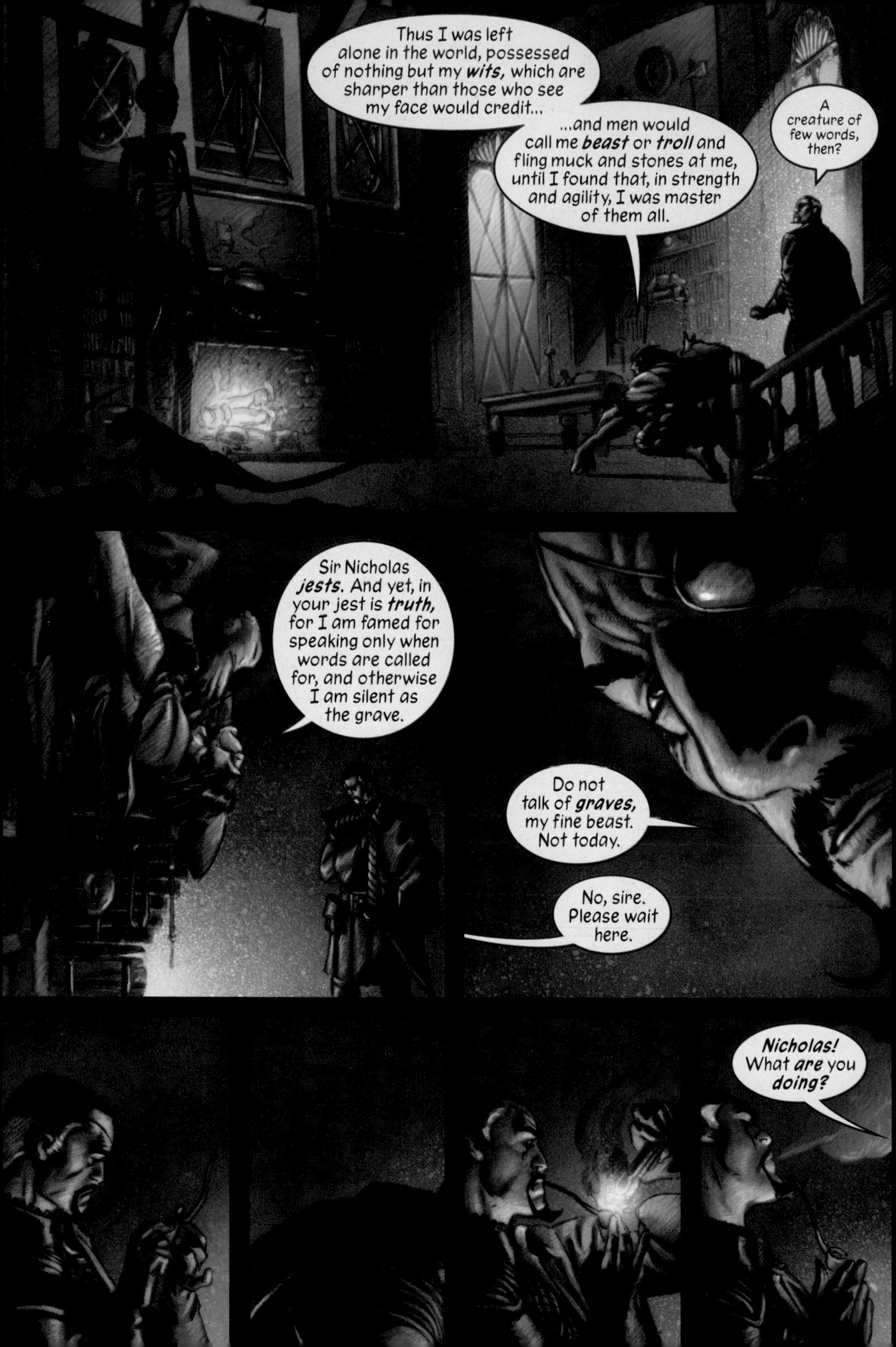

Thus I was left alone in the world, possessed of nothing but my *wits,* which are sharper than those who see my face would credit...
...and men would call me *beast* or *troll* and fling muck and stones at me, until I found that, in strength and agility, I was master of them all.
A creature of few words, then?
Sir Nicholas *jests.* And yet, in your jest is *truth,* for I am famed for speaking only when words are called for, and otherwise I am silent as the grave.
Do not talk of *graves,* my fine beast. Not today.
No, sire. Please wait here.
Nicholas! What *are* you *doing?*

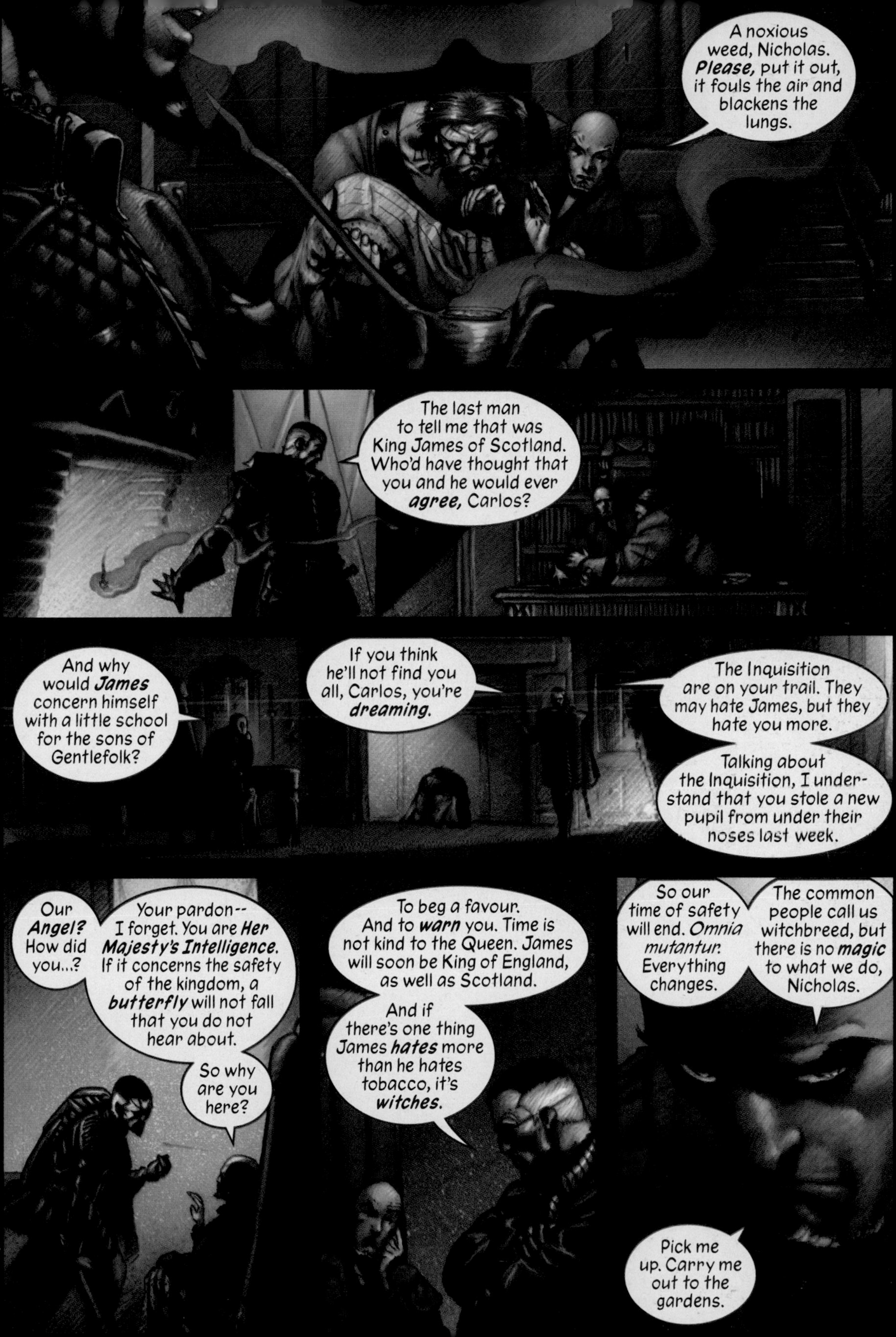
A noxious weed, Nicholas. **Please,** put it out, it fouls the air and blackens the lungs.
The last man to tell me that was King James of Scotland. Who'd have thought that you and he would ever **agree,** Carlos?
And why would **James** concern himself with a little school for the sons of Gentlefolk?
If you think he'll not find you all, Carlos, you're **dreaming.**
The Inquisition are on your trail. They may hate James, but they hate you more.
Talking about the Inquisition, I understand that you stole a new pupil from under their noses last week.
Our **Angel?** How did you...?
Your pardon-- I forget. You are **Her Majesty's Intelligence.** If it concerns the safety of the kingdom, a **butterfly** will not fall that you do not hear about.
So why are you here?
To beg a favour. And to **warn** you. Time is not kind to the Queen. James will soon be King of England, as well as Scotland.
And if there's one thing James **hates** more than he hates tobacco, it's **witches.**
So our time of safety will end. *Omnia mutantur.* Everything changes.
The common people call us witchbreed, but there is no **magic** to what we do, Nicholas.
Pick me up. Carry me out to the gardens.

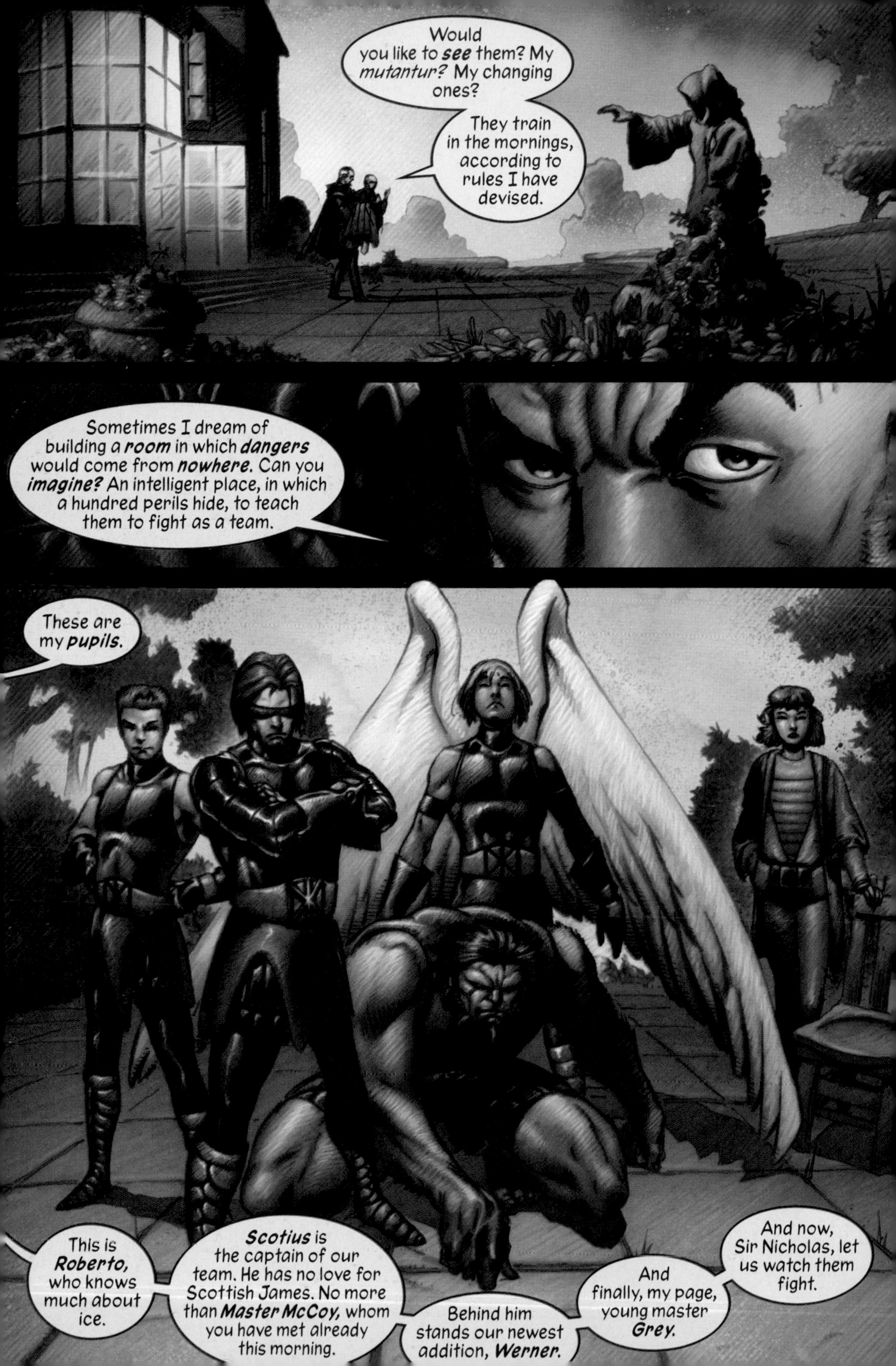
Would you like to *see* them? My *mutantur?* My changing ones?
They train in the mornings, according to rules I have devised.
Sometimes I dream of building a ***room*** in which ***dangers*** would come from ***nowhere***. Can you ***imagine?*** An intelligent place, in which a hundred perils hide, to teach them to fight as a team.
These are my ***pupils***.
This is ***Roberto,*** who knows much about ice.
Scotius is the captain of our team. He has no love for Scottish James. No more than ***Master McCoy,*** whom you have met already this morning.
Behind him stands our newest addition, ***Werner***.
And finally, my page, young master ***Grey***.
And now, Sir Nicholas, let us watch them fight.

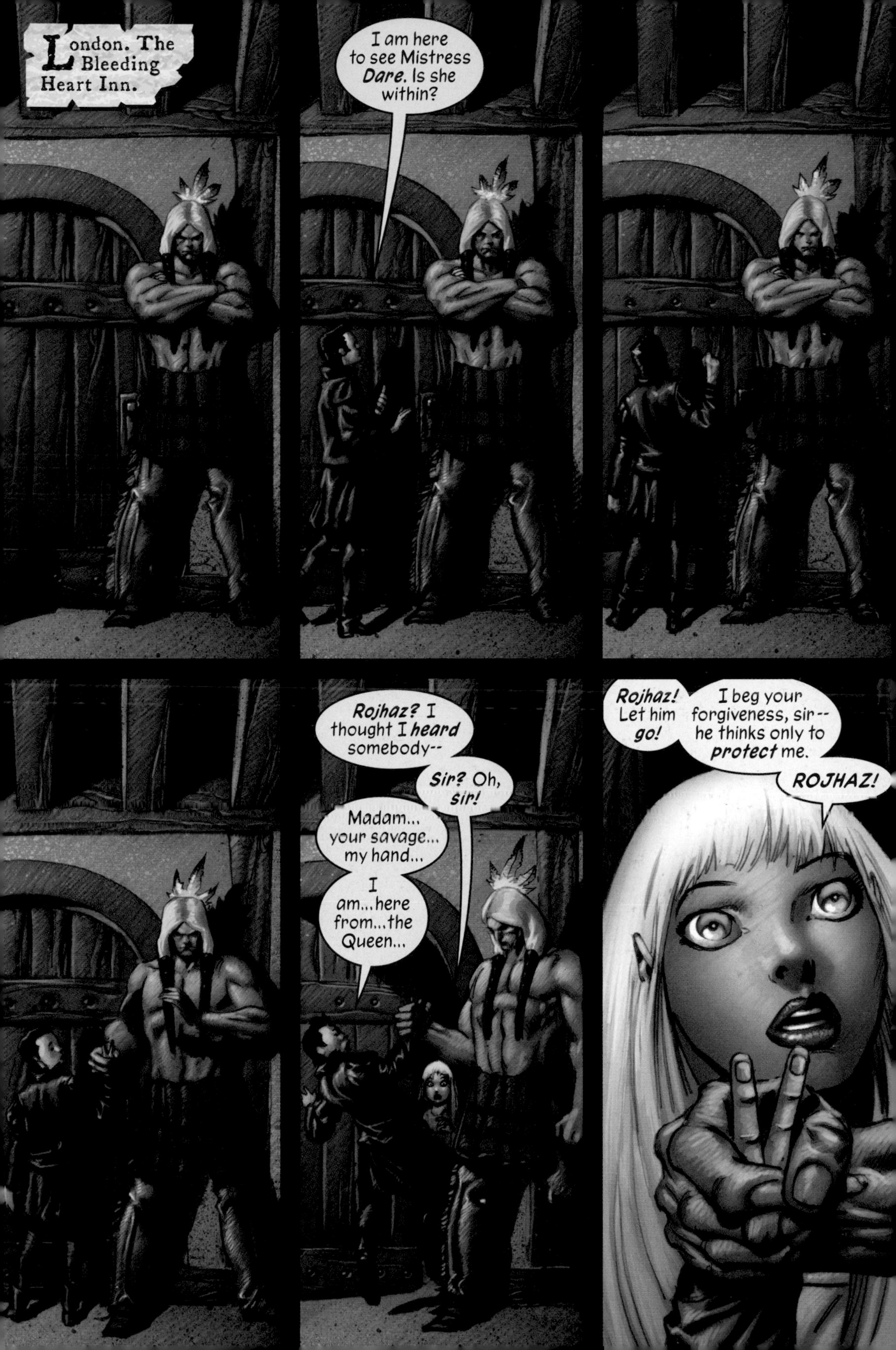
London. The Bleeding Heart Inn.
I am here to see Mistress *Dare*. Is she within?
Rojhaz? I thought I *heard* somebody--
Sir? Oh, *sir!*
Madam... your savage... my hand...
I am... here from... the Queen...
Rojhaz! Let him *go!*
I beg your forgiveness, sir-- he thinks only to *protect* me.
ROJHAZ!

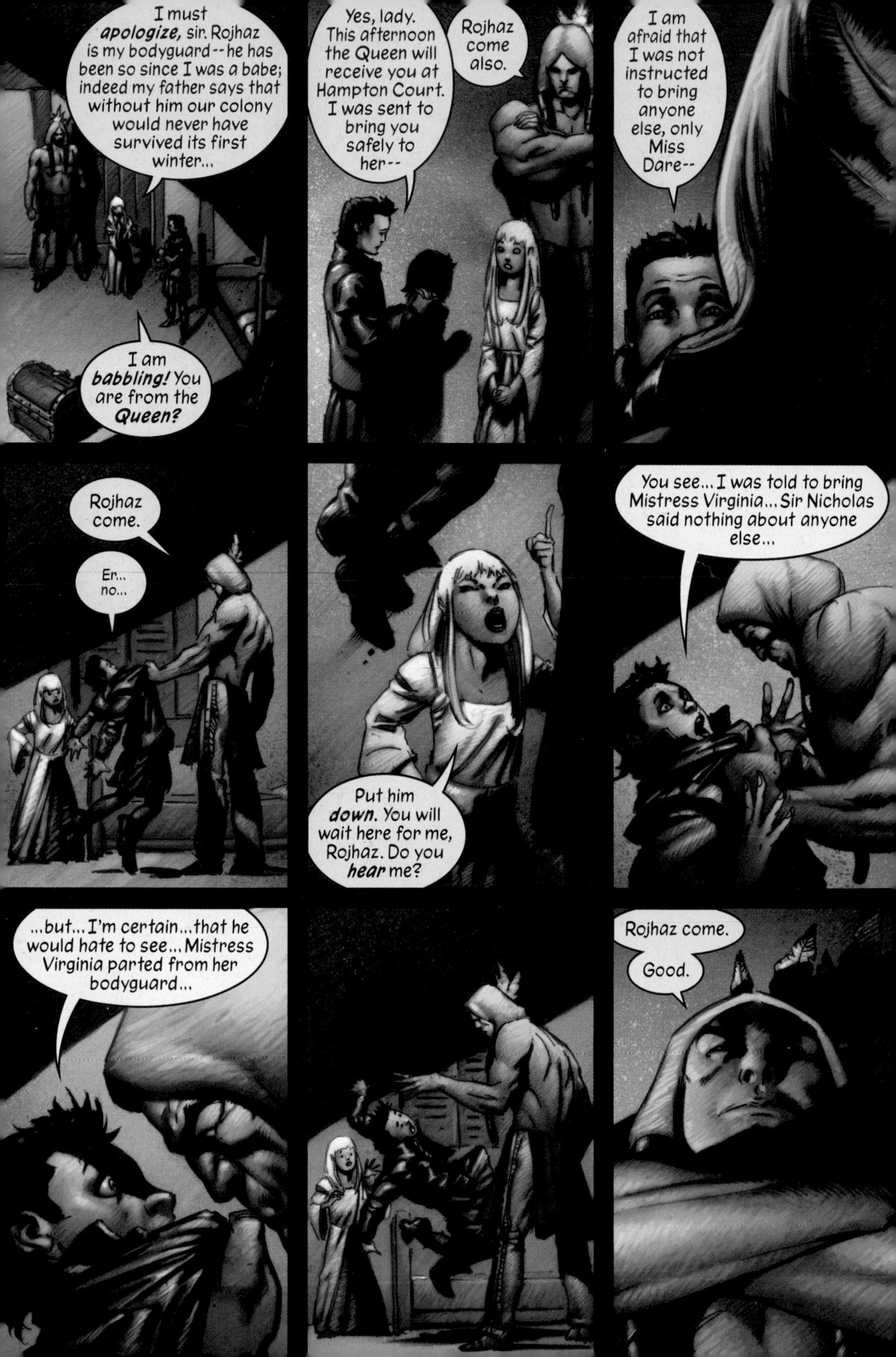
I must apologize, sir. Rojhaz is my bodyguard -- he has been so since I was a babe; indeed my father says that without him our colony would never have survived its first winter...
I am babbling! You are from the Queen?
Yes, lady. This afternoon the Queen will receive you at Hampton Court. I was sent to bring you safely to her--
Rojhaz come also.
I am afraid that I was not instructed to bring anyone else, only Miss Dare--
Rojhaz come.
Er... no...
Put him down. You will wait here for me, Rojhaz. Do you hear me?
You see... I was told to bring Mistress Virginia... Sir Nicholas said nothing about anyone else...
...but... I'm certain... that he would hate to see... Mistress Virginia parted from her bodyguard...
Rojhaz come.
Good.

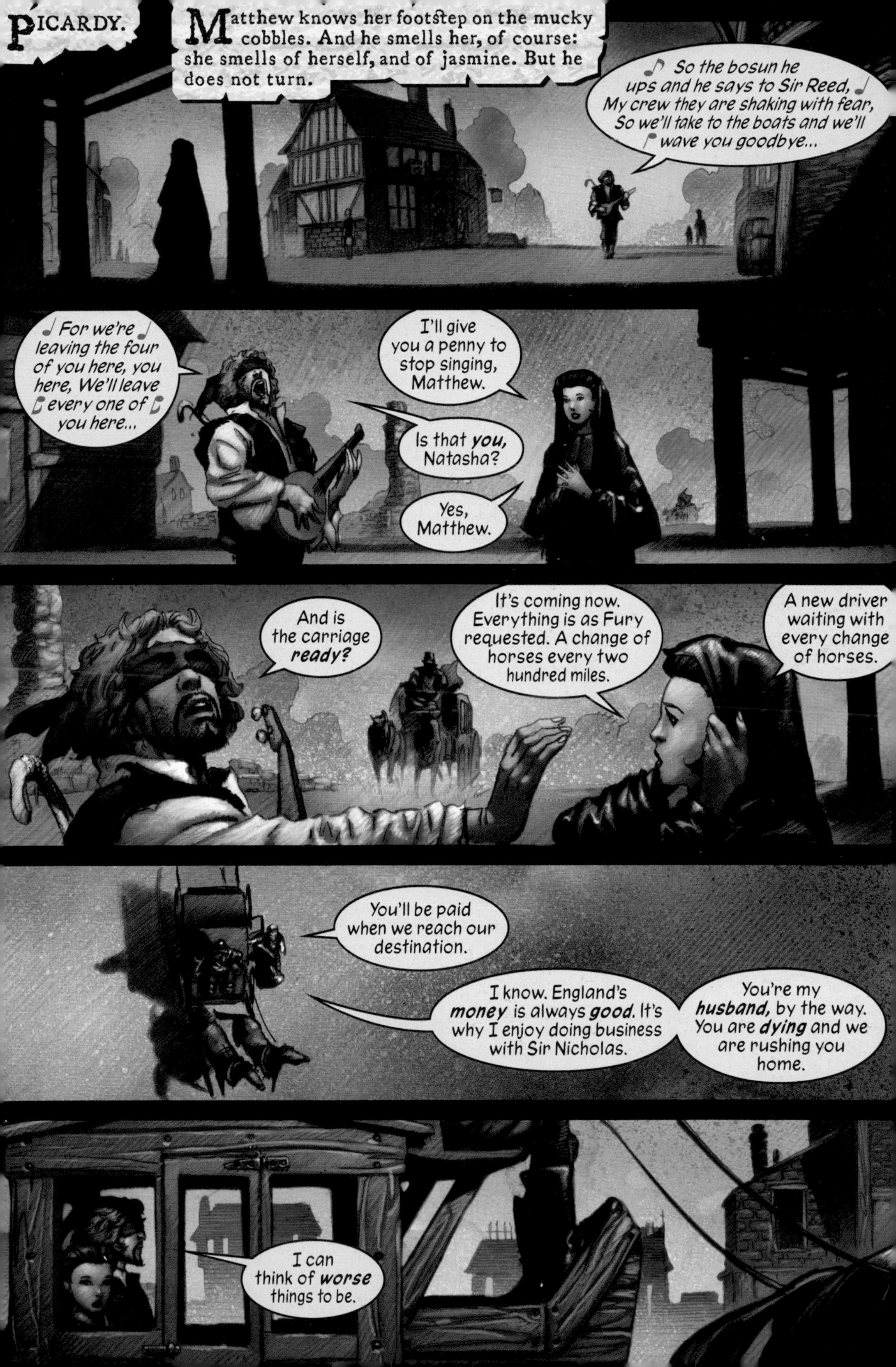
PICARDY.
Matthew knows her footstep on the mucky cobbles. And he smells her, of course: she smells of herself, and of jasmine. But he does not turn.
So the bosun he ups and he says to Sir Reed, My crew they are shaking with fear, So we'll take to the boats and we'll wave you goodbye...
For we're leaving the four of you here, you here, We'll leave every one of you here...
I'll give you a penny to stop singing, Matthew.
Is that *you,* Natasha?
Yes, Matthew.
And is the carriage ***ready?***
It's coming now. Everything is as Fury requested. A change of horses every two hundred miles.
A new driver waiting with every change of horses.
You'll be paid when we reach our destination.
I know. England's ***money*** is always ***good.*** It's why I enjoy doing business with Sir Nicholas.
You're my ***husband,*** by the way. You are ***dying*** and we are rushing you home.
I can think of ***worse*** things to be.

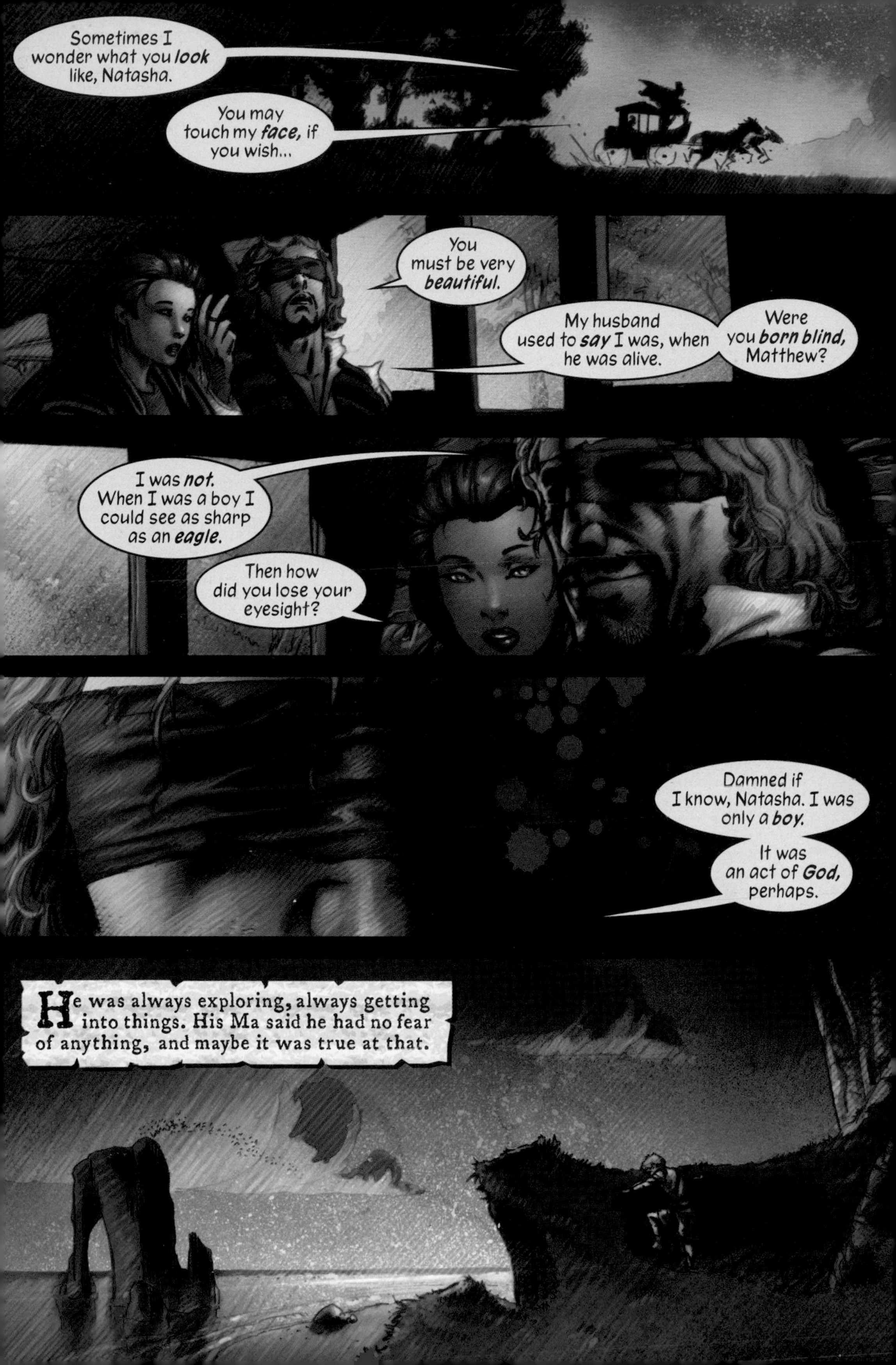
Sometimes I wonder what you *look* like, Natasha.
You may touch my *face,* if you wish...
You must be very *beautiful.*
My husband used to *say* I was, when he was alive.
Were you *born blind,* Matthew?
I was *not.* When I was a boy I could see as sharp as an *eagle.*
Then how did you lose your eyesight?
Damned if I know, Natasha. I was only a *boy.*
It was an act of *God,* perhaps.
He was always exploring, always getting into things. His Ma said he had no fear of anything, and maybe it was true at that.

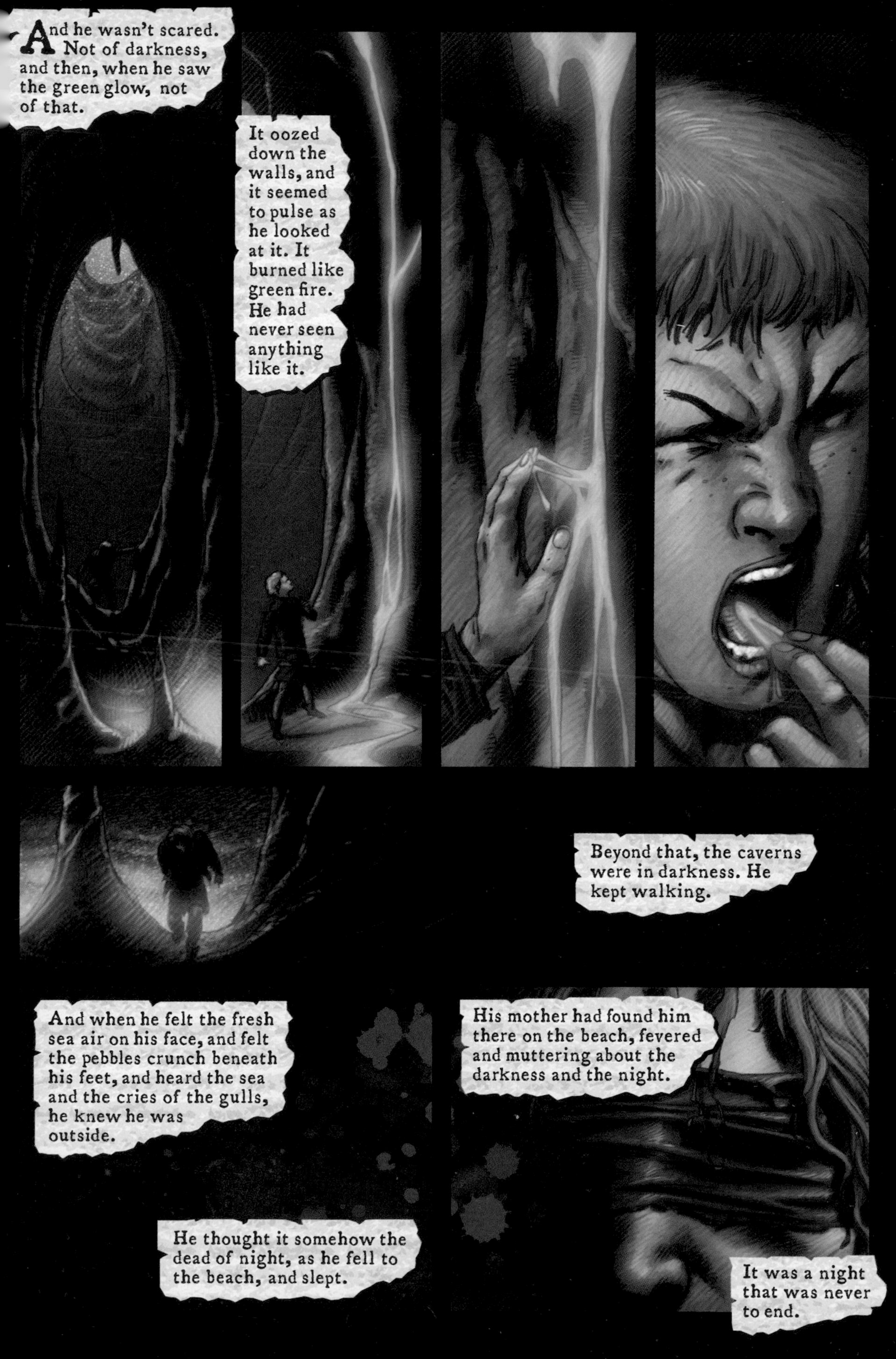
And he wasn't scared. Not of darkness, and then, when he saw the green glow, not of that.
It oozed down the walls, and it seemed to pulse as he looked at it. It burned like green fire. He had never seen anything like it.
Beyond that, the caverns were in darkness. He kept walking.
And when he felt the fresh sea air on his face, and felt the pebbles crunch beneath his feet, and heard the sea and the cries of the gulls, he knew he was outside.
He thought it somehow the dead of night, as he fell to the beach, and slept.
His mother had found him there on the beach, fevered and muttering about the darkness and the night.
It was a night that was never to end.

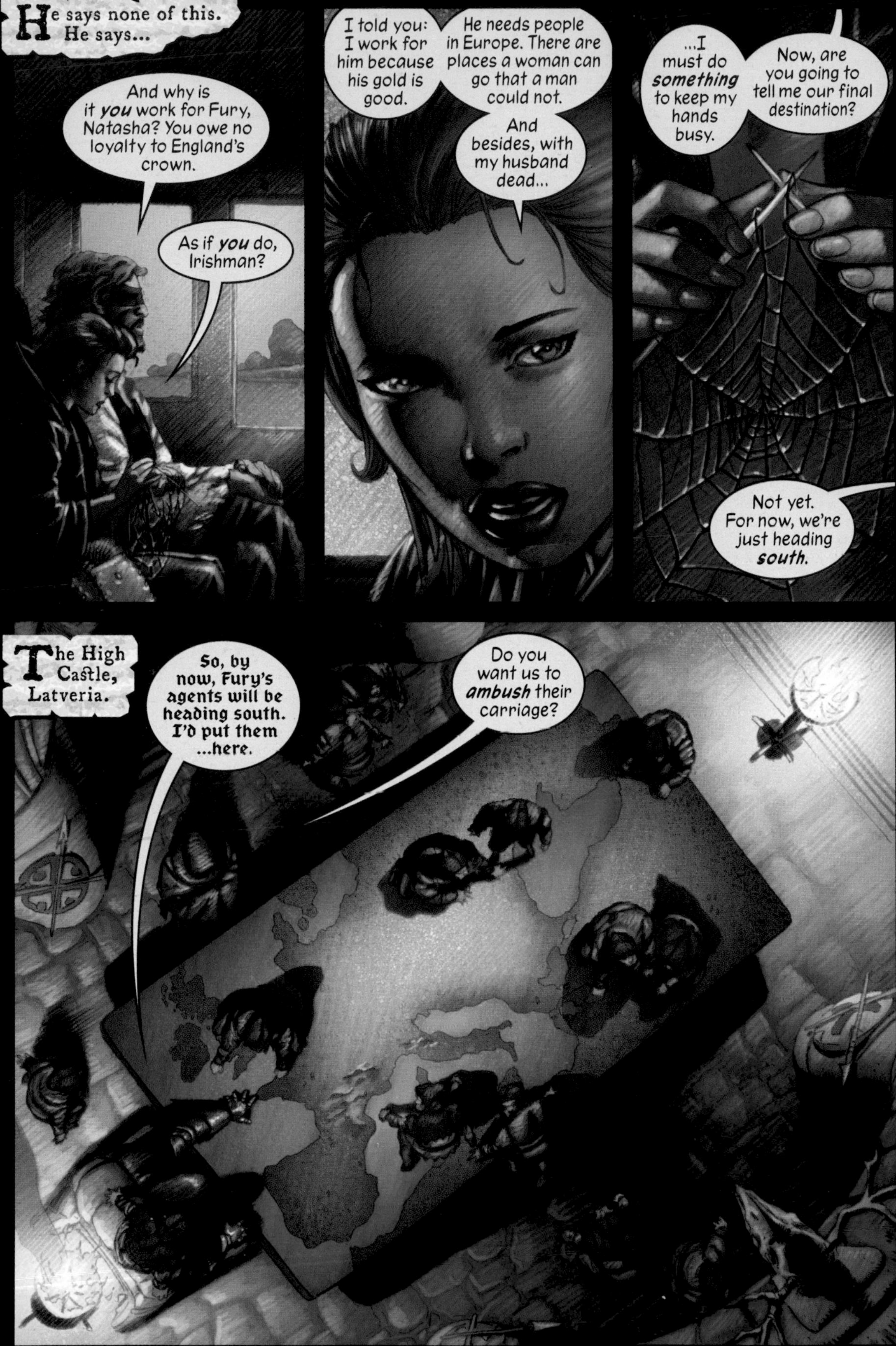
He says none of this. He says...
And why is it *you* work for Fury, Natasha? You owe no loyalty to England's crown.
As if *you* do, Irishman?
I told you: I work for him because his gold is good.
He needs people in Europe. There are places a woman can go that a man could not.
And besides, with my husband dead...
...I must do *something* to keep my hands busy.
Now, are you going to tell me our final destination?
Not yet. For now, we're just heading *south*.
The High Castle, Latveria.
So, by now, Fury's agents will be heading south. I'd put them ...here.
Do you want us to *ambush* their carriage?

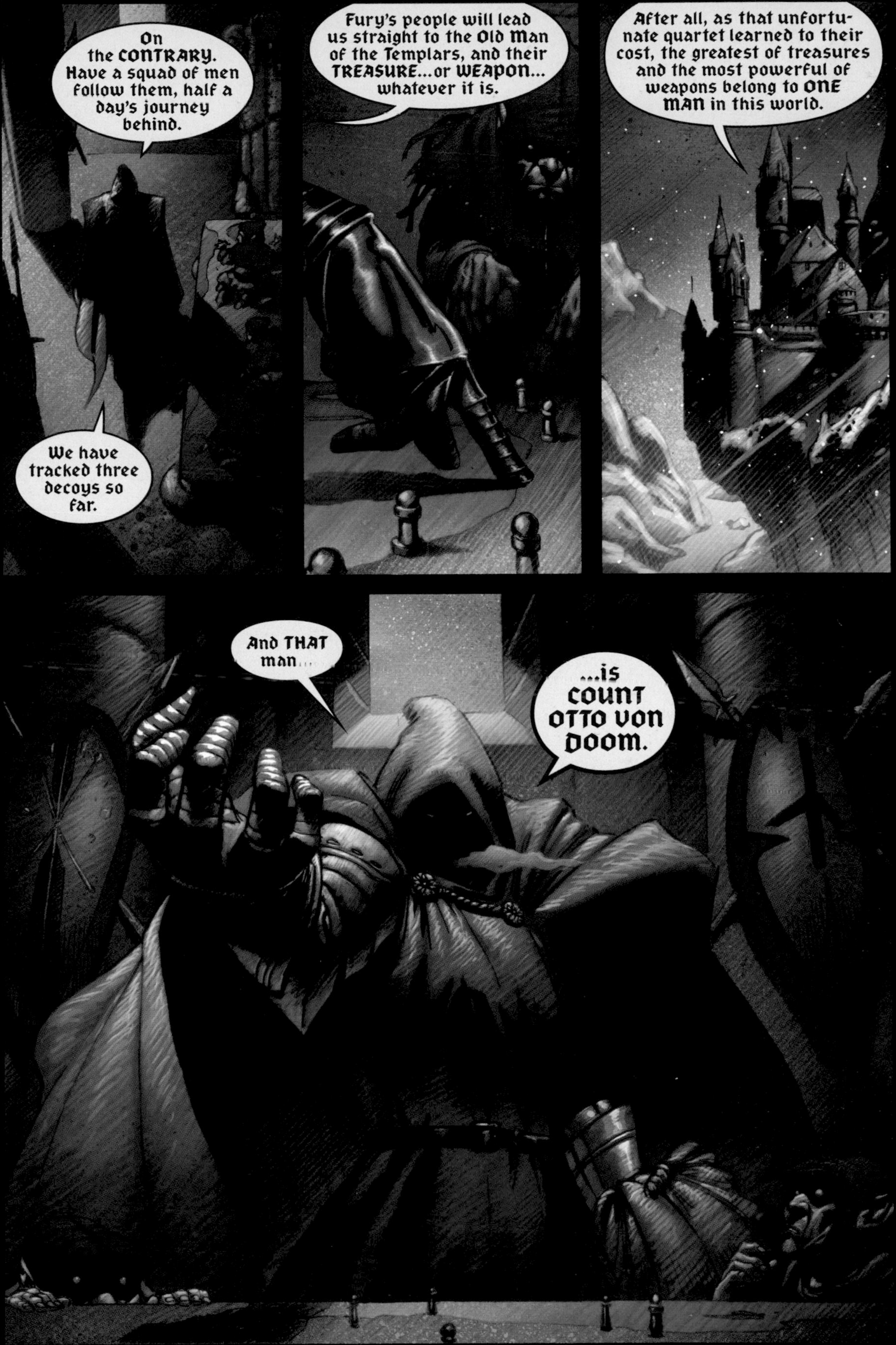
On the CONTRARY. Have a squad of men follow them, half a day's journey behind.
We have tracked three decoys so far.
Fury's people will lead us straight to the OLD MAN of the Templars, and their TREASURE...or WEAPON... whatever it is.
After all, as that unfortunate quartet learned to their cost, the greatest of treasures and the most powerful of weapons belong to ONE MAN in this world.
And THAT man...
...is COUNT OTTO VON DOOM.

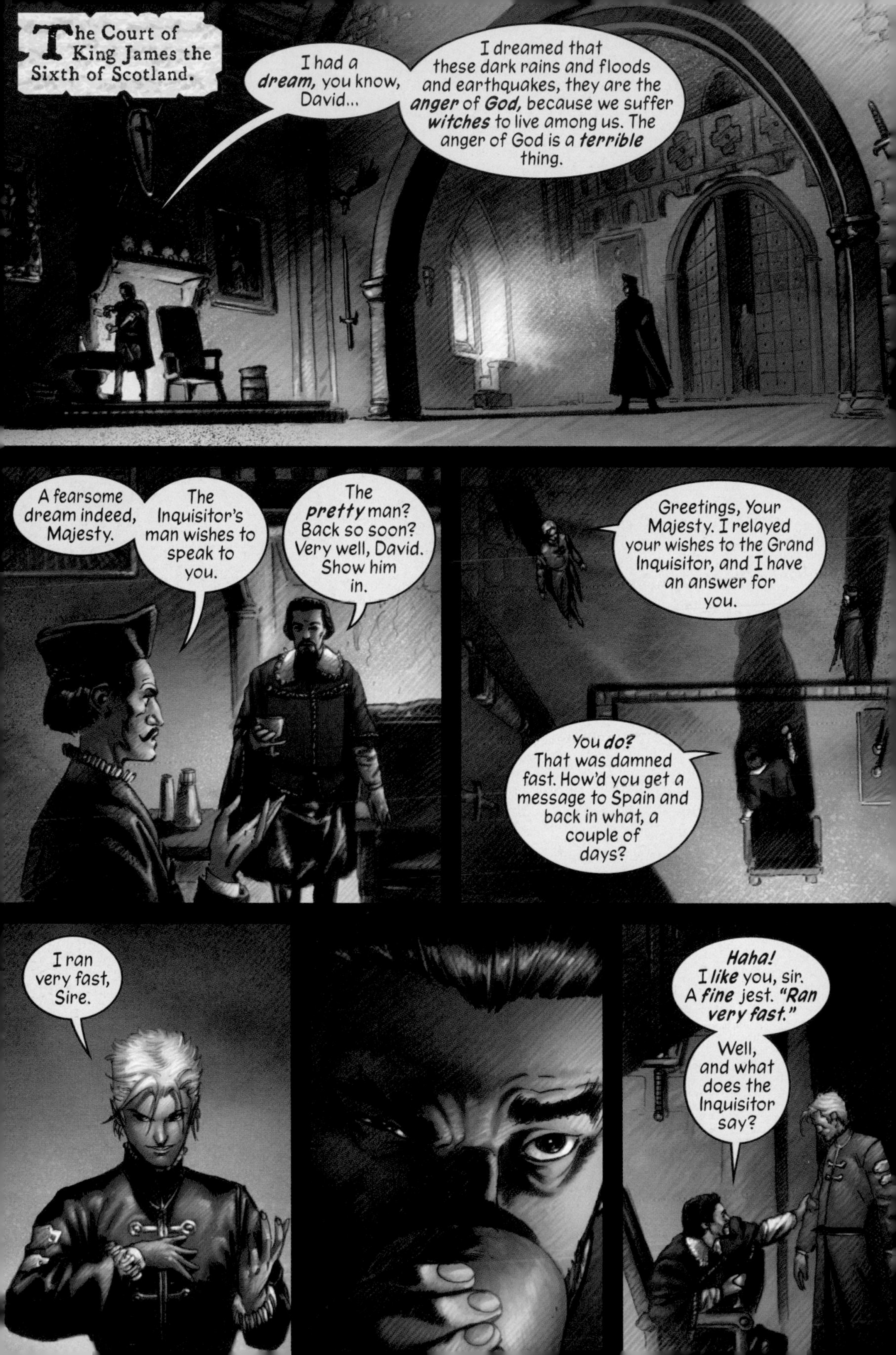
The Court of King James the Sixth of Scotland.
I had a dream, you know, David...
I dreamed that these dark rains and floods and earthquakes, they are the anger of God, because we suffer witches to live among us. The anger of God is a terrible thing.
A fearsome dream indeed, Majesty.
The Inquisitor's man wishes to speak to you.
The pretty man? Back so soon? Very well, David. Show him in.
Greetings, Your Majesty. I relayed your wishes to the Grand Inquisitor, and I have an answer for you.
You do? That was damned fast. How'd you get a message to Spain and back in what, a couple of days?
I ran very fast, Sire.
Haha! I like you, sir. A fine jest. "Ran very fast."
Well, and what does the Inquisitor say?

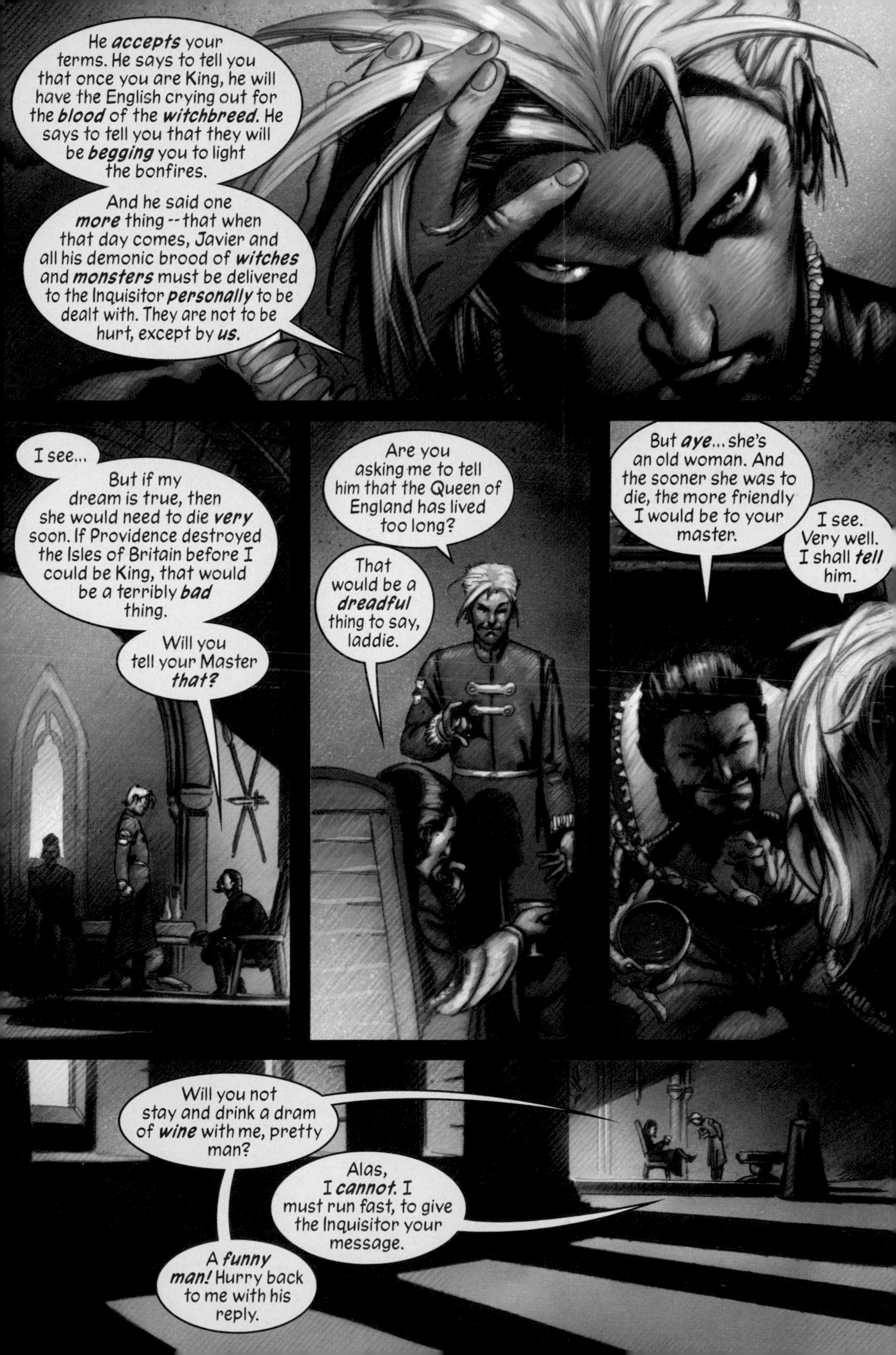
He accepts your terms. He says to tell you that once you are King, he will have the English crying out for the blood of the witchbreed. He says to tell you that they will be begging you to light the bonfires.
And he said one more thing -- that when that day comes, Javier and all his demonic brood of witches and monsters must be delivered to the Inquisitor personally to be dealt with. They are not to be hurt, except by us.
I see...
But if my dream is true, then she would need to die very soon. If Providence destroyed the Isles of Britain before I could be King, that would be a terribly bad thing.
Will you tell your Master that?
Are you asking me to tell him that the Queen of England has lived too long?
That would be a dreadful thing to say, laddie.
But aye... she's an old woman. And the sooner she was to die, the more friendly I would be to your master.
I see. Very well. I shall tell him.
Will you not stay and drink a dram of wine with me, pretty man?
Alas, I cannot. I must run fast, to give the Inquisitor your message.
A funny man! Hurry back to me with his reply.

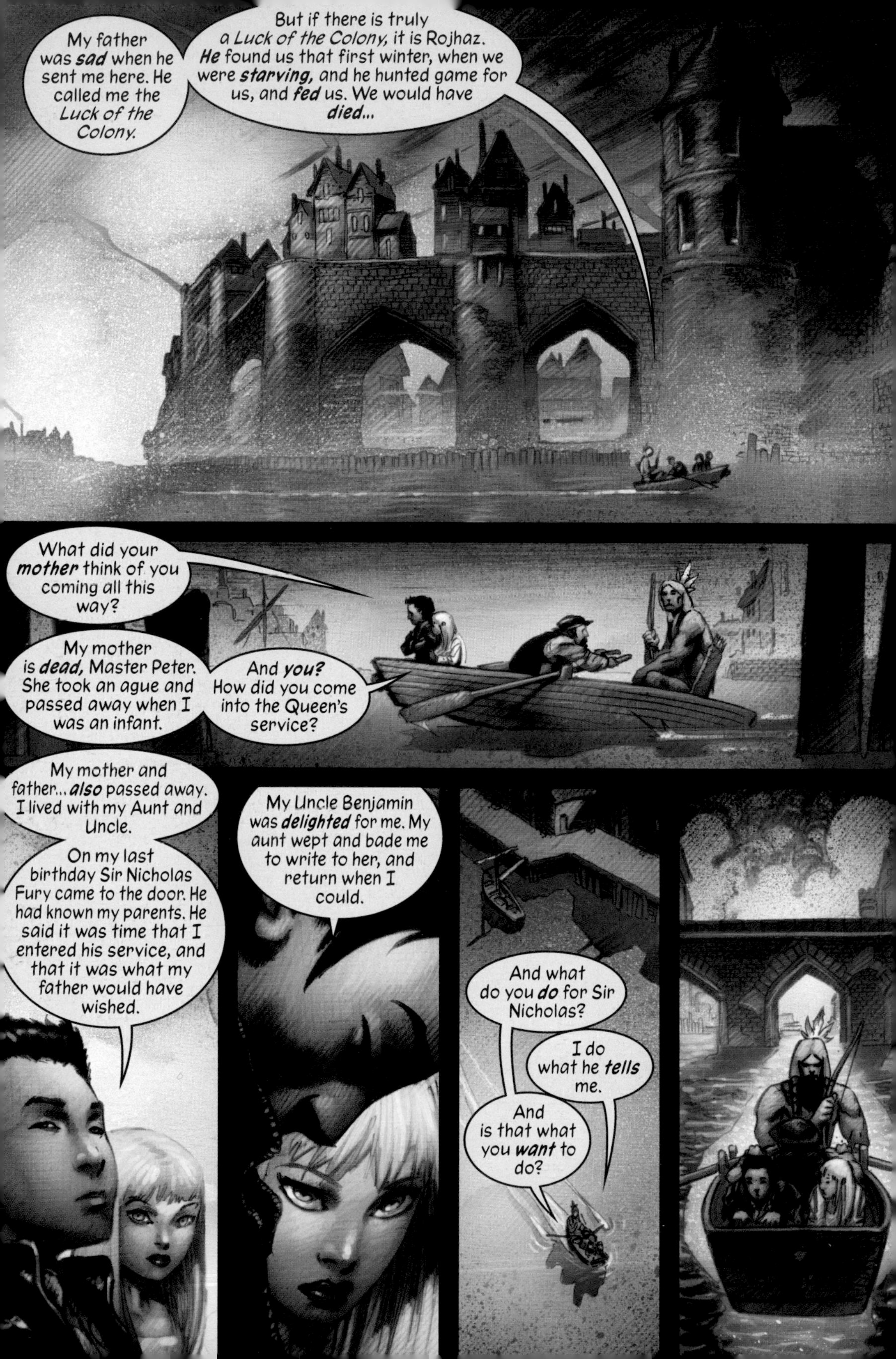
My father was sad when he sent me here. He called me the Luck of the Colony.
But if there is truly a Luck of the Colony, it is Rojhaz. He found us that first winter, when we were starving, and he hunted game for us, and fed us. We would have died...
What did your mother think of you coming all this way?
My mother is dead, Master Peter. She took an ague and passed away when I was an infant.
And you? How did you come into the Queen's service?
My mother and father... also passed away. I lived with my Aunt and Uncle.
On my last birthday Sir Nicholas Fury came to the door. He had known my parents. He said it was time that I entered his service, and that it was what my father would have wished.
My Uncle Benjamin was delighted for me. My aunt wept and bade me to write to her, and return when I could.
And what do you do for Sir Nicholas?
I do what he tells me.
And is that what you want to do?

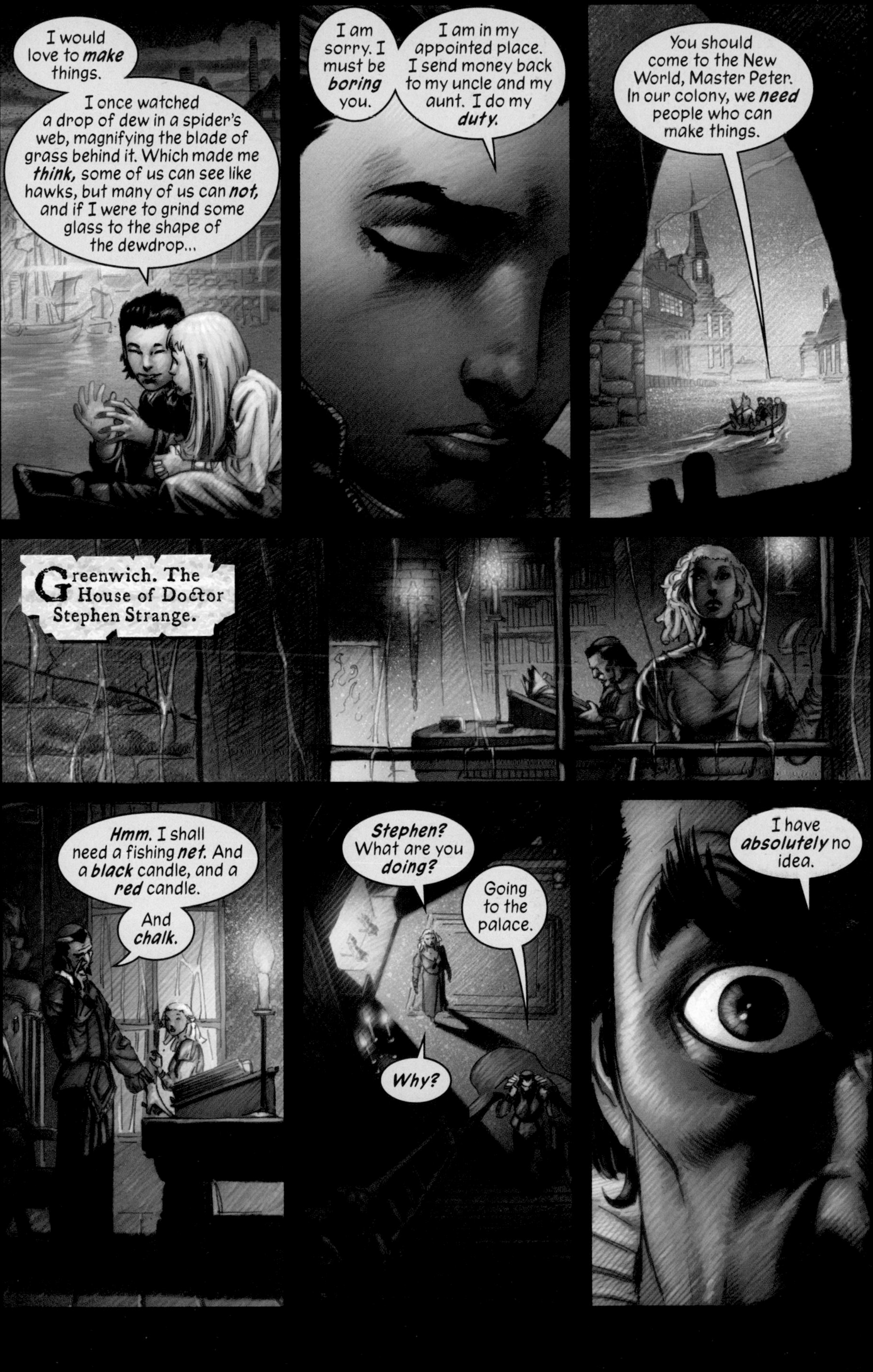
I would love to make things.
I once watched a drop of dew in a spider's web, magnifying the blade of grass behind it. Which made me think, some of us can see like hawks, but many of us can not, and if I were to grind some glass to the shape of the dewdrop...
I am sorry. I must be boring you.
I am in my appointed place. I send money back to my uncle and my aunt. I do my duty.
You should come to the New World, Master Peter. In our colony, we need people who can make things.
Greenwich. The House of Doctor Stephen Strange.
Hmm. I shall need a fishing net. And a black candle, and a red candle.
And chalk.
Stephen? What are you doing?
Going to the palace.
Why?
I have absolutely no idea.

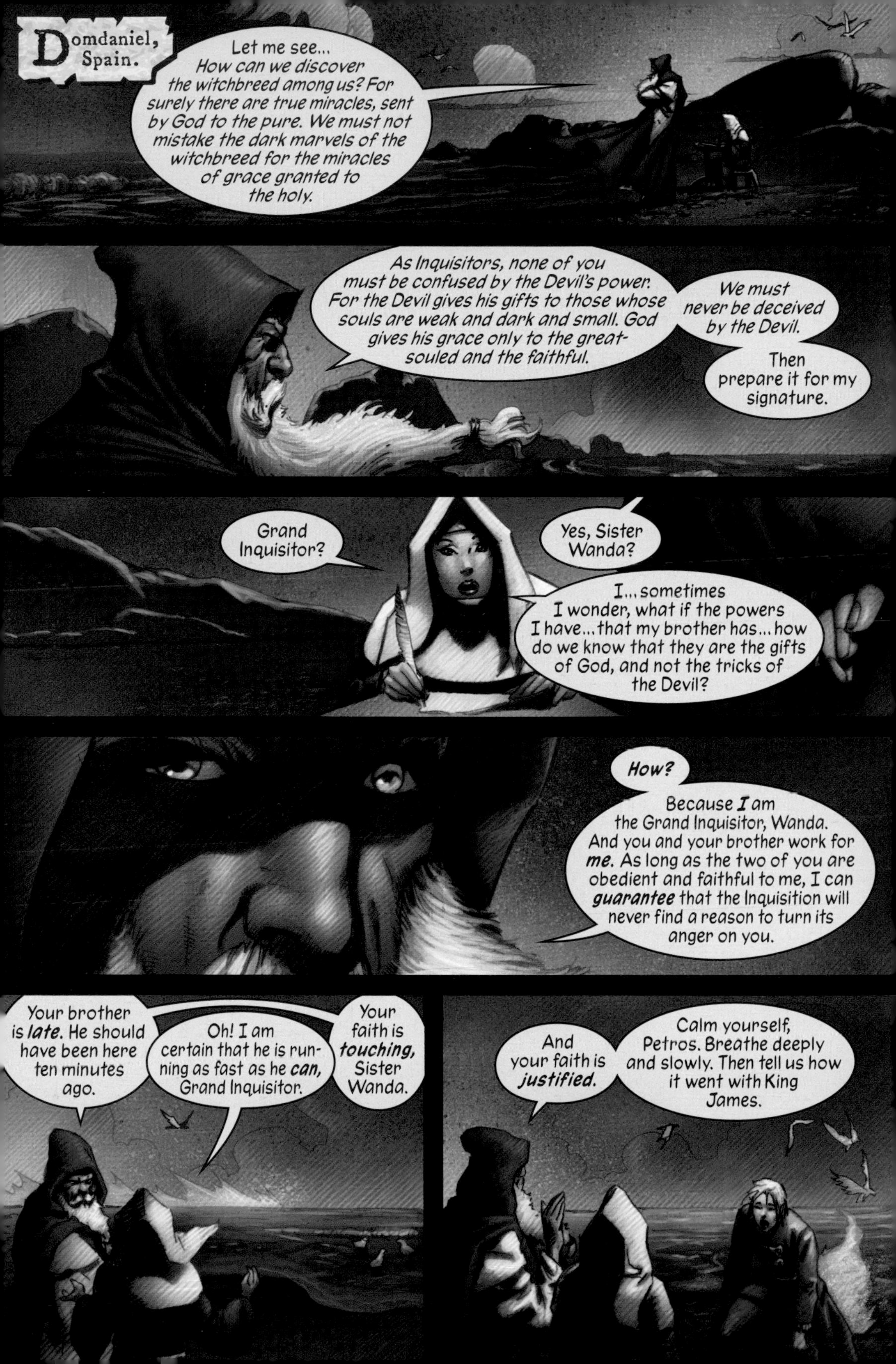
Domdaniel, Spain.
Let me see... How can we discover the witchbreed among us? For surely there are true miracles, sent by God to the pure. We must not mistake the dark marvels of the witchbreed for the miracles of grace granted to the holy.
As Inquisitors, none of you must be confused by the Devil's power. For the Devil gives his gifts to those whose souls are weak and dark and small. God gives his grace only to the great-souled and the faithful.
We must never be deceived by the Devil.
Then prepare it for my signature.
Grand Inquisitor?
Yes, Sister Wanda?
I... sometimes I wonder, what if the powers I have... that my brother has... how do we know that they are the gifts of God, and not the tricks of the Devil?
How?
Because I am the Grand Inquisitor, Wanda. And you and your brother work for me. As long as the two of you are obedient and faithful to me, I can guarantee that the Inquisition will never find a reason to turn its anger on you.
Your brother is late. He should have been here ten minutes ago.
Oh! I am certain that he is running as fast as he can, Grand Inquisitor.
Your faith is touching, Sister Wanda.
And your faith is justified.
Calm yourself, Petros. Breathe deeply and slowly. Then tell us how it went with King James.

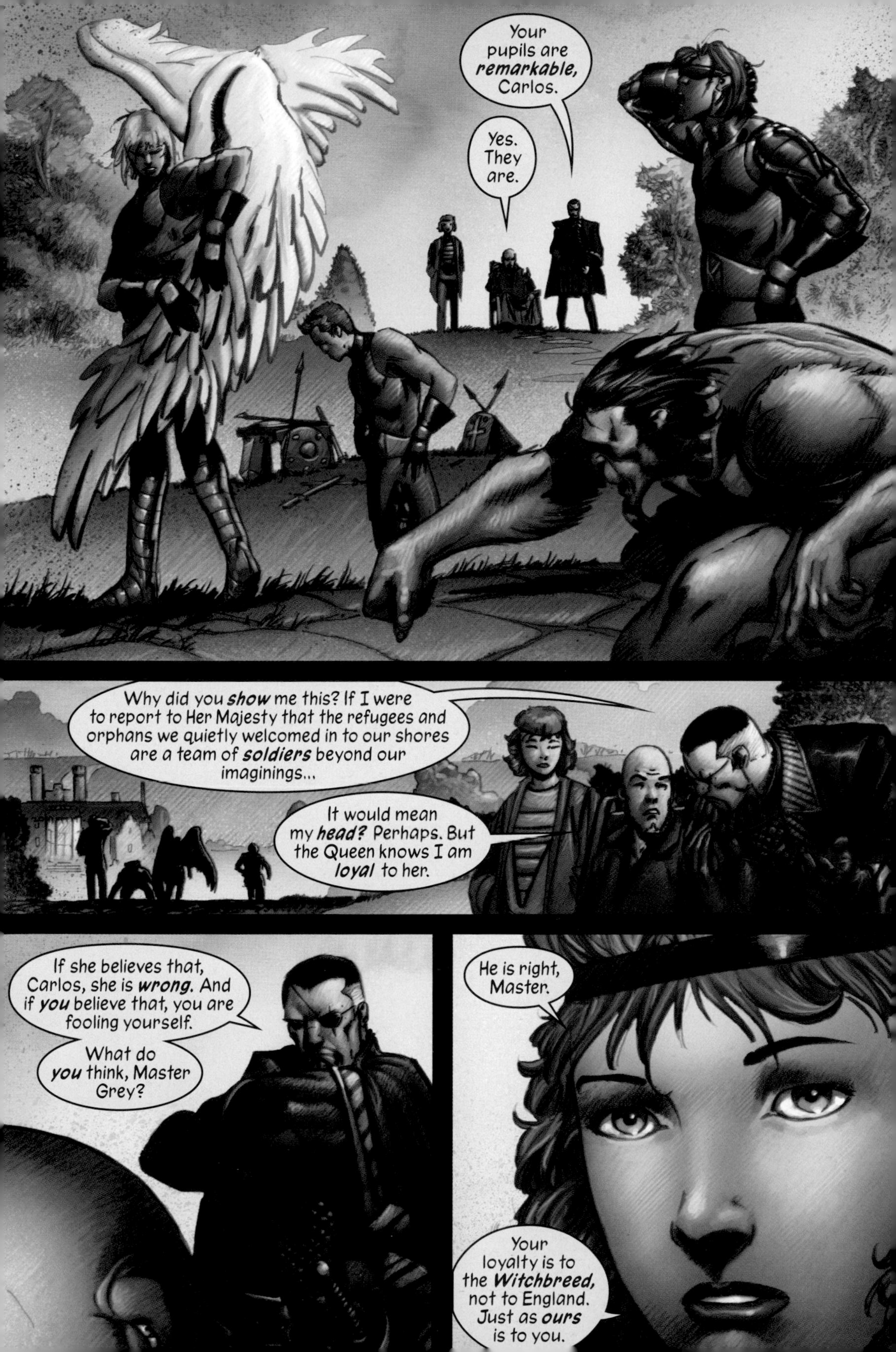

Your pupils are *remarkable,* Carlos.
Yes. They are.
Why did you *show* me this? If I were to report to Her Majesty that the refugees and orphans we quietly welcomed in to our shores are a team of *soldiers* beyond our imaginings...
It would mean my *head?* Perhaps. But the Queen knows I am *loyal* to her.
If she believes that, Carlos, she is *wrong.* And if *you* believe that, you are fooling yourself.
What do *you* think, Master Grey?
He is right, Master.
Your loyalty is to the *Witchbreed,* not to England. Just as *ours* is to you.

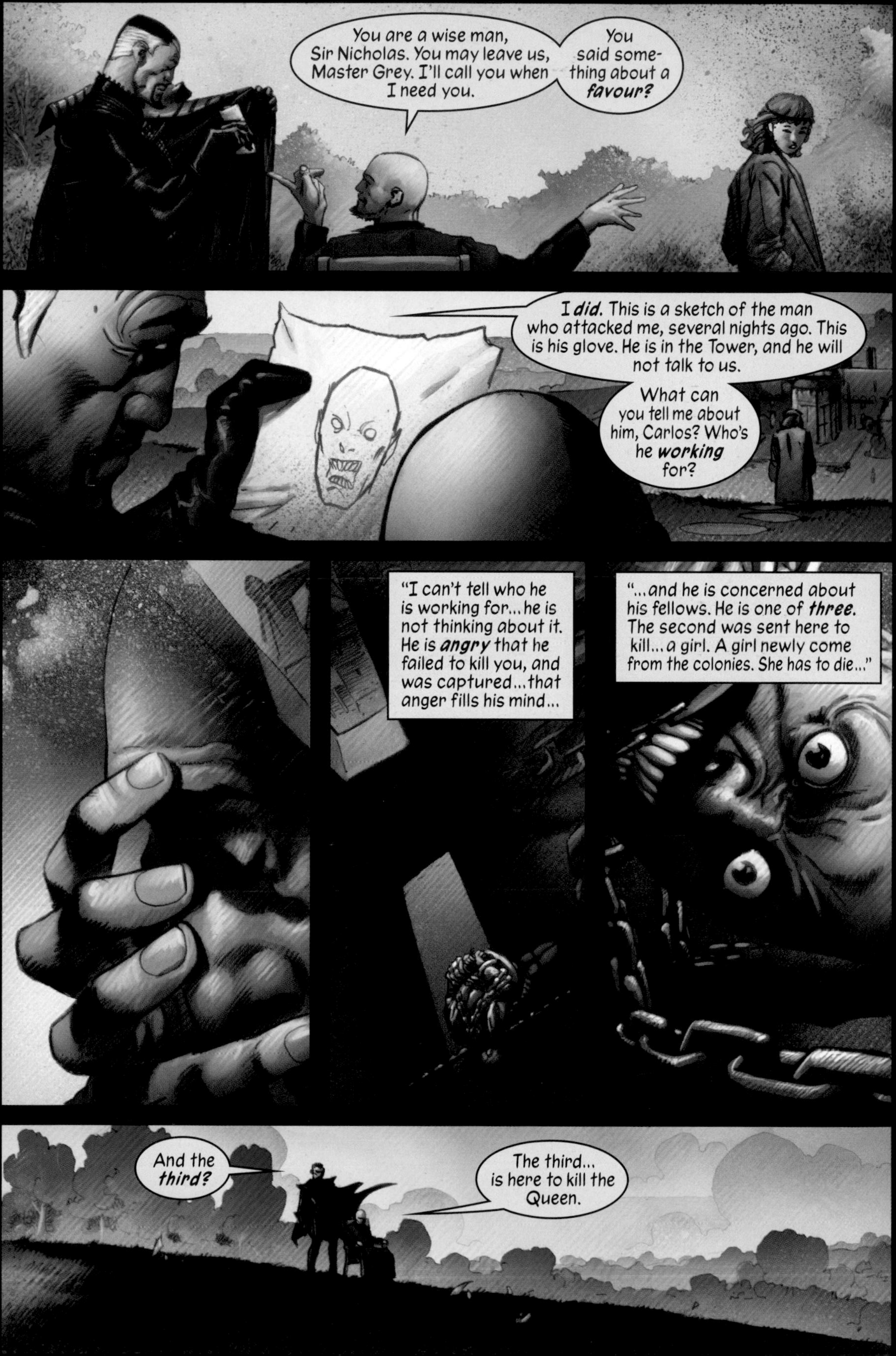
You are a wise man, Sir Nicholas. You may leave us, Master Grey. I'll call you when I need you.
You said something about a *favour?*
I *did.* This is a sketch of the man who attacked me, several nights ago. This is his glove. He is in the Tower, and he will not talk to us.
What can you tell me about him, Carlos? Who's he *working* for?
"I can't tell who he is working for... he is not thinking about it. He is *angry* that he failed to kill you, and was captured... that anger fills his mind...
"...and he is concerned about his fellows. He is one of *three.* The second was sent here to kill... a girl. A girl newly come from the colonies. She has to die..."
And the *third?*
The third... is here to kill the Queen.

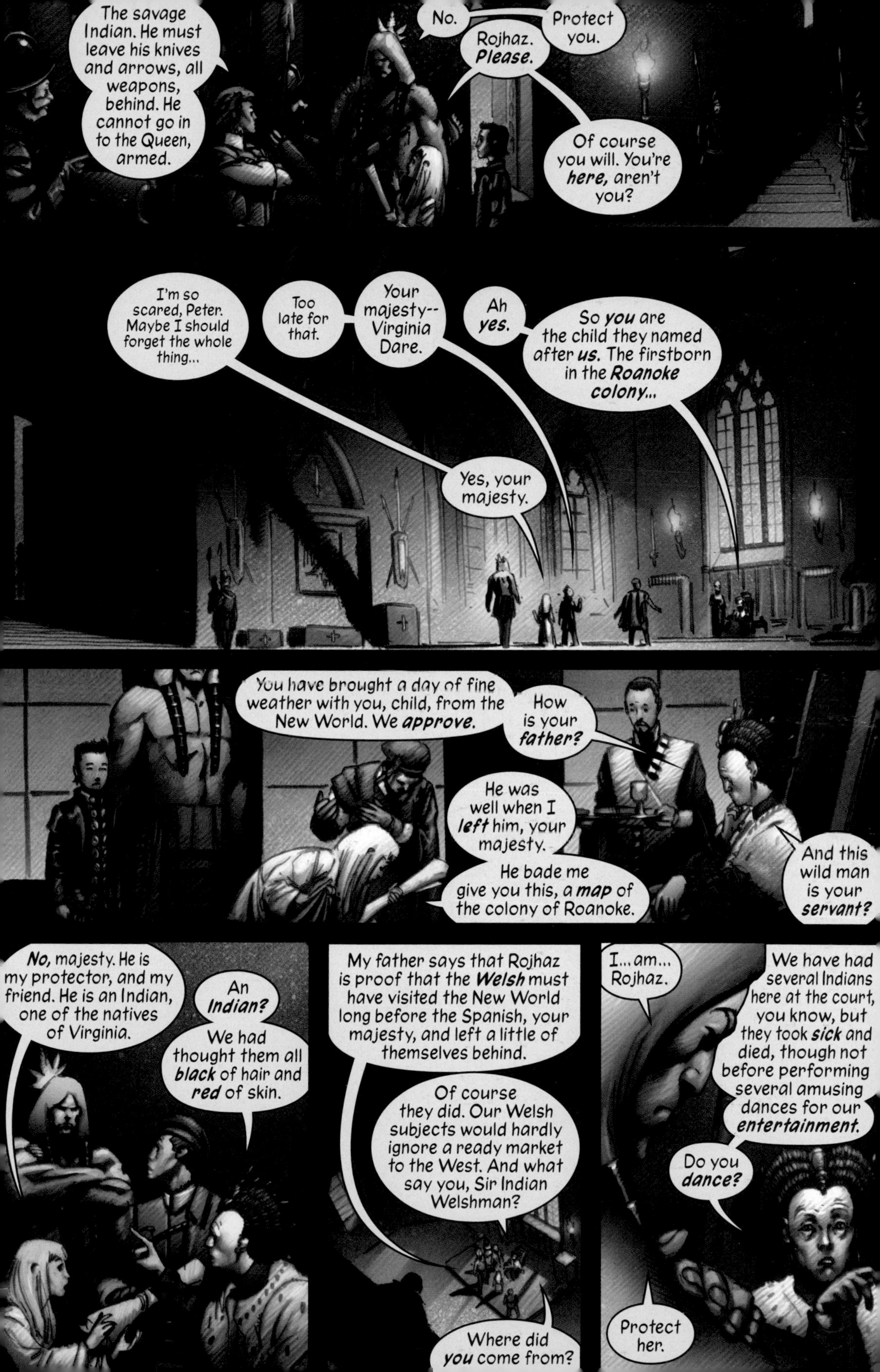
The savage Indian. He must leave his knives and arrows, all weapons, behind. He cannot go in to the Queen, armed.
No.
Protect you.
Rojhaz. *Please.*
Of course you will. You're *here,* aren't you?
I'm so scared, Peter. Maybe I should forget the whole thing...
Too late for that.
Your majesty-- Virginia Dare.
Ah *yes.*
So *you* are the child they named after *us.* The firstborn in the *Roanoke colony...*
Yes, your majesty.
You have brought a day of fine weather with you, child, from the New World. We *approve.*
How is your *father?*
He was well when I *left* him, your majesty.
He bade me give you this, a *map* of the colony of Roanoke.
And this wild man is your *servant?*
No, majesty. He is my protector, and my friend. He is an Indian, one of the natives of Virginia.
An *Indian?*
We had thought them all *black* of hair and *red* of skin.
My father says that Rojhaz is proof that the *Welsh* must have visited the New World long before the Spanish, your majesty, and left a little of themselves behind.
Of course they did. Our Welsh subjects would hardly ignore a ready market to the West. And what say you, Sir Indian Welshman?
Where did *you* come from?
I... am... Rojhaz.
We have had several Indians here at the court, you know, but they took *sick* and died, though not before performing several amusing dances for our *entertainment.*
Do you *dance?*
Protect her.

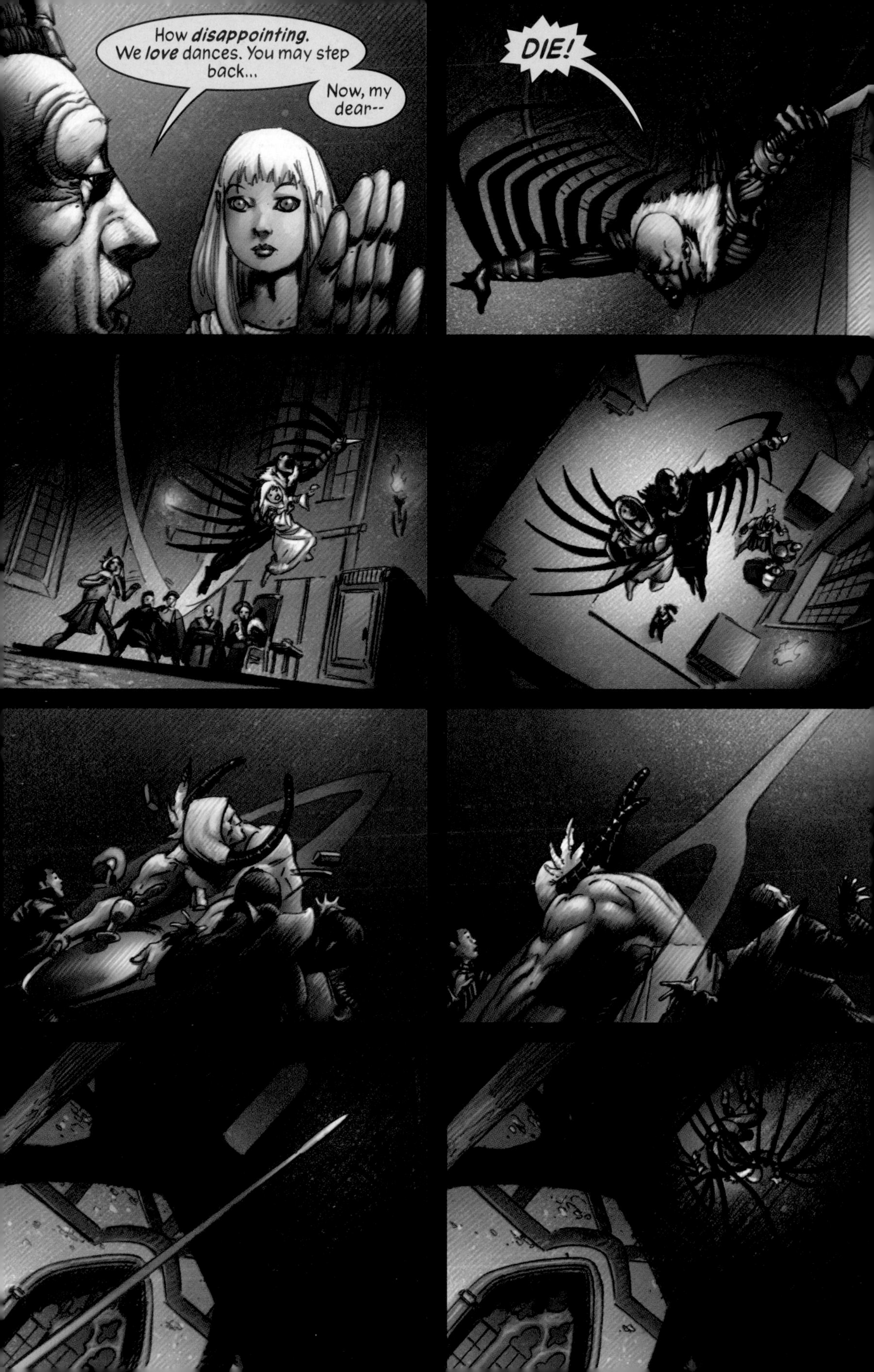
How *disappointing.* We *love* dances. You may step back...
Now, my dear--
DIE!

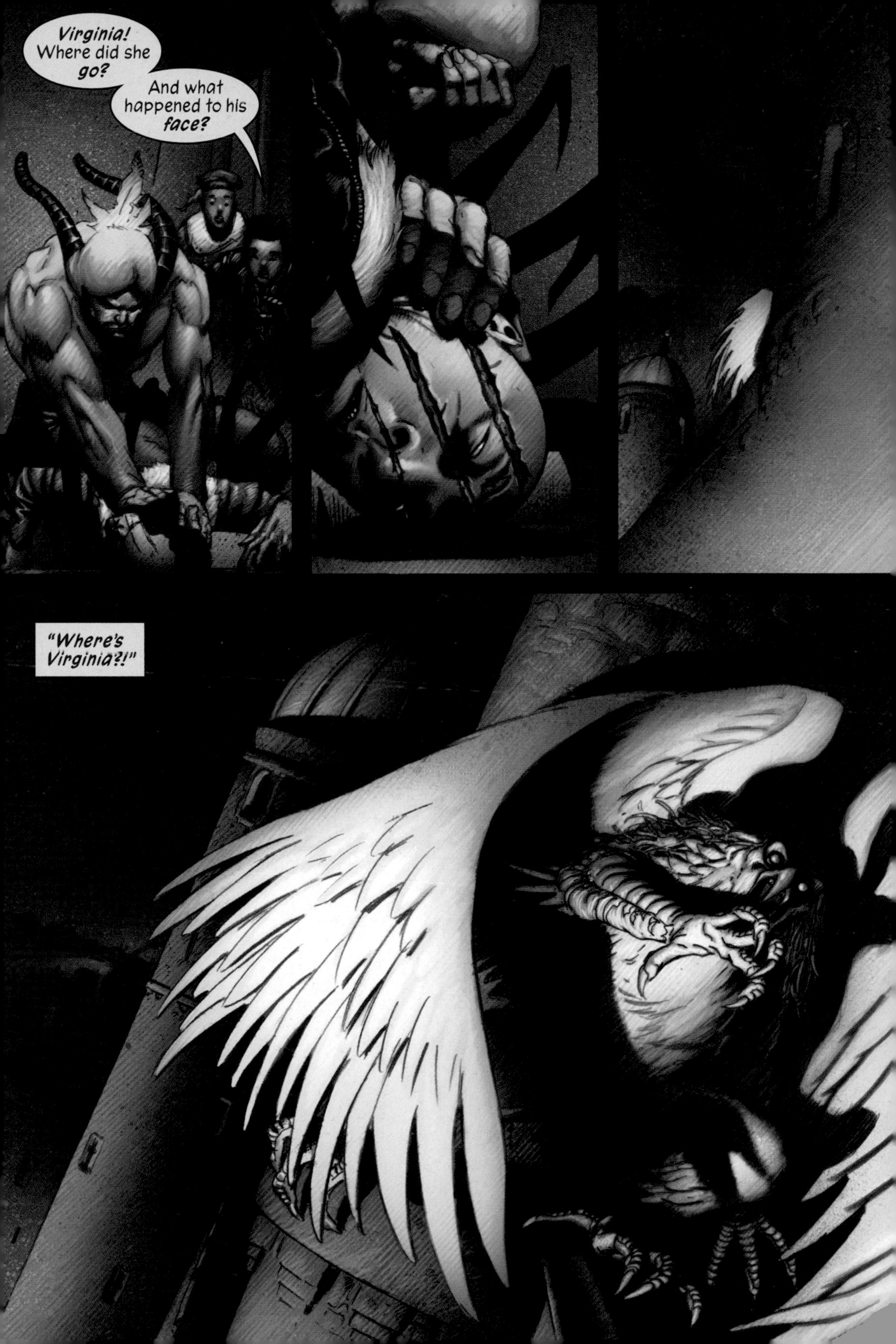
Virginia! Where did she go?
And what happened to his face?
"Where's Virginia?!"

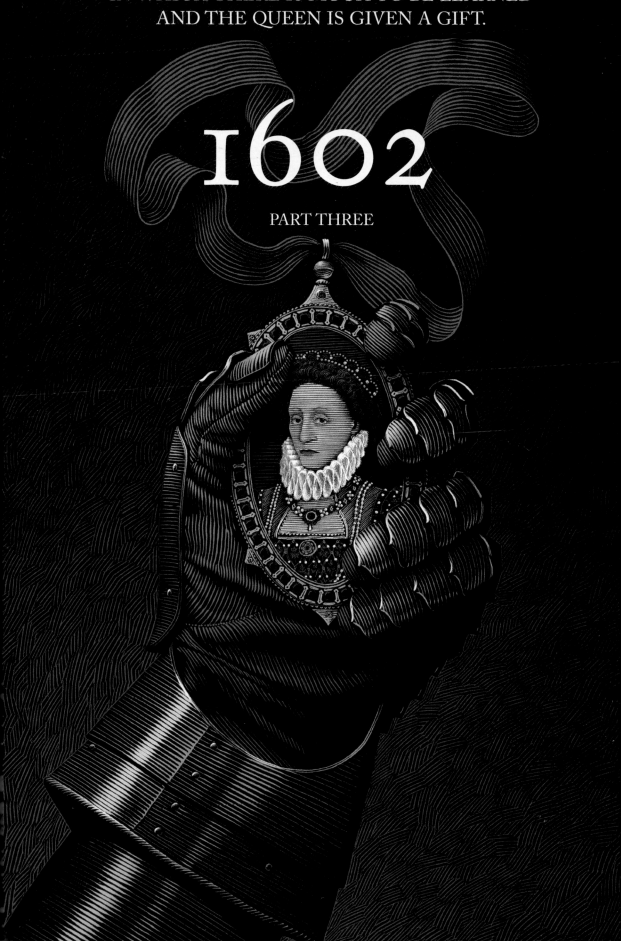

IN WHICH THERE IS MUCH TO BE LEARNED
AND THE QUEEN IS GIVEN A GIFT.

1602

PART THREE

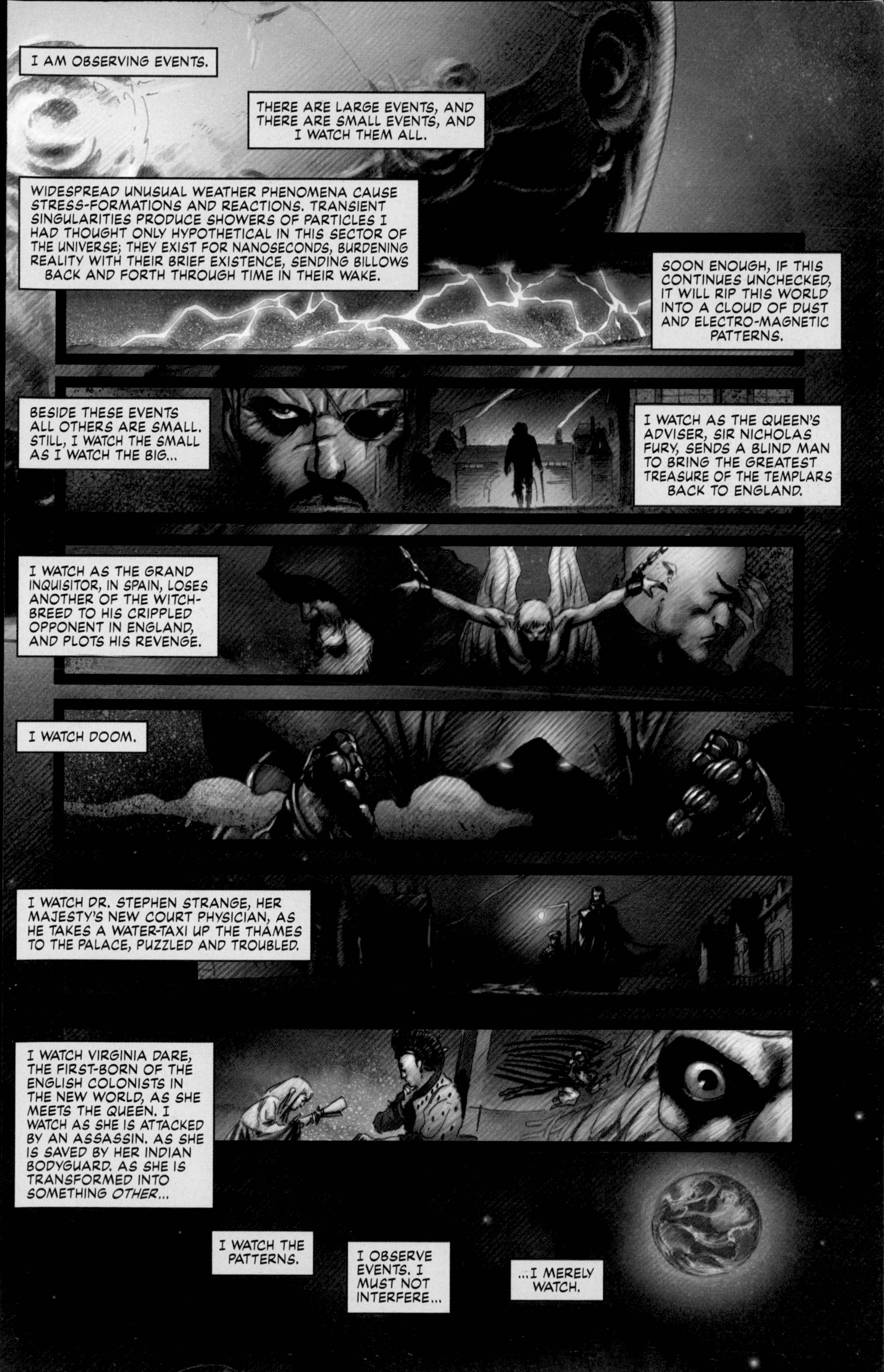
I AM OBSERVING EVENTS.
THERE ARE LARGE EVENTS, AND THERE ARE SMALL EVENTS, AND I WATCH THEM ALL.
WIDESPREAD UNUSUAL WEATHER PHENOMENA CAUSE STRESS-FORMATIONS AND REACTIONS. TRANSIENT SINGULARITIES PRODUCE SHOWERS OF PARTICLES I HAD THOUGHT ONLY HYPOTHETICAL IN THIS SECTOR OF THE UNIVERSE; THEY EXIST FOR NANOSECONDS, BURDENING REALITY WITH THEIR BRIEF EXISTENCE, SENDING BILLOWS BACK AND FORTH THROUGH TIME IN THEIR WAKE.
SOON ENOUGH, IF THIS CONTINUES UNCHECKED, IT WILL RIP THIS WORLD INTO A CLOUD OF DUST AND ELECTRO-MAGNETIC PATTERNS.
BESIDE THESE EVENTS ALL OTHERS ARE SMALL. STILL, I WATCH THE SMALL AS I WATCH THE BIG...
I WATCH AS THE QUEEN'S ADVISER, SIR NICHOLAS FURY, SENDS A BLIND MAN TO BRING THE GREATEST TREASURE OF THE TEMPLARS BACK TO ENGLAND.
I WATCH AS THE GRAND INQUISITOR, IN SPAIN, LOSES ANOTHER OF THE WITCH-BREED TO HIS CRIPPLED OPPONENT IN ENGLAND, AND PLOTS HIS REVENGE.
I WATCH DOOM.
I WATCH DR. STEPHEN STRANGE, HER MAJESTY'S NEW COURT PHYSICIAN, AS HE TAKES A WATER-TAXI UP THE THAMES TO THE PALACE, PUZZLED AND TROUBLED.
I WATCH VIRGINIA DARE, THE FIRST-BORN OF THE ENGLISH COLONISTS IN THE NEW WORLD, AS SHE MEETS THE QUEEN. I WATCH AS SHE IS ATTACKED BY AN ASSASSIN. AS SHE IS SAVED BY HER INDIAN BODYGUARD. AS SHE IS TRANSFORMED INTO SOMETHING *OTHER*...
I WATCH THE PATTERNS.
I OBSERVE EVENTS. I MUST NOT INTERFERE...
...I MERELY WATCH.

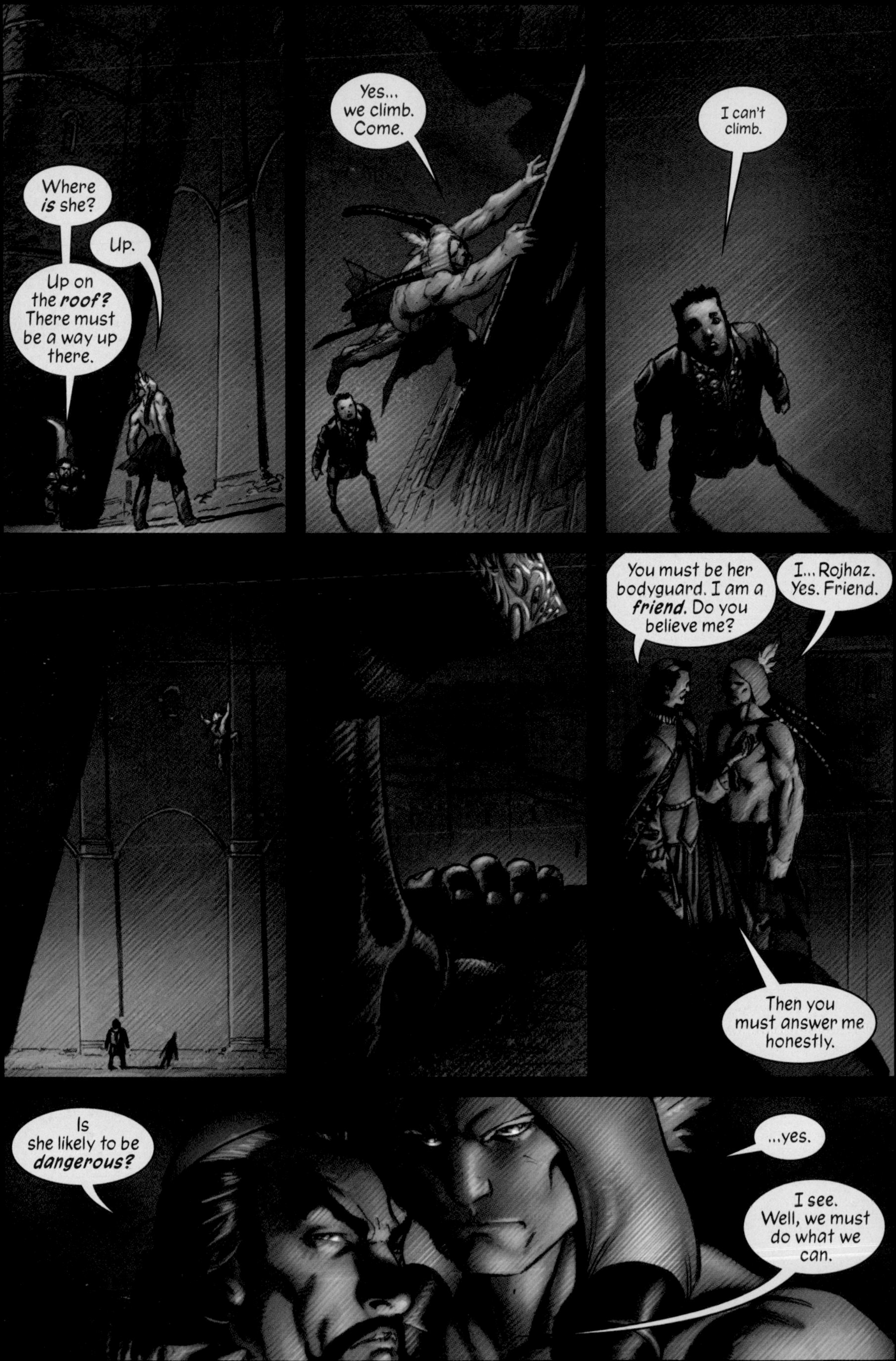

Where *is* she?
Up.
Up on the ***roof?*** There must be a way up there.
Yes... we climb. Come.
I can't climb.
You must be her bodyguard. I am a ***friend.*** Do you believe me?
I... Rojhaz. Yes. Friend.
Then you must answer me honestly.
Is she likely to be ***dangerous?***
...yes.
I see. Well, we must do what we can.

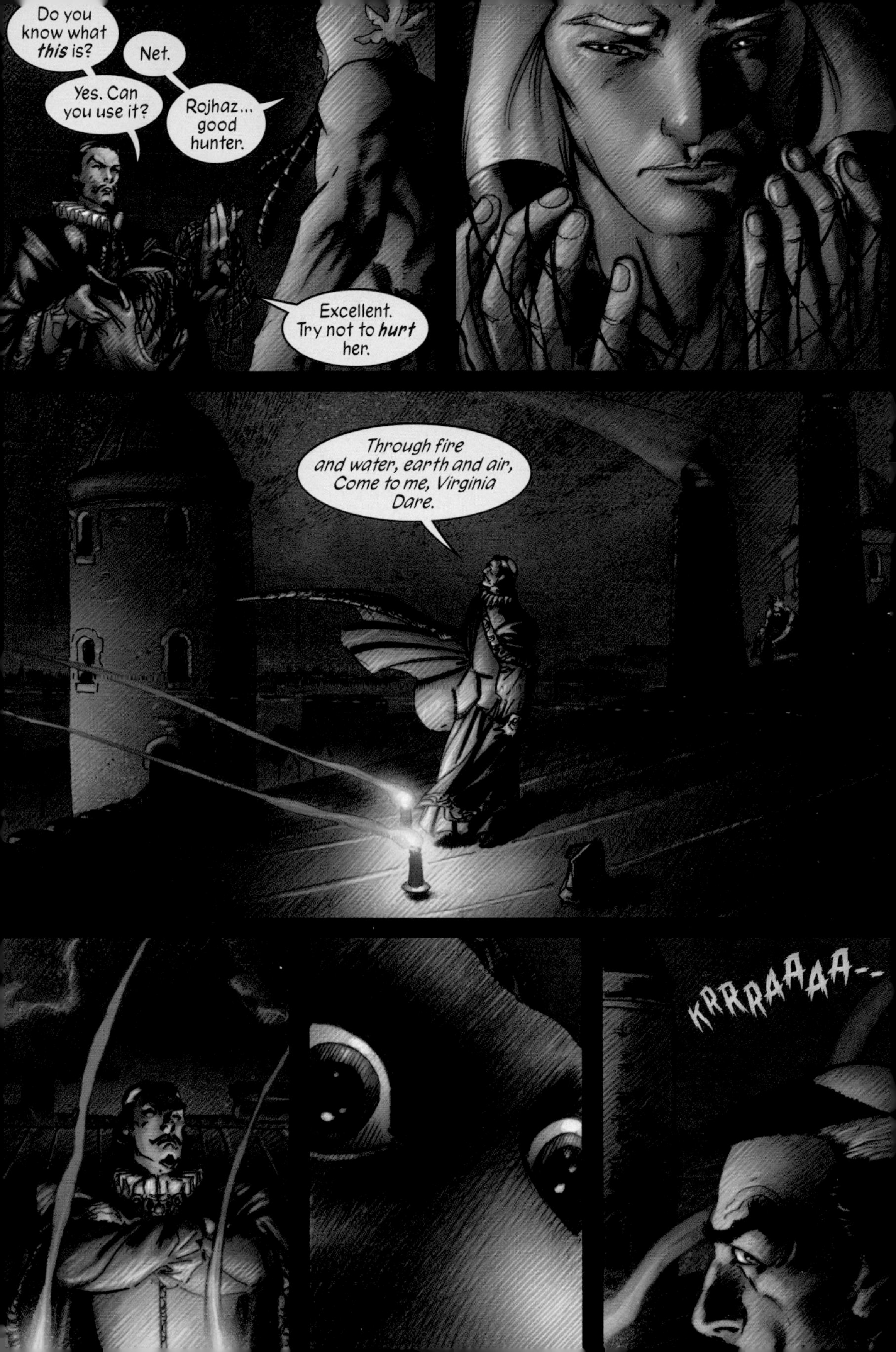
Do you know what *this* is?
Net.
Yes. Can you use it?
Rojhaz... good hunter.
Excellent. Try not to ***hurt*** her.
Through fire and water, earth and air, Come to me, Virginia Dare.
KRRAAAAA--

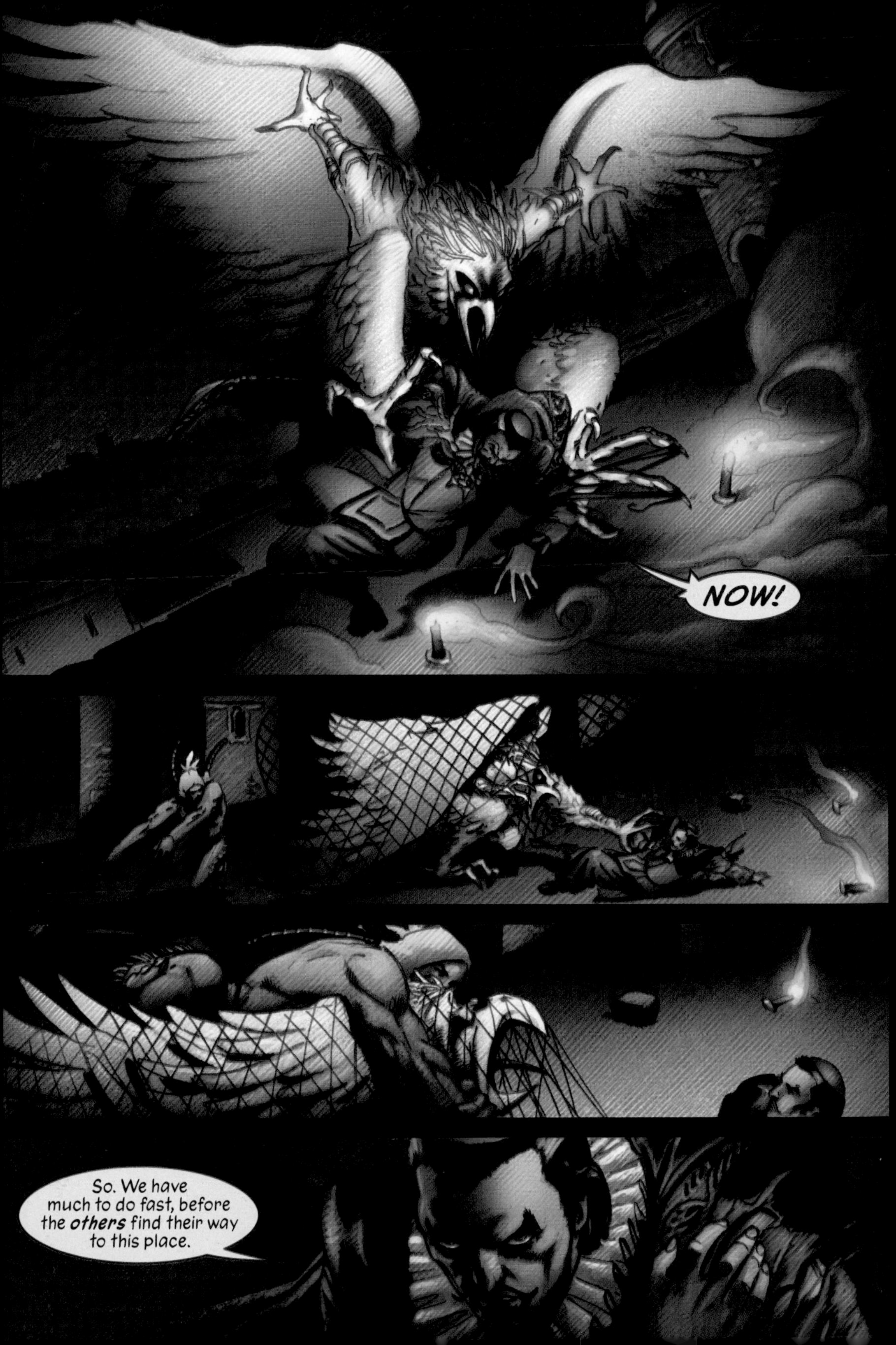
NOW!
So. We have much to do fast, before the *others* find their way to this place.

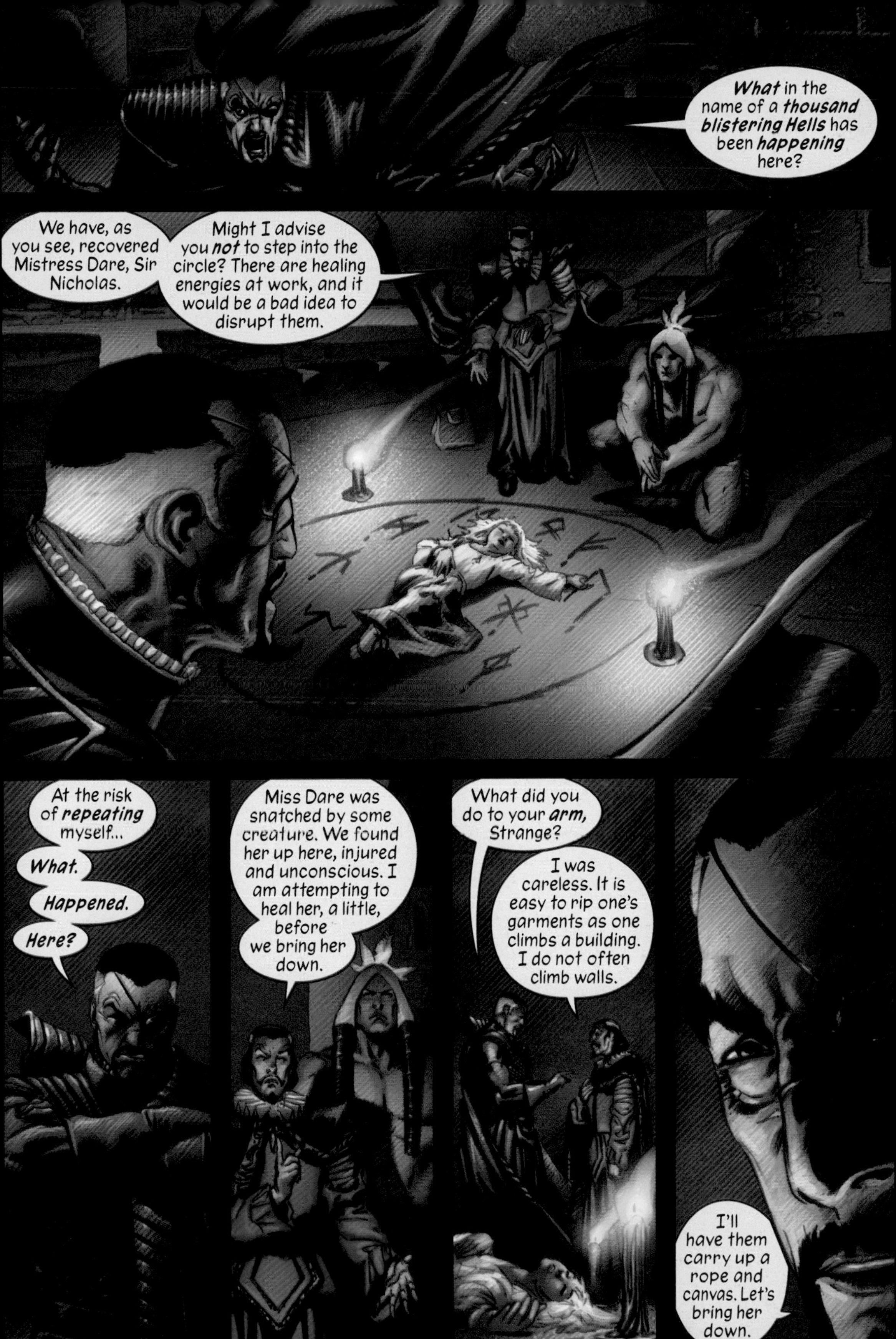
What in the name of a thousand blistering Hells has been happening here?
We have, as you see, recovered Mistress Dare, Sir Nicholas.
Might I advise you not to step into the circle? There are healing energies at work, and it would be a bad idea to disrupt them.
At the risk of repeating myself...
What.
Happened.
Here?
Miss Dare was snatched by some creature. We found her up here, injured and unconscious. I am attempting to heal her, a little, before we bring her down.
What did you do to your arm, Strange?
I was careless. It is easy to rip one's garments as one climbs a building. I do not often climb walls.
I'll have them carry up a rope and canvas. Let's bring her down.

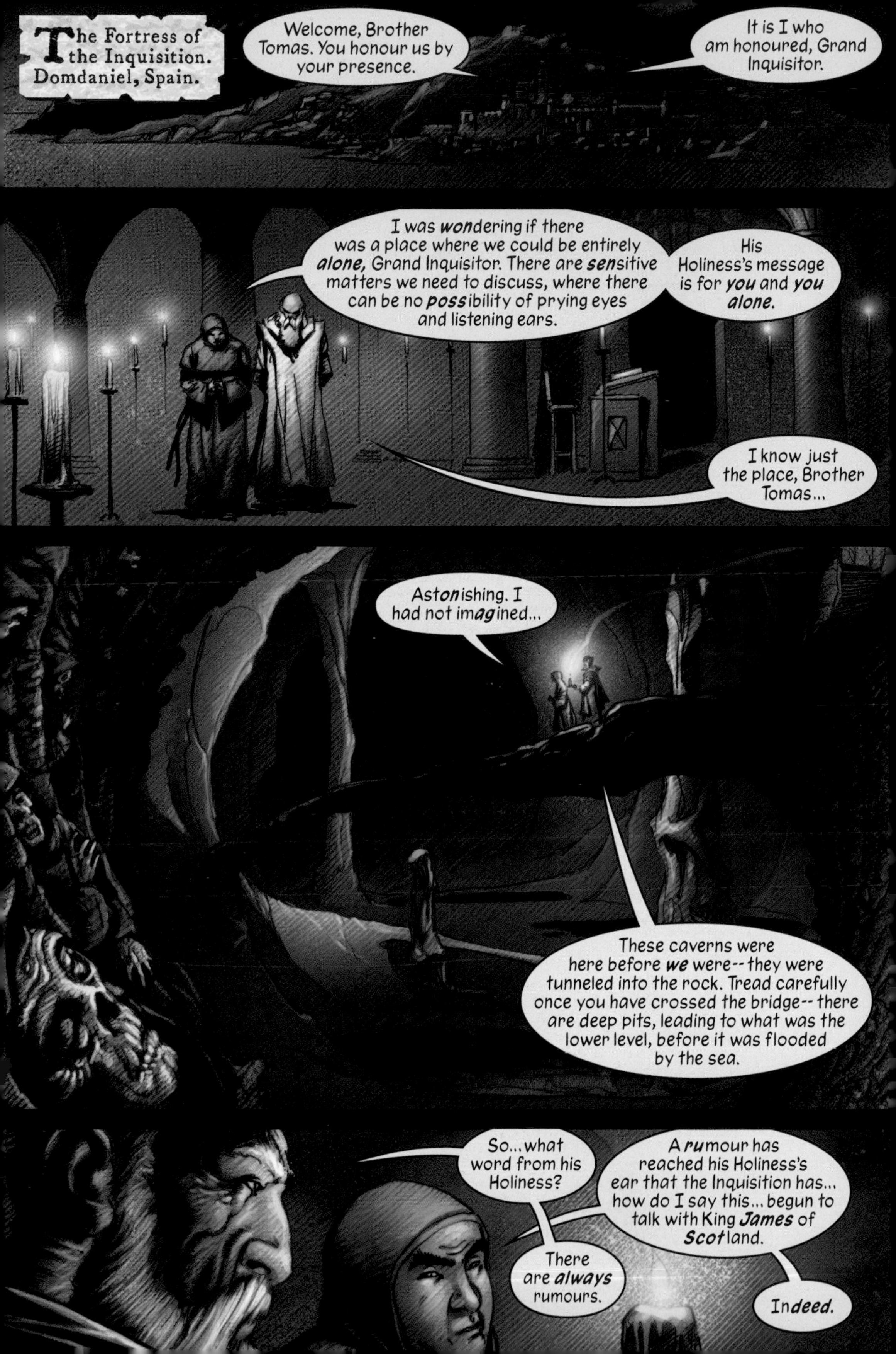
The Fortress of the Inquisition. Domdaniel, Spain.
Welcome, Brother Tomas. You honour us by your presence.
It is I who am honoured, Grand Inquisitor.
I was wondering if there was a place where we could be entirely alone, Grand Inquisitor. There are sensitive matters we need to discuss, where there can be no possibility of prying eyes and listening ears.
His Holiness's message is for you and you alone.
I know just the place, Brother Tomas...
Astonishing. I had not imagined...
These caverns were here before we were-- they were tunneled into the rock. Tread carefully once you have crossed the bridge-- there are deep pits, leading to what was the lower level, before it was flooded by the sea.
So... what word from his Holiness?
A rumour has reached his Holiness's ear that the Inquisition has... how do I say this... begun to talk with King James of Scotland.
There are always rumours.
Indeed.

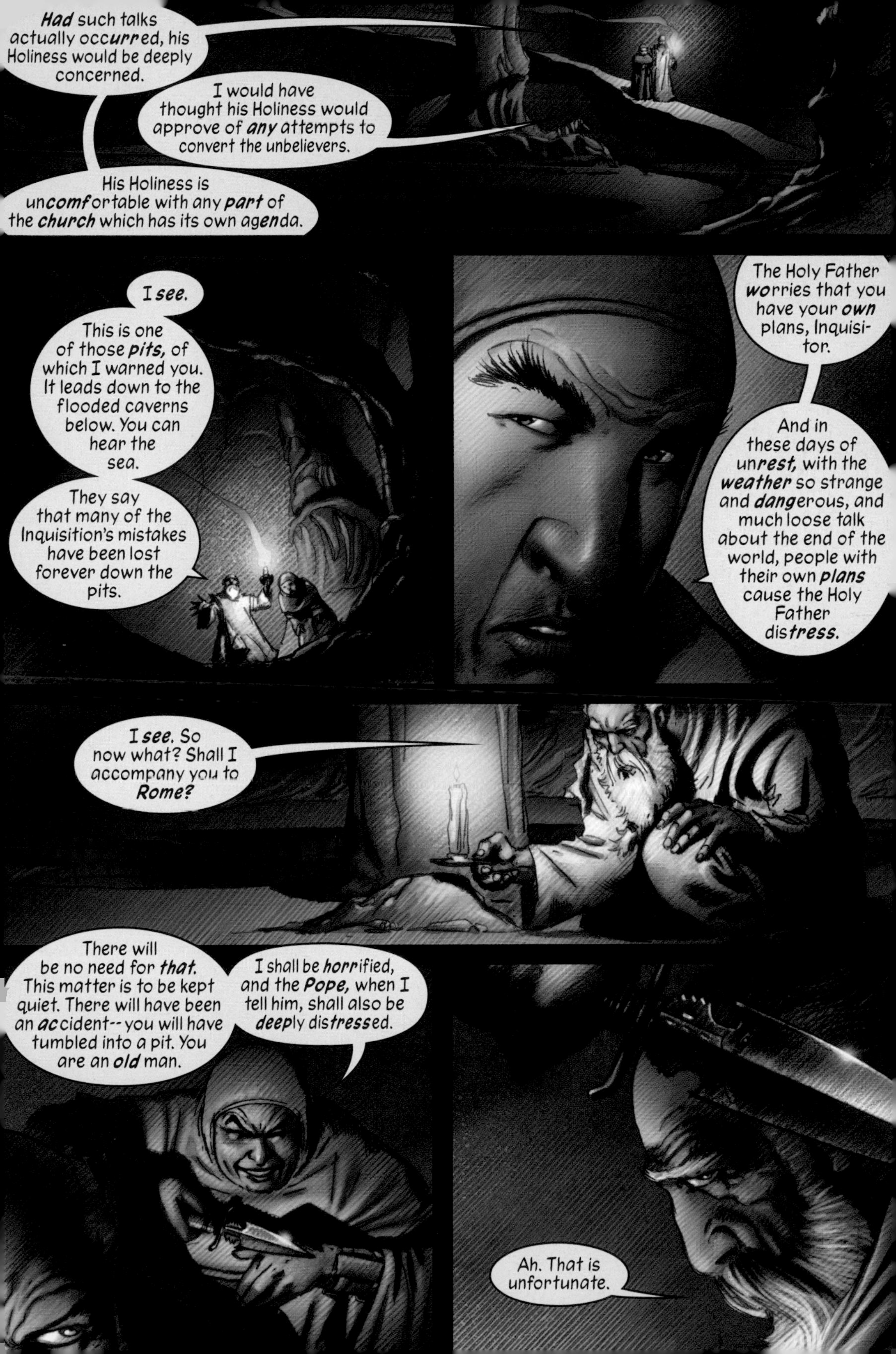

Had such talks actually occurred, his Holiness would be deeply concerned.
I would have thought his Holiness would approve of any attempts to convert the unbelievers.
His Holiness is uncomfortable with any part of the church which has its own agenda.
I see.
This is one of those pits, of which I warned you. It leads down to the flooded caverns below. You can hear the sea.
They say that many of the Inquisition's mistakes have been lost forever down the pits.
The Holy Father worries that you have your own plans, Inquisitor.
And in these days of unrest, with the weather so strange and dangerous, and much loose talk about the end of the world, people with their own plans cause the Holy Father distress.
I see. So now what? Shall I accompany you to Rome?
There will be no need for that. This matter is to be kept quiet. There will have been an accident-- you will have tumbled into a pit. You are an old man.
I shall be horrified, and the Pope, when I tell him, shall also be deeply distressed.
Ah. That is unfortunate.

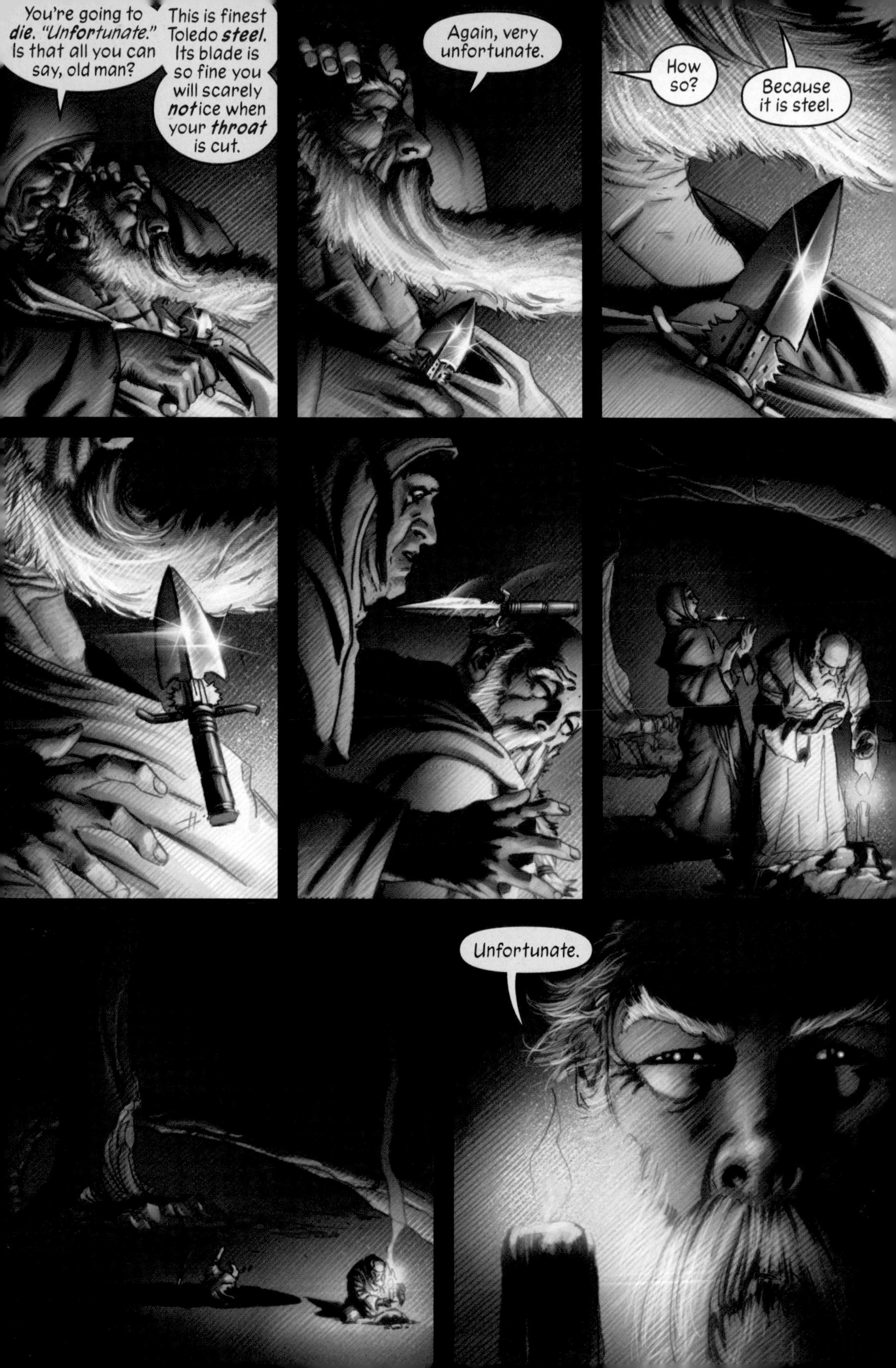
You're going to *die*. "*Unfortunate*." Is that all you can say, old man?
This is finest Toledo ***steel***. Its blade is so fine you will scarely ***not***ice when your ***throat*** is cut.
Again, very unfortunate.
How so?
Because it is steel.
Unfortunate.

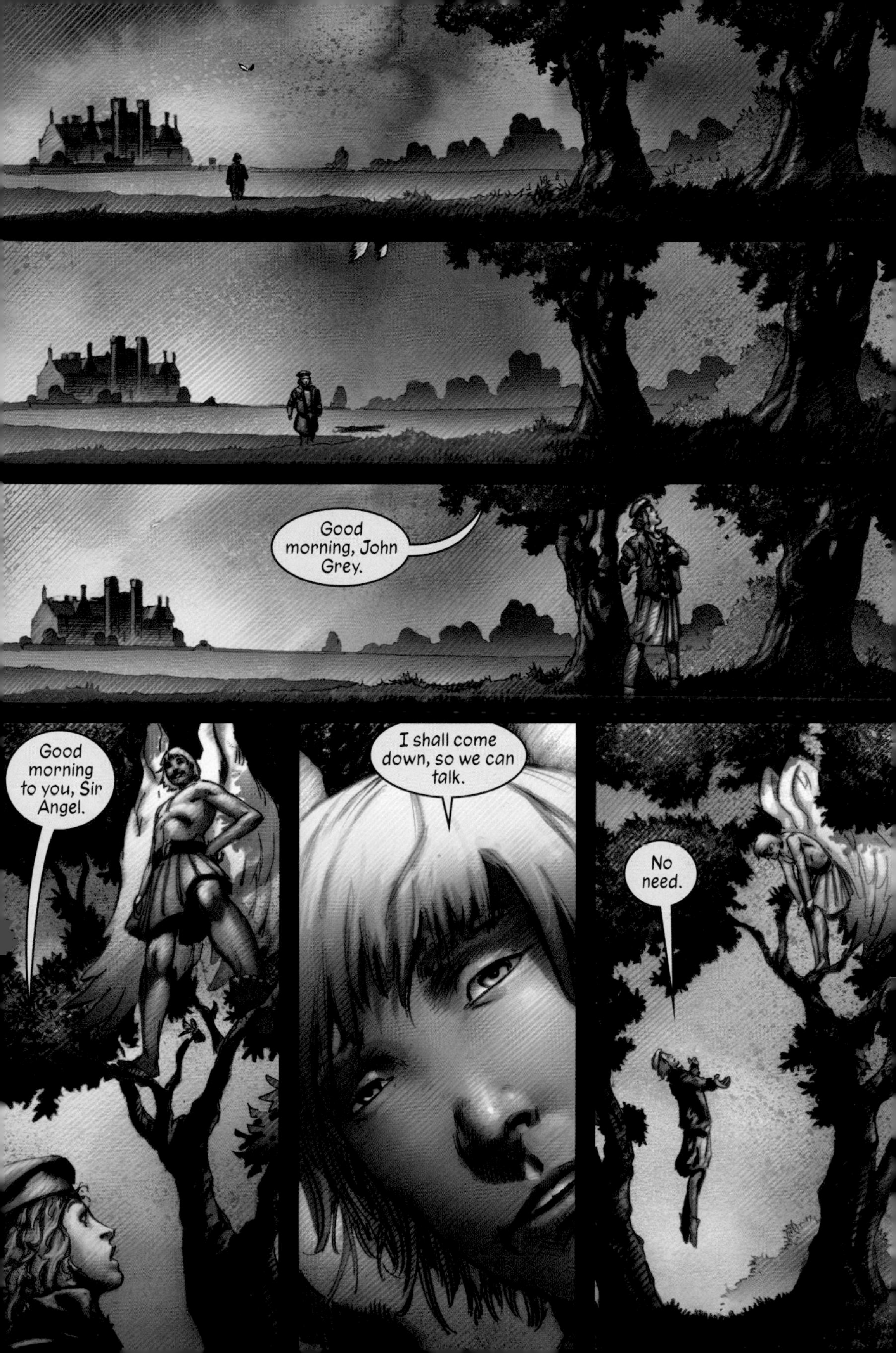
Good morning, John Grey.
Good morning to you, Sir Angel.
I shall come down, so we can talk.
No need.

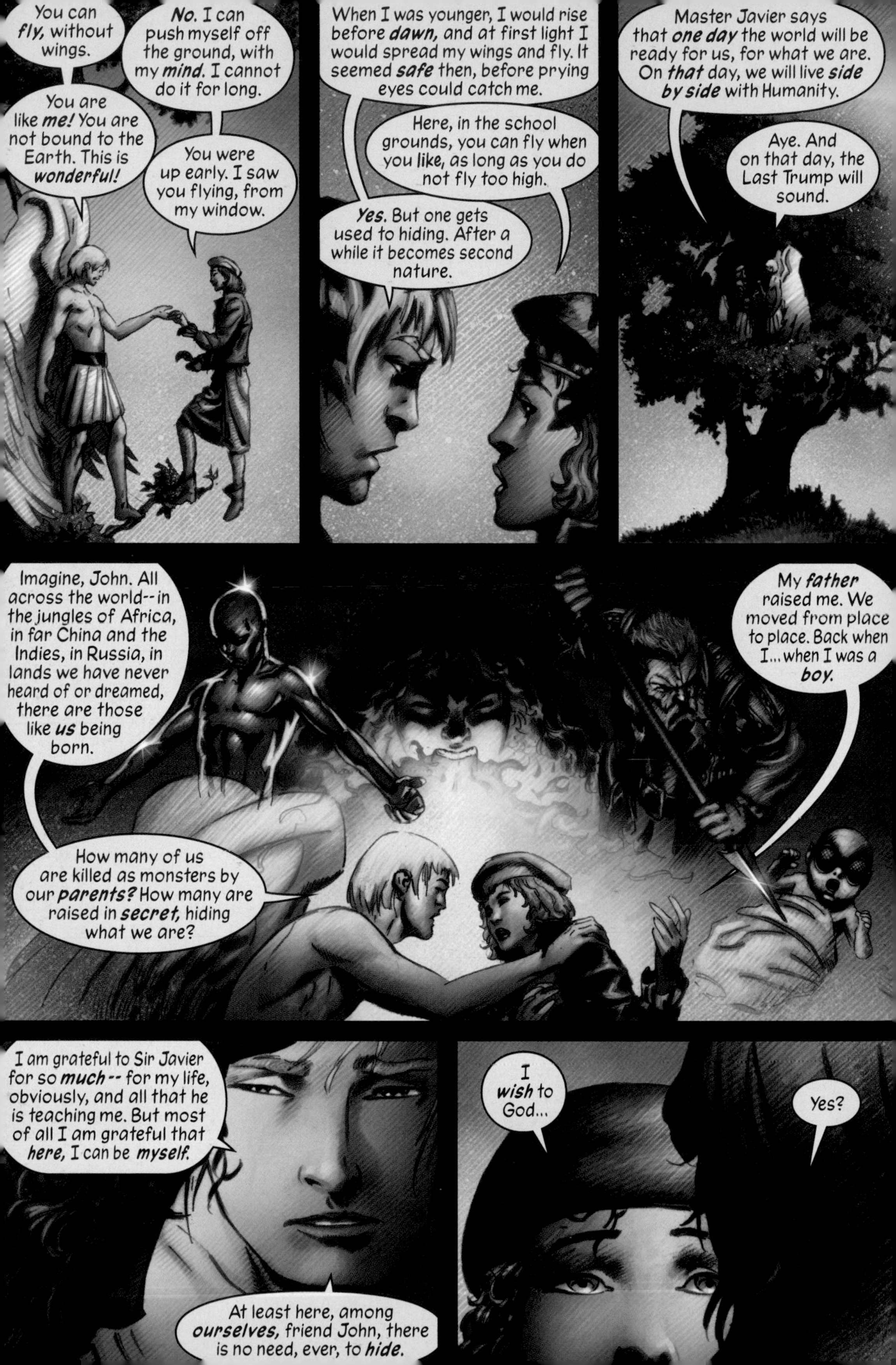
You can fly, without wings.
No. I can push myself off the ground, with my mind. I cannot do it for long.
You are like me! You are not bound to the Earth. This is wonderful!
You were up early. I saw you flying, from my window.
When I was younger, I would rise before dawn, and at first light I would spread my wings and fly. It seemed safe then, before prying eyes could catch me.
Here, in the school grounds, you can fly when you like, as long as you do not fly too high.
Yes. But one gets used to hiding. After a while it becomes second nature.
Master Javier says that one day the world will be ready for us, for what we are. On that day, we will live side by side with Humanity.
Aye. And on that day, the Last Trump will sound.
Imagine, John. All across the world--in the jungles of Africa, in far China and the Indies, in Russia, in lands we have never heard of or dreamed, there are those like us being born.
My father raised me. We moved from place to place. Back when I... when I was a boy.
How many of us are killed as monsters by our parents? How many are raised in secret, hiding what we are?
I am grateful to Sir Javier for so much -- for my life, obviously, and all that he is teaching me. But most of all I am grateful that here, I can be myself.
At least here, among ourselves, friend John, there is no need, ever, to hide.
I wish to God...
Yes?

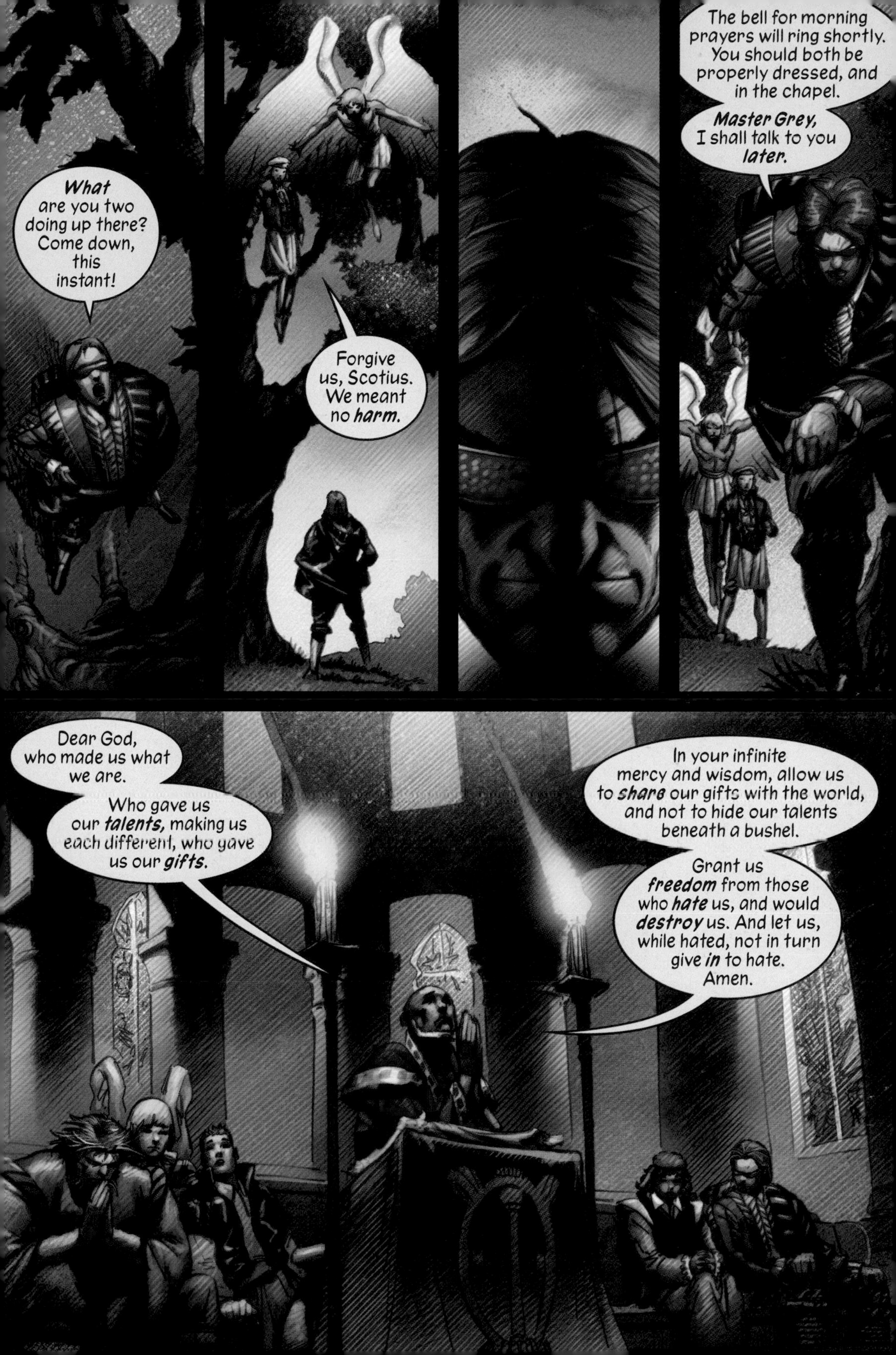
What are you two doing up there? Come down, this instant!
Forgive us, Scotius. We meant no harm.
The bell for morning prayers will ring shortly. You should both be properly dressed, and in the chapel.
Master Grey, I shall talk to you later.
Dear God, who made us what we are.
Who gave us our talents, making us each different, who gave us our gifts.
In your infinite mercy and wisdom, allow us to share our gifts with the world, and not to hide our talents beneath a bushel.
Grant us freedom from those who hate us, and would destroy us. And let us, while hated, not in turn give in to hate. Amen.

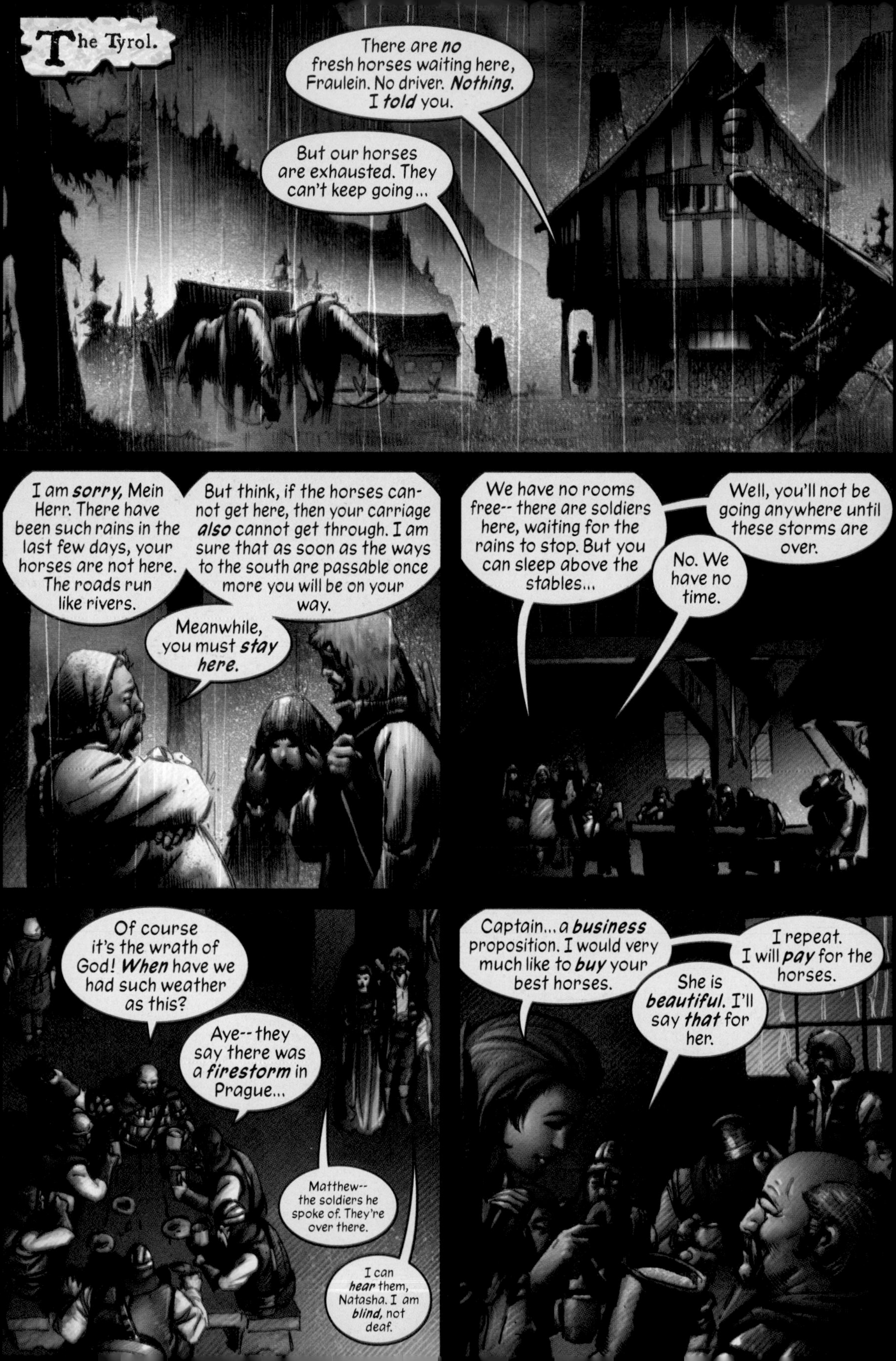
The Tyrol.
There are no fresh horses waiting here, Fraulein. No driver. Nothing. I told you.
But our horses are exhausted. They can't keep going...
I am sorry, Mein Herr. There have been such rains in the last few days, your horses are not here. The roads run like rivers.
But think, if the horses cannot get here, then your carriage also cannot get through. I am sure that as soon as the ways to the south are passable once more you will be on your way.
Meanwhile, you must stay here.
We have no rooms free-- there are soldiers here, waiting for the rains to stop. But you can sleep above the stables...
Well, you'll not be going anywhere until these storms are over.
No. We have no time.
Of course it's the wrath of God! When have we had such weather as this?
Aye-- they say there was a firestorm in Prague...
Matthew-- the soldiers he spoke of. They're over there.
I can hear them, Natasha. I am blind, not deaf.
Captain... a business proposition. I would very much like to buy your best horses.
I repeat. I will pay for the horses.
She is beautiful. I'll say that for her.

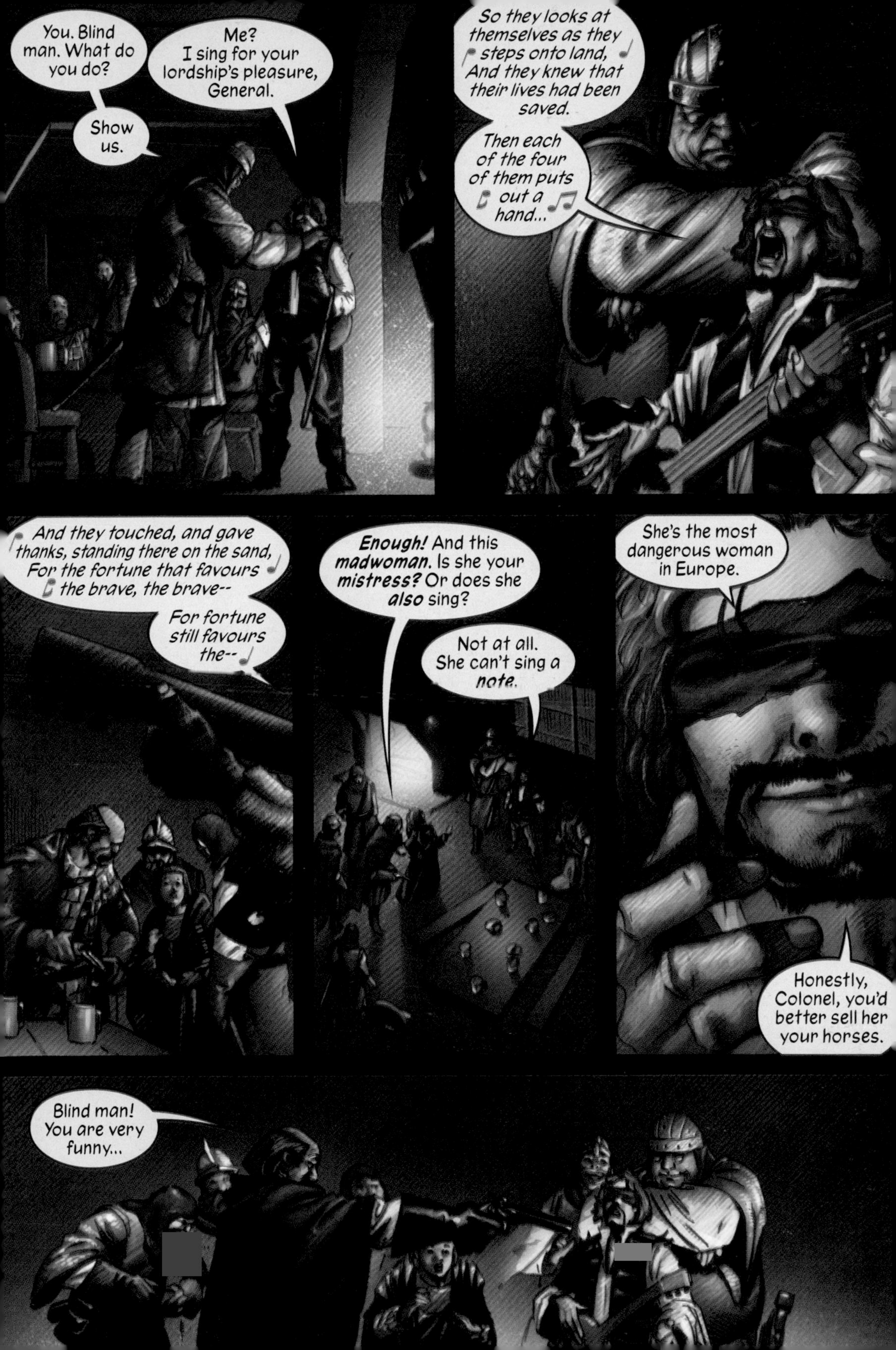
You. Blind man. What do you do?
Me? I sing for your lordship's pleasure, General.
Show us.
So they looks at themselves as they steps onto land, And they knew that their lives had been saved.
Then each of the four of them puts out a hand...
And they touched, and gave thanks, standing there on the sand, For the fortune that favours the brave, the brave--
For fortune still favours the--
Enough! And this madwoman. Is she your mistress? Or does she also sing?
Not at all. She can't sing a note.
She's the most dangerous woman in Europe.
Honestly, Colonel, you'd better sell her your horses.
Blind man! You are very funny...

I *would* have *paid* them. I was perfectly *willing* to pay.

I *know*. I *heard* you.

We'll take the forest paths heading south...we should be all right if we keep to the high ground.

Do you *really* think I'm the most dangerous woman in Europe?

Well, I've not met them *all*. But I can't imagine anyone more dangerous.

That's very *sweet* of you. Hold tight.

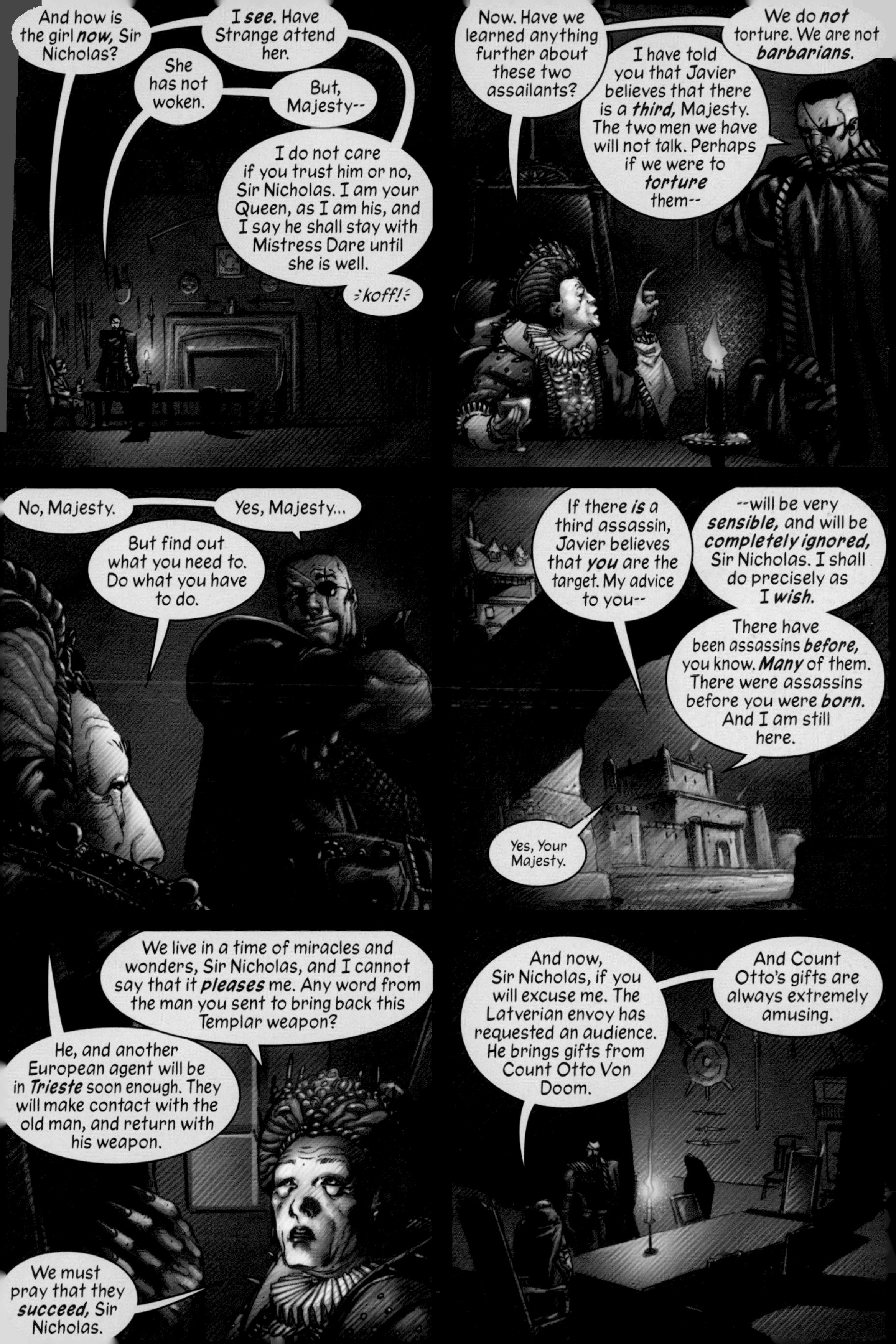
And how is the girl now, Sir Nicholas?
I see. Have Strange attend her.
She has not woken.
But, Majesty--
I do not care if you trust him or no, Sir Nicholas. I am your Queen, as I am his, and I say he shall stay with Mistress Dare until she is well.
koff!
Now. Have we learned anything further about these two assailants?
We do not torture. We are not barbarians.
I have told you that Javier believes that there is a third, Majesty. The two men we have will not talk. Perhaps if we were to torture them--
No, Majesty.
Yes, Majesty...
But find out what you need to. Do what you have to do.
If there is a third assassin, Javier believes that you are the target. My advice to you--
--will be very sensible, and will be completely ignored, Sir Nicholas. I shall do precisely as I wish.
There have been assassins before, you know. Many of them. There were assassins before you were born. And I am still here.
Yes, Your Majesty.
We live in a time of miracles and wonders, Sir Nicholas, and I cannot say that it pleases me. Any word from the man you sent to bring back this Templar weapon?
He, and another European agent will be in Trieste soon enough. They will make contact with the old man, and return with his weapon.
We must pray that they succeed, Sir Nicholas.
And now, Sir Nicholas, if you will excuse me. The Latverian envoy has requested an audience. He brings gifts from Count Otto Von Doom.
And Count Otto's gifts are always extremely amusing.

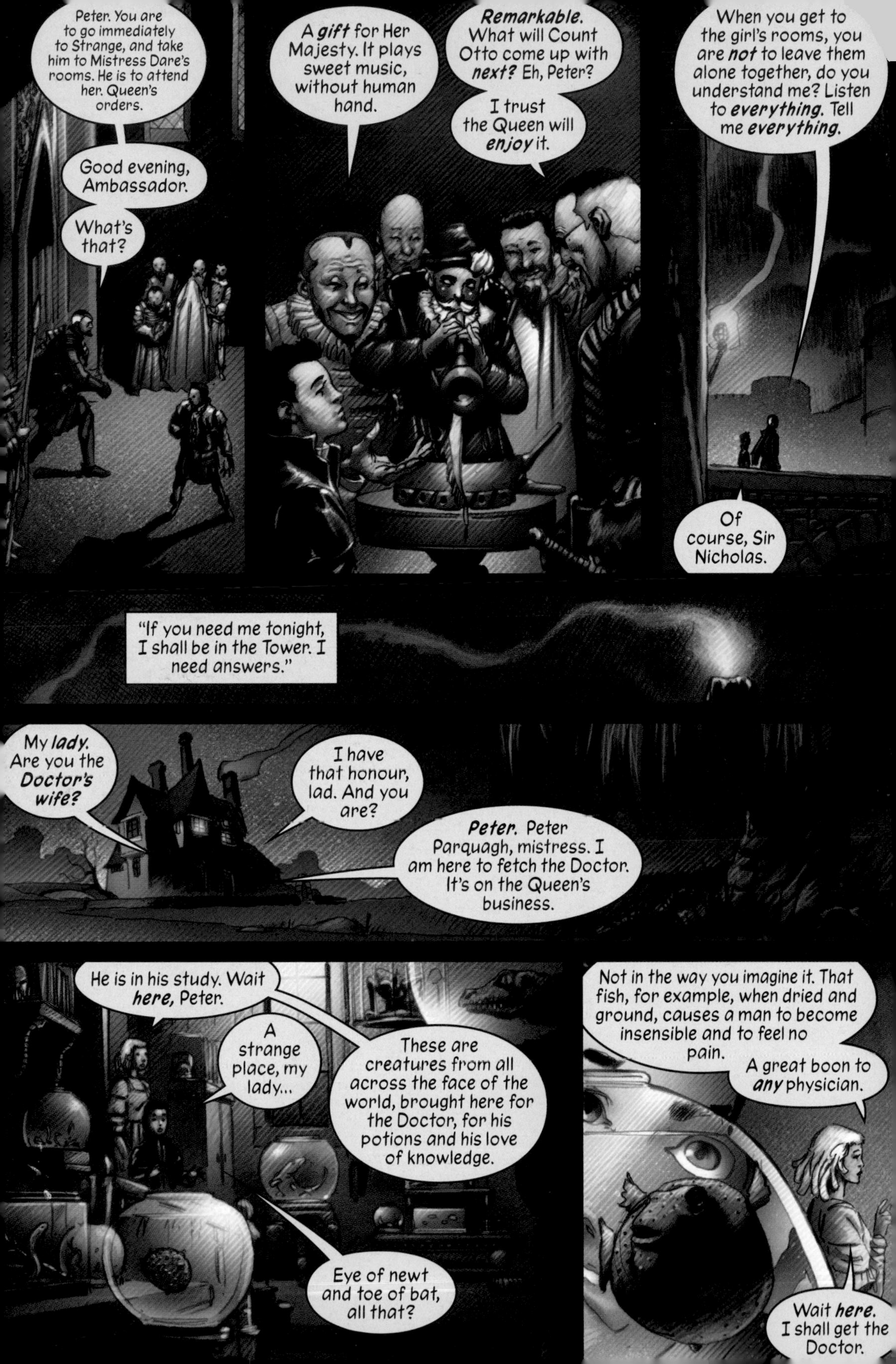
Peter. You are to go immediately to Strange, and take him to Mistress Dare's rooms. He is to attend her. Queen's orders.
Good evening, Ambassador.
What's that?
A *gift* for Her Majesty. It plays sweet music, without human hand.
Remarkable. What will Count Otto come up with *next?* Eh, Peter?
I trust the Queen will *enjoy* it.
When you get to the girl's rooms, you are *not* to leave them alone together, do you understand me? Listen to *everything.* Tell me *everything.*
Of course, Sir Nicholas.
"If you need me tonight, I shall be in the Tower. I need answers."
My *lady.* Are you the *Doctor's wife?*
I have that honour, lad. And you are?
Peter. Peter Parquagh, mistress. I am here to fetch the Doctor. It's on the Queen's business.
He is in his study. Wait *here,* Peter.
A strange place, my lady...
These are creatures from all across the face of the world, brought here for the Doctor, for his potions and his love of knowledge.
Eye of newt and toe of bat, all that?
Not in the way you imagine it. That fish, for example, when dried and ground, causes a man to become insensible and to feel no pain.
A great boon to *any* physician.
Wait *here.* I shall get the Doctor.

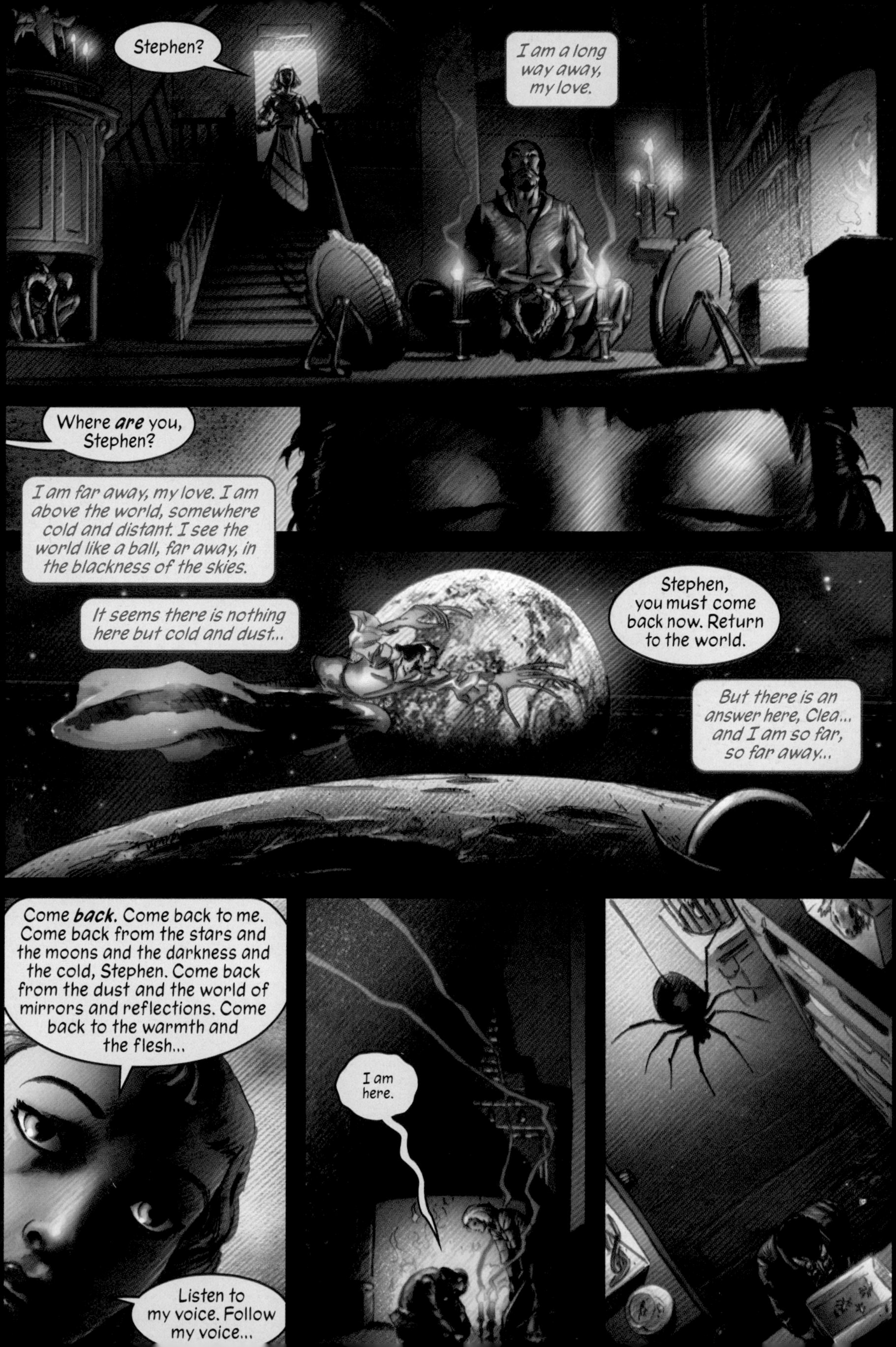
Stephen?
I am a long way away, my love.
Where are you, Stephen?
I am far away, my love. I am above the world, somewhere cold and distant. I see the world like a ball, far away, in the blackness of the skies.
It seems there is nothing here but cold and dust...
Stephen, you must come back now. Return to the world.
But there is an answer here, Clea... and I am so far, so far away...
Come back. Come back to me. Come back from the stars and the moons and the darkness and the cold, Stephen. Come back from the dust and the world of mirrors and reflections. Come back to the warmth and the flesh...
Listen to my voice. Follow my voice...
I am here.

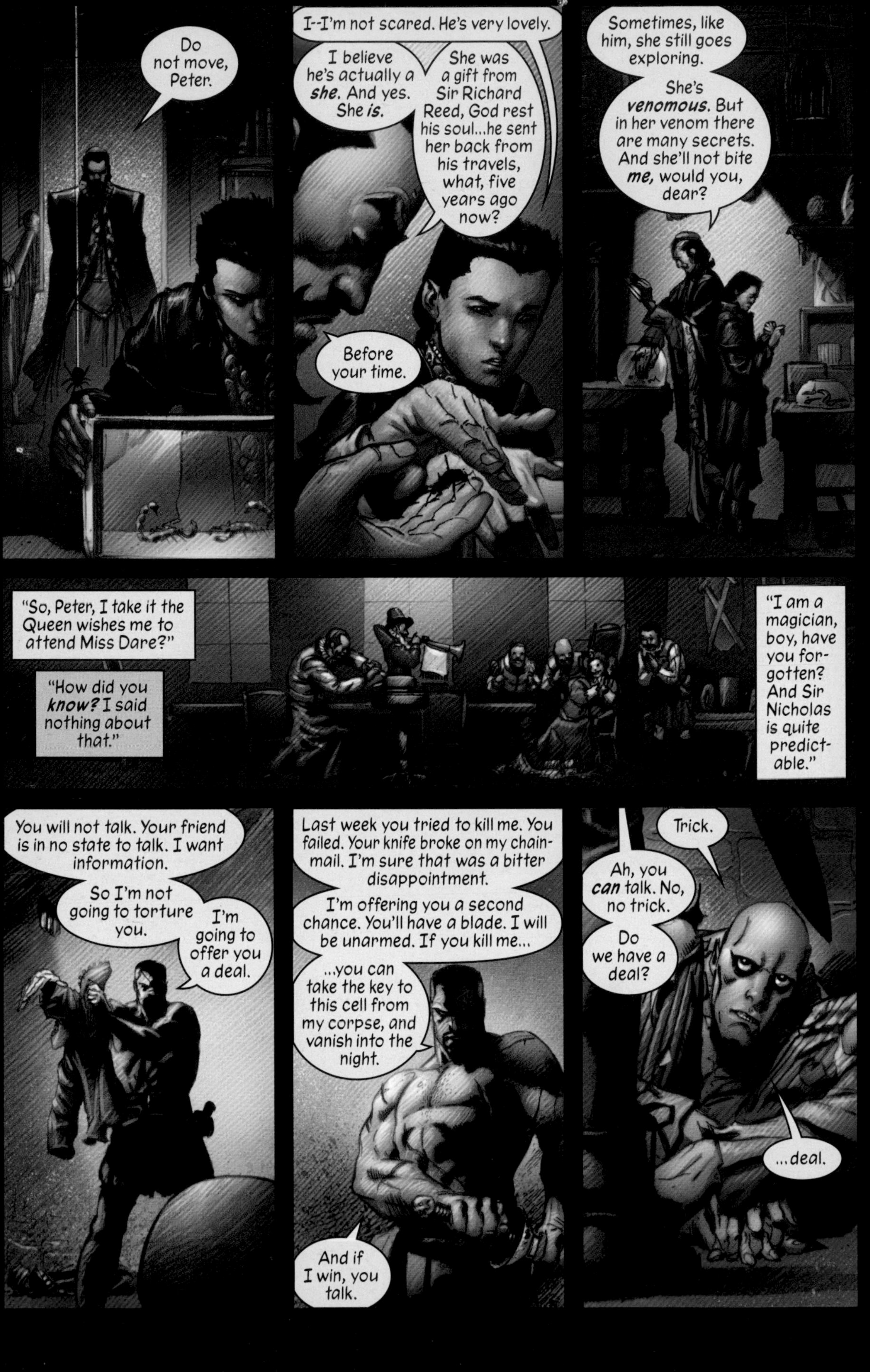
Do not move, Peter.
I--I'm not scared. He's very lovely.
I believe he's actually a *she*. And yes. She *is*.
She was a gift from Sir Richard Reed, God rest his soul...he sent her back from his travels, what, five years ago now?
Before your time.
Sometimes, like him, she still goes exploring.
She's *venomous*. But in her venom there are many secrets. And she'll not bite *me*, would you, dear?
"So, Peter, I take it the Queen wishes me to attend Miss Dare?"
"How did you *know?* I said nothing about that."
"I am a magician, boy, have you forgotten? And Sir Nicholas is quite predictable."
You will not talk. Your friend is in no state to talk. I want information.
So I'm not going to torture you.
I'm going to offer you a deal.
Last week you tried to kill me. You failed. Your knife broke on my chain-mail. I'm sure that was a bitter disappointment.
I'm offering you a second chance. You'll have a blade. I will be unarmed. If you kill me...
...you can take the key to this cell from my corpse, and vanish into the night.
And if I win, you talk.
Trick.
Ah, you *can* talk. No, no trick.
Do we have a deal?
...deal.

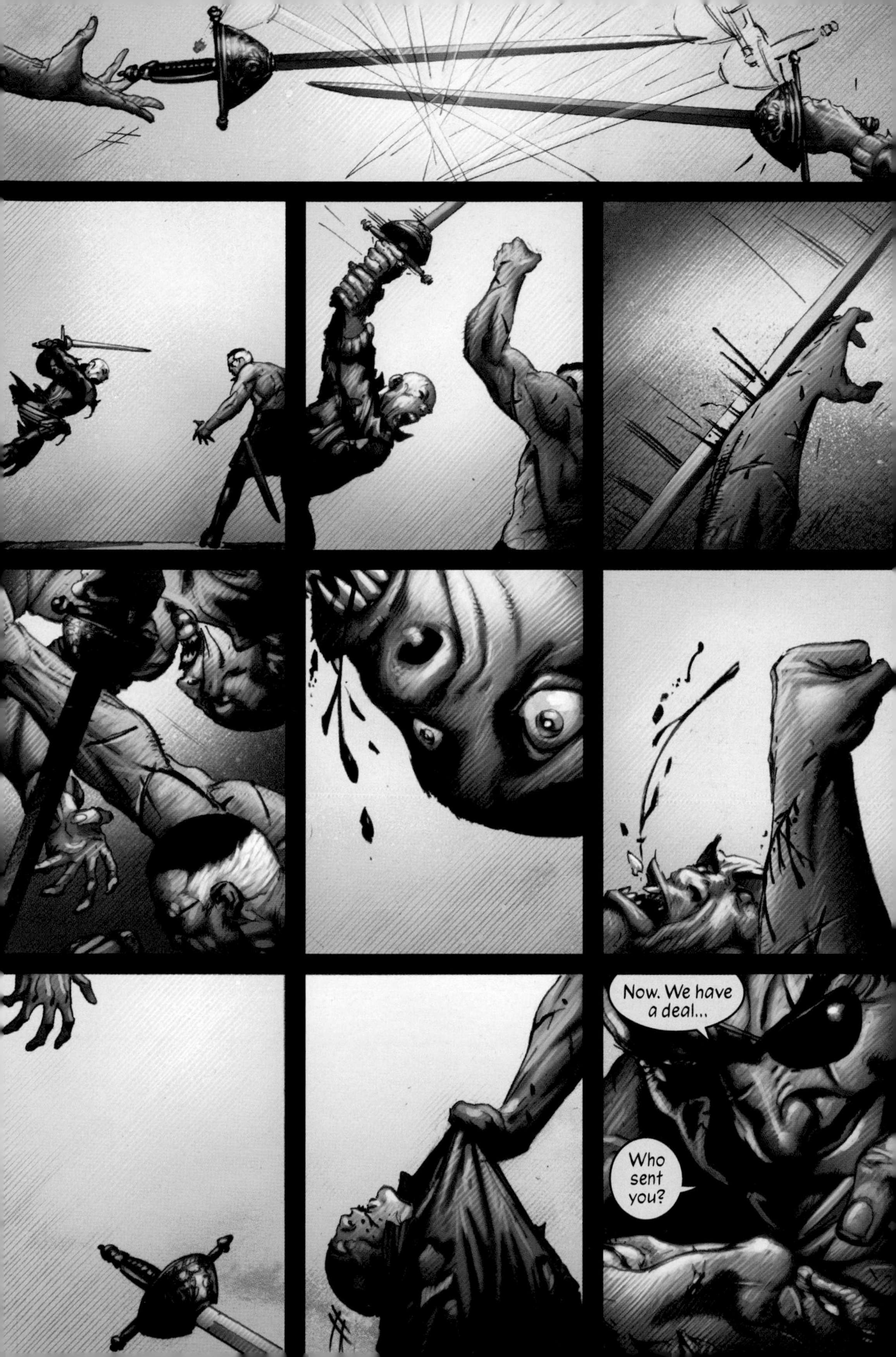
Now. We have a deal...
Who sent you?

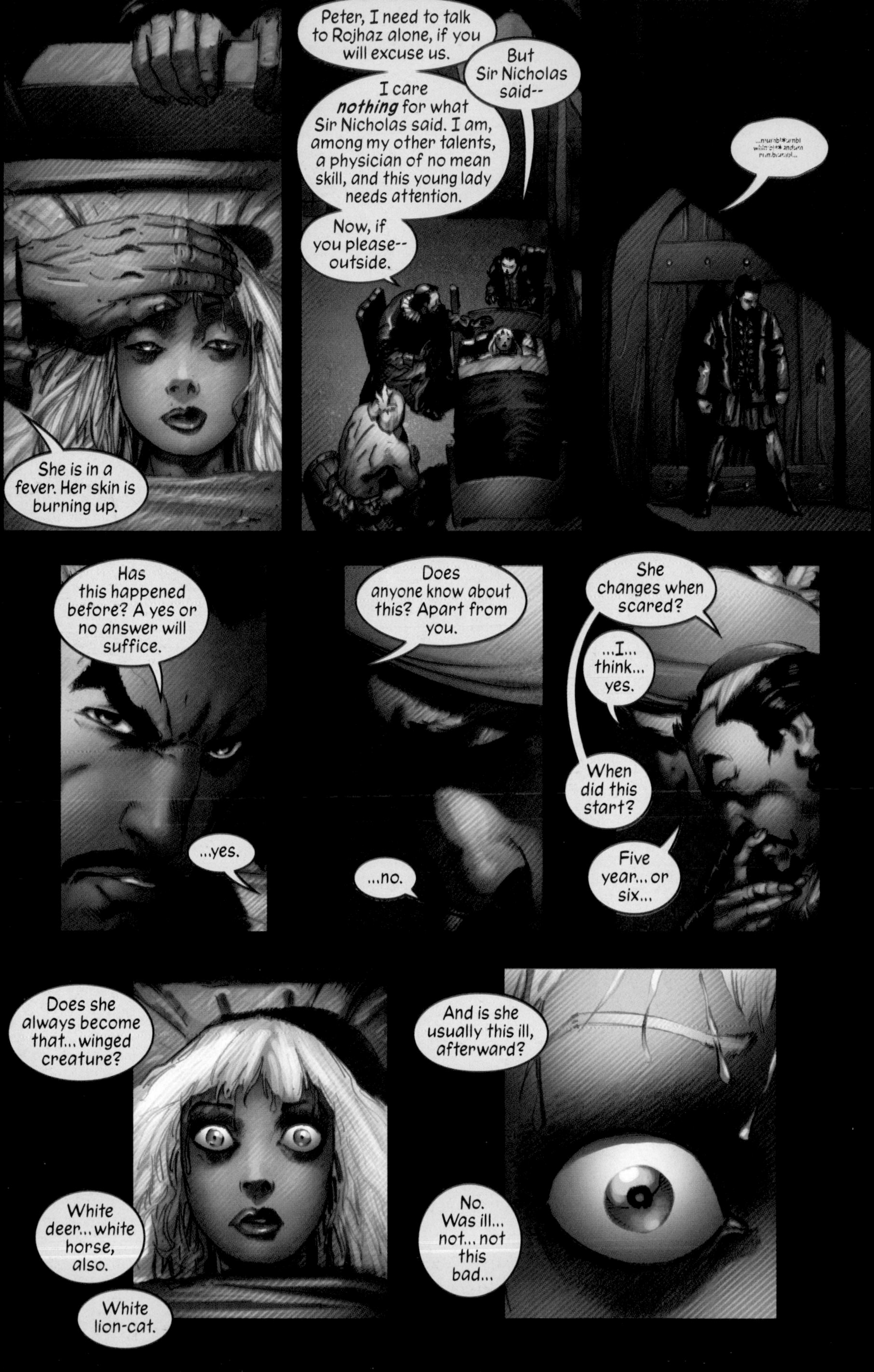
She is in a fever. Her skin is burning up.
Peter, I need to talk to Rojhaz alone, if you will excuse us.
But Sir Nicholas said--
I care ***nothing*** for what Sir Nicholas said. I am, among my other talents, a physician of no mean skill, and this young lady needs attention.
Now, if you please--outside.
Has this happened before? A yes or no answer will suffice.
...yes.
Does anyone know about this? Apart from you.
...no.
She changes when scared?
...I... think... yes.
When did this start?
Five year... or six...
Does she always become that... winged creature?
White deer... white horse, also.
White lion-cat.
And is she usually this ill, afterward?
No. Was ill... not... not this bad...

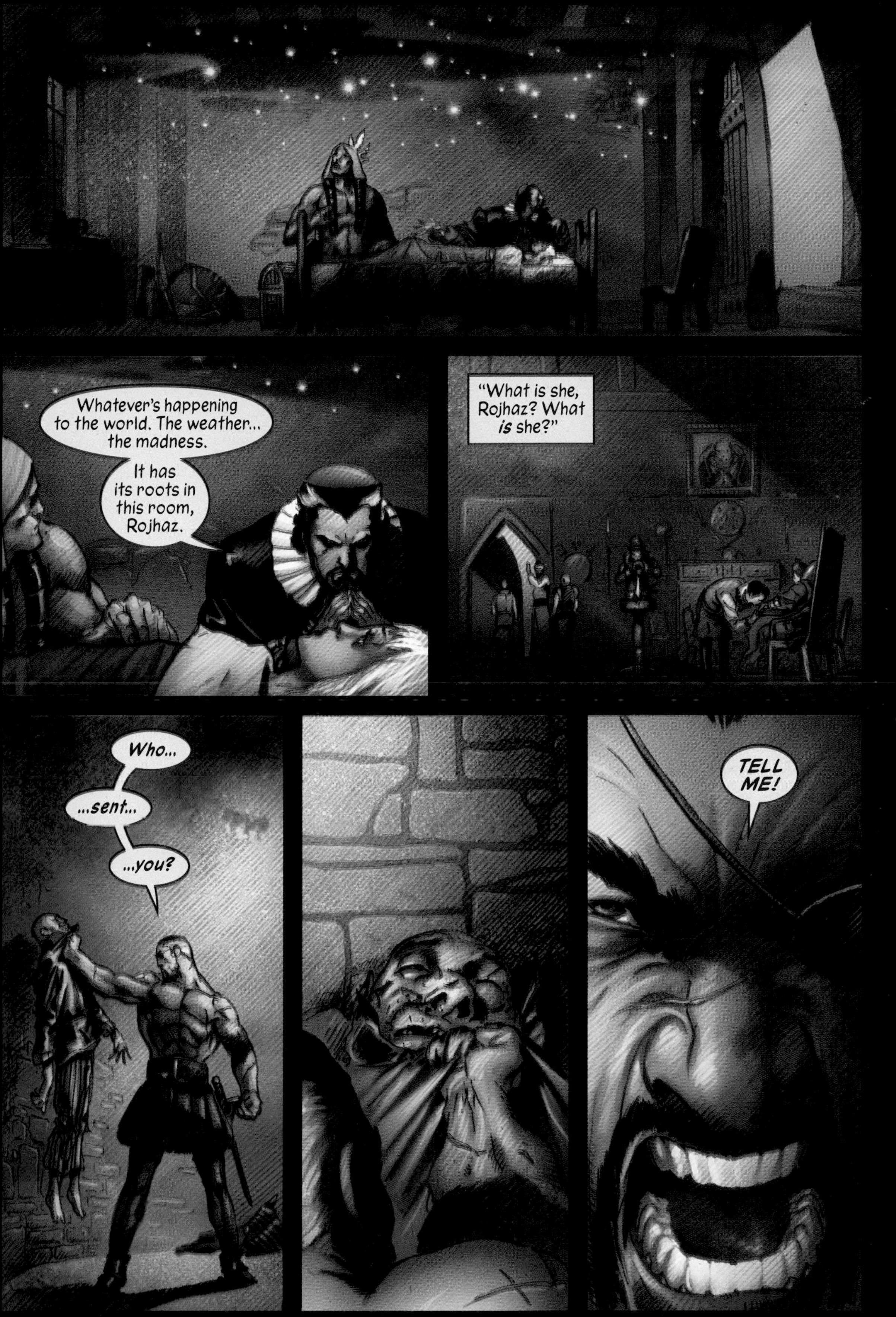
Whatever's happening to the world. The weather... the madness.
It has its roots in this room, Rojhaz.
"What is she, Rojhaz? What *is* she?"
Who...
...sent...
...you?
TELL ME!

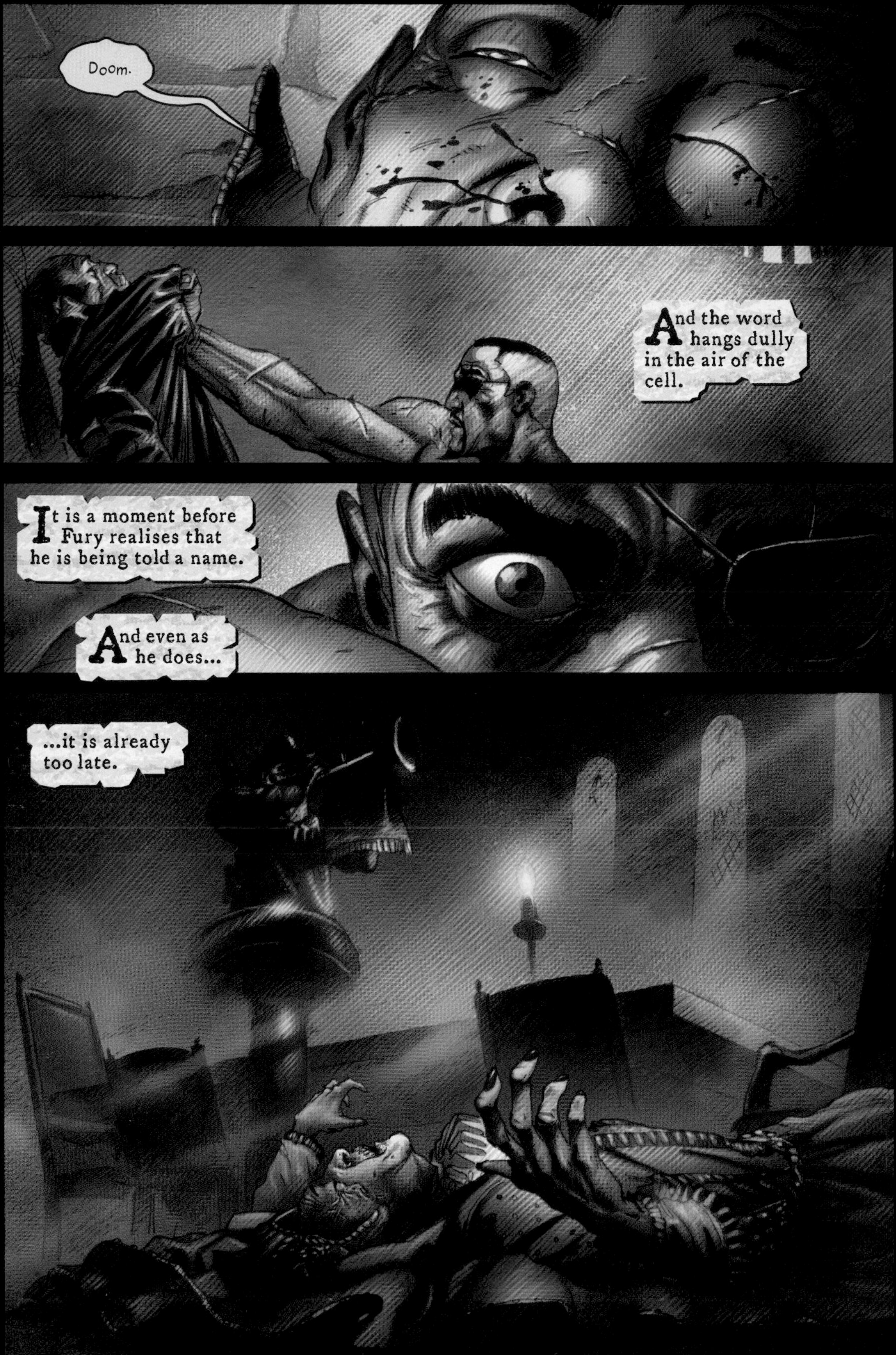
Doom.
And the word hangs dully in the air of the cell.
It is a moment before Fury realises that he is being told a name.
And even as he does...
...it is already too late.

IN WHICH MUCH IS EXPLAINED AND THINGS DO NOT ALWAYS WORK OUT FOR THE BEST.

1602

PART FOUR

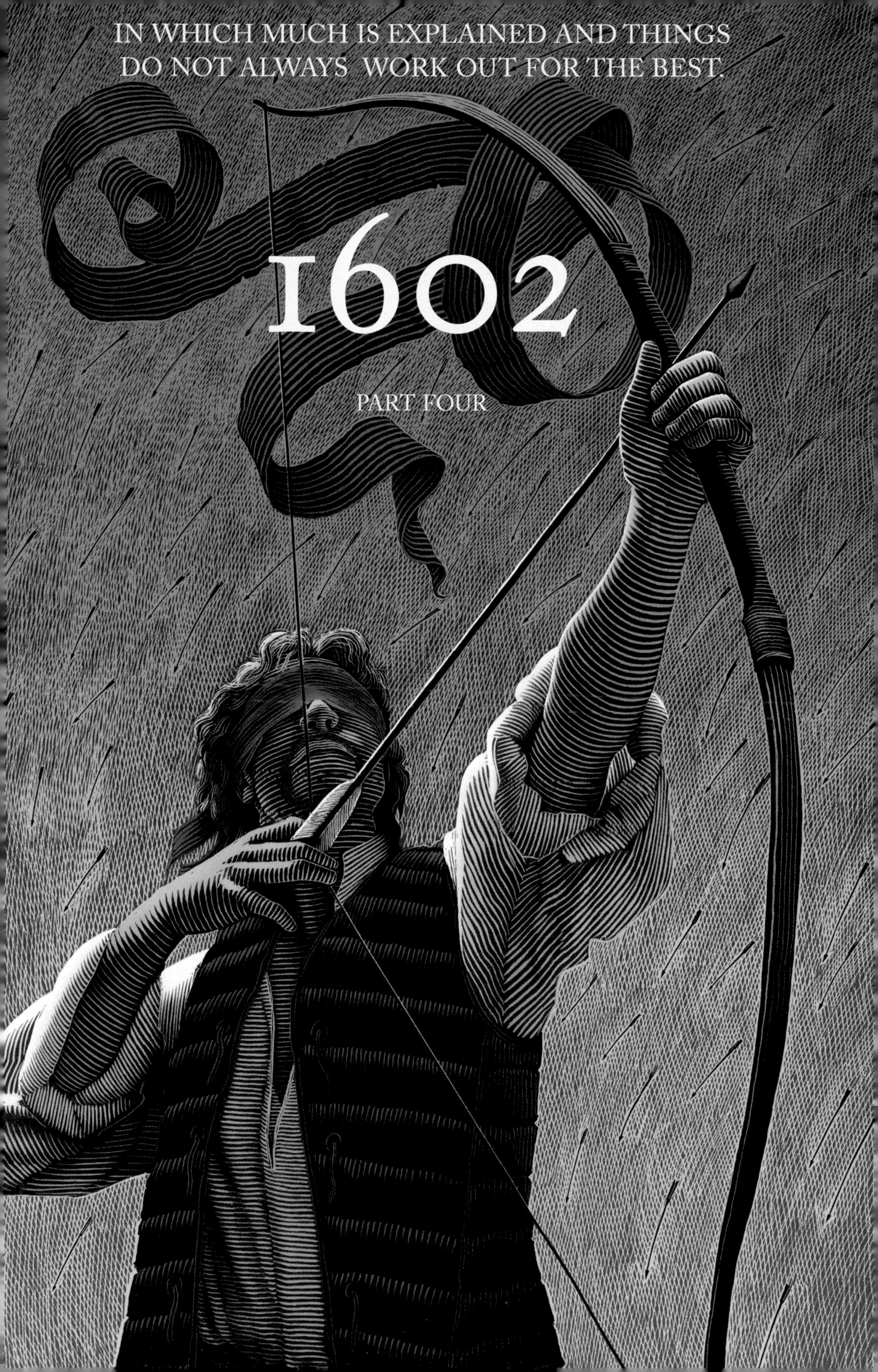

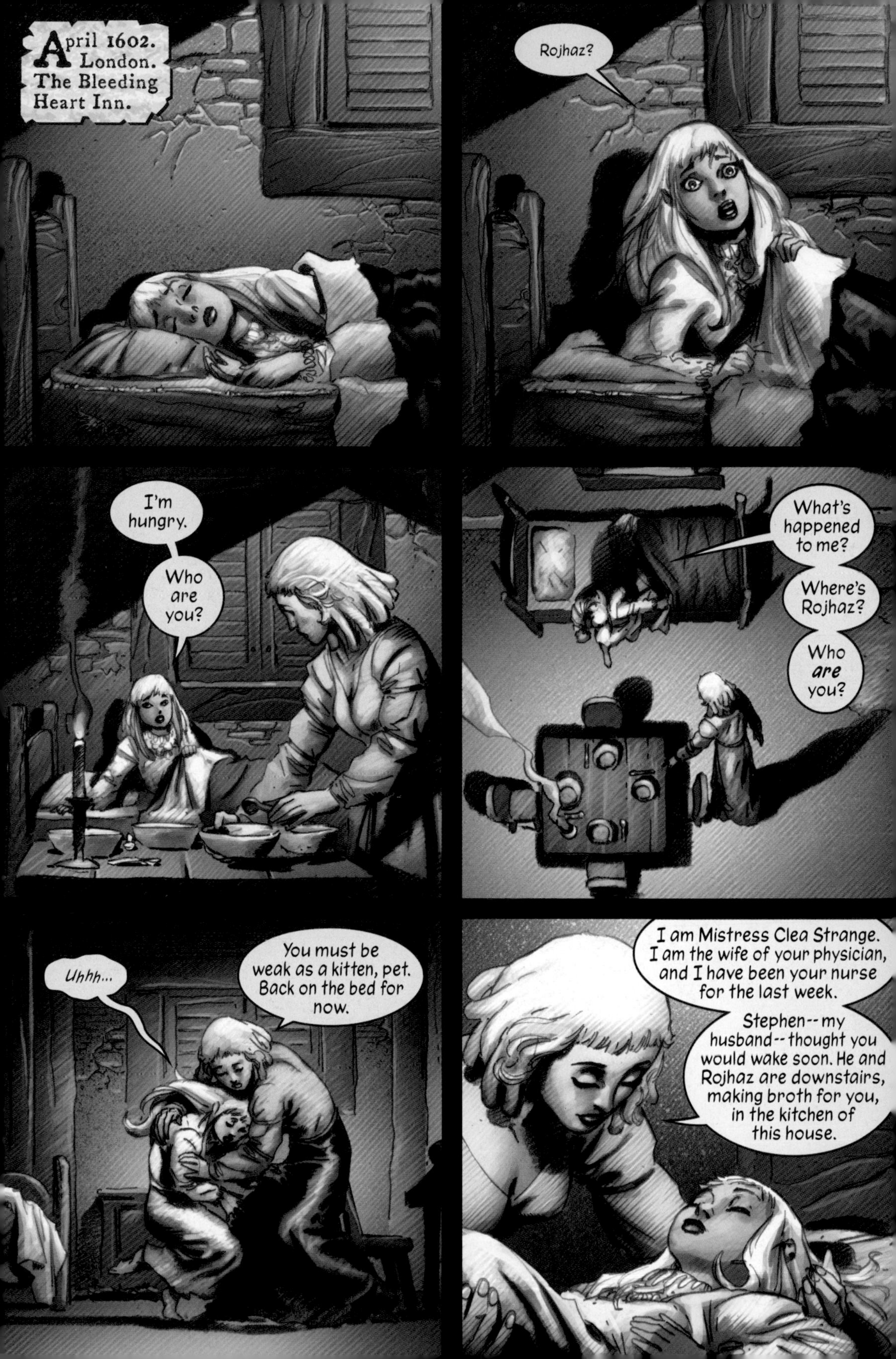
April 1602. London. The Bleeding Heart Inn.
Rojhaz?
I'm hungry.
Who are you?
What's happened to me?
Where's Rojhaz?
Who *are* you?
Uhhh...
You must be weak as a kitten, pet. Back on the bed for now.
I am Mistress Clea Strange. I am the wife of your physician, and I have been your nurse for the last week.
Stephen-- my husband-- thought you would wake soon. He and Rojhaz are downstairs, making broth for you, in the kitchen of this house.

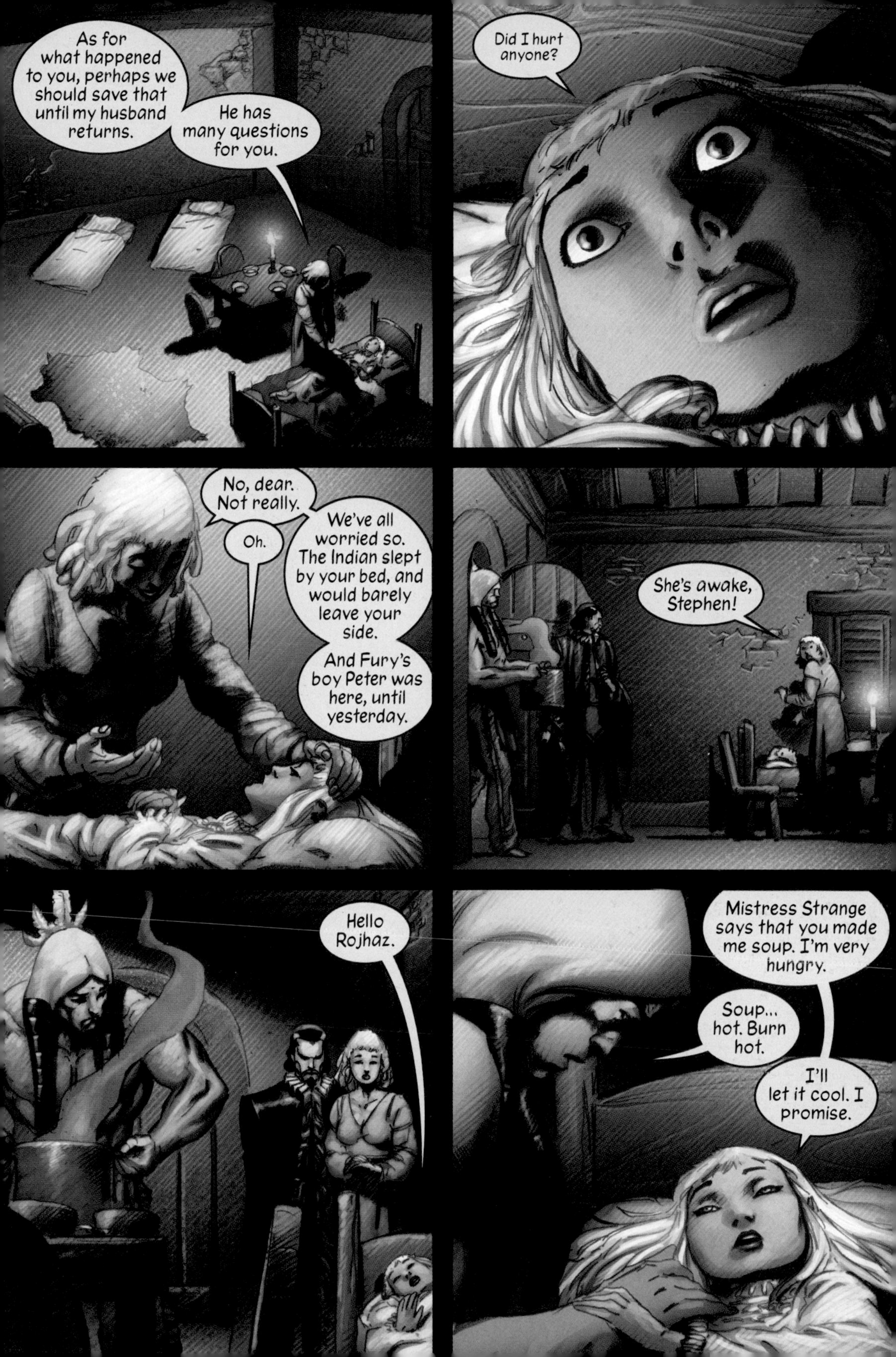
As for what happened to you, perhaps we should save that until my husband returns.
He has many questions for you.
Did I hurt anyone?
No, dear. Not really.
Oh.
We've all worried so. The Indian slept by your bed, and would barely leave your side.
And Fury's boy Peter was here, until yesterday.
She's awake, Stephen!
Hello Rojhaz.
Mistress Strange says that you made me soup. I'm very hungry.
Soup... hot. Burn hot.
I'll let it cool. I promise.

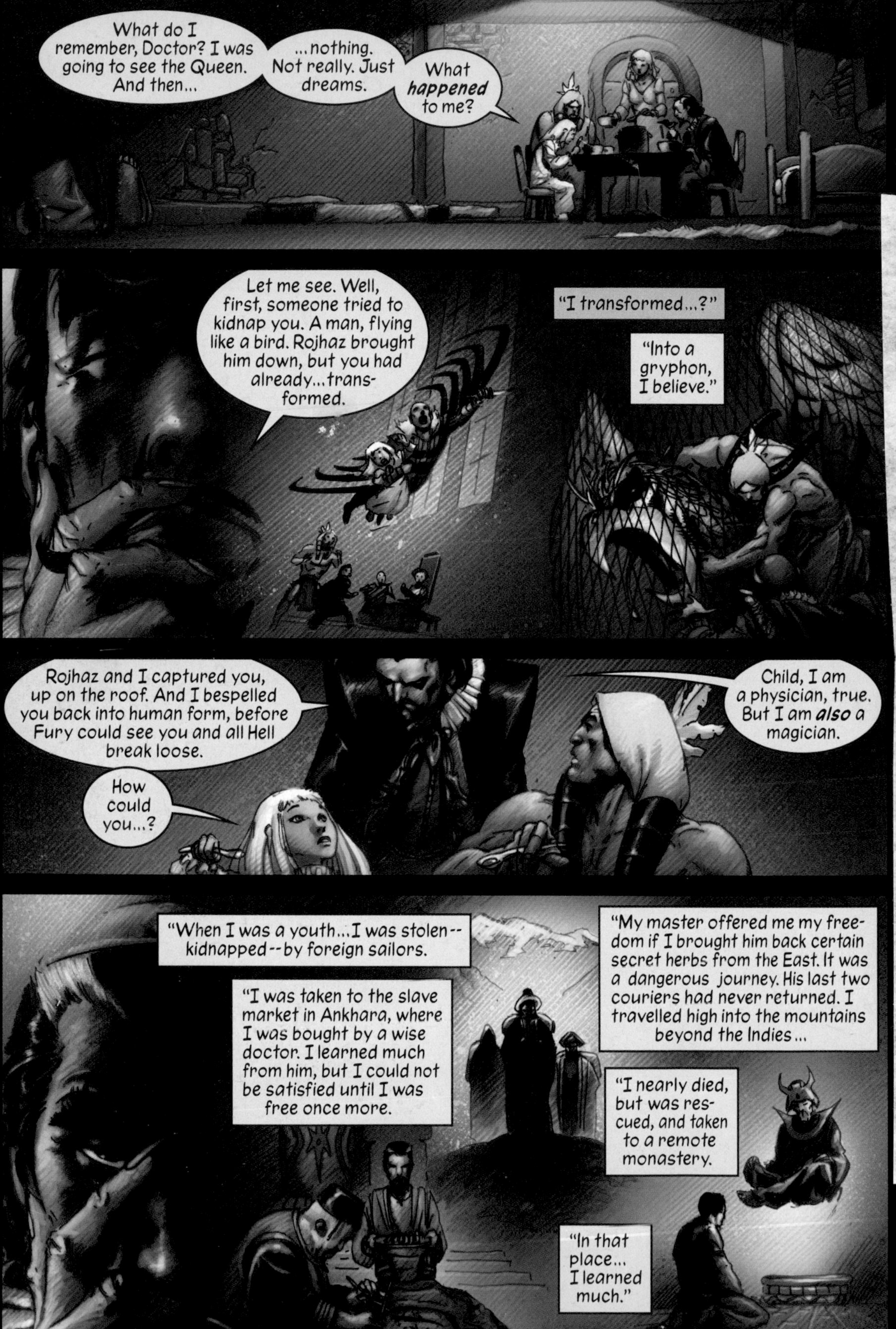

What do I remember, Doctor? I was going to see the Queen. And then...
...nothing. Not really. Just dreams.
What *happened* to me?
Let me see. Well, first, someone tried to kidnap you. A man, flying like a bird. Rojhaz brought him down, but you had already...trans-formed.
"I transformed...?"
"Into a gryphon, I believe."
Rojhaz and I captured you, up on the roof. And I bespelled you back into human form, before Fury could see you and all Hell break loose.
How could you...?
Child, I am a physician, true. But I am *also* a magician.
"When I was a youth...I was stolen--kidnapped--by foreign sailors.
"I was taken to the slave market in Ankhara, where I was bought by a wise doctor. I learned much from him, but I could not be satisfied until I was free once more.
"My master offered me my free-dom if I brought him back certain secret herbs from the East. It was a dangerous journey. His last two couriers had never returned. I travelled high into the mountains beyond the Indies...
"I nearly died, but was res-cued, and taken to a remote monastery.
"In that place... I learned much."

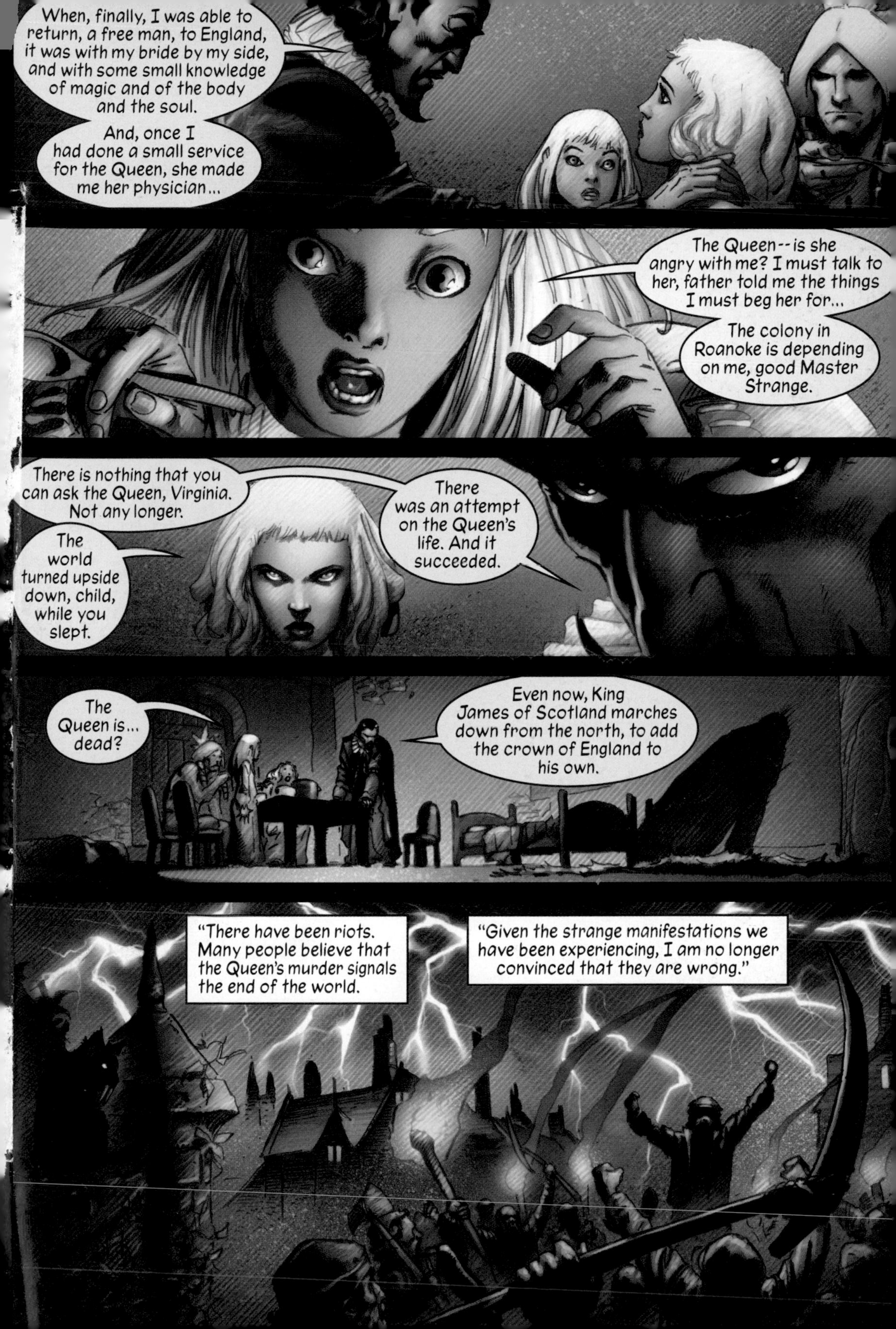
When, finally, I was able to return, a free man, to England, it was with my bride by my side, and with some small knowledge of magic and of the body and the soul.
And, once I had done a small service for the Queen, she made me her physician...
The Queen--is she angry with me? I must talk to her, father told me the things I must beg her for...
The colony in Roanoke is depending on me, good Master Strange.
There is nothing that you can ask the Queen, Virginia. Not any longer.
The world turned upside down, child, while you slept.
There was an attempt on the Queen's life. And it succeeded.
The Queen is... dead?
Even now, King James of Scotland marches down from the north, to add the crown of England to his own.
"There have been riots. Many people believe that the Queen's murder signals the end of the world.
"Given the strange manifestations we have been experiencing, I am no longer convinced that they are wrong."

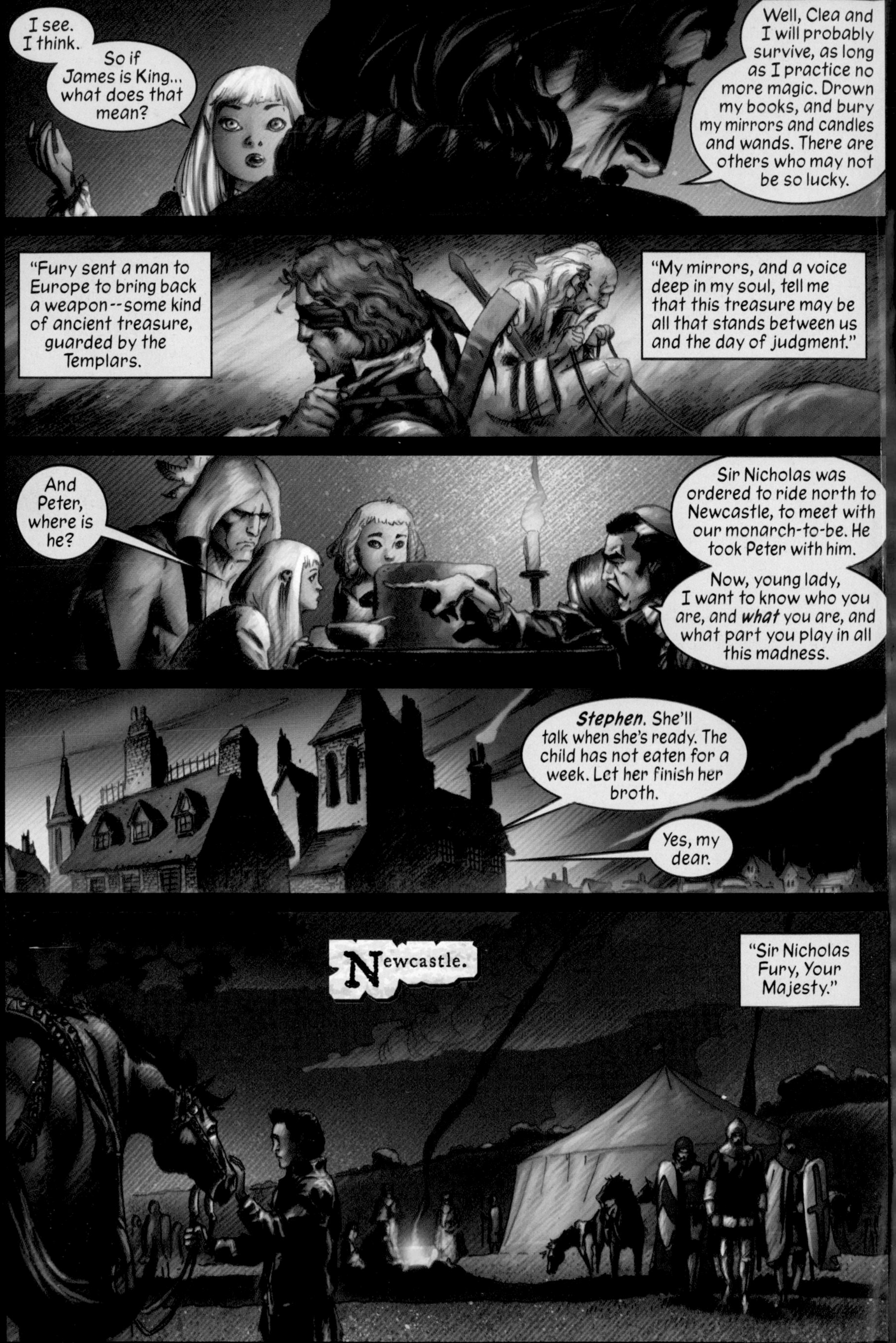
I see. I think.
So if James is King... what does that mean?
Well, Clea and I will probably survive, as long as I practice no more magic. Drown my books, and bury my mirrors and candles and wands. There are others who may not be so lucky.
"Fury sent a man to Europe to bring back a weapon--some kind of ancient treasure, guarded by the Templars.
"My mirrors, and a voice deep in my soul, tell me that this treasure may be all that stands between us and the day of judgment."
And Peter, where is he?
Sir Nicholas was ordered to ride north to Newcastle, to meet with our monarch-to-be. He took Peter with him.
Now, young lady, I want to know who you are, and *what* you are, and what part you play in all this madness.
Stephen. She'll talk when she's ready. The child has not eaten for a week. Let her finish her broth.
Yes, my dear.
Newcastle.
"Sir Nicholas Fury, Your Majesty."

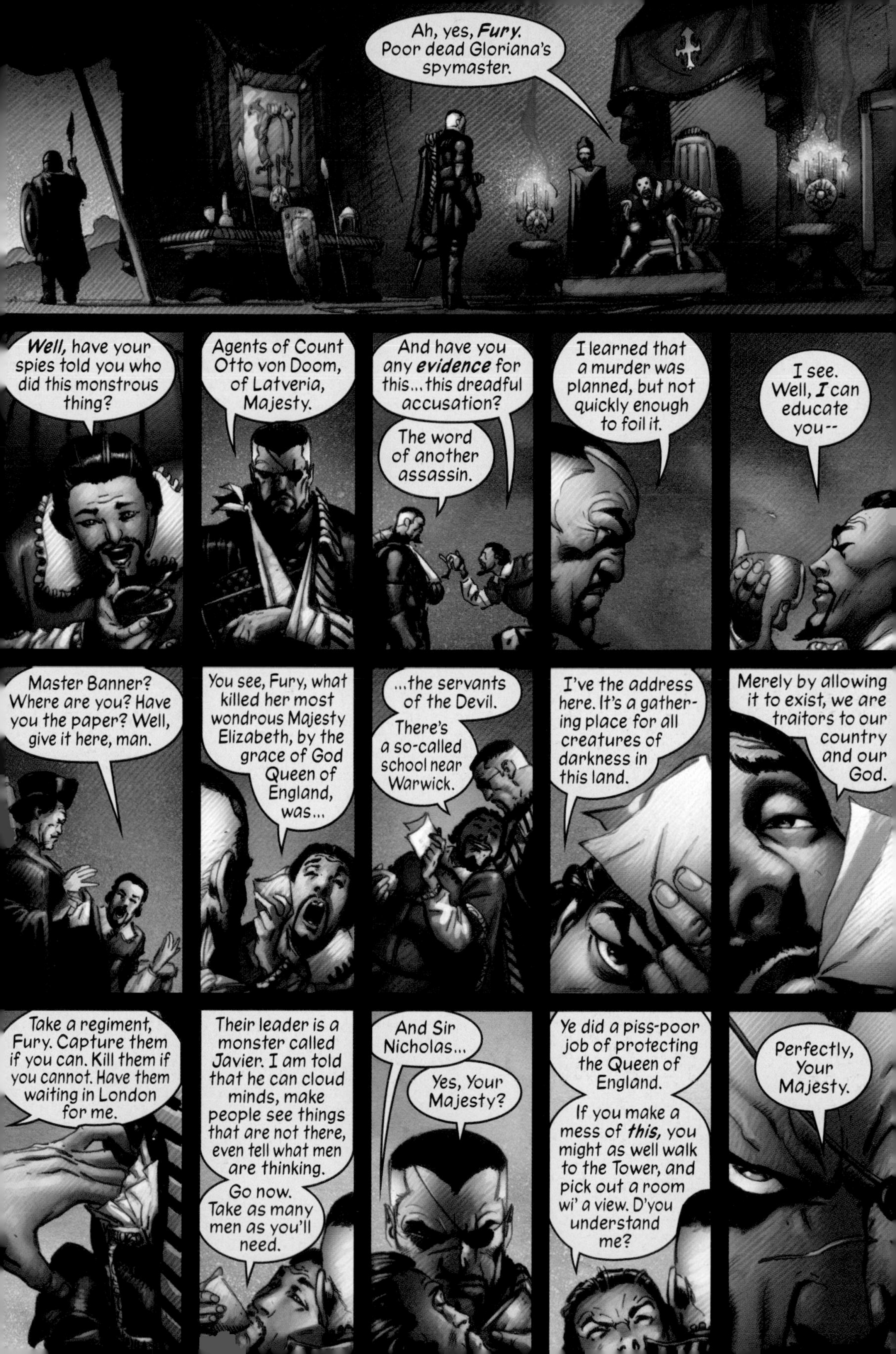
Ah, yes, Fury. Poor dead Gloriana's spymaster.
Well, have your spies told you who did this monstrous thing?
Agents of Count Otto von Doom, of Latveria, Majesty.
And have you any evidence for this... this dreadful accusation?
The word of another assassin.
I learned that a murder was planned, but not quickly enough to foil it.
I see. Well, I can educate you--
Master Banner? Where are you? Have you the paper? Well, give it here, man.
You see, Fury, what killed her most wondrous Majesty Elizabeth, by the grace of God Queen of England, was...
...the servants of the Devil.
There's a so-called school near Warwick.
I've the address here. It's a gathering place for all creatures of darkness in this land.
Merely by allowing it to exist, we are traitors to our country and our God.
Take a regiment, Fury. Capture them if you can. Kill them if you cannot. Have them waiting in London for me.
Their leader is a monster called Javier. I am told that he can cloud minds, make people see things that are not there, even tell what men are thinking.
Go now. Take as many men as you'll need.
And Sir Nicholas...
Yes, Your Majesty?
Ye did a piss-poor job of protecting the Queen of England.
If you make a mess of this, you might as well walk to the Tower, and pick out a room wi' a view. D'you understand me?
Perfectly, Your Majesty.

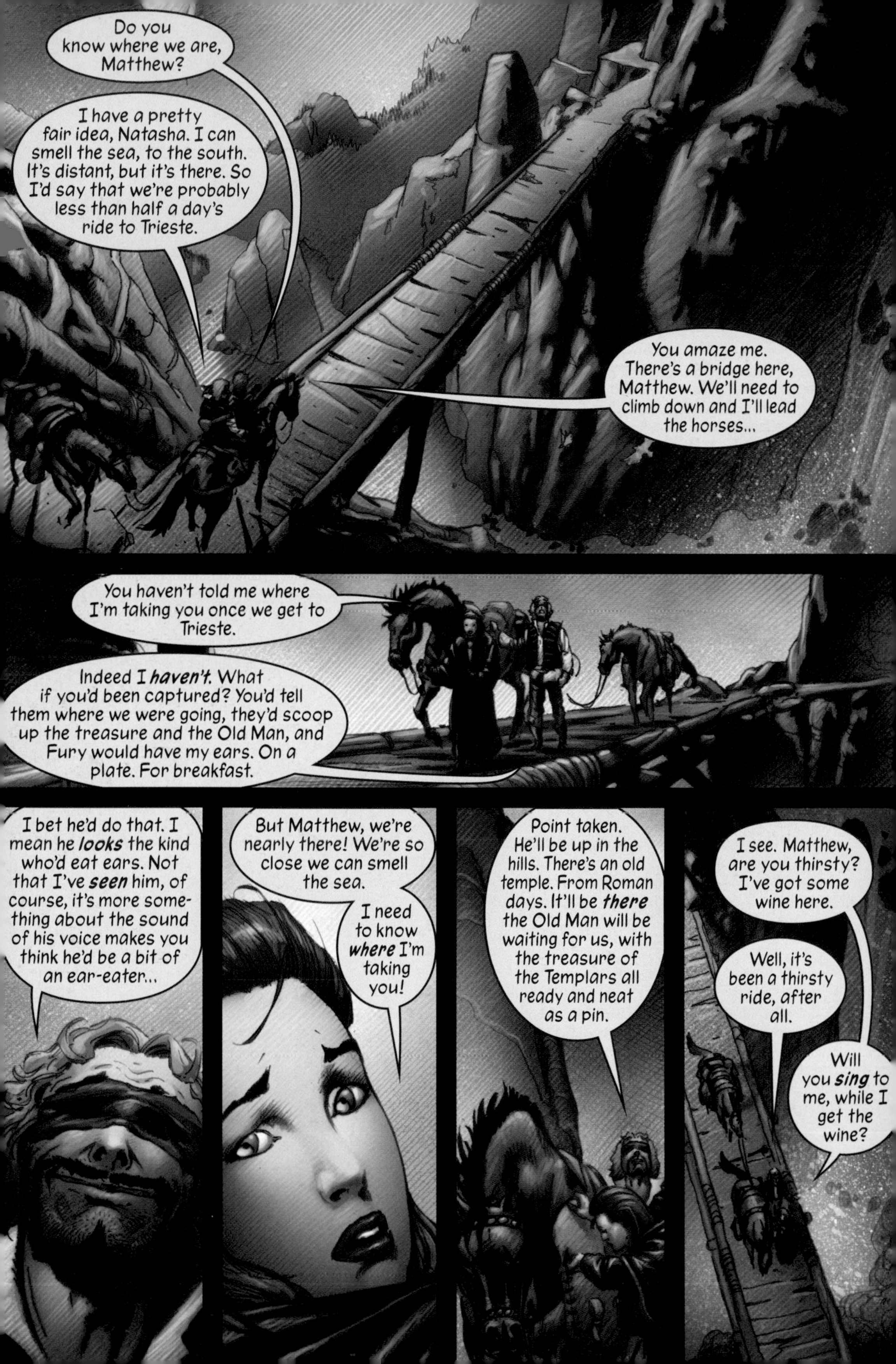
Do you know where we are, Matthew?
I have a pretty fair idea, Natasha. I can smell the sea, to the south. It's distant, but it's there. So I'd say that we're probably less than half a day's ride to Trieste.
You amaze me. There's a bridge here, Matthew. We'll need to climb down and I'll lead the horses...
You haven't told me where I'm taking you once we get to Trieste.
Indeed I *haven't*. What if you'd been captured? You'd tell them where we were going, they'd scoop up the treasure and the Old Man, and Fury would have my ears. On a plate. For breakfast.
I bet he'd do that. I mean he *looks* the kind who'd eat ears. Not that I've *seen* him, of course, it's more something about the sound of his voice makes you think he'd be a bit of an ear-eater...
But Matthew, we're nearly there! We're so close we can smell the sea.
I need to know *where* I'm taking you!
Point taken. He'll be up in the hills. There's an old temple. From Roman days. It'll be *there* the Old Man will be waiting for us, with the treasure of the Templars all ready and neat as a pin.
I see. Matthew, are you thirsty? I've got some wine here.
Well, it's been a thirsty ride, after all.
Will you *sing* to me, while I get the wine?

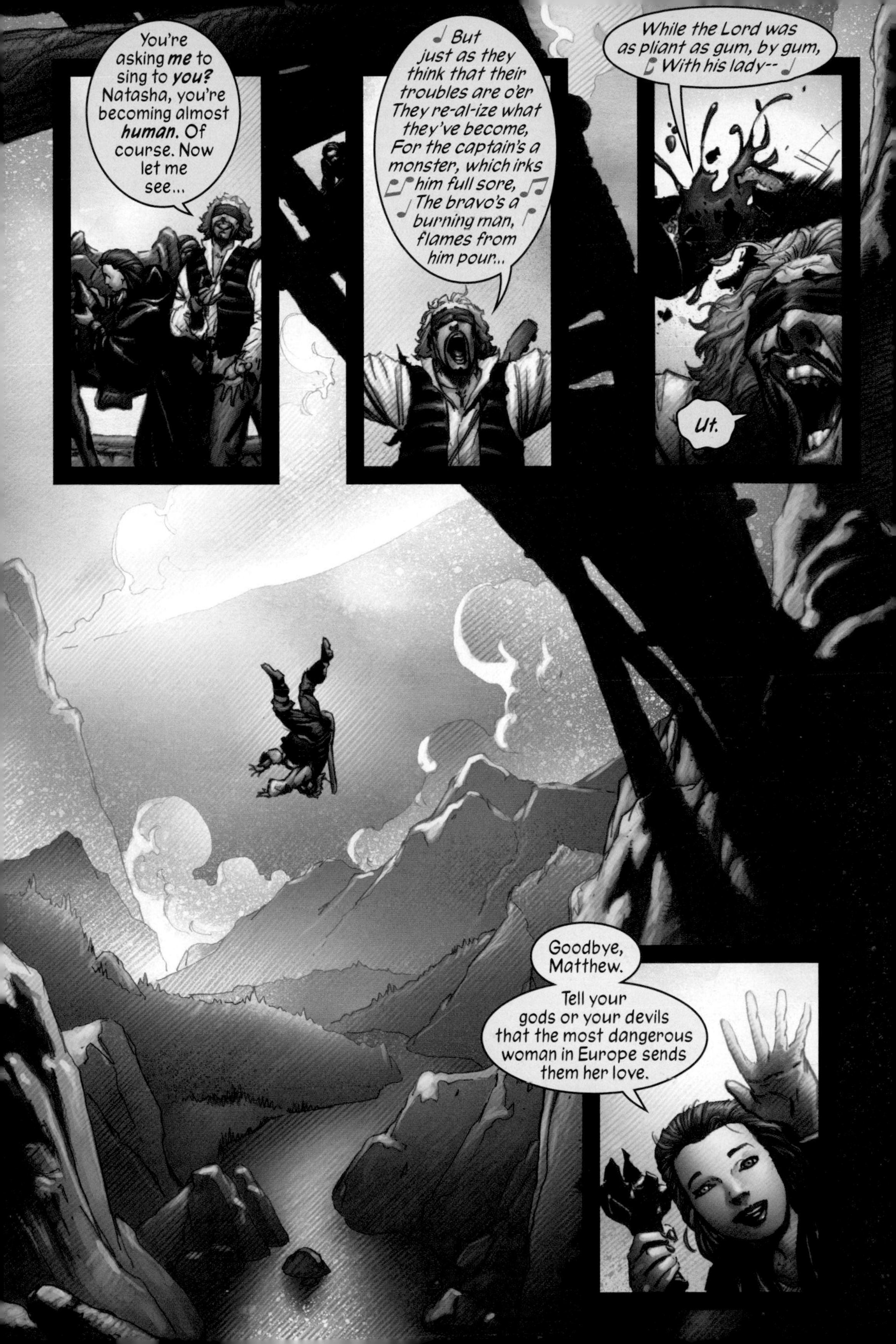
You're asking **me** to sing to **you?** Natasha, you're becoming almost **human**. Of course. Now let me see...
♩ But just as they think that their troubles are o'er They re-al-ize what they've become, For the captain's a monster, which irks ♫ him full sore, ♫ ♩ The bravo's a burning man, ♪ flames from him pour...
While the Lord was as pliant as gum, by gum, ♫ With his lady-- ♩
Ut.
Goodbye, Matthew.
Tell your gods or your devils that the most dangerous woman in Europe sends them her love.

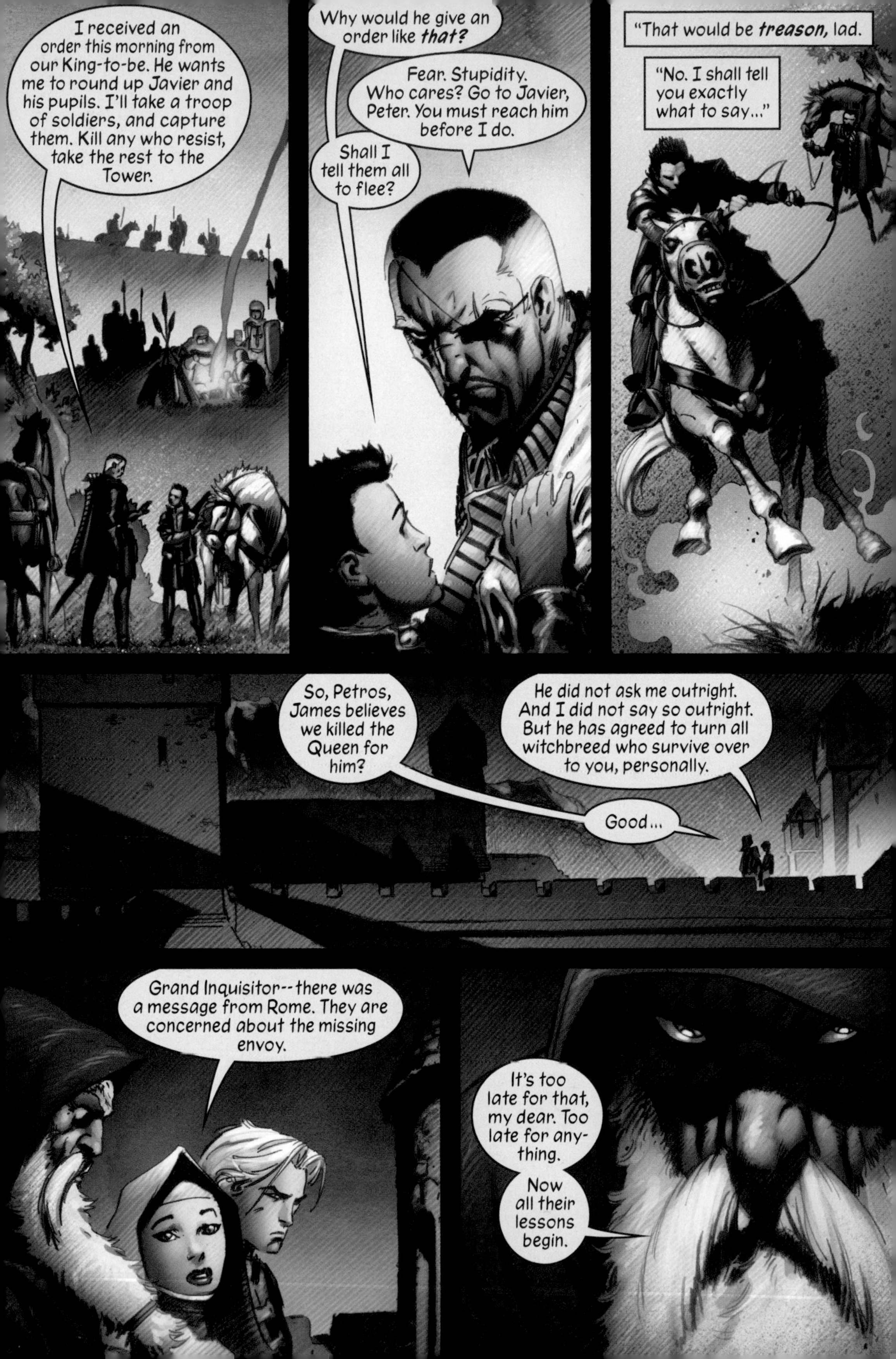

I received an order this morning from our King-to-be. He wants me to round up Javier and his pupils. I'll take a troop of soldiers, and capture them. Kill any who resist, take the rest to the Tower.
Why would he give an order like *that?*
Fear. Stupidity. Who cares? Go to Javier, Peter. You must reach him before I do.
Shall I tell them all to flee?
"That would be ***treason,*** lad.
"No. I shall tell you exactly what to say..."
So, Petros, James believes we killed the Queen for him?
He did not ask me outright. And I did not say so outright. But he has agreed to turn all witchbreed who survive over to you, personally.
Good...
Grand Inquisitor--there was a message from Rome. They are concerned about the missing envoy.
It's too late for that, my dear. Too late for anything.
Now all their lessons begin.

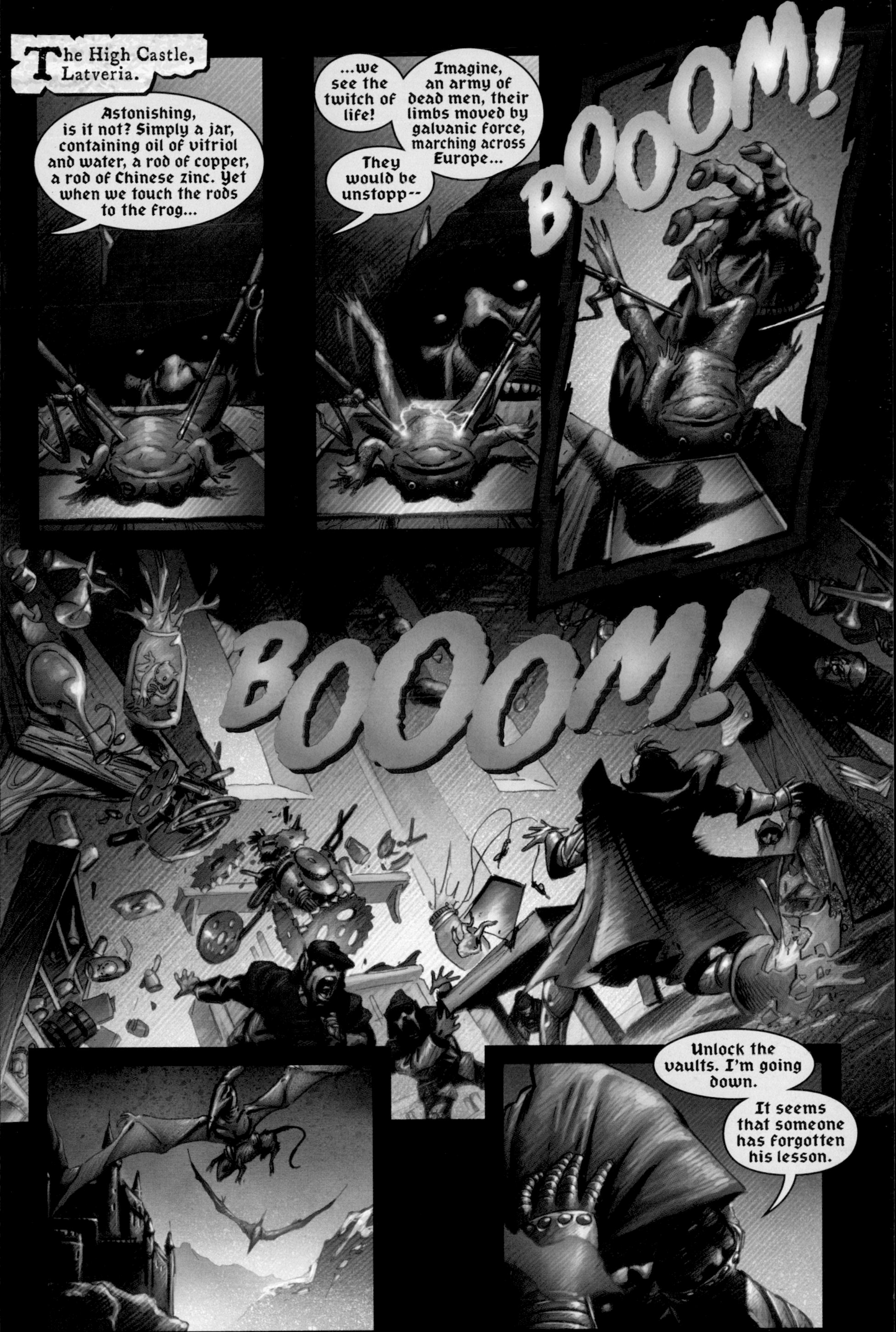
The High Castle, Latveria.
Astonishing, is it not? Simply a jar, containing oil of vitriol and water, a rod of copper, a rod of Chinese zinc. Yet when we touch the rods to the frog...
...we see the twitch of life!
Imagine, an army of dead men, their limbs moved by galvanic force, marching across Europe...
They would be unstopp--
BOOOOM!
BOOOM!
Unlock the vaults. I'm going down.
It seems that someone has forgotten his lesson.

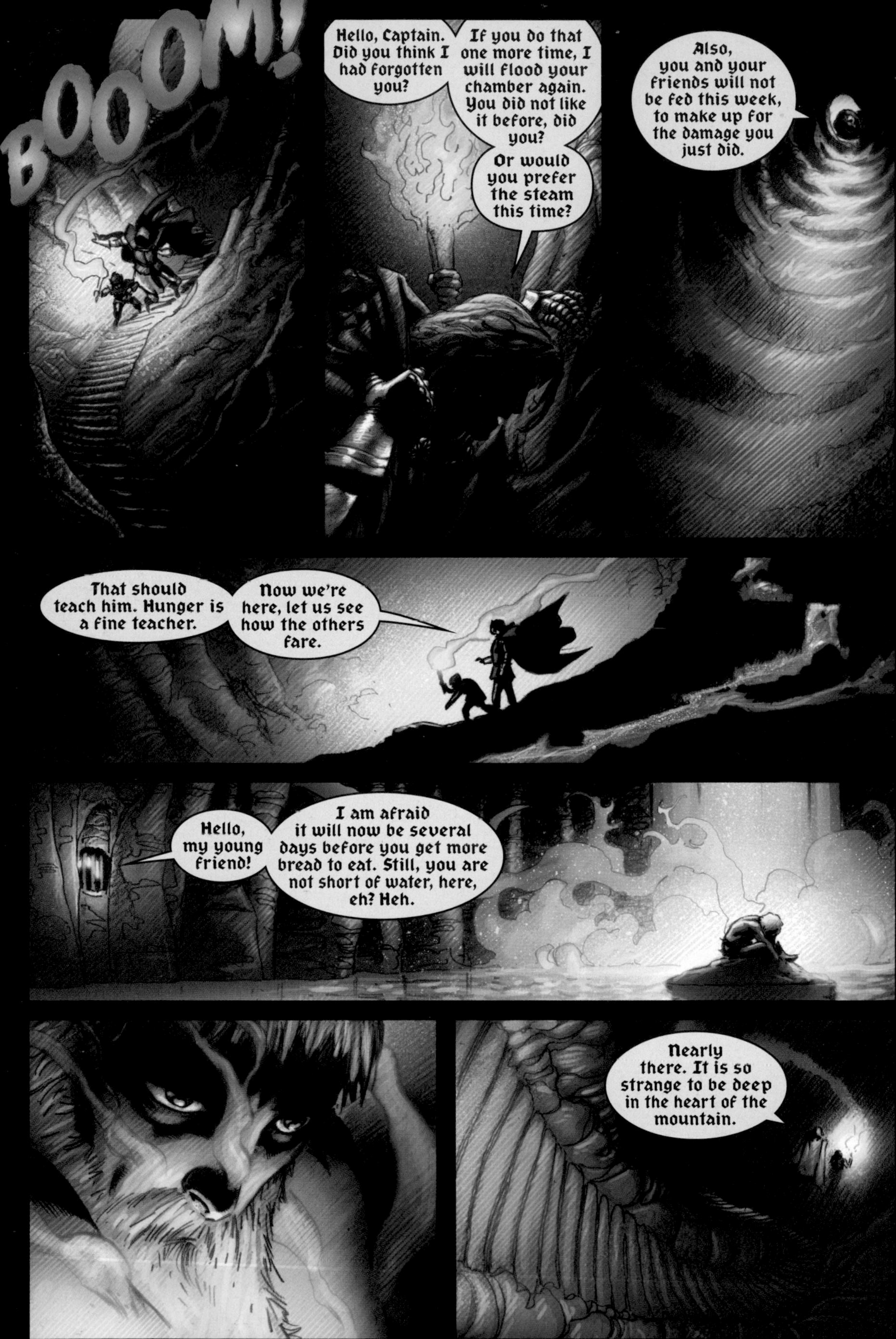
BOOOM!
Hello, Captain. Did you think I had forgotten you?
If you do that one more time, I will flood your chamber again. You did not like it before, did you?
Or would you prefer the steam this time?
Also, you and your friends will not be fed this week, to make up for the damage you just did.
That should teach him. Hunger is a fine teacher.
Now we're here, let us see how the others fare.
Hello, my young friend!
I am afraid it will now be several days before you get more bread to eat. Still, you are not short of water, here, eh? Heh.
Nearly there. It is so strange to be deep in the heart of the mountain.

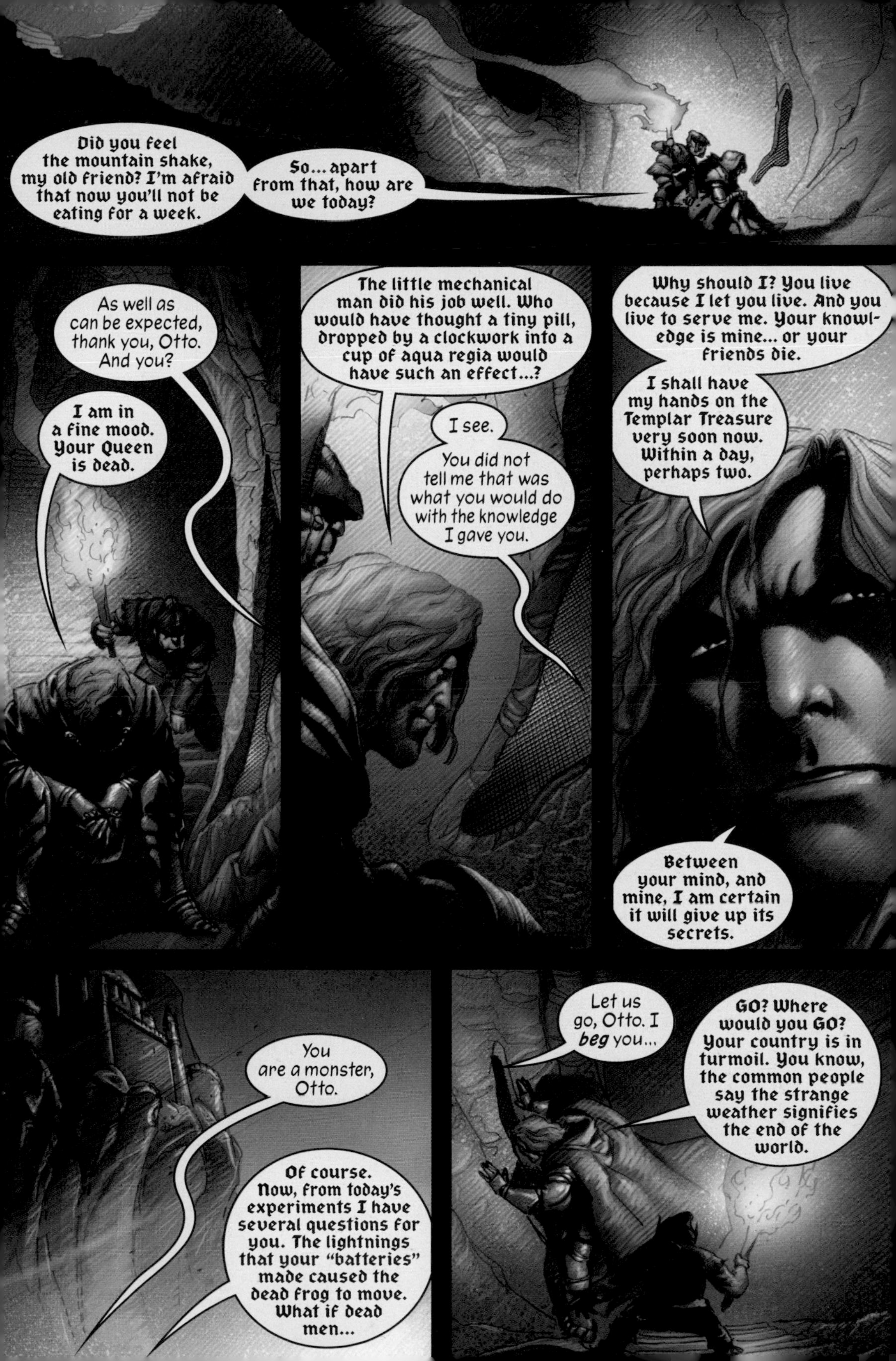
Did you feel the mountain shake, my old friend? I'm afraid that now you'll not be eating for a week.
So... apart from that, how are we today?
As well as can be expected, thank you, Otto. And you?
I am in a fine mood. Your Queen is dead.
The little mechanical man did his job well. Who would have thought a tiny pill, dropped by a clockwork into a cup of aqua regia would have such an effect...?
I see.
You did not tell me that was what you would do with the knowledge I gave you.
Why should I? You live because I let you live. And you live to serve me. Your knowledge is mine... or your friends die.
I shall have my hands on the Templar Treasure very soon now. Within a day, perhaps two.
Between your mind, and mine, I am certain it will give up its secrets.
You are a monster, Otto.
Of course. Now, from today's experiments I have several questions for you. The lightnings that your "batteries" made caused the dead frog to move. What if dead men...
Let us go, Otto. I *beg* you...
GO? Where would you GO? Your country is in turmoil. You know, the common people say the strange weather signifies the end of the world.

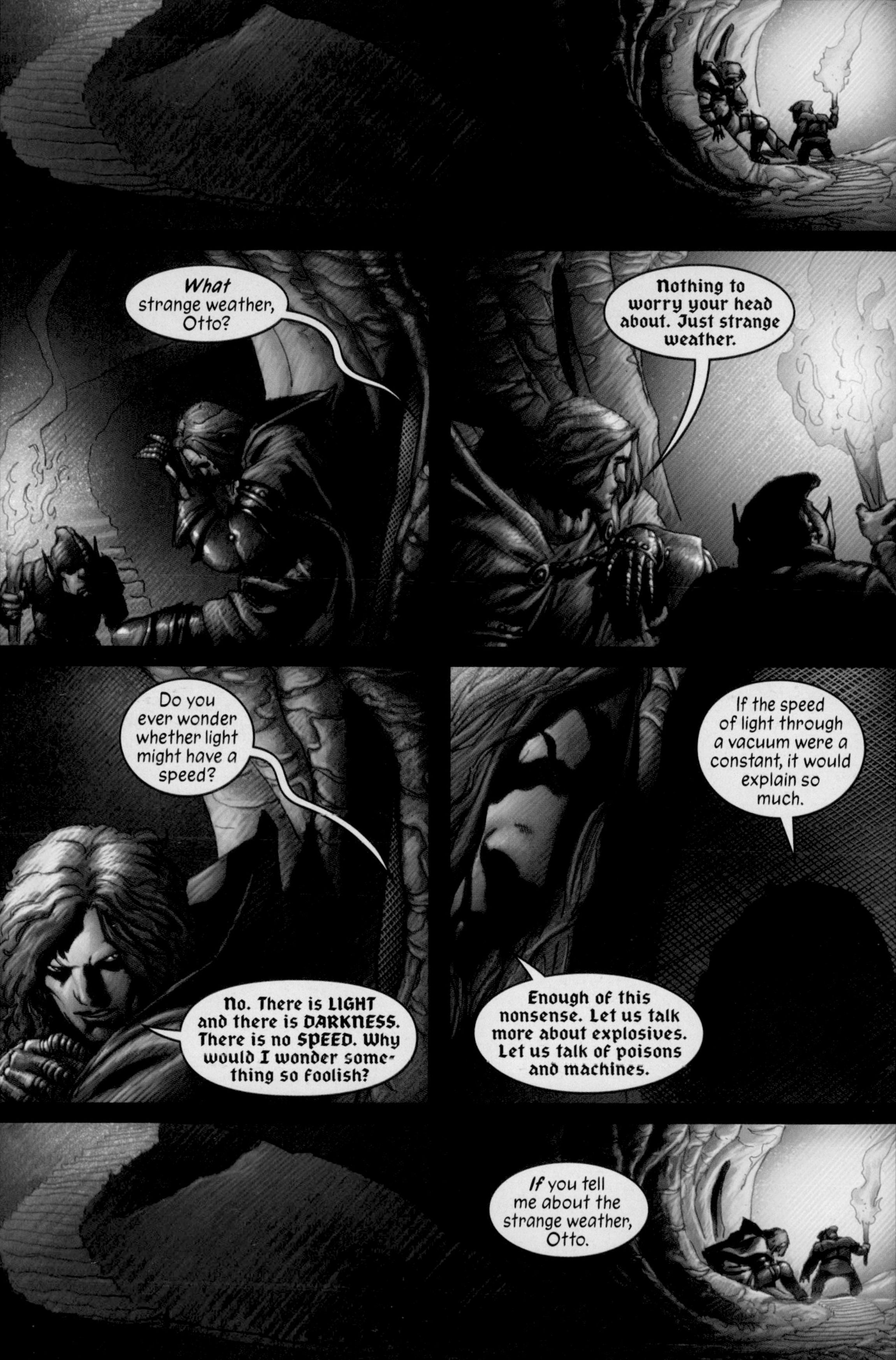
What strange weather, Otto?
Nothing to worry your head about. Just strange weather.
Do you ever wonder whether light might have a speed?
No. There is LIGHT and there is DARKNESS. There is no SPEED. Why would I wonder something so foolish?
If the speed of light through a vacuum were a constant, it would explain so much.
Enough of this nonsense. Let us talk more about explosives. Let us talk of poisons and machines.
If you tell me about the strange weather, Otto.

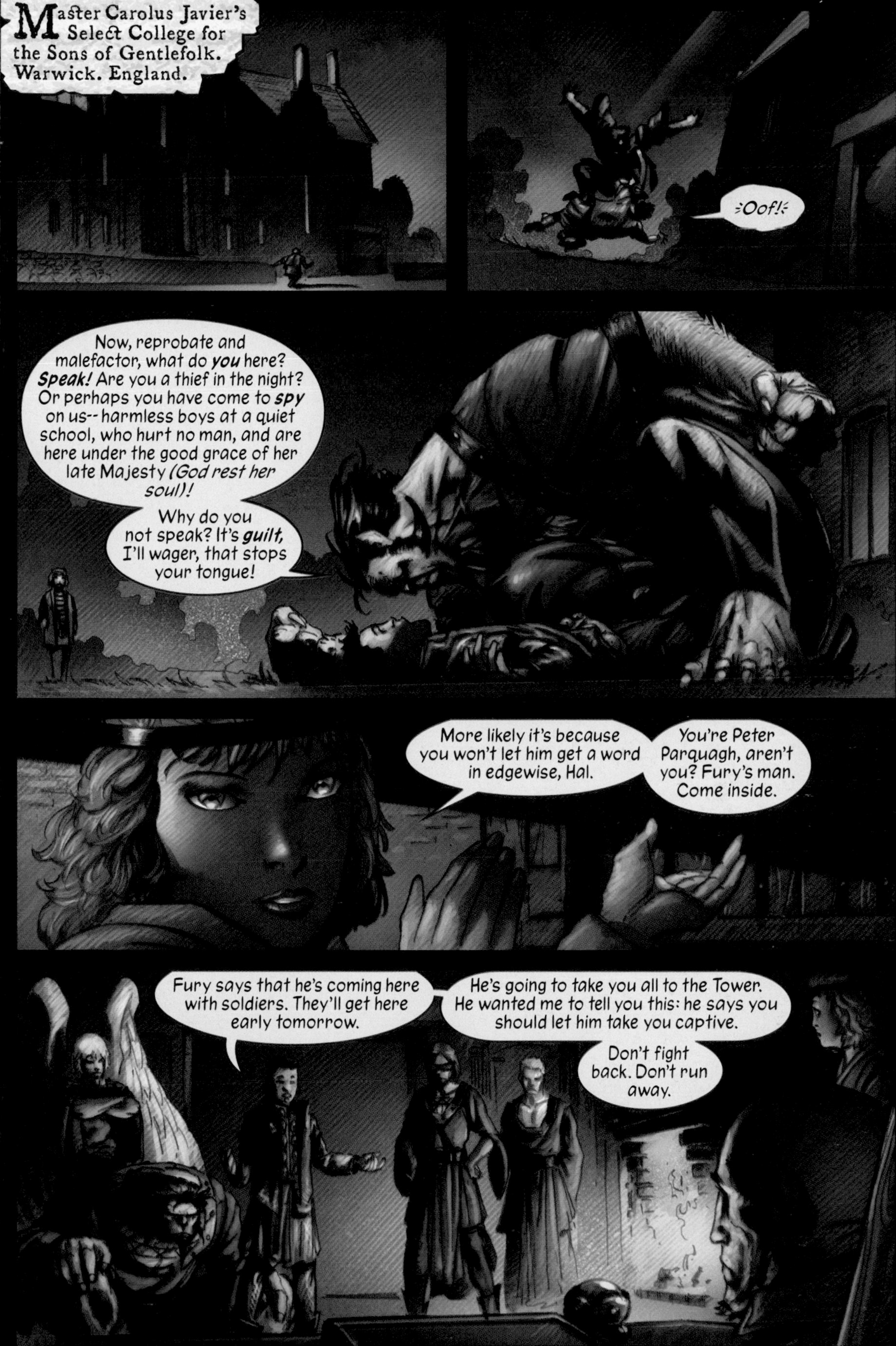
Master Carolus Javier's Select College for the Sons of Gentlefolk. Warwick. England.
Oof!
Now, reprobate and malefactor, what do *you* here? ***Speak!*** Are you a thief in the night? Or perhaps you have come to ***spy*** on us-- harmless boys at a quiet school, who hurt no man, and are here under the good grace of her late Majesty *(God rest her soul)!*
Why do you not speak? It's ***guilt,*** I'll wager, that stops your tongue!
More likely it's because you won't let him get a word in edgewise, Hal.
You're Peter Parquagh, aren't you? Fury's man. Come inside.
Fury says that he's coming here with soldiers. They'll get here early tomorrow.
He's going to take you all to the Tower. He wanted me to tell you this: he says you should let him take you captive.
Don't fight back. Don't run away.

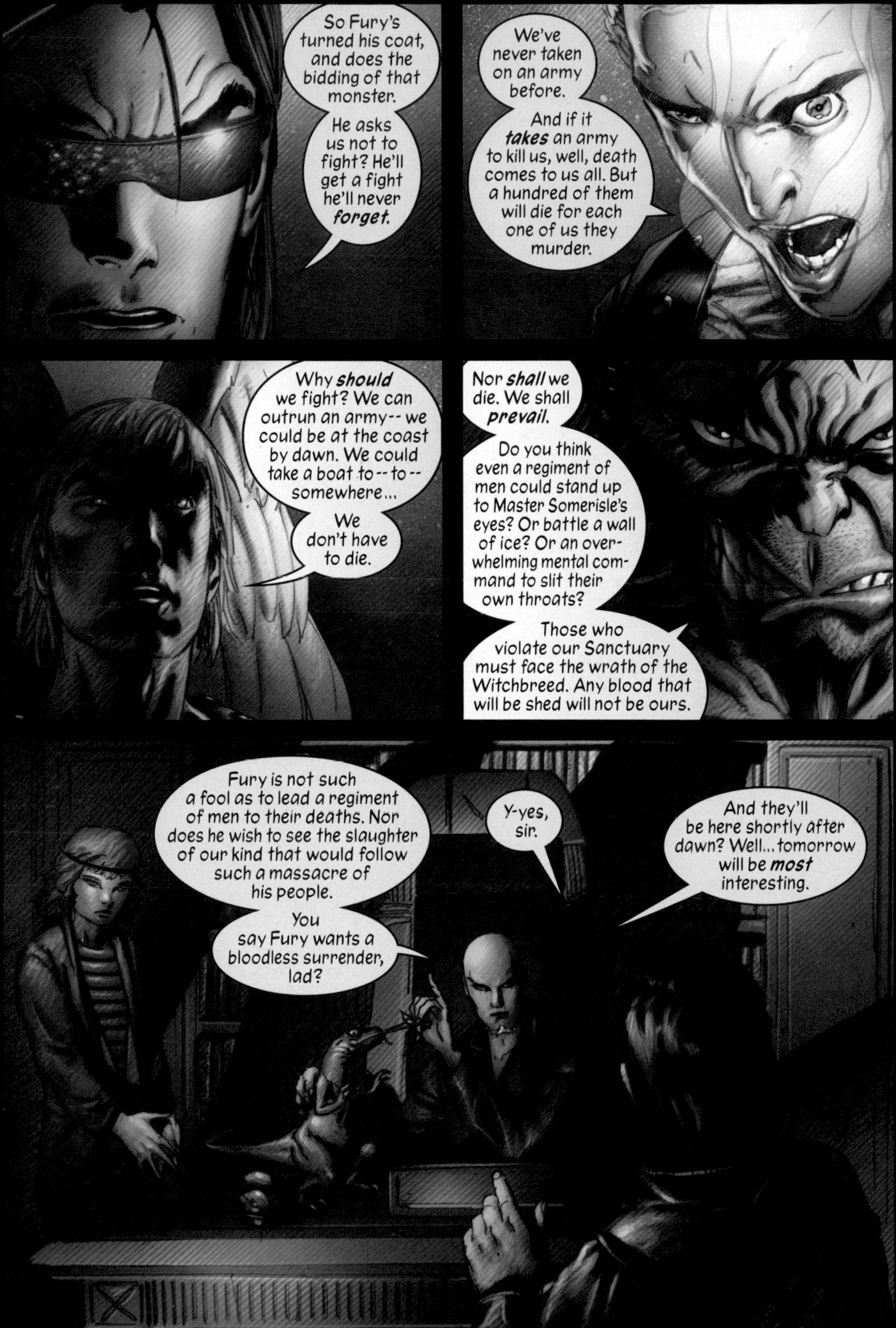
So Fury's turned his coat, and does the bidding of that monster.
He asks us not to fight? He'll get a fight he'll never *forget.*
We've never taken on an army before.
And if it *takes* an army to kill us, well, death comes to us all. But a hundred of them will die for each one of us they murder.
Why *should* we fight? We can outrun an army -- we could be at the coast by dawn. We could take a boat to -- to -- somewhere...
We don't have to die.
Nor *shall* we die. We shall *prevail.*
Do you think even a regiment of men could stand up to Master Somerisle's eyes? Or battle a wall of ice? Or an overwhelming mental command to slit their own throats?
Those who violate our Sanctuary must face the wrath of the Witchbreed. Any blood that will be shed will not be ours.
Fury is not such a fool as to lead a regiment of men to their deaths. Nor does he wish to see the slaughter of our kind that would follow such a massacre of his people.
You say Fury wants a bloodless surrender, lad?
Y-yes, sir.
And they'll be here shortly after dawn? Well... tomorrow will be *most* interesting.

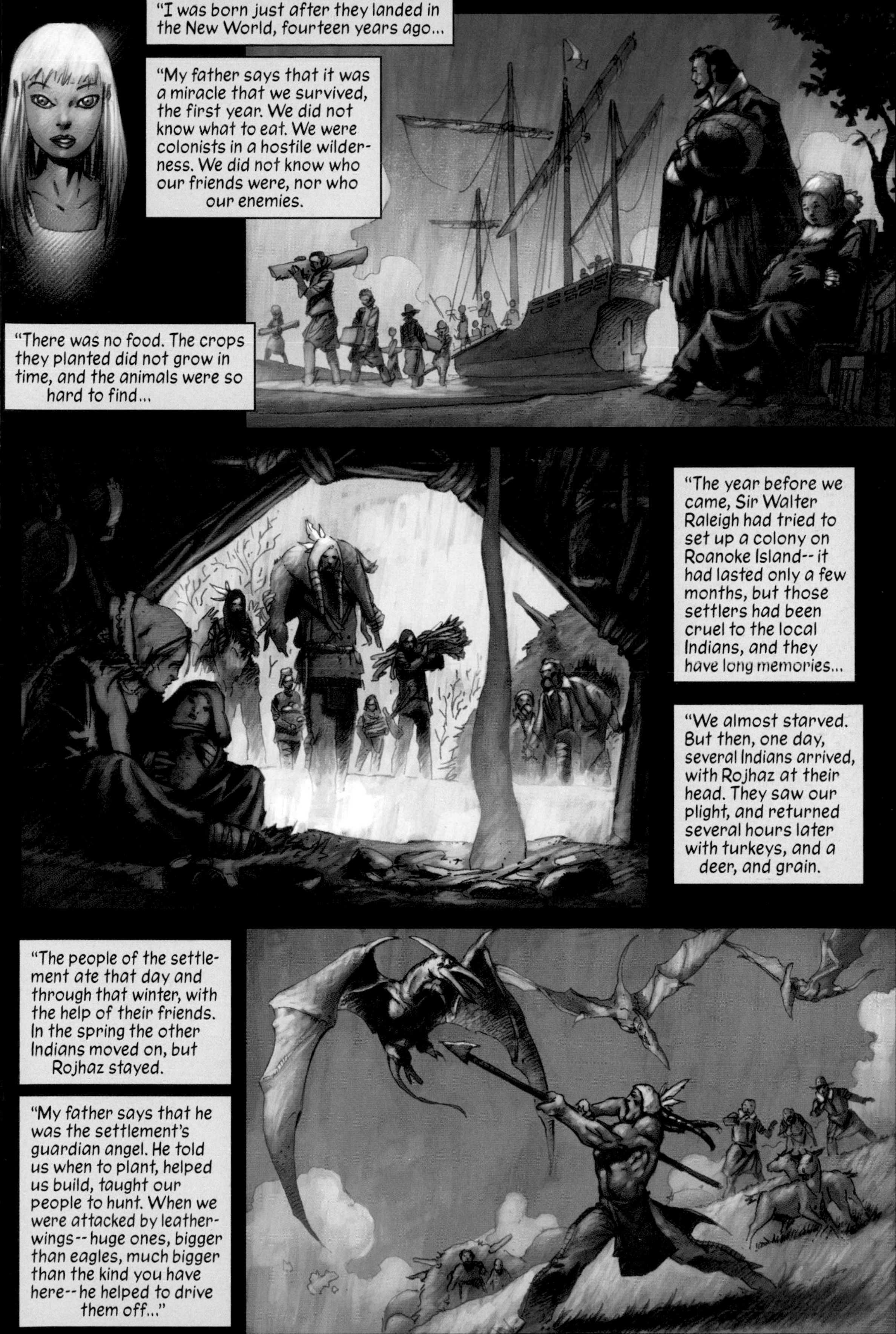
"I was born just after they landed in the New World, fourteen years ago...
"My father says that it was a miracle that we survived, the first year. We did not know what to eat. We were colonists in a hostile wilderness. We did not know who our friends were, nor who our enemies.
"There was no food. The crops they planted did not grow in time, and the animals were so hard to find...
"The year before we came, Sir Walter Raleigh had tried to set up a colony on Roanoke Island-- it had lasted only a few months, but those settlers had been cruel to the local Indians, and they have long memories...
"We almost starved. But then, one day, several Indians arrived, with Rojhaz at their head. They saw our plight, and returned several hours later with turkeys, and a deer, and grain.
"The people of the settlement ate that day and through that winter, with the help of their friends. In the spring the other Indians moved on, but Rojhaz stayed.
"My father says that he was the settlement's guardian angel. He told us when to plant, helped us build, taught our people to hunt. When we were attacked by leather-wings-- huge ones, bigger than eagles, much bigger than the kind you have here-- he helped to drive them off..."

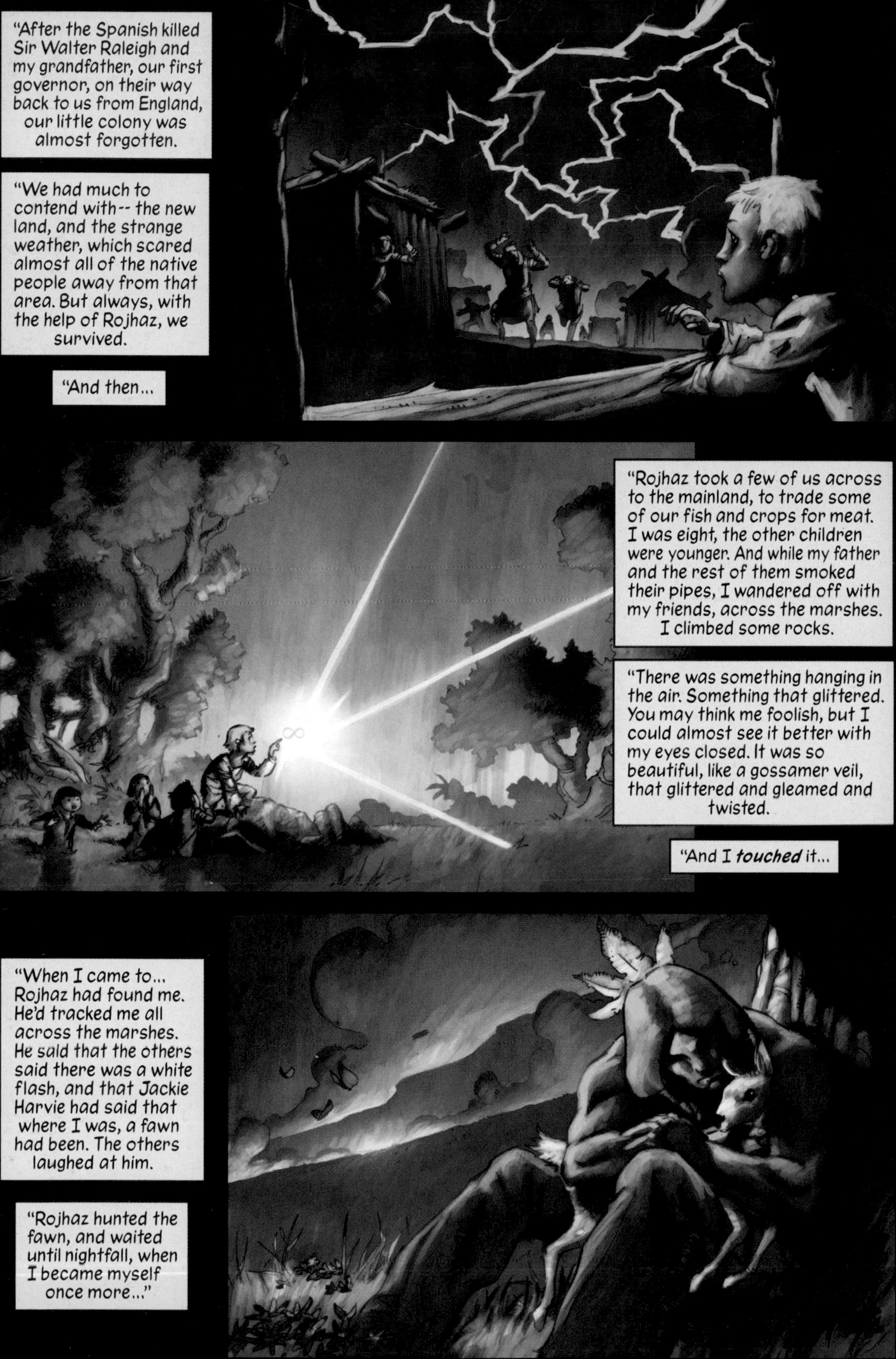
"After the Spanish killed Sir Walter Raleigh and my grandfather, our first governor, on their way back to us from England, our little colony was almost forgotten.
"We had much to contend with-- the new land, and the strange weather, which scared almost all of the native people away from that area. But always, with the help of Rojhaz, we survived.
"And then...
"Rojhaz took a few of us across to the mainland, to trade some of our fish and crops for meat. I was eight, the other children were younger. And while my father and the rest of them smoked their pipes, I wandered off with my friends, across the marshes. I climbed some rocks.
"There was something hanging in the air. Something that glittered. You may think me foolish, but I could almost see it better with my eyes closed. It was so beautiful, like a gossamer veil, that glittered and gleamed and twisted.
"And I *touched* it...
"When I came to... Rojhaz had found me. He'd tracked me all across the marshes. He said that the others said there was a white flash, and that Jackie Harvie had said that where I was, a fawn had been. The others laughed at him.
"Rojhaz hunted the fawn, and waited until nightfall, when I became myself once more..."

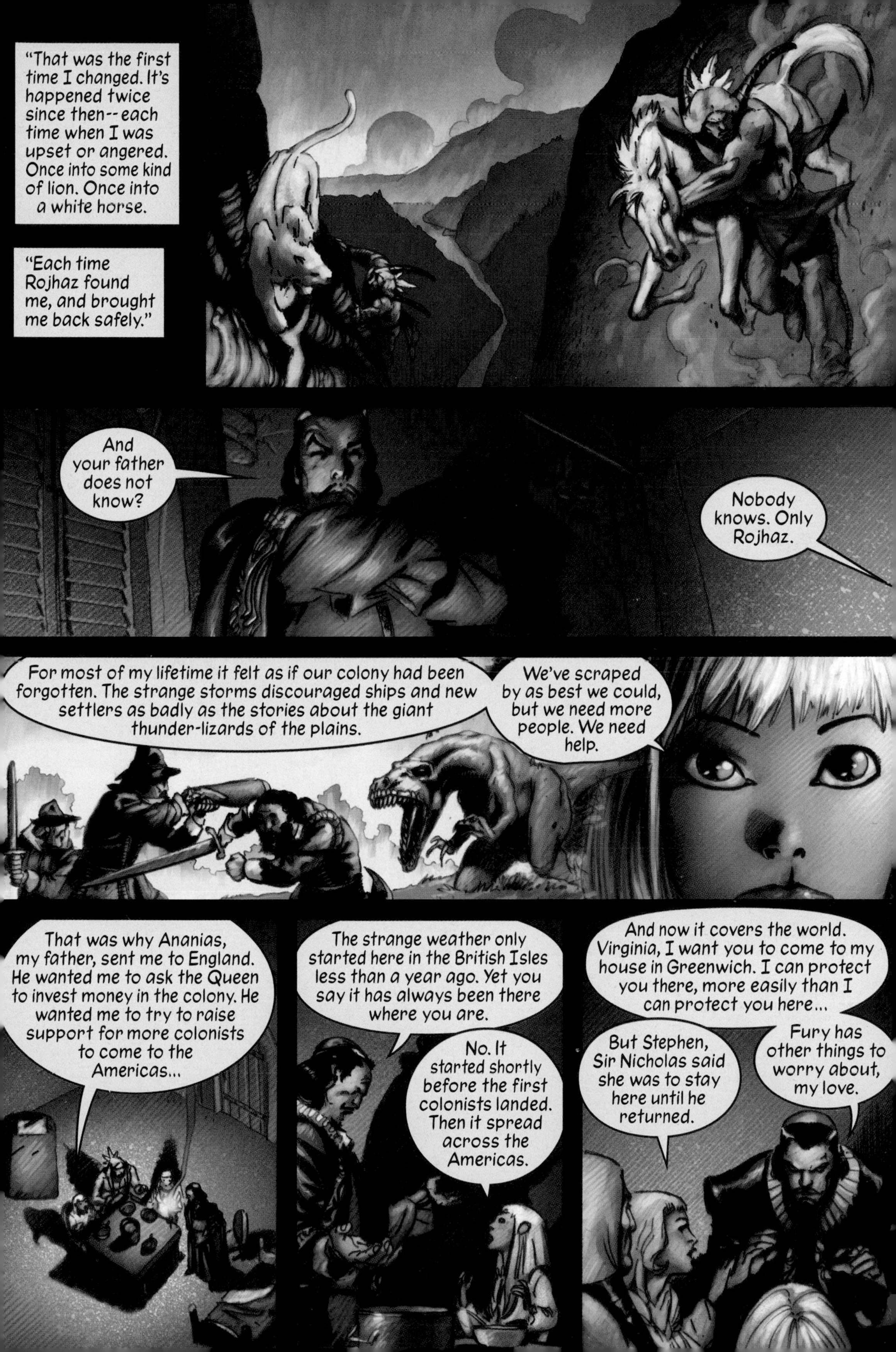
"That was the first time I changed. It's happened twice since then-- each time when I was upset or angered. Once into some kind of lion. Once into a white horse.
"Each time Rojhaz found me, and brought me back safely."
And your father does not know?
Nobody knows. Only Rojhaz.
For most of my lifetime it felt as if our colony had been forgotten. The strange storms discouraged ships and new settlers as badly as the stories about the giant thunder-lizards of the plains.
We've scraped by as best we could, but we need more people. We need help.
That was why Ananias, my father, sent me to England. He wanted me to ask the Queen to invest money in the colony. He wanted me to try to raise support for more colonists to come to the Americas...
The strange weather only started here in the British Isles less than a year ago. Yet you say it has always been there where you are.
No. It started shortly before the first colonists landed. Then it spread across the Americas.
And now it covers the world. Virginia, I want you to come to my house in Greenwich. I can protect you there, more easily than I can protect you here...
But Stephen, Sir Nicholas said she was to stay here until he returned.
Fury has other things to worry about, my love.

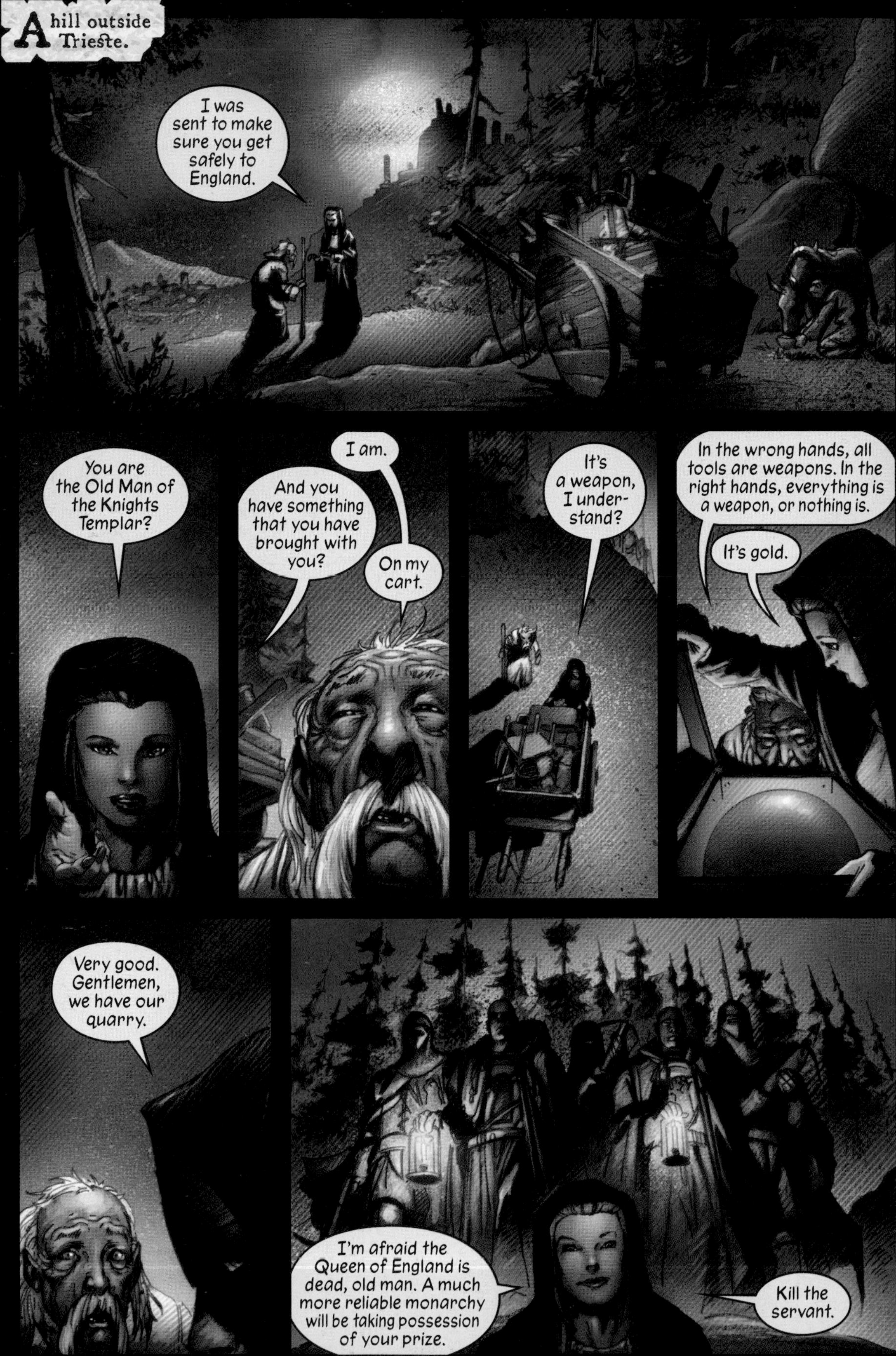
A hill outside Trieste.
I was sent to make sure you get safely to England.
You are the Old Man of the Knights Templar?
I am.
And you have something that you have brought with you?
On my cart.
It's a weapon, I understand?
In the wrong hands, all tools are weapons. In the right hands, everything is a weapon, or nothing is.
It's gold.
Very good. Gentlemen, we have our quarry.
I'm afraid the Queen of England is dead, old man. A much more reliable monarchy will be taking possession of your prize.
Kill the servant.

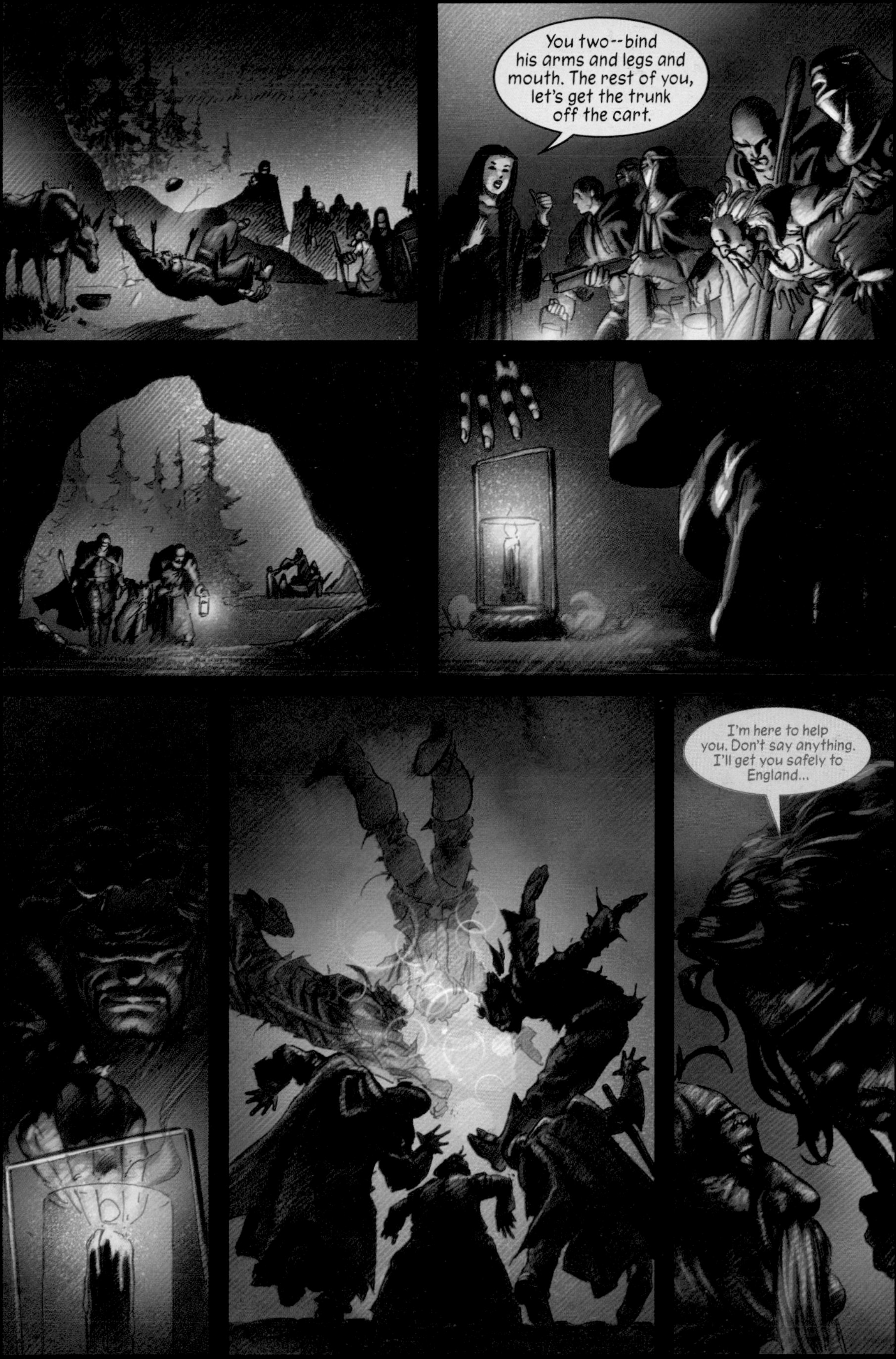
You two--bind his arms and legs and mouth. The rest of you, let's get the trunk off the cart.
I'm here to help you. Don't say anything. I'll get you safely to England...

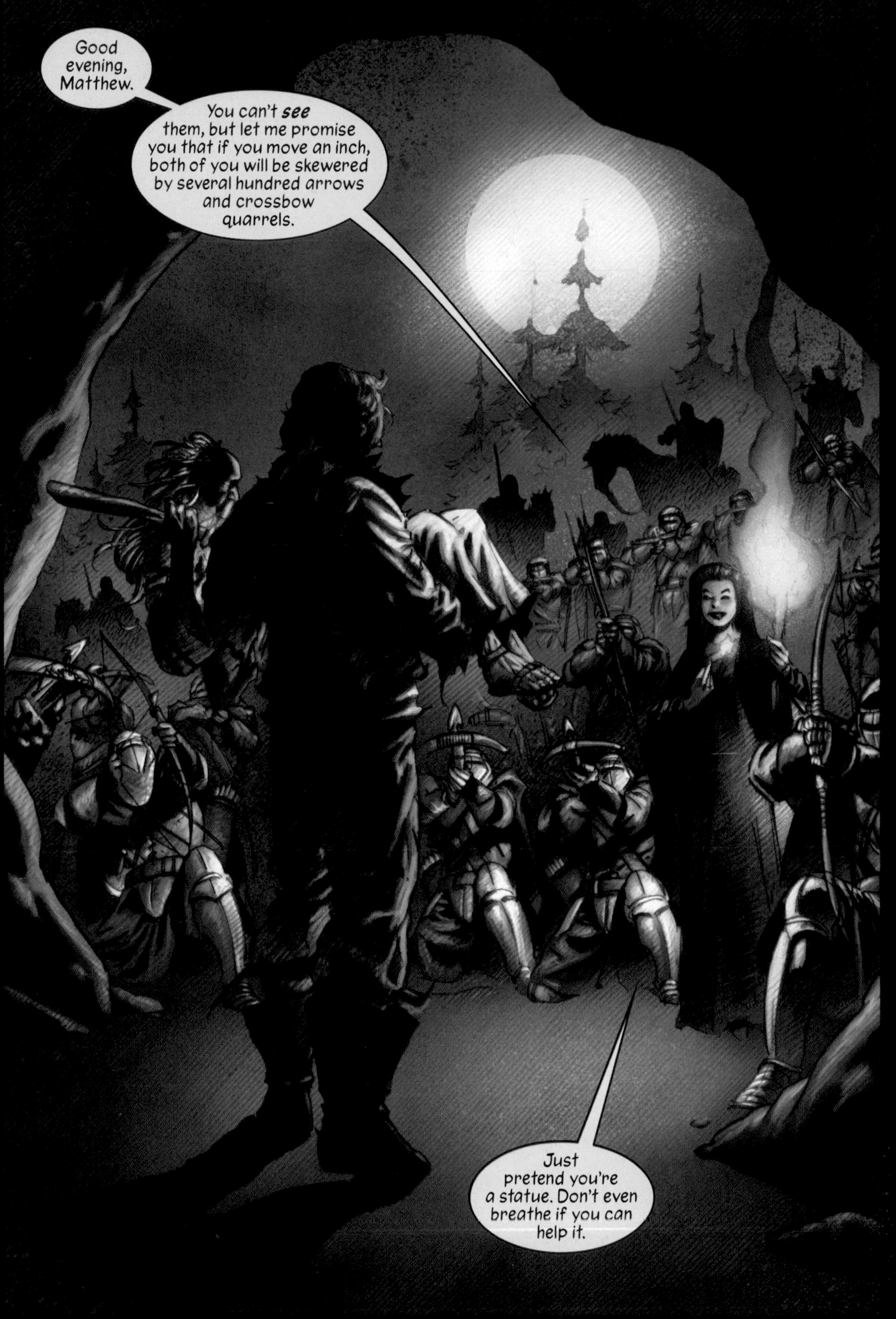
Good evening, Matthew.
You can't ***see*** them, but let me promise you that if you move an inch, both of you will be skewered by several hundred arrows and crossbow quarrels.
Just pretend you're a statue. Don't even breathe if you can help it.

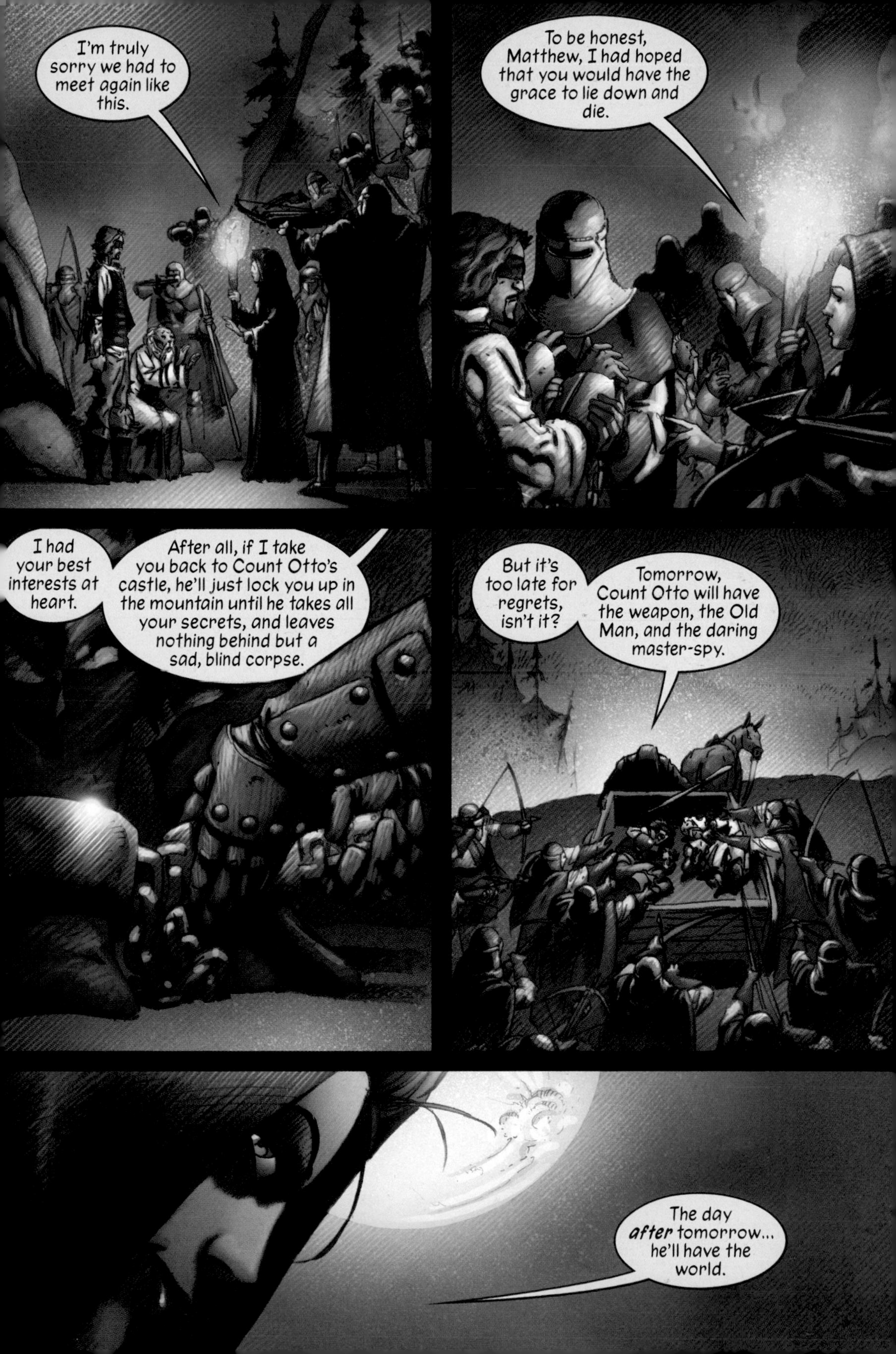
I'm truly sorry we had to meet again like this.
To be honest, Matthew, I had hoped that you would have the grace to lie down and die.
I had your best interests at heart.
After all, if I take you back to Count Otto's castle, he'll just lock you up in the mountain until he takes all your secrets, and leaves nothing behind but a sad, blind corpse.
But it's too late for regrets, isn't it?
Tomorrow, Count Otto will have the weapon, the Old Man, and the daring master-spy.
The day *after* tomorrow... he'll have the world.

IN WHICH A TREACHEROUS COURSE IS PLOTTED

1602

PART FIVE

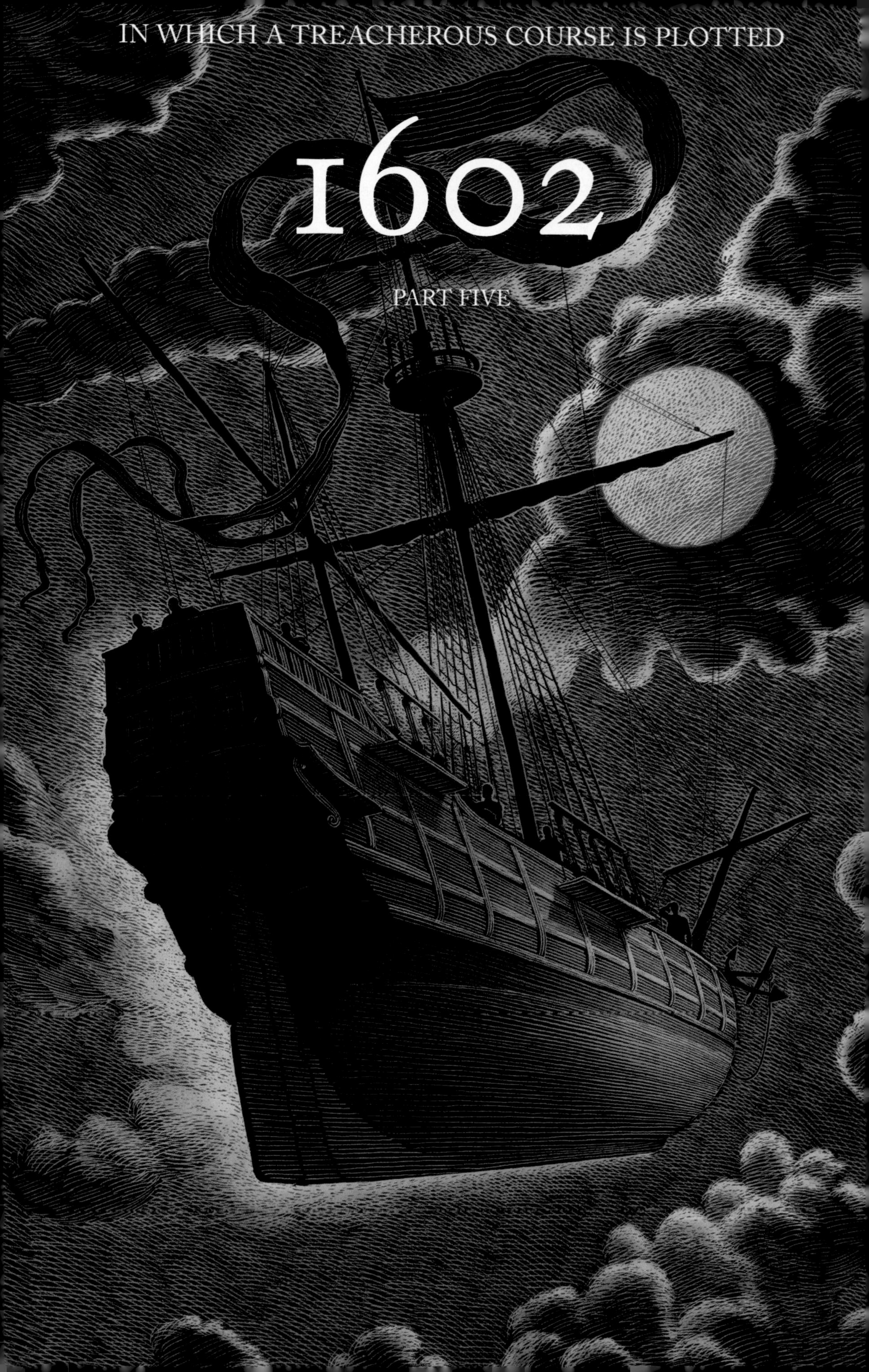

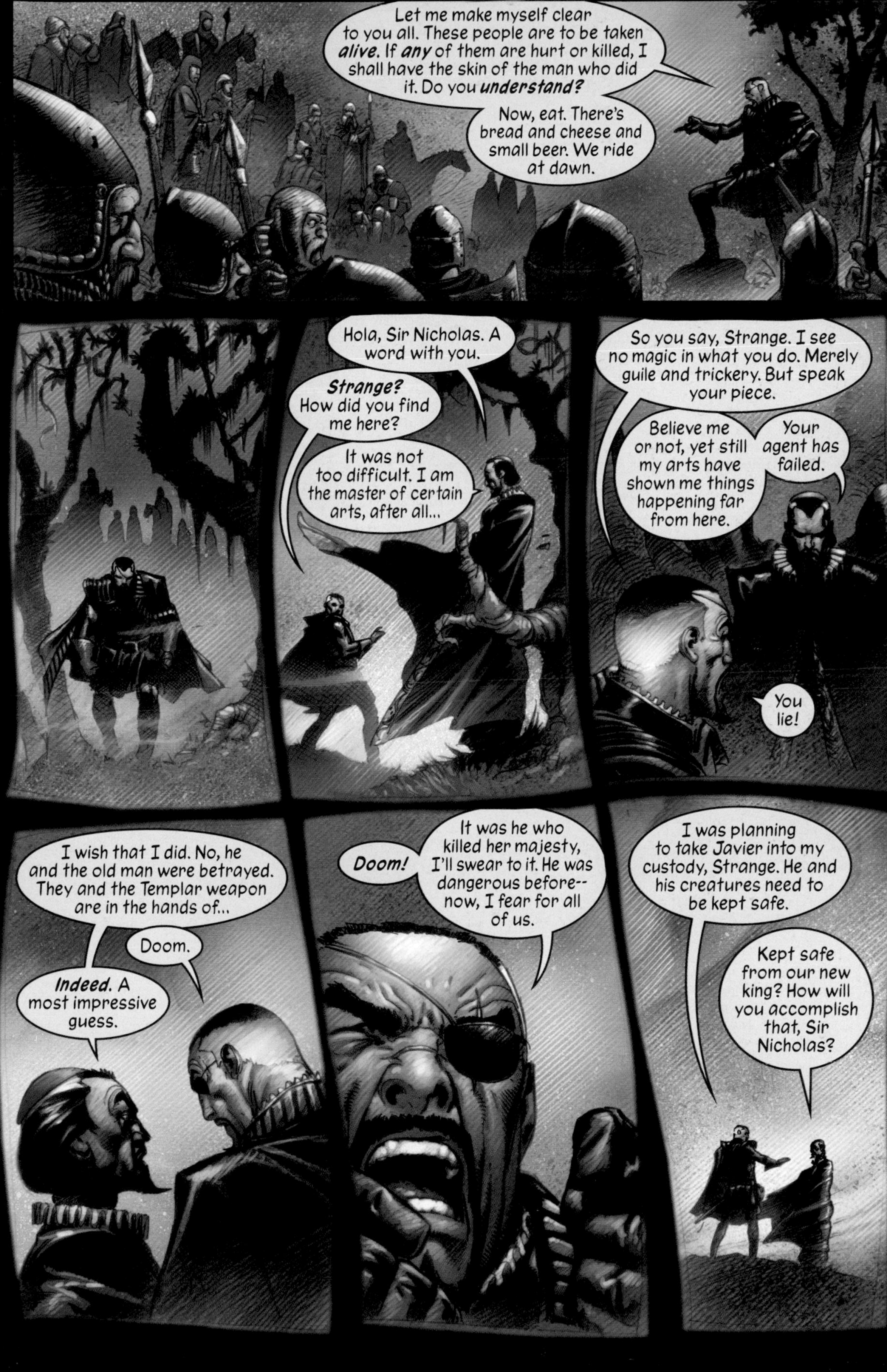
Let me make myself clear to you all. These people are to be taken *alive*. If *any* of them are hurt or killed, I shall have the skin of the man who did it. Do you *understand?*
Now, eat. There's bread and cheese and small beer. We ride at dawn.
Hola, Sir Nicholas. A word with you.
Strange? How did you find me here?
It was not too difficult. I am the master of certain arts, after all...
So you say, Strange. I see no magic in what you do. Merely guile and trickery. But speak your piece.
Believe me or not, yet still my arts have shown me things happening far from here.
Your agent has failed.
You lie!
I wish that I did. No, he and the old man were betrayed. They and the Templar weapon are in the hands of...
Doom.
Indeed. A most impressive guess.
Doom!
It was he who killed her majesty, I'll swear to it. He was dangerous before-- now, I fear for all of us.
I was planning to take Javier into my custody, Strange. He and his creatures need to be kept safe.
Kept safe from our new king? How will you accomplish that, Sir Nicholas?

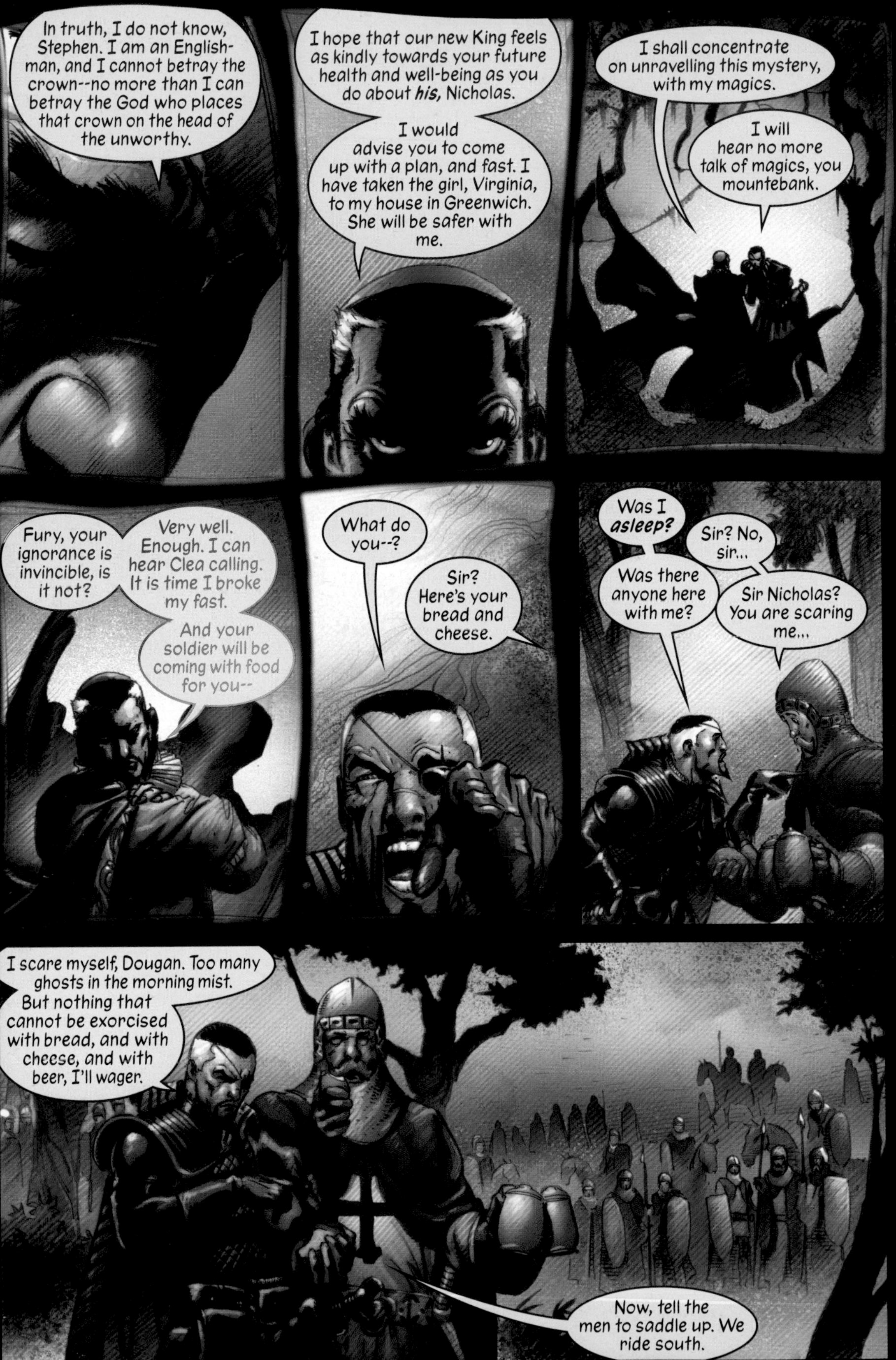
In truth, I do not know, Stephen. I am an Englishman, and I cannot betray the crown--no more than I can betray the God who places that crown on the head of the unworthy.
I hope that our new King feels as kindly towards your future health and well-being as you do about *his,* Nicholas.
I would advise you to come up with a plan, and fast. I have taken the girl, Virginia, to my house in Greenwich. She will be safer with me.
I shall concentrate on unravelling this mystery, with my magics.
I will hear no more talk of magics, you mountebank.
Fury, your ignorance is invincible, is it not?
Very well. Enough. I can hear Clea calling. It is time I broke my fast.
And your soldier will be coming with food for you--
What do you--?
Sir? Here's your bread and cheese.
Was I *asleep?*
Was there anyone here with me?
Sir? No, sir...
Sir Nicholas? You are scaring me...
I scare myself, Dougan. Too many ghosts in the morning mist.
But nothing that cannot be exorcised with bread, and with cheese, and with beer, I'll wager.
Now, tell the men to saddle up. We ride south.

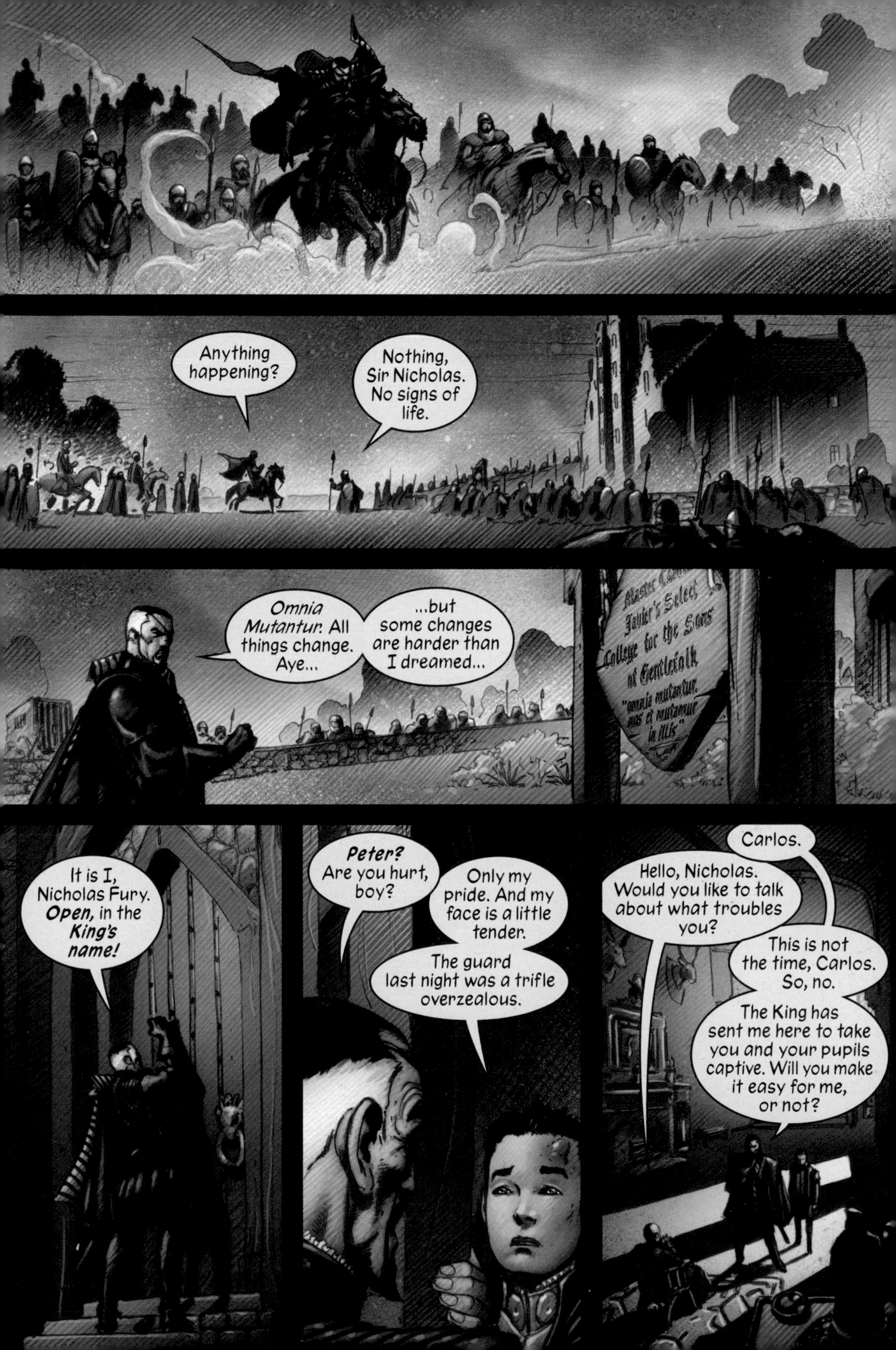
Anything happening?
Nothing, Sir Nicholas. No signs of life.
Omnia Mutantur. All things change. Aye...
...but some changes are harder than I dreamed...
Xavier's Select College for the Sons of Gentlefolk
"omnia mutantur, nos et mutamur in illis"
It is I, Nicholas Fury. ***Open,*** in the ***King's name!***
Peter? Are you hurt, boy?
Only my pride. And my face is a little tender.
The guard last night was a trifle overzealous.
Carlos.
Hello, Nicholas. Would you like to talk about what troubles you?
This is not the time, Carlos. So, no.
The King has sent me here to take you and your pupils captive. Will you make it easy for me, or not?

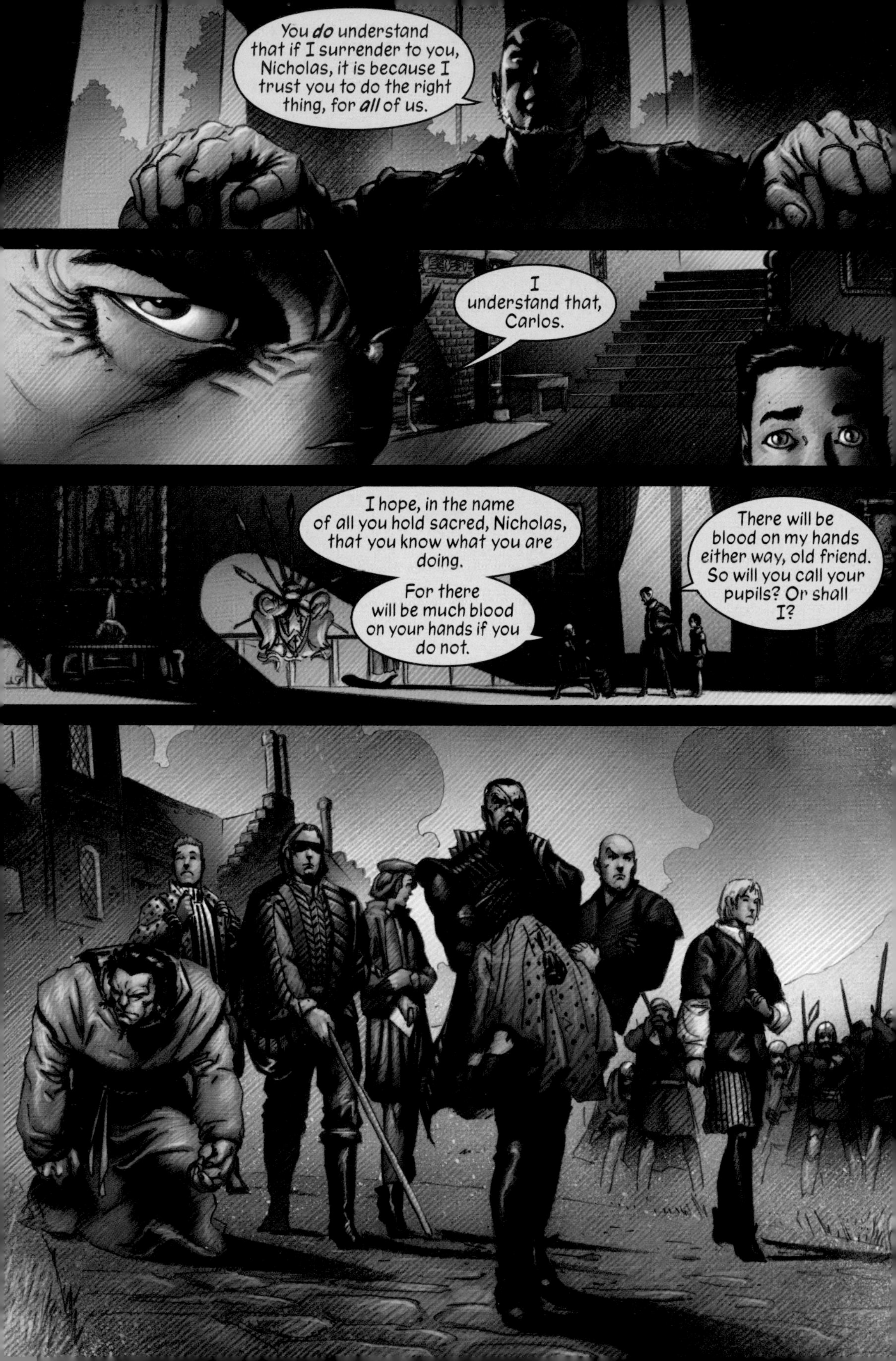

You *do* understand that if I surrender to you, Nicholas, it is because I trust you to do the right thing, for *all* of us.
I understand that, Carlos.
I hope, in the name of all you hold sacred, Nicholas, that you know what you are doing.
For there will be much blood on your hands if you do not.
There will be blood on my hands either way, old friend. So will you call your pupils? Or shall I?

Oh my sweet lord Jesus protect us.

And whatever would be upsetting *you*, soldier-boy?

Have you never seen an Orkneyman before?

Ah, *yes*. I've been expecting you, young Petros.

And what message have you for me today?

The Inquisitor commends you on taking Javier and his monsters captive, and wishes to remind you of the second part of your obligation, Your Majesty--

--to turn the creatures over to the Inquisition.

My obligation? **MY OBLIGATION?**

I am the King of Scotland, soon to be crowned the rightful King of England. My obligation is to my conscience and to my God. Not to some Spanish offal-eater.

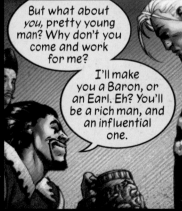

But what about *you*, pretty young man? Why don't you come and work for me?

I'll make you a Baron, or an Earl. Eh? You'll be a rich man, and an influential one.

Now *tell* me--*how* does the Inquisitor know that Javier has been captured? I have given the order, true...

Perhaps a little bird told him, Your Majesty.

And I hope that you will not take it amiss if, for now, at least, I keep my current position.

Well, Banner. The pretty young man left in quite a hurry.

Yes, Your Majesty.

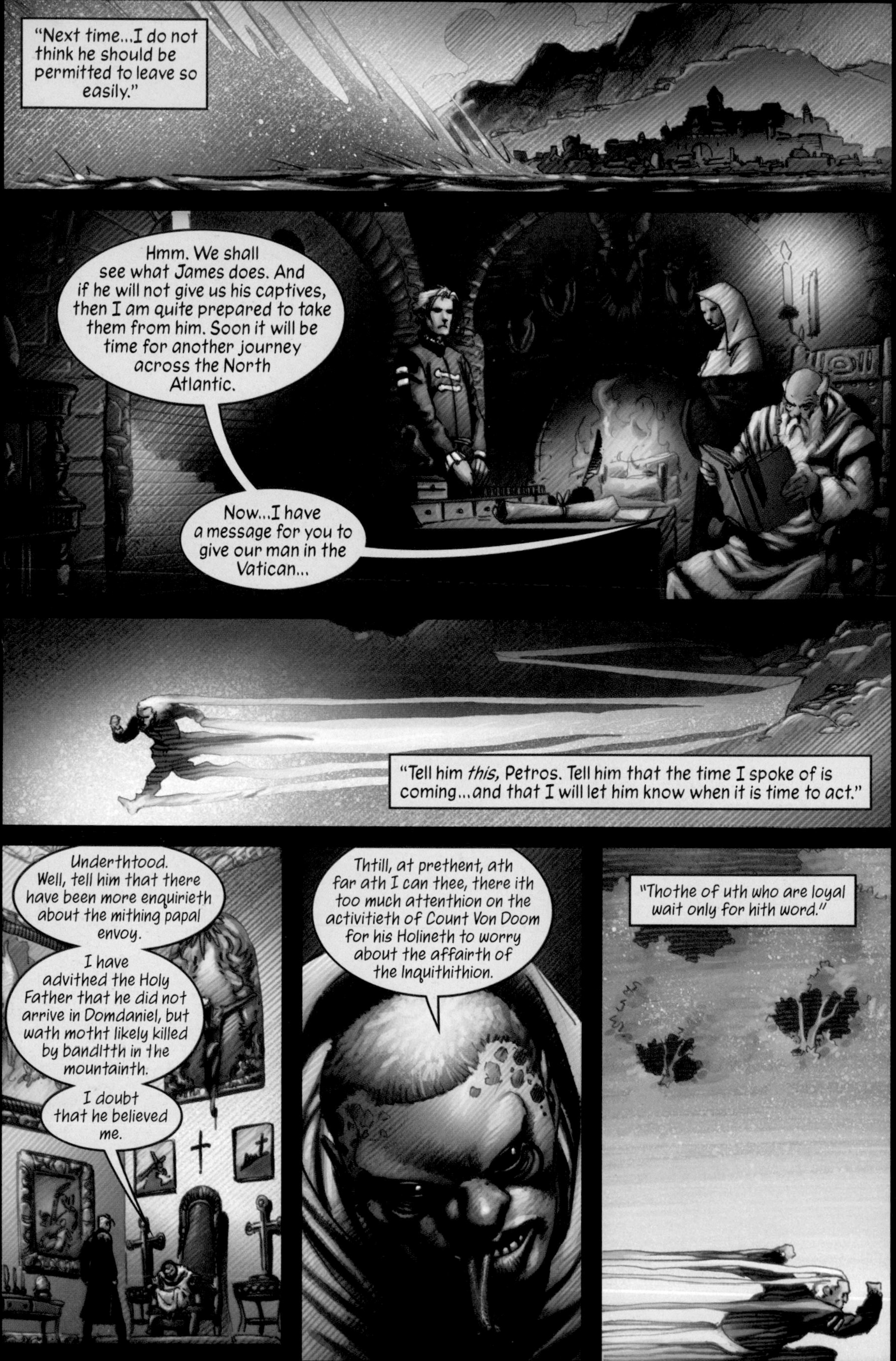

"Next time...I do not think he should be permitted to leave so easily."
Hmm. We shall see what James does. And if he will not give us his captives, then I am quite prepared to take them from him. Soon it will be time for another journey across the North Atlantic.
Now...I have a message for you to give our man in the Vatican...
"Tell him *this,* Petros. Tell him that the time I spoke of is coming...and that I will let him know when it is time to act."
Underthtood. Well, tell him that there have been more enquirieth about the mithing papal envoy.
I have advithed the Holy Father that he did not arrive in Domdaniel, but wath motht likely killed by bandItth in the mountainth.
I doubt that he believed me.
Thtill, at prethent, ath far ath I can thee, there ith too much attenthion on the activitieth of Count Von Doom for his Holineth to worry about the affairth of the Inquithithion.
"Thothe of uth who are loyal wait only for hith word."

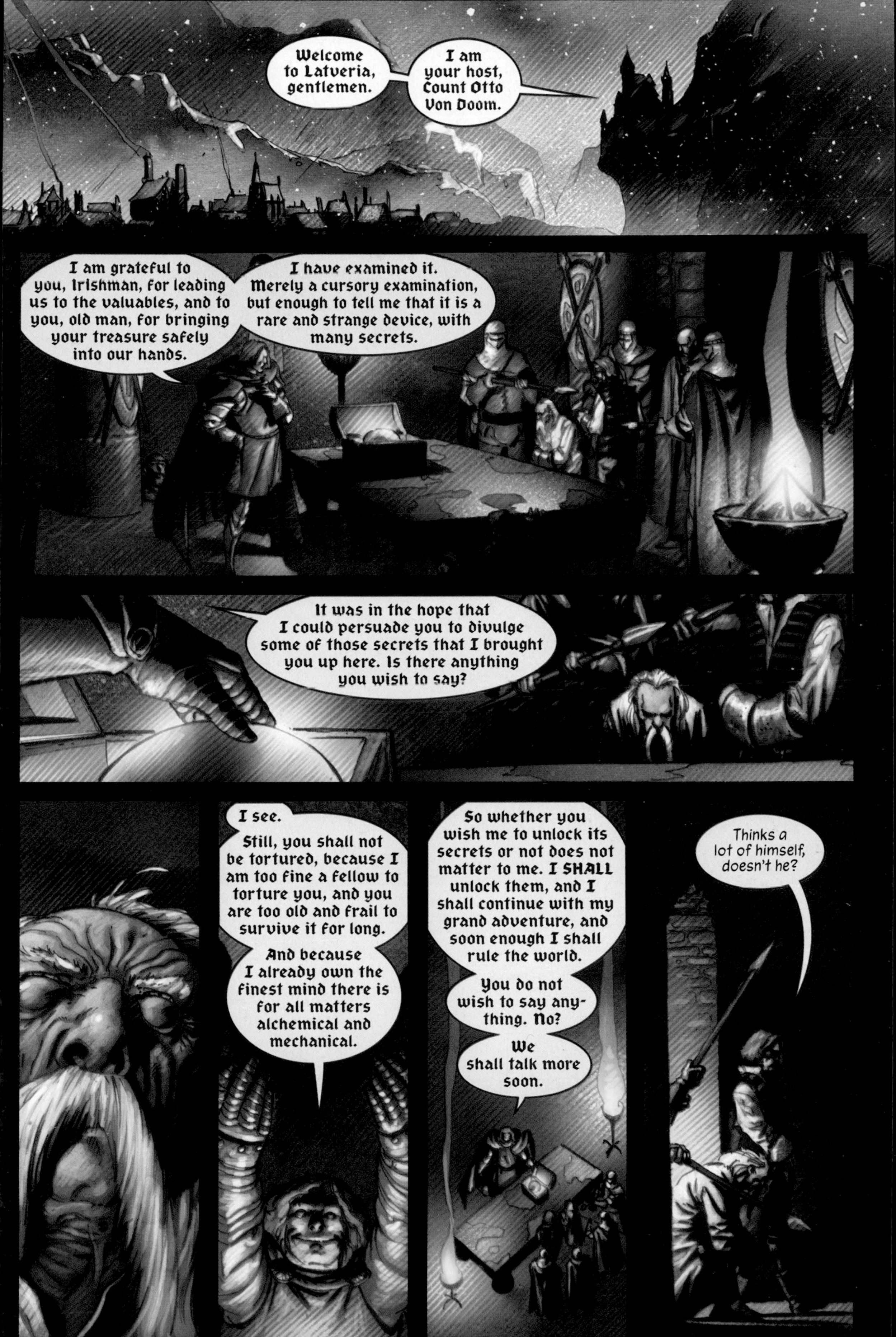
Welcome to Latveria, gentlemen.
I am your host, Count Otto Von Doom.
I am grateful to you, Irishman, for leading us to the valuables, and to you, old man, for bringing your treasure safely into our hands.
I have examined it. Merely a cursory examination, but enough to tell me that it is a rare and strange device, with many secrets.
It was in the hope that I could persuade you to divulge some of those secrets that I brought you up here. Is there anything you wish to say?
I see.
Still, you shall not be tortured, because I am too fine a fellow to torture you, and you are too old and frail to survive it for long.
And because I already own the finest mind there is for all matters alchemical and mechanical.
So whether you wish me to unlock its secrets or not does not matter to me. I SHALL unlock them, and I shall continue with my grand adventure, and soon enough I shall rule the world.
You do not wish to say anything. No?
We shall talk more soon.
Thinks a lot of himself, doesn't he?

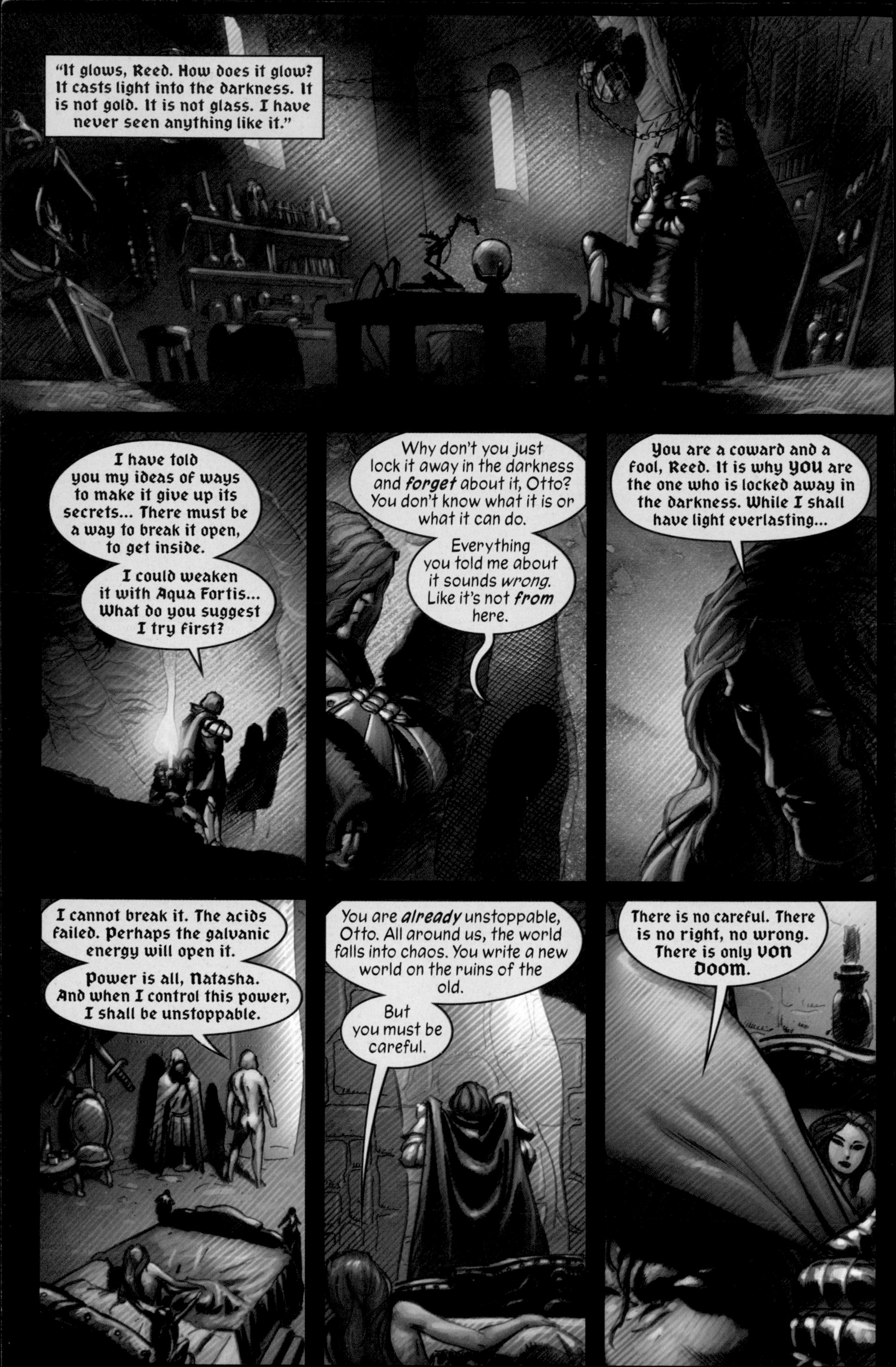
"It glows, Reed. How does it glow? It casts light into the darkness. It is not gold. It is not glass. I have never seen anything like it."
I have told you my ideas of ways to make it give up its secrets... There must be a way to break it open, to get inside.
I could weaken it with Aqua Fortis... What do you suggest I try first?
Why don't you just lock it away in the darkness and *forget* about it, Otto? You don't know what it is or what it can do.
Everything you told me about it sounds *wrong.* Like it's not *from* here.
You are a coward and a fool, Reed. It is why **YOU** are the one who is locked away in the darkness. While I shall have light everlasting...
I cannot break it. The acids failed. Perhaps the galvanic energy will open it.
Power is all, Natasha. And when I control this power, I shall be unstoppable.
You are ***already*** unstoppable, Otto. All around us, the world falls into chaos. You write a new world on the ruins of the old.
But you must be careful.
There is no careful. There is no right, no wrong. There is only **VON DOOM**.

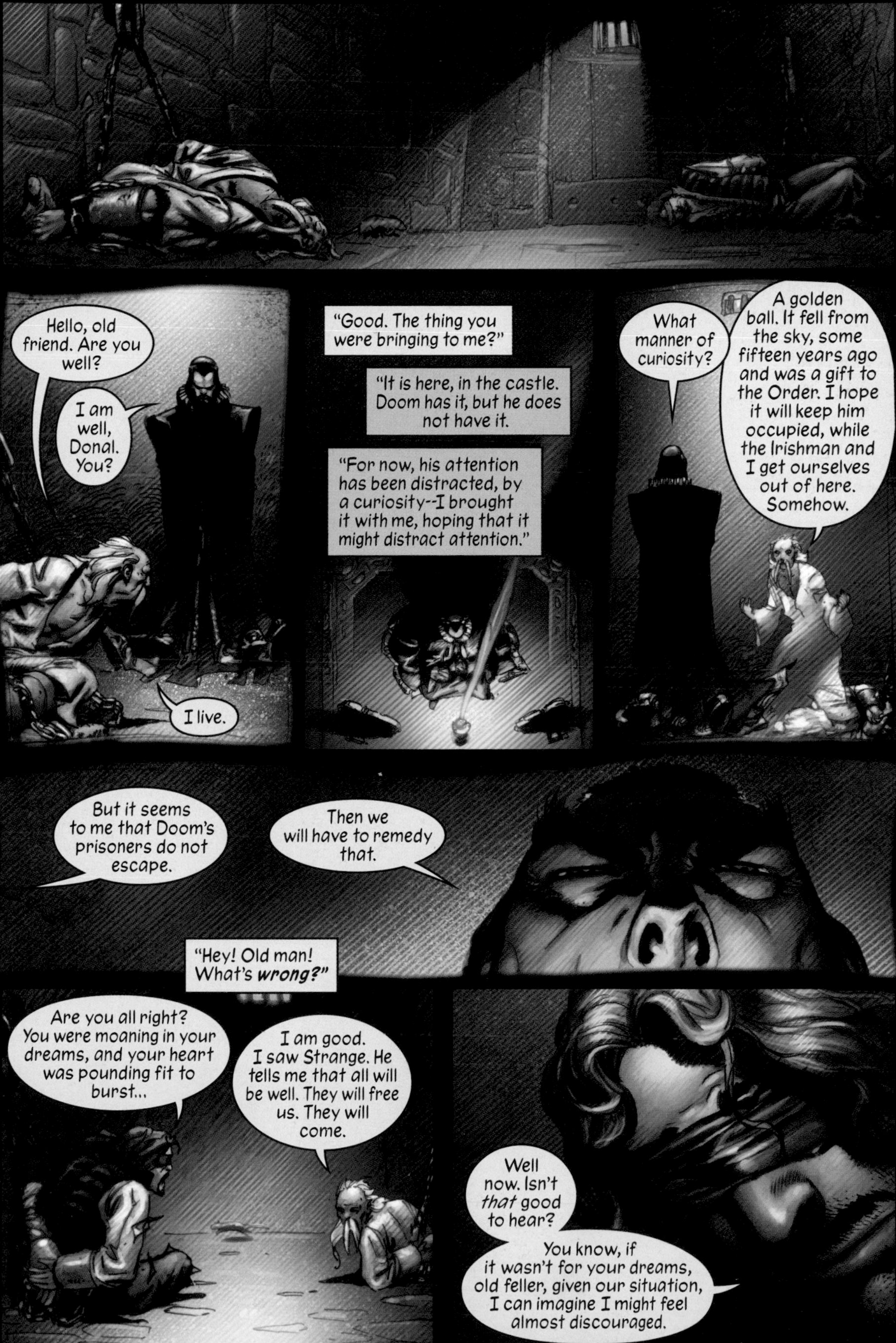
Hello, old friend. Are you well?
I am well, Donal. You?
I live.
"Good. The thing you were bringing to me?"
"It is here, in the castle. Doom has it, but he does not have it.
"For now, his attention has been distracted, by a curiosity--I brought it with me, hoping that it might distract attention."
What manner of curiosity?
A golden ball. It fell from the sky, some fifteen years ago and was a gift to the Order. I hope it will keep him occupied, while the Irishman and I get ourselves out of here. Somehow.
But it seems to me that Doom's prisoners do not escape.
Then we will have to remedy that.
"Hey! Old man! What's *wrong?*"
Are you all right? You were moaning in your dreams, and your heart was pounding fit to burst...
I am good. I saw Strange. He tells me that all will be well. They will free us. They will come.
Well now. Isn't *that* good to hear?
You know, if it wasn't for your dreams, old feller, given our situation, I can imagine I might feel almost discouraged.

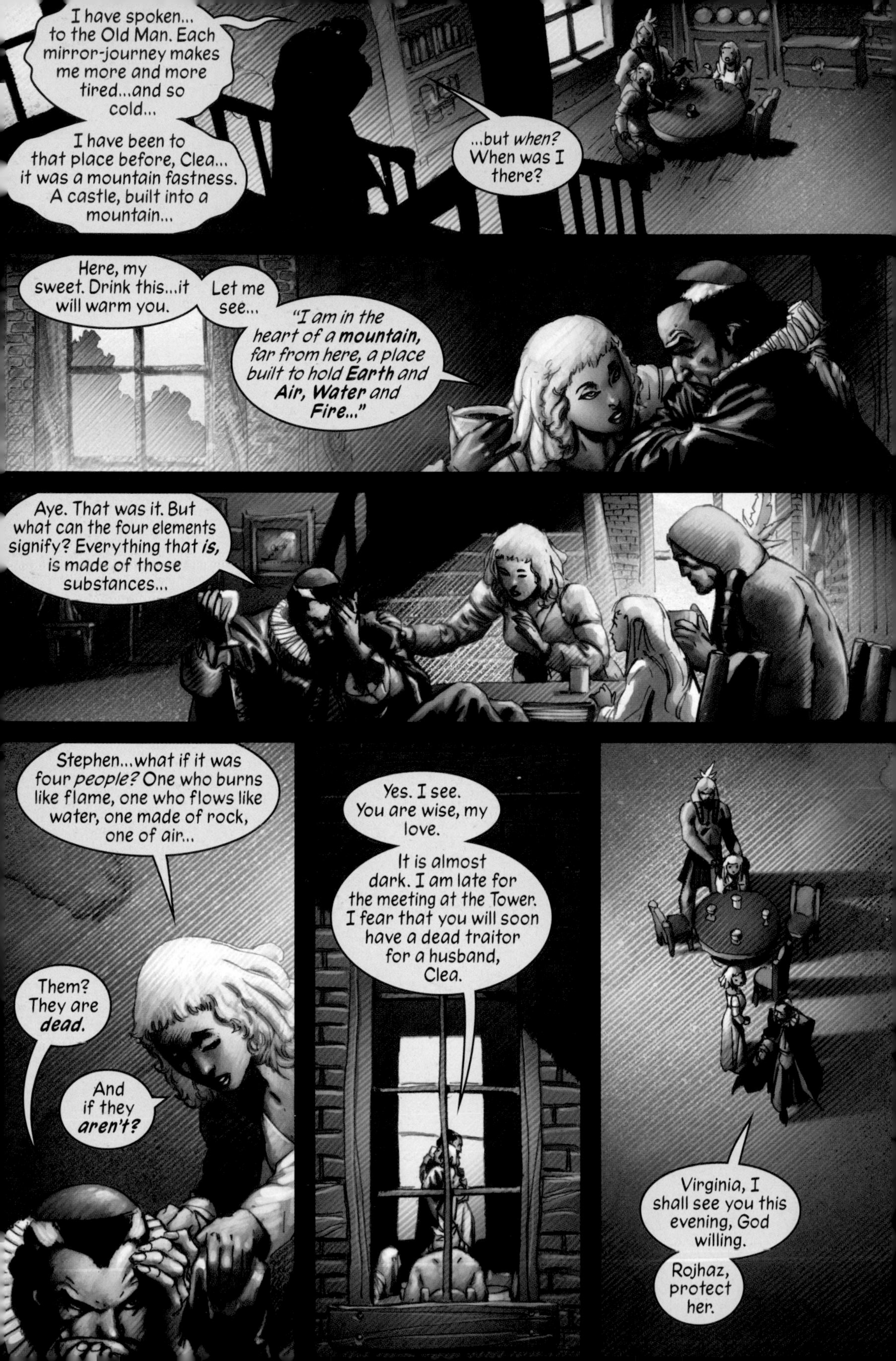
I have spoken... to the Old Man. Each mirror-journey makes me more and more tired...and so cold...
I have been to that place before, Clea... it was a mountain fastness. A castle, built into a mountain...
...but *when?* When was I there?
Here, my sweet. Drink this...it will warm you.
Let me see...
*"I am in the heart of a **mountain,** far from here, a place built to hold **Earth** and **Air, Water** and **Fire...**"*
Aye. That was it. But what can the four elements signify? Everything that *is,* is made of those substances...
Stephen...what if it was four *people?* One who burns like flame, one who flows like water, one made of rock, one of air...
Them? They are ***dead.***
And if they ***aren't?***
Yes. I see. You are wise, my love.
It is almost dark. I am late for the meeting at the Tower. I fear that you will soon have a dead traitor for a husband, Clea.
Virginia, I shall see you this evening, God willing.
Rojhaz, protect her.

Mistress **Clea?** Can I ask what you were talking about? The people who were elements...?

Certainly, Virginia. Let me see...

Sir Richard Reed was one of the most brilliant men who ever walked.

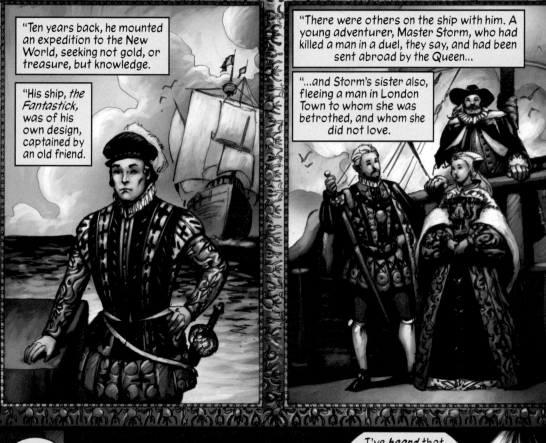

"Ten years back, he mounted an expedition to the New World, seeking not gold, or treasure, but knowledge.

"His ship, *the Fantastick*, was of his own design, captained by an old friend.

"There were others on the ship with him. A young adventurer, Master Storm, who had killed a man in a duel, they say, and had been sent abroad by the Queen...

"...and Storm's sister also, fleeing a man in London Town to whom she was betrothed, and whom she did not love.

There is a song the people sing. Let me see...

There were four brave souls rode the oceans abroad, T'was on the Fantastick they'd sail... ♪

I've **heard** that song! The sailors on the *Virginia Maid* used to sing it! I could never understand the *story*.

Something about a light which changed them, and saving people from a huge monster or something.

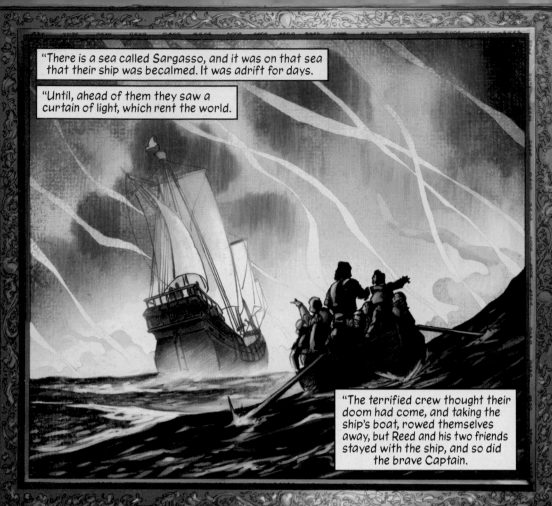

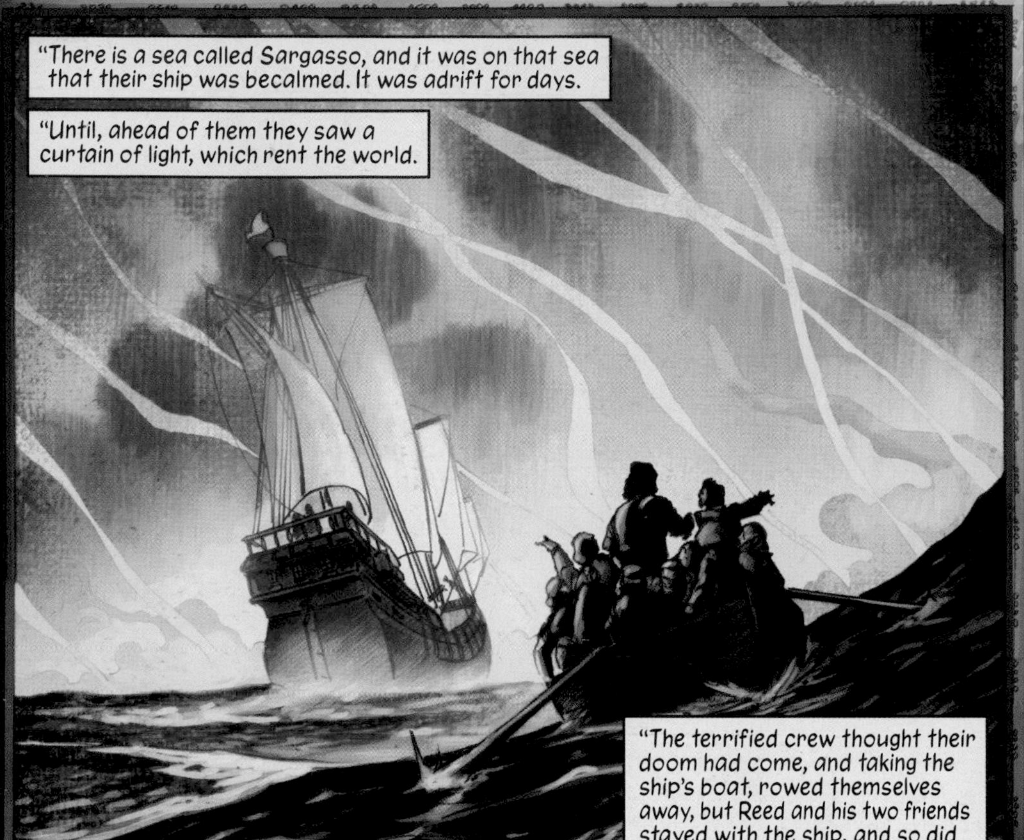
"There is a sea called Sargasso, and it was on that sea that their ship was becalmed. It was adrift for days.
"Until, ahead of them they saw a curtain of light, which rent the world.
"The terrified crew thought their doom had come, and taking the ship's boat, rowed themselves away, but Reed and his two friends stayed with the ship, and so did the brave Captain.

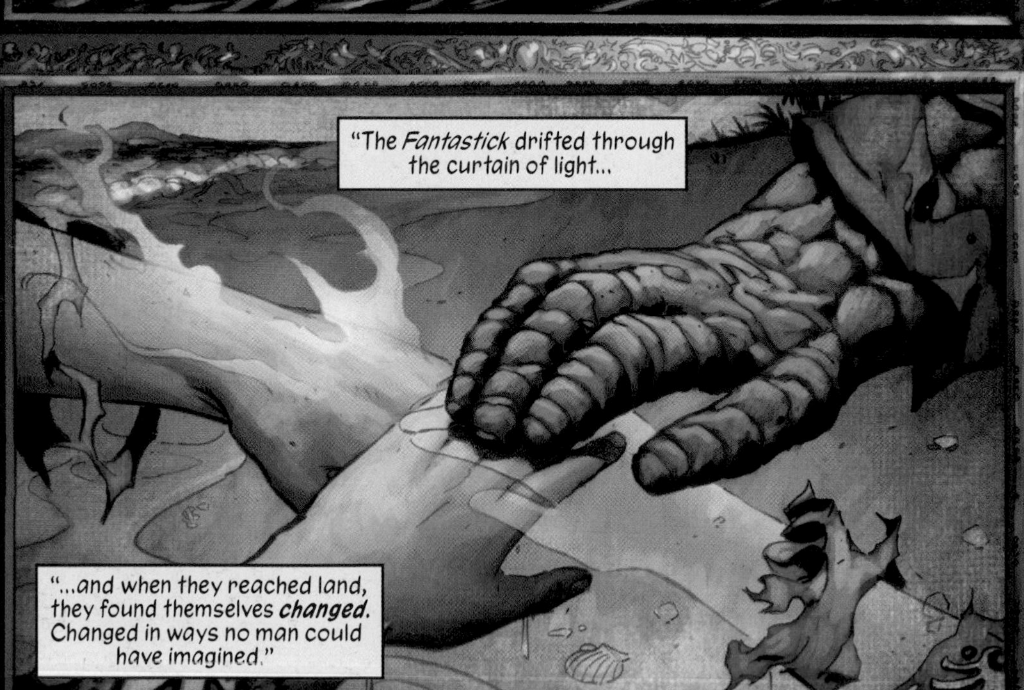
"The *Fantastick* drifted through the curtain of light...
"...and when they reached land, they found themselves ***changed***. Changed in ways no man could have imagined."

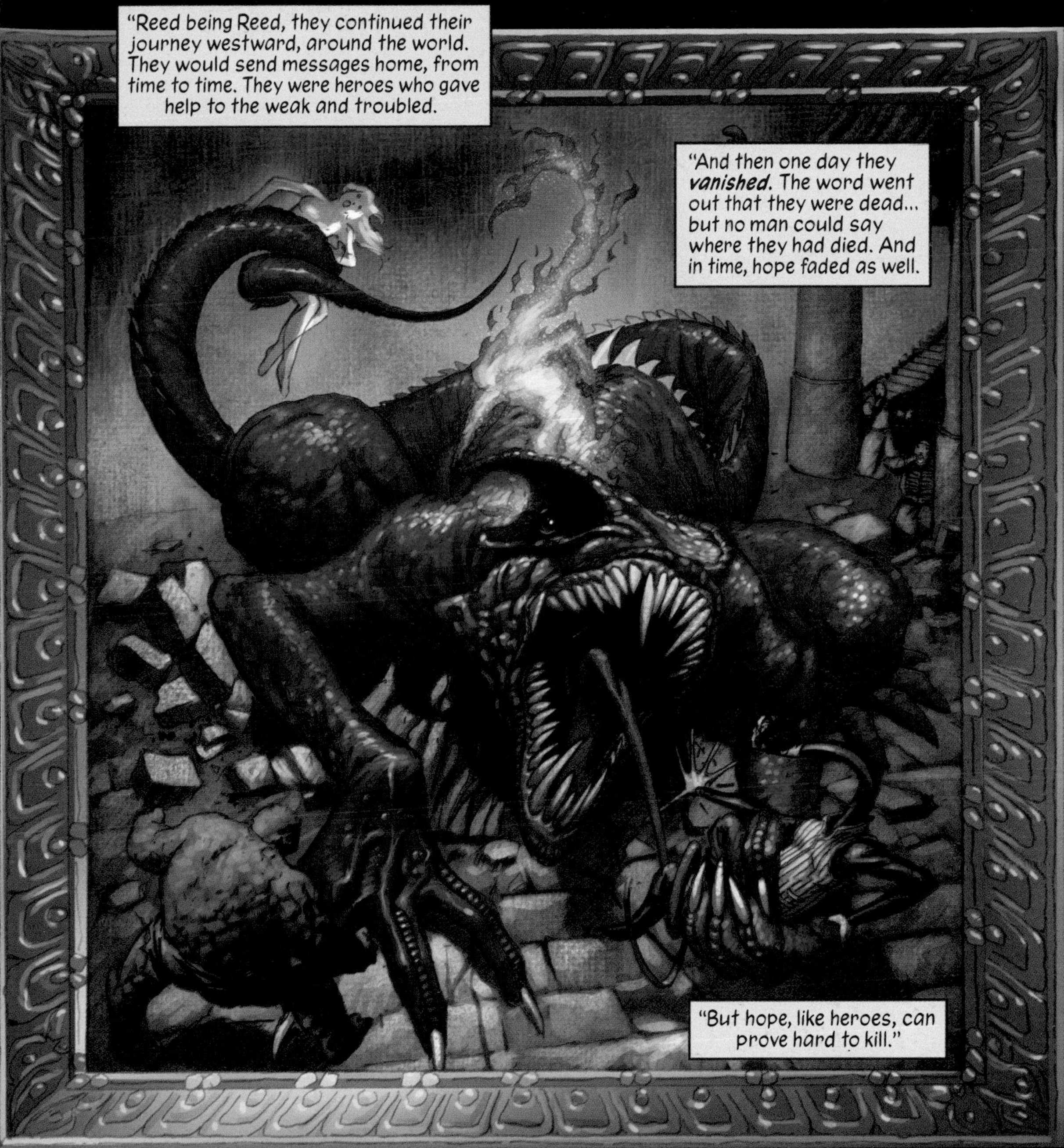
"Reed being Reed, they continued their journey westward, around the world. They would send messages home, from time to time. They were heroes who gave help to the weak and troubled.
"And then one day they ***vanished.*** The word went out that they were dead... but no man could say where they had died. And in time, hope faded as well.
"But hope, like heroes, can prove hard to kill."

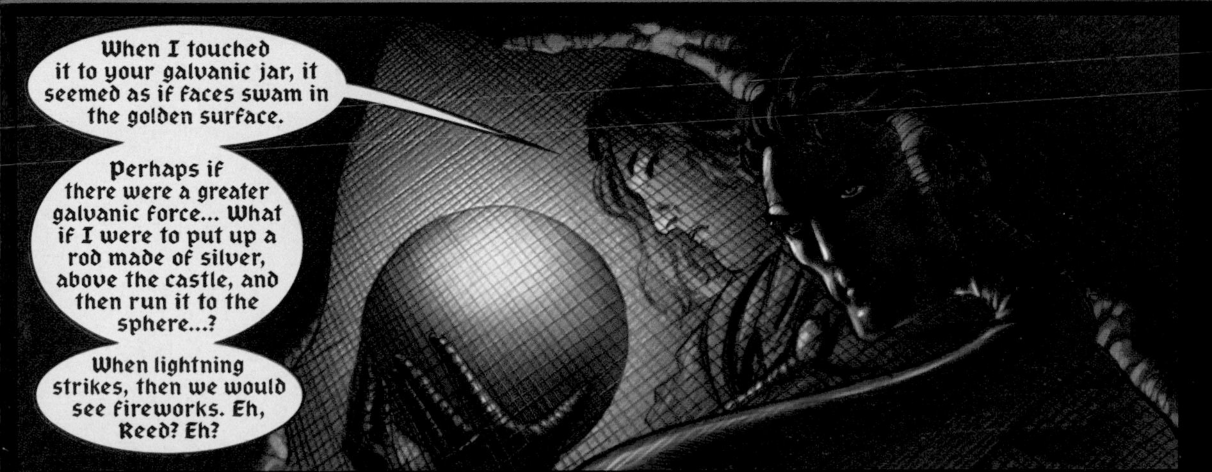
When I touched it to your galvanic jar, it seemed as if faces swam in the golden surface.
Perhaps if there were a greater galvanic force... What if I were to put up a rod made of silver, above the castle, and then run it to the sphere...?
When lightning strikes, then we would see fireworks. Eh, Reed? Eh?

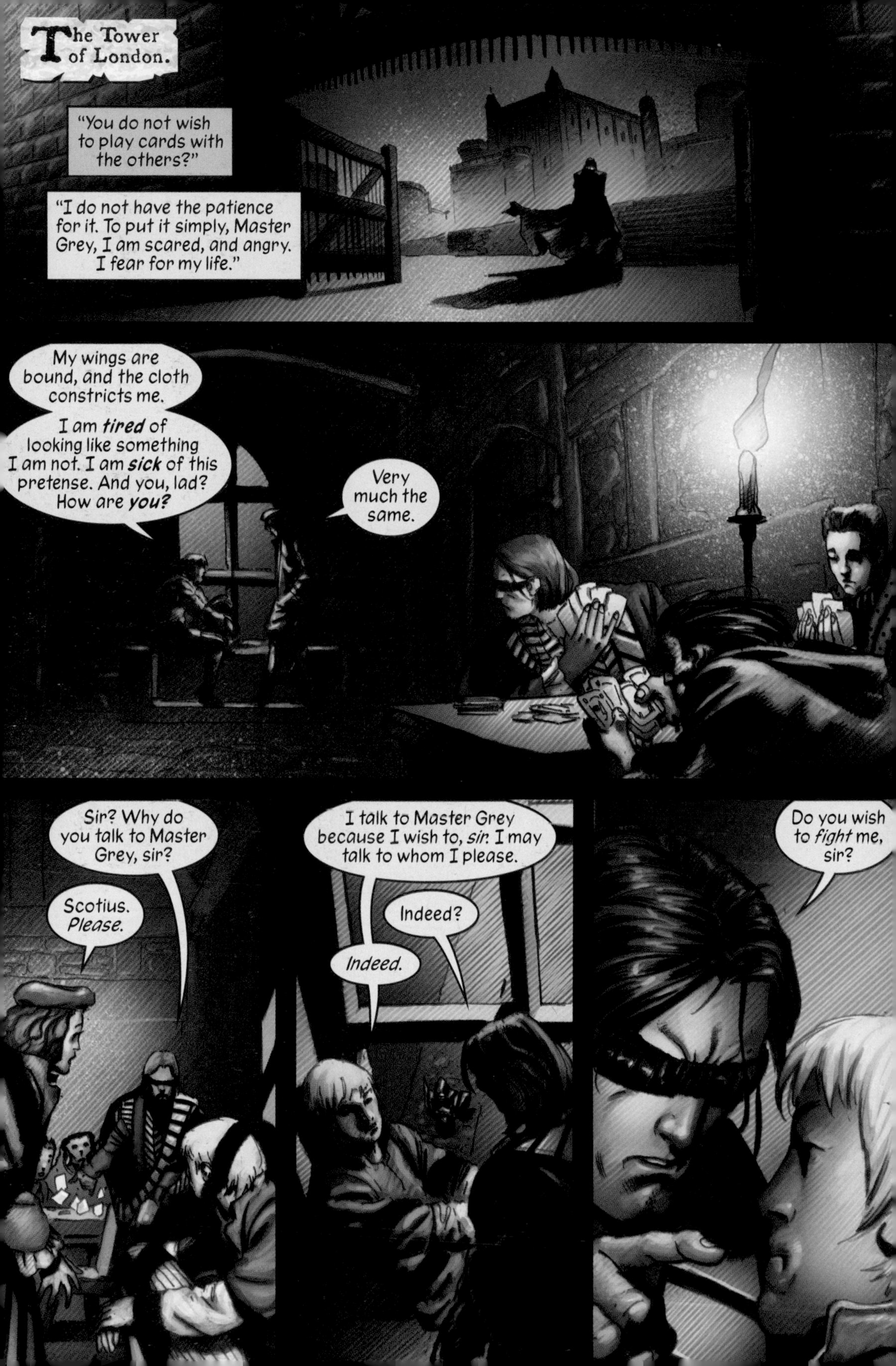
The Tower of London.
"You do not wish to play cards with the others?"
"I do not have the patience for it. To put it simply, Master Grey, I am scared, and angry. I fear for my life."
My wings are bound, and the cloth constricts me.
I am *tired* of looking like something I am not. I am *sick* of this pretense. And you, lad? How are *you?*
Very much the same.
Sir? Why do you talk to Master Grey, sir?
Scotius. *Please.*
I talk to Master Grey because I wish to, *sir.* I may talk to whom I please.
Indeed?
Indeed.
Do you wish to *fight* me, sir?

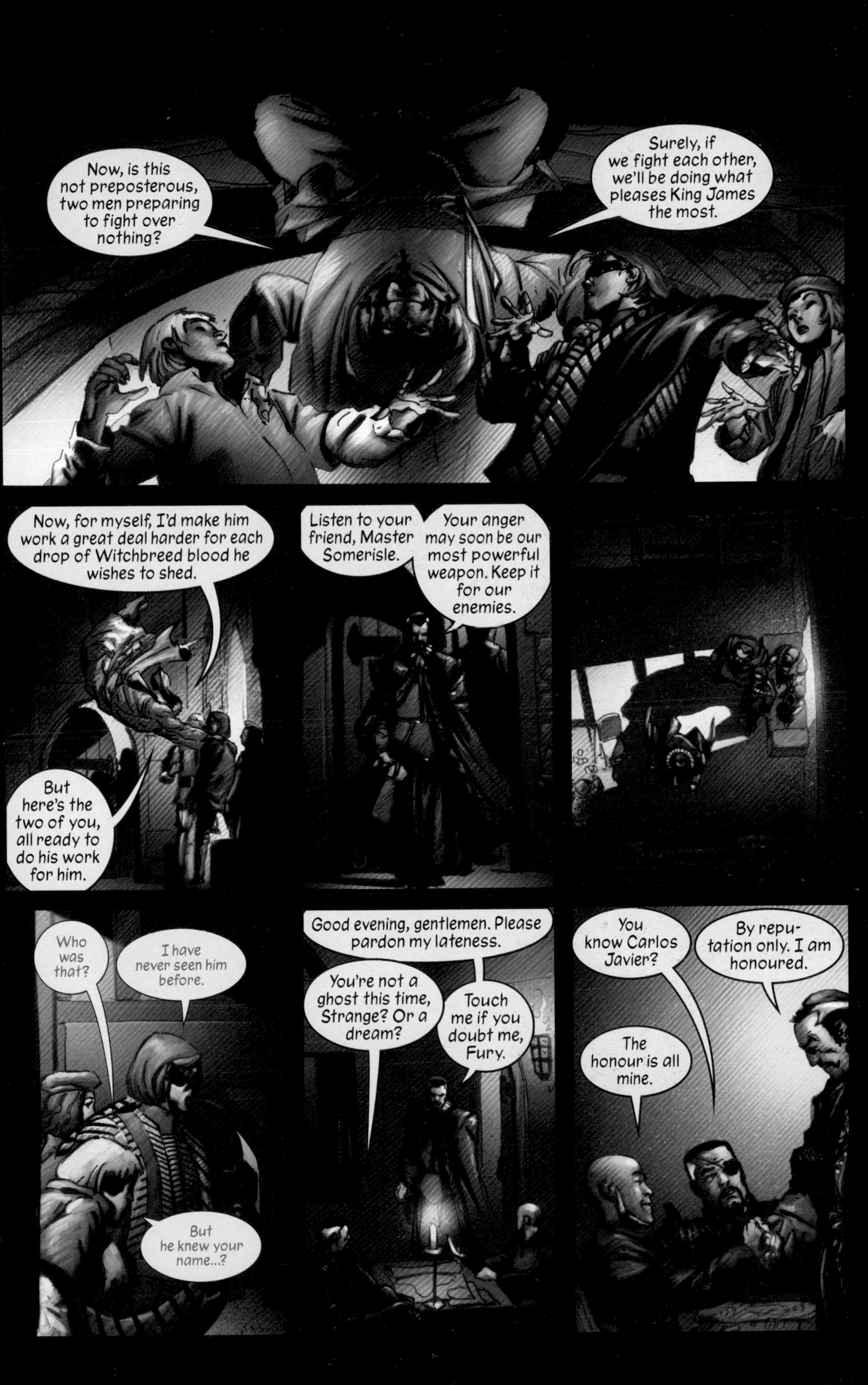
Now, is this not preposterous, two men preparing to fight over nothing?
Surely, if we fight each other, we'll be doing what pleases King James the most.
Now, for myself, I'd make him work a great deal harder for each drop of Witchbreed blood he wishes to shed.
But here's the two of you, all ready to do his work for him.
Listen to your friend, Master Somerisle.
Your anger may soon be our most powerful weapon. Keep it for our enemies.
Who was that?
I have never seen him before.
But he knew your name...?
Good evening, gentlemen. Please pardon my lateness.
You're not a ghost this time, Strange? Or a dream?
Touch me if you doubt me, Fury.
You know Carlos Javier?
By repu-tation only. I am honoured.
The honour is all mine.

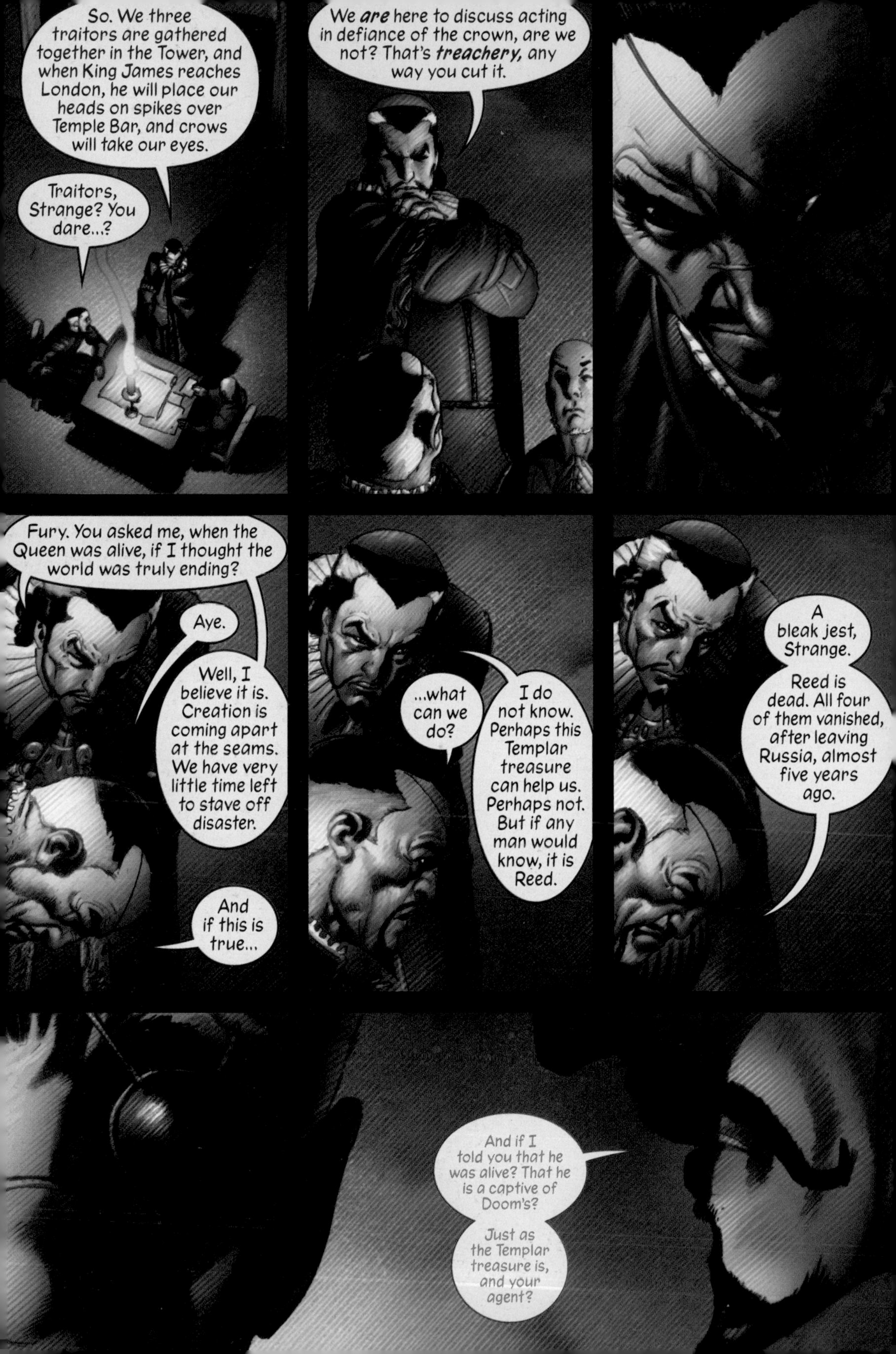
So. We three traitors are gathered together in the Tower, and when King James reaches London, he will place our heads on spikes over Temple Bar, and crows will take our eyes.
Traitors, Strange? You dare...?
We *are* here to discuss acting in defiance of the crown, are we not? That's ***treachery,*** any way you cut it.
Fury. You asked me, when the Queen was alive, if I thought the world was truly ending?
Aye.
Well, I believe it is. Creation is coming apart at the seams. We have very little time left to stave off disaster.
And if this is true...
...what can we do?
I do not know. Perhaps this Templar treasure can help us. Perhaps not. But if any man would know, it is Reed.
A bleak jest, Strange.
Reed is dead. All four of them vanished, after leaving Russia, almost five years ago.
And if I told you that he was alive? That he is a captive of Doom's?
Just as the Templar treasure is, and your agent?

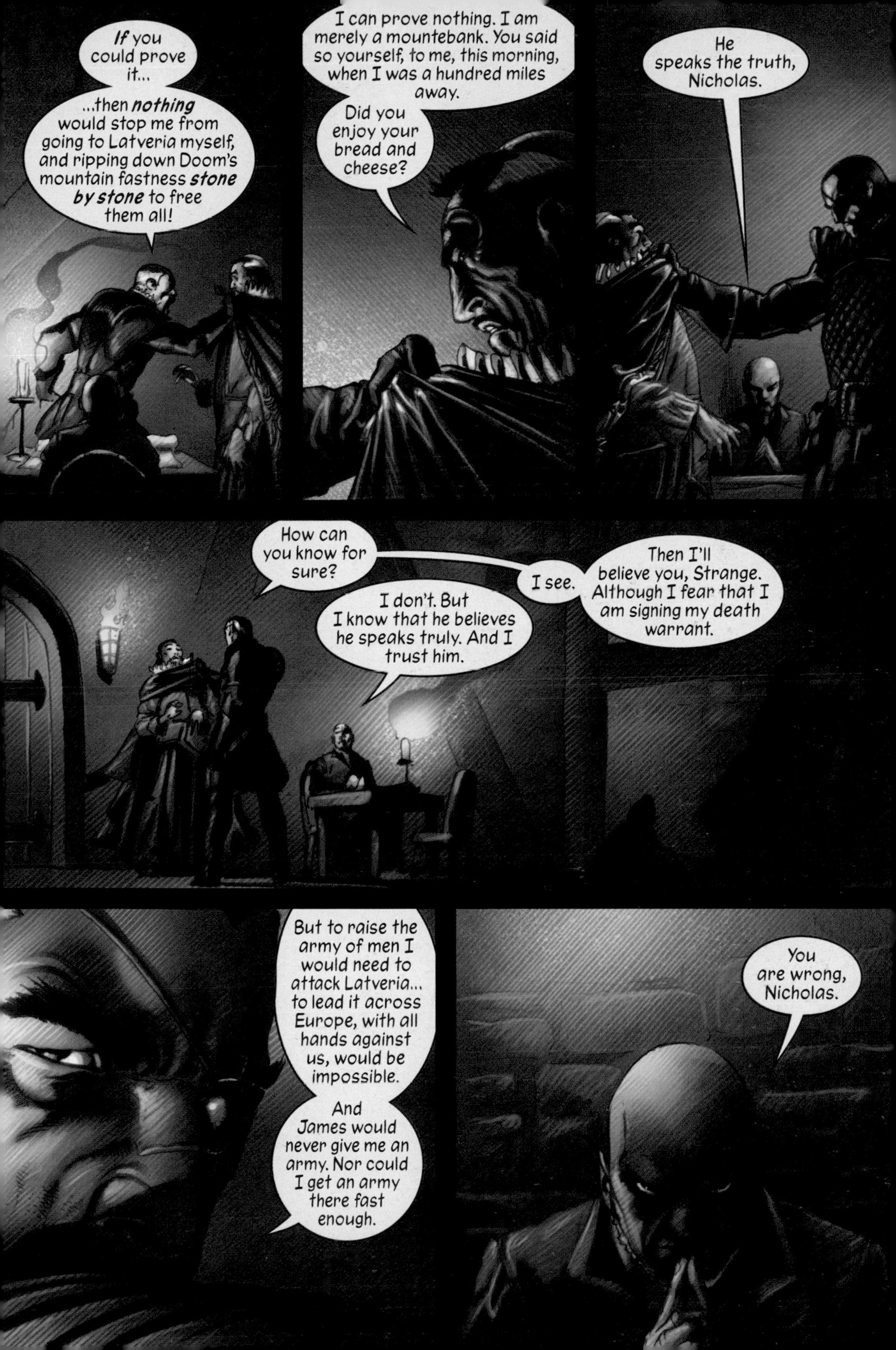
If you could prove it...
...then ***nothing*** would stop me from going to Latveria myself, and ripping down Doom's mountain fastness ***stone by stone*** to free them all!
I can prove nothing. I am merely a mountebank. You said so yourself, to me, this morning, when I was a hundred miles away.
Did you enjoy your bread and cheese?
He speaks the truth, Nicholas.
How can you know for sure?
I don't. But I know that he believes he speaks truly. And I trust him.
I see.
Then I'll believe you, Strange. Although I fear that I am signing my death warrant.
But to raise the army of men I would need to attack Latveria... to lead it across Europe, with all hands against us, would be impossible.
And James would never give me an army. Nor could I get an army there fast enough.
You are wrong, Nicholas.

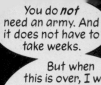

You do **not** need an army. And it does not have to take weeks.

But when this is over, I want your word that you will find a safe place for my people. Somewhere neither James nor the Church will be able to harm us... those of us who are still alive.

And if we help you, then every hand will be against us all. My people, and yours.

You understand that, Nicholas? We will be traitors and fugitives and monsters forever.

I do not believe that the world is ending, Carlos. I neither like nor trust Doctor Stephen Strange. I failed to protect my Queen, and now I find myself betraying my new King.

But Reed was my friend. And **you** are my friend.

You have my word.

Then I'll need a ship, the strongest, fastest that you have.

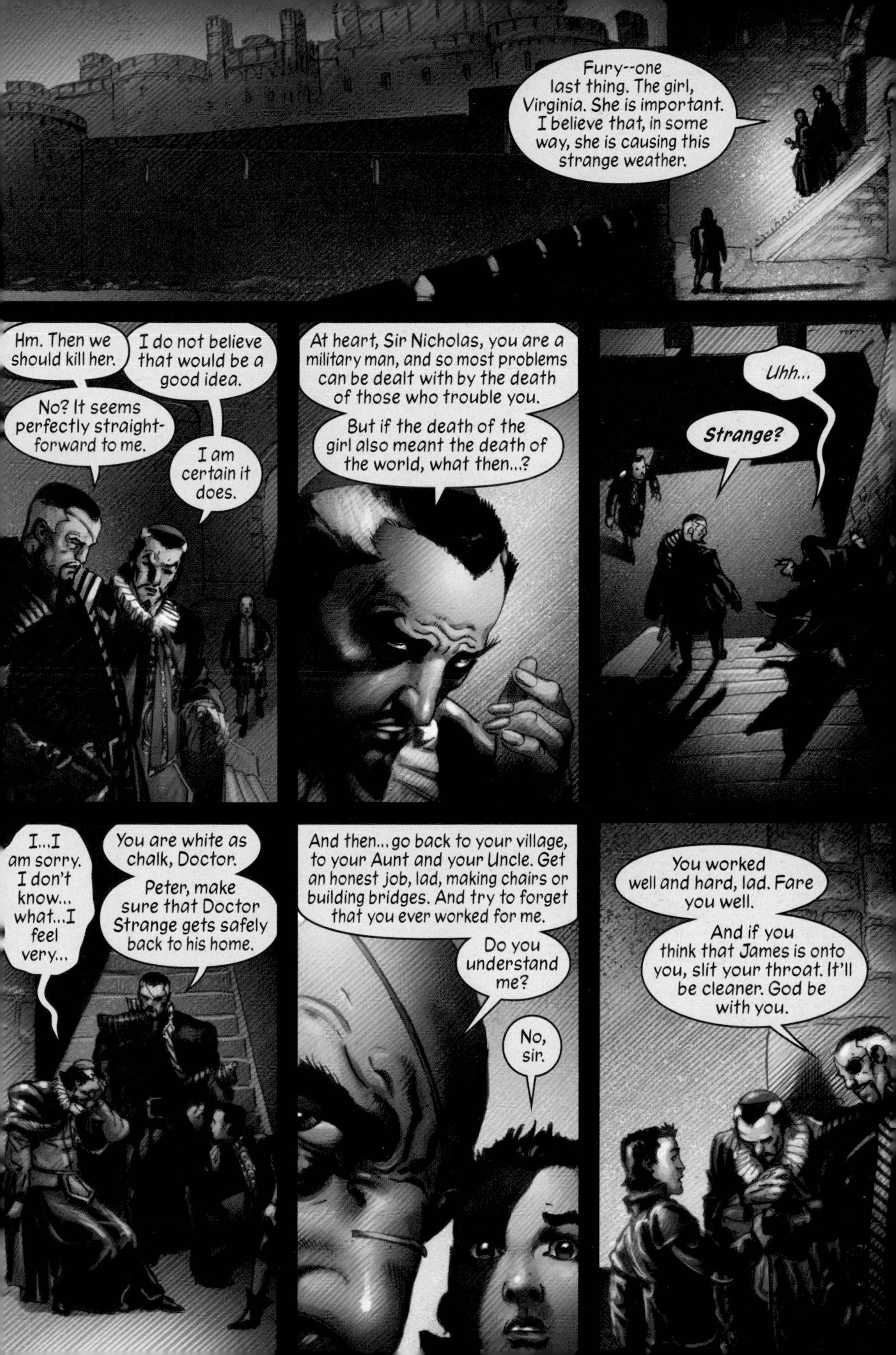
Fury--one last thing. The girl, Virginia. She is important. I believe that, in some way, she is causing this strange weather.
Hm. Then we should kill her.
I do not believe that would be a good idea.
No? It seems perfectly straight-forward to me.
I am certain it does.
At heart, Sir Nicholas, you are a military man, and so most problems can be dealt with by the death of those who trouble you.
But if the death of the girl also meant the death of the world, what then...?
Uhh...
Strange?
I...I am sorry. I don't know... what...I feel very...
You are white as chalk, Doctor.
Peter, make sure that Doctor Strange gets safely back to his home.
And then... go back to your village, to your Aunt and your Uncle. Get an honest job, lad, making chairs or building bridges. And try to forget that you ever worked for me.
Do you understand me?
No, sir.
You worked well and hard, lad. Fare you well.
And if you think that James is onto you, slit your throat. It'll be cleaner. God be with you.

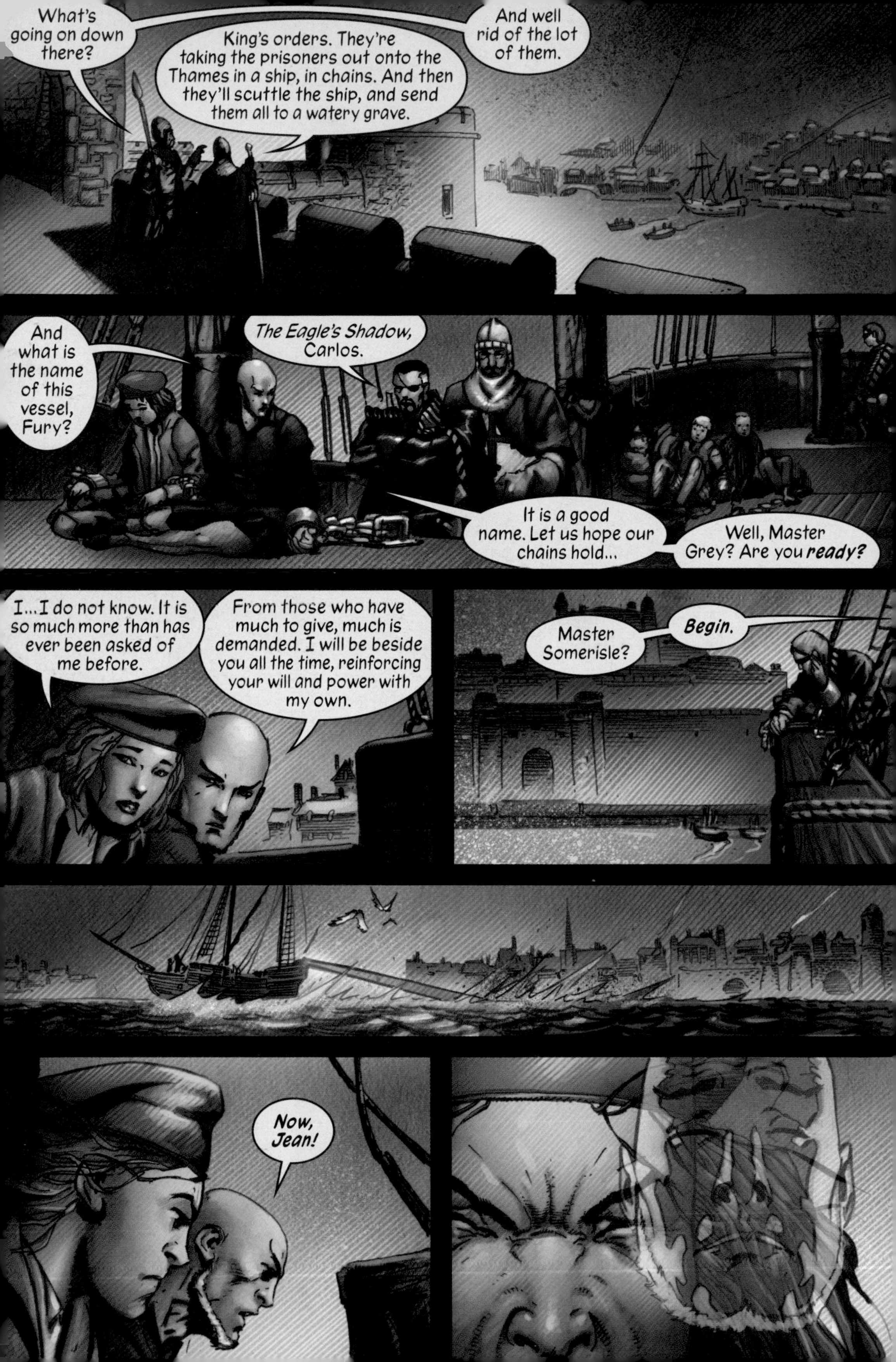
What's going on down there?
King's orders. They're taking the prisoners out onto the Thames in a ship, in chains. And then they'll scuttle the ship, and send them all to a watery grave.
And well rid of the lot of them.
And what is the name of this vessel, Fury?
The Eagle's Shadow, Carlos.
It is a good name. Let us hope our chains hold...
Well, Master Grey? Are you ***ready?***
I...I do not know. It is so much more than has ever been asked of me before.
From those who have much to give, much is demanded. I will be beside you all the time, reinforcing your will and power with my own.
Master Somerisle?
Begin.
Now, Jean!

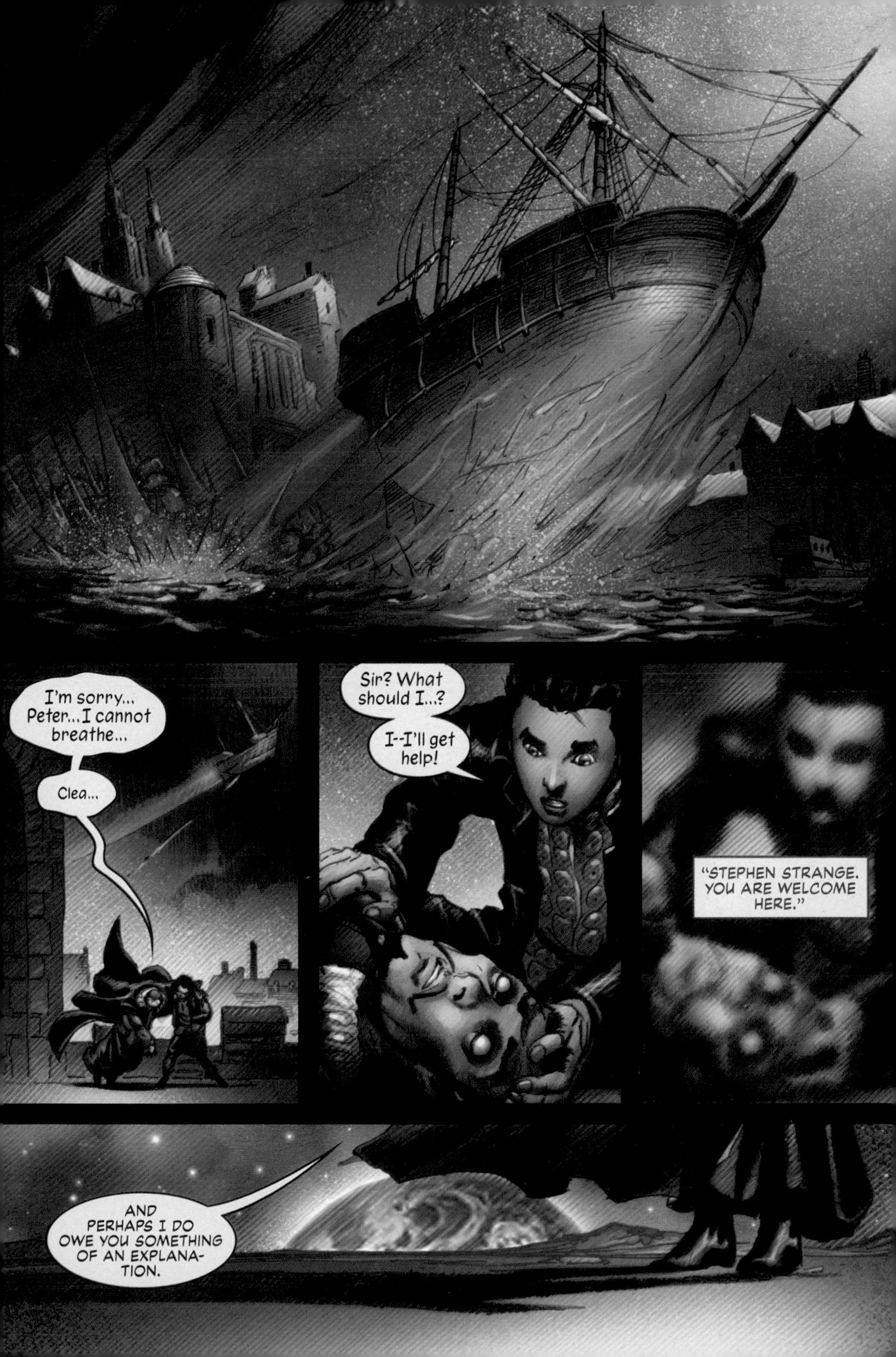
I'm sorry... Peter...I cannot breathe...
Clea...
Sir? What should I...?
I--I'll get help!
"STEPHEN STRANGE. YOU ARE WELCOME HERE."
AND PERHAPS I DO OWE YOU SOMETHING OF AN EXPLANATION.

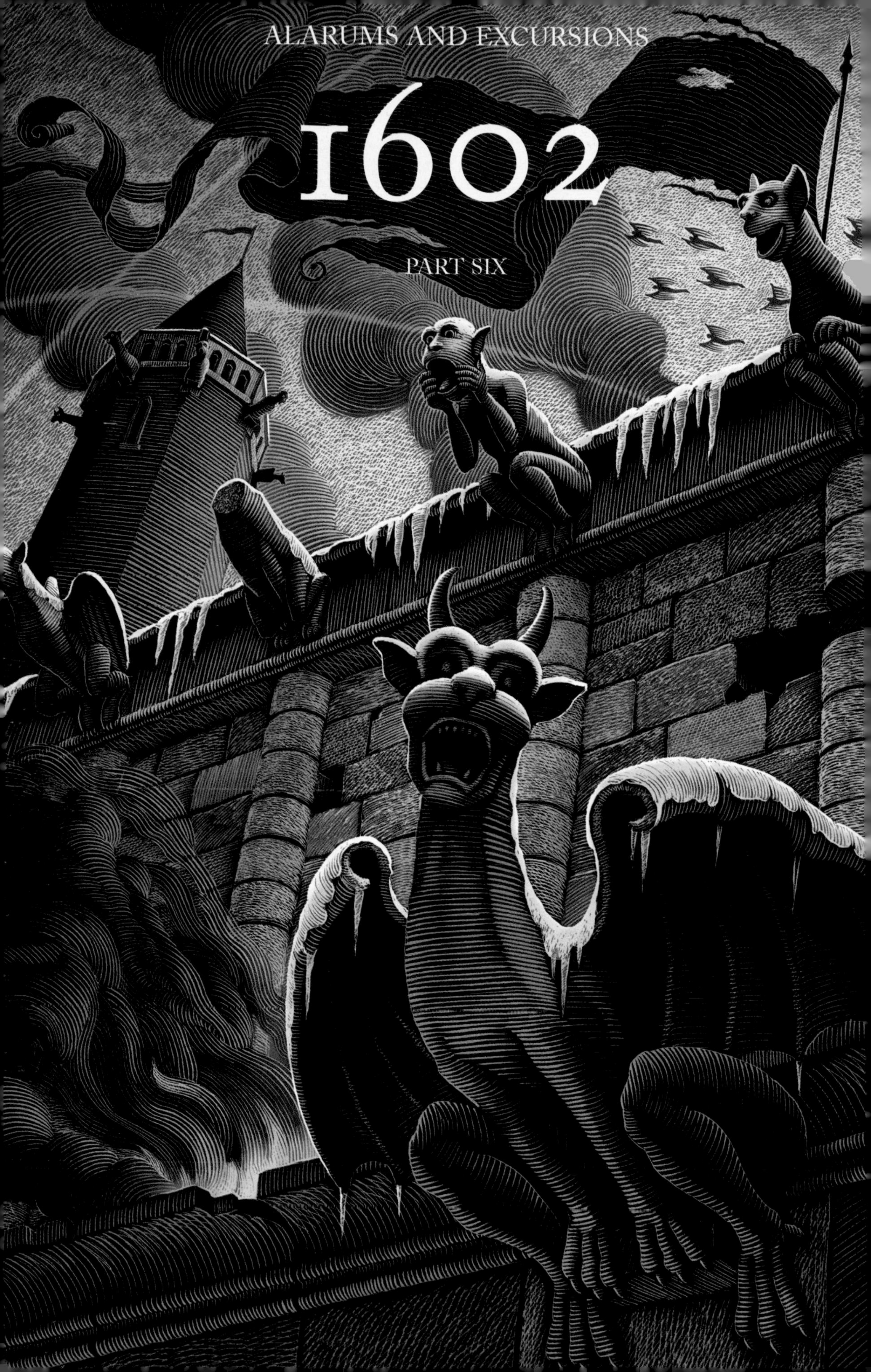
ALARUMS AND EXCURSIONS
1602
PART SIX

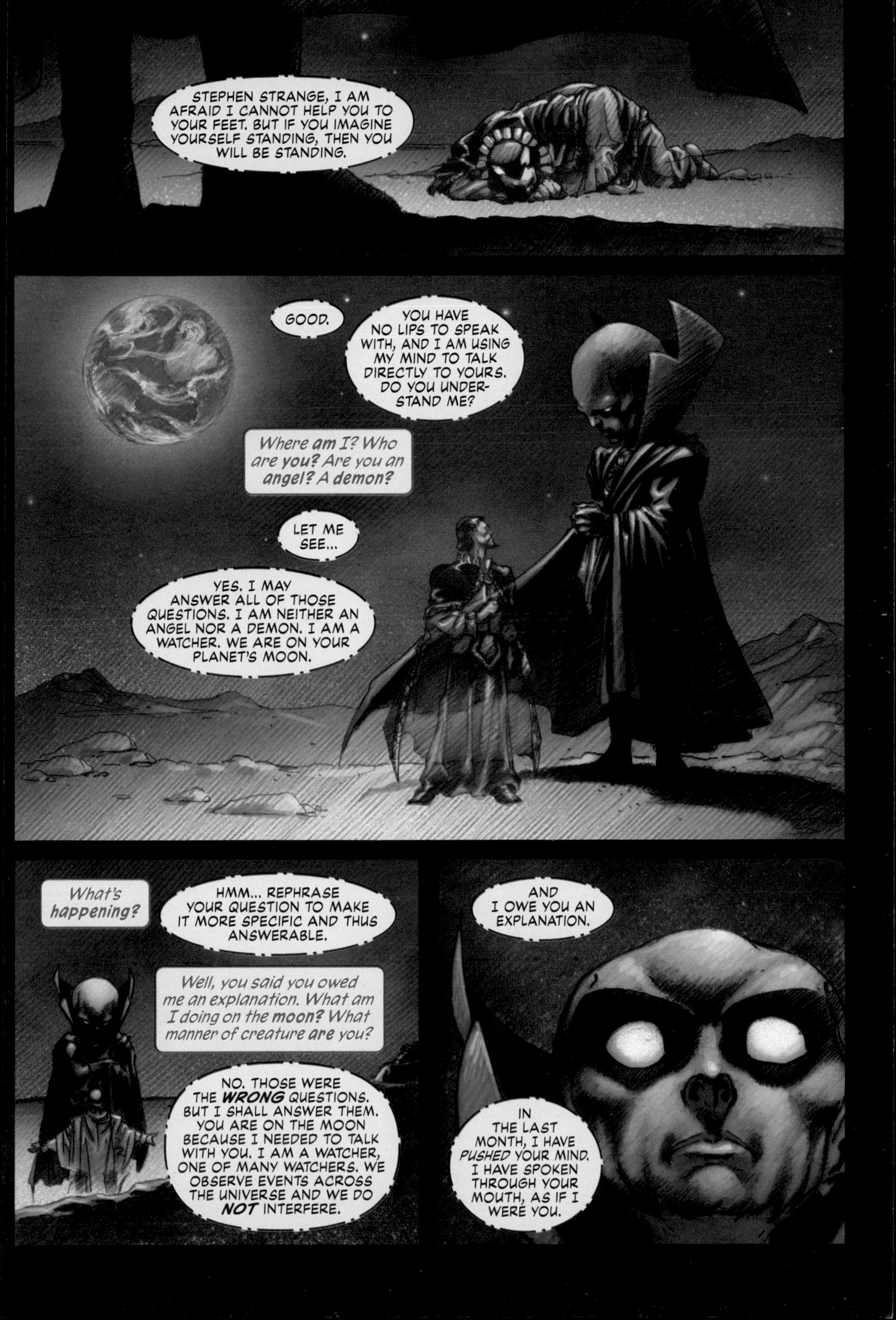
STEPHEN STRANGE, I AM AFRAID I CANNOT HELP YOU TO YOUR FEET. BUT IF YOU IMAGINE YOURSELF STANDING, THEN YOU WILL BE STANDING.
GOOD.
YOU HAVE NO LIPS TO SPEAK WITH, AND I AM USING MY MIND TO TALK DIRECTLY TO YOURS. DO YOU UNDER-STAND ME?
Where am I? Who are you? Are you an angel? A demon?
LET ME SEE...
YES. I MAY ANSWER ALL OF THOSE QUESTIONS. I AM NEITHER AN ANGEL NOR A DEMON. I AM A WATCHER. WE ARE ON YOUR PLANET'S MOON.
What's happening?
HMM... REPHRASE YOUR QUESTION TO MAKE IT MORE SPECIFIC AND THUS ANSWERABLE.
Well, you said you owed me an explanation. What am I doing on the moon? What manner of creature are you?
NO. THOSE WERE THE WRONG QUESTIONS. BUT I SHALL ANSWER THEM. YOU ARE ON THE MOON BECAUSE I NEEDED TO TALK WITH YOU. I AM A WATCHER, ONE OF MANY WATCHERS. WE OBSERVE EVENTS ACROSS THE UNIVERSE AND WE DO NOT INTERFERE.
AND I OWE YOU AN EXPLANATION.
IN THE LAST MONTH, I HAVE PUSHED YOUR MIND. I HAVE SPOKEN THROUGH YOUR MOUTH, AS IF I WERE YOU.

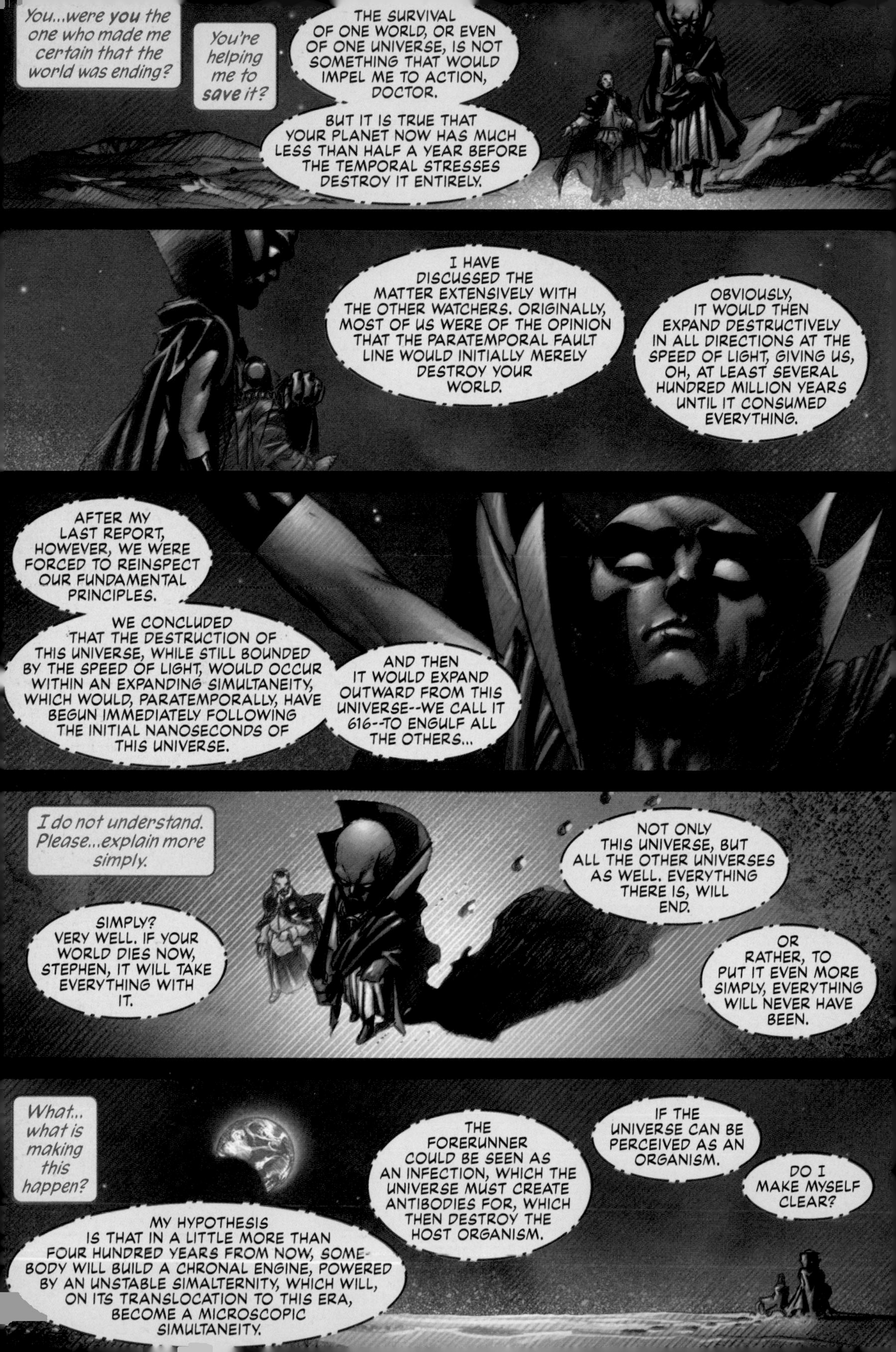
You...were *you* the one who made me certain that the world was ending?
You're helping me to *save* it?
THE SURVIVAL OF ONE WORLD, OR EVEN OF ONE UNIVERSE, IS NOT SOMETHING THAT WOULD IMPEL ME TO ACTION, DOCTOR.
BUT IT IS TRUE THAT YOUR PLANET NOW HAS MUCH LESS THAN HALF A YEAR BEFORE THE TEMPORAL STRESSES DESTROY IT ENTIRELY.
I HAVE DISCUSSED THE MATTER EXTENSIVELY WITH THE OTHER WATCHERS. ORIGINALLY, MOST OF US WERE OF THE OPINION THAT THE PARATEMPORAL FAULT LINE WOULD INITIALLY MERELY DESTROY YOUR WORLD.
OBVIOUSLY, IT WOULD THEN EXPAND DESTRUCTIVELY IN ALL DIRECTIONS AT THE SPEED OF LIGHT, GIVING US, OH, AT LEAST SEVERAL HUNDRED MILLION YEARS UNTIL IT CONSUMED EVERYTHING.
AFTER MY LAST REPORT, HOWEVER, WE WERE FORCED TO REINSPECT OUR FUNDAMENTAL PRINCIPLES.
WE CONCLUDED THAT THE DESTRUCTION OF THIS UNIVERSE, WHILE STILL BOUNDED BY THE SPEED OF LIGHT, WOULD OCCUR WITHIN AN EXPANDING SIMULTANEITY, WHICH WOULD, PARATEMPORALLY, HAVE BEGUN IMMEDIATELY FOLLOWING THE INITIAL NANOSECONDS OF THIS UNIVERSE.
AND THEN IT WOULD EXPAND OUTWARD FROM THIS UNIVERSE--WE CALL IT 616--TO ENGULF ALL THE OTHERS...
I do not understand. Please...explain more simply.
SIMPLY? VERY WELL. IF YOUR WORLD DIES NOW, STEPHEN, IT WILL TAKE EVERYTHING WITH IT.
NOT ONLY THIS UNIVERSE, BUT ALL THE OTHER UNIVERSES AS WELL. EVERYTHING THERE IS, WILL END.
OR RATHER, TO PUT IT EVEN MORE SIMPLY, EVERYTHING WILL NEVER HAVE BEEN.
What... what is making this happen?
MY HYPOTHESIS IS THAT IN A LITTLE MORE THAN FOUR HUNDRED YEARS FROM NOW, SOME-BODY WILL BUILD A CHRONAL ENGINE, POWERED BY AN UNSTABLE SIMALTERNITY, WHICH WILL, ON ITS TRANSLOCATION TO THIS ERA, BECOME A MICROSCOPIC SIMULTANEITY.
THE FORERUNNER COULD BE SEEN AS AN INFECTION, WHICH THE UNIVERSE MUST CREATE ANTIBODIES FOR, WHICH THEN DESTROY THE HOST ORGANISM.
IF THE UNIVERSE CAN BE PERCEIVED AS AN ORGANISM.
DO I MAKE MYSELF CLEAR?

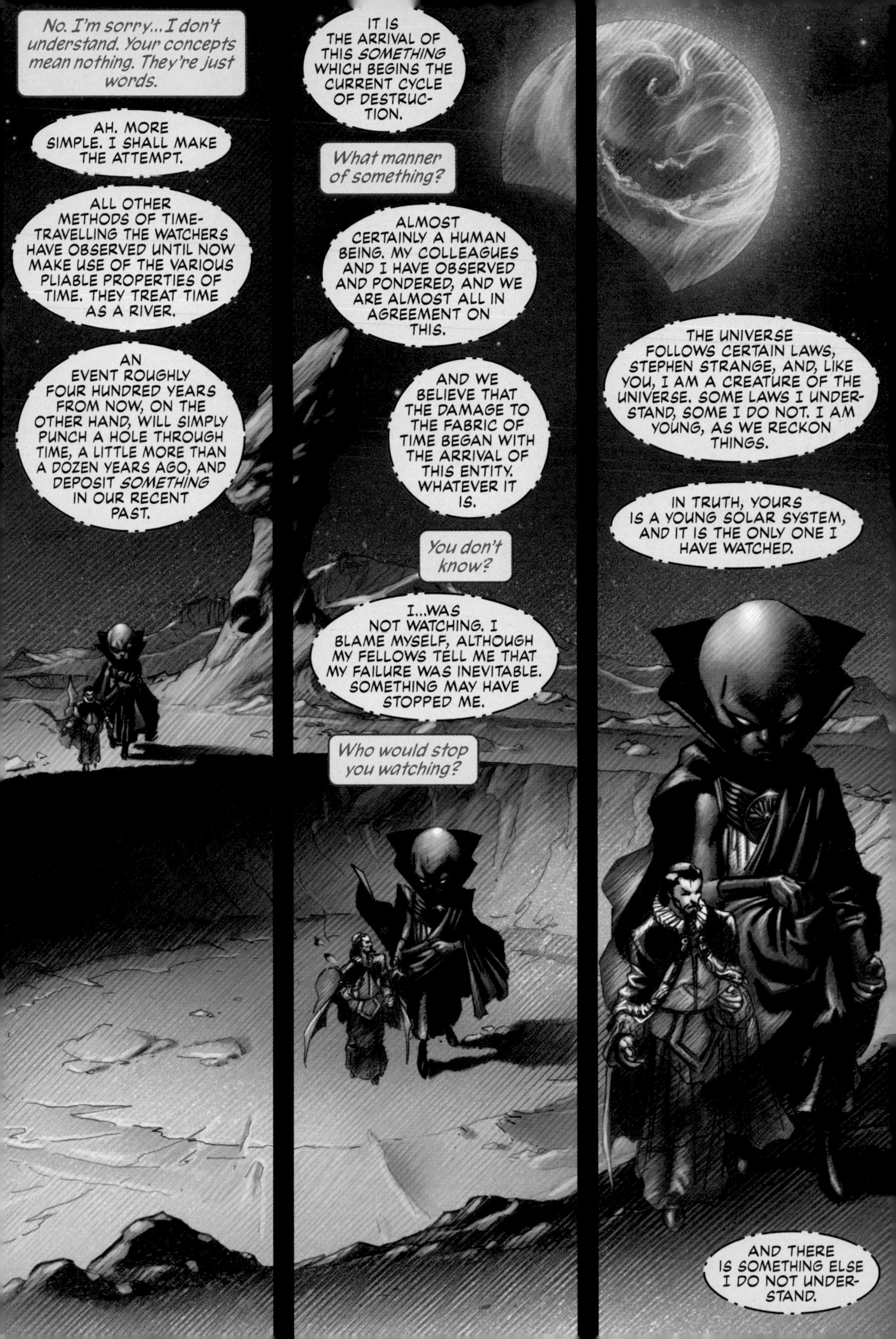
No. I'm sorry... I don't understand. Your concepts mean nothing. They're just words.
AH. MORE SIMPLE. I SHALL MAKE THE ATTEMPT.
ALL OTHER METHODS OF TIME-TRAVELLING THE WATCHERS HAVE OBSERVED UNTIL NOW MAKE USE OF THE VARIOUS PLIABLE PROPERTIES OF TIME. THEY TREAT TIME AS A RIVER.
AN EVENT ROUGHLY FOUR HUNDRED YEARS FROM NOW, ON THE OTHER HAND, WILL SIMPLY PUNCH A HOLE THROUGH TIME, A LITTLE MORE THAN A DOZEN YEARS AGO, AND DEPOSIT *SOMETHING* IN OUR RECENT PAST.
IT IS THE ARRIVAL OF THIS *SOMETHING* WHICH BEGINS THE CURRENT CYCLE OF DESTRUCTION.
What manner of something?
ALMOST CERTAINLY A HUMAN BEING. MY COLLEAGUES AND I HAVE OBSERVED AND PONDERED, AND WE ARE ALMOST ALL IN AGREEMENT ON THIS.
AND WE BELIEVE THAT THE DAMAGE TO THE FABRIC OF TIME BEGAN WITH THE ARRIVAL OF THIS ENTITY. WHATEVER IT IS.
You don't know?
I...WAS NOT WATCHING. I BLAME MYSELF, ALTHOUGH MY FELLOWS TELL ME THAT MY FAILURE WAS INEVITABLE. SOMETHING MAY HAVE STOPPED ME.
Who would stop you watching?
THE UNIVERSE FOLLOWS CERTAIN LAWS, STEPHEN STRANGE, AND, LIKE YOU, I AM A CREATURE OF THE UNIVERSE. SOME LAWS I UNDERSTAND, SOME I DO NOT. I AM YOUNG, AS WE RECKON THINGS.
IN TRUTH, YOURS IS A YOUNG SOLAR SYSTEM, AND IT IS THE ONLY ONE I HAVE WATCHED.
AND THERE IS SOMETHING ELSE I DO NOT UNDERSTAND.

EVERYTHING HAS ITS SEASON. IN SPRING, THE WORLD BRINGS FORTH BLOSSOMS. IN CHERRY SEASON, YOU GET CHERRIES.

BUT A SEASON HAS DAWNED OVER THREE HUNDRED YEARS EARLY: A SEASON OF HEROES AND MARVELS. MY OWN CONCLUSION--SEVERAL OF MY COLLEAGUES LAUGH AT ME--IS THAT THE TWO ARE CONNECTED.

THAT THE UNIVERSE FIGHTS TO SAVE ITSELF.

TO SAVE EVERYTHING, THE HEROES HAVE COME.

THE HYPOTHESIS MY STAIDER COLLEAGUES PREFER IS THAT THE ARRIVAL OF THE ENTITY THEY REFER TO AS THE FORERUNNER IS, IN ITSELF, THE SIGNAL TO THE UNIVERSE FOR THE SEASON OF MARVELS TO BEGIN.

AND THAT ENTITY'S ARRIVAL ALSO CREATED THE SIMULTANEITY.

You said you were not permitted to interfere. Yes?

THAT IS CORRECT.

But you brought me here, and told me this.

You are obviously interfering. Why?

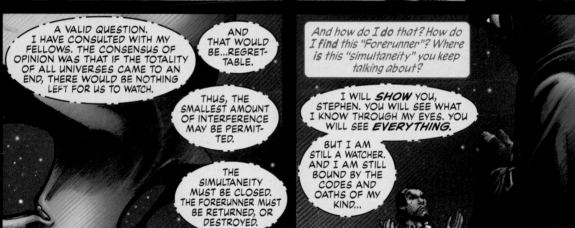

A VALID QUESTION. I HAVE CONSULTED WITH MY FELLOWS. THE CONSENSUS OF OPINION WAS THAT IF THE TOTALITY OF ALL UNIVERSES CAME TO AN END, THERE WOULD BE NOTHING LEFT FOR US TO WATCH.

AND THAT WOULD BE...REGRET-TABLE.

THUS, THE SMALLEST AMOUNT OF INTERFERENCE MAY BE PERMIT-TED.

THE SIMULTANEITY MUST BE CLOSED. THE FORERUNNER MUST BE RETURNED, OR DESTROYED.

And how do I do that? How do I find this "Forerunner"? Where is this "simultaneity" you keep talking about?

I WILL *SHOW* YOU, STEPHEN. YOU WILL SEE WHAT I KNOW THROUGH MY EYES. YOU WILL SEE *EVERYTHING*.

BUT I AM STILL A WATCHER. AND I AM STILL BOUND BY THE CODES AND OATHS OF MY KIND...

"THERE IS ONLY ONE INJUNCTION I MUST LAY UPON YOU, STEPHEN. IT IS THIS:

"WHILE YOU LIVE, YOU MAY SAY NOTHING OF WHAT YOU KNOW TO ANY SOUL. YOU MAY NOT ACT IN ANY WAY UPON WHAT YOU KNOW.

"LIKE ME, YOU ARE CONDEMNED ONLY TO WATCH."

...only to watch...

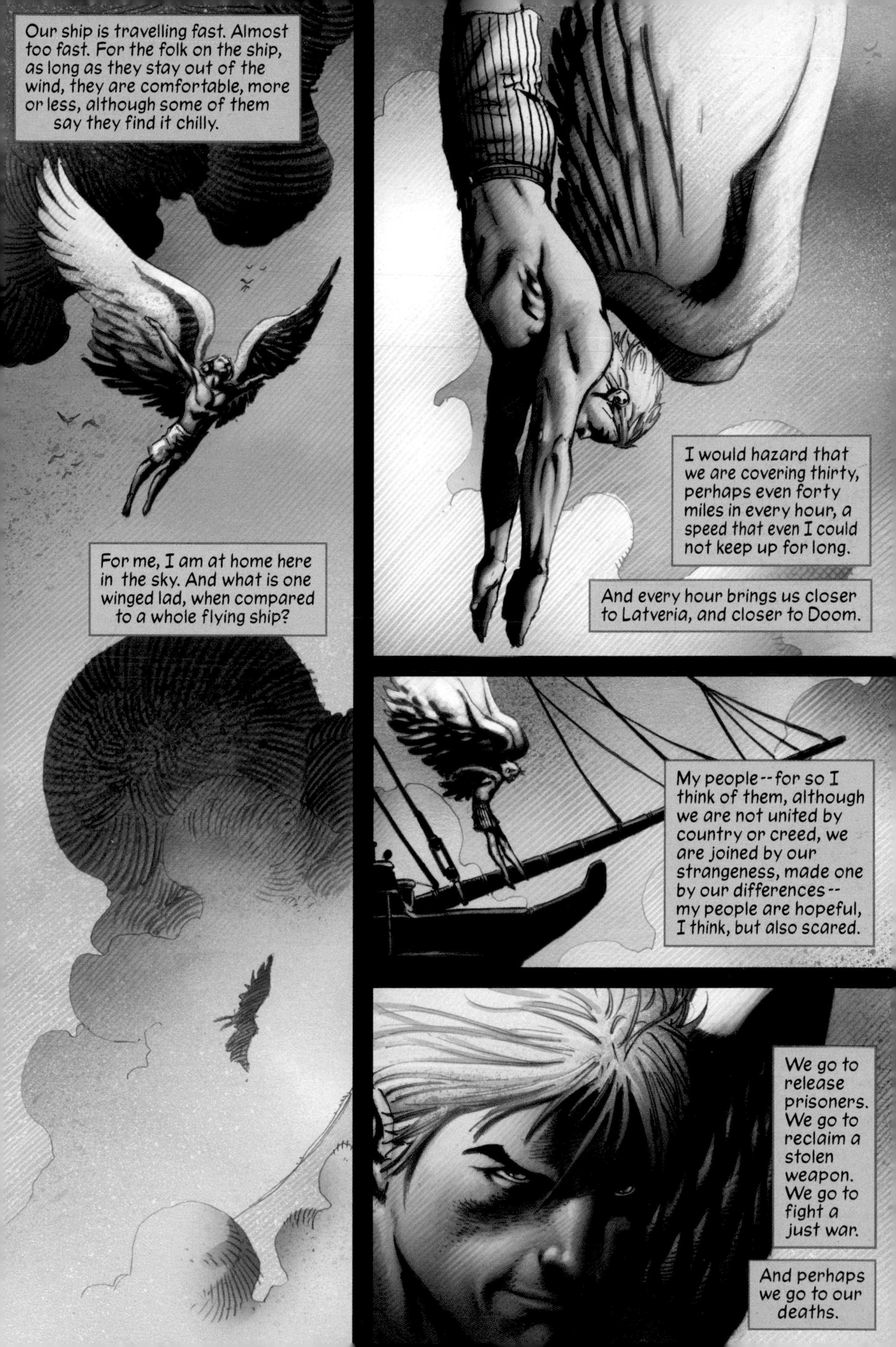
Our ship is travelling fast. Almost too fast. For the folk on the ship, as long as they stay out of the wind, they are comfortable, more or less, although some of them say they find it chilly.
For me, I am at home here in the sky. And what is one winged lad, when compared to a whole flying ship?
I would hazard that we are covering thirty, perhaps even forty miles in every hour, a speed that even I could not keep up for long.
And every hour brings us closer to Latveria, and closer to Doom.
My people--for so I think of them, although we are not united by country or creed, we are joined by our strangeness, made one by our differences--my people are hopeful, I think, but also scared.
We go to release prisoners. We go to reclaim a stolen weapon. We go to fight a just war.
And perhaps we go to our deaths.

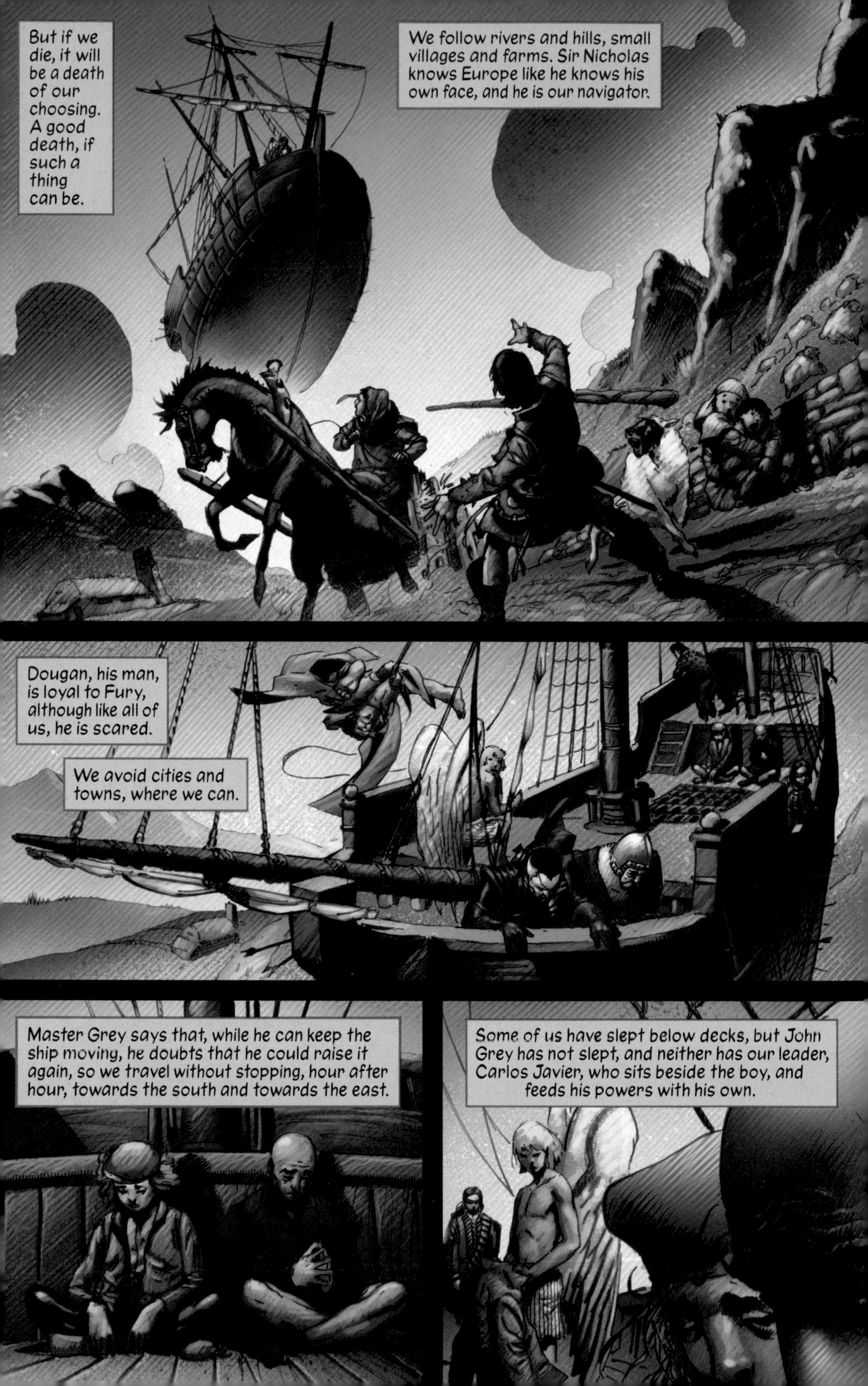
But if we die, it will be a death of our choosing. A good death, if such a thing can be.
We follow rivers and hills, small villages and farms. Sir Nicholas knows Europe like he knows his own face, and he is our navigator.
Dougan, his man, is loyal to Fury, although like all of us, he is scared.
We avoid cities and towns, where we can.
Master Grey says that, while he can keep the ship moving, he doubts that he could raise it again, so we travel without stopping, hour after hour, towards the south and towards the east.
Some of us have slept below decks, but John Grey has not slept, and neither has our leader, Carlos Javier, who sits beside the boy, and feeds his powers with his own.

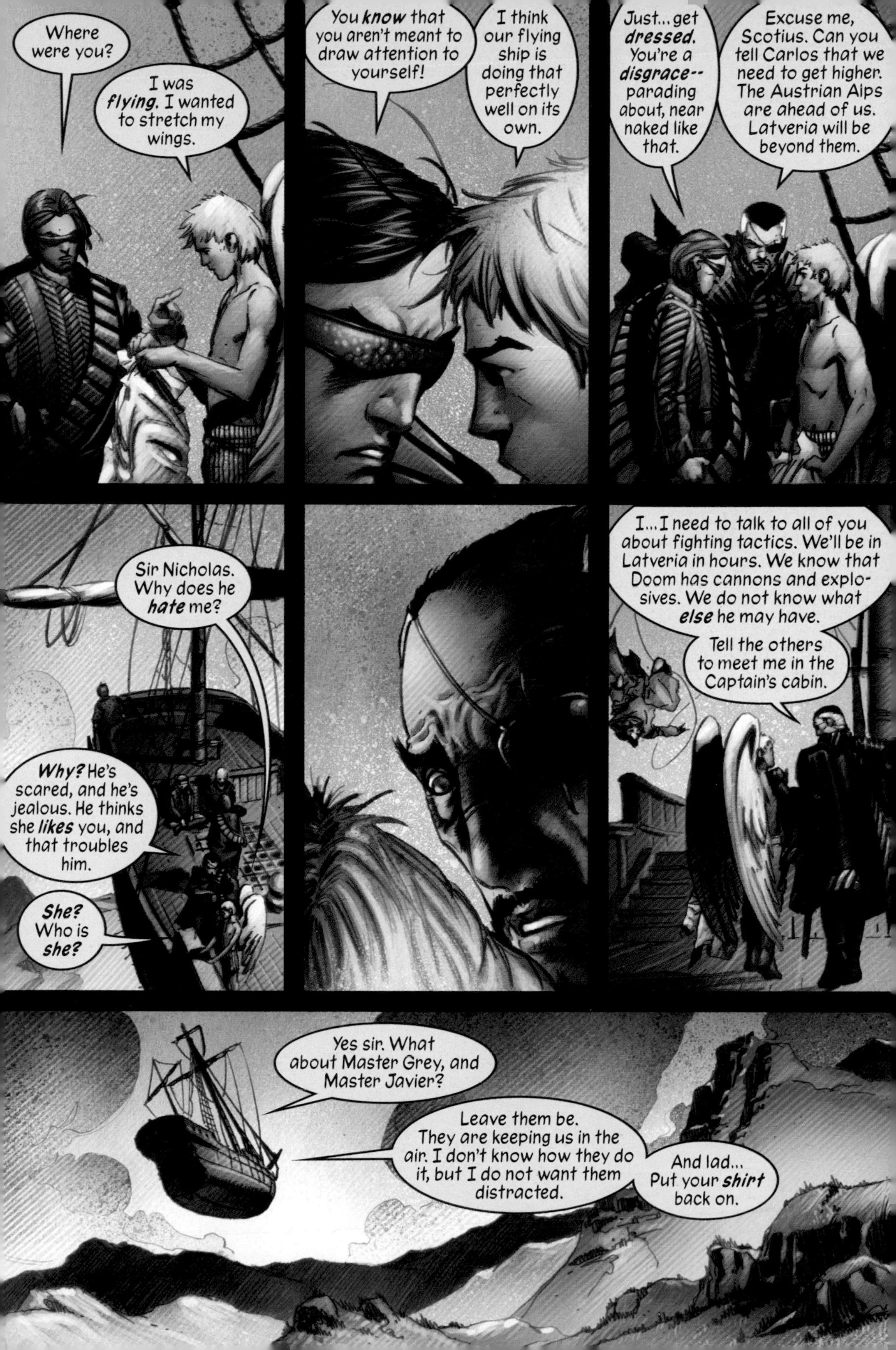
Where were you?
I was *flying.* I wanted to stretch my wings.
You *know* that you aren't meant to draw attention to yourself!
I think our flying ship is doing that perfectly well on its own.
Just... get *dressed.* You're a *disgrace*-- parading about, near naked like that.
Excuse me, Scotius. Can you tell Carlos that we need to get higher. The Austrian Alps are ahead of us. Latveria will be beyond them.
Sir Nicholas. Why does he *hate* me?
Why? He's scared, and he's jealous. He thinks she *likes* you, and that troubles him.
She? Who is *she?*
I... I need to talk to all of you about fighting tactics. We'll be in Latveria in hours. We know that Doom has cannons and explosives. We do not know what *else* he may have.
Tell the others to meet me in the Captain's cabin.
Yes sir. What about Master Grey, and Master Javier?
Leave them be. They are keeping us in the air. I don't know how they do it, but I do not want them distracted.
And lad... Put your *shirt* back on.

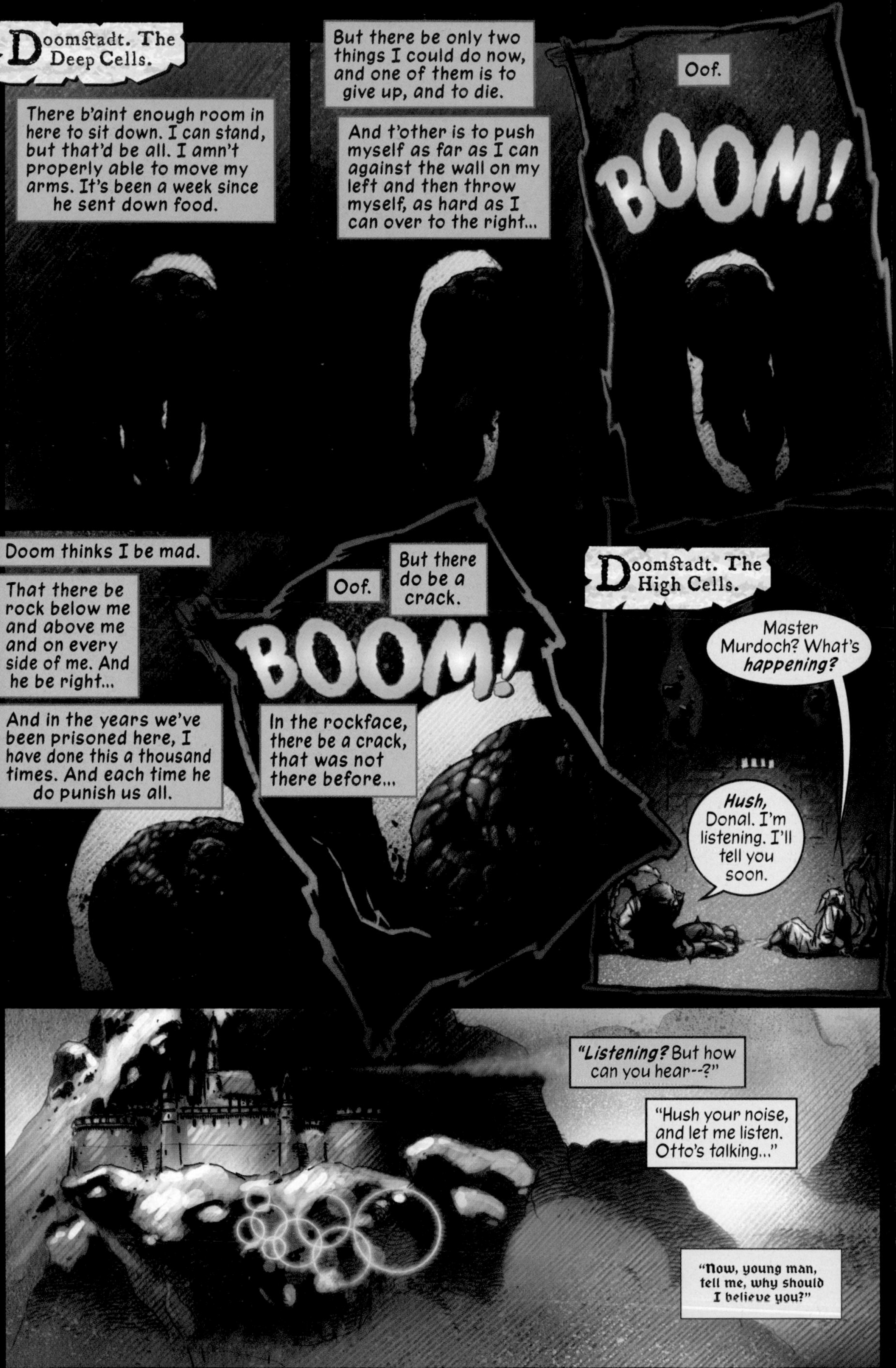
Doomstadt. The Deep Cells.
There b'aint enough room in here to sit down. I can stand, but that'd be all. I amn't properly able to move my arms. It's been a week since he sent down food.
But there be only two things I could do now, and one of them is to give up, and to die.
And t'other is to push myself as far as I can against the wall on my left and then throw myself, as hard as I can over to the right...
Oof.
BOOM!
Doom thinks I be mad.
That there be rock below me and above me and on every side of me. And he be right...
And in the years we've been prisoned here, I have done this a thousand times. And each time he do punish us all.
Oof.
But there do be a crack.
BOOM!
In the rockface, there be a crack, that was not there before...
Doomstadt. The High Cells.
Master Murdoch? What's *happening?*
Hush, Donal. I'm listening. I'll tell you soon.
"*Listening?* But how can you hear--?"
"Hush your noise, and let me listen. Otto's talking..."
"Now, young man, tell me, why should I believe you?"

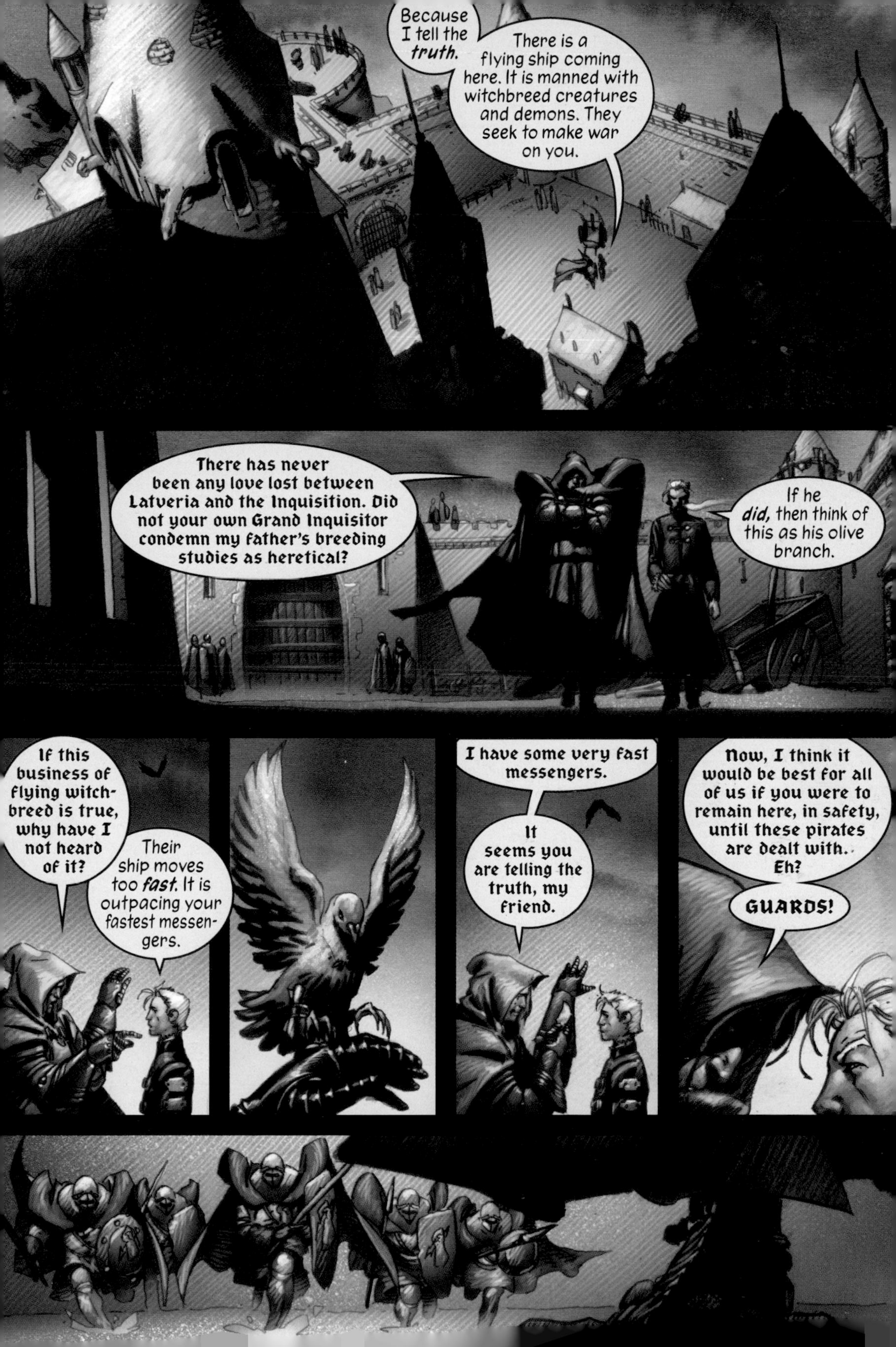
Because I tell the *truth.*
There is a flying ship coming here. It is manned with witchbreed creatures and demons. They seek to make war on you.
There has never been any love lost between Latveria and the Inquisition. Did not your own Grand Inquisitor condemn my father's breeding studies as heretical?
If he *did,* then think of this as his olive branch.
If this business of flying witch-breed is true, why have I not heard of it?
Their ship moves too *fast.* It is outpacing your fastest messen-gers.
I have some very fast messengers.
It seems you are telling the truth, my friend.
Now, I think it would be best for all of us if you were to remain here, in safety, until these pirates are dealt with. Eh?
GUARDS!

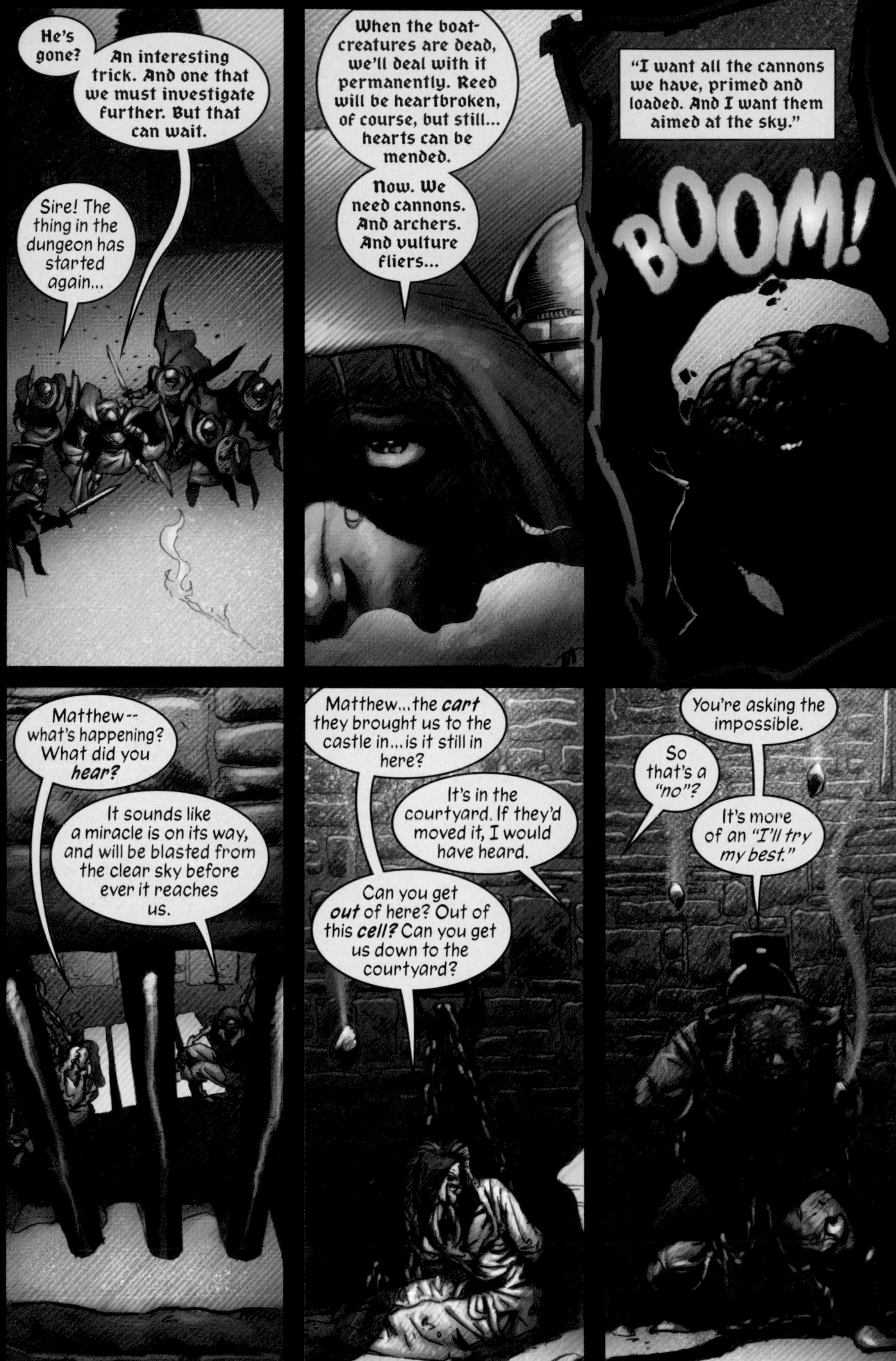
He's gone?
An interesting trick. And one that we must investigate further. But that can wait.
Sire! The thing in the dungeon has started again...
When the boat-creatures are dead, we'll deal with it permanently. Reed will be heartbroken, of course, but still... hearts can be mended.
Now. We need cannons. And archers. And vulture fliers...
"I want all the cannons we have, primed and loaded. And I want them aimed at the sky."
BOOM!
Matthew--what's happening? What did you *hear?*
It sounds like a miracle is on its way, and will be blasted from the clear sky before ever it reaches us.
Matthew...the *cart* they brought us to the castle in...is it still in here?
It's in the courtyard. If they'd moved it, I would have heard.
Can you get *out* of here? Out of this *cell?* Can you get us down to the courtyard?
You're asking the impossible.
So that's a *"no"*?
It's more of an *"I'll try my best."*

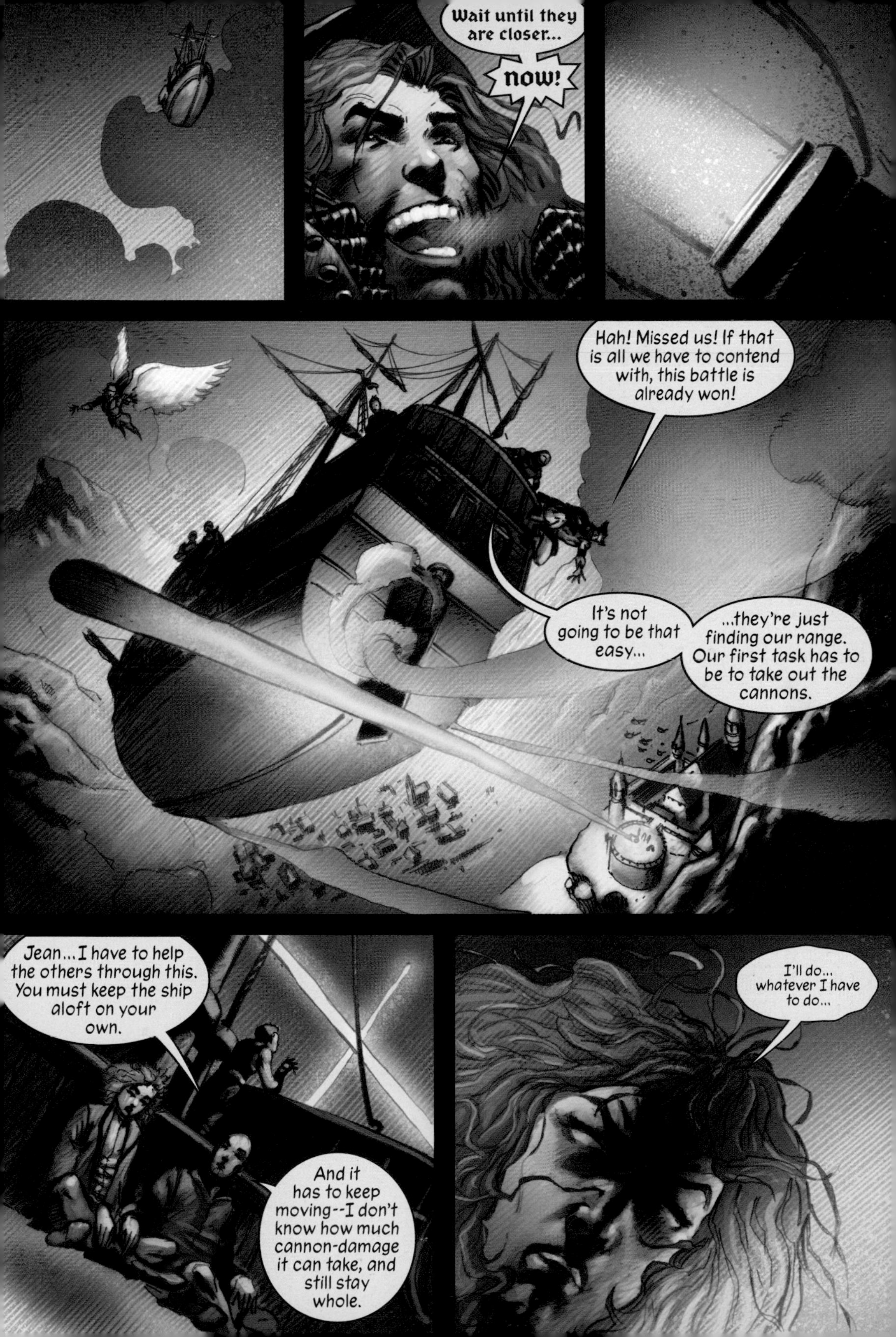
Wait until they are closer...
now!
Hah! Missed us! If that is all we have to contend with, this battle is already won!
It's not going to be that easy...
...they're just finding our range. Our first task has to be to take out the cannons.
Jean... I have to help the others through this. You must keep the ship aloft on your own.
And it has to keep moving--I don't know how much cannon-damage it can take, and still stay whole.
I'll do... whatever I have to do...

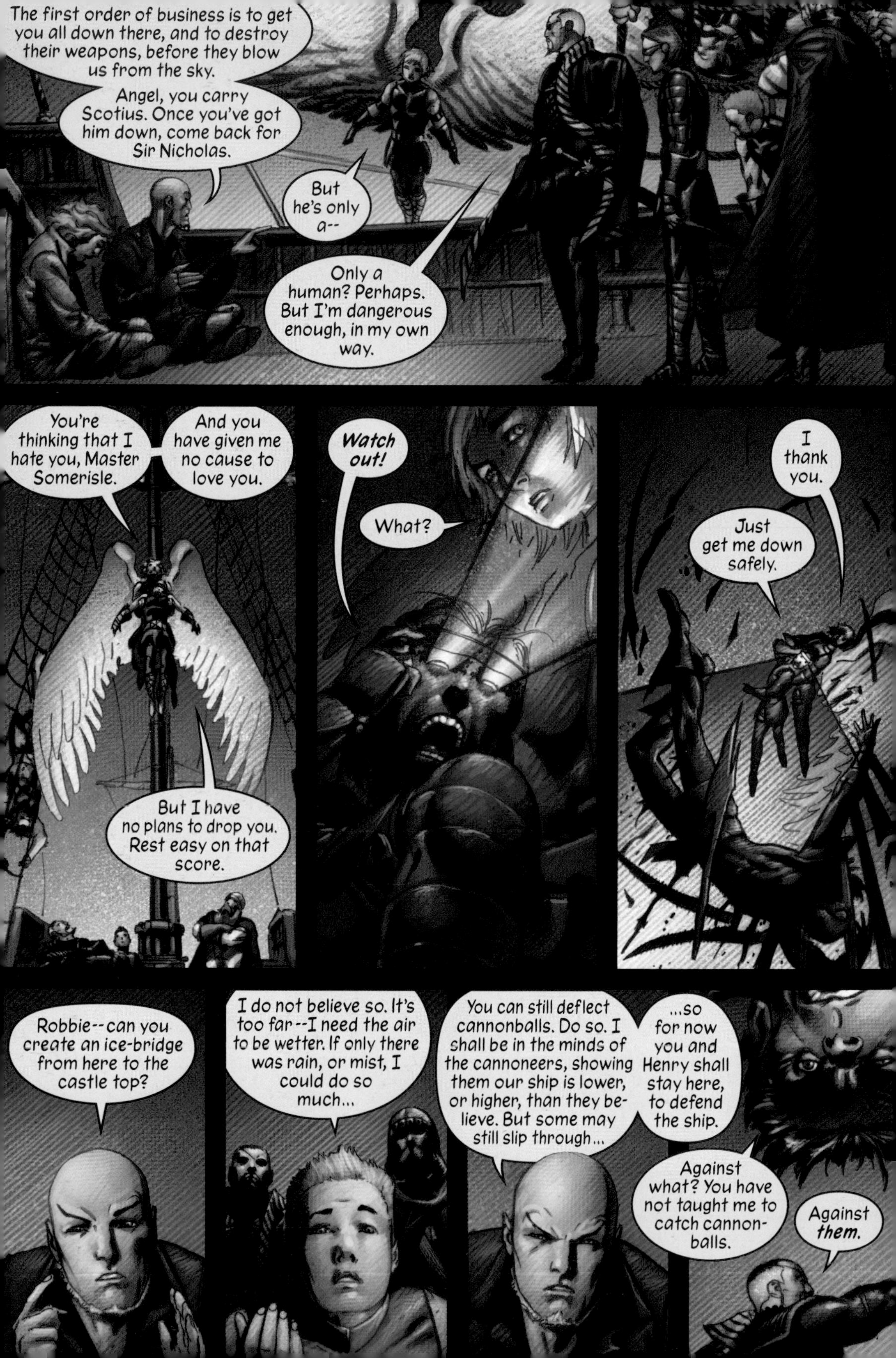
The first order of business is to get you all down there, and to destroy their weapons, before they blow us from the sky.
Angel, you carry Scotius. Once you've got him down, come back for Sir Nicholas.
But he's only a--
Only a human? Perhaps. But I'm dangerous enough, in my own way.
You're thinking that I hate you, Master Somerisle.
And you have given me no cause to love you.
But I have no plans to drop you. Rest easy on that score.
Watch out!
What?
I thank you.
Just get me down safely.
Robbie--can you create an ice-bridge from here to the castle top?
I do not believe so. It's too far--I need the air to be wetter. If only there was rain, or mist, I could do so much...
You can still deflect cannonballs. Do so. I shall be in the minds of the cannoneers, showing them our ship is lower, or higher, than they believe. But some may still slip through...
...so for now you and Henry shall stay here, to defend the ship.
Against what? You have not taught me to catch cannonballs.
Against them.

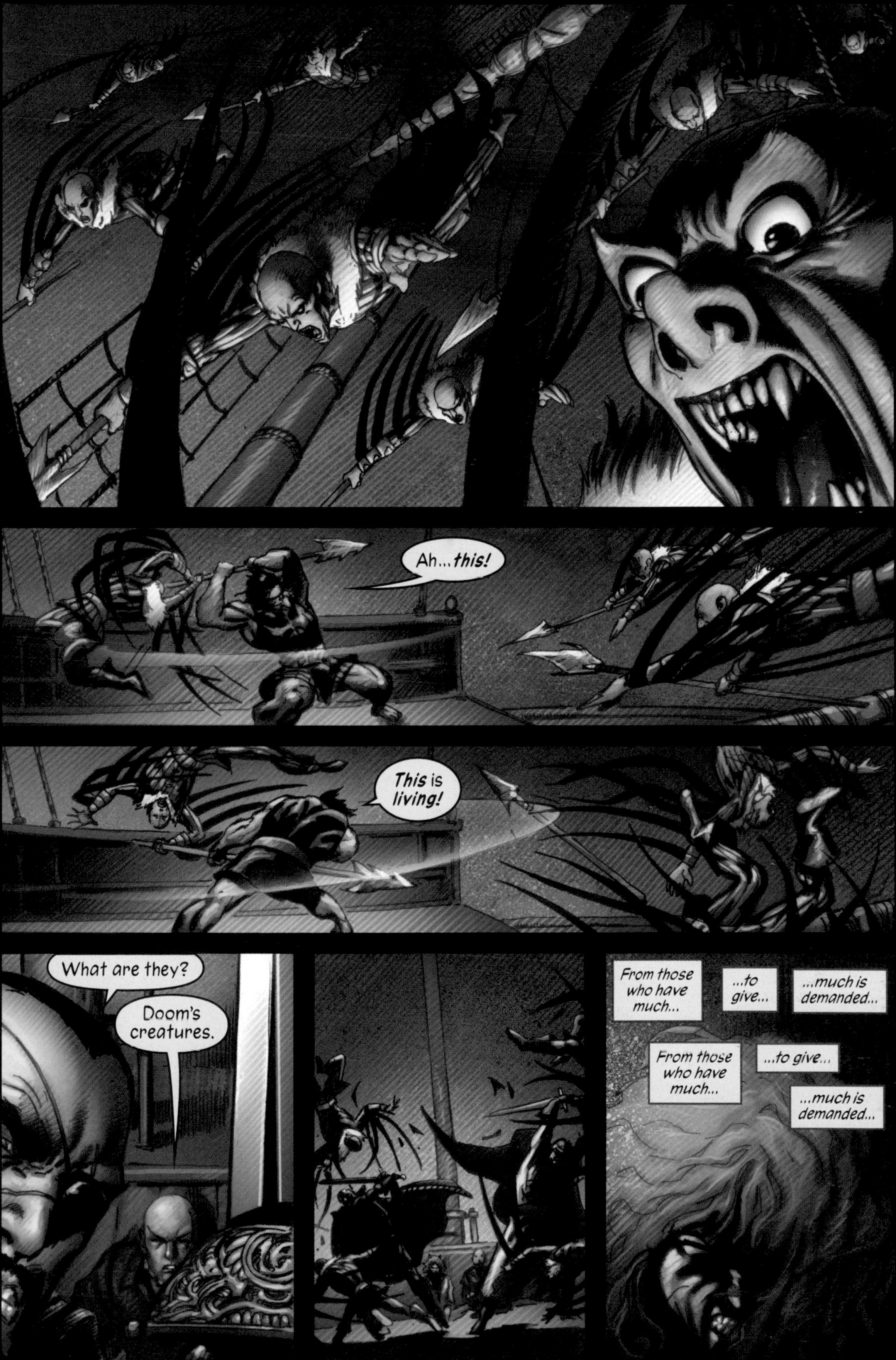
Ah... this!
This is living!
What are they?
Doom's creatures.
From those who have much...
...to give...
...much is demanded...
From those who have much...
...to give...
...much is demanded...

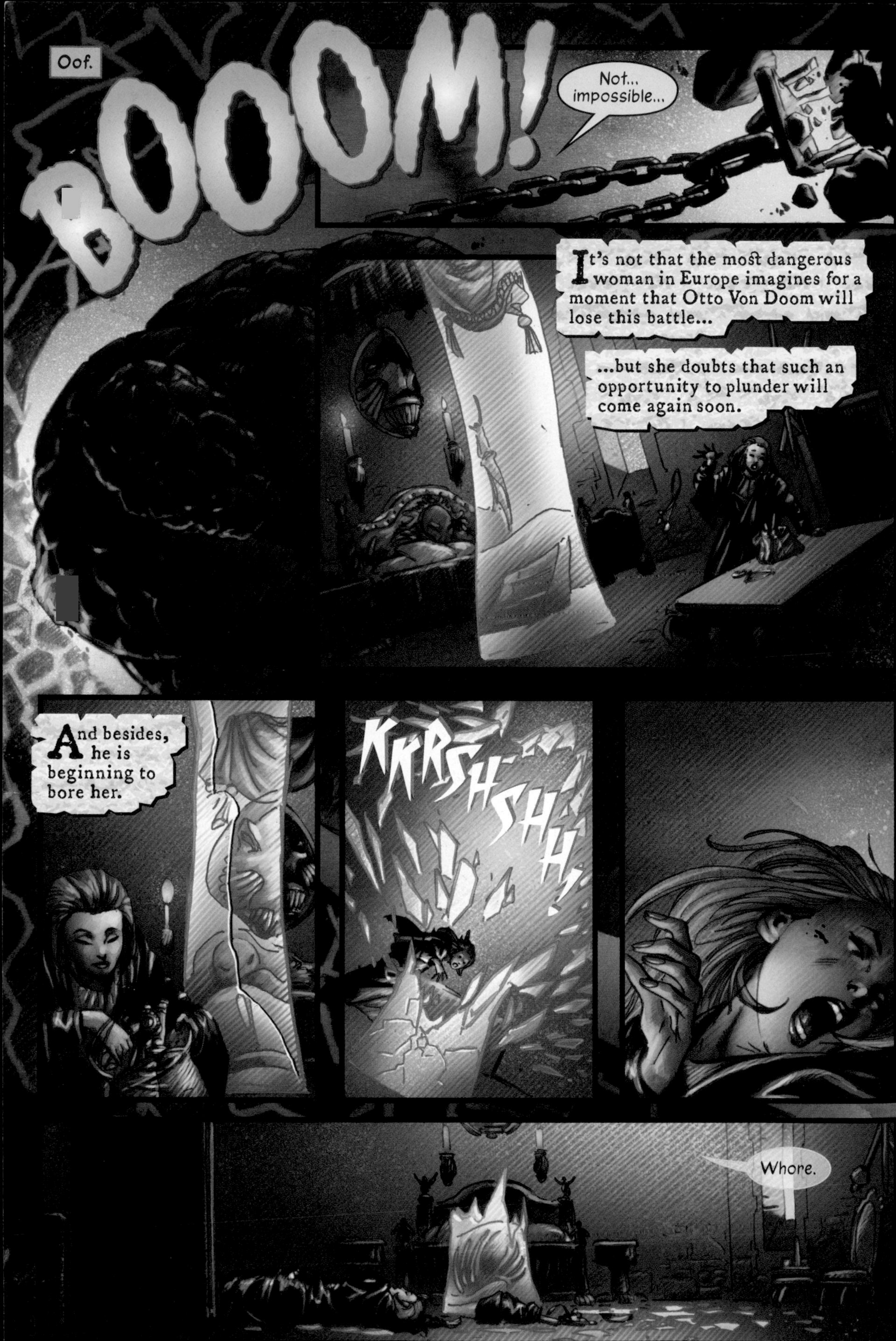
Oof.
BOOOM!
Not... impossible...
It's not that the most dangerous woman in Europe imagines for a moment that Otto Von Doom will lose this battle...
...but she doubts that such an opportunity to plunder will come again soon.
And besides, he is beginning to bore her.
KKRSHSHH!
Whore.

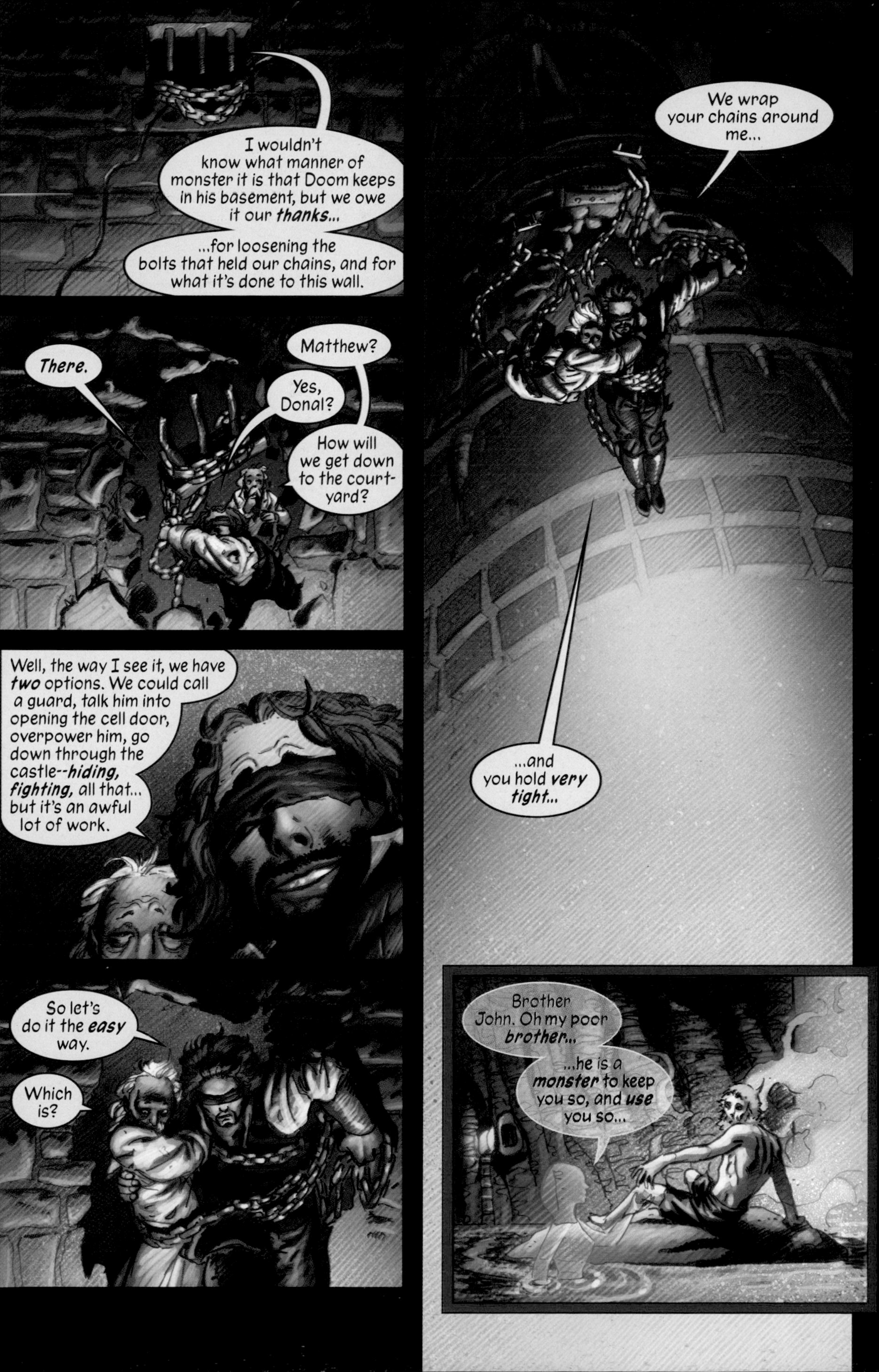
I wouldn't know what manner of monster it is that Doom keeps in his basement, but we owe it our *thanks*...
...for loosening the bolts that held our chains, and for what it's done to this wall.
There.
Matthew?
Yes, Donal?
How will we get down to the court-yard?
Well, the way I see it, we have *two* options. We could call a guard, talk him into opening the cell door, overpower him, go down through the castle--*hiding, fighting,* all that... but it's an awful lot of work.
So let's do it the *easy* way.
Which is?
We wrap your chains around me...
...and you hold *very tight*...
Brother John. Oh my poor *brother*...
...he is a *monster* to keep you so, and *use* you so...

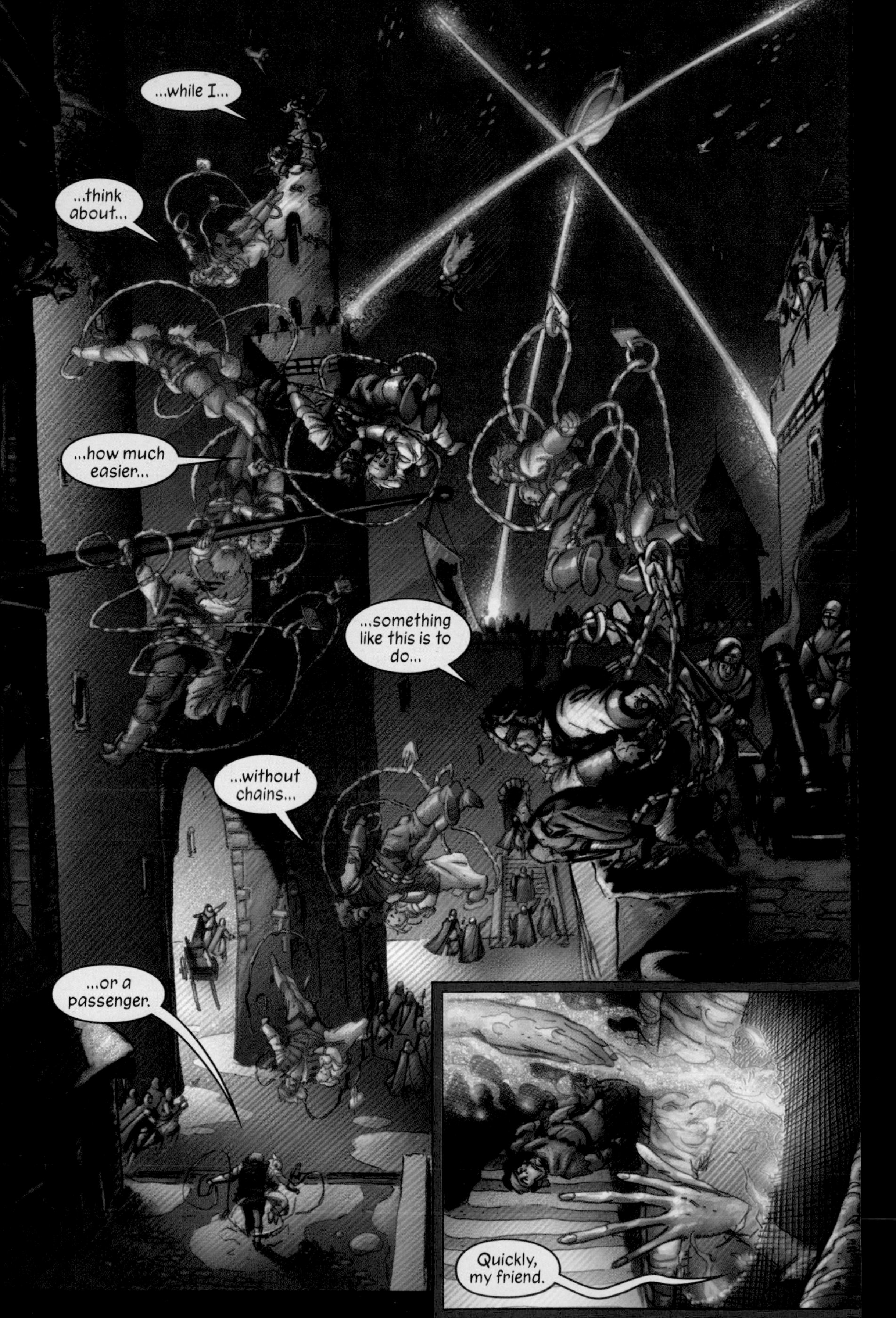
...while I...
...think about...
...how much easier...
...something like this is to do...
...without chains...
...or a passenger.
Quickly, my friend.

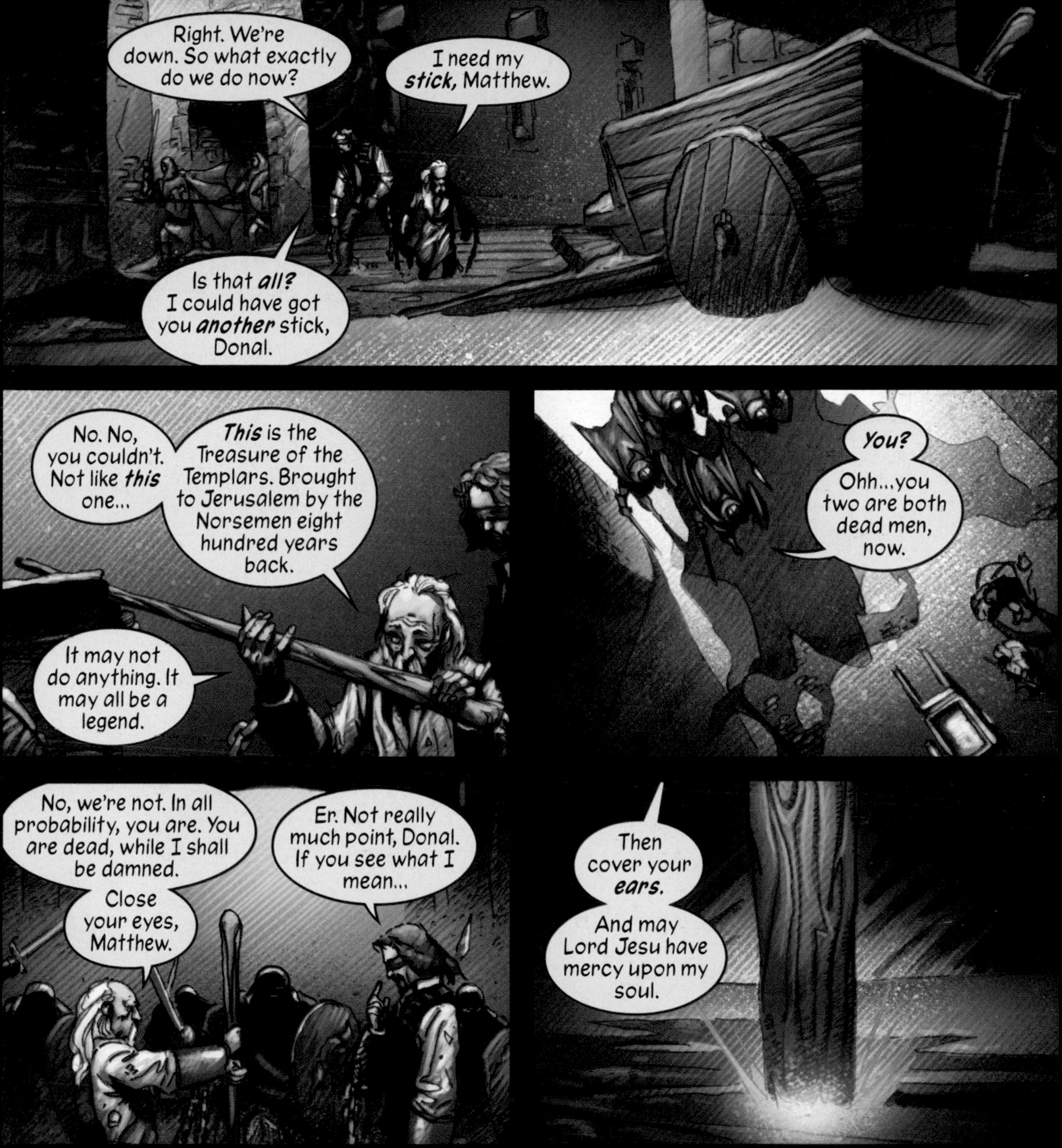
Right. We're down. So what exactly do we do now?
I need my ***stick,*** Matthew.
Is that ***all?*** I could have got you ***another*** stick, Donal.
No. No, you couldn't. Not like ***this*** one...
This is the Treasure of the Templars. Brought to Jerusalem by the Norsemen eight hundred years back.
It may not do anything. It may all be a legend.
You?
Ohh...you two are both dead men, now.
No, we're not. In all probability, you are. You are dead, while I shall be damned.
Close your eyes, Matthew.
Er. Not really much point, Donal. If you see what I mean...
Then cover your ***ears.***
And may Lord Jesu have mercy upon my soul.

Even with his ears covered, the crash of thunder is deafening: louder than the cannons, louder than the monster in the dungeon...

...it leaves him disoriented, although he can still smell the ozone lightning flash.

That was close, he thinks, as the rain begins to pour from a previously cloudless sky...

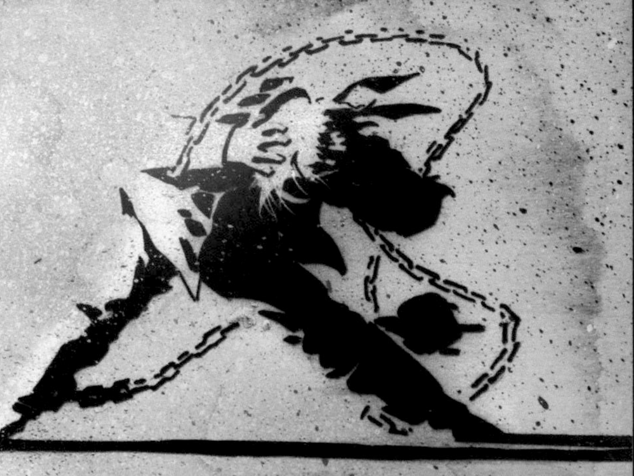

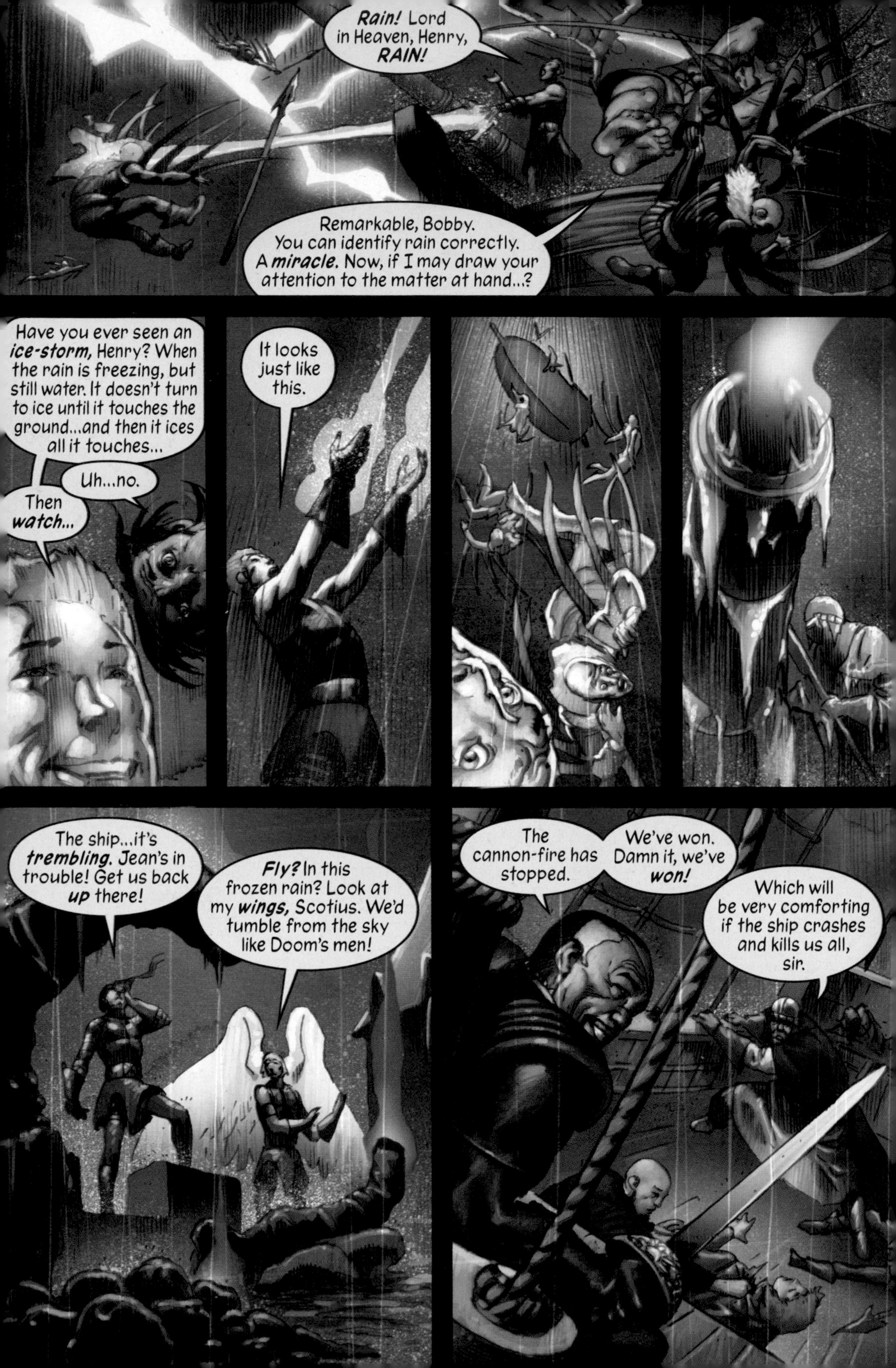
Rain! Lord in Heaven, Henry, RAIN!
Remarkable, Bobby. You can identify rain correctly. A miracle. Now, if I may draw your attention to the matter at hand...?
Have you ever seen an ice-storm, Henry? When the rain is freezing, but still water. It doesn't turn to ice until it touches the ground...and then it ices all it touches...
Uh...no.
Then watch...
It looks just like this.
The ship...it's trembling. Jean's in trouble! Get us back up there!
Fly? In this frozen rain? Look at my wings, Scotius. We'd tumble from the sky like Doom's men!
...
The cannon-fire has stopped.
We've won. Damn it, we've won!
Which will be very comforting if the ship crashes and kills us all, sir.

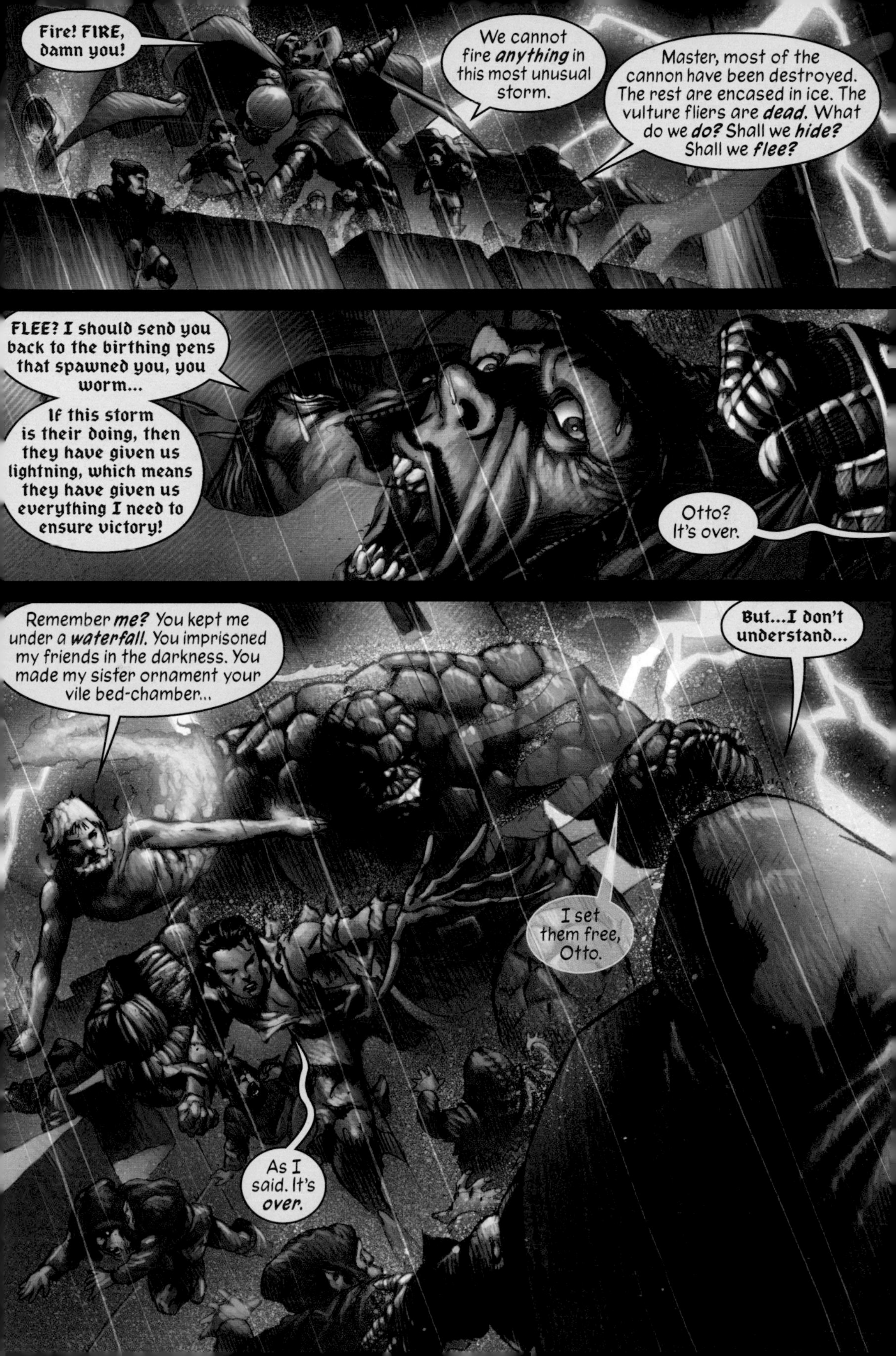

Fire! FIRE, damn you!
We cannot fire anything in this most unusual storm.
Master, most of the cannon have been destroyed. The rest are encased in ice. The vulture fliers are dead. What do we do? Shall we hide? Shall we flee?
FLEE? I should send you back to the birthing pens that spawned you, you worm...
If this storm is their doing, then they have given us lightning, which means they have given us everything I need to ensure victory!
Otto? It's over.
Remember me? You kept me under a waterfall. You imprisoned my friends in the darkness. You made my sister ornament your vile bed-chamber...
But...I don't understand...
I set them free, Otto.
As I said. It's over.

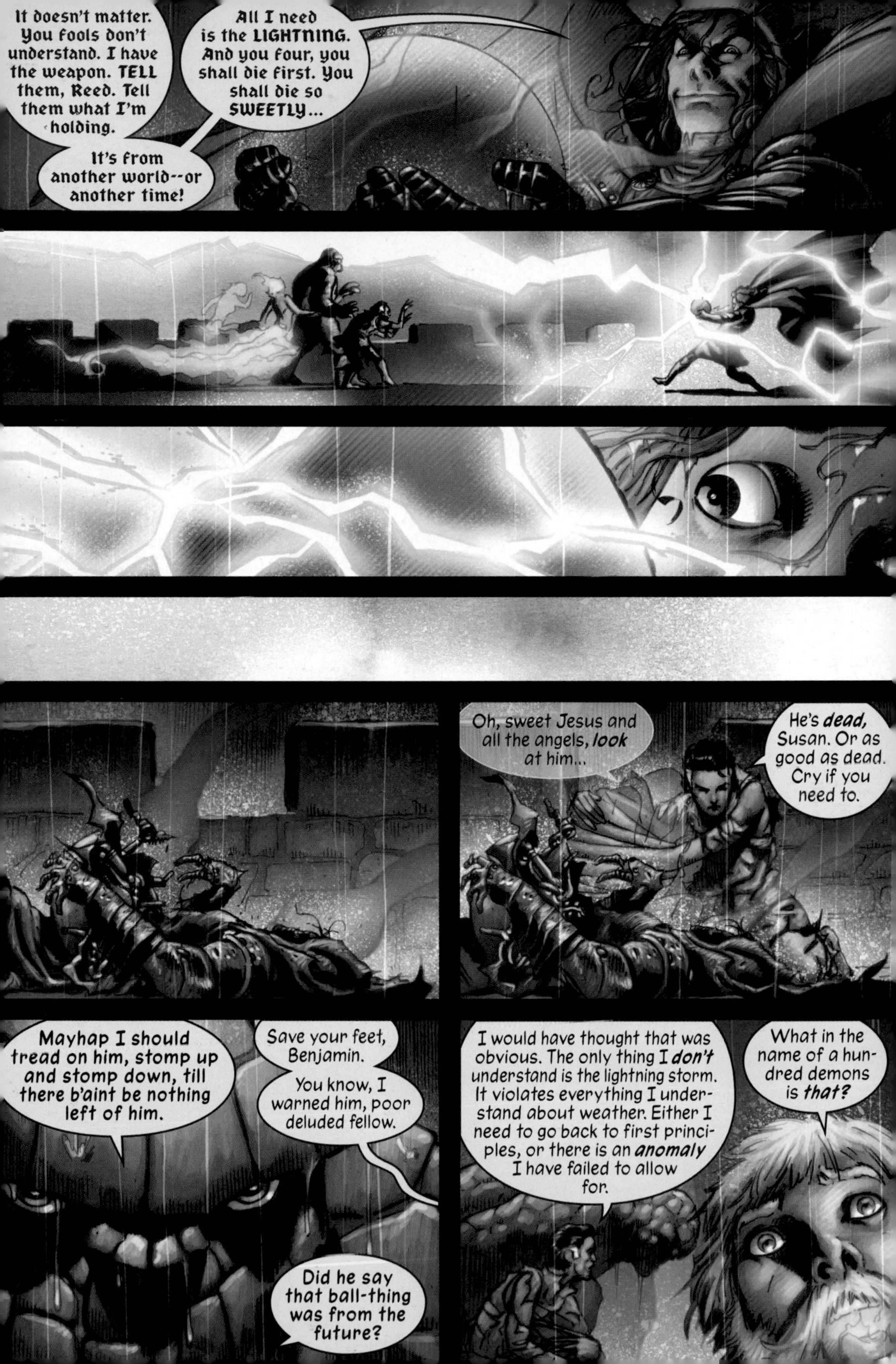
It doesn't matter. You fools don't understand. I have the weapon. TELL them, Reed. Tell them what I'm holding.
It's from another world--or another time!
All I need is the LIGHTNING. And you four, you shall die first. You shall die so SWEETLY...
Oh, sweet Jesus and all the angels, look at him...
He's dead, Susan. Or as good as dead. Cry if you need to.
Mayhap I should tread on him, stomp up and stomp down, till there b'aint be nothing left of him.
Save your feet, Benjamin.
You know, I warned him, poor deluded fellow.
Did he say that ball-thing was from the future?
I would have thought that was obvious. The only thing I don't understand is the lightning storm. It violates everything I understand about weather. Either I need to go back to first principles, or there is an anomaly I have failed to allow for.
What in the name of a hundred demons is that?

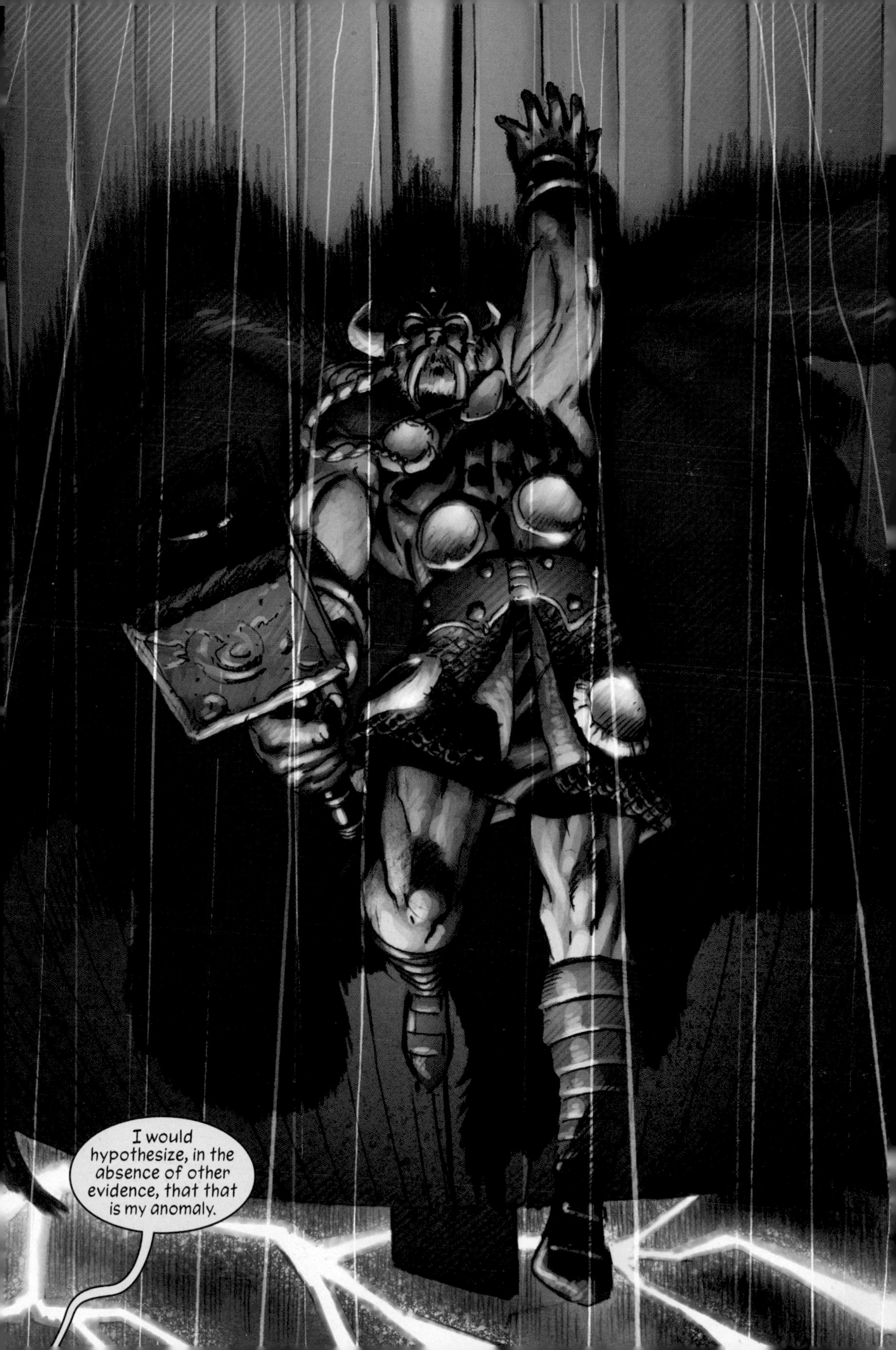
I would hypothesize, in the absence of other evidence, that that is my anomaly.

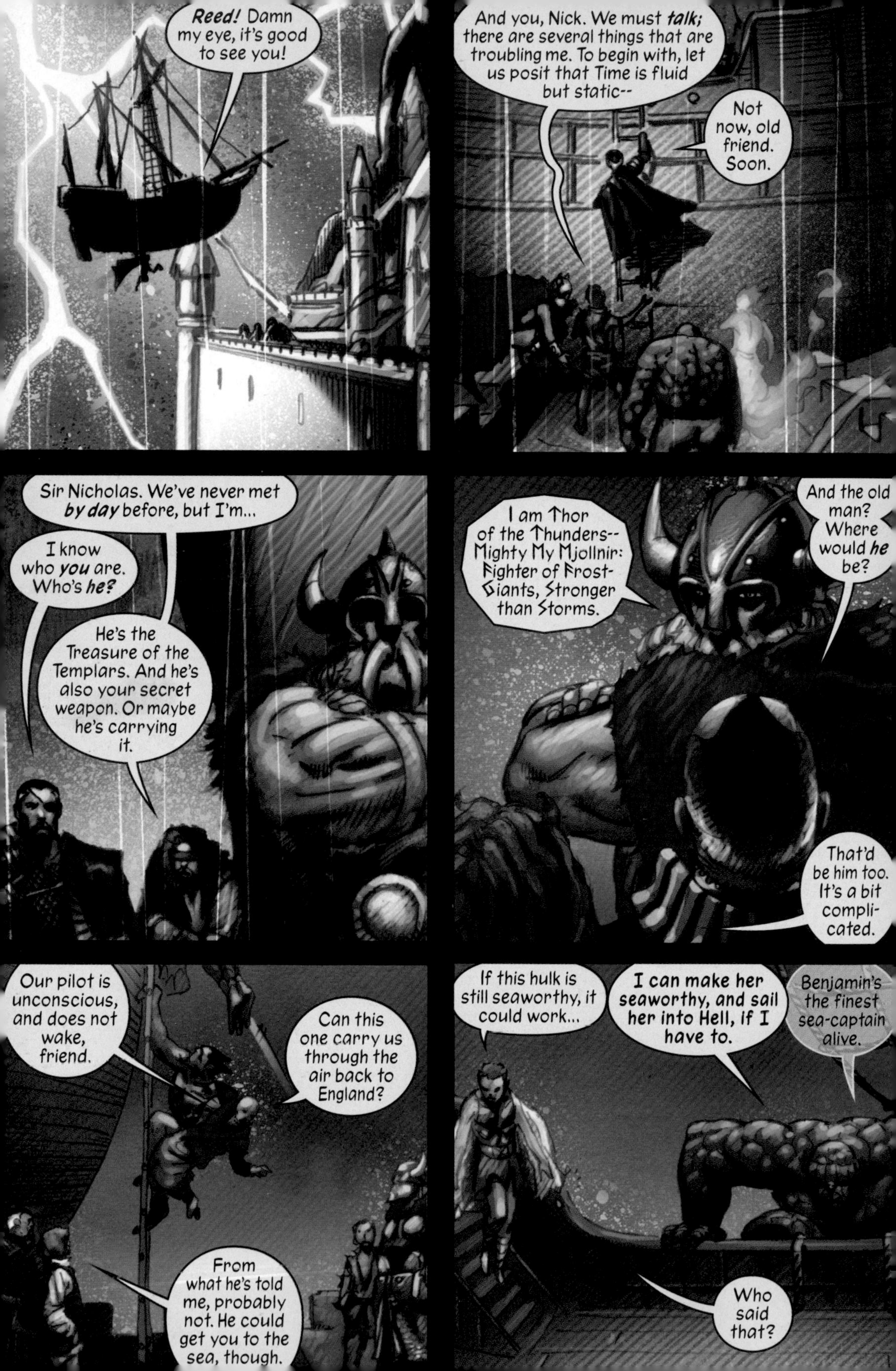
Reed! Damn my eye, it's good to see you!
And you, Nick. We must talk; there are several things that are troubling me. To begin with, let us posit that Time is fluid but static--
Not now, old friend. Soon.
Sir Nicholas. We've never met by day before, but I'm...
I know who you are. Who's he?
He's the Treasure of the Templars. And he's also your secret weapon. Or maybe he's carrying it.
I am Thor of the Thunders-- Mighty My Mjollnir: Fighter of Frost-Giants, Stronger than Storms.
And the old man? Where would he be?
That'd be him too. It's a bit compli-cated.
Our pilot is unconscious, and does not wake, friend.
Can this one carry us through the air back to England?
From what he's told me, probably not. He could get you to the sea, though.
If this hulk is still seaworthy, it could work...
I can make her seaworthy, and sail her into Hell, if I have to.
Benjamin's the finest sea-captain alive.
Who said that?

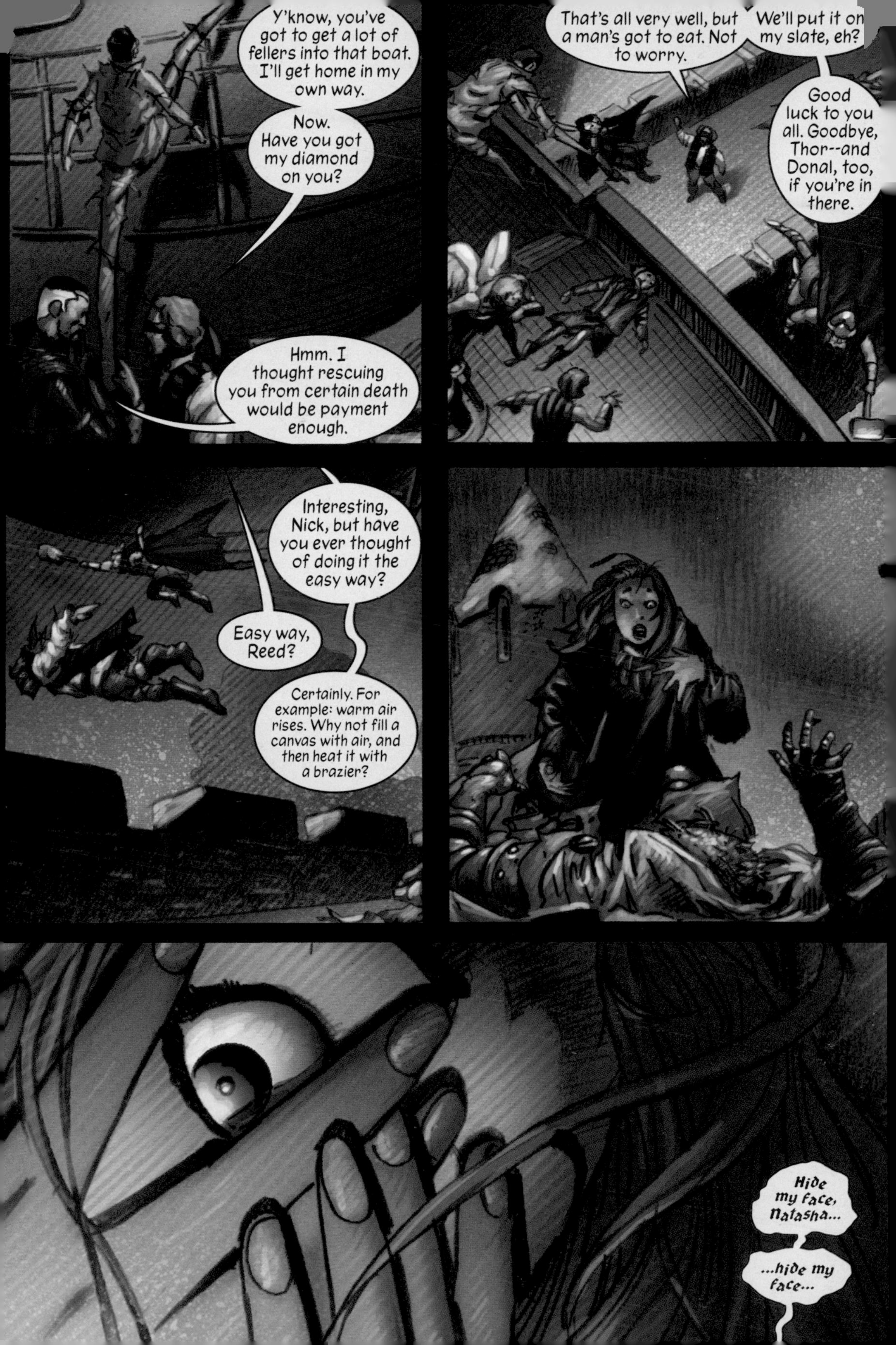
Y'know, you've got to get a lot of fellers into that boat. I'll get home in my own way.
Now. Have you got my diamond on you?
Hmm. I thought rescuing you from certain death would be payment enough.
That's all very well, but a man's got to eat. Not to worry.
We'll put it on my slate, eh?
Good luck to you all. Goodbye, Thor--and Donal, too, if you're in there.
Interesting, Nick, but have you ever thought of doing it the easy way?
Easy way, Reed?
Certainly. For example: warm air rises. Why not fill a canvas with air, and then heat it with a brazier?
Hide my face, Natasha...
...hide my face...

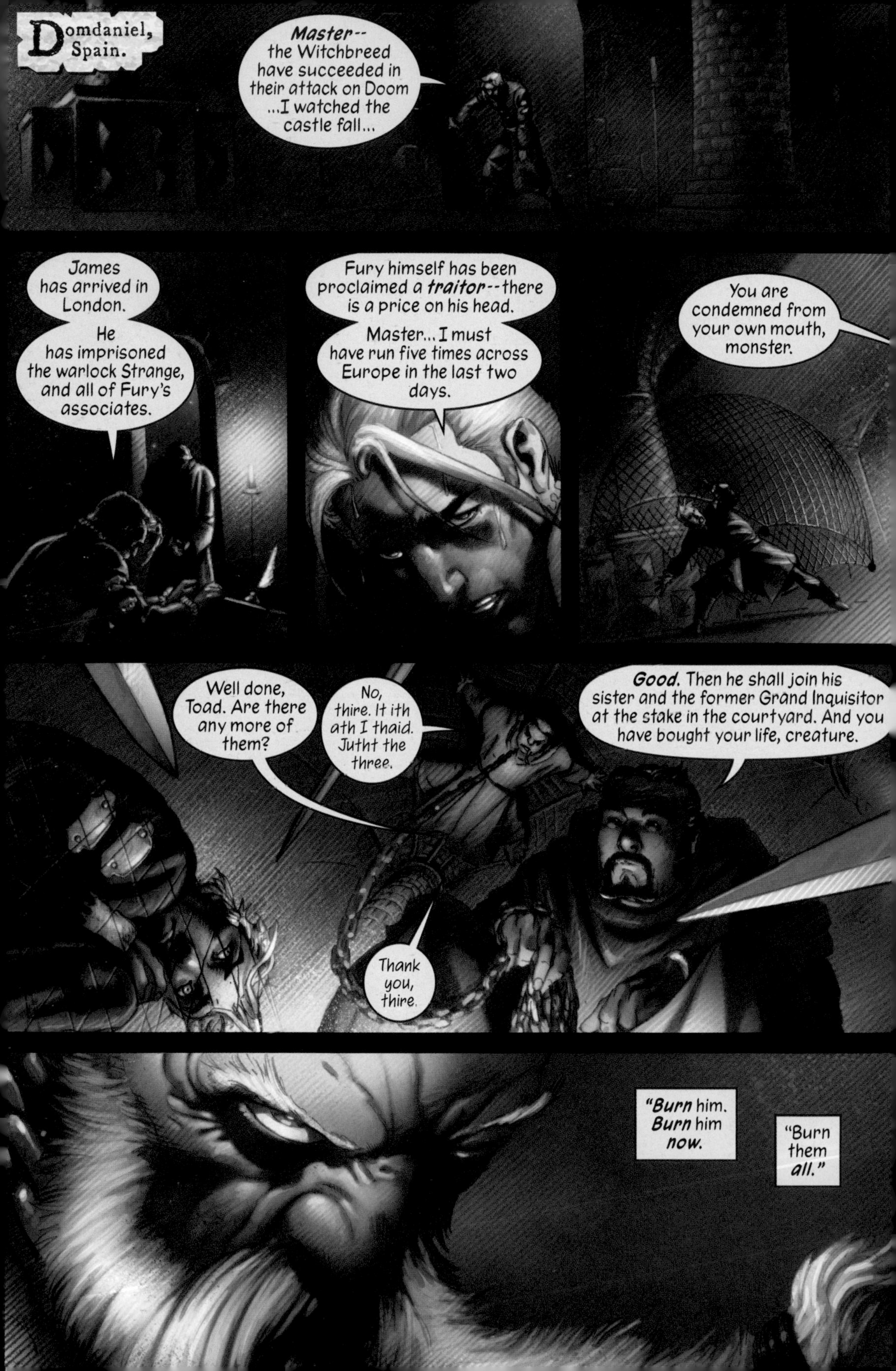
Domdaniel, Spain.
Master-- the Witchbreed have succeeded in their attack on Doom ...I watched the castle fall...
James has arrived in London.
He has imprisoned the warlock Strange, and all of Fury's associates.
Fury himself has been proclaimed a traitor--there is a price on his head.
Master... I must have run five times across Europe in the last two days.
You are condemned from your own mouth, monster.
Well done, Toad. Are there any more of them?
No, thire. It ith ath I thaid. Jutht the three.
Good. Then he shall join his sister and the former Grand Inquisitor at the stake in the courtyard. And you have bought your life, creature.
Thank you, thire.
"Burn him. Burn him now.
"Burn them all."

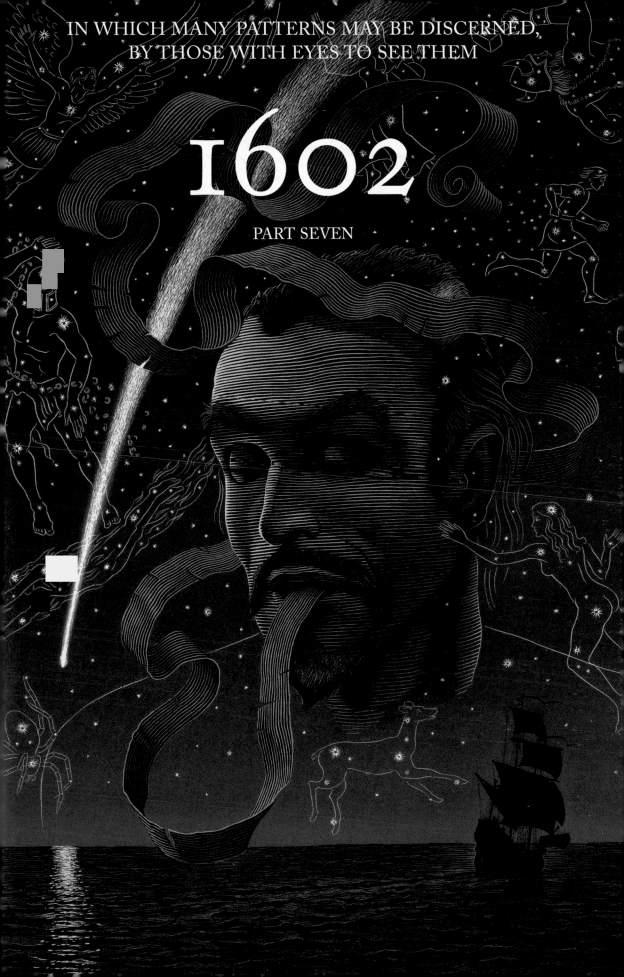

IN WHICH MANY PATTERNS MAY BE DISCERNED,
BY THOSE WITH EYES TO SEE THEM

1602

PART SEVEN

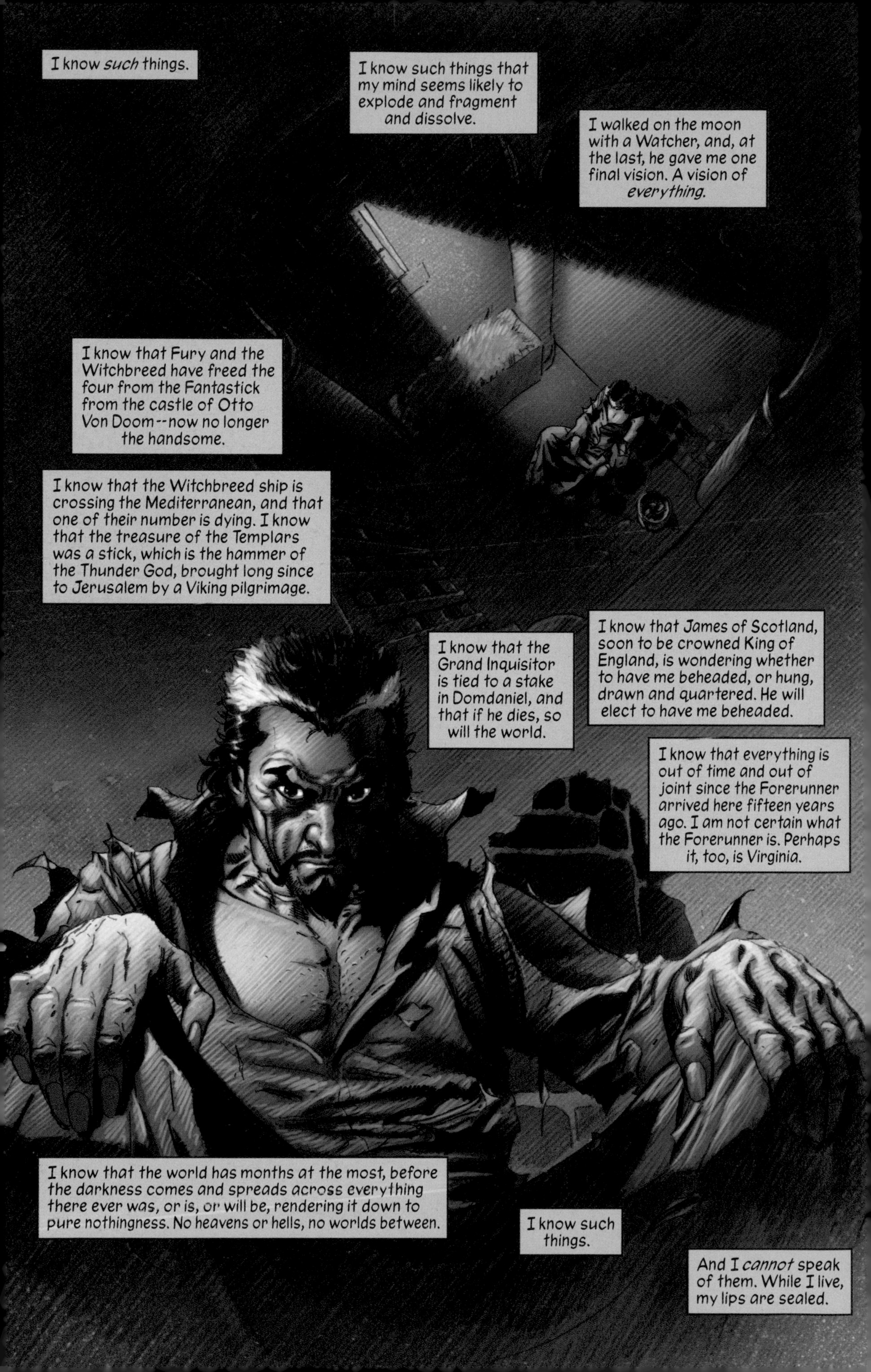
I know *such* things.
I know such things that my mind seems likely to explode and fragment and dissolve.
I walked on the moon with a Watcher, and, at the last, he gave me one final vision. A vision of *everything.*
I know that Fury and the Witchbreed have freed the four from the Fantastick from the castle of Otto Von Doom--now no longer the handsome.
I know that the Witchbreed ship is crossing the Mediterranean, and that one of their number is dying. I know that the treasure of the Templars was a stick, which is the hammer of the Thunder God, brought long since to Jerusalem by a Viking pilgrimage.
I know that the Grand Inquisitor is tied to a stake in Domdaniel, and that if he dies, so will the world.
I know that James of Scotland, soon to be crowned King of England, is wondering whether to have me beheaded, or hung, drawn and quartered. He will elect to have me beheaded.
I know that everything is out of time and out of joint since the Forerunner arrived here fifteen years ago. I am not certain what the Forerunner is. Perhaps it, too, is Virginia.
I know that the world has months at the most, before the darkness comes and spreads across everything there ever was, or is, or will be, rendering it down to pure nothingness. No heavens or hells, no worlds between.
I know such things.
And I *cannot* speak of them. While I live, my lips are sealed.

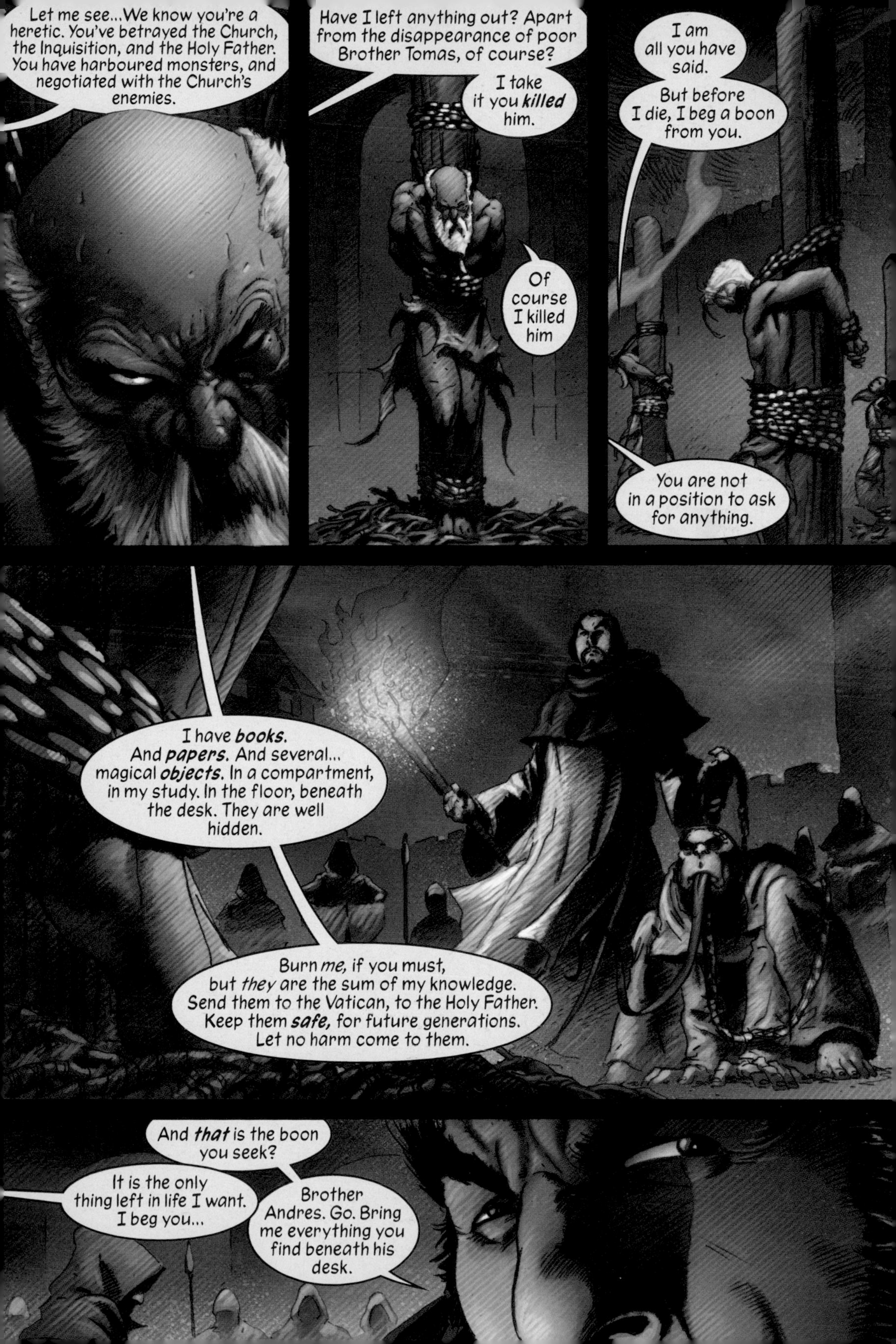
Let me see...We know you're a heretic. You've betrayed the Church, the Inquisition, and the Holy Father. You have harboured monsters, and negotiated with the Church's enemies.
Have I left anything out? Apart from the disappearance of poor Brother Tomas, of course?
I take it you *killed* him.
Of course I killed him
I am all you have said.
But before I die, I beg a boon from you.
You are not in a position to ask for anything.
I have **books**. And **papers**. And several... magical **objects**. In a compartment, in my study. In the floor, beneath the desk. They are well hidden.
Burn *me,* if you must, but *they* are the sum of my knowledge. Send them to the Vatican, to the Holy Father. Keep them **safe,** for future generations. Let no harm come to them.
And **that** is the boon you seek?
It is the only thing left in life I want. I beg you...
Brother Andres. Go. Bring me everything you find beneath his desk.

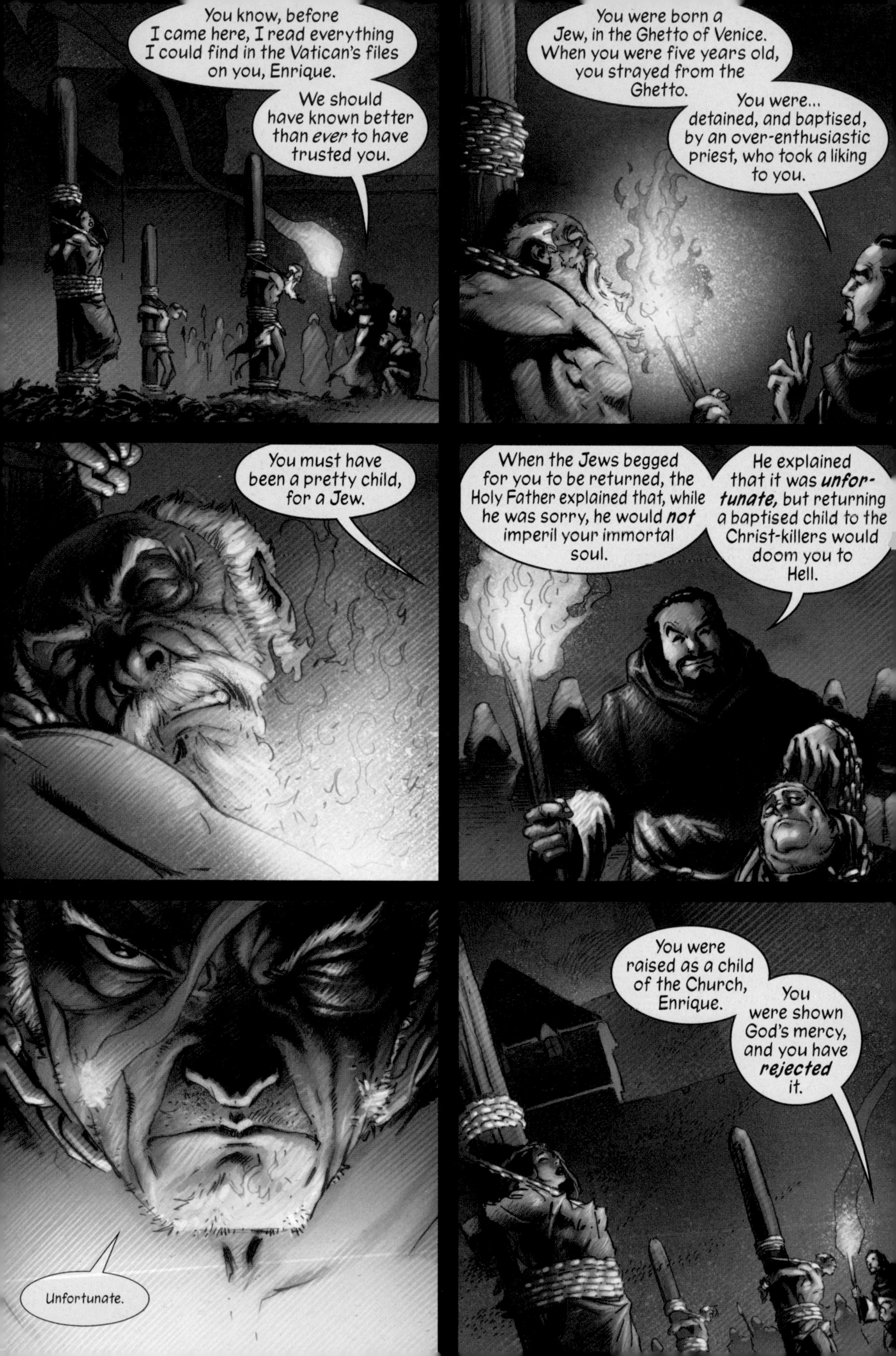

You know, before I came here, I read everything I could find in the Vatican's files on you, Enrique.
We should have known better than *ever* to have trusted you.
You were born a Jew, in the Ghetto of Venice. When you were five years old, you strayed from the Ghetto.
You were... detained, and baptised, by an over-enthusiastic priest, who took a liking to you.
You must have been a pretty child, for a Jew.
When the Jews begged for you to be returned, the Holy Father explained that, while he was sorry, he would ***not*** imperil your immortal soul.
He explained that it was ***unfortunate,*** but returning a baptised child to the Christ-killers would doom you to Hell.
Unfortunate.
You were raised as a child of the Church, Enrique.
You were shown God's mercy, and you have ***rejected*** it.

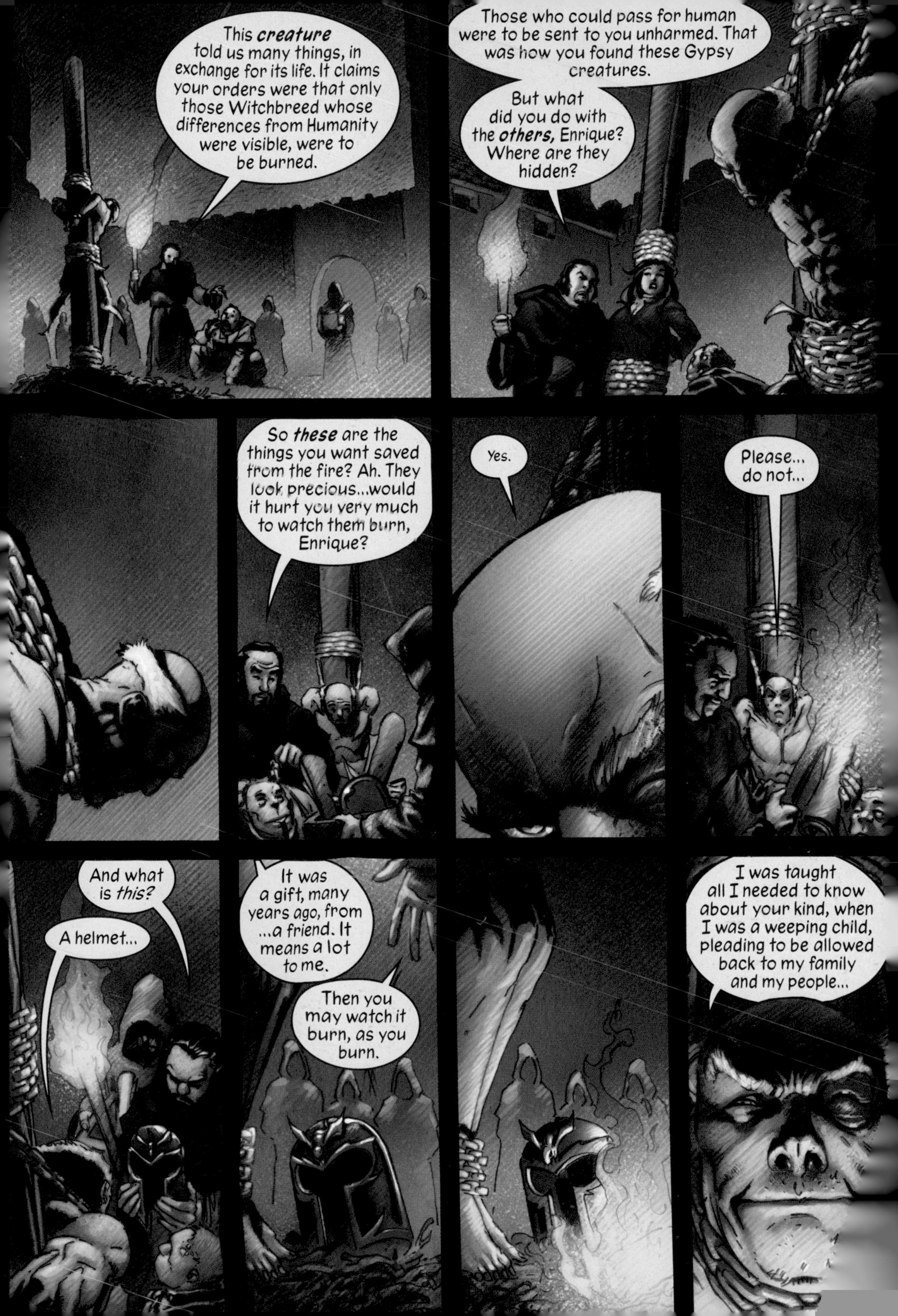
This *creature* told us many things, in exchange for its life. It claims your orders were that only those Witchbreed whose differences from Humanity were visible, were to be burned.
Those who could pass for human were to be sent to you unharmed. That was how you found these Gypsy creatures.
But what did you do with the *others,* Enrique? Where are they hidden?
So *these* are the things you want saved from the fire? Ah. They look precious...would it hurt you very much to watch them burn, Enrique?
Yes.
Please... do not...
And what is *this?*
A helmet...
It was a gift, many years ago, from ...a friend. It means a lot to me.
Then you may watch it burn, as you burn.
I was taught all I needed to know about your kind, when I was a weeping child, pleading to be allowed back to my family and my people...

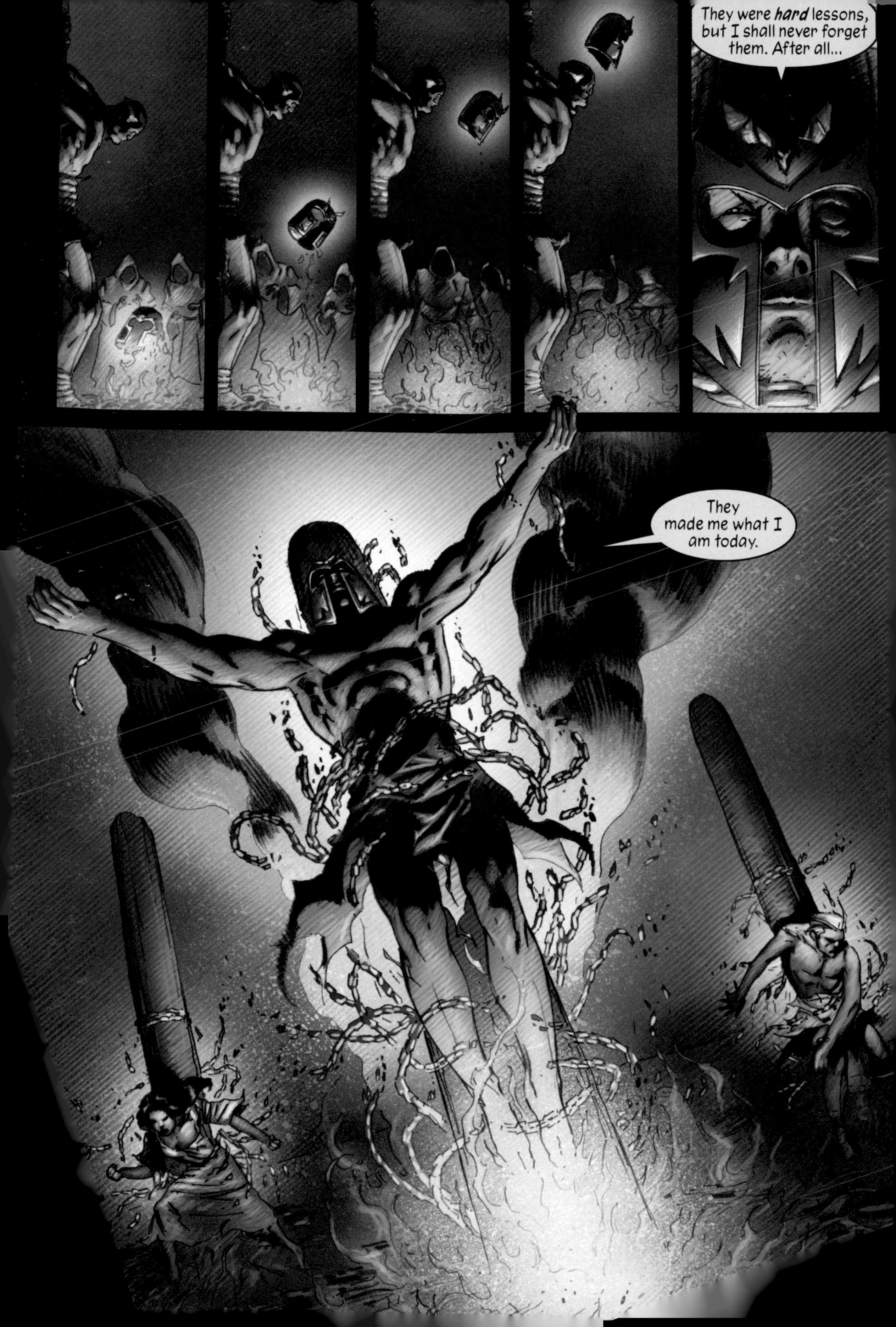
They were **hard** lessons, but I shall never forget them. After all...
They made me what I am today.

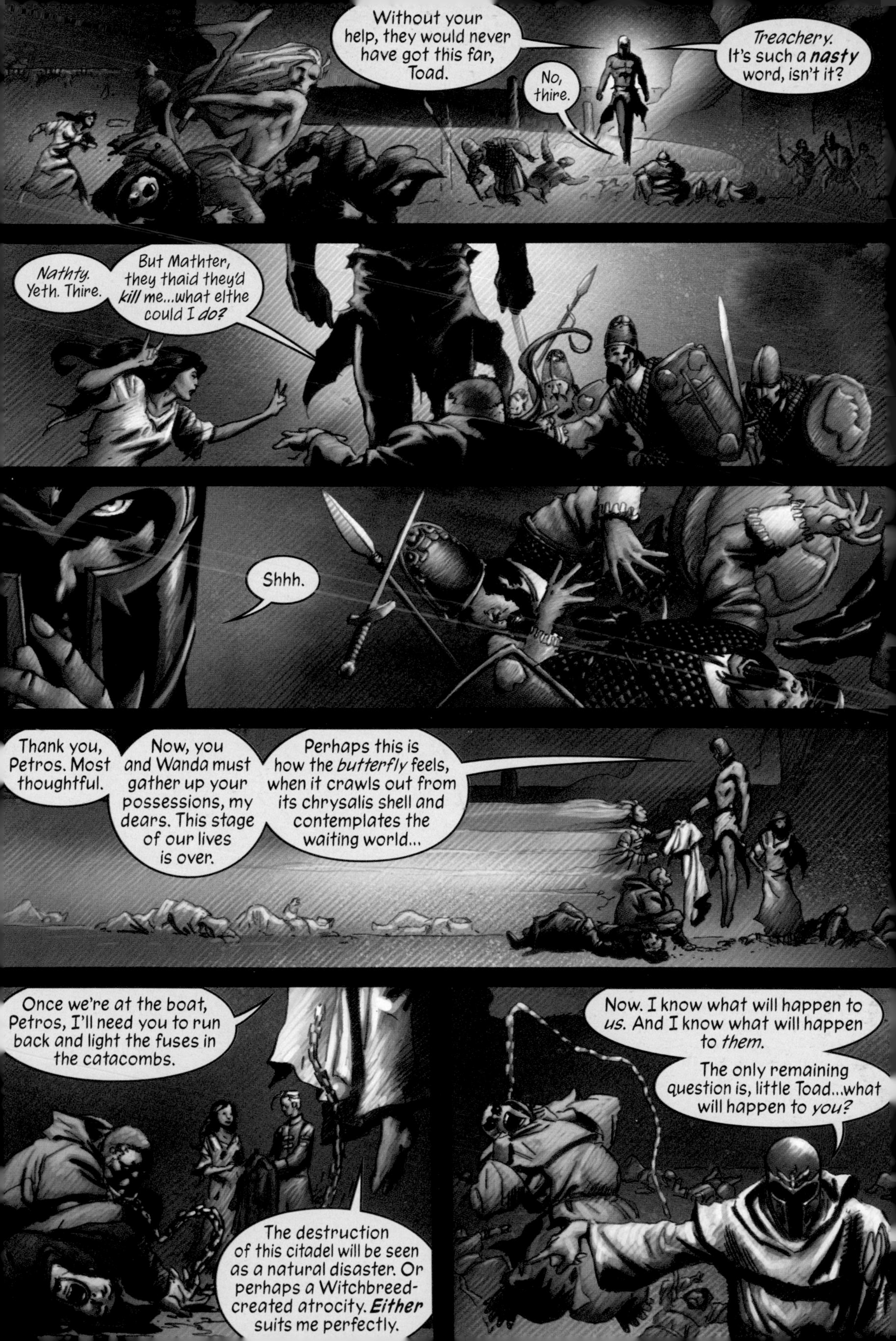
Without your help, they would never have got this far, Toad.
No, thire.
Treachery. It's such a ***nasty*** word, isn't it?
Nathty. Yeth. Thire.
But Mathter, they thaid they'd ***kill*** me...what elthe could I *do?*
Shhh.
Thank you, Petros. Most thoughtful.
Now, you and Wanda must gather up your possessions, my dears. This stage of our lives is over.
Perhaps this is how the *butterfly* feels, when it crawls out from its chrysalis shell and contemplates the waiting world...
Once we're at the boat, Petros, I'll need you to run back and light the fuses in the catacombs.
The destruction of this citadel will be seen as a natural disaster. Or perhaps a Witchbreed-created atrocity. ***Either*** suits me perfectly.
Now. I know what will happen to *us.* And I know what will happen to *them.*
The only remaining question is, little Toad...what will happen to *you?*

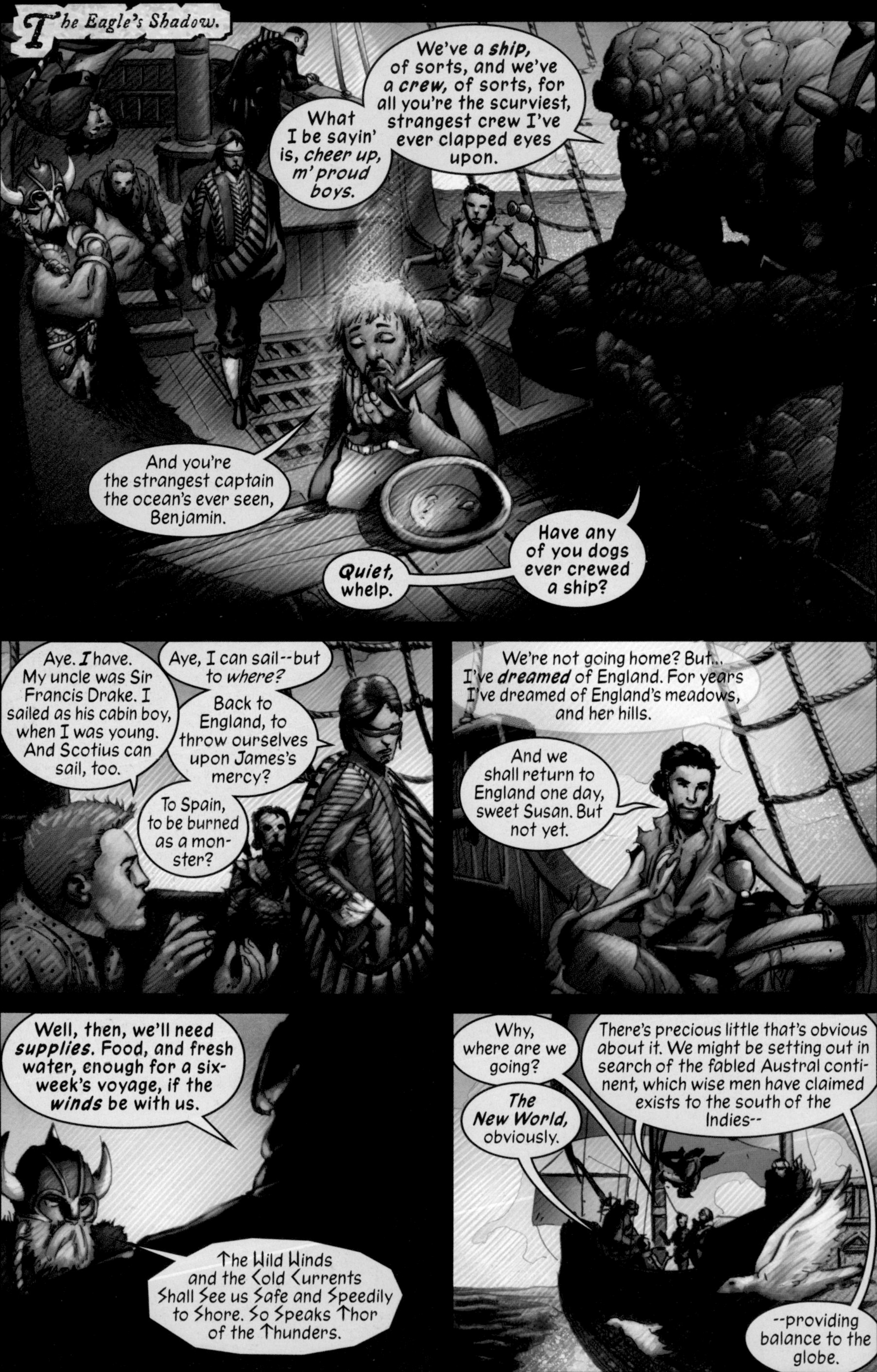
The Eagle's Shadow.
What I be sayin' is, cheer up, m' proud boys.
We've a ship, of sorts, and we've a crew, of sorts, for all you're the scurviest, strangest crew I've ever clapped eyes upon.
And you're the strangest captain the ocean's ever seen, Benjamin.
Quiet, whelp.
Have any of you dogs ever crewed a ship?
Aye. I have. My uncle was Sir Francis Drake. I sailed as his cabin boy, when I was young. And Scotius can sail, too.
Aye, I can sail--but to where?
Back to England, to throw ourselves upon James's mercy?
To Spain, to be burned as a monster?
We're not going home? But... I've dreamed of England. For years I've dreamed of England's meadows, and her hills.
And we shall return to England one day, sweet Susan. But not yet.
Well, then, we'll need supplies. Food, and fresh water, enough for a six-week's voyage, if the winds be with us.
The Wild Winds and the Cold Currents Shall See us Safe and Speedily to Shore. So Speaks Thor of the Thunders.
Why, where are we going?
The New World, obviously.
There's precious little that's obvious about it. We might be setting out in search of the fabled Austral continent, which wise men have claimed exists to the south of the Indies--
--providing balance to the globe.

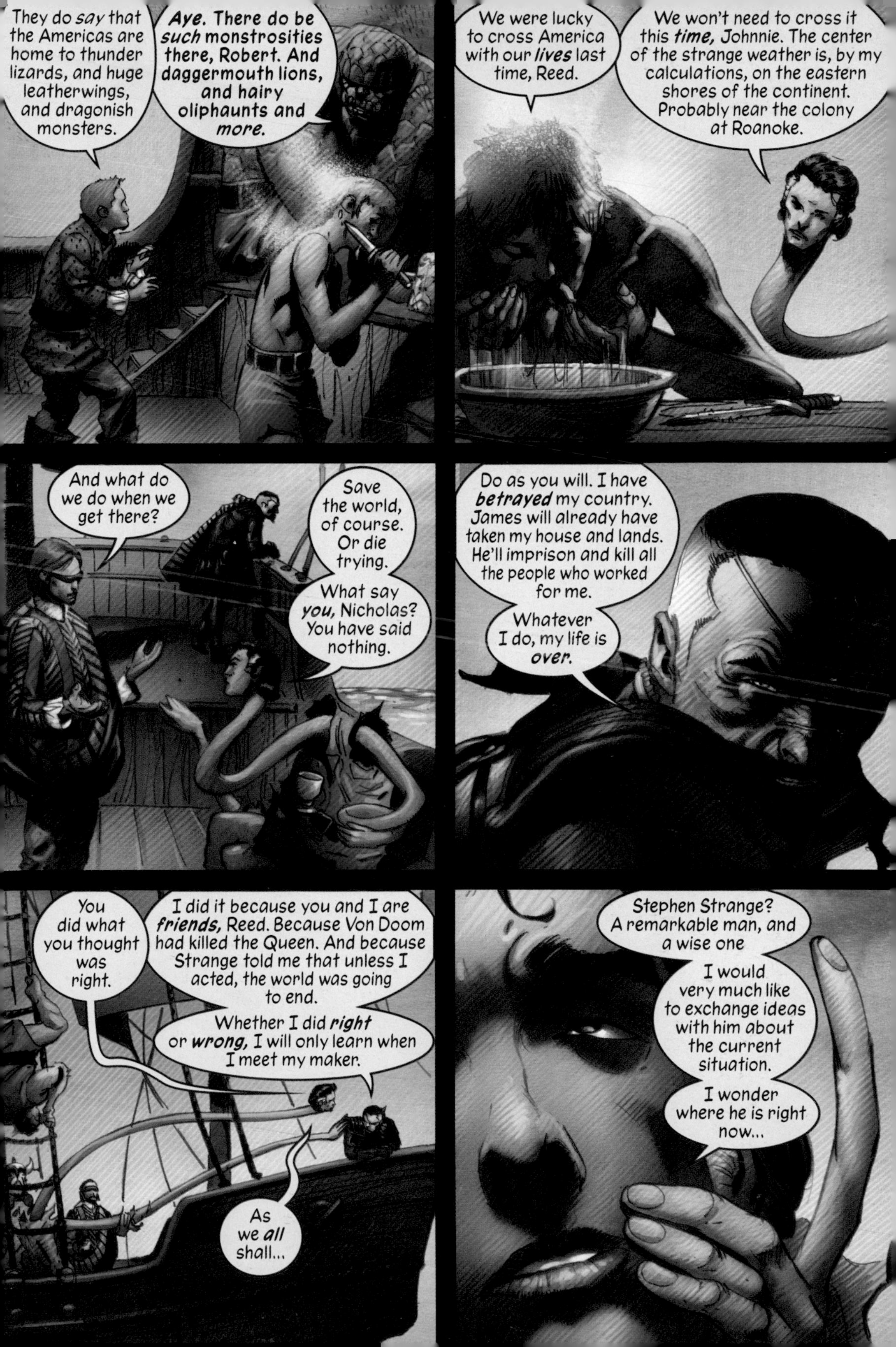
They do *say* that the Americas are home to thunder lizards, and huge leatherwings, and dragonish monsters.
Aye. **There do be** ***such*** **monstrosities there, Robert. And daggermouth lions, and hairy oliphaunts and** ***more.***
We were lucky to cross America with our ***lives*** last time, Reed.
We won't need to cross it this ***time,*** Johnnie. The center of the strange weather is, by my calculations, on the eastern shores of the continent. Probably near the colony at Roanoke.
And what do we do when we get there?
Save the world, of course. Or die trying.
What say ***you,*** Nicholas? You have said nothing.
Do as you will. I have ***betrayed*** my country. James will already have taken my house and lands. He'll imprison and kill all the people who worked for me.
Whatever I do, my life is ***over.***
You did what you thought was right.
I did it because you and I are ***friends,*** Reed. Because Von Doom had killed the Queen. And because Strange told me that unless I acted, the world was going to end.
Whether I did ***right*** or ***wrong,*** I will only learn when I meet my maker.
As we ***all*** shall...
Stephen Strange? A remarkable man, and a wise one
I would very much like to exchange ideas with him about the current situation.
I wonder where he is right now...

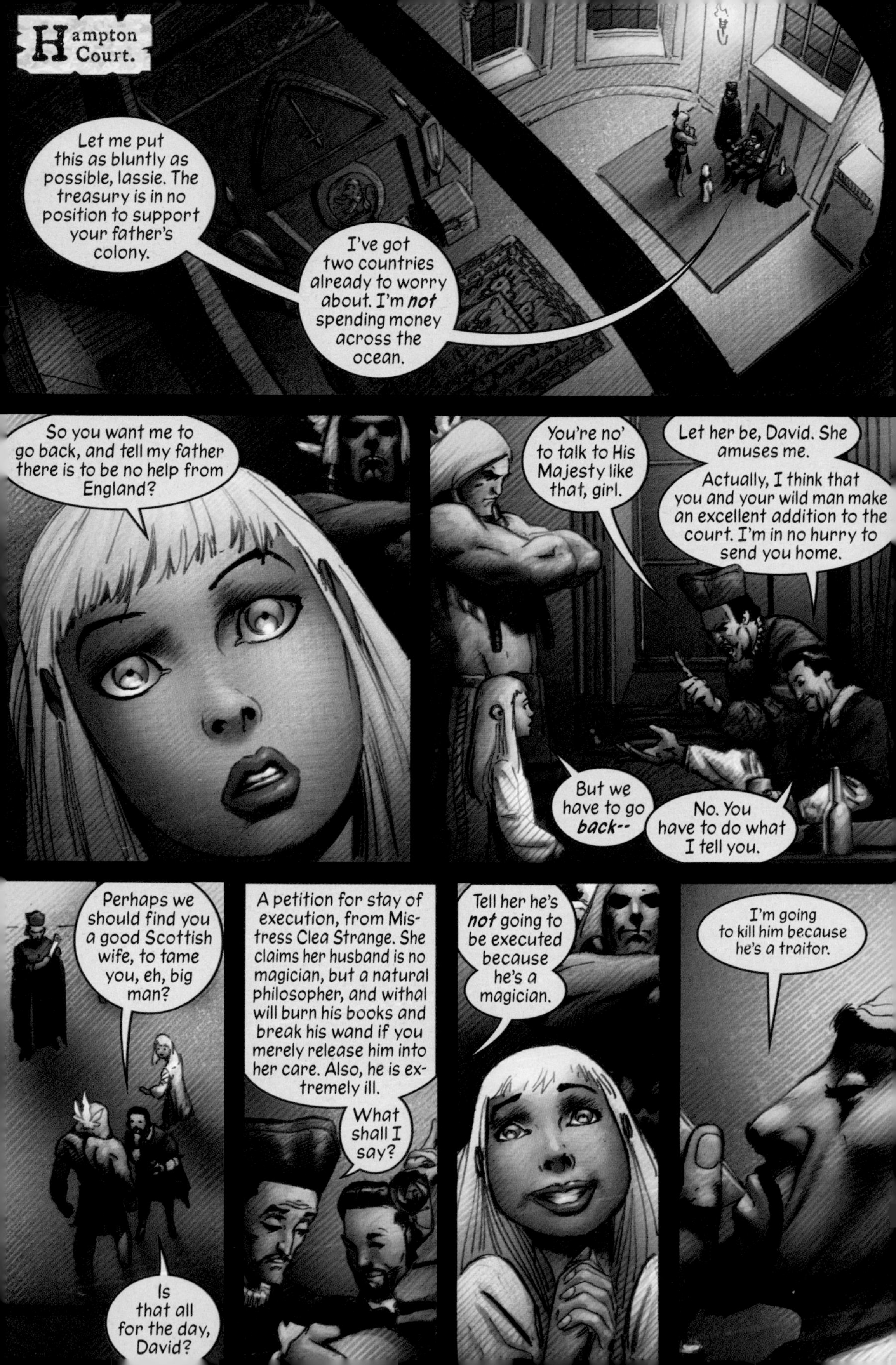
Hampton Court.
Let me put this as bluntly as possible, lassie. The treasury is in no position to support your father's colony.
I've got two countries already to worry about. I'm *not* spending money across the ocean.
So you want me to go back, and tell my father there is to be no help from England?
You're no' to talk to His Majesty like that, girl.
Let her be, David. She amuses me.
Actually, I think that you and your wild man make an excellent addition to the court. I'm in no hurry to send you home.
But we have to go *back*--
No. You have to do what I tell you.
Perhaps we should find you a good Scottish wife, to tame you, eh, big man?
Is that all for the day, David?
A petition for stay of execution, from Mistress Clea Strange. She claims her husband is no magician, but a natural philosopher, and withal will burn his books and break his wand if you merely release him into her care. Also, he is extremely ill.
What shall I say?
Tell her he's *not* going to be executed because he's a magician.
I'm going to kill him because he's a traitor.

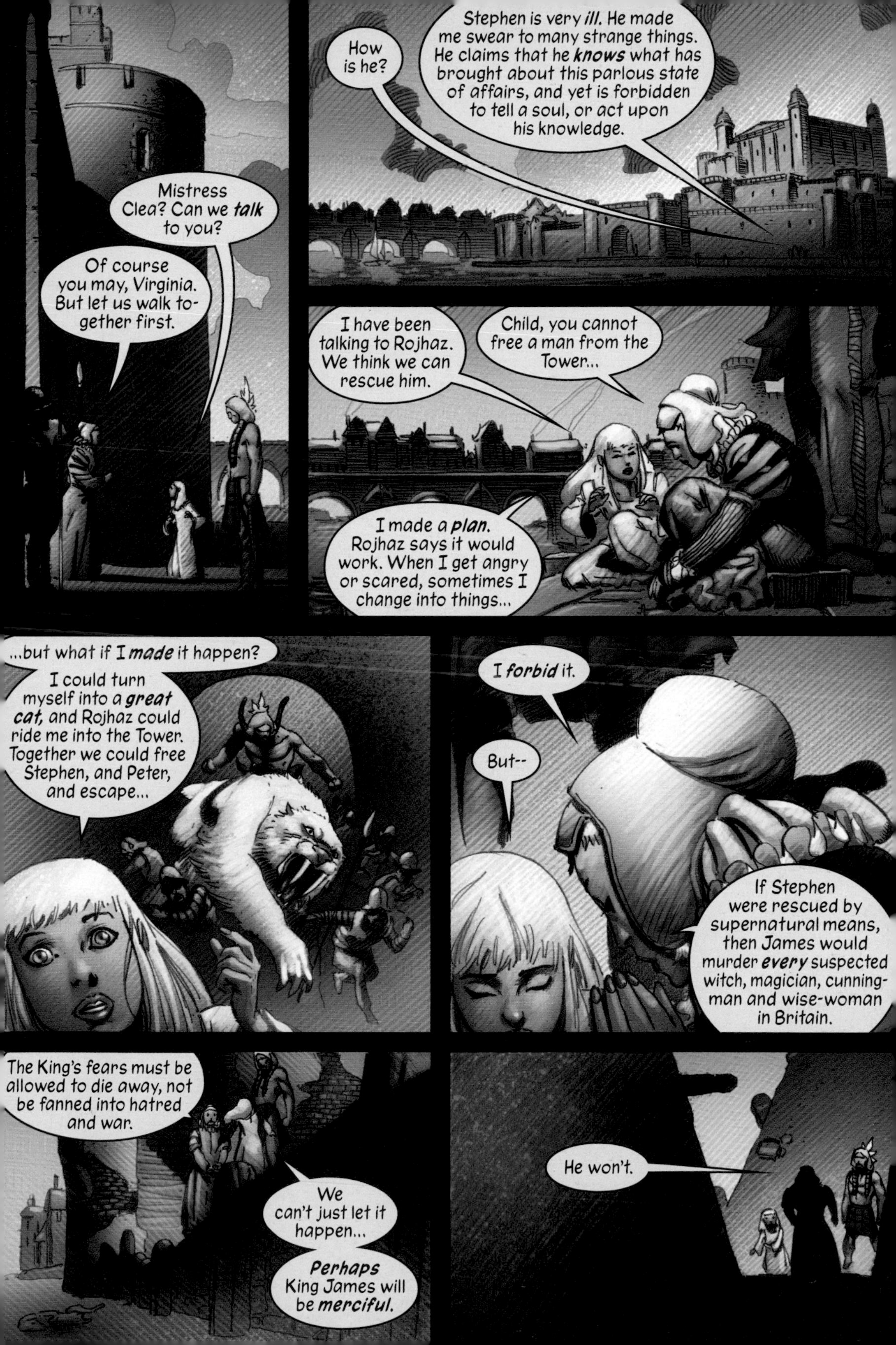
Mistress Clea? Can we *talk* to you?
Of course you may, Virginia. But let us walk together first.
How is he?
Stephen is very *ill*. He made me swear to many strange things. He claims that he ***knows*** what has brought about this parlous state of affairs, and yet is forbidden to tell a soul, or act upon his knowledge.
I have been talking to Rojhaz. We think we can rescue him.
Child, you cannot free a man from the Tower...
I made a ***plan***. Rojhaz says it would work. When I get angry or scared, sometimes I change into things...
...but what if I ***made*** it happen?
I could turn myself into a ***great cat,*** and Rojhaz could ride me into the Tower. Together we could free Stephen, and Peter, and escape...
I ***forbid*** it.
But--
If Stephen were rescued by supernatural means, then James would murder ***every*** suspected witch, magician, cunning-man and wise-woman in Britain.
The King's fears must be allowed to die away, not be fanned into hatred and war.
We can't just let it happen...
Perhaps King James will be ***merciful***.
He won't.

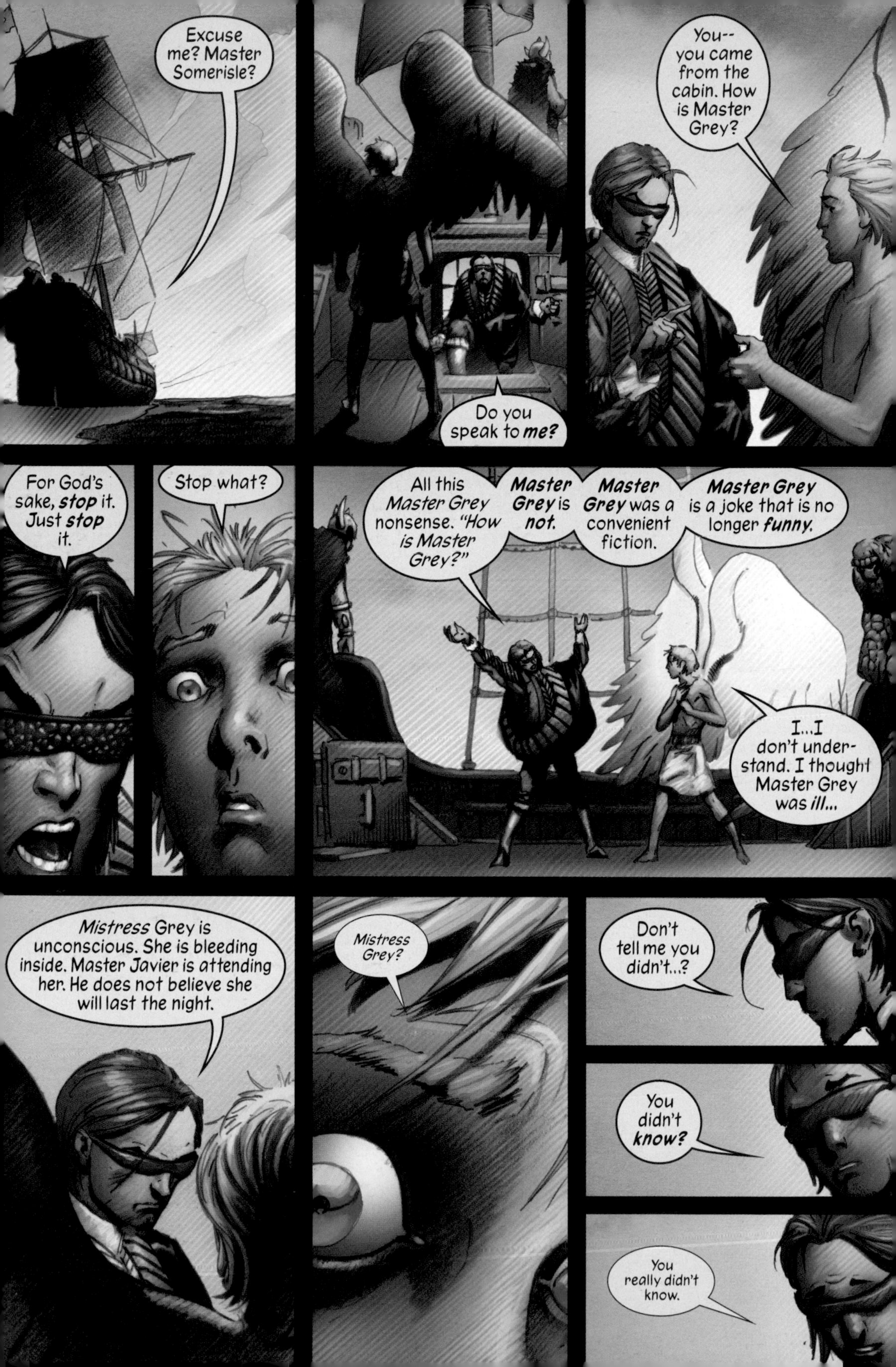

Excuse me? Master Somerisle?
Do you speak to *me?*
You-- you came from the cabin. How is Master Grey?
For God's sake, *stop* it. Just *stop* it.
Stop what?
All this *Master Grey* nonsense. *"How is Master Grey?"*
Master Grey is ***not.***
Master Grey was a convenient fiction.
Master Grey is a joke that is no longer ***funny.***
I...I don't under-stand. I thought Master Grey was *ill...*
Mistress Grey is unconscious. She is bleeding inside. Master Javier is attending her. He does not believe she will last the night.
Mistress Grey?
Don't tell me you didn't...?
You didn't ***know?***
You really didn't know.

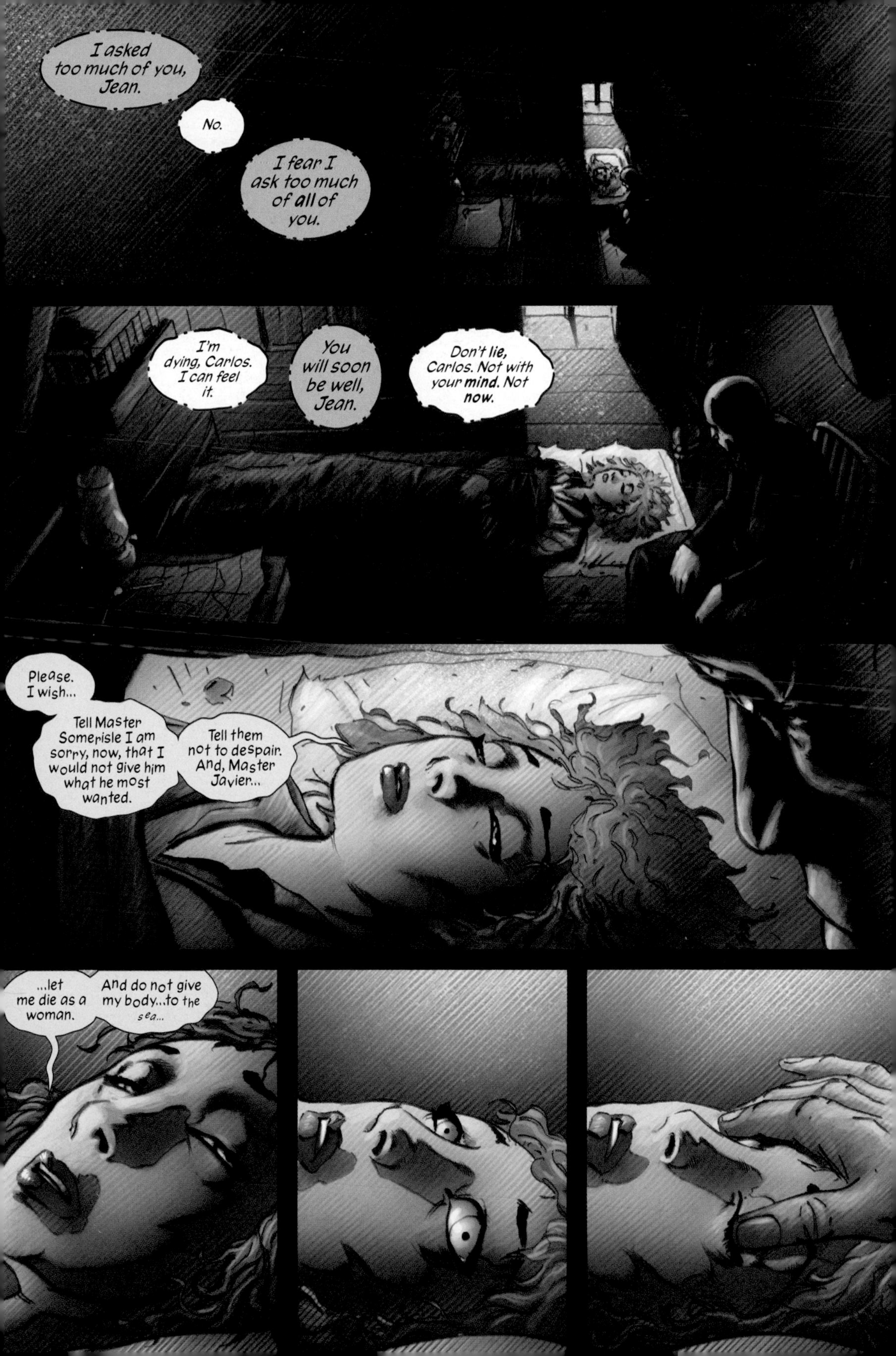
I asked too much of you, Jean.
No.
I fear I ask too much of all of you.
I'm dying, Carlos. I can feel it.
You will soon be well, Jean.
Don't lie, Carlos. Not with your mind. Not now.
Please. I wish...
Tell Master Somerisle I am sorry, now, that I would not give him what he most wanted.
Tell them not to despair. And, Master Javier...
...let me die as a woman.
And do not give my body...to the sea...

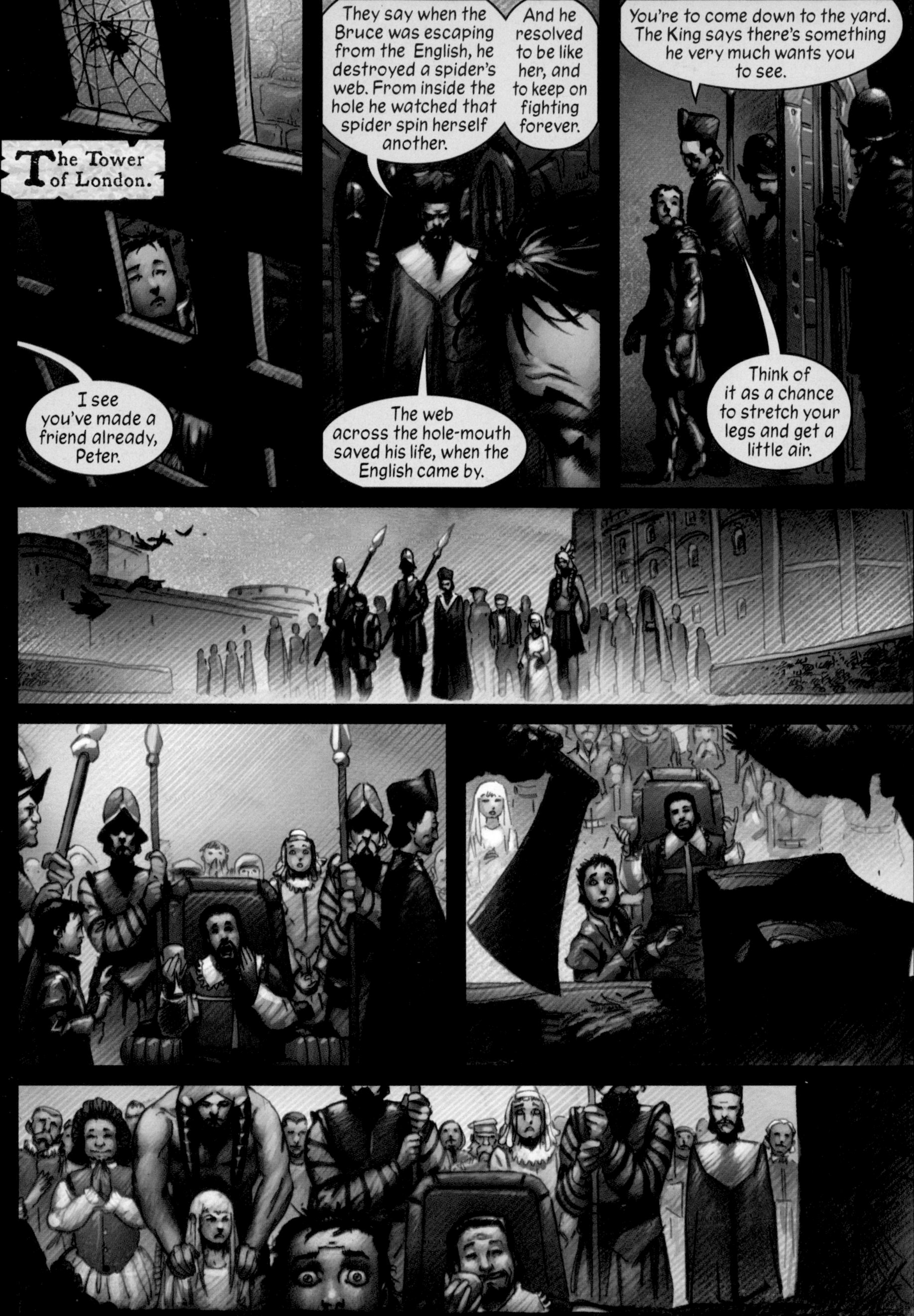
The Tower of London.
I see you've made a friend already, Peter.
They say when the Bruce was escaping from the English, he destroyed a spider's web. From inside the hole he watched that spider spin herself another.
And he resolved to be like her, and to keep on fighting forever.
The web across the hole-mouth saved his life, when the English came by.
You're to come down to the yard. The King says there's something he very much wants you to see.
Think of it as a chance to stretch your legs and get a little air.

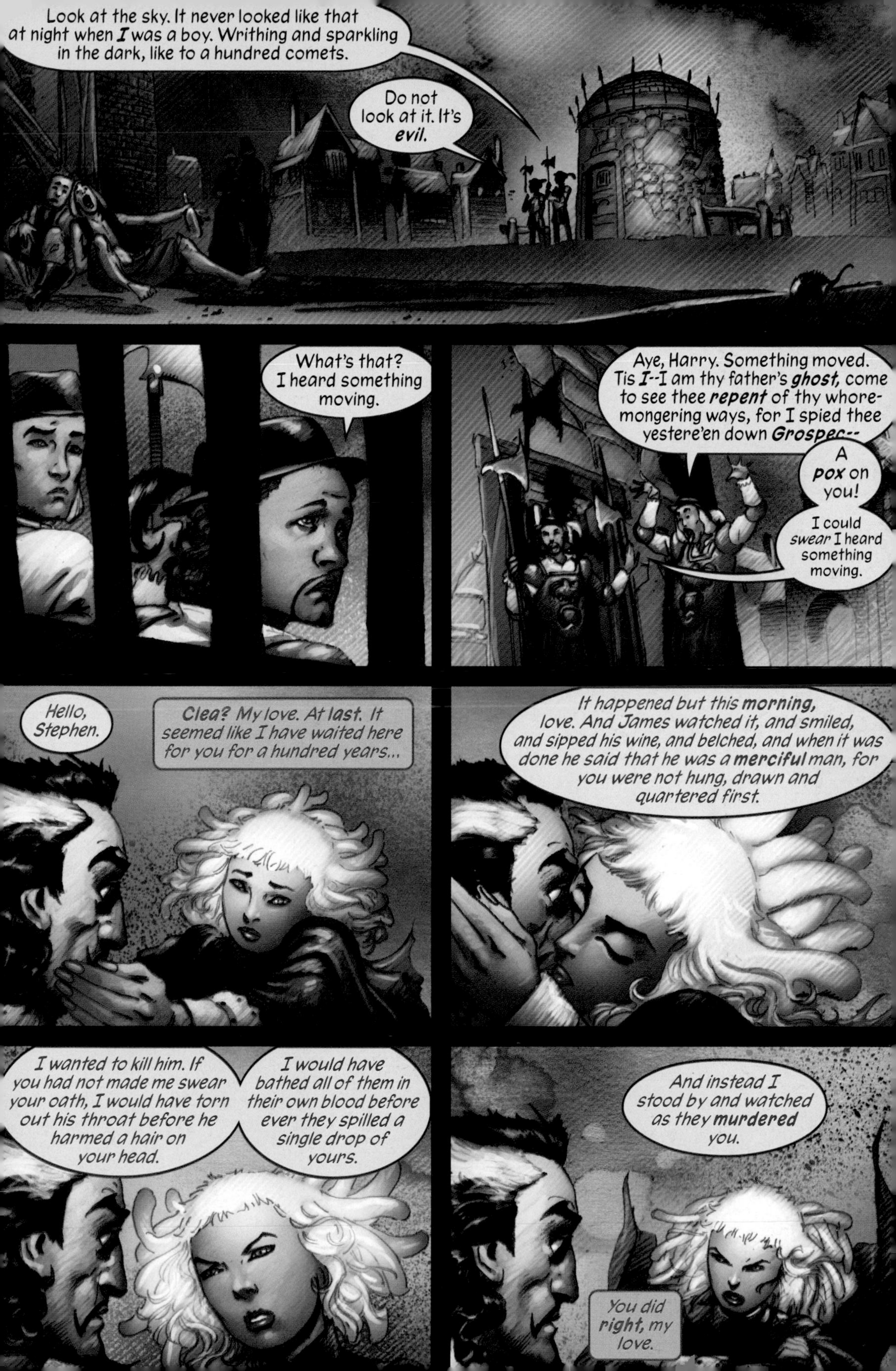
Look at the sky. It never looked like that at night when I was a boy. Writhing and sparkling in the dark, like to a hundred comets.
Do not look at it. It's evil.
What's that? I heard something moving.
Aye, Harry. Something moved. Tis I--I am thy father's ghost, come to see thee repent of thy whore-mongering ways, for I spied thee yestere'en down Grospec--
A pox on you!
I could swear I heard something moving.
Hello, Stephen.
Clea? My love. At last. It seemed like I have waited here for you for a hundred years...
It happened but this morning, love. And James watched it, and smiled, and sipped his wine, and belched, and when it was done he said that he was a merciful man, for you were not hung, drawn and quartered first.
I wanted to kill him. If you had not made me swear your oath, I would have torn out his throat before he harmed a hair on your head.
I would have bathed all of them in their own blood before ever they spilled a single drop of yours.
And instead I stood by and watched as they murdered you.
You did right, my love.

You made me swear. And I **swore**, Stephen, as I swore I would be yours when you freed me, far beyond the veils of this world.

But it hurt me more than anything has ever hurt me.

And I would follow you into the darkness, now. I do not **wish** to stay.

Clea. There is but little time before the darkness takes me... There was a ...**compulsion** placed upon my lips--that I could not speak of what I learned, while I lived.

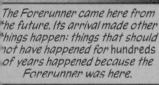

The Forerunner came here from the future. Its arrival made other things happen: things that should not have happened for hundreds of years happened because the Forerunner was here.

As a stone, dropped into a pond, creates ripples that spread, so the Forerunner's presence cast its influence into the past and the future.

The Forerunner is the first. We all follow it...even you. Even me.

You must send the Forerunner back.

When I was a Queen, far from here...

...my people said the dead would speak only in riddles, Stephen.

I am speaking as clearly as I can. It came here from another time. The machine that brought it has already been destroyed.

It must be returned, by the same gate it came through...

You must take it back to America.

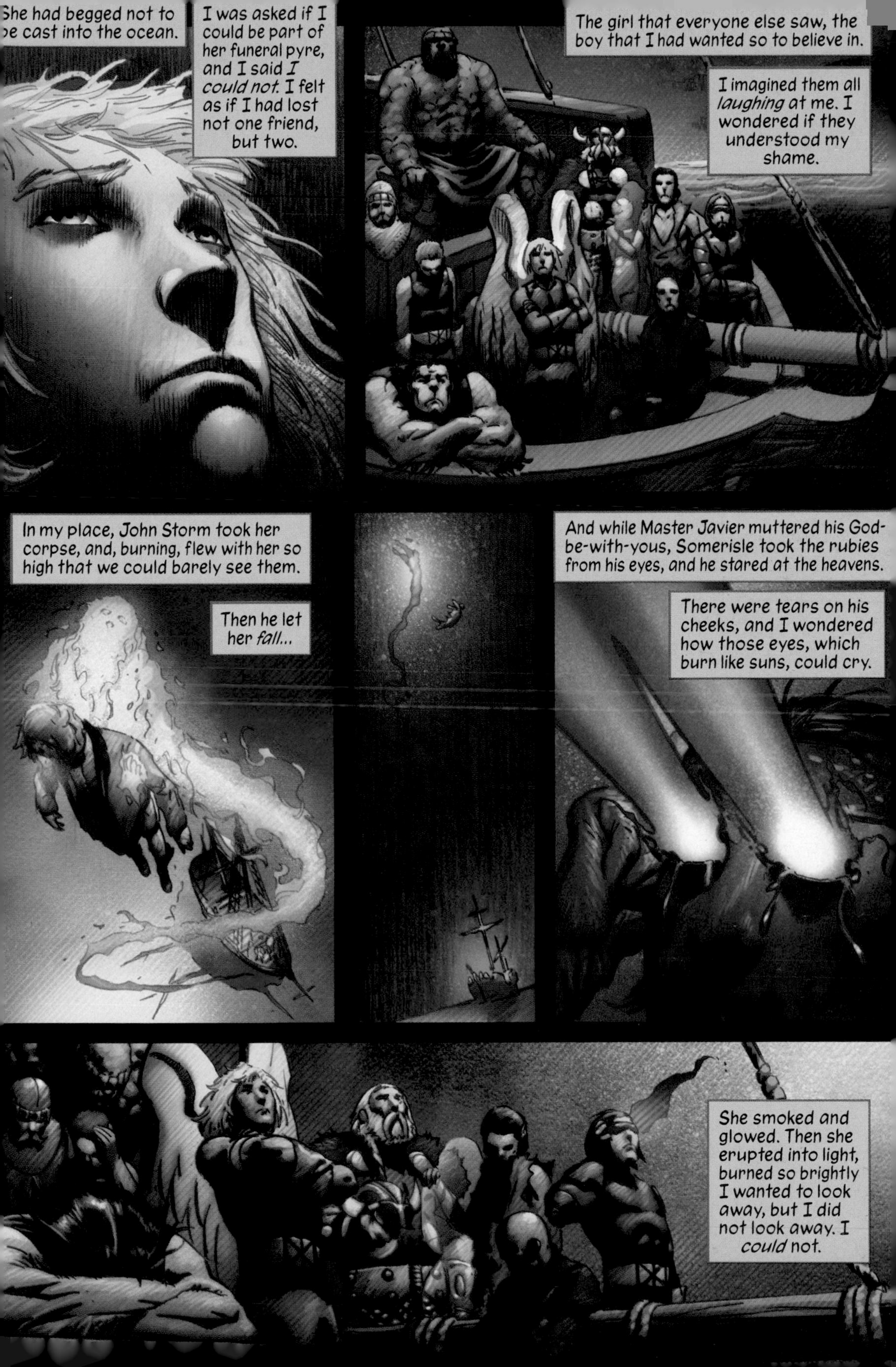
She had begged not to be cast into the ocean.
I was asked if I could be part of her funeral pyre, and I said *I could not.* I felt as if I had lost not one friend, but two.
The girl that everyone else saw, the boy that I had wanted so to believe in.
I imagined them all *laughing* at me. I wondered if they understood my shame.
In my place, John Storm took her corpse, and, burning, flew with her so high that we could barely see them.
Then he let her *fall...*
And while Master Javier muttered his God-be-with-yous, Somerisle took the rubies from his eyes, and he stared at the heavens.
There were tears on his cheeks, and I wondered how those eyes, which burn like suns, could cry.
She smoked and glowed. Then she erupted into light, burned so brightly I wanted to look away, but I did not look away. I *could* not.

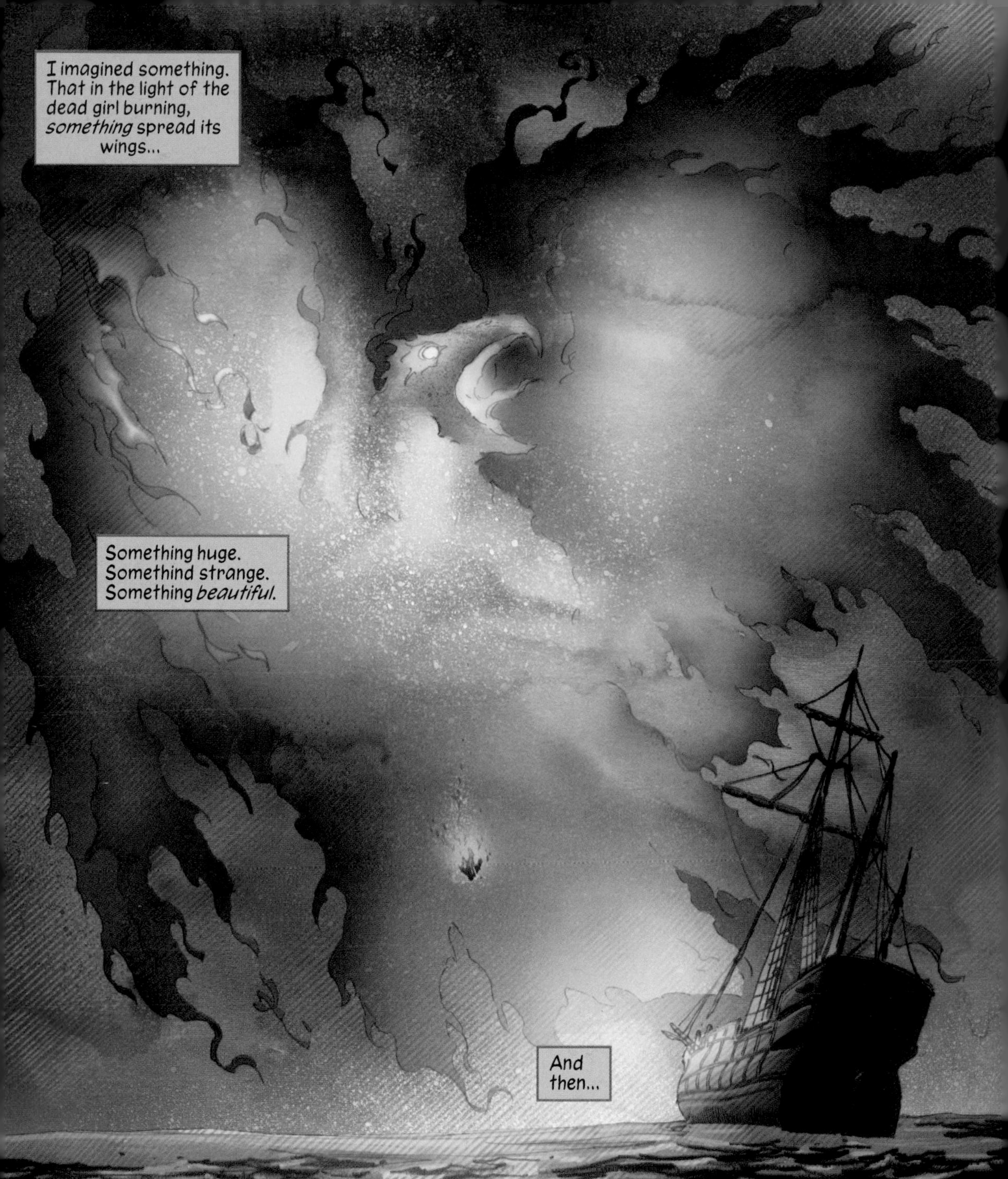
I imagined something. That in the light of the dead girl burning, *something* spread its wings...
Something huge. Somethind strange. Something *beautiful*.
And then...

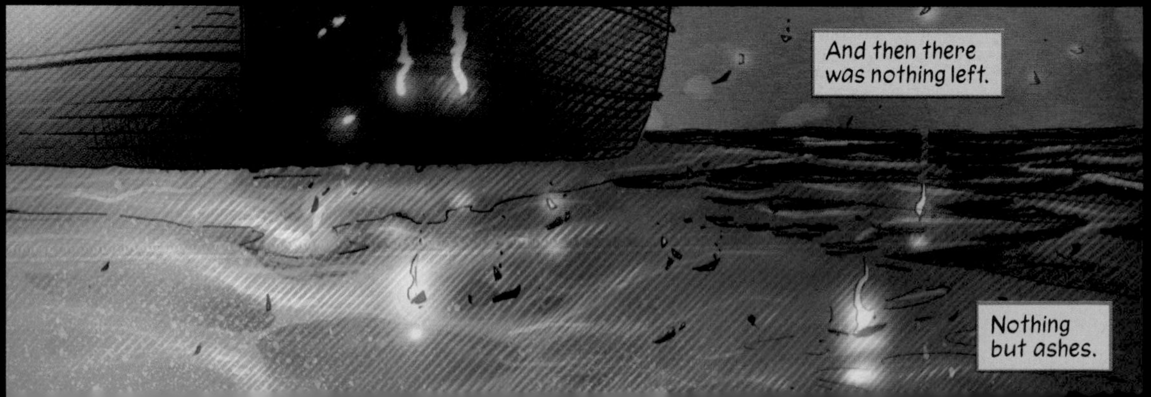
And then there was nothing left.
Nothing but ashes.

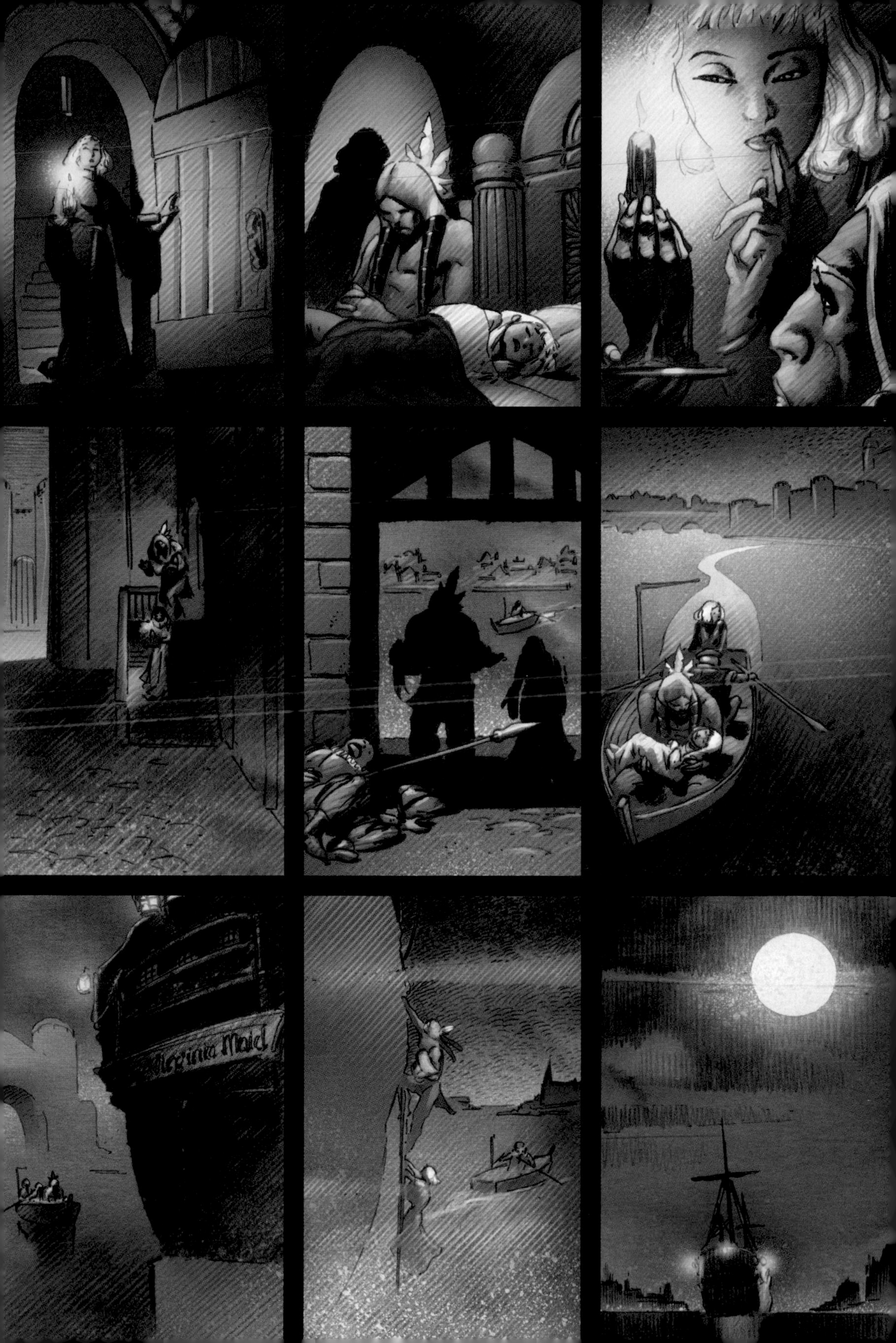
Virginia Maid

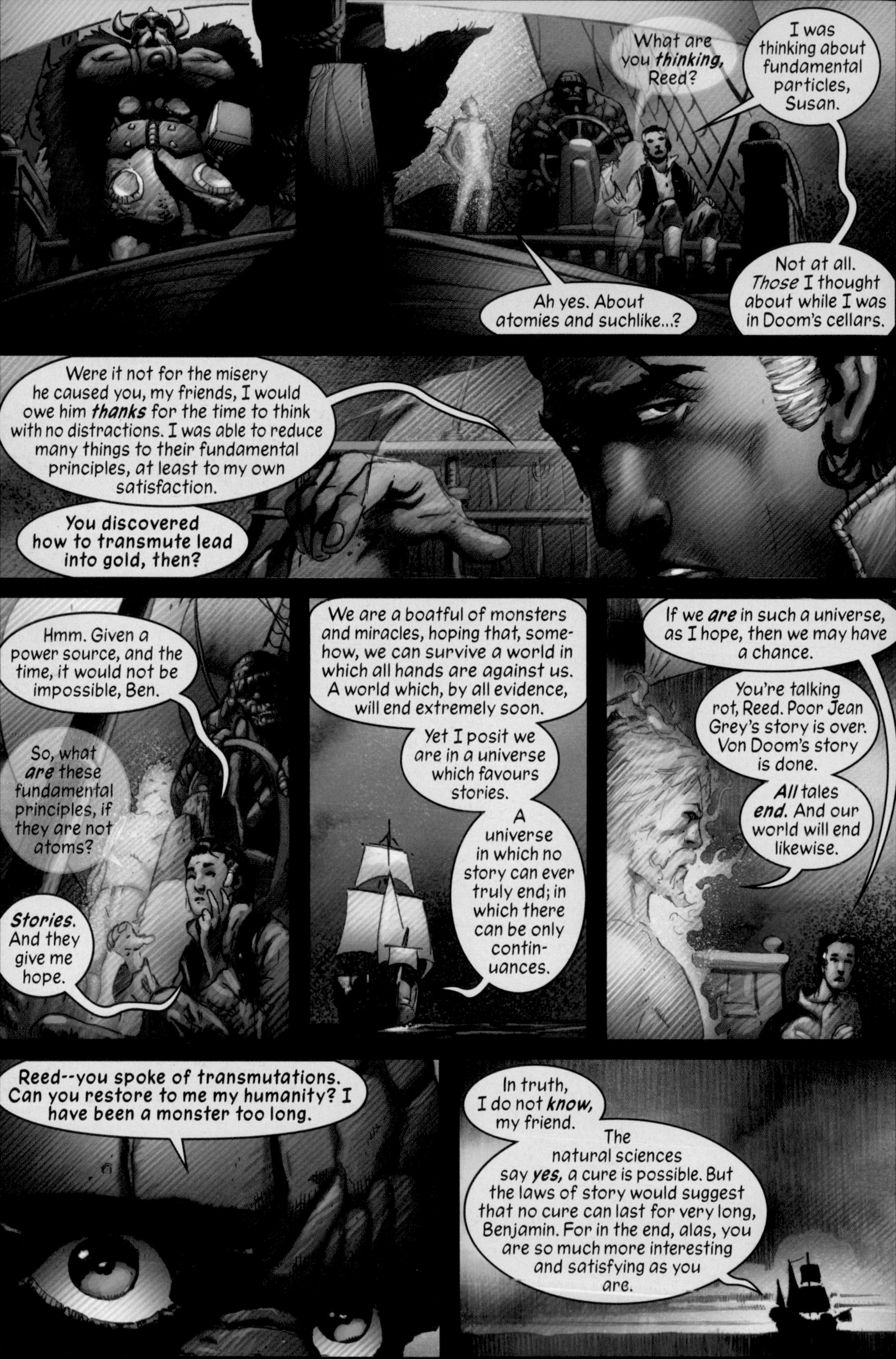
What are you *thinking,* Reed?
I was thinking about fundamental particles, Susan.
Ah yes. About atomies and suchlike...?
Not at all. *Those* I thought about while I was in Doom's cellars.
Were it not for the misery he caused you, my friends, I would owe him **thanks** for the time to think with no distractions. I was able to reduce many things to their fundamental principles, at least to my own satisfaction.
You discovered how to transmute lead into gold, then?
Hmm. Given a power source, and the time, it would not be impossible, Ben.
So, what *are* these fundamental principles, if they are not atoms?
Stories. And they give me hope.
We are a boatful of monsters and miracles, hoping that, somehow, we can survive a world in which all hands are against us. A world which, by all evidence, will end extremely soon.
Yet I posit we are in a universe which favours stories.
A universe in which no story can ever truly end; in which there can be only continuances.
If we *are* in such a universe, as I hope, then we may have a chance.
You're talking rot, Reed. Poor Jean Grey's story is over. Von Doom's story is done.
All tales ***end.*** And our world will end likewise.
Reed--you spoke of transmutations. Can you restore to me my humanity? I have been a monster too long.
In truth, I do not *know,* my friend.
The natural sciences say *yes,* a cure is possible. But the laws of story would suggest that no cure can last for very long, Benjamin. For in the end, alas, you are so much more interesting and satisfying as you are.

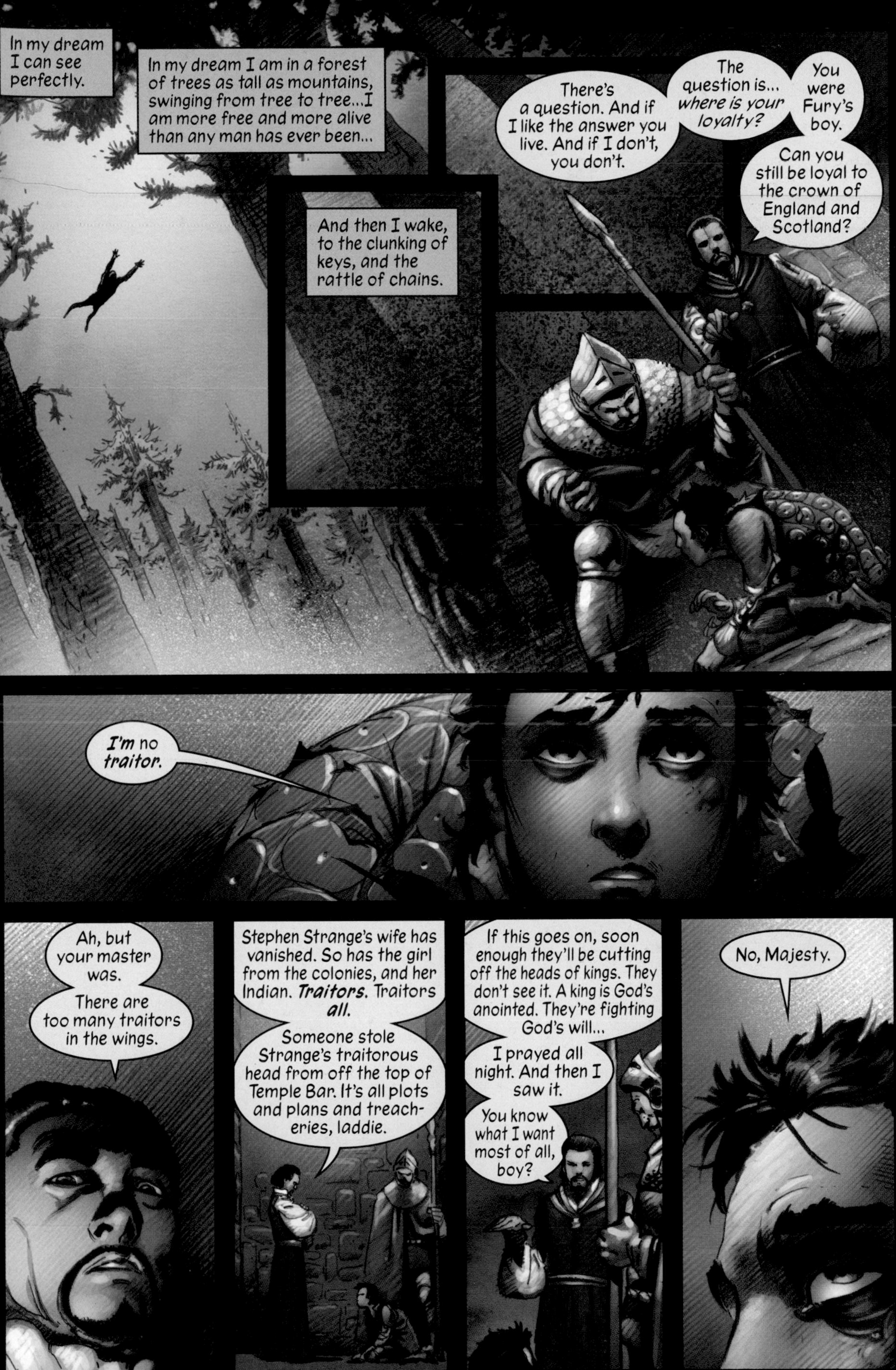

In my dream I can see perfectly.
In my dream I am in a forest of trees as tall as mountains, swinging from tree to tree...I am more free and more alive than any man has ever been...
And then I wake, to the clunking of keys, and the rattle of chains.
There's a question. And if I like the answer you live. And if I don't, you don't.
The question is... *where is your loyalty?*
You were Fury's boy.
Can you still be loyal to the crown of England and Scotland?
I'm no ***traitor.***
Ah, but your master was.
There are too many traitors in the wings.
Stephen Strange's wife has vanished. So has the girl from the colonies, and her Indian. ***Traitors.*** Traitors ***all.***
Someone stole Strange's traitorous head from off the top of Temple Bar. It's all plots and plans and treacheries, laddie.
If this goes on, soon enough they'll be cutting off the heads of kings. They don't see it. A king is God's anointed. They're fighting God's will...
I prayed all night. And then I saw it.
You know what I want most of all, boy?
No, Majesty.

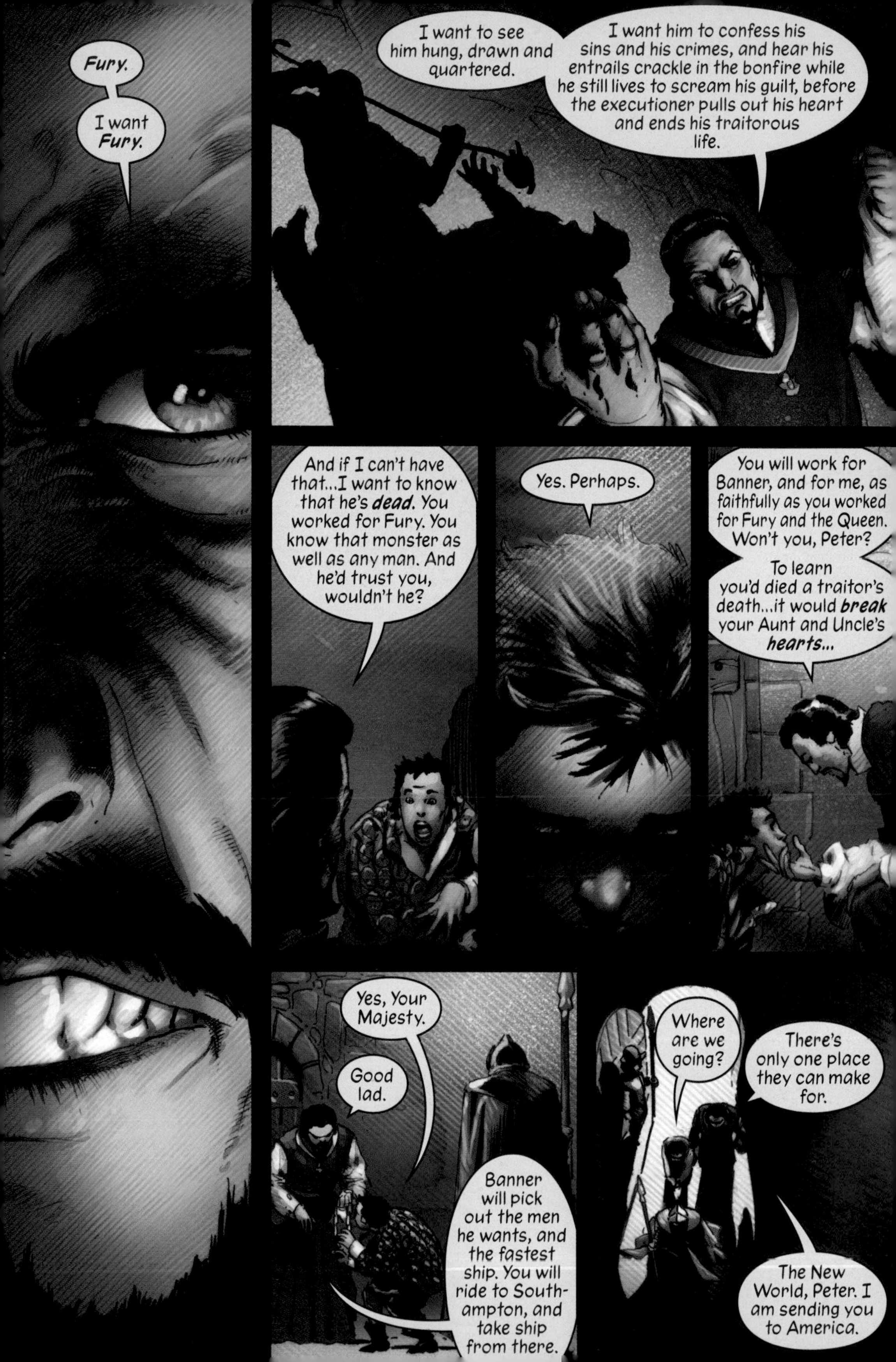

Fury.
I want *Fury.*
I want to see him hung, drawn and quartered.
I want him to confess his sins and his crimes, and hear his entrails crackle in the bonfire while he still lives to scream his guilt, before the executioner pulls out his heart and ends his traitorous life.
And if I can't have that...I want to know that he's ***dead.*** You worked for Fury. You know that monster as well as any man. And he'd trust you, wouldn't he?
Yes. Perhaps.
You will work for Banner, and for me, as faithfully as you worked for Fury and the Queen. Won't you, Peter?
To learn you'd died a traitor's death...it would ***break*** your Aunt and Uncle's ***hearts...***
Yes, Your Majesty.
Good lad.
Banner will pick out the men he wants, and the fastest ship. You will ride to South-ampton, and take ship from there.
Where are we going?
There's only one place they can make for.
The New World, Peter. I am sending you to America.

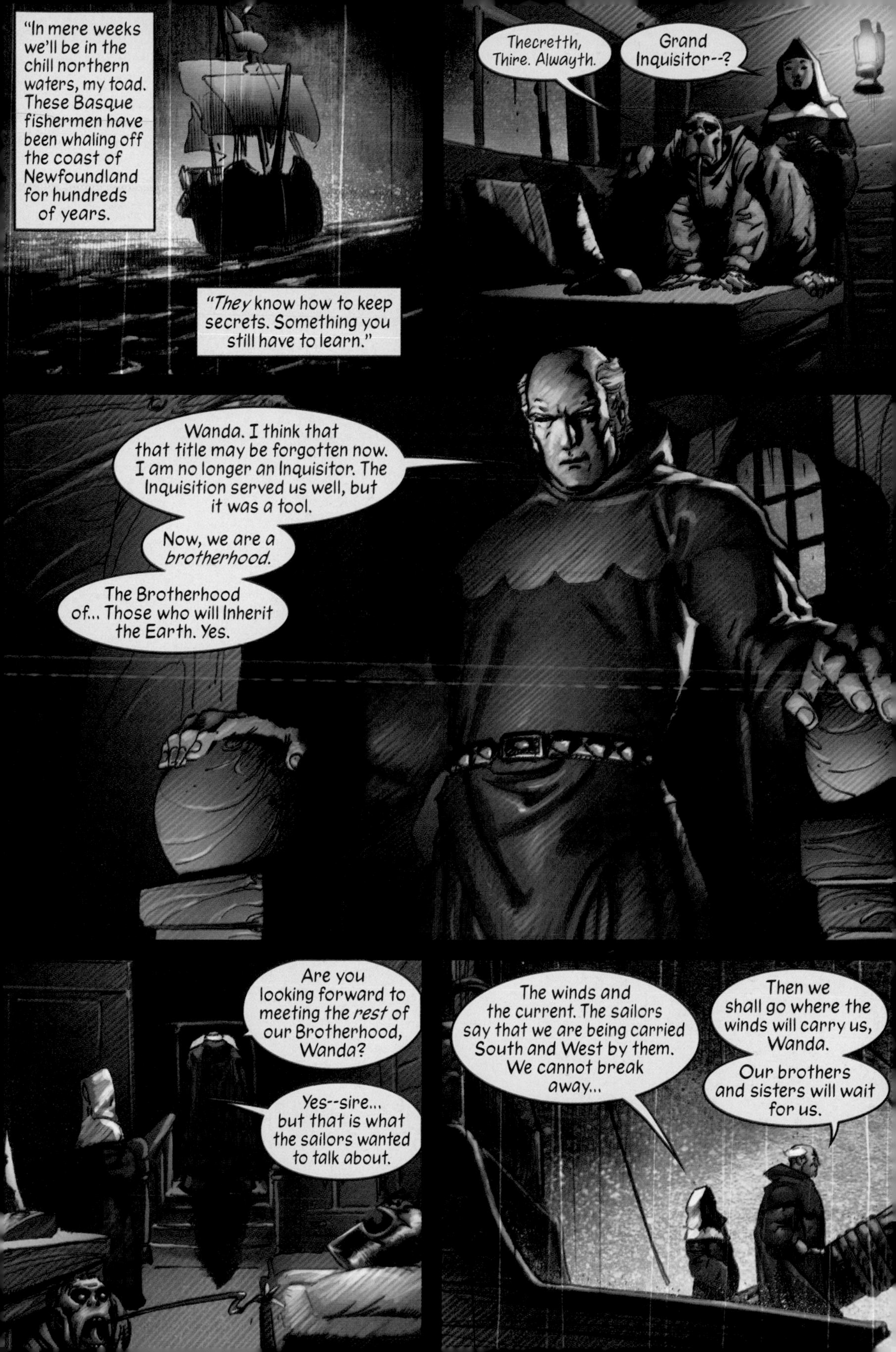
"In mere weeks we'll be in the chill northern waters, my toad. These Basque fishermen have been whaling off the coast of Newfoundland for hundreds of years.
"*They* know how to keep secrets. Something you still have to learn."
Thecretth, Thire. Alwayth.
Grand Inquisitor--?
Wanda. I think that that title may be forgotten now. I am no longer an Inquisitor. The Inquisition served us well, but it was a tool.
Now, we are a *brotherhood*.
The Brotherhood of... Those who will Inherit the Earth. Yes.
Are you looking forward to meeting the *rest* of our Brotherhood, Wanda?
Yes--sire... but that is what the sailors wanted to talk about.
The winds and the current. The sailors say that we are being carried South and West by them. We cannot break away...
Then we shall go where the winds will carry us, Wanda.
Our brothers and sisters will wait for us.

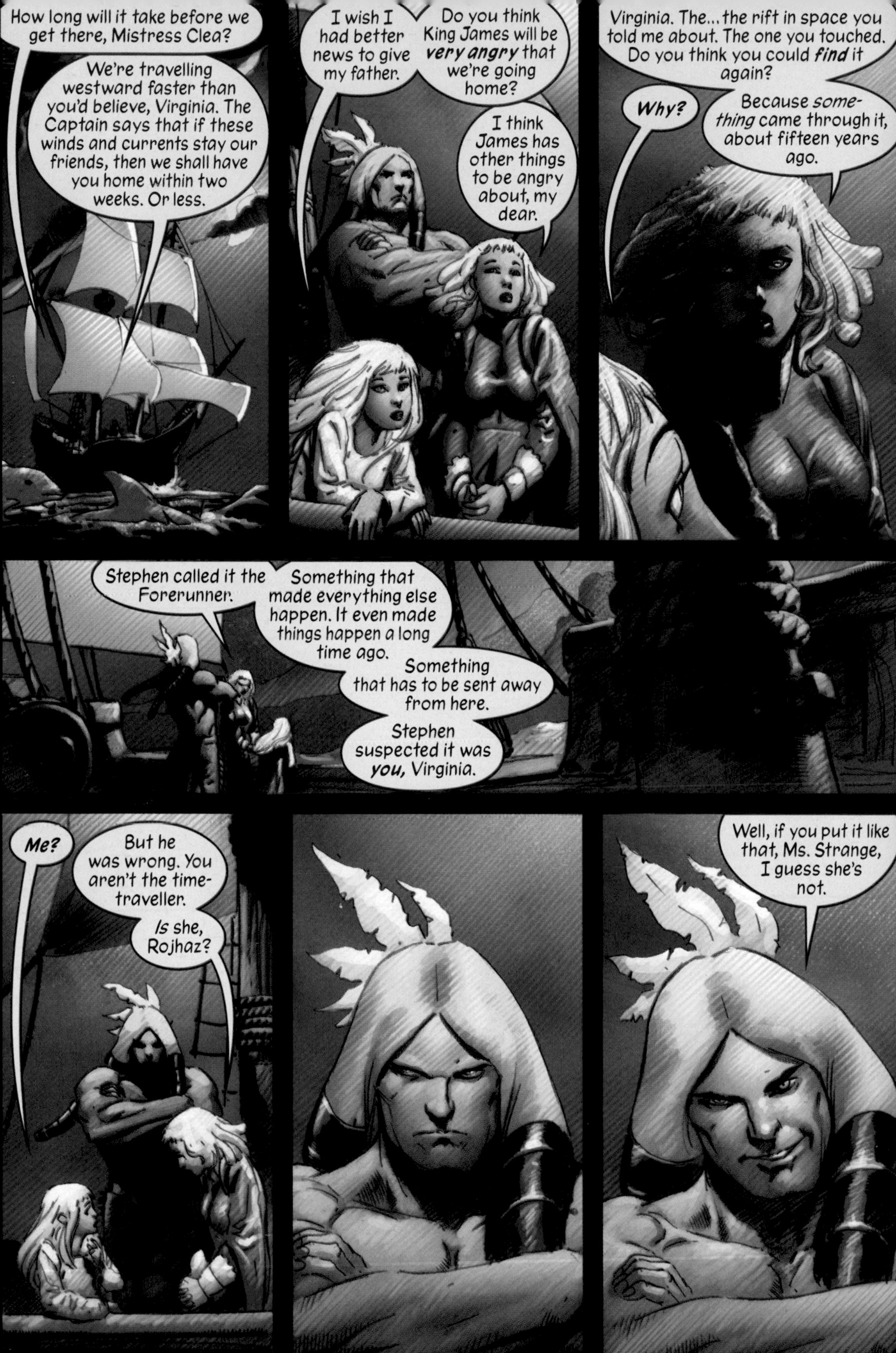
How long will it take before we get there, Mistress Clea?
We're travelling westward faster than you'd believe, Virginia. The Captain says that if these winds and currents stay our friends, then we shall have you home within two weeks. Or less.
I wish I had better news to give my father.
Do you think King James will be *very angry* that we're going home?
I think James has other things to be angry about, my dear.
Virginia. The... the rift in space you told me about. The one you touched. Do you think you could *find* it again?
Why?
Because *some-thing* came through it, about fifteen years ago.
Stephen called it the Forerunner.
Something that made everything else happen. It even made things happen a long time ago.
Something that has to be sent away from here.
Stephen suspected it was *you,* Virginia.
Me?
But he was wrong. You aren't the time-traveller.
Is she, Rojhaz?
Well, if you put it like that, Ms. Strange, I guess she's not.

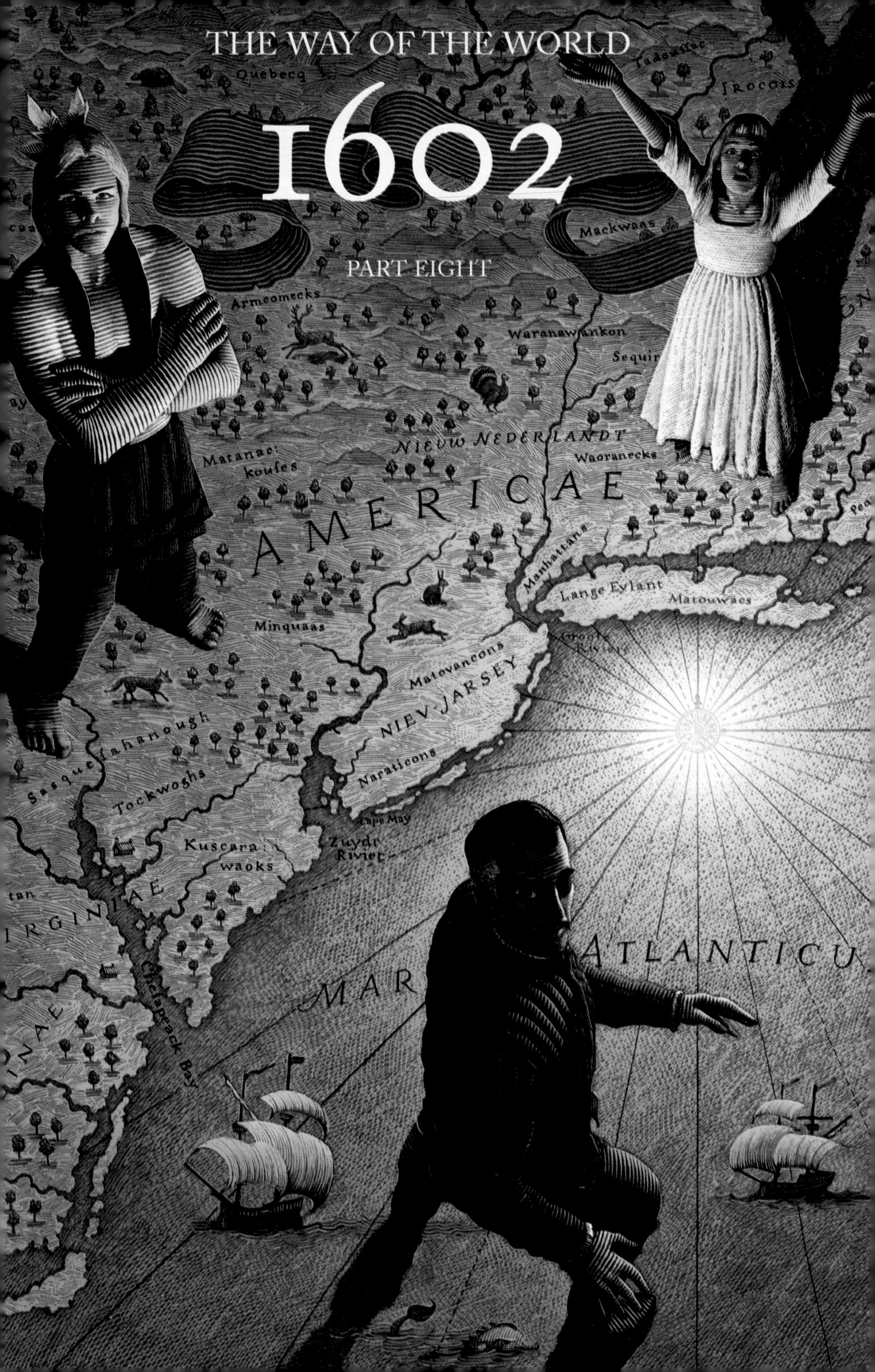
THE WAY OF THE WORLD
1602
PART EIGHT
Quebecq
Mackwaas
Armeomecks
Waranawankon
NIEUW NEDERLANDT
Waeranecks
Matanae: koufes
AMERICAE
Manhattans
Lange Eylant
Matouwaes
Minquaas
Matovancons
NIEV JARSEY
Tockwoghs
Naraticons
Cape May
Kuscarawaoks
Zuydr Riviet
Chesapeack Bay
MAR
ATLANTICU

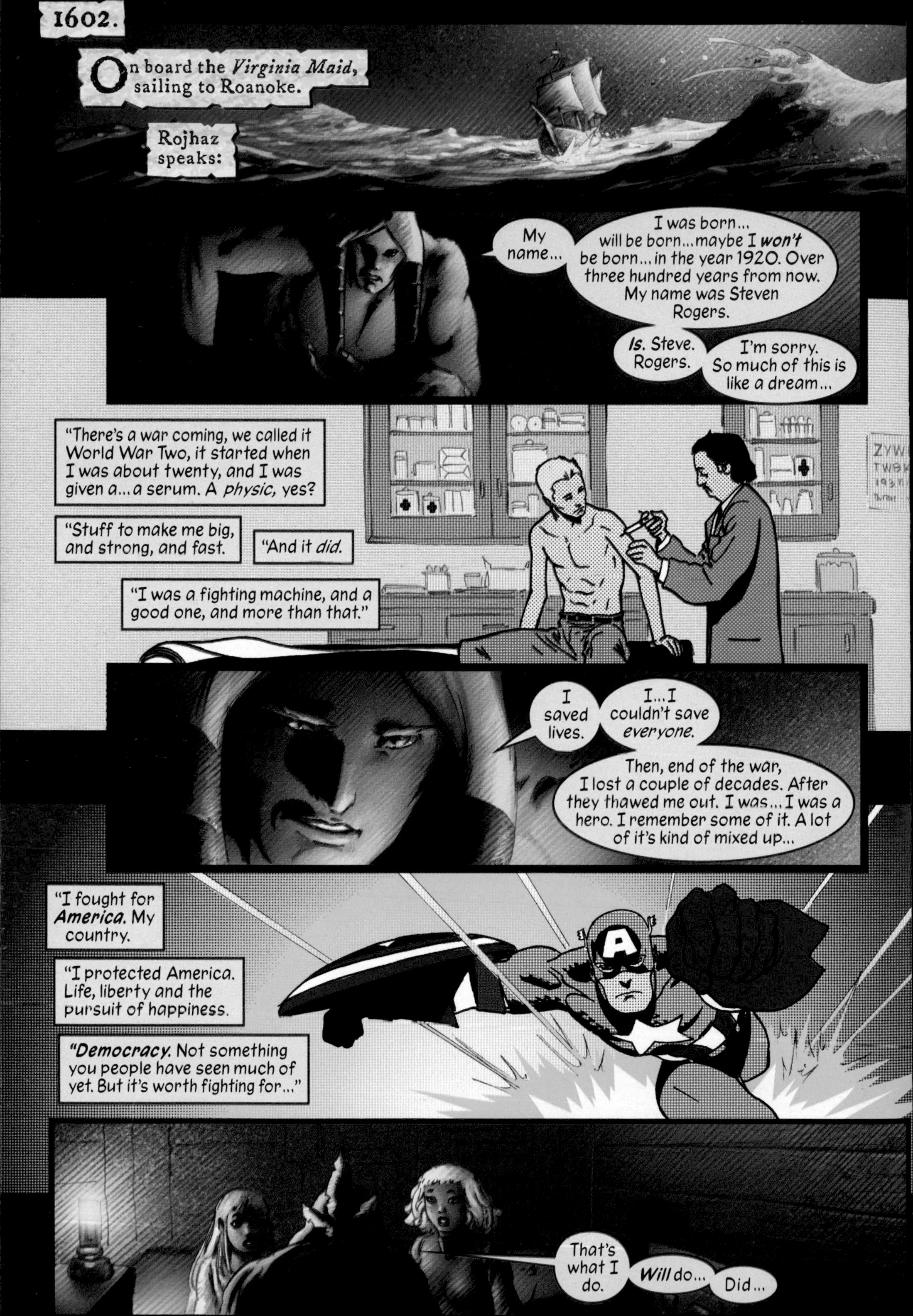
1602.
On board the Virginia Maid, sailing to Roanoke.
Rojhaz speaks:
My name...
I was born... will be born... maybe I won't be born... in the year 1920. Over three hundred years from now. My name was Steven Rogers.
Is. Steve. Rogers.
I'm sorry. So much of this is like a dream...
"There's a war coming, we called it World War Two, it started when I was about twenty, and I was given a... a serum. A physic, yes?
"Stuff to make me big, and strong, and fast.
"And it did.
"I was a fighting machine, and a good one, and more than that."
I saved lives.
I... I couldn't save everyone.
Then, end of the war, I lost a couple of decades. After they thawed me out. I was... I was a hero. I remember some of it. A lot of it's kind of mixed up...
"I fought for America. My country.
"I protected America. Life, liberty and the pursuit of happiness.
"Democracy. Not something you people have seen much of yet. But it's worth fighting for..."
That's what I do.
Will do...
Did...

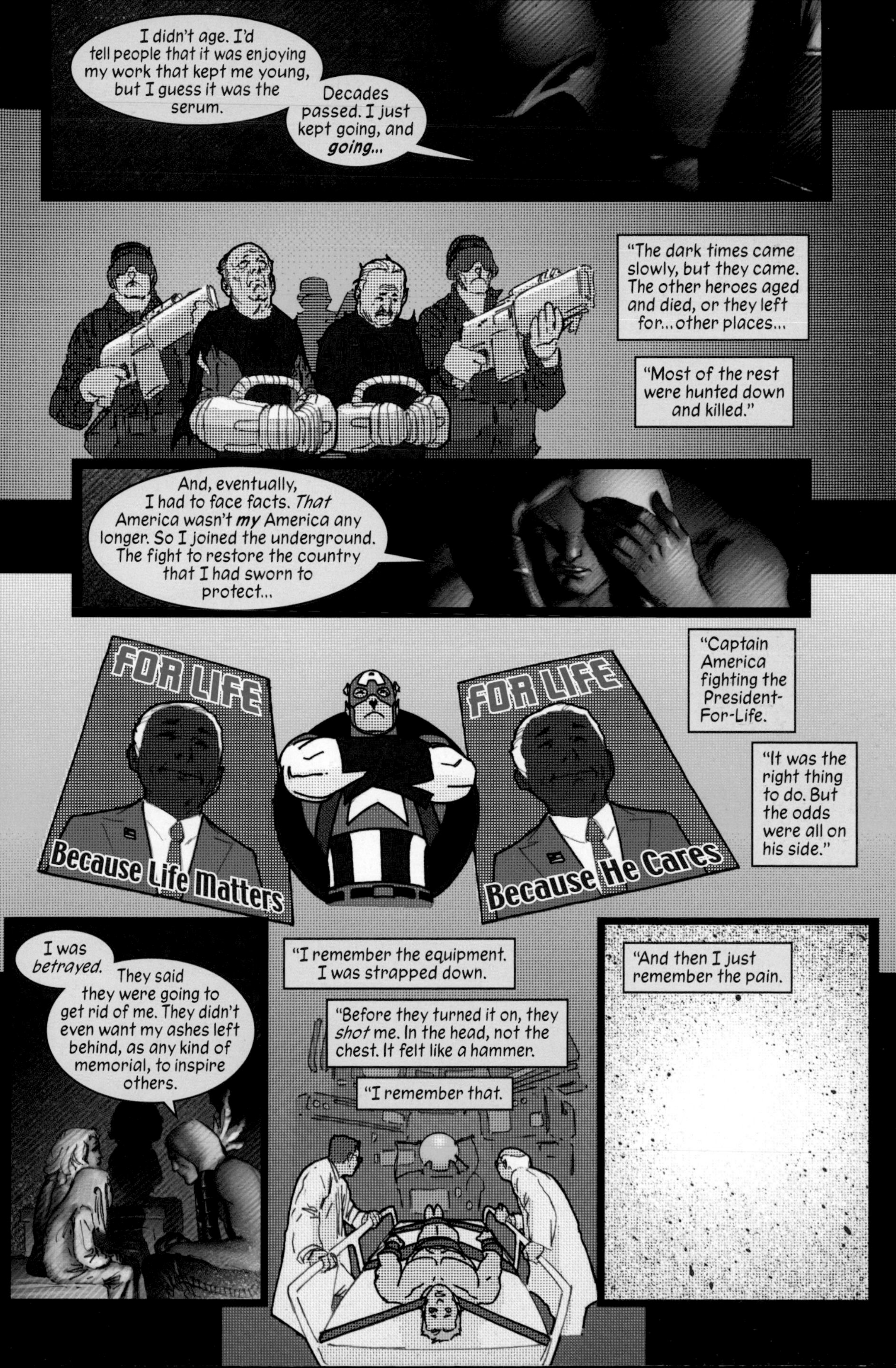
I didn't age. I'd tell people that it was enjoying my work that kept me young, but I guess it was the serum.
Decades passed. I just kept going, and *going*...
"The dark times came slowly, but they came. The other heroes aged and died, or they left for...other places...
"Most of the rest were hunted down and killed."
And, eventually, I had to face facts. *That* America wasn't *my* America any longer. So I joined the underground. The fight to restore the country that I had sworn to protect...
FOR LIFE
Because Life Matters
FOR LIFE
Because He Cares
"Captain America fighting the President-For-Life.
"It was the right thing to do. But the odds were all on his side."
I was *betrayed.* They said they were going to get rid of me. They didn't even want my ashes left behind, as any kind of memorial, to inspire others.
"I remember the equipment. I was strapped down.
"Before they turned it on, they *shot* me. In the head, not the chest. It felt like a hammer.
"I remember that.
"And then I just remember the pain.

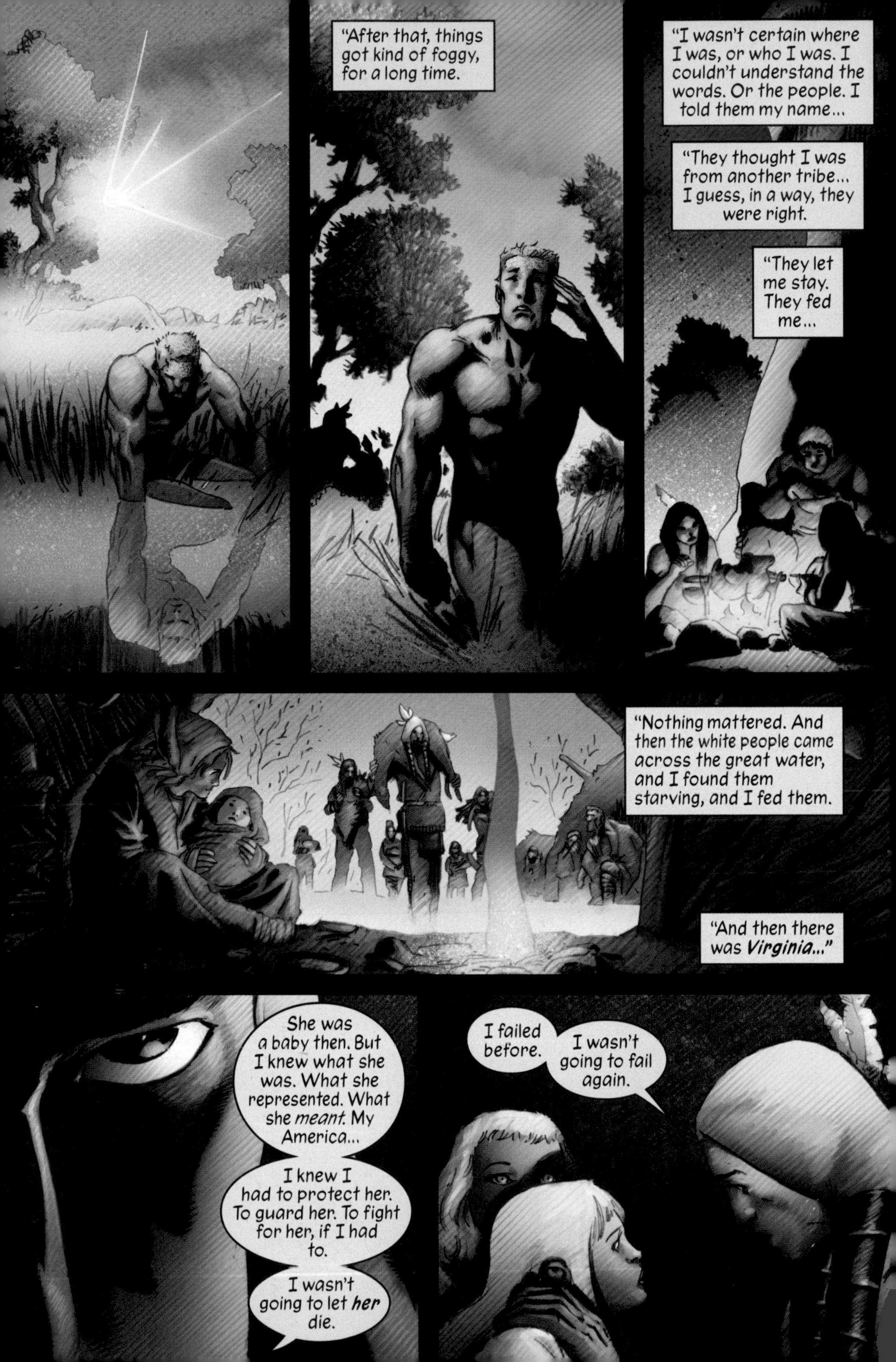
"After that, things got kind of foggy, for a long time.
"I wasn't certain where I was, or who I was. I couldn't understand the words. Or the people. I told them my name...
"They thought I was from another tribe... I guess, in a way, they were right.
"They let me stay. They fed me...
"Nothing mattered. And then the white people came across the great water, and I found them starving, and I fed them.
"And then there was *Virginia...*"
She was a baby then. But I knew what she was. What she represented. What she *meant.* My America...
I knew I had to protect her. To guard her. To fight for her, if I had to.
I wasn't going to let *her* die.
I failed before.
I wasn't going to fail again.

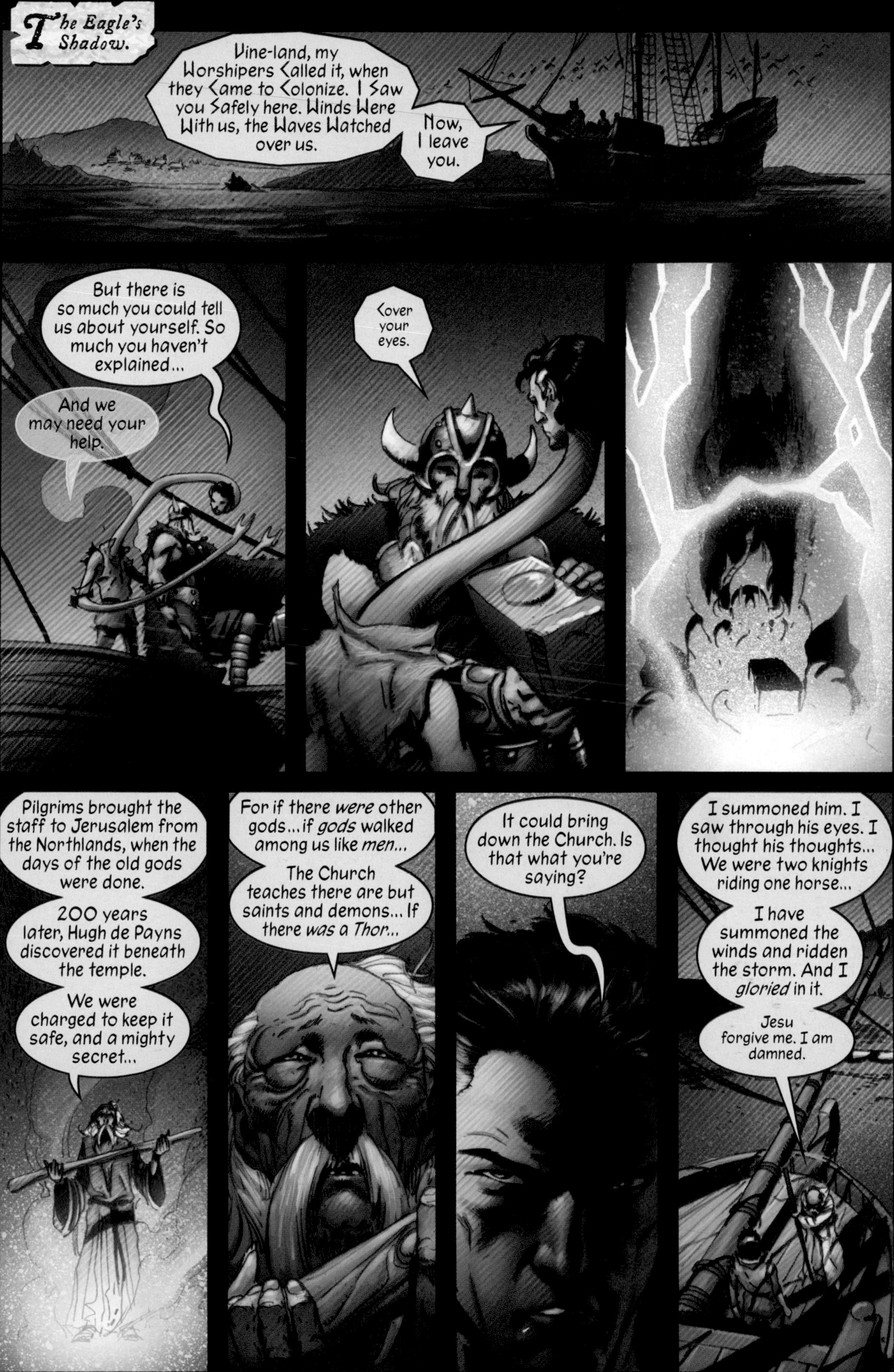
The Eagle's Shadow.
Vine-land, my Worshipers Called it, when they Came to Colonize. I Saw you Safely here. Winds Were With us, the Waves Watched over us.
Now, I leave you.
But there is so much you could tell us about yourself. So much you haven't explained...
And we may need your help.
Cover your eyes.
Pilgrims brought the staff to Jerusalem from the Northlands, when the days of the old gods were done.
200 years later, Hugh de Payns discovered it beneath the temple.
We were charged to keep it safe, and a mighty secret...
For if there *were* other gods... if *gods* walked among us like *men*...
The Church teaches there are but saints and demons... If there *was a Thor*...
It could bring down the Church. Is that what you're saying?
I summoned him. I saw through his eyes. I thought his thoughts... We were two knights riding one horse...
I have summoned the winds and ridden the storm. And I *gloried* in it.
Jesu forgive me. I am damned.

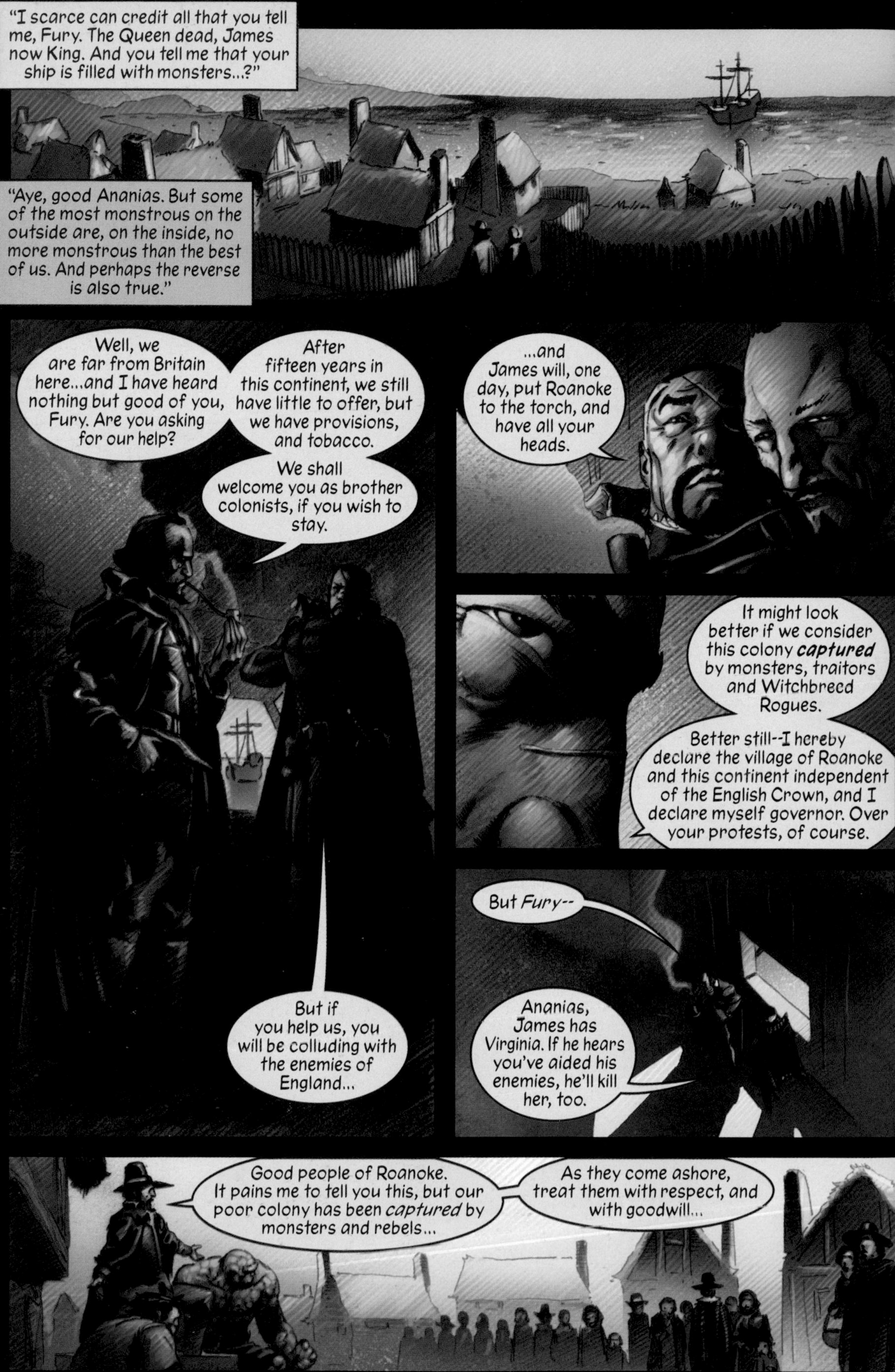
"I scarce can credit all that you tell me, Fury. The Queen dead, James now King. And you tell me that your ship is filled with monsters...?"
"Aye, good Ananias. But some of the most monstrous on the outside are, on the inside, no more monstrous than the best of us. And perhaps the reverse is also true."
Well, we are far from Britain here...and I have heard nothing but good of you, Fury. Are you asking for our help?
After fifteen years in this continent, we still have little to offer, but we have provisions, and tobacco.
We shall welcome you as brother colonists, if you wish to stay.
But if you help us, you will be colluding with the enemies of England...
...and James will, one day, put Roanoke to the torch, and have all your heads.
It might look better if we consider this colony *captured* by monsters, traitors and Witchbreed Rogues.
Better still--I hereby declare the village of Roanoke and this continent independent of the English Crown, and I declare myself governor. Over your protests, of course.
But *Fury*--
Ananias, James has Virginia. If he hears you've aided his enemies, he'll kill her, too.
Good people of Roanoke. It pains me to tell you this, but our poor colony has been *captured* by monsters and rebels...
As they come ashore, treat them with respect, and with goodwill...

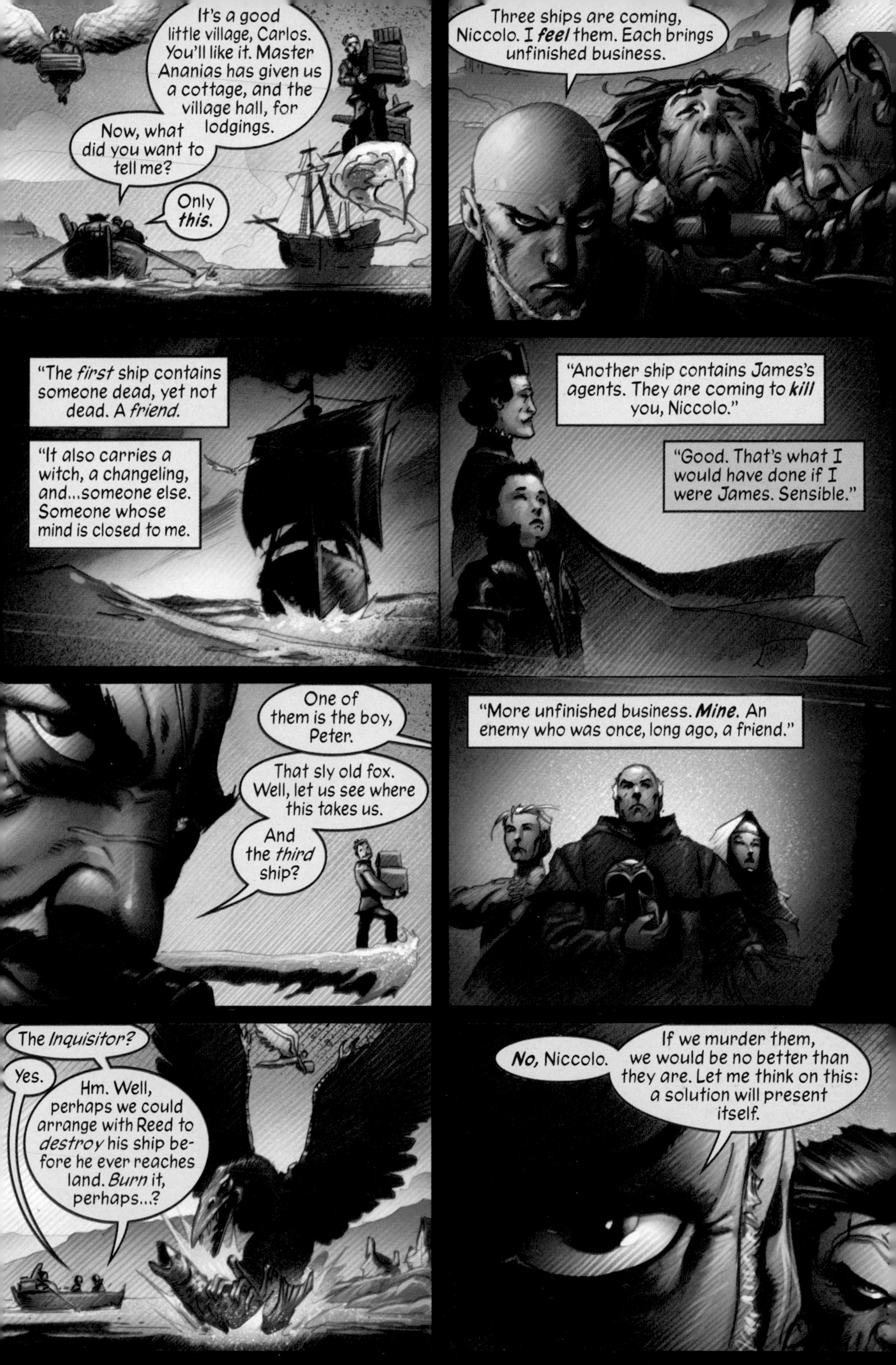
It's a good little village, Carlos. You'll like it. Master Ananias has given us a cottage, and the village hall, for lodgings.
Now, what did you want to tell me?
Only *this.*
Three ships are coming, Niccolo. I *feel* them. Each brings unfinished business.
"The *first* ship contains someone dead, yet not dead. A *friend.*
"It also carries a witch, a changeling, and...someone else. Someone whose mind is closed to me.
"Another ship contains James's agents. They are coming to ***kill*** you, Niccolo."
"Good. That's what I would have done if I were James. Sensible."
One of them is the boy, Peter.
That sly old fox. Well, let us see where this takes us.
And the *third* ship?
"More unfinished business. ***Mine.*** An enemy who was once, long ago, a friend."
The *Inquisitor?*
Yes.
Hm. Well, perhaps we could arrange with Reed to *destroy* his ship before he ever reaches land. *Burn* it, perhaps...?
No, Niccolo.
If we murder them, we would be no better than they are. Let me think on this: a solution will present itself.

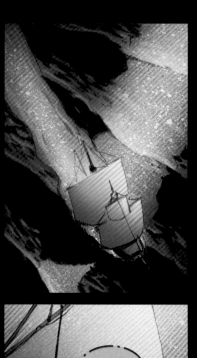

Wake up, Enrico.

Hello, Carlos. You must be close, to be so loud in my head.

So. You did not destroy the helmet I made you.

No.

I presume that you are coming here to kill us. Or do you still dream of persuading me to help you in your madness?

I do not come to kill you, Carlos.

I was on my own voyage for my own purposes when the currents pulled me here.

And you expect me to believe that?

Believe what you like.

Tell me, Carlos. Have the *mondani* embraced you, yet? Proclaimed you and your breed their superiors? Or do they hate you more than ever?

Enrico, you are like a lute player, who only knows one tune and plays it over and over.

Has your church yet realized that the man who they trust to seek out and burn their Witchbreed only burns those it suits him to burn?

I am afraid the answer to that is yes. They found out.

Petros! Wake your sister. They're *trying* something. Javier and his damned breed. Get up on deck...

I am afraid it is too late for that, Enrico.

Cold. Tho cold. Thleepy...

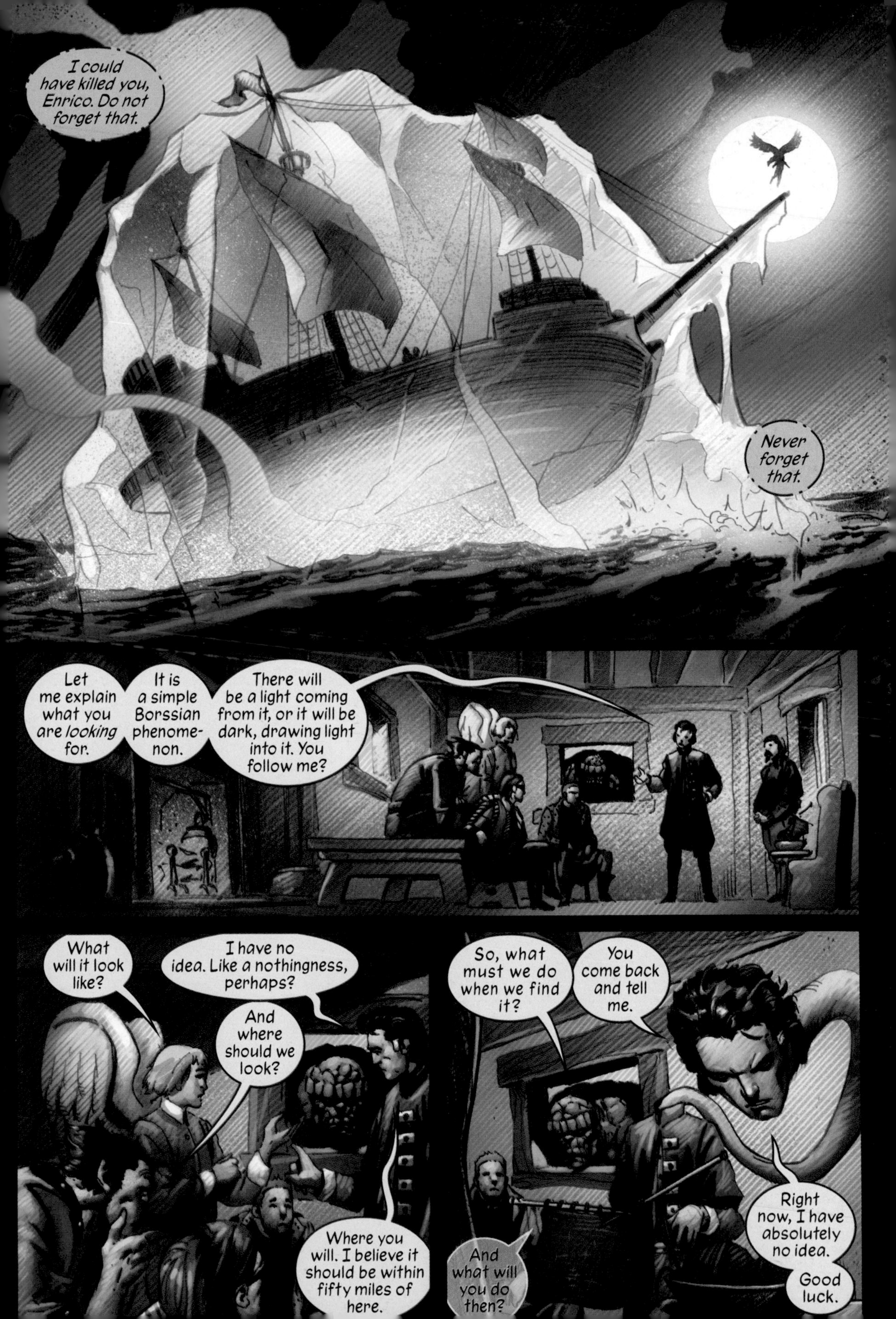
I could have killed you, Enrico. Do not forget that.
Never forget that.
Let me explain what you are *looking* for.
It is a simple Borssian phenomenon.
There will be a light coming from it, or it will be dark, drawing light into it. You follow me?
What will it look like?
I have no idea. Like a nothingness, perhaps?
And where should we look?
Where you will. I believe it should be within fifty miles of here.
So, what must we do when we find it?
You come back and tell me.
And what will you do then?
Right now, I have absolutely no idea.
Good luck.

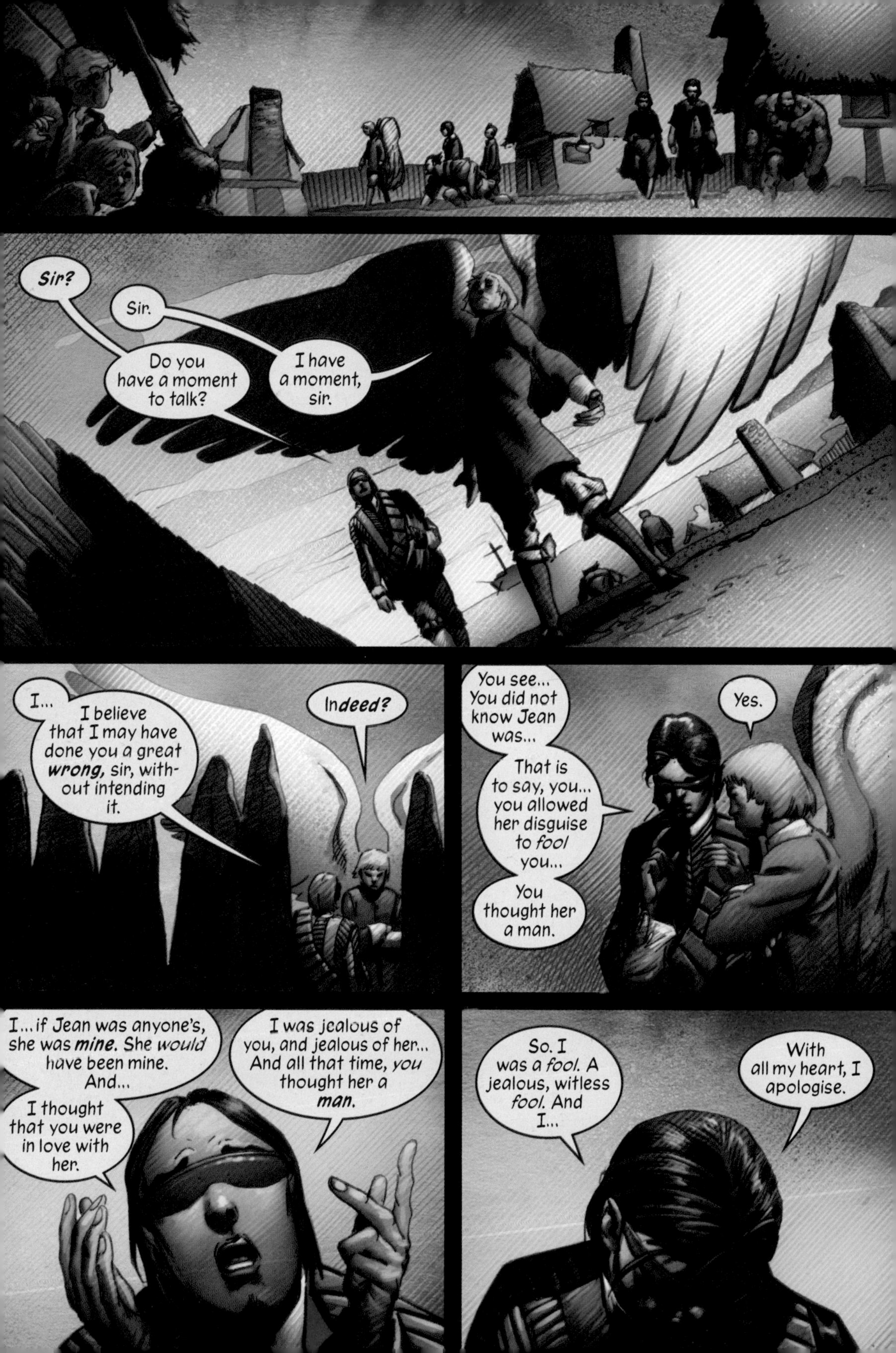
Sir?
Sir.
Do you have a moment to talk?
I have a moment, sir.
I...
I believe that I may have done you a great **wrong**, sir, without intending it.
In*deed?*
You see... You did not know Jean was...
Yes.
That is to say, you... you allowed her disguise to *fool* you...
You thought her a man.
I... if Jean was anyone's, she was **mine.** She *would* have been mine. And...
I thought that you were in love with her.
I was jealous of you, and jealous of her... And all that time, *you* thought her a ***man.***
So. I was a *fool.* A jealous, witless *fool.* And I...
With all my heart, I apologise.

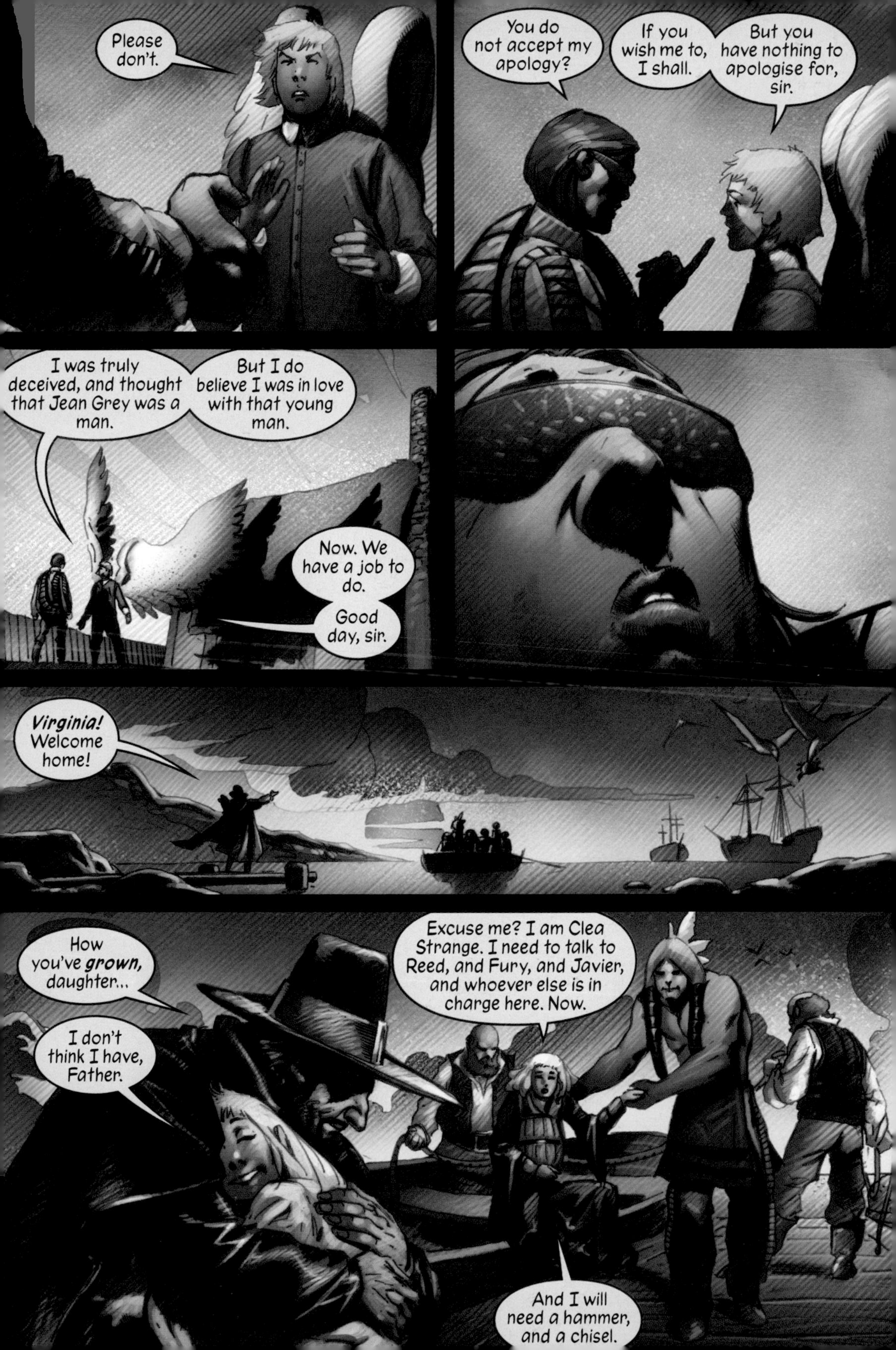
Please don't.
You do not accept my apology?
If you wish me to, I shall.
But you have nothing to apologise for, sir.
I was truly deceived, and thought that Jean Grey was a man.
But I do believe I was in love with that young man.
Now. We have a job to do.
Good day, sir.
Virginia! Welcome home!
How you've ***grown,*** daughter...
I don't think I have, Father.
Excuse me? I am Clea Strange. I need to talk to Reed, and Fury, and Javier, and whoever else is in charge here. Now.
And I will need a hammer, and a chisel.

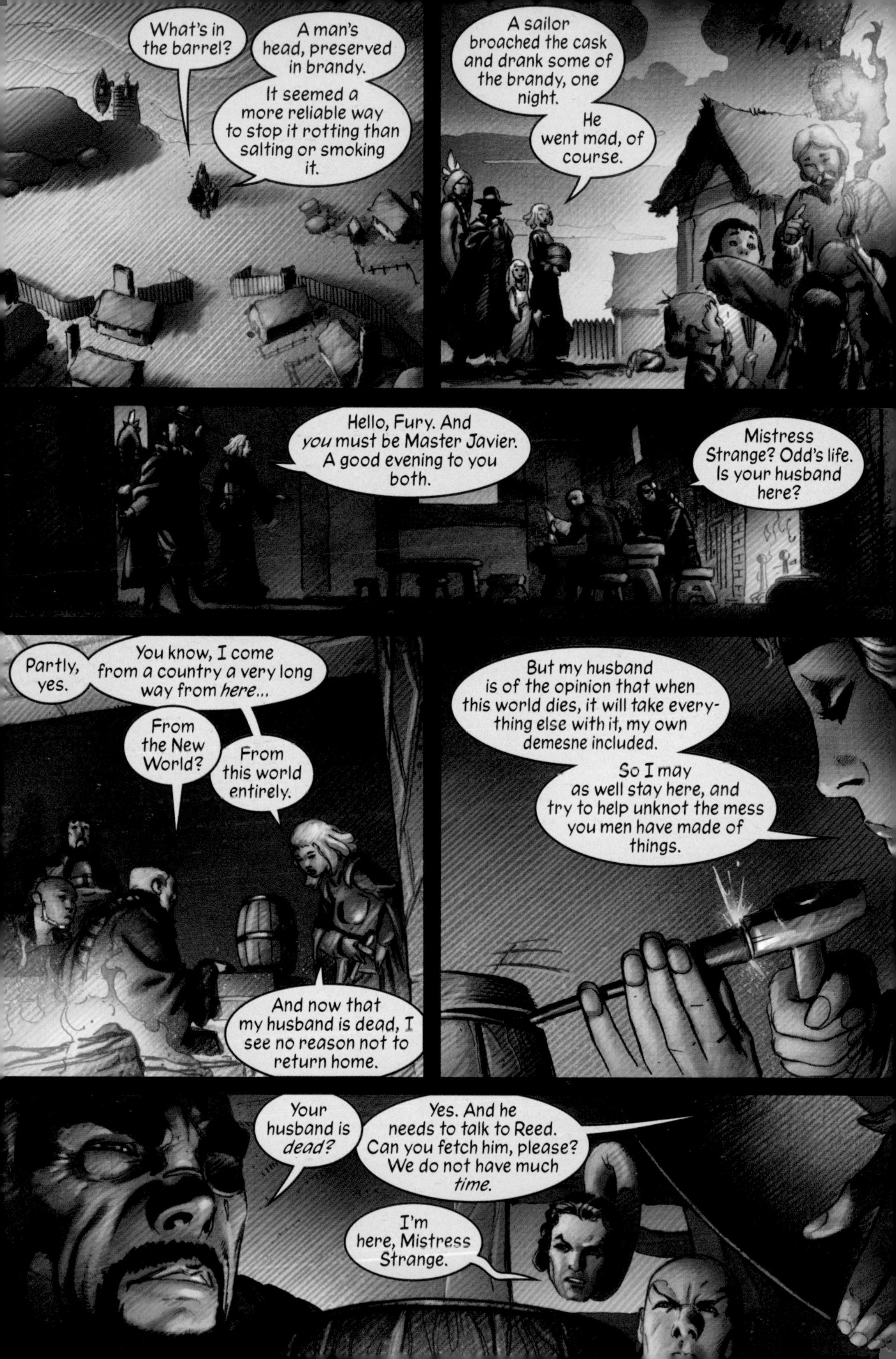

What's in the barrel?
A man's head, preserved in brandy.
It seemed a more reliable way to stop it rotting than salting or smoking it.
A sailor broached the cask and drank some of the brandy, one night.
He went mad, of course.
Hello, Fury. And *you* must be Master Javier. A good evening to you both.
Mistress Strange? Odd's life. Is your husband here?
Partly, yes.
You know, I come from a country a very long way from *here*...
From the New World?
From this world entirely.
And now that my husband is dead, I see no reason not to return home.
But my husband is of the opinion that when this world dies, it will take everything else with it, my own demesne included.
So I may as well stay here, and try to help unknot the mess you men have made of things.
Your husband is *dead?*
Yes. And he needs to talk to Reed. Can you fetch him, please? We do not have much *time.*
I'm here, Mistress Strange.

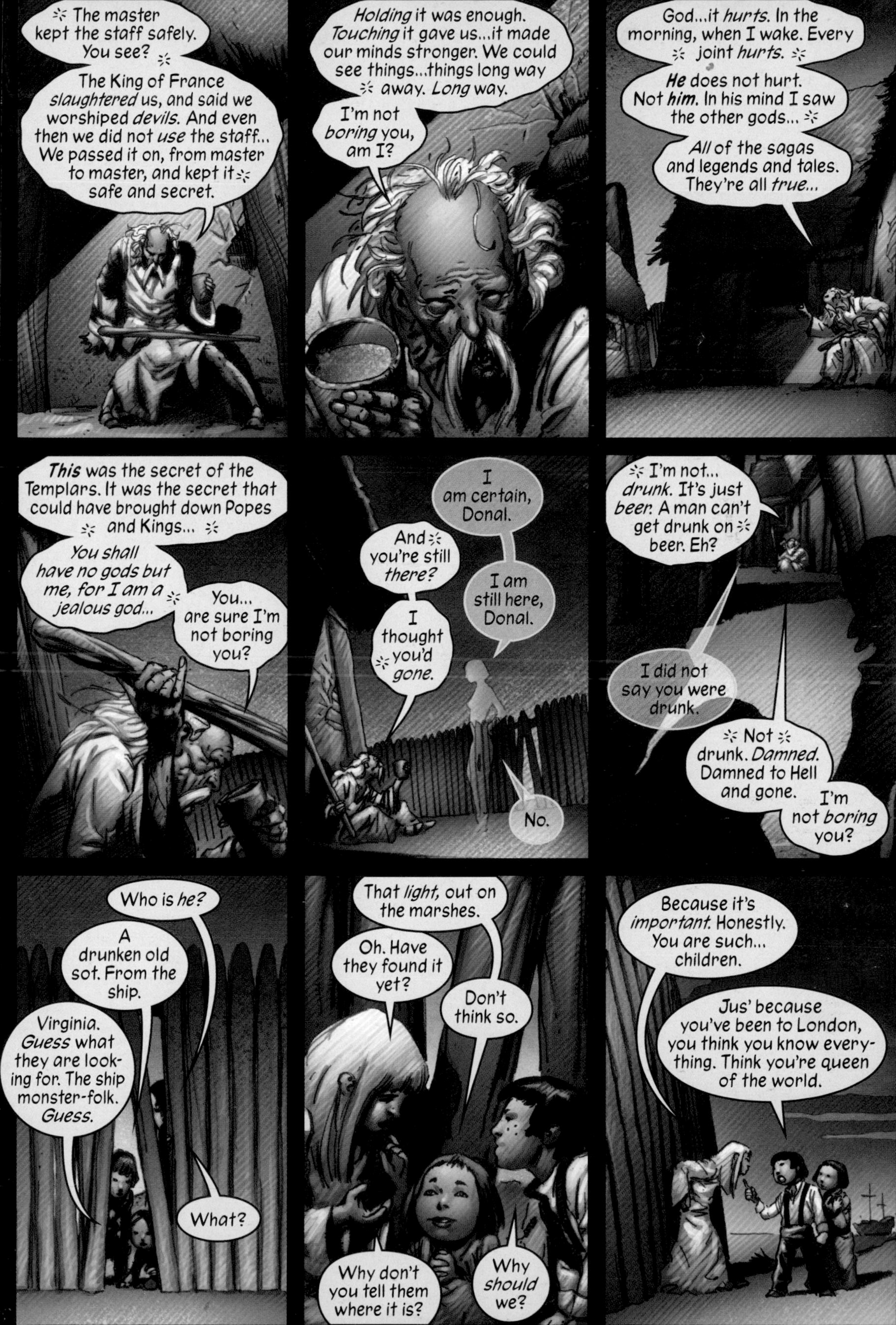

The master kept the staff safely. You see?
The King of France *slaughtered* us, and said we worshiped *devils*. And even then we did not *use* the staff... We passed it on, from master to master, and kept it safe and secret.
Holding it was enough. *Touching* it gave us...it made our minds stronger. We could see things...things long way away. *Long* way.
I'm not *boring* you, am I?
God...it *hurts*. In the morning, when I wake. Every joint *hurts*.
He does not hurt. Not *him*. In his mind I saw the other gods...
All of the sagas and legends and tales. They're all *true*...
This was the secret of the Templars. It was the secret that could have brought down Popes and Kings...
You shall have no gods but me, for I am a jealous god...
You... are sure I'm not boring you?
I am certain, Donal.
And you're still *there*?
I am still here, Donal.
I thought you'd *gone*.
No.
I'm not... *drunk*. It's just *beer*. A man can't get drunk on beer. Eh?
I did not say you were drunk.
Not drunk. *Damned*. Damned to Hell and gone.
I'm not *boring* you?
Who is *he*?
A drunken old sot. From the ship.
Virginia. *Guess* what they are looking for. The ship monster-folk. *Guess*.
What?
That *light*, out on the marshes.
Oh. Have they found it yet?
Don't think so.
Why don't you tell them where it is?
Why *should* we?
Because it's *important*. Honestly. You are such... children.
Jus' because you've been to London, you think you know everything. Think you're queen of the world.

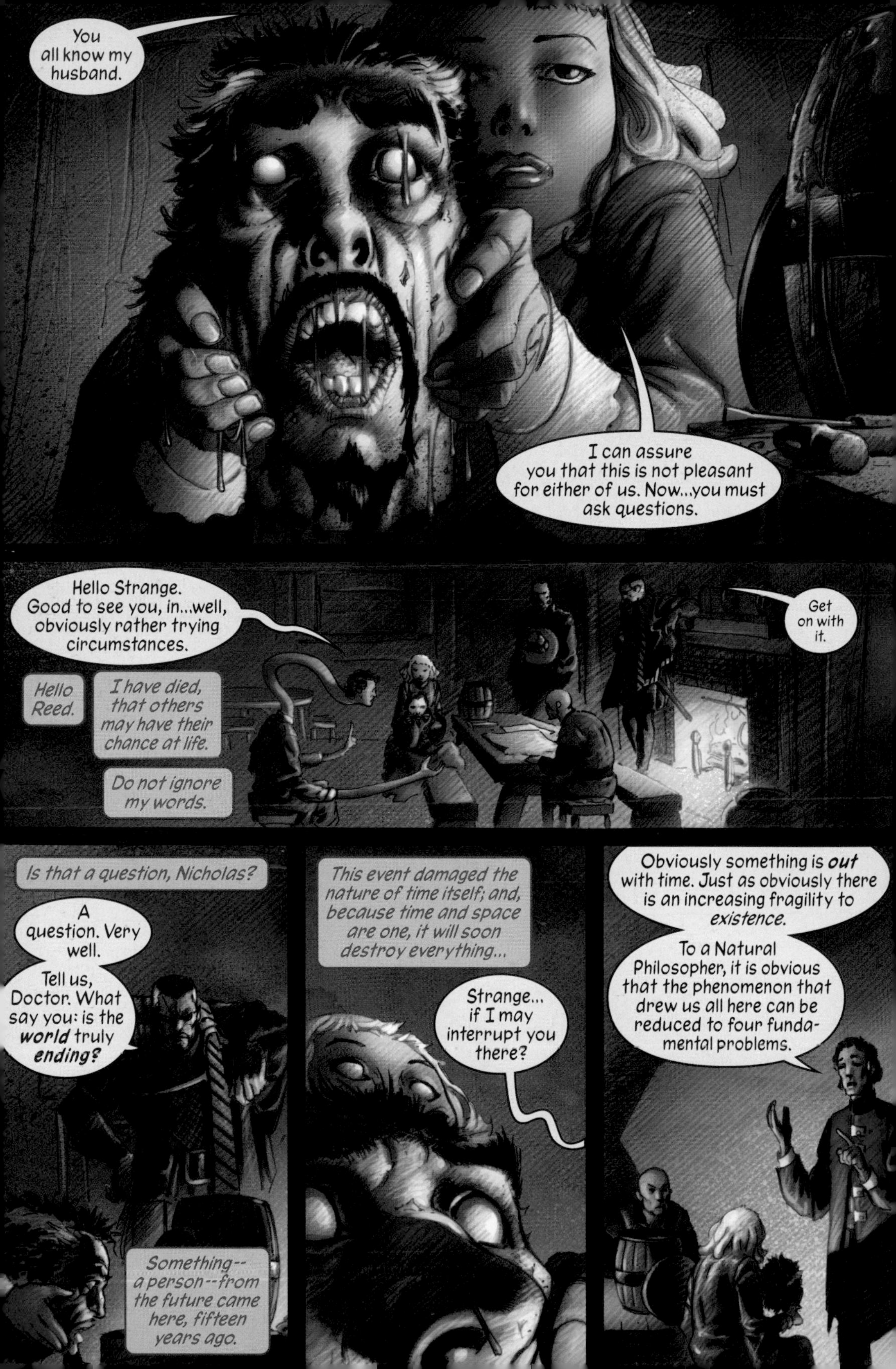

You all know my husband.
I can assure you that this is not pleasant for either of us. Now...you must ask questions.
Hello Strange. Good to see you, in...well, obviously rather trying circumstances.
Get on with it.
Hello Reed.
I have died, that others may have their chance at life.
Do not ignore my words.
Is that a question, Nicholas?
A question. Very well.
Tell us, Doctor. What say you: is the **world** truly **ending?**
Something--a person--from the future came here, fifteen years ago.
This event damaged the nature of time itself; and, because time and space are one, it will soon destroy everything...
Strange... if I may interrupt you there?
Obviously something is ***out*** with time. Just as obviously there is an increasing fragility to *existence.*
To a Natural Philosopher, it is obvious that the phenomenon that drew us all here can be reduced to four fundamental problems.

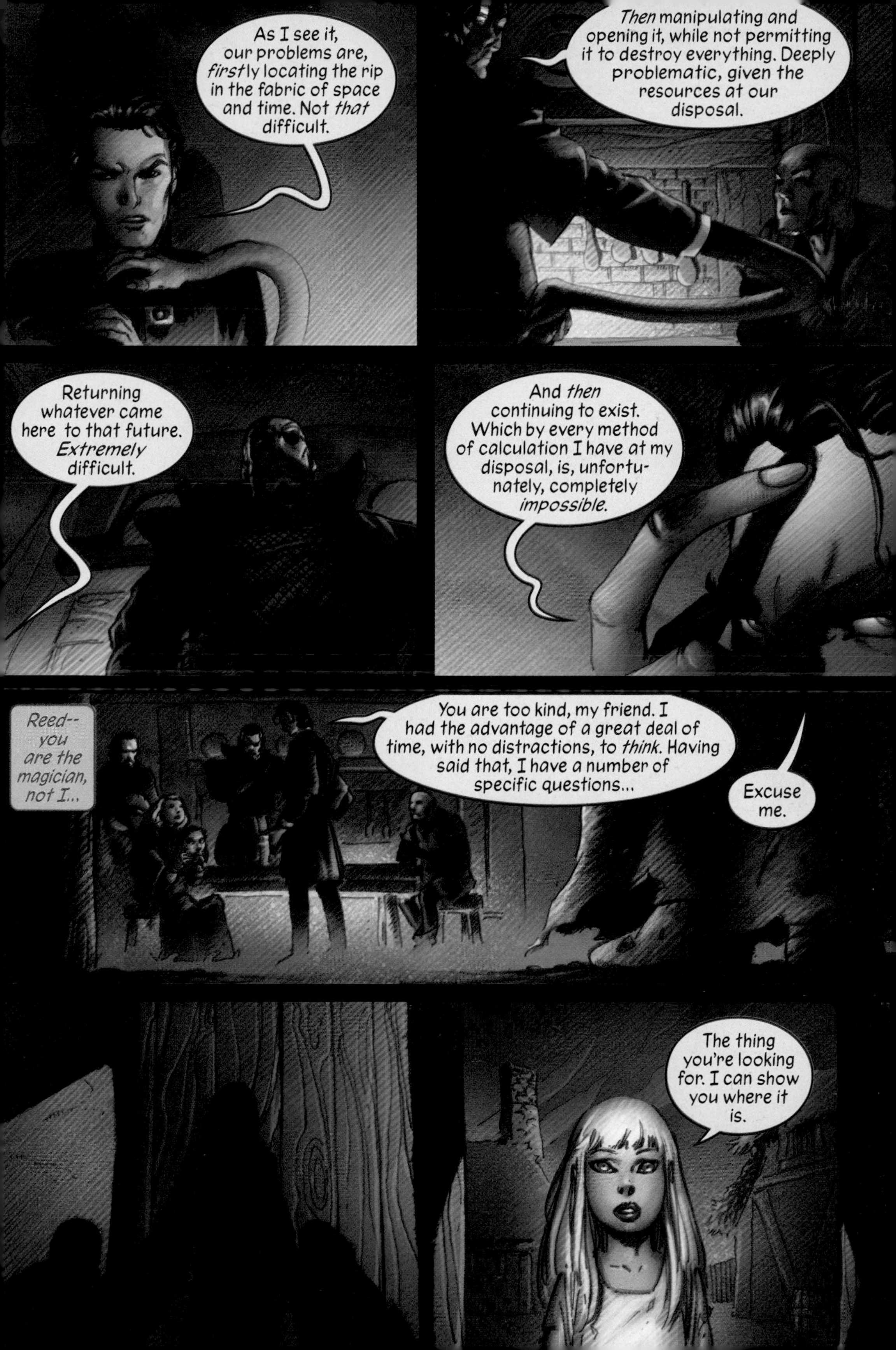
As I see it, our problems are, *firstly* locating the rip in the fabric of space and time. Not *that* difficult.
Then manipulating and opening it, while not permitting it to destroy everything. Deeply problematic, given the resources at our disposal.
Returning whatever came here to that future. *Extremely* difficult.
And *then* continuing to exist. Which by every method of calculation I have at my disposal, is, unfortunately, completely *impossible*.
Reed--you are the magician, not I...
You are too kind, my friend. I had the advantage of a great deal of time, with no distractions, to *think*. Having said that, I have a number of specific questions...
Excuse me.
The thing you're looking for. I can show you where it is.

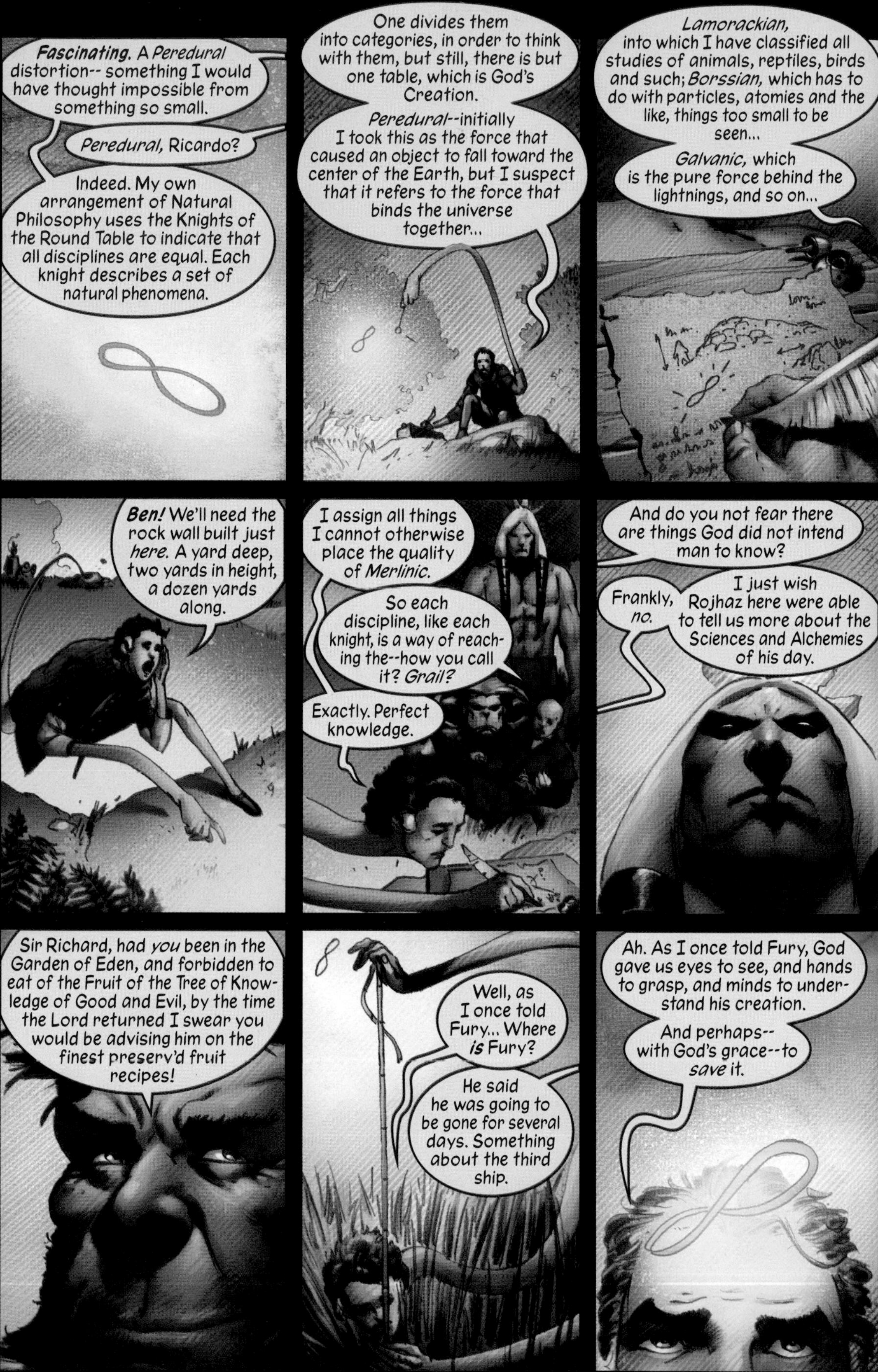
Fascinating. A *Peredural* distortion-- something I would have thought impossible from something so small.
Peredural, Ricardo?
Indeed. My own arrangement of Natural Philosophy uses the Knights of the Round Table to indicate that all disciplines are equal. Each knight describes a set of natural phenomena.
One divides them into categories, in order to think with them, but still, there is but one table, which is God's Creation.
Peredural--initially I took this as the force that caused an object to fall toward the center of the Earth, but I suspect that it refers to the force that binds the universe together...
Lamorackian, into which I have classified all studies of animals, reptiles, birds and such; *Borssian,* which has to do with particles, atomies and the like, things too small to be seen...
Galvanic, which is the pure force behind the lightnings, and so on...
Ben! We'll need the rock wall built just *here.* A yard deep, two yards in height, a dozen yards along.
I assign all things I cannot otherwise place the quality of *Merlinic.*
So each discipline, like each knight, is a way of reaching the--how you call it? *Grail?*
Exactly. Perfect knowledge.
And do you not fear there are things God did not intend man to know?
Frankly, *no.*
I just wish Rojhaz here were able to tell us more about the Sciences and Alchemies of his day.
Sir Richard, had *you* been in the Garden of Eden, and forbidden to eat of the Fruit of the Tree of Knowledge of Good and Evil, by the time the Lord returned I swear you would be advising him on the finest preserv'd fruit recipes!
Well, as I once told Fury... Where *is* Fury?
He said he was going to be gone for several days. Something about the third ship.
Ah. As I once told Fury, God gave us eyes to see, and hands to grasp, and minds to understand his creation.
And perhaps-- with God's grace--to *save* it.

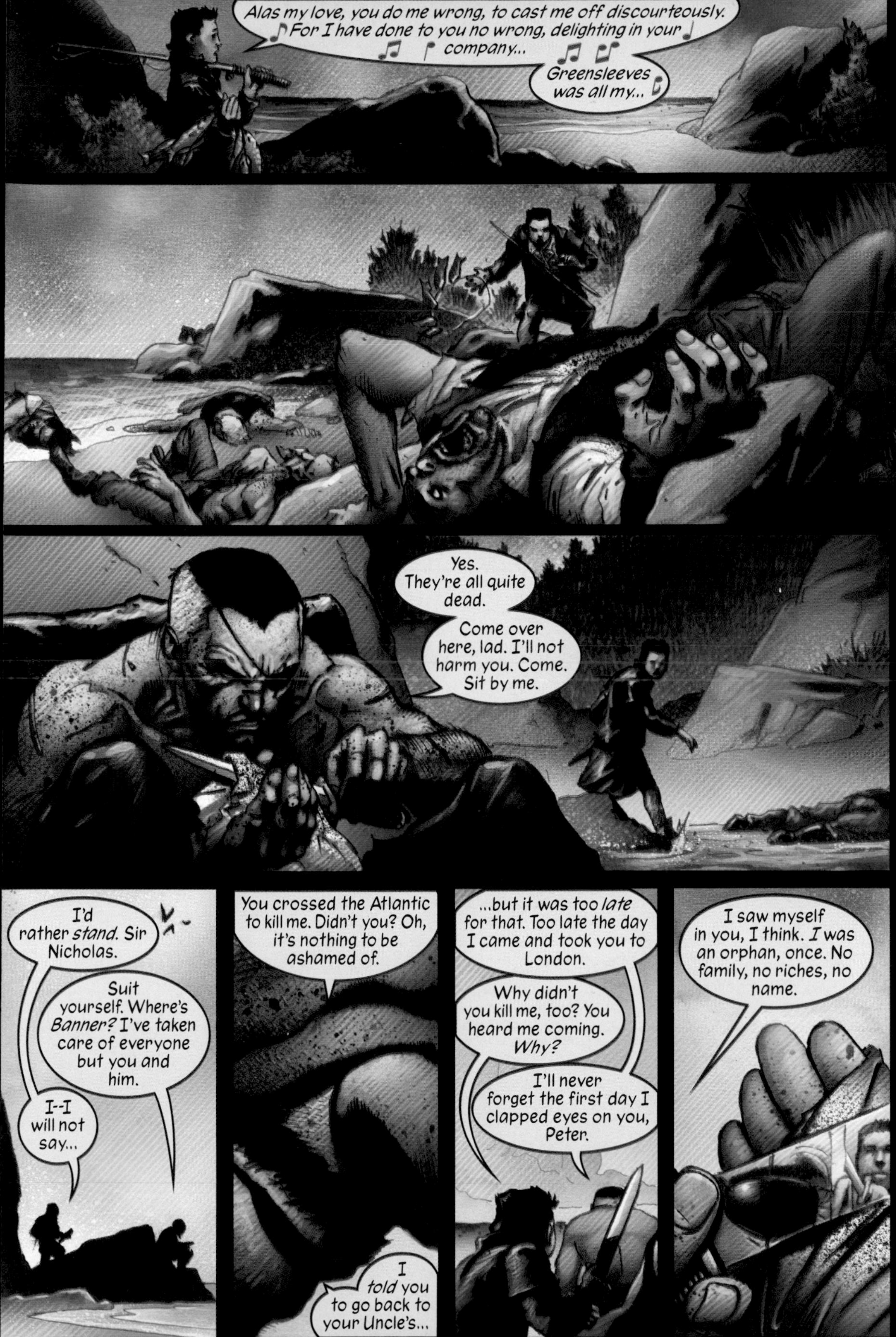
Alas my love, you do me wrong, to cast me off discourteously. For I have done to you no wrong, delighting in your company...
Greensleeves was all my...
Yes. They're all quite dead.
Come over here, lad. I'll not harm you. Come. Sit by me.
I'd rather *stand*. Sir Nicholas.
Suit yourself. Where's *Banner?* I've taken care of everyone but you and him.
I--I will not say...
You crossed the Atlantic to kill me. Didn't you? Oh, it's nothing to be ashamed of.
I *told* you to go back to your Uncle's...
...but it was too *late* for that. Too late the day I came and took you to London.
Why didn't you kill me, too? You heard me coming. *Why?*
I'll never forget the first day I clapped eyes on you, Peter.
I saw myself in you, I think. *I* was an orphan, once. No family, no riches, no name.

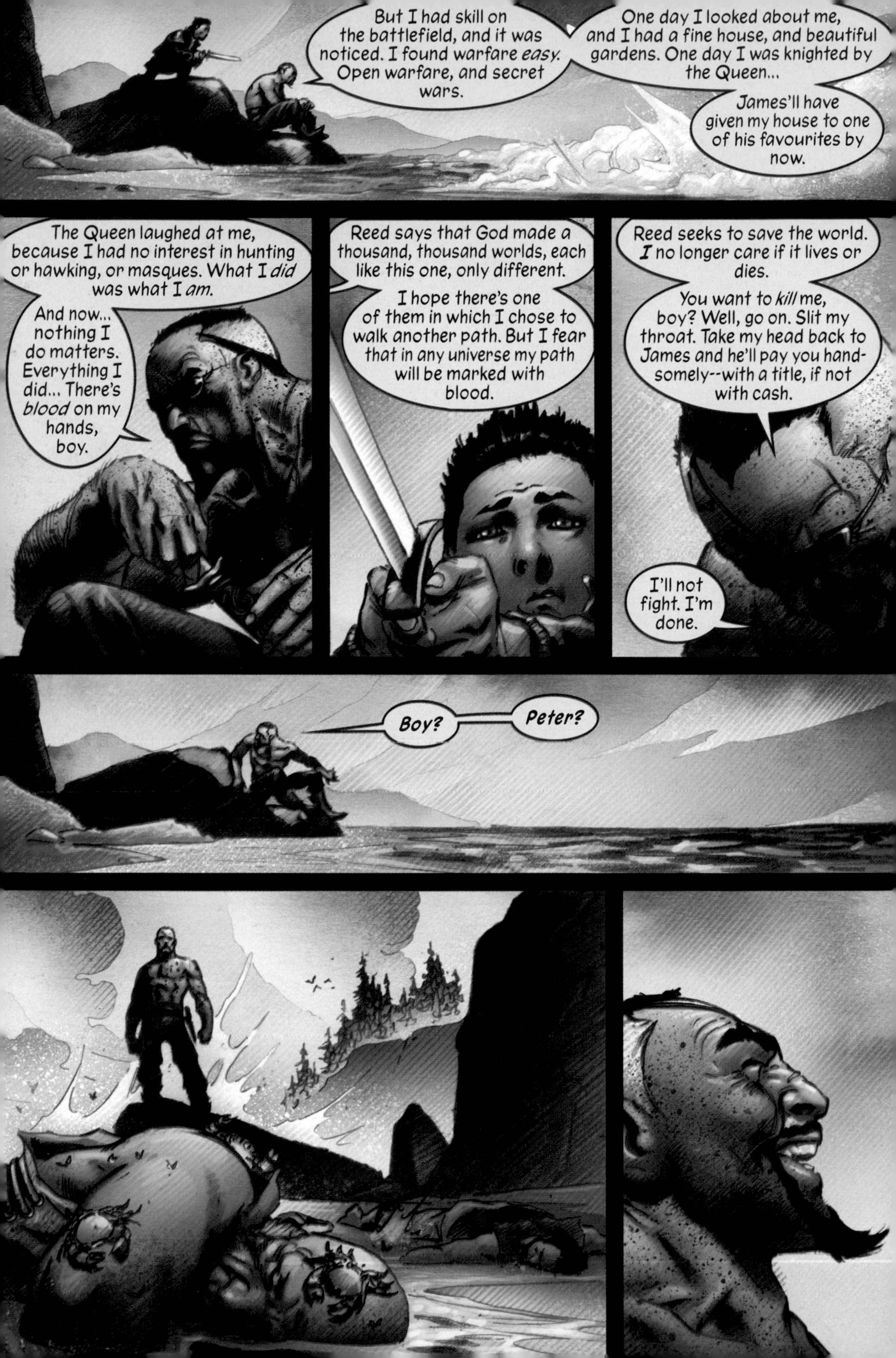
But I had skill on the battlefield, and it was noticed. I found warfare *easy*. Open warfare, and secret wars.
One day I looked about me, and I had a fine house, and beautiful gardens. One day I was knighted by the Queen...
James'll have given my house to one of his favourites by now.
The Queen laughed at me, because I had no interest in hunting or hawking, or masques. What I *did* was what I *am*.
And now... nothing I do matters. Everything I did... There's *blood* on my hands, boy.
Reed says that God made a thousand, thousand worlds, each like this one, only different.
I hope there's one of them in which I chose to walk another path. But I fear that in any universe my path will be marked with blood.
Reed seeks to save the world. *I* no longer care if it lives or dies.
You want to *kill* me, boy? Well, go on. Slit my throat. Take my head back to James and he'll pay you handsomely--with a title, if not with cash.
I'll not fight. I'm done.
Boy?
Peter?

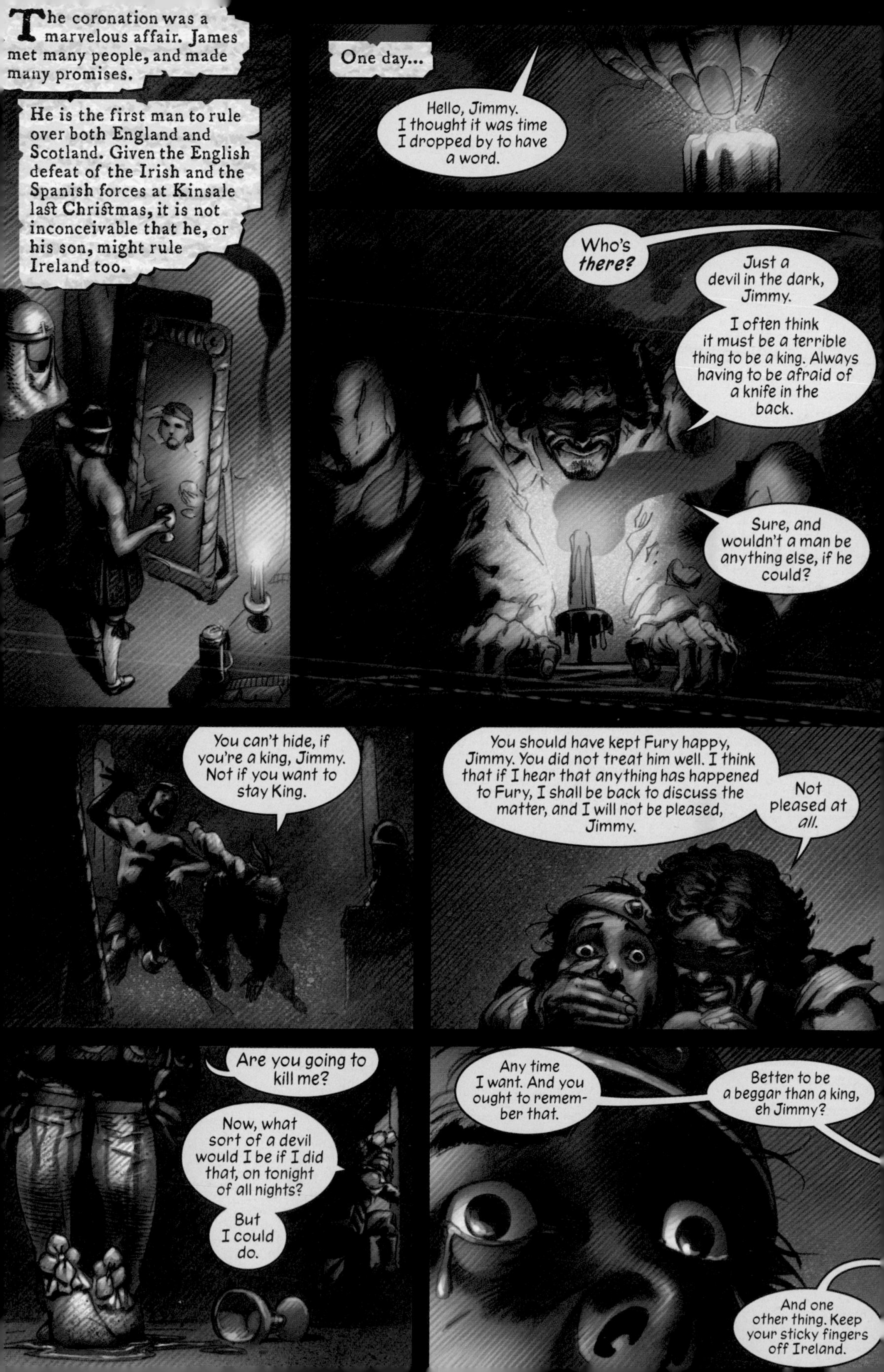

The coronation was a marvelous affair. James met many people, and made many promises.
He is the first man to rule over both England and Scotland. Given the English defeat of the Irish and the Spanish forces at Kinsale last Christmas, it is not inconceivable that he, or his son, might rule Ireland too.
One day...
Hello, Jimmy. I thought it was time I dropped by to have a word.
Who's *there?*
Just a devil in the dark, Jimmy.
I often think it must be a terrible thing to be a king. Always having to be afraid of a knife in the back.
Sure, and wouldn't a man be anything else, if he could?
You can't hide, if you're a king, Jimmy. Not if you want to stay King.
You should have kept Fury happy, Jimmy. You did not treat him well. I think that if I hear that anything has happened to Fury, I shall be back to discuss the matter, and I will not be pleased, Jimmy.
Not pleased at *all.*
Are you going to kill me?
Now, what sort of a devil would I be if I did that, on tonight of all nights?
But I could do.
Any time I want. And you ought to remember that.
Better to be a beggar than a king, eh Jimmy?
And one other thing. Keep your sticky fingers off Ireland.

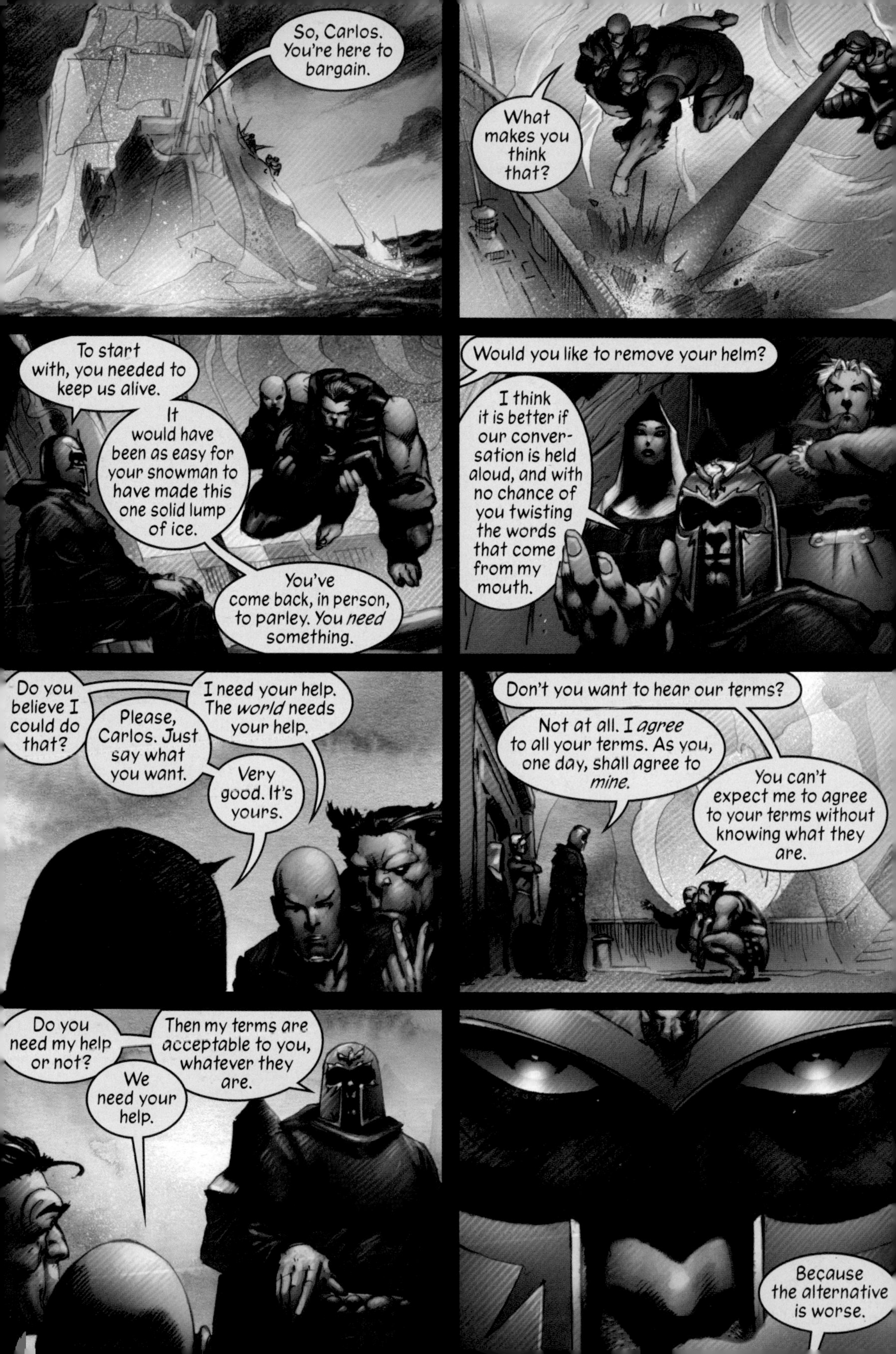
So, Carlos. You're here to bargain.
What makes you think that?
To start with, you needed to keep us alive.
It would have been as easy for your snowman to have made this one solid lump of ice.
You've come back, in person, to parley. You *need* something.
Would you like to remove your helm?
I think it is better if our conversation is held aloud, and with no chance of you twisting the words that come from my mouth.
Do you believe I could do that?
I need your help. The *world* needs your help.
Please, Carlos. Just say what you want.
Very good. It's yours.
Don't you want to hear our terms?
Not at all. I *agree* to all your terms. As you, one day, shall agree to *mine.*
You can't expect me to agree to your terms without knowing what they are.
Do you need my help or not?
Then my terms are acceptable to you, whatever they are.
We need your help.
Because the alternative is worse.

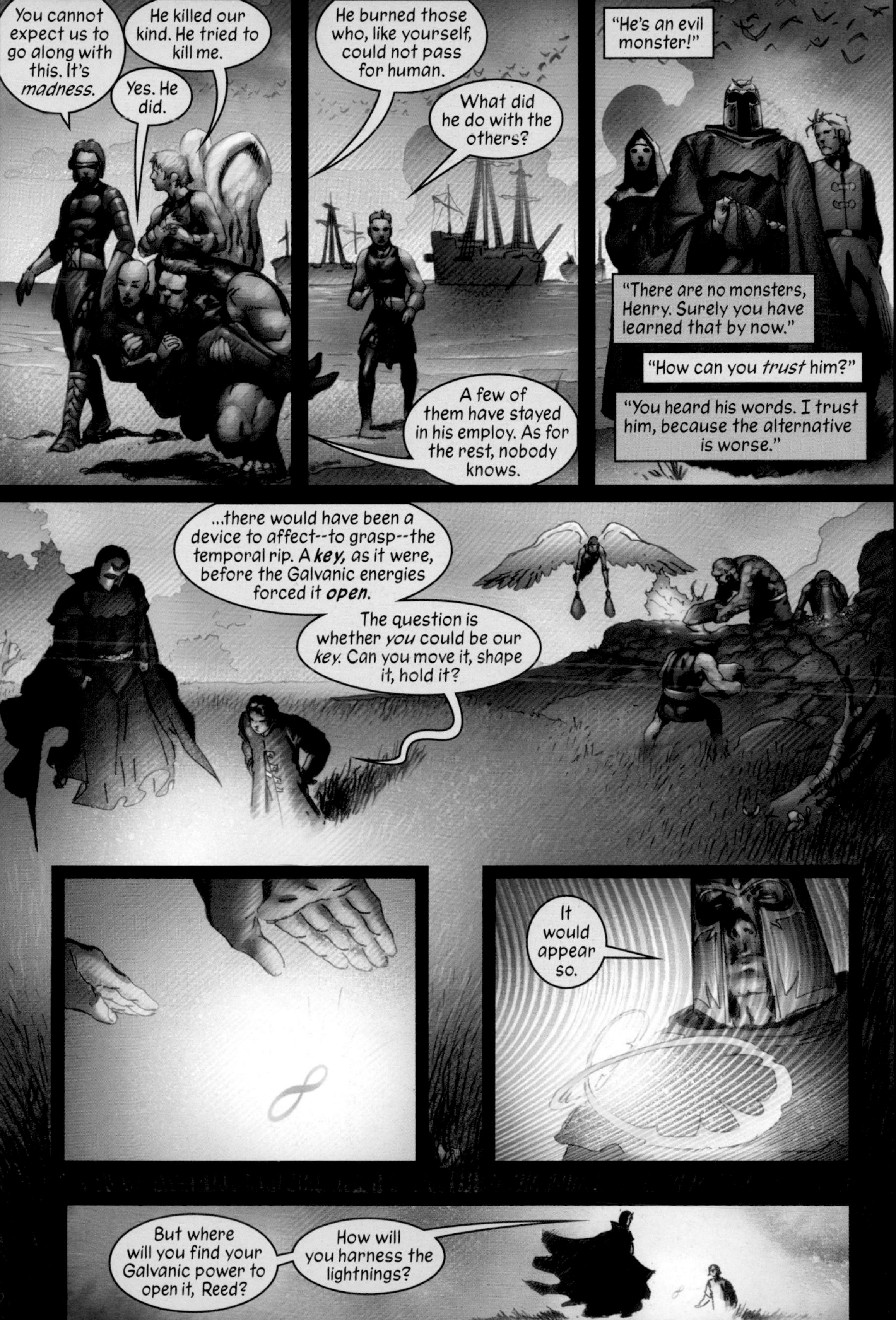
You cannot expect us to go along with this. It's *madness.*
He killed our kind. He tried to kill me.
Yes. He did.
He burned those who, like yourself, could not pass for human.
What did he do with the others?
A few of them have stayed in his employ. As for the rest, nobody knows.
"He's an evil monster!"
"There are no monsters, Henry. Surely you have learned that by now."
"How can you *trust* him?"
"You heard his words. I trust him, because the alternative is worse."
...there would have been a device to affect--to grasp--the temporal rip. A ***key,*** as it were, before the Galvanic energies forced it ***open.***
The question is whether *you* could be our *key.* Can you move it, shape it, hold it?
It would appear so.
But where will you find your Galvanic power to open it, Reed?
How will you harness the lightnings?

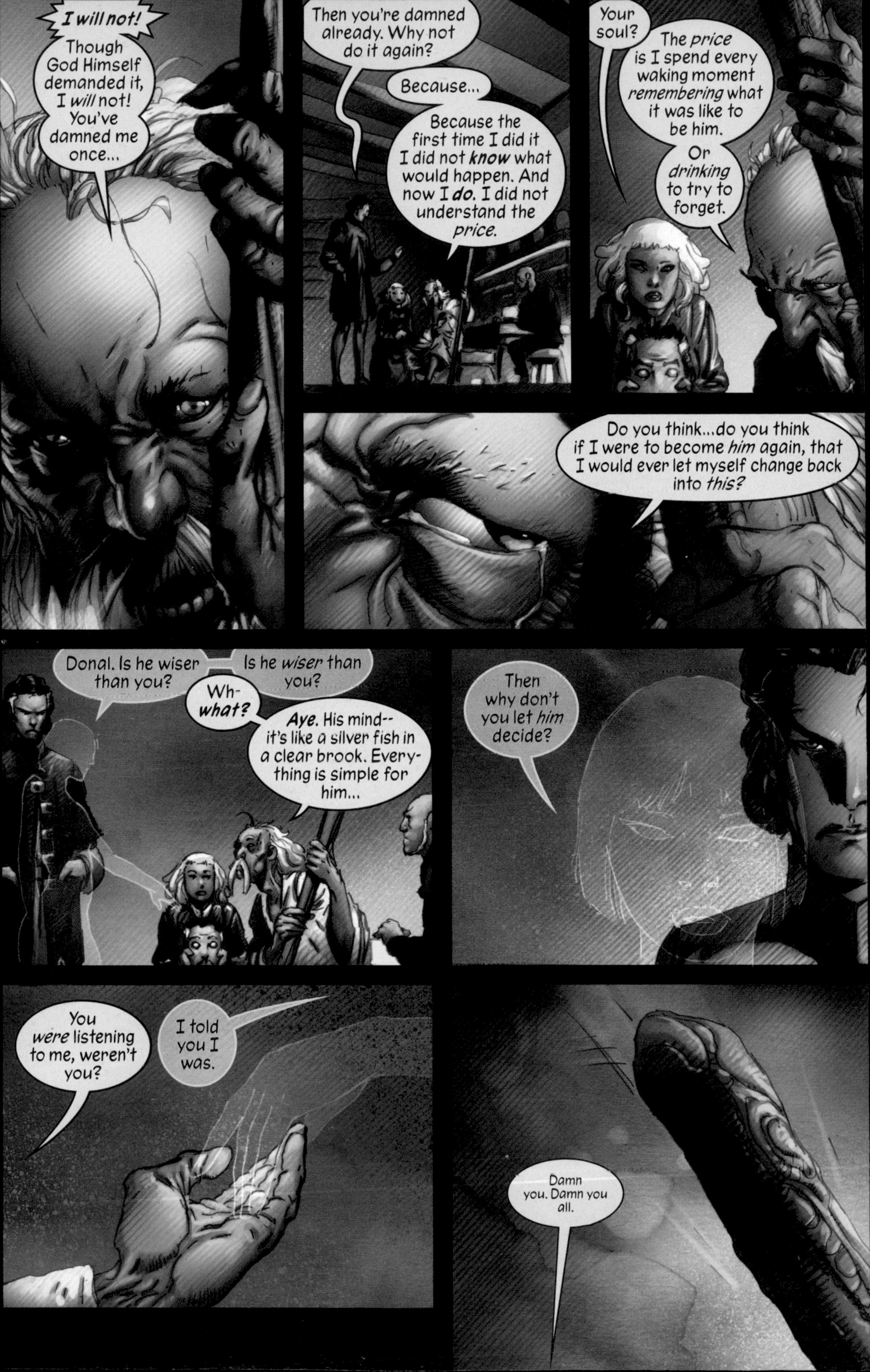
I will not!
Though God Himself demanded it, I *will* not! You've damned me once...
Then you're damned already. Why not do it again?
Because...
Because the first time I did it I did not **know** what would happen. And now I **do**. I did not understand the *price*.
Your soul?
The *price* is I spend every waking moment *remembering* what it was like to be him.
Or *drinking* to try to forget.
Do you think...do you think if I were to become *him* again, that I would ever let myself change back into *this*?
Donal. Is he wiser than you?
Is he *wiser* than you?
Wh- *what?*
Aye. His mind-- it's like a silver fish in a clear brook. Everything is simple for him...
Then why don't you let *him* decide?
You *were* listening to me, weren't you?
I told you I was.
Damn you. Damn you all.

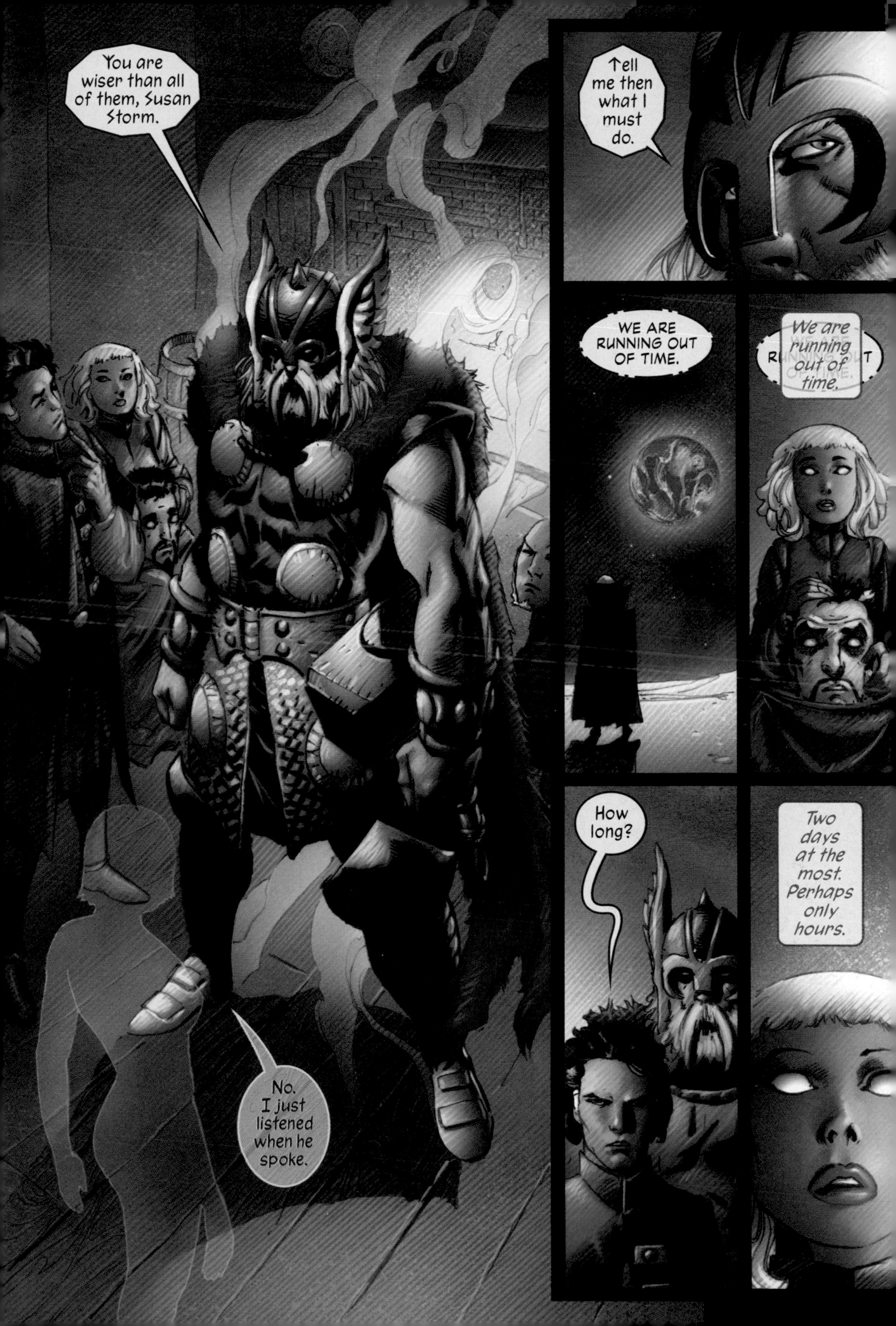
You are wiser than all of them, Susan Storm.
No. I just listened when he spoke.
Tell me then what I must do.
WE ARE RUNNING OUT OF TIME.
We are running out of time.
How long?
Two days at the most. Perhaps only hours.

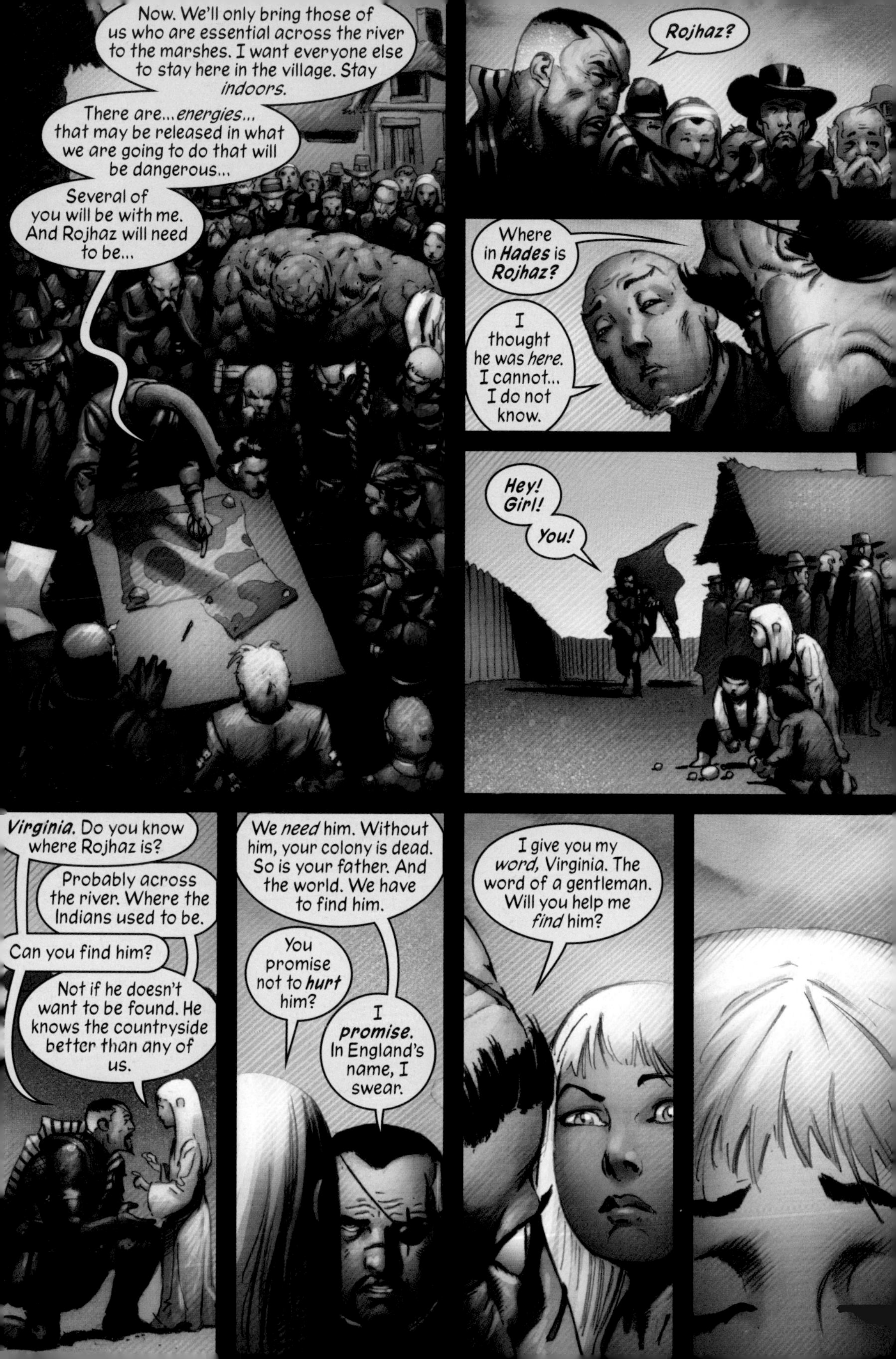
Now. We'll only bring those of us who are essential across the river to the marshes. I want everyone else to stay here in the village. Stay *indoors.*
There are... *energies*... that may be released in what we are going to do that will be dangerous...
Several of you will be with me. And Rojhaz will need to be...
Rojhaz?
Where in *Hades* is *Rojhaz?*
I thought he was *here.* I cannot... I do not know.
Hey! Girl!
You!
Virginia. Do you know where Rojhaz is?
Probably across the river. Where the Indians used to be.
Can you find him?
Not if he doesn't want to be found. He knows the countryside better than any of us.
We *need* him. Without him, your colony is dead. So is your father. And the world. We have to find him.
You promise not to *hurt* him?
I *promise.* In England's name, I swear.
I give you my *word,* Virginia. The word of a gentleman. Will you help me *find* him?

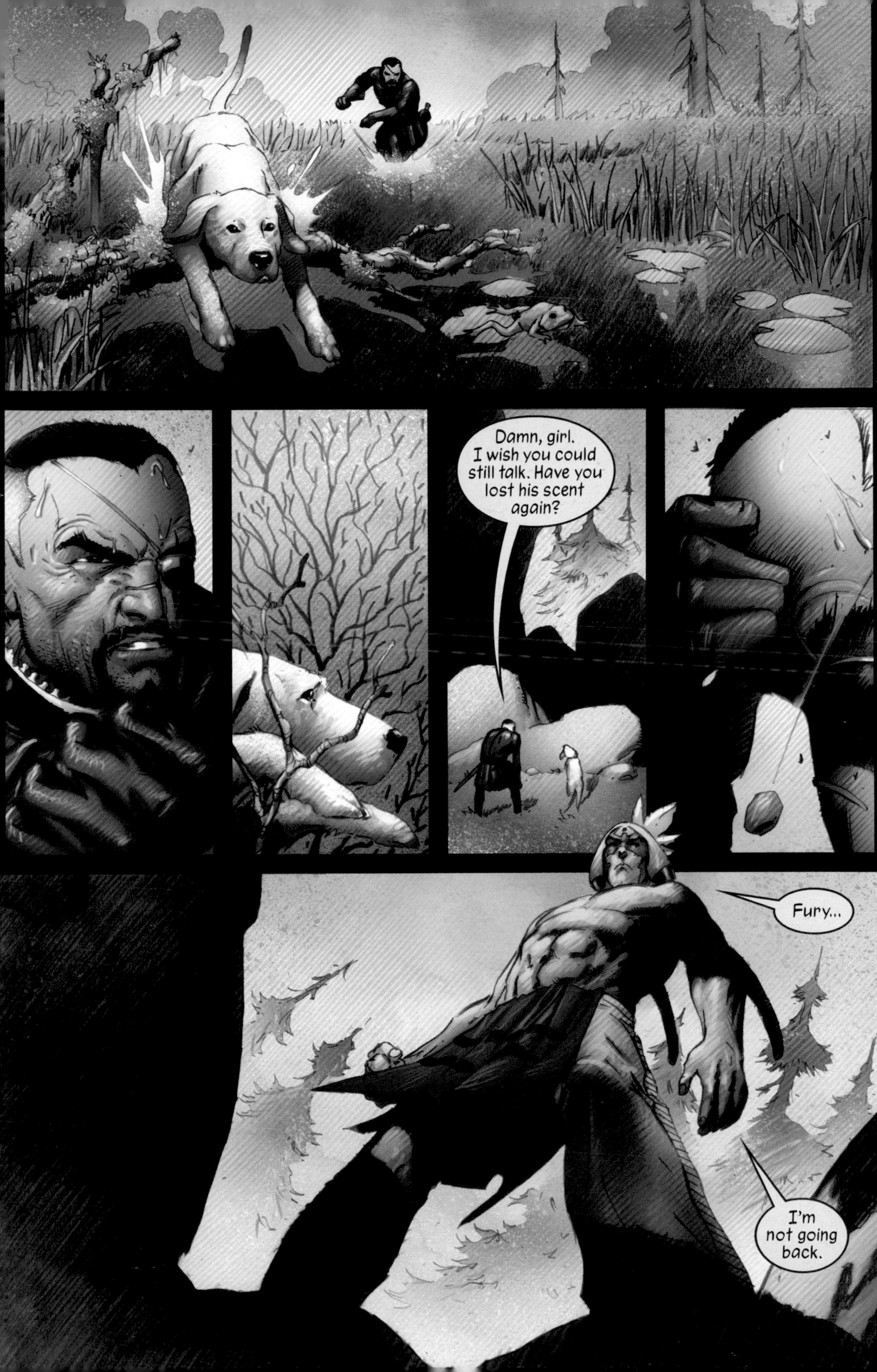
Damn, girl. I wish you could still talk. Have you lost his scent again?
Fury...
I'm not going back.

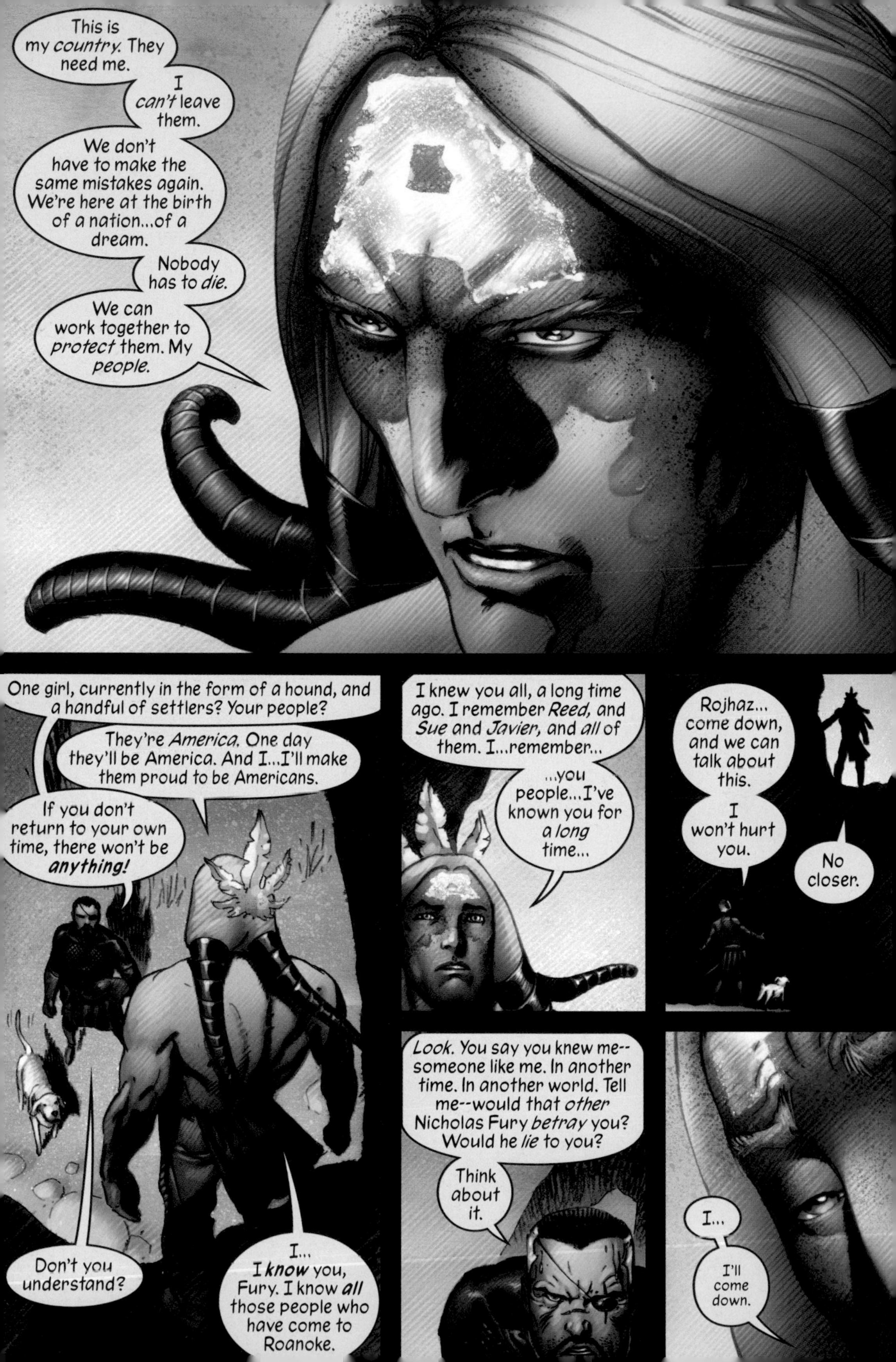
This is my *country*. They need me.
I *can't* leave them.
We don't have to make the same mistakes again. We're here at the birth of a nation...of a dream.
Nobody has to *die*.
We can work together to *protect* them. My *people*.
One girl, currently in the form of a hound, and a handful of settlers? Your people?
They're *America*. One day they'll be America. And I...I'll make them proud to be Americans.
If you don't return to your own time, there won't be ***anything!***
Don't you understand?
I... I ***know*** you, Fury. I know ***all*** those people who have come to Roanoke.
I knew you all, a long time ago. I remember *Reed,* and *Sue* and *Javier,* and *all* of them. I...remember...
...you people...I've known you for *a long* time...
Rojhaz... come down, and we can talk about this.
I won't hurt you.
No closer.
Look. You say you knew me--someone like me. In another time. In another world. Tell me--would that *other* Nicholas Fury *betray* you? Would he *lie* to you?
Think about it.
I...
I'll come down.

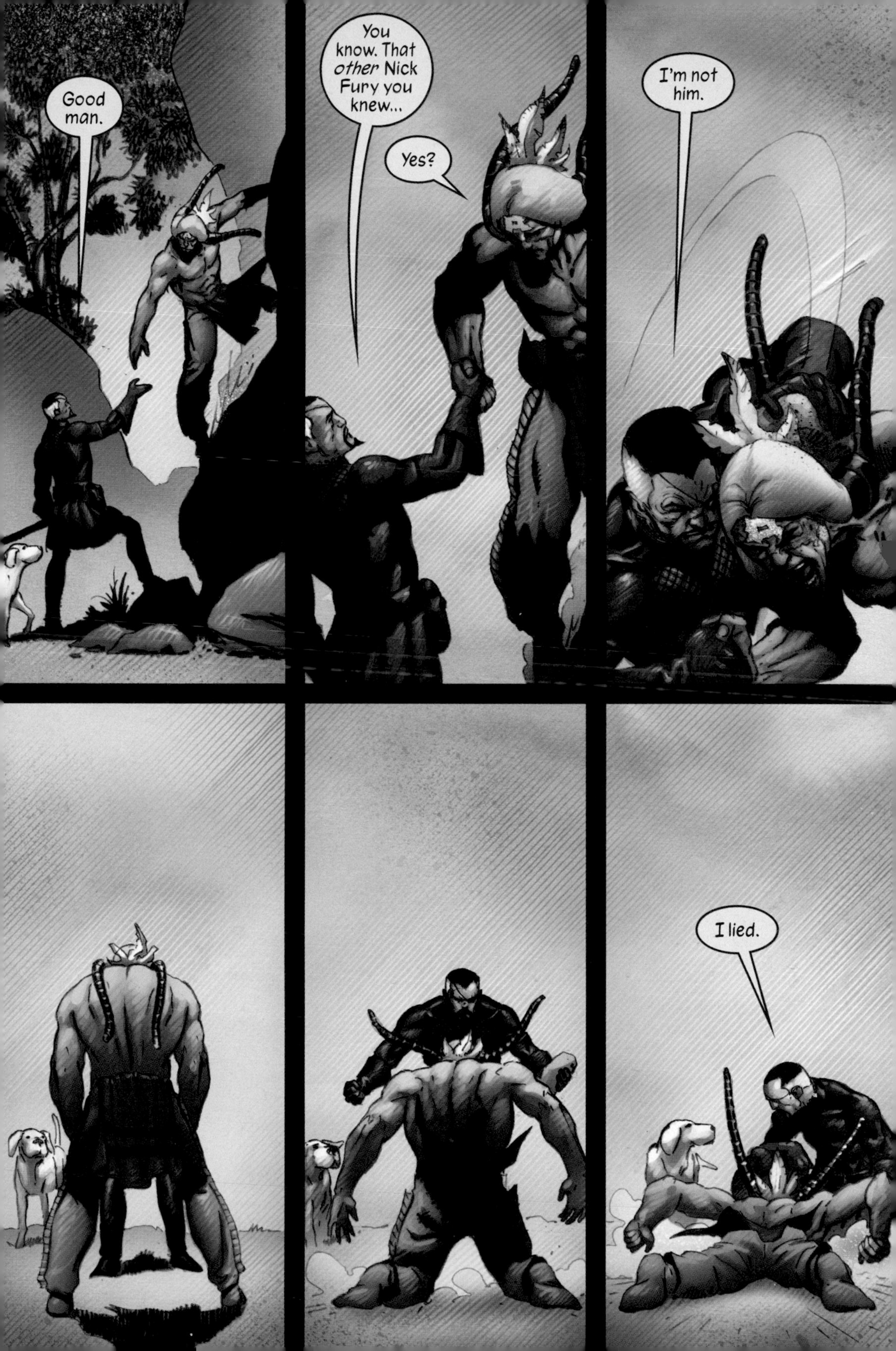
Good man.
You know. That *other* Nick Fury you knew...
Yes?
I'm not him.
I lied.

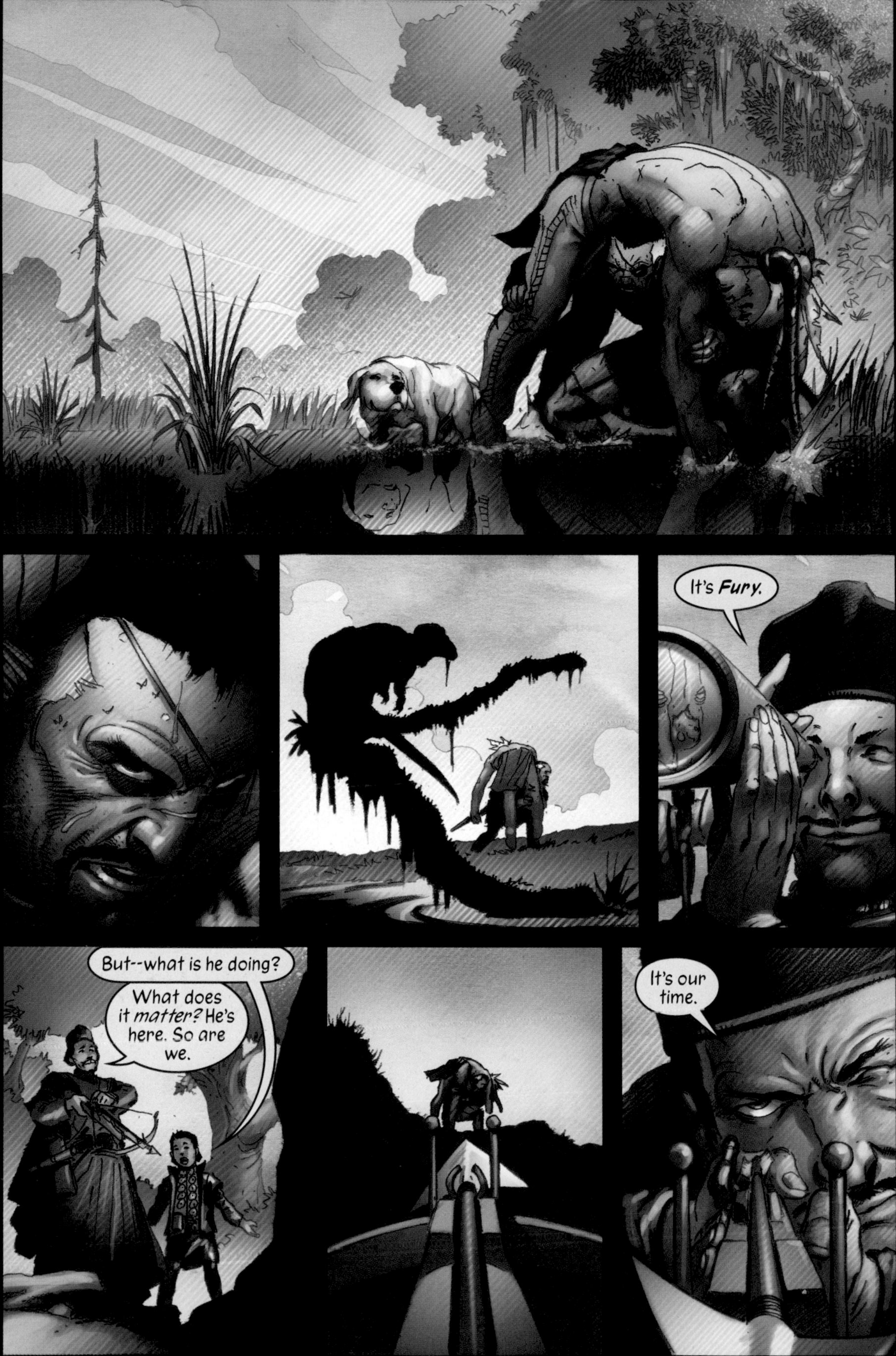
It's *Fury.*
But--what is he doing?
What does it *matter?* He's here. So are we.
It's our time.

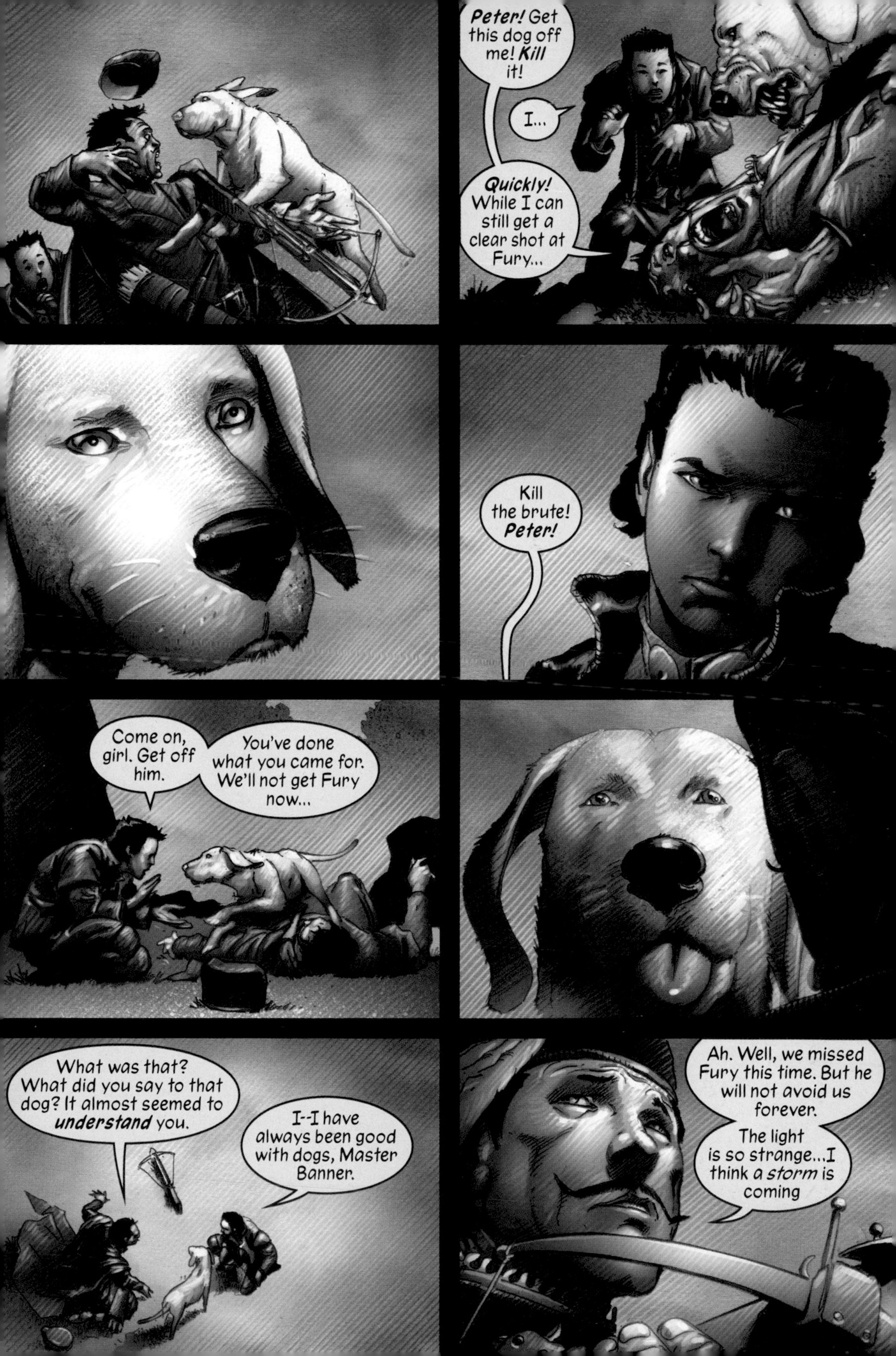

Peter! Get this dog off me! Kill it!
I...
Quickly! While I can still get a clear shot at Fury...
Kill the brute! Peter!
Come on, girl. Get off him.
You've done what you came for. We'll not get Fury now...
What was that? What did you say to that dog? It almost seemed to understand you.
I--I have always been good with dogs, Master Banner.
Ah. Well, we missed Fury this time. But he will not avoid us forever.
The light is so strange...I think a storm is coming

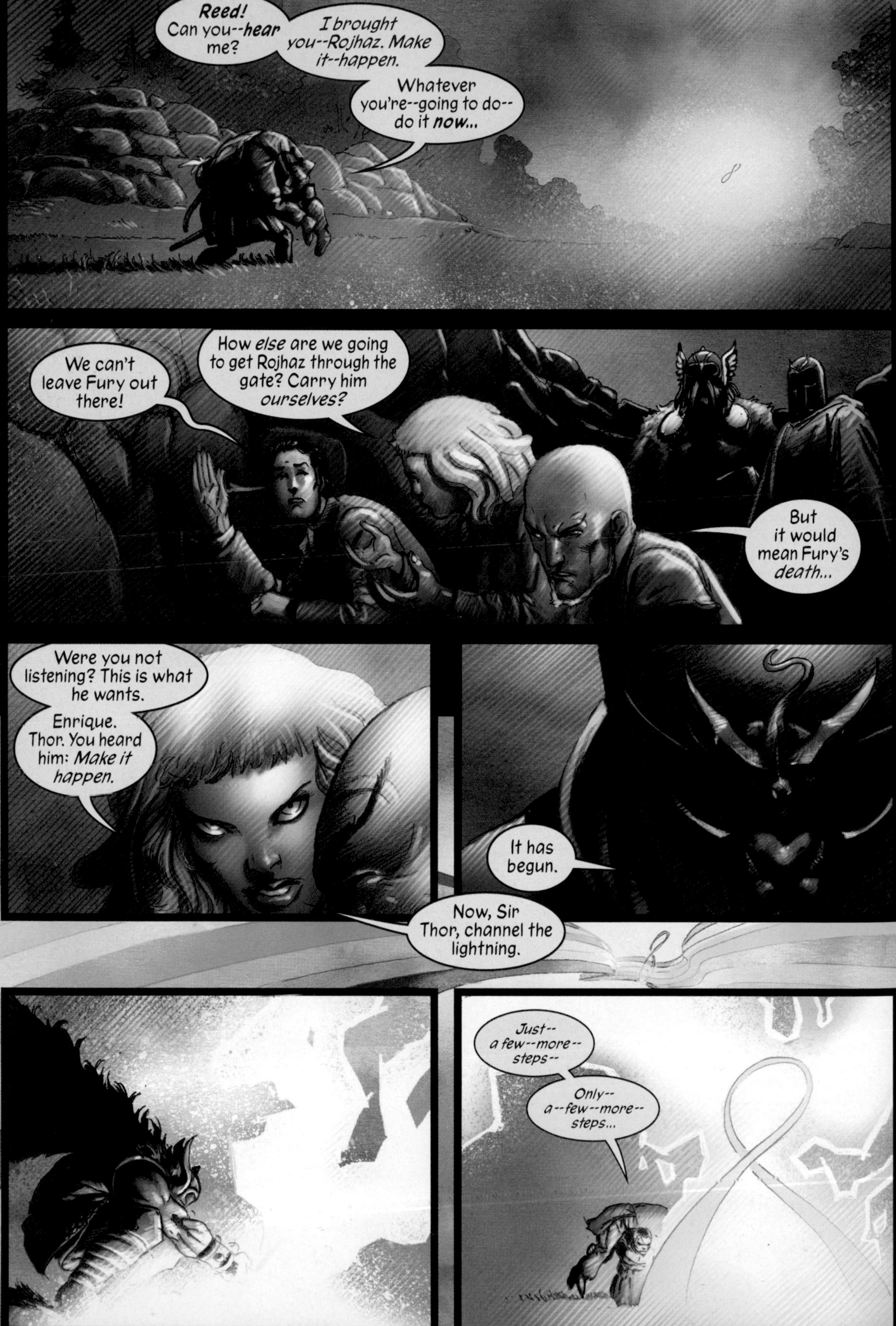
Reed! Can you--hear me?
I brought you--Rojhaz. Make it--happen.
Whatever you're--going to do--do it now...
We can't leave Fury out there!
How else are we going to get Rojhaz through the gate? Carry him ourselves?
But it would mean Fury's death...
Were you not listening? This is what he wants.
Enrique. Thor. You heard him: Make it happen.
It has begun.
Now, Sir Thor, channel the lightning.
Just--a few--more--steps--
Only--a--few--more--steps...

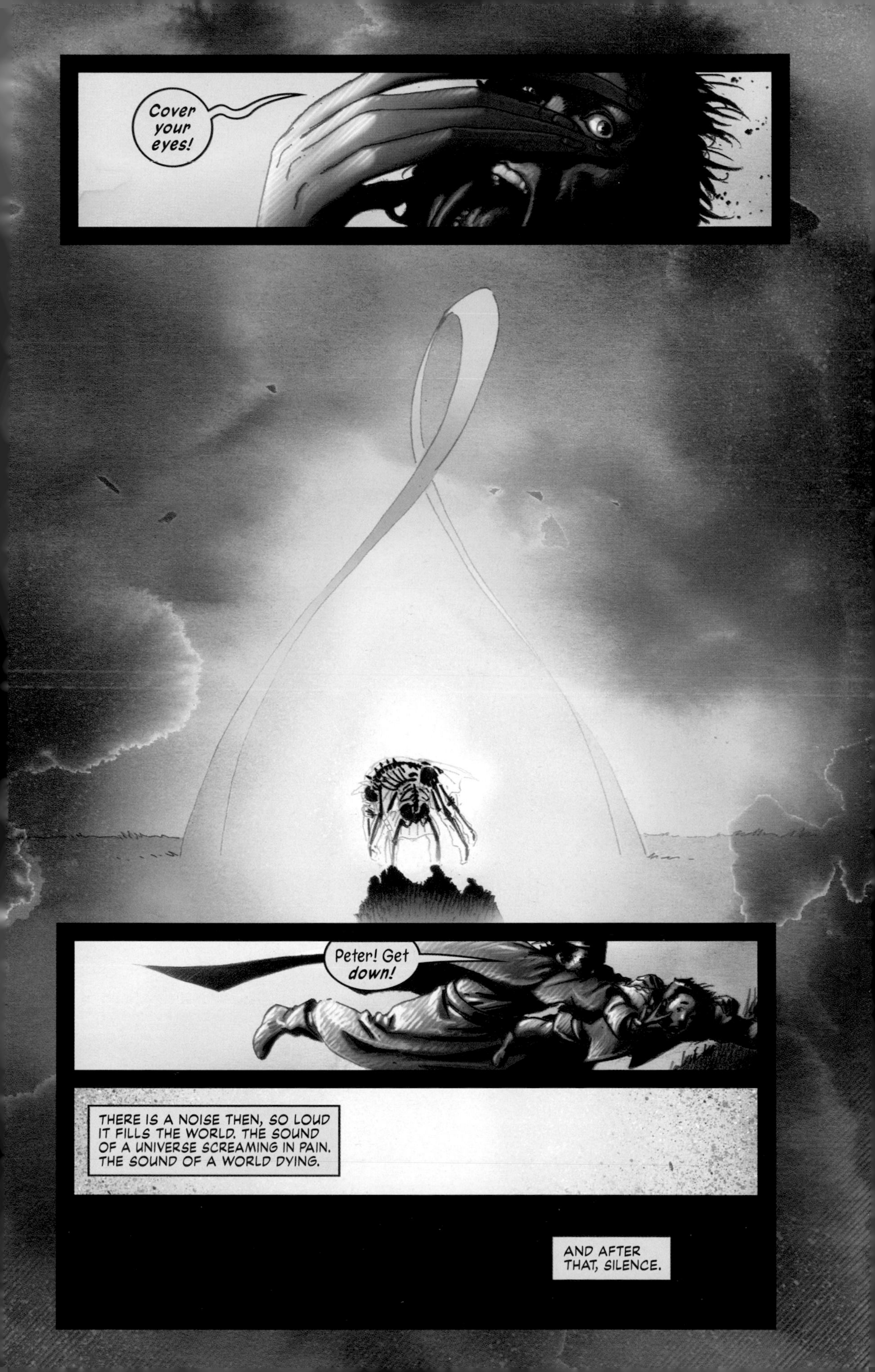
Cover your eyes!
Peter! Get down!
THERE IS A NOISE THEN, SO LOUD IT FILLS THE WORLD. THE SOUND OF A UNIVERSE SCREAMING IN PAIN. THE SOUND OF A WORLD DYING.
AND AFTER THAT, SILENCE.

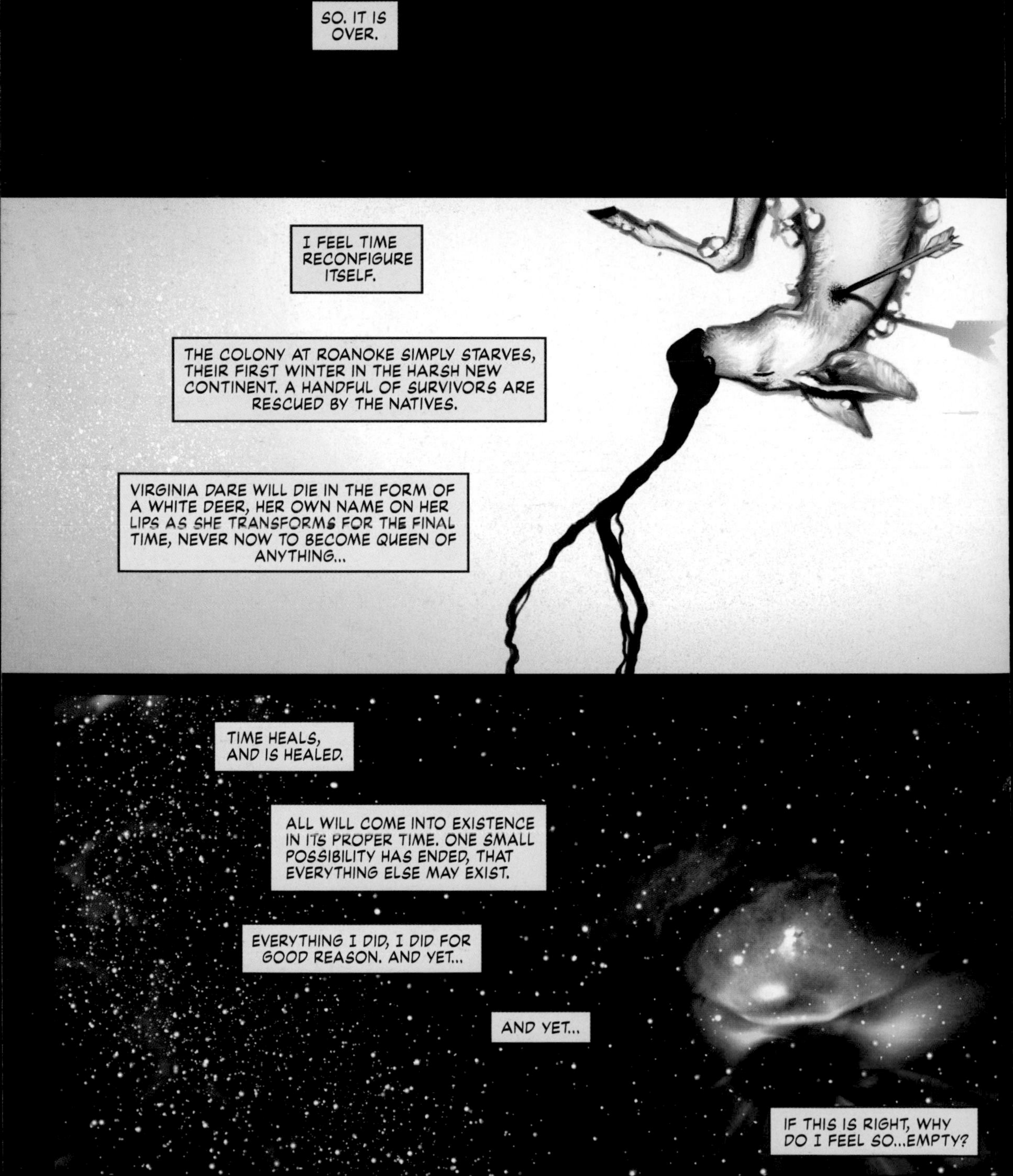
SO. IT IS OVER.
I FEEL TIME RECONFIGURE ITSELF.
THE COLONY AT ROANOKE SIMPLY STARVES, THEIR FIRST WINTER IN THE HARSH NEW CONTINENT. A HANDFUL OF SURVIVORS ARE RESCUED BY THE NATIVES.
VIRGINIA DARE WILL DIE IN THE FORM OF A WHITE DEER, HER OWN NAME ON HER LIPS AS SHE TRANSFORMS FOR THE FINAL TIME, NEVER NOW TO BECOME QUEEN OF ANYTHING...
TIME HEALS, AND IS HEALED.
ALL WILL COME INTO EXISTENCE IN ITS PROPER TIME. ONE SMALL POSSIBILITY HAS ENDED, THAT EVERYTHING ELSE MAY EXIST.
EVERYTHING I DID, I DID FOR GOOD REASON. AND YET...
AND YET...
IF THIS IS RIGHT, WHY DO I FEEL SO...EMPTY?

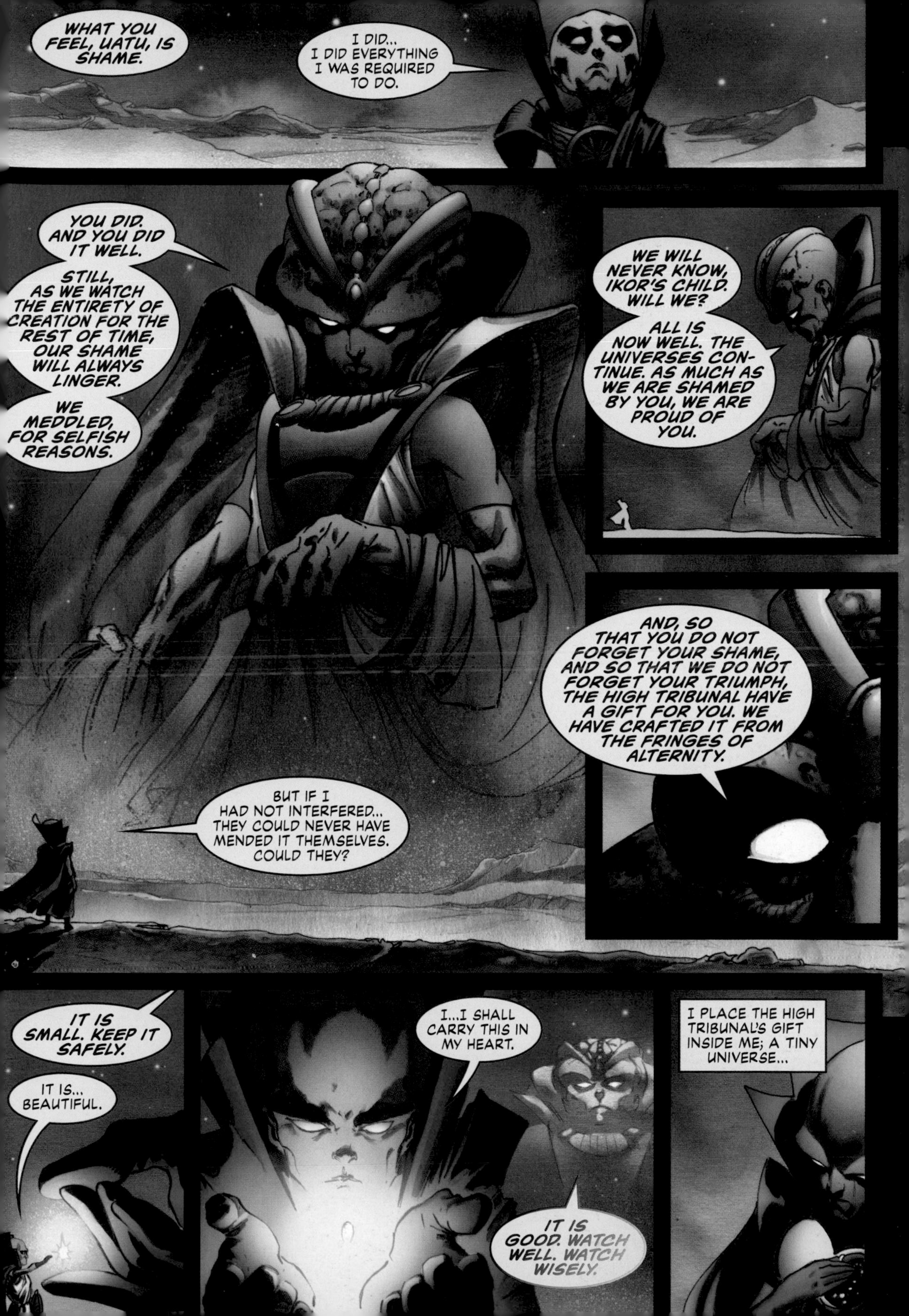
WHAT YOU FEEL, UATU, IS SHAME.
I DID... I DID EVERYTHING I WAS REQUIRED TO DO.
YOU DID. AND YOU DID IT WELL.
STILL, AS WE WATCH THE ENTIRETY OF CREATION FOR THE REST OF TIME, OUR SHAME WILL ALWAYS LINGER.
WE MEDDLED, FOR SELFISH REASONS.
BUT IF I HAD NOT INTERFERED... THEY COULD NEVER HAVE MENDED IT THEMSELVES. COULD THEY?
WE WILL NEVER KNOW, IKOR'S CHILD. WILL WE?
ALL IS NOW WELL. THE UNIVERSES CONTINUE. AS MUCH AS WE ARE SHAMED BY YOU, WE ARE PROUD OF YOU.
AND, SO THAT YOU DO NOT FORGET YOUR SHAME, AND SO THAT WE DO NOT FORGET YOUR TRIUMPH, THE HIGH TRIBUNAL HAVE A GIFT FOR YOU. WE HAVE CRAFTED IT FROM THE FRINGES OF ALTERNITY.
IT IS SMALL. KEEP IT SAFELY.
IT IS... BEAUTIFUL.
I...I SHALL CARRY THIS IN MY HEART.
IT IS GOOD. WATCH WELL. WATCH WISELY.
I PLACE THE HIGH TRIBUNAL'S GIFT INSIDE ME; A TINY UNIVERSE...

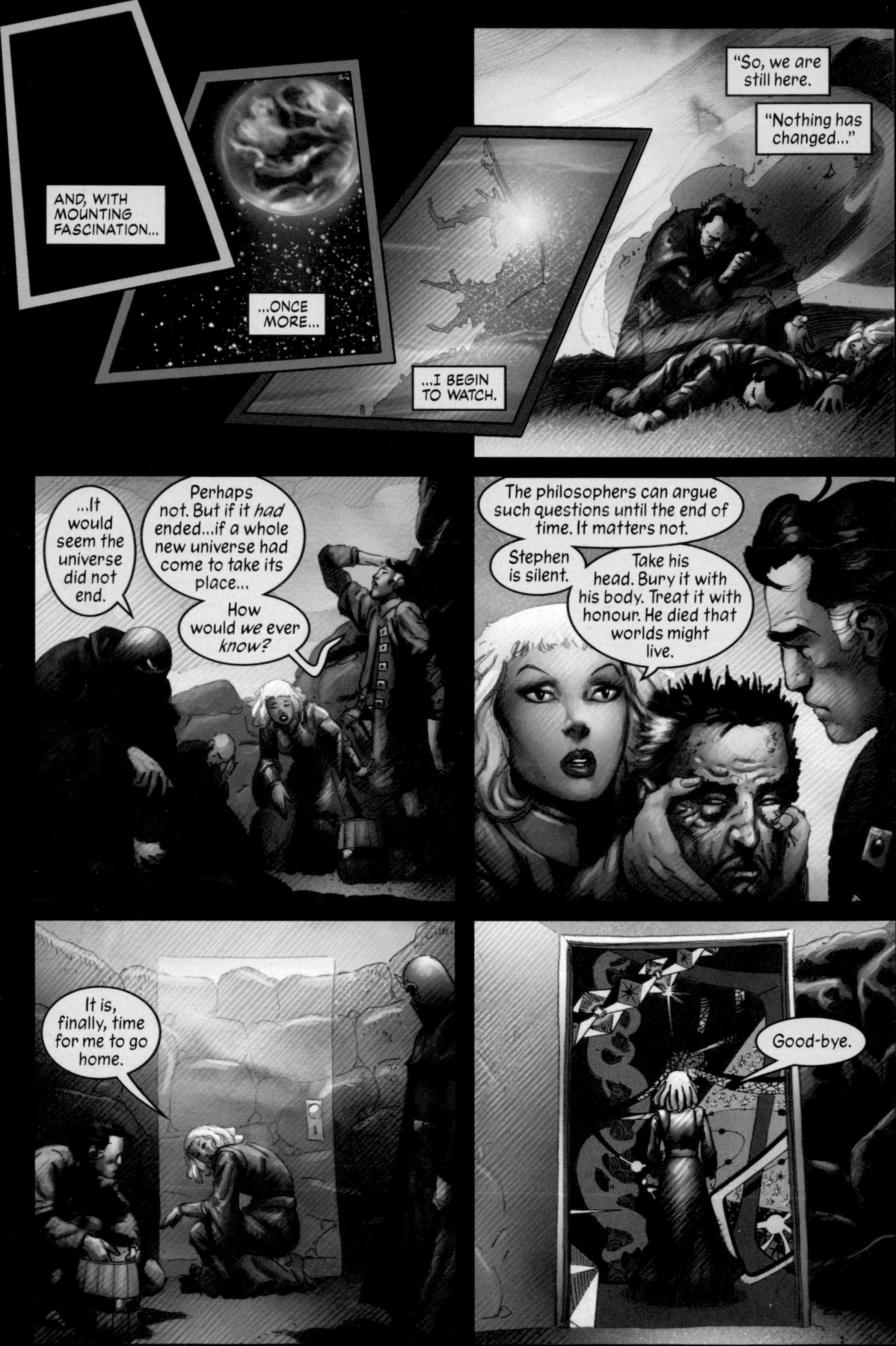

AND, WITH MOUNTING FASCINATION...
...ONCE MORE...
...I BEGIN TO WATCH.
"So, we are still here.
"Nothing has changed..."
...It would seem the universe did not end.
Perhaps not. But if it *had* ended...if a whole new universe had come to take its place...
How would *we* ever *know?*
The philosophers can argue such questions until the end of time. It matters not.
Stephen is silent.
Take his head. Bury it with his body. Treat it with honour. He died that worlds might live.
It is, finally, time for me to go home.
Good-bye.

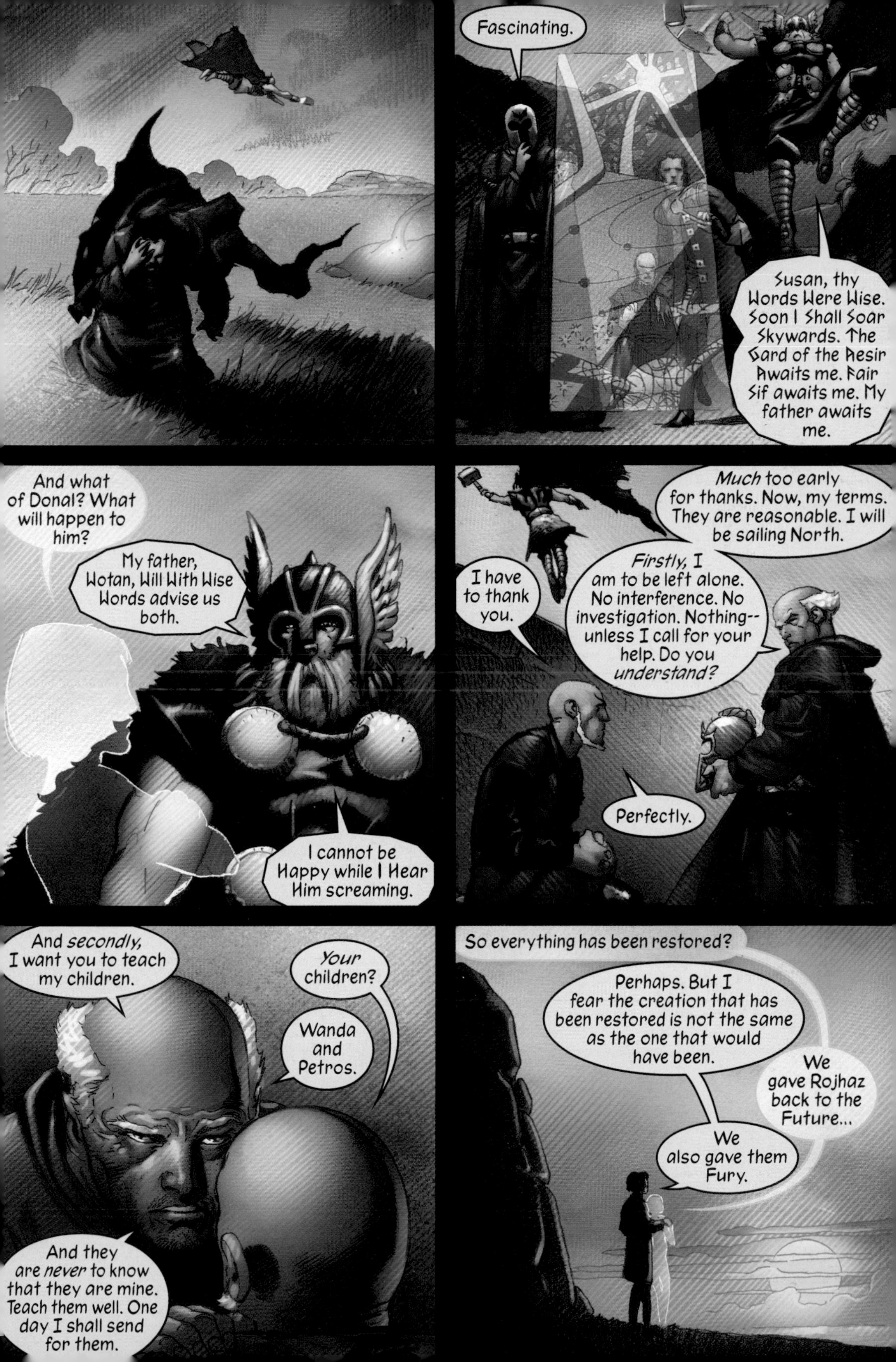
Fascinating.
Susan, thy Words Were Wise. Soon I Shall Soar Skywards. The Gard of the Aesir Awaits me. Fair Sif awaits me. My father awaits me.
And what of Donal? What will happen to him?
My father, Wotan, Will With Wise Words advise us both.
I cannot be Happy while I Hear Him screaming.
I have to thank you.
Much too early for thanks. Now, my terms. They are reasonable. I will be sailing North.
Firstly, I am to be left alone. No interference. No investigation. Nothing-- unless I call for your help. Do you *understand?*
Perfectly.
And *secondly,* I want you to teach my children.
Your children?
Wanda and Petros.
And they are *never* to know that they are mine. Teach them well. One day I shall send for them.
So everything has been restored?
Perhaps. But I fear the creation that has been restored is not the same as the one that would have been.
We gave Rojhaz back to the Future...
We also gave them Fury.

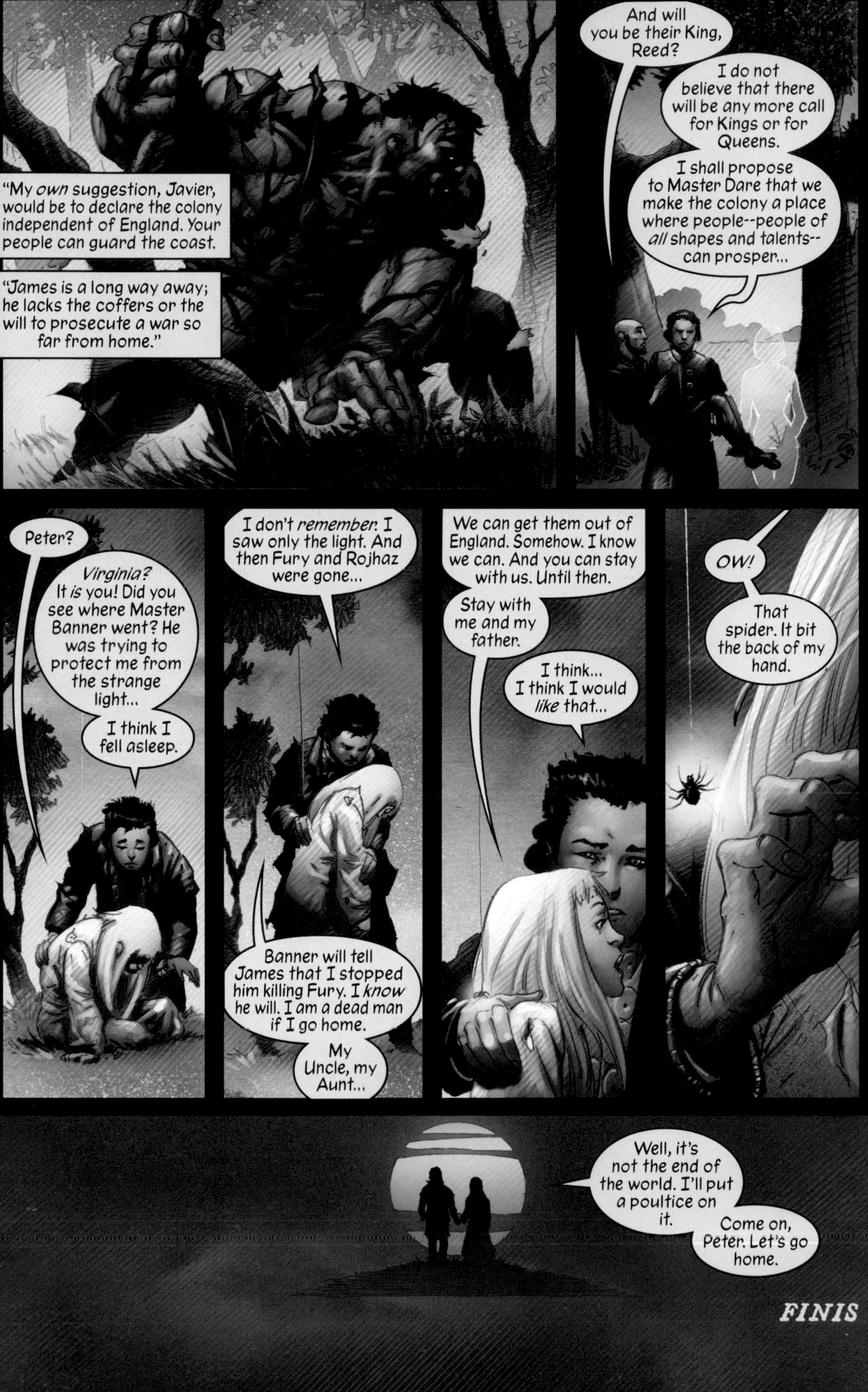
"My *own* suggestion, Javier, would be to declare the colony independent of England. Your people can guard the coast.
"James is a long way away; he lacks the coffers or the will to prosecute a war so far from home."
And will you be their King, Reed?
I do not believe that there will be any more call for Kings or for Queens.
I shall propose to Master Dare that we make the colony a place where people--people of *all* shapes and talents--can prosper...
Peter?
Virginia? It *is* you! Did you see where Master Banner went? He was trying to protect me from the strange light...
I think I fell asleep.
I don't *remember*. I saw only the light. And then Fury and Rojhaz were gone...
Banner will tell James that I stopped him killing Fury. I *know* he will. I am a dead man if I go home.
My Uncle, my Aunt...
We can get them out of England. Somehow. I know we can. And you can stay with us. Until then.
Stay with me and my father.
I think... I think I would *like* that...
OW!
That spider. It bit the back of my hand.
Well, it's not the end of the world. I'll put a poultice on it.
Come on, Peter. Let's go home.
FINIS

Afterword

It being a beautiful day today, and seeing that I am now, in all honesty, too big to comfortably clamber about beneath a porch and I do not possess a treehouse, I put all eight copies of the *1602* comic, along with a pen and a pad of yellow Post-it notes, into a plastic bag then clambered into a small boat, which I paddled into the middle of the lake. Once I was a very long way away from anywhere, I opened the bag, and took out the first issue.

There are places to read the comics of summer, and a small boat, in the middle of a large lake, on a sunny day, with a soft breeze down on water level, is one of them. It's the kind of day when, as a boy in Sussex, I'd take my comics down into a local field, by a pond, near a stand of bulrushes, and I'd read.

I was about six years old when I met the Marvel characters. It was 1967 and an English publisher started the "Power Comics" line (five comics altogether: Wham! Smash! Pow! Fantastic! and Terrific!), and while the first three comics included the Leo Baxendale created strips The Man from BUNGLE, and its spin-off, Grimly Feendish, and such home-grown super heroes as Rubber Man – condemned by the magic of an Indian Fakir (whatever that was, I'd think each week) to be rubbery, the last two comics were devoted exclusively to reprints, in black and white with a third colour, normally blue or red, of Marvel titles.

So although at this point the Stan Lee Jack Kirby Steve Ditko Marvel Universe was already five years old, I got to experience it from the beginning. I met the X-Men in the same way as Jean Grey, arriving at Professor X's School for Gifted Teenagers; I encountered Thor just as poor crippled Dr. Don Blake did, in a cave in Norway, as he picked up a stick he found in a cave, transformed into Thor, and immediately foiled an alien invasion....

It was a good way to meet them all, and created a sort of timeless present, in which the events in those comics are still happening. Doctor Strange is still, for me, drawn by Steve Ditko. He is promising to save a stranger from evil dreams, or he is rescuing Clea from the dread Dormammu. The Fantastic Four are at this moment discovering that a homeless man in New York is in reality the Sub-Mariner...

I viewed the Marvel Universe as a real place. Everyone knew everyone. Everyone had mistakenly fought everyone, everyone had rescued everyone. The mid-sixties American Marvels I was able to find confirmed this impression: I delighted in the Inhumans, in the arrival of the Silver Surfer (not to mention Galactus). I caught up with Daredevil and Spider-Man. I found out what these characters looked like in colour.

It was magic.

When Joe Quesada became Marvel's Editor in Chief, he hunted me down in whatever hotel I was in in New York, and told me he wanted me to write a Marvel Comic. Eventually, events conspired to make it a certainty that I would. So, in the Autumn of 2001, I agreed to write a Marvel Comic. I wasn't sure what it would contain, though.

And then September the 11th happened, and while I wasn't certain what I wanted in there, I suddenly knew what I didn't want. No planes. No skyscrapers. No bombs. No guns. I didn't want it to be a war story, and I didn't want to write a story in which might made right – or in which might made anything.

A week later, I was in Venice. It was chilly, and there were few tourists (the planes had begun flying again the previous day. Friends had begged me not to cross the Atlantic, as if unimaginable dangers waited for me in Europe) and the past seemed very close at hand.

I came home from that trip knowing exactly what kind of story I wanted to tell.

I wanted to write a comic with the same sense of playfulness, and of being part of a world a-borning, that I had seen in those early Marvel comics. To write something that would not be a pastiche, but which Stan Lee or Jack Kirby or Steve Ditko would have recognized.

A Marvel universe that had started, for its own reasons, four hundred years early...

I found myself playing with correspondences, building things up. I sent an outline with some character descriptions to artist Andy Kubert, watched in delight as he sent me back drawings of the people I had imagined.

Writing it was odd – I'd not written comics for half a decade, and needed to find my feet; and then the story, which had been envisaged as six 36-page chapters, needed to be reshaped on the fly for 8 parts, as the page count dropped to 22 pages, and I found myself moving things around, tossing out entire plotlines. I cursed myself several times an issue for having thought that a story with about thirty major characters was a good idea.

But then I'd see the pencilled pages that Andy Kubert would send back, or Scott's remarkable scratchboard covers, and I'd smile.

We did our best to finish the whole book before the first part was published, and confined our publicity efforts to not telling people what it was we were doing, mostly because we figured it would take the best part of two years to produce, and we didn't want people getting bored with it before it had come out. This turned out to be an astonishingly effective promotional strategy.

And then it came out. Entertainment Weekly loved it. Time Magazine immediately proclaimed it the worst comic of the year (although the journalist who created the list rather ruined the effect some months later, by explaining that when he said it was the worst comic of the year, he didn't actually mean it was the worst comic of the year, which I thought extremely wishy-washy of him). People bought it, and they argued about it. Most of them liked it. Some of them didn't, and those who didn't really didn't. There was, I learned, from both sides a definite consensus that it was not Sandman, which I found rather a relief, as I had been trying quite hard not to write Sandman.

It's easy to forget the amount of work that goes on behind the scenes on something like this. Joe Quesada edited the first issue, and then, probably because he thought we all knew what we were doing, he let us get on with it, so the editorial chores were, in the main, carried out with cheerful aplomb by Nick Lowe (not the one who was in Brinsley Schwartz); Andy Kubert drew it with enthusiasm and skill, and often waited patiently for pages while I did strange things like direct a movie or contract meningitis; Richard Isanove took Andy's pencils and made them look like little paintings; and Todd Klein forever managed to fit too many words into an impossibly small space, and to always come up with ways to make the word balloons magical. I'd like to thank them all.

I just re-read *1602*, for proofreading purposes, this afternoon, in a small boat, drifting across a lake on a sunny day, and I found, to my relief, it was very much the kind of comic I had wanted to write: something for summer, to be read under a porch or in a treehouse; or up on a roof; or in a small field, a long time ago, beside the bulrush patch.

Neil Gaiman
June 30, 2004

1602 I

Script by Neil Gaiman
Sketches by Andy Kubert

And because I always wanted to write this on a script:

CONFIDENTIAL

Hello Andy,

Well, here we are, five hundred years ago. Having fun. We aren't trying to mirror the Marvel Universe here: we're doing something that's more fun than that – we're trying to create it. We get to make up our own.

No costumes – except everyone's in costume, an olden-days, Elizabethan sort of costume, and each of their clothes can be stylised to remind people of what they might be if they were wearing more superheroey clothes.

I'm trying to go for, mainly, fairly straightforward panel grids and layouts here – the kind of things that the eye eats and vanishes. Take a look back at what Dave Gibbons did on Watchmen. We're not doing that here, but it's not a bad thing to keep as an ideal. I was always fascinated by the way that Watchmen looked like the "WRONG WAY TO DO IT" panels from "How to Draw Comics The Marvel Way."

We'll do lots of cool visual stuff, but concentrate most of all on grounding everything in a sense of reality, and the cool stuff will take care of itself.

By part two or part three I'll really be writing for you, with a sense of what you can do and what you like to do. Here at the start, I'm just assuming, from what I've seen you do so far, that you're incredibly competent and can draw anything, and will stop me boring people to death.

Feel free to ignore my suggestions if you can see a better way of doing it. (You are the artist.) The most important thing is the storytelling.

Also, there's an awful lot to cram in here, so let me know if you need more room, and if I'm trying to jam in too much...

And with that, only one real request: have fun. Lots of it.

Neil

Page 1 panel 1

We are looking at Dr Stephen Strange, court magician to Elizabeth the 1st, from behind. He is heading down a corridor. Ahead of him, against the wall, is a guard, with a halberd, staring straight ahead. We can see that Strange has a skullcap and a ruff around his neck, and wears a large cloak – not, however, a classic Dr Strange Design cloak. His hair is longer. It is night.

CAPTION: 1602. March. Hampton Court. England.

CAPTION: "For a whole week the skies over London have been BLOOD RED at noon. We have reports here from all over our KINGDOM. Reports of THUNDERSTORMS, with thunderclaps loud enough to DEAFEN, and LIGHTNINGS that strike churches and towers alike, but not one DROP of rain that falls.

CAPTION: "Look at this – "

Page 1 panel 2

Now, a good look at him as he hesitates before a wooden door. A dark beard and moustache, in something slightly longer than a Vandyke. Good cheek bones. Some streaks of white in the beard, although he's in his late 30s.

CAPTION: "Where did I put it?

CAPTION: "Ah yes. LOOK. Earthquakes tumbled our city of York. The fens are FLOODED. And from what you are saying, such things are happening across Europe – perhaps across the world.'"

Page 1 panel 3

Inside the room: It's a large room, a royal room. Not the throne room – but there is a large wooden table, and seated at the table is her majesty, Elizabeth the first: an old woman in a red wig, her teeth little brown nubs, her cheeks sunken, her eyes still bright. She will die very soon. She wears a huge dress, a large ruff, and the dress is cut low, pushing her old breasts up and out: she was proud of them. Standing beside her is a tall man with greying hair and white temples. He has an eyepatch over one eye, a squarish jaw, and reminds us, a little, of Nick Fury, Agent of SHIELD. He also has a scar running down the side of the face with the missing eye. He's in his late fifties. He wears black clothes, with a white ruff, and black gloves. His is standing beside the queen, and they are looking at a number of papers.

The door behind them has opened, and Dr Stephen Strange is walking in. We need a feeling here of a long room, of night, of two people conferring by candlelight.

FURY: Yes, Majesty. I believe so.

QUEEN: You understand, Sir Nicholas, there are those in court who say that this – coff! coff! – means we are entering the final days. That the world will end in fire and darkness soon enough. What do you say to that? Eh?

FURY: I'm afraid Armageddon is rather outside my department, Majesty.

Page 1 panel 4

Close up on the queen, an ancient grotesque, her red wig slightly askew. She is dabbing at her lips with a lace-edged handkerchief, and looking up at us and asking:

QUEEN: Ah, the good Doctor. Right on time.

What say you then, good sir Doctor? Is the world truly ending?

Page 2 panel 1

Okay: good shot of Dr Strange – or rather, someone who might be his great-great grandfather's grandfather: not the same man, but someone like him. Both his ears have small gold rings in them. He spreads his hands as he looks down at this tiny old woman.

STRANGE: Majesty. It is certain that something untoward is in the air. Whether it be the Day of Judgement or not is not for me to say.

No man shall know the day or the hour, eh?

Page 2 panel 2

Pull back. Strange and Fury are next to each other, still standing, one on each side of the queen. The queen is sitting.

QUEEN: If it is not yours to say, then we are paying you for nothing, and the royal purse is not inexhaustible, Doctor.

Have you two met before?

STRANGE: I cannot say that we have that honour –

Page 2 panel 3

The Queen, and Dr Strange beside her. He has folded his hands across his chest, bowed his head slightly. It's a gesture you don't see any more, but it shows up in pictures of old academics. She is pointing to him with one of the documents, rolled into a scroll.

QUEEN: No. But you know each other, I have no doubt.

Doctor Stephen Strange, master of the Queen's magics, meet Sir Nicholas Fury, who is – what is your official title, Sir Nicholas? No, be quiet. You'll tell us we do not pay you enough.

Page 2 panel 4

Our first good shot of Nick Fury. Again, lit by firelight. He's an Elizabethan spymaster, subtle, but no stranger to the knife or the sword. He's fought in wars, and sailed the seas. I think he's probably cleanshaven, or has a very thin Vandyke beard.

QUEEN: Sir Nicholas is our intelligencer, Doctor. All the plots and counterplots, all the words whispered and knives in the dark are his to unravel and employ. He does his job well – that I am still queen, and have not been assassinated a hundred times over, is his fault.

FURY: I am proud to serve, Majesty.

Page 2 panel 5

The queen herself, dabbing at her mouth with her handkerchief.

QUEEN: Pride comes before a fall, Sir Nicholas.

Koff Koff Koff...

Page 2 panel 6

Pull back. She is pushing herself unsteadily to her feet, reaching out to take Dr Strange's arm to steady herself.

Queen Elizabeth

"We live in a time of miracles and wonders and I cannot say that it pleases me."

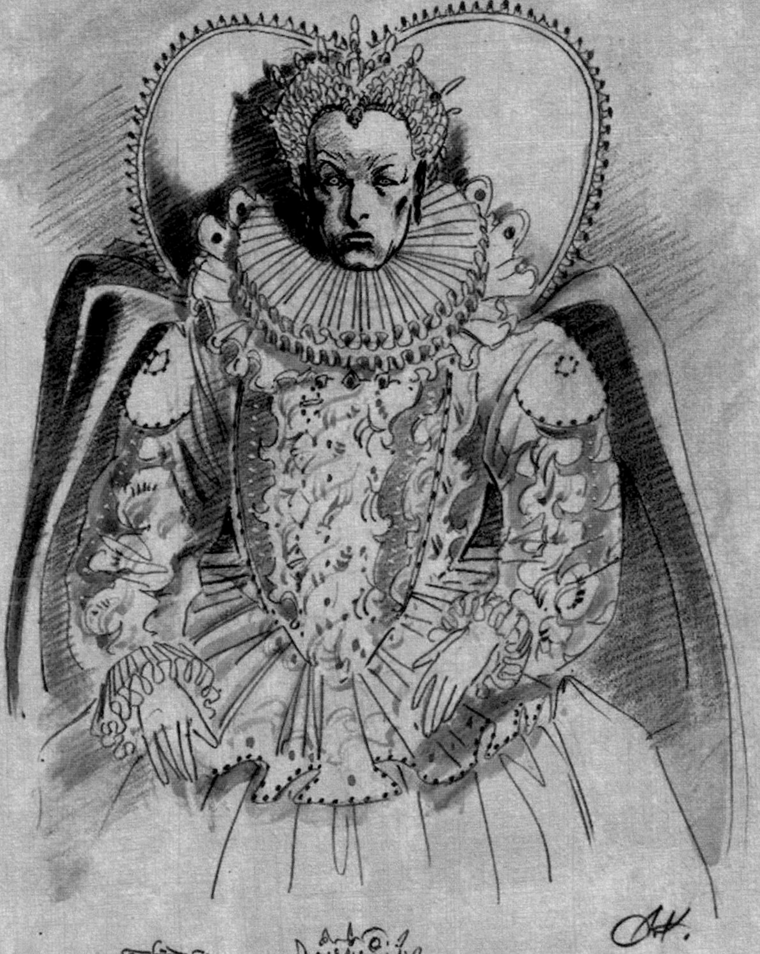

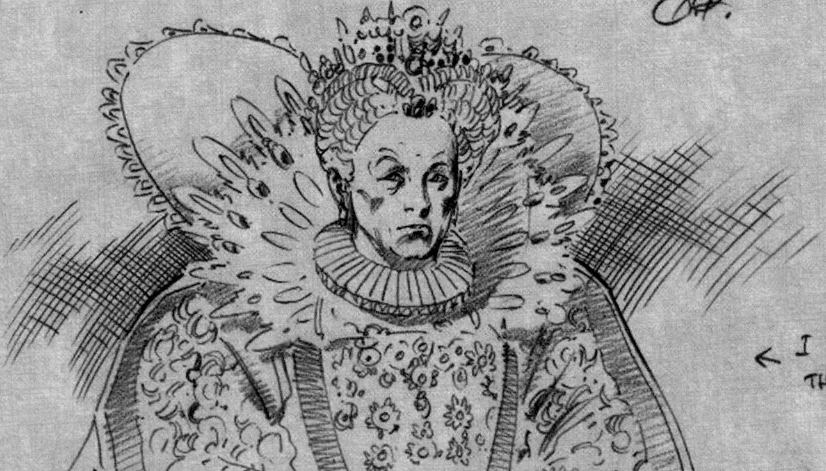

← I LIKE THIS FACE

There is blood on the handkerchief.

QUEEN: Doctor, tell Sir Nicholas what you communicated to the palace this morning.

STRANGE: Yes, Majesty.

Page 3 panel 1

Strange is now facing Fury; the Queen is walking away from them, taking a few steps back, so she's no longer between them. Fury is taller, more powerful than Strange, Strange more precise, more focussed. Strange has made a steeple of his forefingers and placed them beneath his lower lip as he talks, mysteriously... Fury is not impressed by this.

STRANGE: First, I should say that there are certain lines of communication open to those who, like myself, study the mystic arts. I cannot reveal these –

Page 3 panel 2

Head to head, in profile. Strange is irritated.

FURY: Good Sir Doctor, I can tell you every foreigner you have spoken to in the last five years.

STRANGE: There are many kinds of speech, Sir Nicholas, and not all of them can be overheard by your spies and cutthroats.

Page 3 panel 3

A slim panel. The Queen herself is irritated, – she may be a sick old woman, but she is also the queen — and she barks out:

QUEEN: Enough, Strange. Tell him what you told me.

Page 3 panel 4

Close in: Strange's eyes, staring out at us, from across the middle of the page.

STRANGE: There is something – I am not certain what, but something... powerful. Something dangerous, I believe. In Jerusalem, the Holy City. It has been offered to me to guard, and I have accepted.

If it were to fall into the wrong hands, it could mean disaster for England. Perhaps disaster for the world.

Page 3 panel 5

Fury facing us, Strange in profile.

FURY: You do not know what manner of thing this is?

STRANGE: A weapon, I believe. I am not certain. But it must be kept safe on its way here.

Page 3 panel 6

Fury in close up. He is smiling, ever-so slightly.

FURY: We can do that.

Page 3 panel 7

And the Queen is smiling, and talking, and holding her handkerchief.

QUEEN: Very well. We are done. Koff. Koff... And let us hope that the world does not end, eh, Sir Nicholas? Eh, good Doctor?

At least, let it not end before I do.

QUEEN: Good night to you both.

Page 4 panel 1

Strange and Fury are walking together out of the palace. For reference, I'd suggest *Shakespeare in Love*, and, to a lesser extent, *Elizabeth*, as films that give a feeling for the manners, clothes and customs of the time – and you'll see a lot of water taxis in *Shakespeare in Love*, and a fair number of big important houses. Now they look less strained, less formal. It cannot have been easy in there with the queen. There are flaming lanterns on each side of the path. The palace is behind them. The moon is out – a crescent-moon.

FURY: There are those who say that Her Majesty is simply frightened by a few bad storms.

STRANGE: Are you one of them?

FURY: I have not yet made up my mind. And what about you, Doctor?

Page 4 panel 2

Now we're behind them: The water, with flaming lamps along the side, is ahead of them. Boats wait to take them back.

STRANGE: These storms are far from natural.

FURY: Hmm. If the world is indeed ending, can your Templar treasure protect us?

STRANGE: I did not mention the Templars, Sir Nicholas.

FURY: No. Nor did you mention that the old man himself would be bringing you this treasure.

Page 4 panel 3

Now move back in for a medium shot. Fury is grinning, and resting his hand on Strange's upper arm, a gesture of reassurance.

FURY: See? My spies and cutthroats are good for something.

But if I know, then I can wager you the Spanish and the Portuguese and the Russians also know. None of them know what it is, but they know that they want it.

Page 4 panel 4

They are ready to part company. Perhaps a boatman or courtier waiting at the dock is helping Fury into a boat. Fury, looking back at Strange...

FURY: I go to Westminster, where I shall talk to the man whose task it shall be to bring your mystery box safely back to London.

STRANGE: And I to my home in the village of Greenwich. Good night.

Page 4 panel 5

End on Strange's face, his arms crossed, staring at Fury.

STRANGE: (Small) I have questions to ask my mirror.

Page 5

Now, there are a couple of ways to do this page, Andy. It's

Dr. Stephen Strange

"I know such things that my mind seems likely to explode and fragment and dissolve."

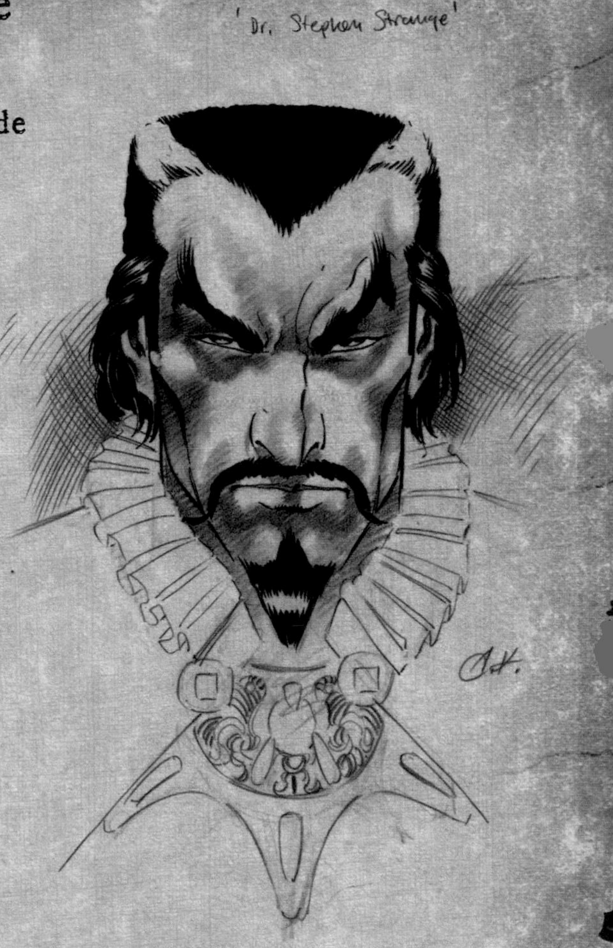

'Dr. Stephen Strange'

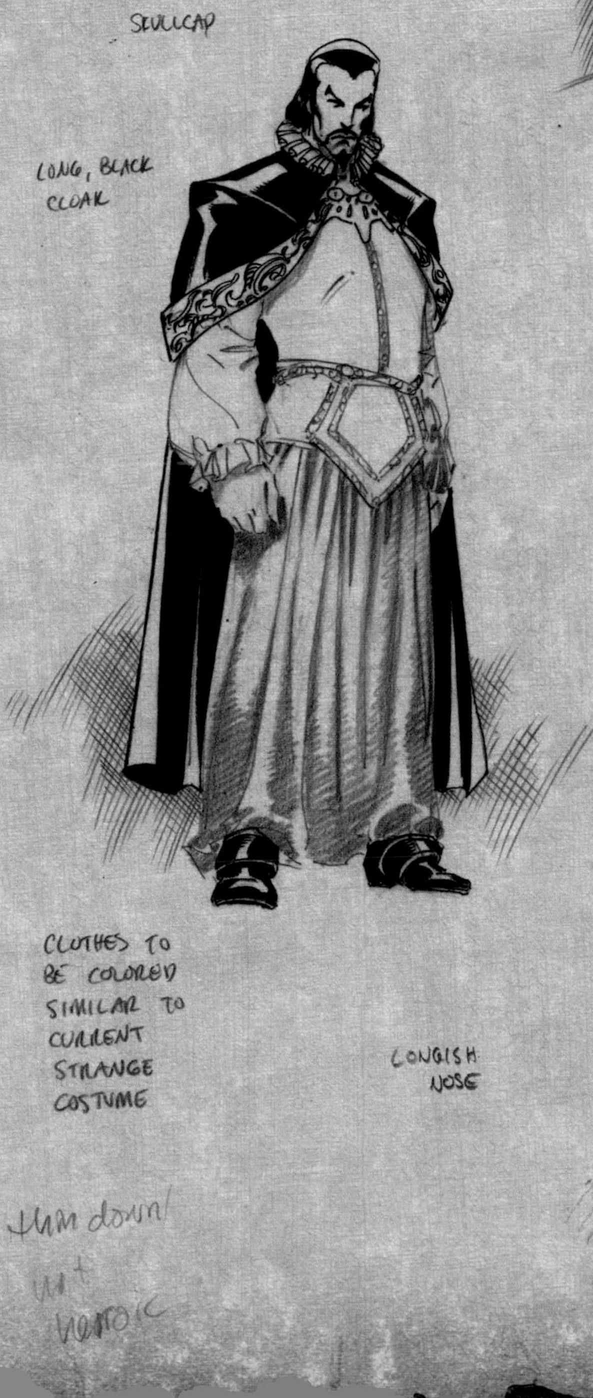

SKULLCAP
LONG, BLACK CLOAK
CLOTHES TO BE COLORED SIMILAR TO CURRENT STRANGE COSTUME
thin down!
not heroic

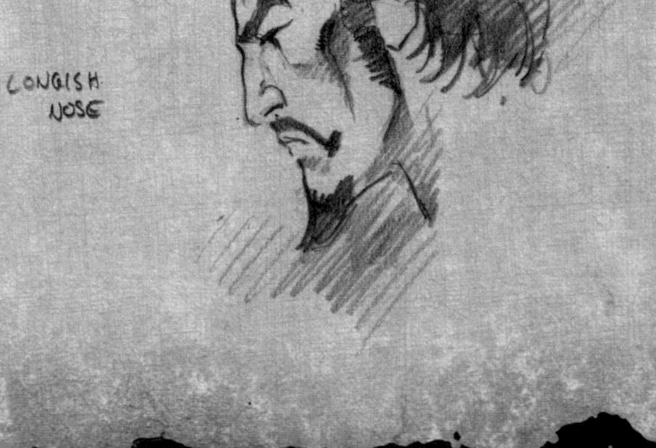

LONGISH NOSE

your call. Either we could do it as a set of small shots, starting on the tower, then in on his face, then slowly pulling back, in strips running horizontally across the page, that slowly add up to a whole; or do a splash page, and then just arrange our captions around it to lead the eye and make sure it gets read. I tend to want to go for the splash – which would be an image of a young man, blonde hair, clean-shaven as he's too young to shave, wearing ragged britches and nothing else, chained to a wall. The only illumination is moonlight, which gives this a really Frank Millery feeling in my head, all harsh blacks made into a picture by thin whites. The young man has feathery angel-wings. He is chained so that his body is in an X-shape, and his wings are closed behind him. (Second thoughts: let's do this page as small images – a hand chained, a bare foot with an iron shackle around it, part of a face, all that, and then go over the page to a shot of the whole thing.)

CAPTION: The High Tower in the Palace of the Inquisition. Domdaniel. Spain.

ANGEL CAPTION: Yesterday, they burned a Jew. He was a secret Jew – his grandfathers had converted to Christianity to stay in Spain – but still, he did not work on the Sabbath, and he ate no pork, which was how they found him out.

ANGEL CAPTION: I could smell him burning from up here.

ANGEL CAPTION: A stench of woodsmoke and burning hair, then a smell of meat, cooking. There were screams. He called on his God to protect him.

ANGEL CAPTION: Last night – my captors told me as if it was not important – a heretic died, being tortured. They were disappointed. A waste of a death.

ANGEL CAPTION: They have not tortured me. Not physically.

ANGEL CAPTION: I have been left here, chained in this tower, able to feel the winds on my face and skin. Sometimes they ask me questions.

ANGEL CAPTION: They ask as friends, enquiring after my health and livelihood:

ANGEL CAPTION: Who hid me as I grew? Who protected me? Did I kiss the Devil's rump before I grew my wings? Do I have friends who are Witchbreed?

Page 6

Now a full page shot of him chained to the wall, in shadows.

ANGEL CAPTION: I have lived for almost 17 years. I die tomorrow. And this is what hurts the most: that I shall die on the ground. That I shall never take to the skies again, to dance, to laugh, to fly...

ANGEL CAPTION: Or rather, that when I take to the skies, for one last time, it will be as ashes.

Page 7 panel 1

A pub in Westminster: Again, look at *Shakespeare in Love*, and the various Tavern sequences. A huge fire is burning, brands against the wall give some light, a pot-girl is balancing a tray of mugs filled with ale... Large panel: establishing shot.

And there are a number of people in the room, but only two of them are important: young Peter Parquaugh, Fury's assistant, and a red-headed Irish ballad singer, blind and big, with a white cane and a rag bandage over his eyes. Peter is sitting at a table, his hand cradling something interesting he's found, and examining it. There are a bunch of other people at the table, but they are all calling to the ballad singer. Imagine Matt Murdoch (The Gene Colan one, I suppose, but he's stayed pretty consistent over the years) with longer, badly-cut hair, dressed in poor clothes and accompanying himself on a battered lute, and you'll have an idea what this Matthew Murdoch is like. For young master Parquaugh, think of Ditko's version of Peter Parker (not Romita's — I want that slight angularity of face). Then lose the spectacles, because they didn't really have them then, which means our young man is pretty shortsighted. Let the hair grow longer, and put him in Elizabethan clothes. He's an Elizabethan Nerd. There should also be someone who looks like a sailor.

CAPTION: The Moor's Head. A Tavern in Westminster.

MAN 1: Another song!

MATTHEW: Certainly, good masters. Is there any song in particular you'd be after?

MAN 2: D'ye know the Ballad of the Fantastick?

MATTHEW: And what kind of a balladeer would I be, if I did not?

There were four brave souls rode the oceans abroad. T'was on the Fantastick they sailed...

Page 7 panel 2

Now, let's look at Peter – who in the last panel was just one of the crowd. He's barely listening to the song. Now he's looking down at the wooden table, upon which we can see a rather attractive spider, at least, for those who like spiders. The ballad singer carries on singing...

MATTHEW: And one was the captain, and one was a lord, And one a young hothead who carried a sword, and the last was a maiden so pale — so pale...

Page 7 panel 3

Right – pull back. The sailor's grabbed blind Matt's arm, while his friend tries to pull him off. The Sailor's talking to Matt, the friend to the sailor.

MATTHEW: The last was a maiden so pale.

SAILOR: Hoy! Matthew! I'll give you a groat not to sing that ballad! It's a song of ill-omen, you damned fool.

FRIEND: Leave the poor blind bog-trotter alone. He's just trying to make enough for a bed for the night.

Page 7 panel 4

Back again to Peter, at his table, where a number of drunken conversations are going on. Peter's neighbour, a fat man holding a large tankard, has caught sight of Peter's spider.

MAN 1: I say again, if the Queen had had issue, the world would not be in the parlous state it is.

MAN 2: If you say so.

MAN 1: I do say so.

FAT MAN: Hey, lad. What's that you've found?

Page 7 panel 5

Thin panel, as Peter smiles enthusiastically. He points to the spider, sitting on the table in front of him.

PETER: A spider, sir. And such an interesting beast it is. Why, see how its carapace glitters –

FAT MAN: Faugh!

Page 7 panel 6

Repeat the panel, only now the fat man's tankard has been smashed down on the place where the spider was.

FX: Bam!

Page 7 panel 7

Peter is staring in complete shock at the fat man and his tankard. Fury stands behind Peter and rests his hand on Peter's shoulder.

FURY: Peter? Is the room ready?

PETER: Uh.... Yes, Sir Nicholas.

Page 8 panel 1

Okay. Now the tavern owner is walking, with Peter and Fury up the stairs, in the background. In the foreground, the blind Irish ballad singer has slung the lute over his back, and, with his thin cane, is tapping ahead of him. He's announcing, angrily, to the room:

MATTHEW: Aye. Well, if there's no song you gentlemen would like to hear, I'll be off in search of a tavern where they'd actually be grateful for a little music.

Page 8 panel 2

Up on the next floor. Fury is handing the Tavernkeeper a golden coin. Peter's opening the door to an upstairs room.

TAVERNKEEPER: There's no fire in there, Sir, just like he said.

FURY: Well done, Jack. We do not wish to be disturbed.

Page 8 panel 3

Outside the tavern, in an alleyway. Matthew the ballad singer, with the rags over his eyes, is putting down his stick and his lute against the wall. Above him is an open window. It's dark in the alleyway, so we could do this panel in the classic Daredevil way, with concentric circles centring on the man's head. We can see the open window in the upper floor, and the word balloons coming from it:

FURY: There. Now bar the door, I'll shutter the lanterns.

PETER: But sir? If the door is barred, how will our man come to us?

FURY: Don't worry yourself about that. He'll be here.

Page 8 panel 4

Now, one of those acrobatic Daredevil panels: still in concentric circles, as, by an amazing acrobatic feat, we see

him in several frozen outline moments, swinging, jackknifing up and in at the open window.

PETER: Brrr. No-one could come to us up here, sir, unless he was the Devil himself.

Page 8 panel 5

In the dark room. We can see a body between us and the window. Matthew's unruly, slightly curly hair looks like horns in silhouette, black against grey.

MATTHEW: If a Devil is one who dares, when others hold back, then I am happy to play the Devil in this Mystery, boy.

And who would you be?

Page 8 panel 6

Some of these panels are going to be too easy to draw, Andy. This one, for example. It's a black panel. You just need to make sure that Peter and Fury are always on the right of panel, Matthew always on the left.

FURY: His name is Peter Parquagh. He is my new assistant in the department. You may speak in front of him as you would if we were alone.

Page 9 panel 1

Just to keep it interesting visually, you could do dark grey silhouettes against a black background. Or you could leave the panels flat black. Your call.

MATTHEW: So, Fury. There's word on the street something is coming this way from Jerusalem. Something that kings and princes would give their crowns to possess. I take it that's what you're after?

FURY: Of course. Do you know who else is after it?

Page 9 panel 2

Peter's word balloon arrows are beneath Fury's – he's about 9-10 inches shorter, after all.

MATTHEW: We can count on the usual bunch: King of Spain, the Tsar, Count Otto Von Doom –

PETER: The one they call the Handsome?

Page 9 panel 3

MATTHEW: So they say, boy, although I can't say I've ever seen it myself.

FURY: You'll make contact with the Old Man in Trieste, at the port, on the night of the full moon. I want him and his cargo brought safely here.

Page 9 panel 4

MATTHEW: That's only five days from now.

FURY: Then you should move fast. Should you not?

MATTHEW: And my payment?

Page 9 panel 5

FURY: Your usual payment, sir Devil. A diamond the size of a cherry-stone, with its twin to be given to you upon safe delivery of the Old Man and his treasure.

MATTHEW: I'll take the diamond now –

PETER: Do you need light, sir?

Page 9 panel 6

Okay. Do the concentric circles – Daredevil's radar effect – here: Fury and Peter on one side, Matt over by the window, on the other side of the panel. Matt has his hand outstretched, ready to catch the diamond that Fury is tossing.

MATTHEW: If I wanted light, I'd ask for it, boy. Take it in your hand. Now, throw it here, Fury, toward my voice.

Page 10 panel 1

Thin black panel.

No dialogue

Page 10 panel 2

Another thin panel. Now Fury is uncovering a lantern with a burning candle in it.

PETER: (off panel) Is he...?

FURY: Aye. He's gone.

Page 10 panel 3

Outside the building: the alleyway, from the cobbled street, and Matthew is coming out of it, his lute over his shoulder, his rough cane tap-tapping along the street.

PETER CAP: "What – what manner of thing was that, sir?"

FURY CAP: "A man, or so I believe. I have my own ideas about who and what he is, but I daresay they're wrong. And I am merely grateful to the providence that led him to work for me, rather than for the Queen's enemies."

FURY CAP: "I do not seek to ask how a man can catch a diamond in the darkness."

Page 10 panel 4

Peter is unbarring the door. Fury is standing just behind him.

PETER: I know one thing about him, sir.

FURY: What's that, lad?

Page 10 panel 5

Okay: final panel. A moody panel, Matt walking down the cobbled street, his rag-bandaged head raised high.

PETER CAP: "He is not afraid of the dark."

FURY CAP: "No, Peter. Nor anything else, I'll wager."

Page 11 panel 1

The scene shifts to Dr Strange's house in the village of Greenwich, in London. A river mist is coming up, and we're looking at the house, tall and old even then, with narrow high chimneys. A light in the window. Clea, Dr Strange's wife, is talking, and the word balloon can be a caption, or a balloon going to the house.

CAP: Greenwich: A Village East of London. The House of Stephen Strange.

CLEA: How was the Queen, Stephen?

Page 11 panel 2

Inside the house. A sorcerer's room: a dried crocodile hangs from the ceiling, huge dark candles. Shelves covered with huge old leather-bound books. Clea looks like any thirty-year-old Elizabethan lady, but she has that funky black and white thing going on with her hair that the original Clea had, although her hair is up in Elizabethan style. She is holding Strange's arm.

STRANGE: Pragmatic enough to have a court magician, my love. But she grows older and more ill with each day, and my arts can do nothing for her there.

CLEA: And when she dies? Have you thought of that, Stephen?

Page 11 panel 3

Close up on Strange, who looks suddenly very old and very tired.

STRANGE: Aye. I think of little else these days.

Will it be anarchy? Or another Spanish invasion? Or will it be James of Scotland, who has no love for magics, or those who try to master them.

Brrr.

Page 11 panel 4

Flirtatiously, to distract him, she puts her arm around him, from behind, maybe kisses his ear. He is opening a box on the desk.

CLEA: And what did the queen want?

Strange: I think she wants me to do something about the weather.

Page 11 panel 5

He takes out two large polished mirrors, circular, vaguely reminiscent of the Dr Strange Amulet.

CLEA: If I can do anything to help you, you know I shall.

STRANGE: I know. I shall see what there is to be seen. For now, just record my words.

Page 11 panel 6

Strange sits crosslegged on the floor, hands pressed together – it's almost a yoga pose. Clea sits at the desk, with paper and quill pen. Strange is staring into the mirrors, which are facing him, angled, and, between them, a candle, muttering to himself. I know what I want for the word balloon – it may be hard to do without some hand-lettering here: little illegible scribbles as if he's muttering to himself and we can't hear, and then, here and there, a word that's legible.

STRANGE: ...(mutter mutter) Triaseia Ogneia (mutters) Lomeia Zhelteia Neviea (mutters)... Chamodrakaina... (mutters)

... kron, zeves, aris, dennitsa... (mutter)

Page 11 panel 7

Sir Nicholas Fury

"There's blood on my hands, boy."

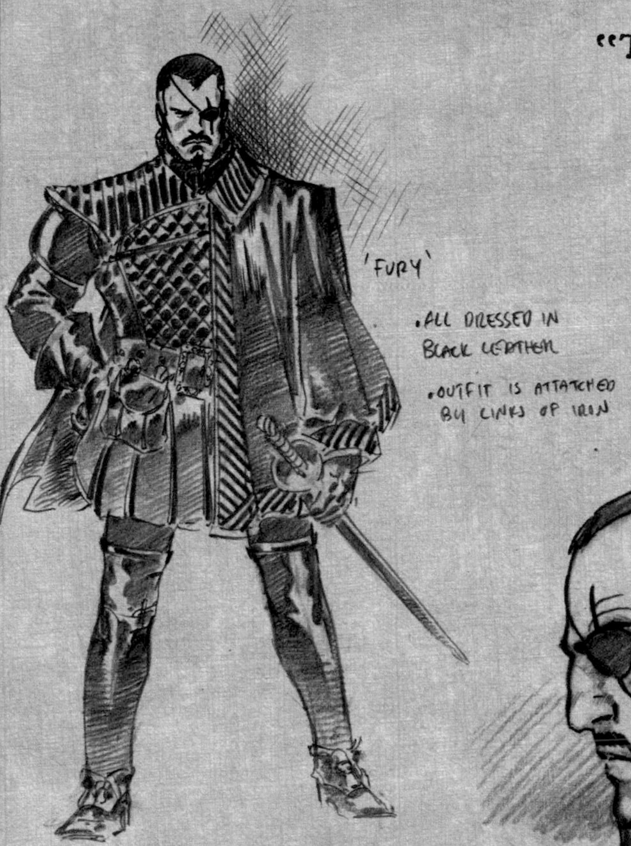
'FURY'
•ALL DRESSED IN BLACK LEATHER
•OUTFIT IS ATTACHED BY LINKS OF IRON

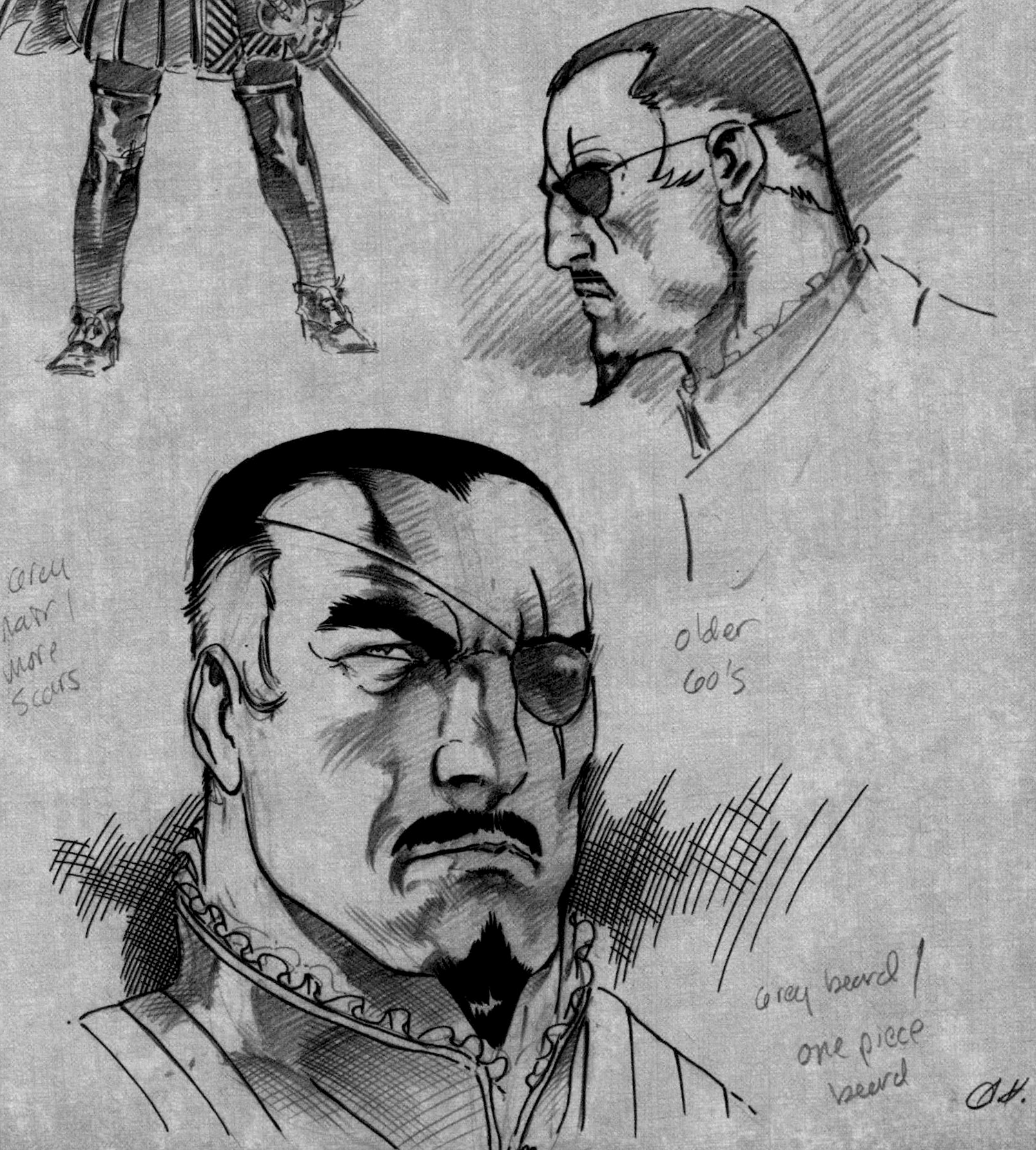
Grey hair / more scars
older 60's
Grey beard / one piece beard

Thin panel: his eyes are now completely white: the pupils have gone. Perhaps they have rolled up in their sockets. His face is dead. Slightly wiggly lettering here, for him in a trance state.

STRANGE: Now: Ask your question.

Page 12 panel 1

A very swirly sort of page — a double page spread for preference: we are in Strange's mind as he astral travels. On the extreme top left, some of Clea's face:

CLEA: The strange weather? What causes it, my love?

Page 12 panel 2

A thin panel. Darkness.

CLEA: Stephen? Stephen? Where are you?

Page 12 panel 3

Images in this can be slightly stylised, less realistic, in colour and everything else. We can see a small ship, sails billowing, as it sails through the night.

STRANGE CAP: "I am flying, like a gull or a nightbird, above a ship. It comes toward us, out of the west.

"There are two people on the deck, in the thin light of the crescent moon."

Page 12 panel 4

Our first sight of Virginia Dare, and her Indian (Native American) bodyguard, Rojhaz. She leans against a wooden railing, he stands a little behind her. She is pale, white-skinned, white-haired. There is something fawn-like about this girl: huge eyes, a haunting beauty — she's about 14 years old, Juliet's age. Rojhaz is huge — seven feet tall, muscled, wearing a buckskin loincloth, his long hair twined with feathers and beads.

CLEA CAP: "The ship's name, Stephen?"

STRANGE CAP: "The Virginia Maid.

STRANGE CAP: "And on the deck I see the maid herself.

STRANGE CAP: "No, there are no answers here."

Page 12 panel 5

Swirly blackness.

STRANGE CAP: "Ask another question, my love?"

CLEA: "How may the darkness be lifted from the land?"

Page 12 panel 6

We are looking at a strange room — it's a cell, carved out of a rock, deep in the earth, and a waterfall tumbles down into it, spray filling the air. There is a young man, naked on a tiny rock in the middle of the water. We cannot see his face: he seems to be steaming gently.

STRANGE CAP: "I am in the heart of a mountain, far from here, a place built to hold Earth and Air, Water and Fire...

STRANGE CAP: "No... it slips away from me. Slips and changes."

Page 13 panel 1

Now, the tower that the Angel is held prisoner in. A tower, inside a walled compound.

STRANGE CAP: "I see a tower. And in the tower there is ... an angel?"

Page 13 panel 2

The angel, as we saw him before, but stranger, and more stylised.

STRANGE CAP: "No. No, I lie. It is a man. A man with wings."

Page 13 panel 3

The square — it's dark but we're seeing it in ghost-vision: Living monks are laying firwood and brushwood around a stake. Meanwhile, ghostly men and women are tied to phantom stakes and are screaming in agony. It's surreal and odd...

STRANGE CAP: "They are piling firewood in the square below. The square is filled with ghosts in pain, who scream in silent voices, trapped in their final moments.."

CLEA: "Who does this thing, Stephen? What is its significance?"

STRANGE CAP: "Would that I knew.."

Page 13 panel 4

Okay. Our first glimpse of Magneto — or our Magneto analogue. I ought to name him, oughtn't I? Very well, he is the Inquisitor. A white-haired gentleman with magnificent eyebrows, in a very bare cell. His hair is shaved into a tonsure. He wears white robes. He is talking to the Scarlet Witch: she is dressed as a nun, of the period, in a fairly simple habit, but deep red in colour. The room is filled with candles. There is another man, the Inquisitor's secretary, but we cannot see his face.

STRANGE CAP: "There is a man here. A priest. In conversation with a nun. Her habit is the red of fresh blood. I would that I could hear them. That I could do more than see.."

Page 13 panel 5

The Scarlet Nun has turned: this beautiful face, looking straight at us...

STRANGE CAP: "She sees me!

"It is impossible... but she senses me, in some way I cannot fathom...."

Page 13 panel 6

The Nun — She raises her hand —

No dialogue

Page 13 panel 7

A thin panel, echoing Page 12 panel 2... Darkness.

Page 13 panel 8

The final image – Strange's face – sweat-soaked, haggard, miserable. His eyes are normal once again. He looks exhausted. His face echoes Clea's as the first panel on page 12....

STRANGE: I can see... no more....

What did I see, Clea? What did I say?

Page 14 panel 1

Three panels across the top tier: Clea is helping Stephen to his feet.

CLEA: Come to bed, my darling. I will tell you when you wake.

STRANGE (SMALL): ...yes.

Page 14 panel 2

In the foreground, the burning candle between the mirrors. Reflected in a mirror, Clea and Strange as they walk away, slightly unsteadily. The balloon arrows go to the people (out of panel) not to their reflections.

CLEA: Stephen?

STRANGE: Yes, love?

CLEA: If the Queen dies, and James of Scotland becomes king....

Well, we shall be all right. Won't we? I mean. Well, how bad can it get?

Page 14 panel 3

The candle goes out... a puff of smoke from the wick...

STRANGE (OFF): I don't know, Clea.

I don't know.

Page 14 panel 4

Big panel for the rest of the page: A scene change. We are looking at a cluster of buildings behind a big wall – we should perhaps recognise the tower as the one that the Angel is being held in. There's a small ship bobbing in the bay. It's pre-dawn – a grey light... In a building, domed possibly, on the far side of the building complex, away from the Tower, one light is burning. The moon has set. There might still be a scattering of stars on the west of the sky...

CAP: The Fortress of the Inquisition. Domdaniel. Spain.

INQUISITOR CAP: "Can you tell me anything else about this presence you say you felt, Sister Wanda?"

Page 15 panel 1

Now, we are back in the room of many candles. It's much more realistic than it was in Strange's vision. There are no crosses in the room. The Inquisitor, in white robes, a man in his fifties, who resembles our own Magneto, but is older, looks like he's lived a harder life. His face is set. He's standing, his hands behind his back. Wanda is a beautiful woman, in a scarlet nun's habit.

WANDA: Nothing, Grand Inquisitor. Perhaps... perhaps I simply imagined it.

INQUISITOR: I doubt it.

No, it was Javier. I have no doubt on that score.

Page 15 panel 2

Sitting at the only desk in the room – there are no other chairs, in this it resembles the queen's room at the start of the story, but only in this, for otherwise it is a small room – is a young man, with slightly odd hair at the front: he is Petros, and he is our Quicksilver analogue, Wanda's brother. He is not dressed as a monk, for he is the Inquisitor's secretary, and his representative into the outside world. The Inquisitor leans over the desk and says,

INQUISITOR: Petros? Send a message to the guard: they must be extra vigilant at tomorrow's burning.

PETROS: Yes sir.

INQUISITOR: You may leave us, Sister Wanda.

Page 15 panel 3

The Inquisitor has linked his hands behind his back, and is walking away from Petros, who is writing at the desk with a quill. Wanda is going out.

INQUISITOR: So tell me, Petros, how was the court of James of Scotland?

PETROS: His majesty sends you his greetings, Inquisitor.

INQUISITOR: And?

Page 15 panel 4

Petros in close-up for the first time, looking up at us. His hair is longer than Quicksilver's, but it goes up into those odd sort of speed-fins at the front. Possibly his clothes are green in colour.

PETROS: While James is of the Protestant Faith, he feels that there is common cause against

'... witches, magicians and the witchbreed, who infest England like lice crawling through a shepherd's crotch?'

His words. Not mine.

Page 15 panel 5

Now, they keep talking, while we follow something else for a moment: There are three people standing by the wall of the Fortress, outside. They are wearing monk's robes. Again, either in caps, or balloons going to the lighted room on the other side of the wall.

INQUISITOR: So is there room for an alliance?

PETROS: He told me that the English have long memories. They have not yet forgotten Queen Mary – they call her Bloody Mary – and her burnings.

He says that any work must be done carefully and quietly – and with public support and approval.

Page 16 panel 1

The Inquisitor smiles, and spreads his arms, he's explaining something very simple.

INQUISITOR: Easily done. Tell him that, when he is King, we shall endeavour to demonstrate that the Witchbreed are plotting against his throne — obviously they wish to blow up the Houses of Parliament in some sort of explosion.

INQUISITOR: If we convince the English of that, they'll be begging us to light the bonfires.

Page 16 panel 2

Now there are two of the figures in the monk's hoods from the page before, running across the deserted courtyard. We can see the face of the one in the front, a little light under the monk's cowl: he has some kind of black band around his face, across his eyes. This will be our Cyclops. He does not look like an X-Man, though. He looks like something slightly inhuman.

PETROS CAP: "And do they really plan to blow up the English Parliament?"

INQUISITOR CAP: "Oh, Petros, your innocence is refreshing."

Page 16 panel 3

The Inquisitor has picked up a candle-snuffer, with which he has started to put out the many candles. He says, over his shoulders to Petros:

INQUISITOR: Before I sleep, I shall send orders to make certain that all is in readiness for today's execution.

Perhaps I should order them to daub his wings with pitch, or wax, so the damned creature will burn like a torch for righteousness.

Page 16 panel 4

And now we're looking in the square: a stake, and brushwood and firewood stacked beneath it. Maybe our shadowy monks hiding behind the pillars at the edge of the courtyard.

INQUISITOR CAP: "Javier and his monsters will not get this poor soul, eh Petros?"

"He burns at Sunrise."

Page 16 panel 5

The last panel. The Inquisitor is smiling, as he puts out the final candle-wick.

INQUISITOR: As they all will burn.

Page 17 panel 1

The ship we saw in Dr Strange's vision, the Virginia Maid. And on the deck, the girl and the huge blonde Indian. He is sitting beside her. They are small figures — the light is grey, pre-dawn.... Andy — we have three scenes on ships or boats in this issue, in different places, so we really need to feel they're all very different..

CAPTION: The Atlantic Ocean. The Virginia Maid.

DARE: Rojhaz? Are you asleep?

ROJHAZ : No, Virginia.

DARE: The sun will be up soon, Rojhaz. Tomorrow if the winds hold, or the next day, we shall dock in Greenwich.

Page 17 panel 2

Move in now on them. The girl in the light of the pre-dawn. She is very pale and very lovely. Rojhaz stands just behind her, enormous and protective....

DARE: Why did Father not come with us? He knows London. He knows the Queen. I feel so young and foolish.

ROJHAZ: You know.

DARE: You mean, "I know why he sent us"?

ROJHAZ: You know.

DARE: I guess I do.

Page 17 panel 3

Virginia Dare smiles shyly. She's a schoolgirl, excited to be going to the city, to meet people. She's going to be the centre of attention. Oh, if only she knew...

DARE: He says "an old colonist will attract precious little attention."

But if he sends his daughter, the first child born in the colonies, and her Indian guard and protector, why then all of London will be buzzing like a hive.

Page 17 panel 4

Rojhaz rests his hand on her shoulder. It's huge, against her pale skin.

DARE: Then Roanoke will see more colonists and investors. He has to look after the colony.

ROJHAZ: Yes.

DARE: I'm scared, Rojhaz.

ROJHAZ: Protect you.

DARE: I know you will.

Rojhaz? How many people do you think there are in London Town? Two hundred? Five hundred?

Page 17 panel 5

She looks up at him affectionately, her hair, like his, blows in the sea-breeze. She holds his tree-trunk-like arm, maybe even swings on it.

ROJHAZ: More. Thousands.

DARE: Silly. There aren't that many people in the world....

Do you think the Queen will be nice to me?

ROJHAZ: Yes.

Page 17 panel 6

And now her mood changes. She bites her lower lip, shivers, lets go of him, and hugs herself. Maybe turns away from him...

DARE: Rojhaz...

What happens if it happens again, when I am in London. What if I change?

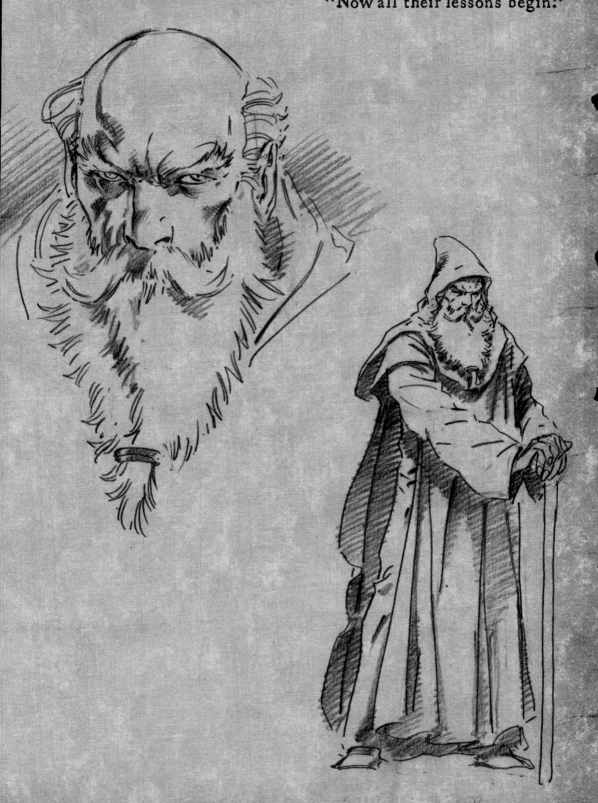

Inquisitor

"Now all their lessons begin."

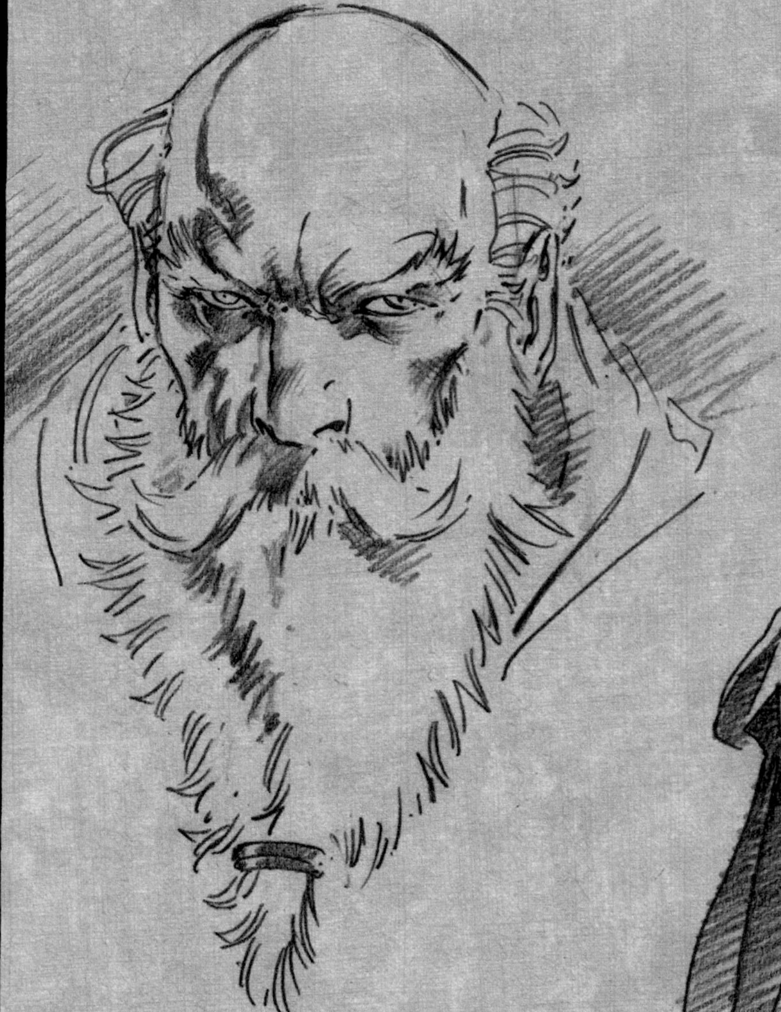

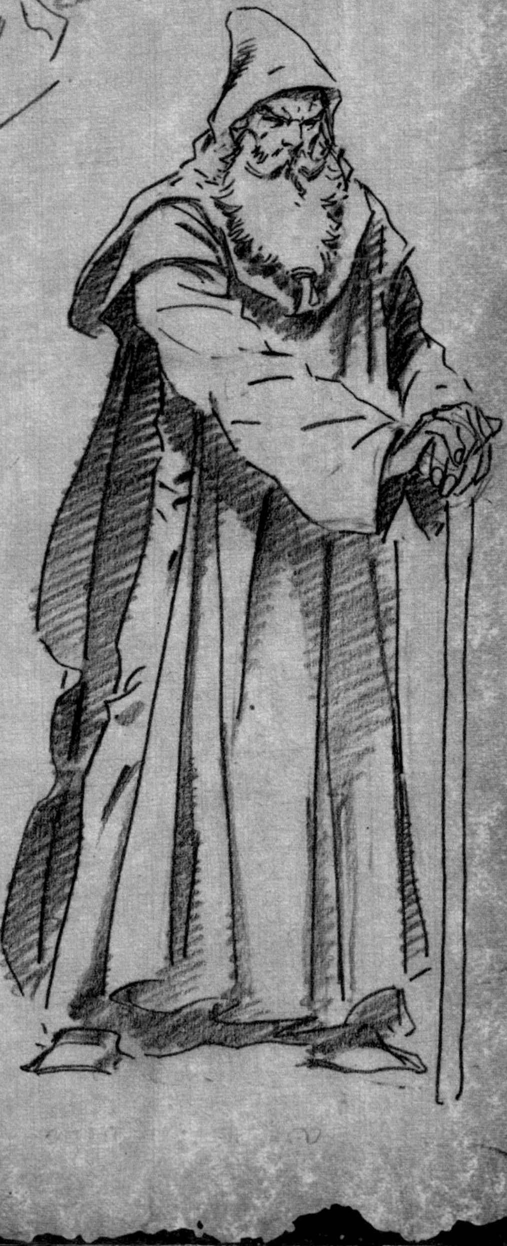

Virginia Dare

"There was something hanging in the air. Something that glittered. And I touched it!"

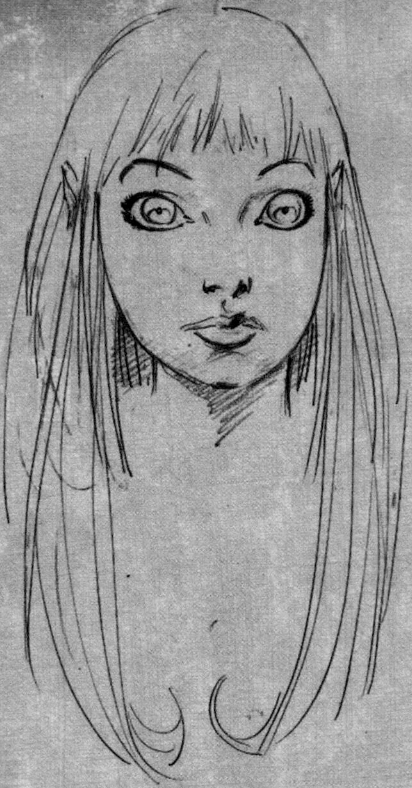

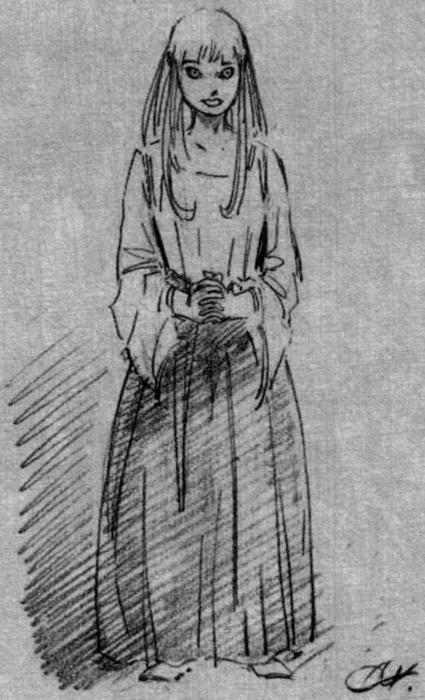

Rojhaz

"I knew I had to protect her. To guard her. To fight for her if I had to!"

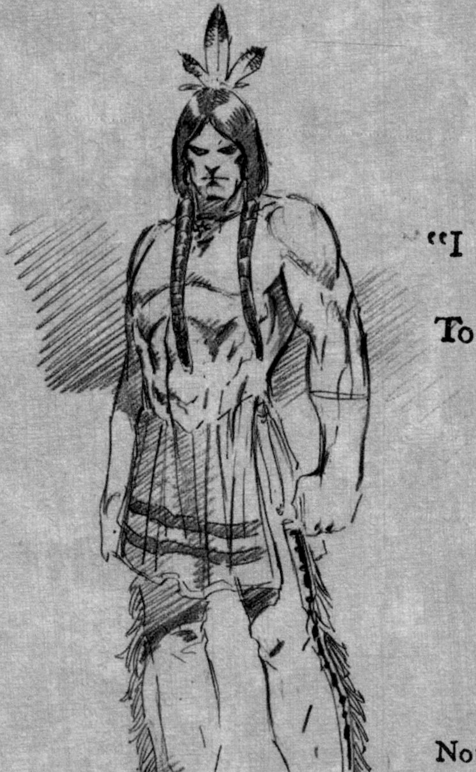

Note: Andy drew this sketch before he knew Rojhaz was Captain America and therefore blond.

ROJHAZ: No one will hurt you.

Page 17 panel 7

Final panel, those slightly strange eyes. Her face in close up, staring out into the distance, straight at us.

DARE: I know. But what if I hurt them?

Page 18 panel 1

We are in an alleyway. Peter Parquaugh carries a lighted brand, which burns as he leads the way, Fury walking behind him. Peter is worried.

CAP: Near The Temple, off Fleet Street. England.

PETER: Why have we come this way, Sir Nicholas? Why are we here?

FURY: Ah. A very profound question, Peter. Why are we here? To suffer, some say. Others claim that this world is a refining fire in which the dross in our souls —

Page 18 panel 2

They've come out beside the Temple, off Fleet Street, a large church. We'll get some reference for you.

PETER: No, I mean, um, here, in the Temple. Should we not be crossing the river?

FURY: Not at all. This is a perfect place to be. We are here for two reasons.

Firstly because it was built by the Templars, four hundred years ago. And what do we know of the Templars, eh, Peter?

Page 18 panel 3

Move closer in on the two of them. Peter is still holding the burning brand. Fury is resting his arm on the boy's shoulder.

PETER: I don't know much about monks and such, Sir Nicholas. Before my time.

FURY: If you are to prosper, in this world of secrets and powers, you must understand many things that happened before your time. How else can we understand our own time, or predict what may come?

Page 18 panel 4

Thin panel. Peter frowning, looking down, trying to figure this one out. Head shot, or head and shoulders, looking down.

PETER: I...

Page 18 panel 5

Same panel, exactly, except now he's raised his head and is saying:

PETER: I see. Yes. Your point is taken, sir.

Please — Who were the Templars?

Page 18 panel 6

No panel border: Fury begins to explain...

FURY: That is a small question, but with as many answers as a hydra has heads.

In brief, they were an order of warrior monks, founded,

some five hundred years ago, to guard the routes to Jerusalem.

Page 19 panel 1

Flashback panel: We have a bunch of warriors, with white surcoats over their chainmail, dusty beards... a couple of them walk forward, while a couple of others haul a huge box forward. All of them have their swords out, as if they're expecting trouble. Daylight, and the background is Jerusalem a long time ago, looking like it does in Monty Python's Life of Brian... monochrome browns, perhaps?

FURY: "Some say they came together to guard a great treasure."

"Within a century they were the most powerful organisation in Christendom, and answerable only to their leader, the Grand Master."

Page 19 panel 2

The Flashback continues. The King of France, his back to us, looks down into a crowded field, filled with people — crippled, tortured, bearded men, burning at stakes. A crowd is back at a safe distance, watching. Again, daylight, maybe monochrome?

FURY: "And a century after that, the King of France and the Pope combined their forces to destroy the Templars, as best they could."

Page 19 panel 3

Okay: now this is our first look at the old man. He has a long white beard, and a walking stick, and a long white robe. He is pointing to a cart, with the hand that isn't leaning on the walking stick, and some men are shouldering a huge box onto the back of the cart.

FURY: "But some fled to England and into Scotland — and there were others who avoided the power of the Inquisition, and the torture chambers, and the bonfires, and stayed in Jerusalem.

"But what treasure the Templars were guarding, in the Holy City, is a secret well-kept to this day."

Page 19 panel 4

Back into the present (well, 500 years ago but you know what I mean). Fury is resting his hand on his sword-hilt, casually. He is stepping away from Peter...

PETER: How — important do we think this treasure will prove?

FURY: We shall see.

PETER: You said there were two reasons we were here. What was the second?

Page 19 panel 5

Fury has his fists closed, and his head raised.

FURY (SMALL): It approaches from behind us.

Step away from me, Peter. Do not turn around.

Page 19 panel 6

An assassin – a smallish man, with a bald head and a slightly pointed face (someone like the original Spidey villain, the Vulture), with a dagger raised comes running at Fury, screaming:

ASSASSIN: Die!

Page 20 panels 1-4

No Dialogue over these panels. Your call on how you tell it, Andy: The man attacks and the dagger is plunged into Fury's back — and Fury spins around and punches the man in the stomach. The Dagger, its point bent, falls to the cobblestones.

Then as the man crumples, Fury knees him in the jaw. The assassin collapses.

Page 20 panel 5

Peter is holding the bent dagger, and staring at it astonished. Fury is grinning. He barely broke a sweat.

PETER: The knife...?

FURY: Leather and chainmail, boy. Nothing magic about it.

The second reason for coming here is because it seemed like a fine place to deal with somebody following us.

Page 21 panel 1

Three panels across the top of the page: Fury is on his knee, and in the light of the brand Peter holds, is tying the assassin's wrists together.

FURY: As to how important the treasure would prove? I would say, important enough to kill for.

I think we shall keep our new friend in the Tower until we find out who he is working for.

PETER: Sir? The gentleman in the dark room mentioned Count Otto Von Doom...

Page 21 panel 2

Start to pull back, as Peter walks out in the front. Fury has thrown the man over his shoulder.

FURY: Otto The Handsome. What of him?

PETER: They say he is a great man. Pious, and learned and wise.

FURY: That's what they say, to be sure.

But in this profession, Peter, you will learn many things about what goes on beneath the surface. Damn, boy, but I wish Sir Reed were still alive.

Page 21 panel 3

Nicholas Fury walks ahead of Peter, a small bald assassin, bound hand and foot, over his shoulder.

FURY: We are the queen's shield. We are the nation's shield. Never forget that.

Now. Let's get him to the tower.

Page 21 Panel 4

I quite like the idea here of changing scene again mid page. We are looking at a small ship, crossing the Channel, navigating by the stars.

CAP: "Master Murdoch?"

CAP: "Aye, Captain Nelson?"

CAP: "Could I ask you a question?"

CAP: "That's a question already. But certainly, ask away. Whether you get an answer or not is another matter."

Page 21 panel 5

Now, Captain "Fog-Bound" Nelson is a chubby fellow, who is standing beside Matthew Murdoch. Murdoch is leaning against the mast, his staff over his back.

NELSON: It's been five years you've been using my ship. I was wondering why you travel.

MATTHEW: I travel to see the sights, Captain.

NELSON: There's some as say that you're a smuggler, Master Murdoch.

MATTHEW: People say all manner of things. But my gold is good.

Page 21 panel 6

Captain Nelson is worried now — he may have said the wrong thing here, but he's going to keep going.

NELSON: And I was wondering... Y'see...

A sailor I met, a lowlander, told me of a time that he and several others tried to rob a blind Irish balladeer, in a port town, at night.

NELSON: He said that they were lucky to escape with their lives.

Page 21 panel 7

Matthew Murdoch, his eyes are hidden, but he grins like a madman as he says:

MATTHEW: Surely, the same can be said of any fellow who asks too many questions, Captain.

Now, is it a song you'll be wanting? To see the dawn in?

Page 22 panel 1

Okay. There is a monk, and two burly guards. The guards are unlocking the Angel's leg shackles. The Monk is saying:

MONK: It is almost Dawn, monster. Are you prepared to repent your heresies, before you reach the cleansing fire?

ANGEL: I am no monster. I am as my creator made me.

MONK: You counterfeit an angel, aye. But your creator is the Devil.

Page 22 panel 2

The Monk, holding a lantern, walks down some winding steps, with a guard behind him. Then comes the angel, with a chain around his waist, going to his arms and around his wings. Then another guard. Each of the guards has a spear pointed at the angel.

MONK: Were you to repent now, we would take mercy on you.

ANGEL: You would save me from the stake?

MONK: Not at all. But we would use wet wood and

Matthew Murdoch

"If a Devil is one who dares, when others hold back, then I am happy to play the Devil in this Mystery, boy."

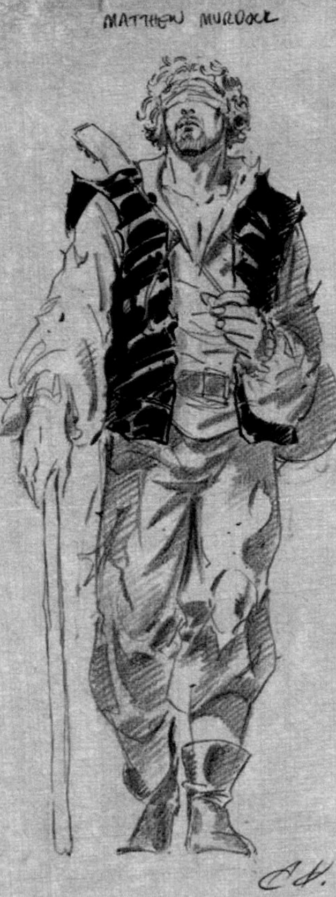
MATTHEW MURDOCK

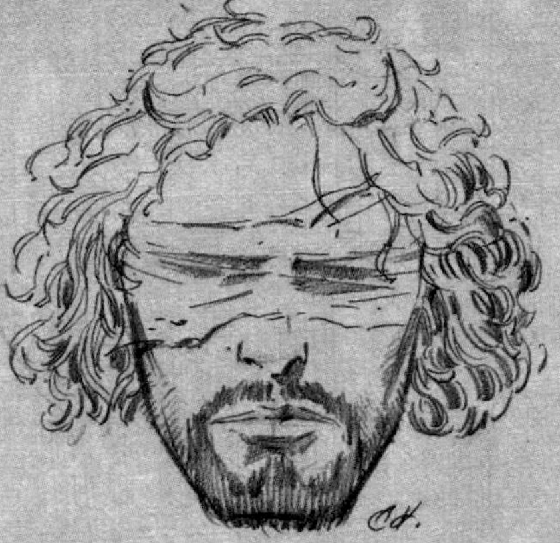

Peter Parquagh

"A spider, sir. And such an interesting beast it is."

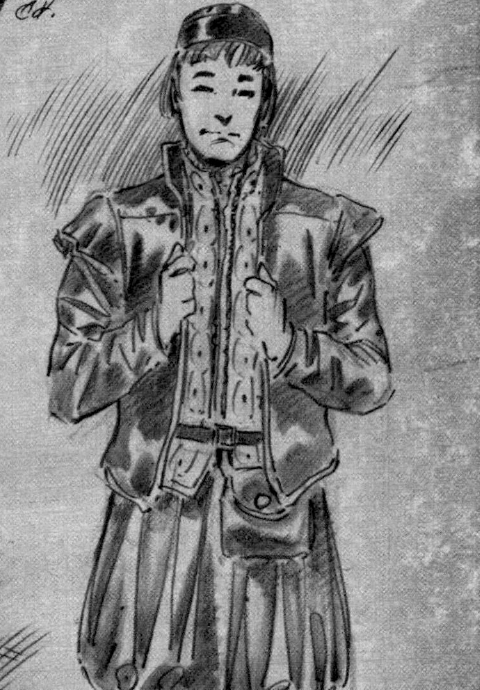

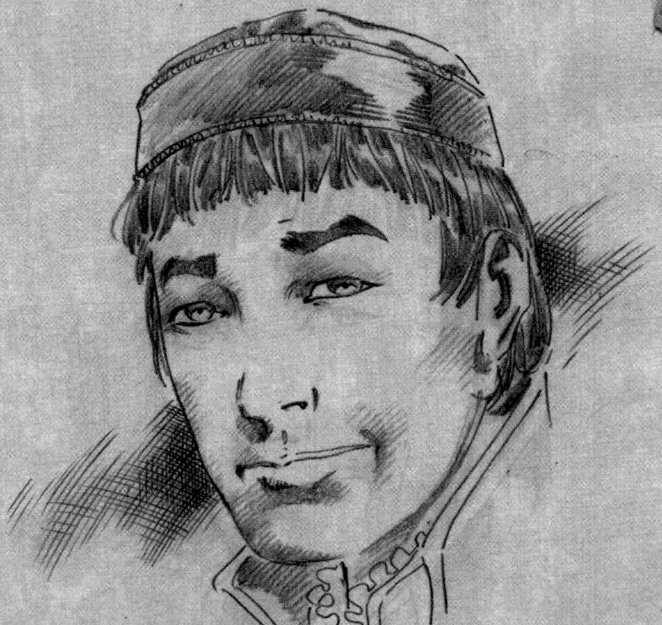

grass, and the smoke would render you unconscious before the flame touched your flesh.

Page 22 panel 3

Angel, close up on his face, dirty and angry.

ANGEL: Your kindness renders me speechless.

Page 22 panel 4

Big panel — In the square. The Angel is tied to the stake. There are a few monks around in a knot over the left of panel. From the right of panel a man approaches with a burning brand.

No dialogue

Page 23 panel 1

Lots of small panels on this page: Think Steranko... Try to get 5 panels on the top tier – really. Angel's face. He stares at the brand in fear.

No dialogue

Page 23 panel 2

The hand with a raised brand, burning.

No Dialogue

Page 23 panel 3

The monks are standing and watching. There are two monks over on one side who are our X-Men...

ROBERT: Quickly now...?
SCOTT: Not yet...

Page 23 panel 4

The brand is touched to the wood...

No dialogue

Page 23 panel 5

Close up on our Cyclops's face as he pushes his hood back and says:

SCOTT: Now.

Page 23 panel 6

Middle tier. Still small panels: The flame goes out, as the brand and the wood touch. A little smoke comes from it.

No Dialogue.

Page 23 panel 7

The Monk holding the brand drops it, shouting:

MONK: It's too cold to touch!! What devil's work is this?

Page 23 panel 8

Angel's face. He starts to grin.

No dialogue.

Page 23 panel 9

The Monk, shouting:

MONK: Kill the monster!

Page 24 panel 1

One of the X-monks, Robert, has just pushed back his cowl and extended his sleeve, and we can see that he is covered with a thin layer of ice. He's extended his arms, and has frozen the air into a wall, with the monks and guards on the other side. Cyclops is heading for the bound angel.

ROBERT: Quickly, friend. The ice won't hold them for long...

Page 24 panel 2

Cyclops has pushed up his visor. His visor is made of various rubies of every shape and size, jammed into a metal frame that covers his eyes. A power blast is coming out of his eyes, and burning through the chains that bind Angel.

ANGEL: Your eyes!
What are you?

Page 24 panel 3

Cyclops, visor back down, pulls the last of the chain apart, or pulls Angel down from the pyre, saying:

SCOTT: I'm witchbreed, boy. Just like you are. We'll explain later.
For now, we just have to get you out of here. Can you fly?

Page 24 panel 4

Angel is brushing down his wings. They are standing next to the wall...

ANGEL: My wings are cramped, but yes.
SCOTT: Then meet us down at the bay. We have a ship waiting there.

Page 24 panel 5

Angel is spreading his wings as wide as they go, which is pretty wide, before he flies, and then he asks Cyclops:

ANGEL: But how will you get out of the fortress? I can fly, but there's a wall between you and the outside.

Page 24 panel 6

Thin panel, no panel border – Cyclops, pushes up his visor one more time, all the way. Energy crackles....

No dialogue

Page 24 panel 7

Long panel. There's a huge hole blasted in the wall beside them. And Cyclops grins and says:

SCOTT: Not anymore.

Page 25 panel 1

Angel

"I have lived for almost 17 years. I die tomorrow.
And this is what hurts the most: that I shall die on the ground.
That I shall never take to the skies again,
to dance, to laugh, to fly..."

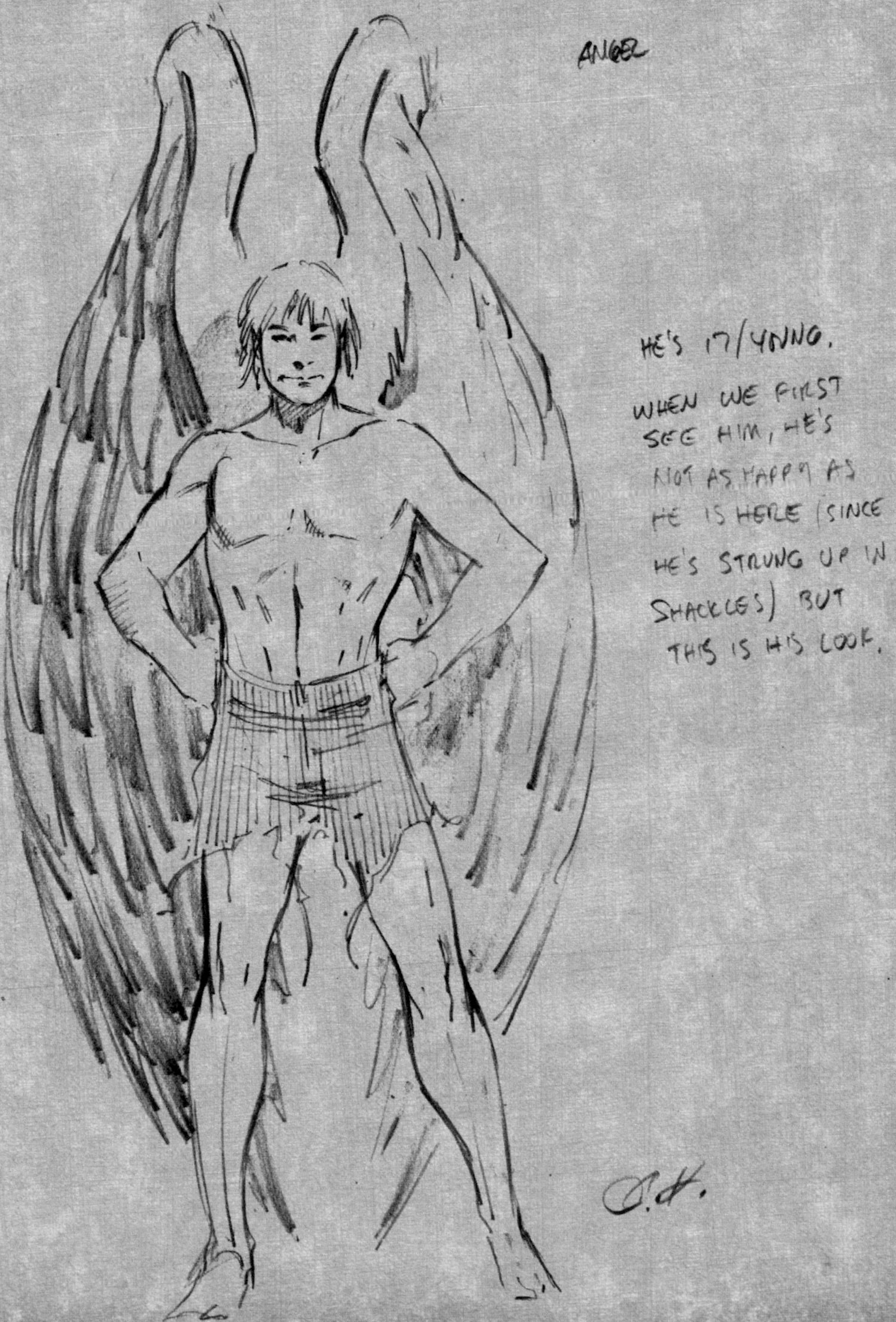
ANGEL
HE'S 17/YOUNG.
WHEN WE FIRST SEE HIM, HE'S NOT AS HAPPY AS HE IS HERE (SINCE HE'S STRUNG UP IN SHACKLES) BUT THIS IS HIS LOOK.

For the last couple of pages, let's do it almost as a story-book, Andy. We've met too many people already in this comic, so let's meet one more. Start with the old Queen: she's almost bald, with thin grey hair, and an old woman's face. Her wig sits on a wooden head, we can see through the open curtains of her four-poster bed.

> CAP: Queen Elizabeth is an old woman, and in pain, and she sleeps poorly. Now she tosses uncomfortably in her bed, and rolls over, and dreams a strange dream.

Page 25 panel 2

Now, we're into a daylight panel. We're seeing something happening a long way away. The old man rattles down a narrow unpaved road, in a crude cart, pulled by a donkey. There is a man sitting on the back of the cart... The old man's walking stick is across his lap.

> CAP: The Old Man left Jerusalem two days ago, in a cart, pulled by a donkey. The back of the cart was piled high with battered furniture – chairs, and pots, and an unremarkable wooden chest – and padded with straw.

Page 25 panel 3

Now we see an expensive cart, with a big serious man driving it, and mounted riders around it. It has a big "treasure chest" box on the back.

> CAP: As he left, three other carts left Jerusalem. The other carts were accompanied by outriders, and guards. They were decoys, although the men who drove them did not know that.
>
> The old man is accompanied only by a member of their order who can pass as a deaf-mute servant.

Page 25 panel 4

Close up on the old man's face. Long white beard, he is looking up, smelling the air, listening to the thunder.

> CAP: The rumble of the storm is now almost continual.
> CAP: He knows much, the old man. He knows many things.

Page 25 panel 5

The same cart we saw in panel 3, only now the horses are dead, and so are the outriders, on the ground. The cart is missing a wheel, and the chest is opened and empty. The big guy who was driving the cart is also dead. Vultures circle. Arrows stick out of people and horses alike.

> CAP: He knows that one of the other three carts has already been seized by enemies, by those who would steal the treasures of their order.
> CAP: He felt them die.

Page 26 panel 1

So the old man rides on. He shades his eyes...

> CAP: He does not know what has begun to tear the world apart, but he recognises the first signs.

Page 26 panel 2

Now pull back. There's a mild earthquake going on... the donkey stumbles, but will keep going....

> CAP: He knows where he needs to go. He knows that the time is upon him, the time his order has guarded their treasure for so patiently, and for so long.
>
> CAP: The ground shakes.

page 26 panel 3

Your call how literal you want to be with this panel.

> CAP: When the rain begins, it rains not water but blood and tiny lizards, which squirm and scream before shrivelling into jelly beneath the wooden wheels of the cart.
> CAP: The old man whips the donkey. It plods on.

Page 26 panel 4

We can see there are old tables and chairs on the back of his cart, and a bale of straw – and a chest... The man who plays a deaf mute sits on the back of the cart. Strange things fall from the skies and the clouds writhe above him. (No, you don't have to draw the clouds writhing, Andy.)

> CAP: He wonders if he has left all this too late.
> CAP: Trieste is a long way. England is much further.
> CAP: And now he begins to worry about his cargo.

Page 26 panel 5

Moody shot of the old man, sitting on his cart, clutching his walking stick for reassurance.

> CAP: He travels with the most powerful thing in the world.
> CAP: He fears it will not be enough.

Page 26 panel 6

And we finish with the Queen, awake, and coughing blood into her handkerchief.

> CAP: Half-waking, the Queen coughs, and before her dreams can vanish into the day she is suddenly and inexplicably afraid....

Page 27 panel 1

This is the new final page, Andy. The Sun is rising. It's real daylight for the first time. We are on a boat – a small fishing boat, which is skidding across the sea-water like a motorboat, attaining unheard-of speeds: thirty, even forty miles per hour... It has a mast, but no sail. Angel is standing in the prow, the front of the boat, his wings spread and back, enjoying the wind and the spray of the water. (The sun is on the right of the boat – we're going north.)

> CAPTION: Off the coast of Spain.

No dialogue

Page 27 panel 2

Our Cyclops, still in his monk's robe, with the strange wire-and-ruby eye-mask contraption over his eyes, walks over to talk to Angel.

> SCOTT: How are you feeling?
> ANGEL: Terrified. And, um, sea-sick.

Wanda

"I sometimes wonder,
what if the powers I have...
how do we know that they are
the gifts of God, and not the
tricks of the Devil?"

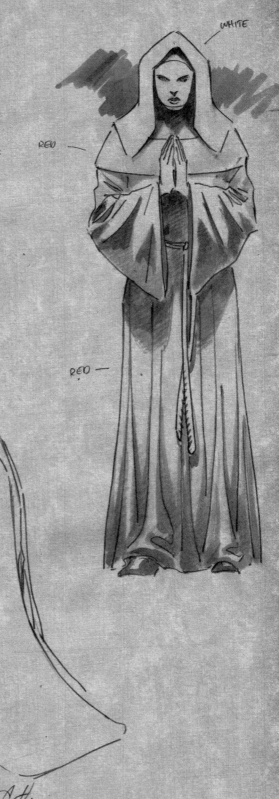

But happy not to have been burned to death.

Page 27 panel 3

Angel has turned suddenly, his wings spreading out huge behind him, flapping against the wind, helping him to keep his balance. He's folded his arms across his chest, and is asking —

> ANGEL: Who are you people? How did you get into the fortress? How do you do that thing with your eyes? And that wall of ice? And why does the boat go so fast, without a sail?
>
> And where are we going?

Page 27 panel 4

Scott is smiling gently, as if Angel's comments are nothing to worry about.

> SCOTT: You are all questions, my friend.
>
> ANGEL: And I would like some answers.
>
> SCOTT: Very well. Who are we? We are witchbreed, like you.

Page 27 panel 5

Scott points to himself with one hand, to the smaller, blonde boy, our Iceman with the other. Iceman is hauling a bag, like a sailor's canvas bag, filled with clothes.

> SCOTT: I am Apprentice Scotius Summerisle, this is journeyman Robert Trefusis, and over there, at the helm of this craft, is Apprentice John Grey.

Page 27 panel 6

A shot of Master Grey — in "his" monk's robe, at the back of the boat. He is smiling, and has raised a hand. "His" hair is short, like a girl's, but c'mon, this has got to be a beautiful red-haired girl in male drag. Scott keeps talking...

> SCOTT (OFF): He speaks but little.
>
> It is he that propels us through these seas, without wind or current.

Page 28 panel 1

Scott has pulled off his monk's robe. He wears breeches underneath, is naked. On his chest is a burn-mark — an X over his heart. Angel stares at it in horror.

> SCOTT: We are almost in English waters. It is time to remove our robes. Monks are not welcome in England. Fishermen, on the other hand, will attract no attention.
>
> ANGEL: Your chest....?
>
> SCOTT: They brand monsters, where I come from,

before they drown them.

Page 28 panel 2

Robert (Iceman) is now dressed as a fisherman — a huge woolen sweater, big jacket, loose, patched trousers, boots. He hands Angel some clothes.

> ROBERT: Can you hide your wings?
>
> ANGEL: I can fold them, to hide beneath my garb. And my mother made me clothes with room for them — she sewed them so cunningly that no man could tell.

Page 28 panel 3

Angel's face. He's looking up, a tragic figure — a young man caught in a nightmarish memory.

> ANGEL: They killed her, you know, when they caught me.
>
> They said, come back, or we kill her, so I came back, but they killed her anyway.

Page 28 panel 4

Scott is now dressed as a fisherman. He's pulled a cap low over his face and head, to hide as much of his eyes, and the things that cover them, as he can. He is on one side of Angel, and Robert, showing Angel the cords that will hide his wings, on the other. Angel has folded his wings across his back.

> SCOTT: I'm sorry.
>
> Robert: We have garb for you, and cords to bind your wings.
>
> SCOTT: Our master thinks of everything. We shall dock by noon, and a horse-cart will be waiting to take us the rest of the way.

Page 28 panel 5

And now Robert is binding the cord around the wings, while Angel pulls on the loose fisherman's trousers, and Scott finishes the lecture. Angel is looking up at Scott...

> SCOTT: As to where we go, we are on our way to a schoolhouse, which we call Sanctuary. And it is there that our master and our teacher will answer the rest of your questions.
>
> ANGEL: And it is there that we shall be safe from the world?

Page 28 panel 6

And we pull way back for the last panel of the issue, to see the boat heading towards England... And Scott saying...

> SCOTT: Aye. Perhaps.
>
> For a little while.

TO BE CONTINUED....

Thor

"I am Thor of the Thunders—
Mighty My Mjolnir: Fighter of Frost-giants,
Stronger than Storms!"

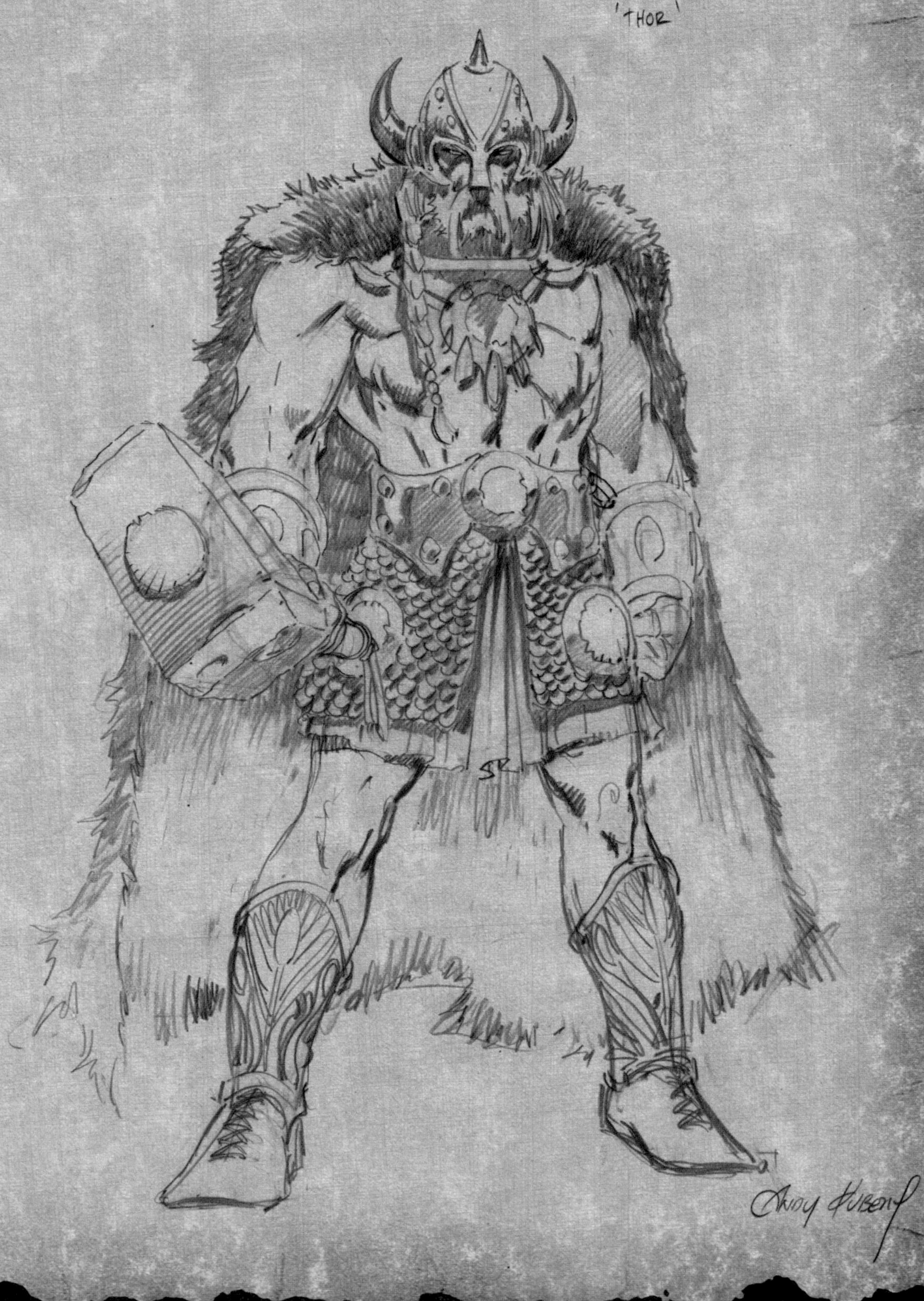
'THOR'
Andy Kubert

Scott McKowen Cover Process

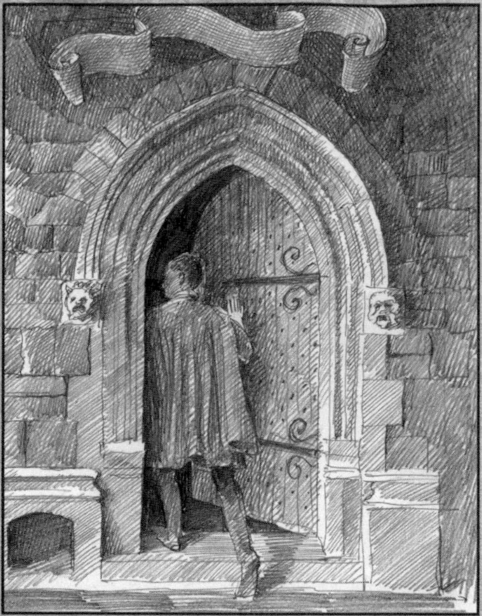

Unused cover sketch for Part 3

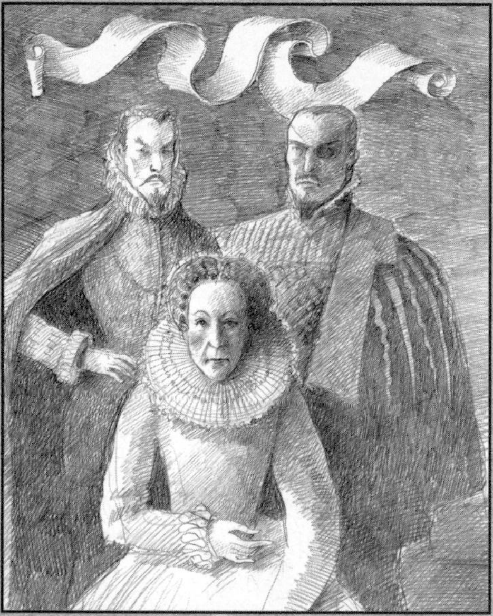

Unused cover sketch for Part 1

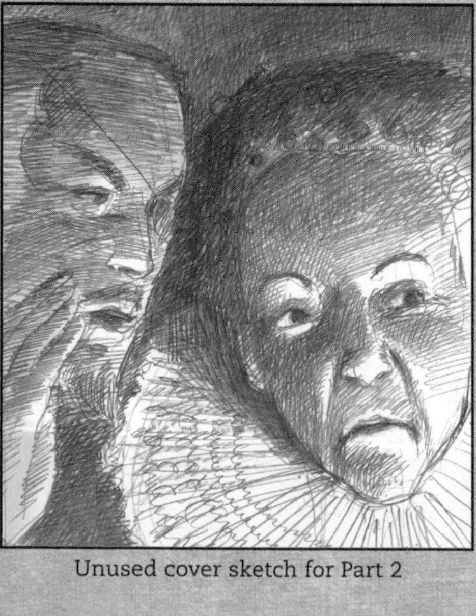

Unused cover sketch for Part 2

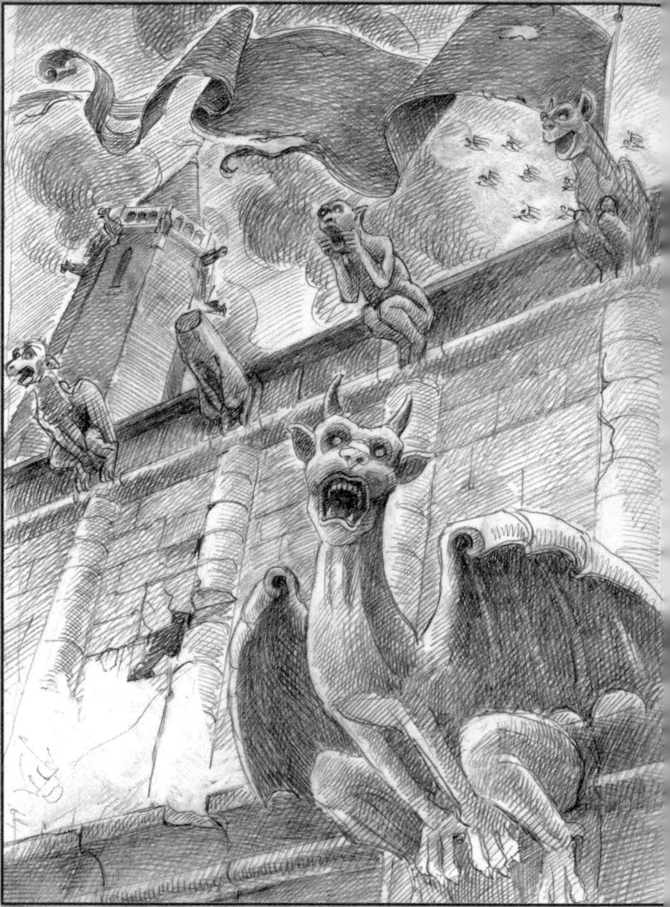

Pencil Drawing for Part 6

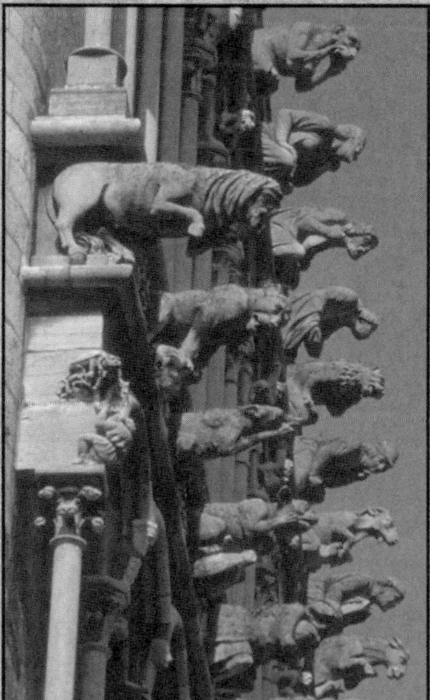

Reference photo (Dijon Cathedral) for Part 6

Nick Lowe, the editor for th project, had noticed my theatr posters in New York, an thought that the engravin "look" of the scratchboar would be interesting for th historical setting of thi story. Scratchboard is not typical medium for comic boo covers, and Marvel liked th idea of a distinctive look fo the world of this story.

My scratchboard illustration are hand-drawn, black an white, line art drawings Scratchboard is a piece o cardboard with a specificall prepared surface of har white chalk. A thin layer o black ink is rolled over th surface, and lines are draw with a sharp knife by scrapin through that ink layer to th white surface underneath — in effect drawing the whit lines into the all-blac surface with the blade. Al the coloring was added later i Photoshop.

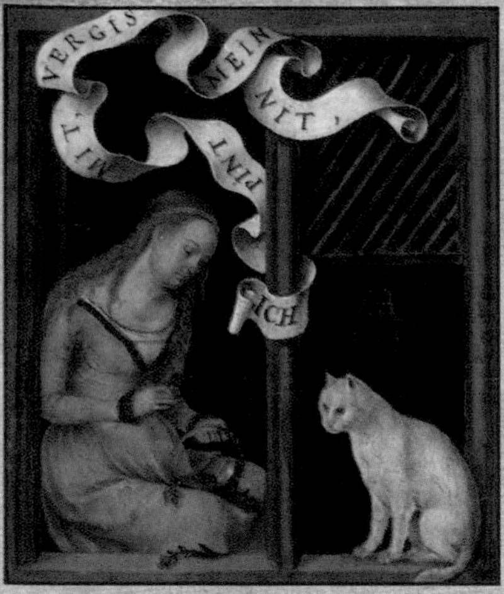
VERGIS
MEIN NIT
ICH

Girl Making a Garland by Hans Seuss von Klumbach. This was one inspiration for the scroll device.

I looked at a lot of seventeenth-century engravings in preparation for this project — Jacques Callot and Stefano della Bella were useful for their wonderful flamboyant storm scenes and threatening skies. My very first sketches were portraits of the main characters in period dress, with an atmosphere of intrigue.

Many Renaissance paintings contain scrolls or banners, often floating in mid air, upon which are written comments about the scene portrayed, or even words which the subject might be saying — an historical precedent for the dialogue balloons in comic books! My assignment included the design of a logotype for the series title. I realized that a floating scroll on each cover would make a great logo device. The scrolls in Renaissance paintings usually involve a trompe-l'oeil treatment of words rendered to look like they are printed "on" the scroll. Because "1602" is such a short title, my treatment became more of a juxtaposition — placing the clean, reverse type OVER the scroll. The scroll on each cover is different — sometimes it's a flag, sometimes a banner.

For the **PART EIGHT** cover, it was important to signal that the final chapter of the story shifts to the New World, so I looked at a lot of maps from the period — I have included a detail scan of a map of Virginia from 1618, and you'll see where the look of the hills, trees, animals and sailing ships came from. I was fascinated by the place names on these seventeenth-century maps — a crazy mix of Latin, Dutch, French and English, reflecting the colonial demographics of the era. All the names and spellings in the illustration come from period sources — including the names of the Native American Indian nations to describe regions and territories.

Many of these period maps include an elaborate, decorative compass rose with lines radiating out to the edges of the oceans. I used the focal point of a compass rose to make reference to the glittering point of light which Neil calls "the singularity" — the rip in time at the center of the story. The compass rose is the light source for the three figures; painting in a "glow" with a feathered brush in Photoshop added a nice surreal touch : The compass rose seemed to float right up off the page! I made individual pencil sketches of the three characters in order to work out their separate light sources; then I incorporated the figures into a final composite pencil sketch.

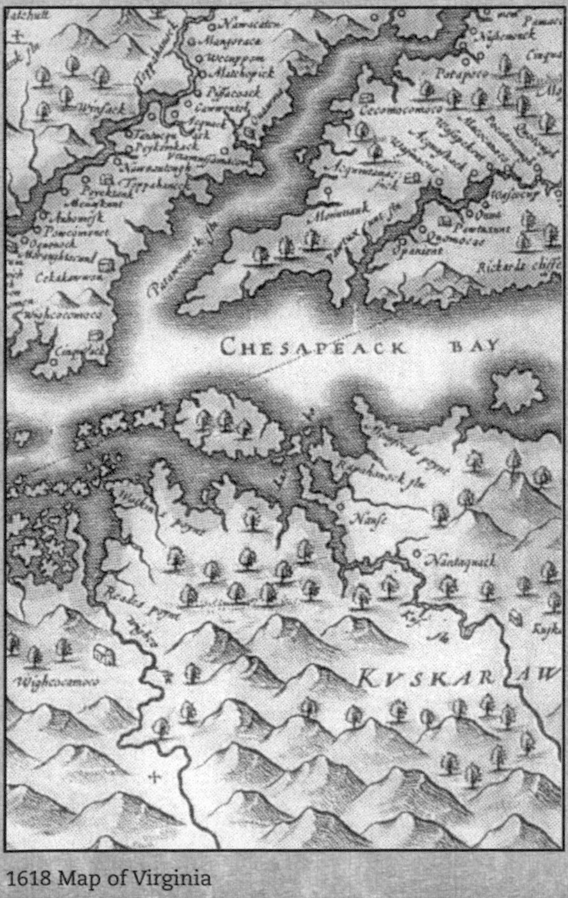
CHESAPEACK BAY
KVSKAR AW

1618 Map of Virginia

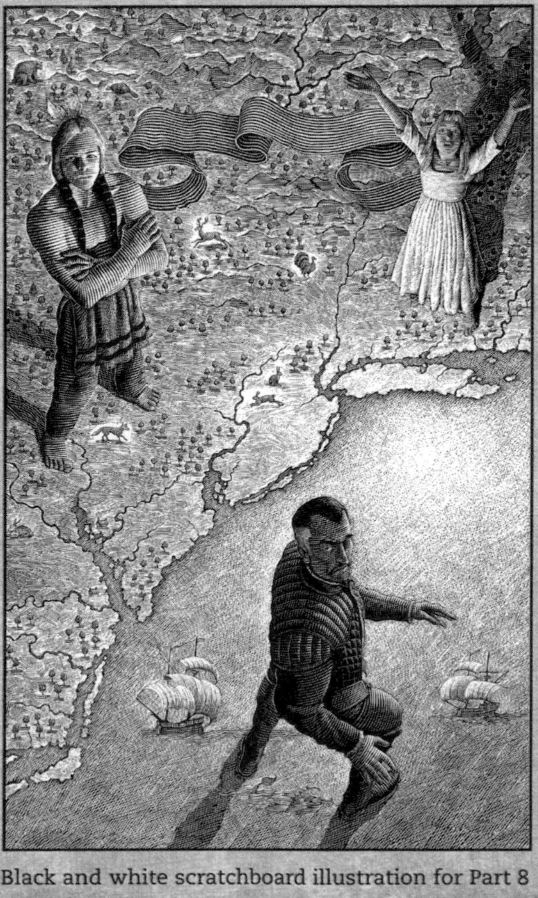

Black and white scratchboard illustration for Part 8

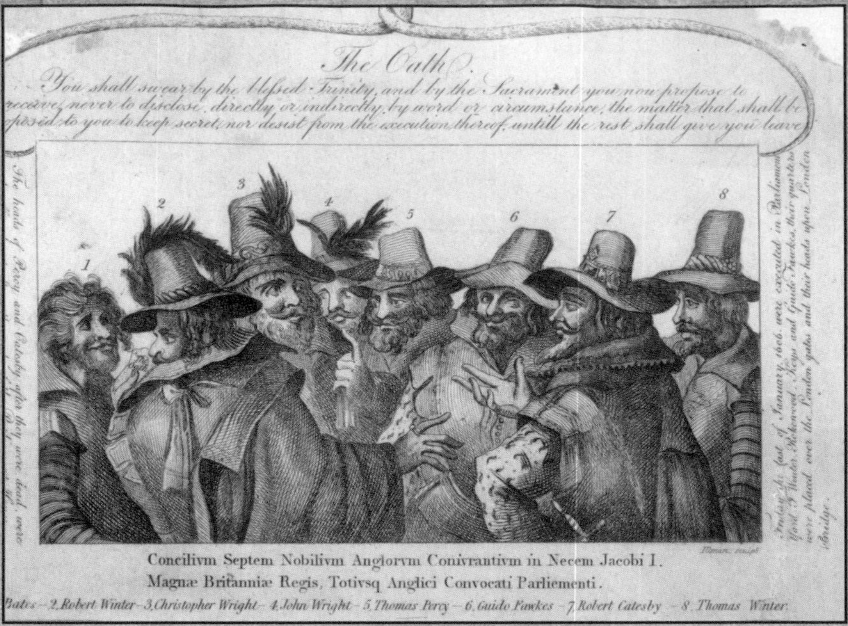
The Oath.
You shall swear by the blessed Trinity, and by the Sacrament you now propose to receive, never to disclose, directly or indirectly, by word or circumstance, the matter that shall be posed to you to keep secret, nor desist from the execution thereof, untill the rest shall give you leave.
1 2 3 4 5 6 7 8
Concilivm Septem Nobilivm Angiorvm Conivrantivm in Necem Jacobi I.
Magnæ Britanniæ Regis, Totivsq Anglici Convocati Parliementi.
Bates – 2. Robert Winter – 3. Christopher Wright – 4. John Wright – 5. Thomas Percy – 6. Guido Fawkes – 7. Robert Catesby – 8. Thomas Winter.

1605 Guy Fawkes Consipirators Engraving

For the dustjacket of the hardcover edition, I couldn't resist one more reference to a piece of art from the period. England under Queen Elizabeth I lived with laws against Catholicism — but when King James VI of Scotland succeeded Elizabeth as King James I of England, many Catholics worried that they would face more severe persecution than ever before. A small group of politically influential Catholics plotted to kill King James by blowing up the House of Lords on the opening day of Parliament — November 5, 1605.

The plot was discovered, however, and the traitors were all captured and executed for treason. The most famous of the "Gunpowder Plot" conspirators was Guy Fawkes — whose name is infamously attached to the annual lighting of bonfires all over England on the Fifth of November, to celebrate the fact that the plot was not successful.

An engraving of the conspirators was made in 1605 — the closest thing to a front-page newspaper photo of the crime of the century. This engraving is reproduced larger-than-life size in one of the London Underground "tube" stations near where the events took place.

Since the characters in 1602 are "outlaws" from the point of view of King James, it occurred to me to use the engraving of the Gunpowder Plot conspirators as the basis for a composition of Neil's characters. The original is a grouping of eight men, which worked nicely for my purposes (if you accept "Master" Jean Gray's disguise). I added Virginia to the middle of this group — and made her the only character who is looking out at us.

Pencil Sketches of Characters

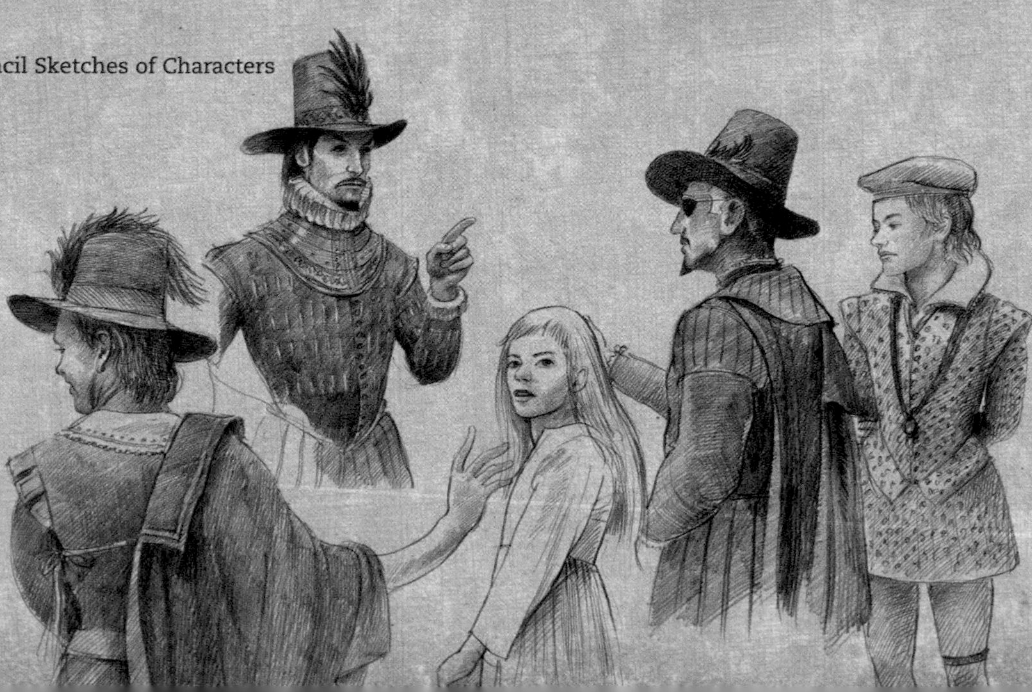

For 1602, Andy Kubert utilized a technique called enhanced pencils. Unlike usual penciled pages (which go to an inker who lays down black areas and lines on the penciled pages), enhanced penciled pages go right to the colorist, so they are usually tighter, more elaborate and more finished. This was a technique Andy used on Origin with great success. These pages then went to Richard Isanove who, utilizing a computer, digitally painted them to look like the interiors you saw in 1602. Here are some of the enhanced pencil pages.

-Nick

Part One: Page 21

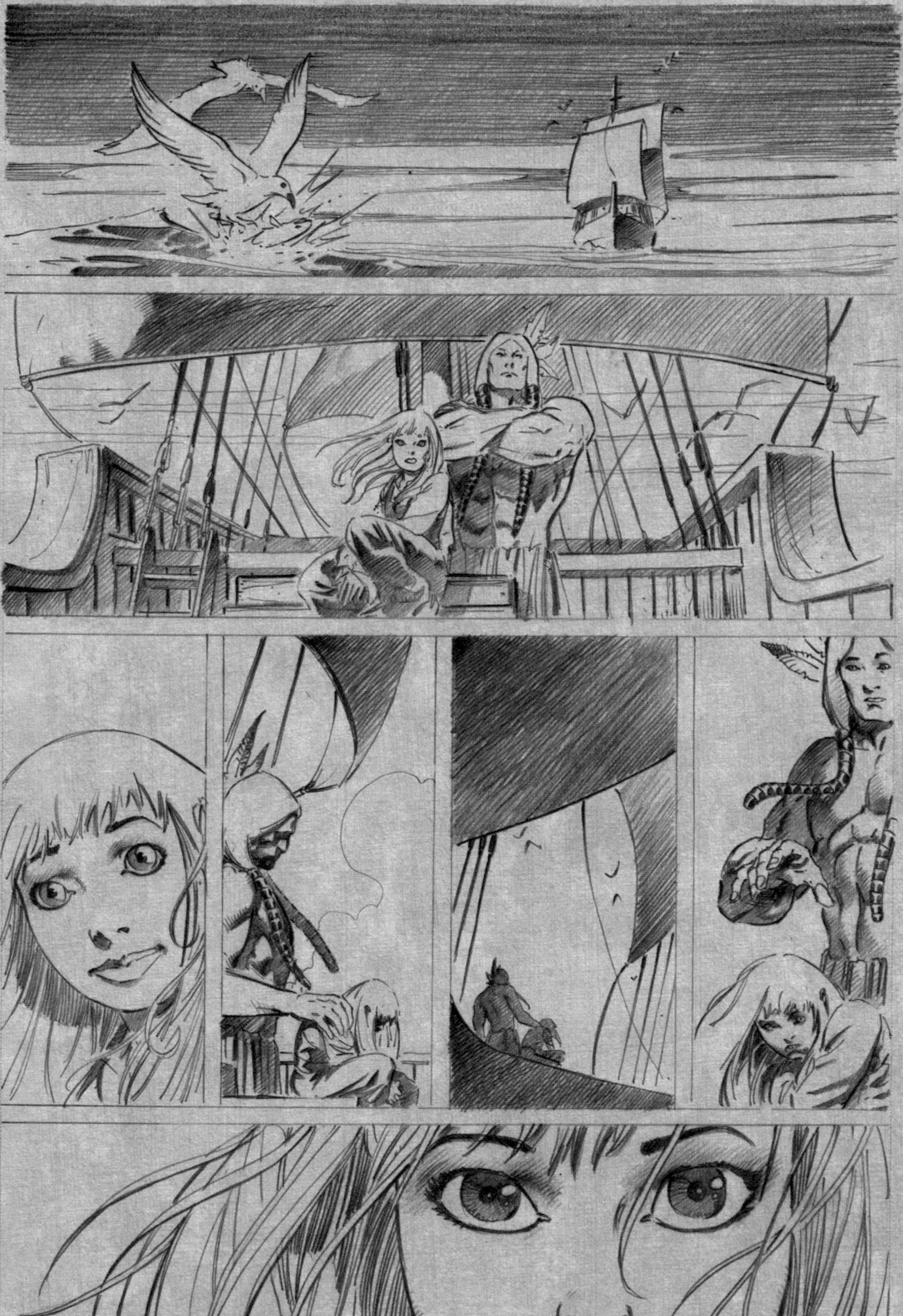

Part Five: Page 14

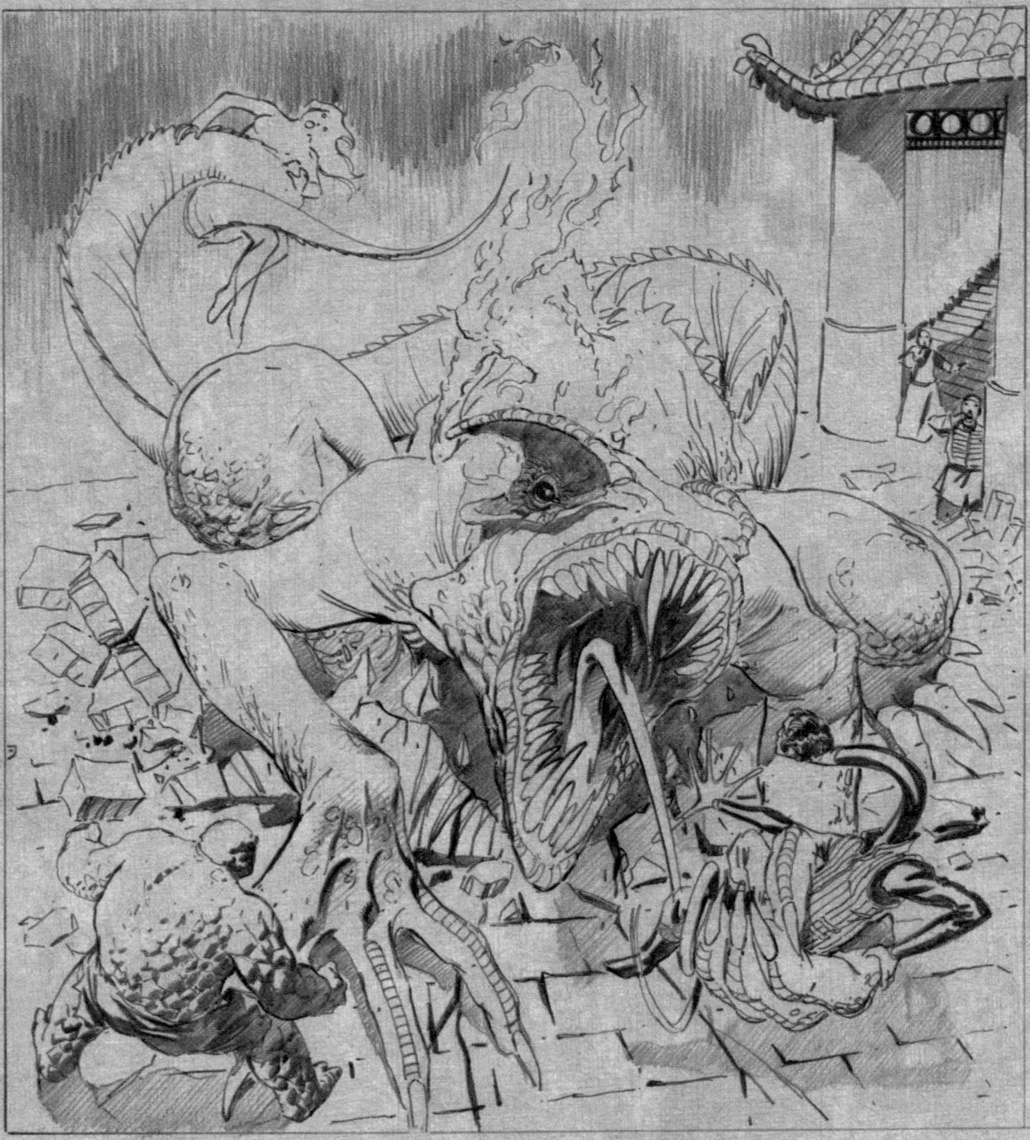

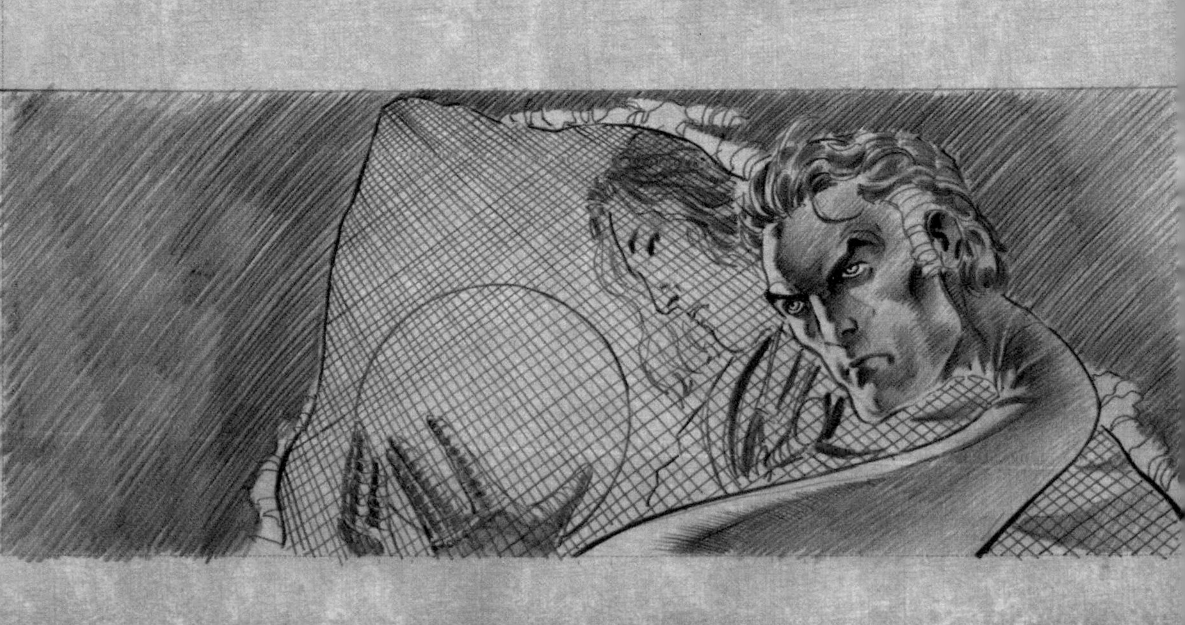

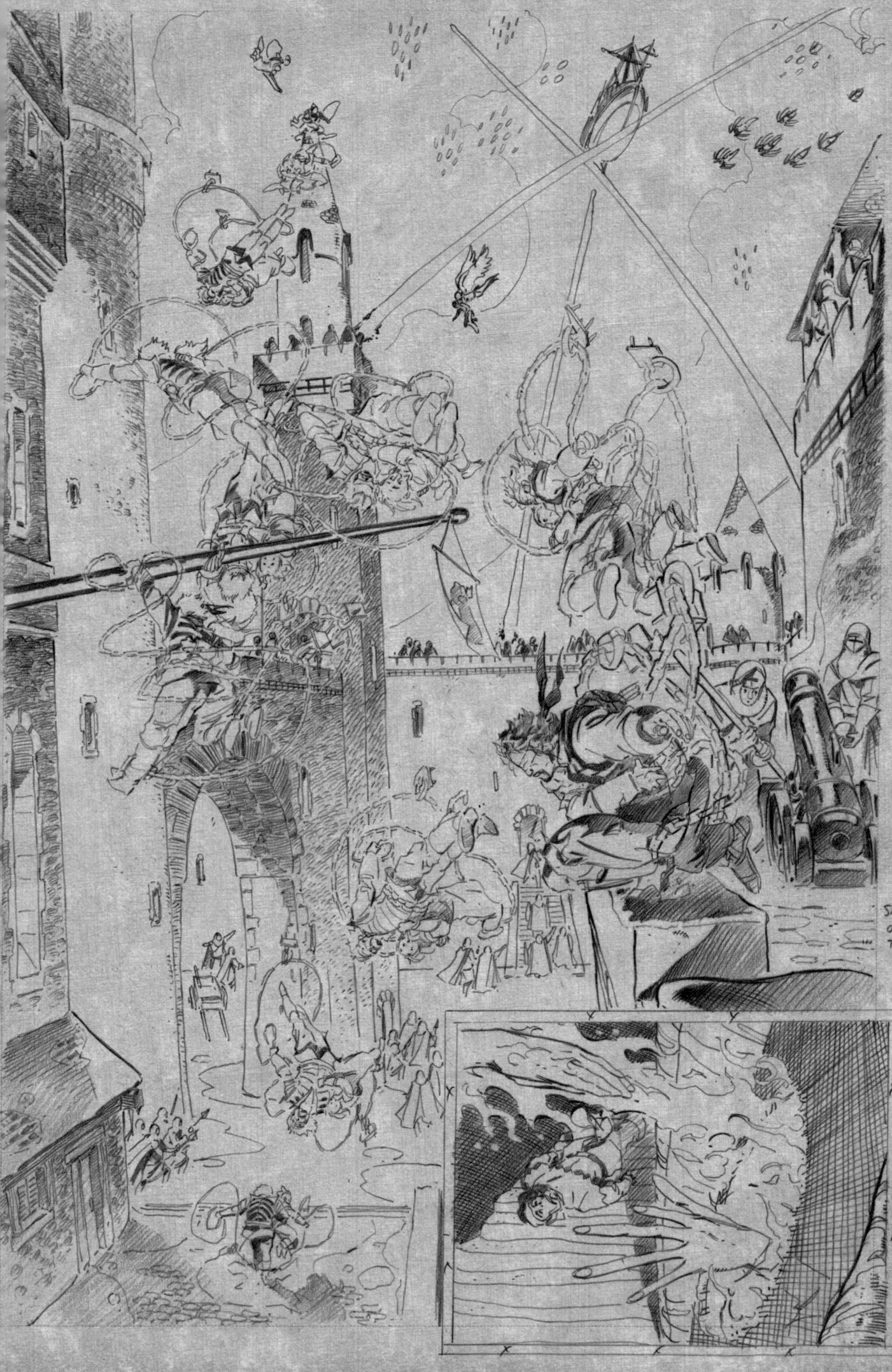

This page was originally used in part 5 to give an introduction to new readers. We reproduce it here for the sake of completeness and to make sure that you (yes, you) saw the great cartoon of Andy and Neil.

-Nick

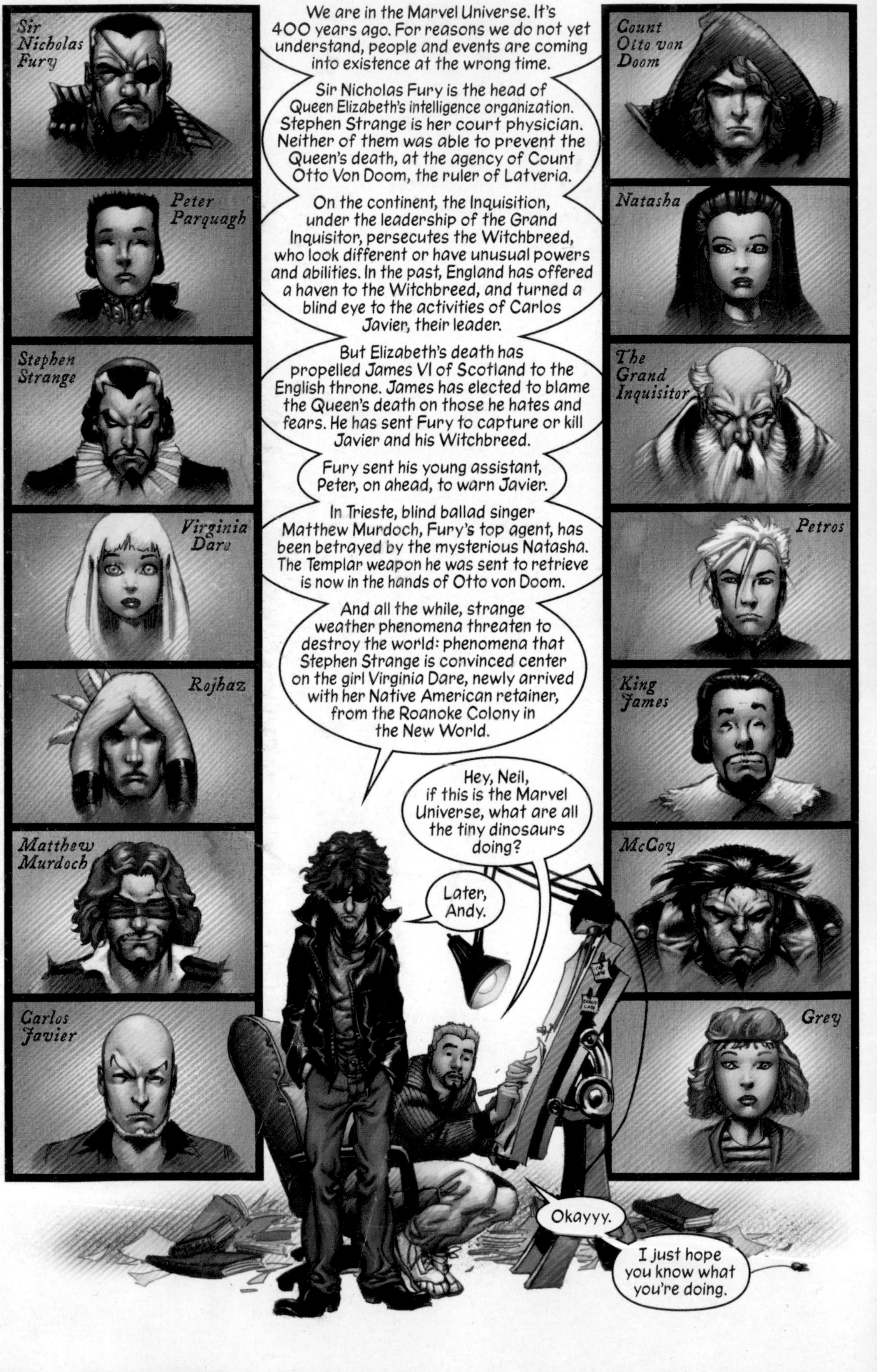
Sir Nicholas Fury
Peter Parquagh
Stephen Strange
Virginia Dare
Rojhaz
Matthew Murdoch
Carlos Javier
We are in the Marvel Universe. It's 400 years ago. For reasons we do not yet understand, people and events are coming into existence at the wrong time.
Sir Nicholas Fury is the head of Queen Elizabeth's intelligence organization. Stephen Strange is her court physician. Neither of them was able to prevent the Queen's death, at the agency of Count Otto Von Doom, the ruler of Latveria.
On the continent, the Inquisition, under the leadership of the Grand Inquisitor, persecutes the Witchbreed, who look different or have unusual powers and abilities. In the past, England has offered a haven to the Witchbreed, and turned a blind eye to the activities of Carlos Javier, their leader.
But Elizabeth's death has propelled James VI of Scotland to the English throne. James has elected to blame the Queen's death on those he hates and fears. He has sent Fury to capture or kill Javier and his Witchbreed.
Fury sent his young assistant, Peter, on ahead, to warn Javier.
In Trieste, blind ballad singer Matthew Murdoch, Fury's top agent, has been betrayed by the mysterious Natasha. The Templar weapon he was sent to retrieve is now in the hands of Otto von Doom.
And all the while, strange weather phenomena threaten to destroy the world: phenomena that Stephen Strange is convinced center on the girl Virginia Dare, newly arrived with her Native American retainer, from the Roanoke Colony in the New World.
Hey, Neil, if this is the Marvel Universe, what are all the tiny dinosaurs doing?
Later, Andy.
Okayyy.
I just hope you know what you're doing.
Count Otto von Doom
Natasha
The Grand Inquisitor
Petros
King James
McCoy
Grey